Immigration, nationality & refugee law handbook

2002 edition

Edited by Duran Seddon

Joint Council for the Welfare of Immigrants

JCWI is an independent national organisation which exists to campaign for justice in immigration, nationality and refugee law and policy. It undertakes strategic casework and acts as an expert training resource for others who work in this field. Our mission is to eliminate discrimination in this sphere.

JCWI's unique experience is distilled in the JCWI Immigration, nationality and refugee law handbook, an indispensable guide to the law and practice. This fifth edition has been completely revised and expanded to incorporate the wide-ranging implications of the Immigration and Asylum Act 1999 and Human Rights Act 1998. This edition also contains details of the forthcoming changes proposed in the Nationality, Immigration and Asylum Bill 2002.

Duran Seddon is a member of the specialist immigration team of barristers at Two Garden Court Chambers, London

© JCWI 2002

ISBN 1 874010 05 6

Editorial coordinator: Tauhid Pasha, Legal, Policy and Information Director, JCWI
Cover design: Sharon Tait
Typesetting: Boldface, 17A Clerkenwell Road, London EC1M 5RD
Printing: Unwin Brothers Ltd, Old Woking, GU22 9LH

The 2002 edition has been financially supported by: The Barrow Cadbury Trust, British Council (for the work carried out in the chapter on students), The Ian Mactaggart Trust and Nadir Dinshaw of the Dinshaw and Spencer Charitable Trust.

JCWI, 115 Old Street, London EC1V 9RT
Tel: 020 7251 8708, Fax: 020 7251 8707
Email: info@jcwi.org.uk

Preface and acknowledgements

Each edition of the *JCWI Handbook* has grown and this 2002 edition is no exception. The Immigration and Asylum Act 1999 and the regulations made under it have had an enormous effect on the way the immigration and asylum system operates. The Act made substantial changes to the structure of immigration control in allowing entry clearances to operate as leave to enter and, in certain circumstances, preventing leave from lapsing when a person departs. In the area of enforcement of controls, the powers of 'deportation' have been eroded in favour of a far swifter administrative process of removal of those who over-stay or otherwise breach their conditions of leave. The appeals system has been overhauled and a 'one-stop' appeals process has been introduced which requires appellants to raise all of their grounds for remaining in the UK in one appeal.

The introduction of the Human Rights Act 1998, at the same time as a right of appeal against immigration decisions alleged to be in breach of human rights, has opened up fresh approaches and new ways of thinking about common immigration problems. The 1999 Act also made far-reaching changes to welfare entitlements and erected a national support scheme for asylum-seekers. Even the giving of immigration advice itself has been made subject to detailed regulation by the Office of the Immigration Services Commissioner.

All of the above developments are covered. However, the phrase 'there is nothing more constant than change' is nowhere more true than in immigration and asylum. During production of this edition, a number of further significant developments have taken place. Towards the end of 2001, the Anti-terrorism, Crime and Security Act 2001 was passed, which allows for the indefinite detention of suspected 'international terrorists' whether or not they can be removed from the UK. In early January 2002, the government brought into force regulations which enabled certain decisions of the Immigration Appellate Authorities to be issued first to the Home Office for it to decide how and when to provide the decision to appellants. At the close of the same month, the Highly Skilled Migrants Programme (HSMP) came into effect. Changes to the 'grace' periods for the continued provision of asylum support were introduced by regulations in early April 2002. In addition, there are constant changes of practice which do not require regulations. For example, on 4 March 2002, without notice, the government announced the abolition of the 'special voucher' scheme with immediate effect. These changes are all accounted for as are the practical changes set out in the government's White Paper *Secure Borders, Safe Haven* (February 2002); for example, the introduction of the new asylum 'Application Registration Cards' (ARC) replacing Standard Acknowledgment Letters for asylum applicants.

However, the White Paper also trails the introduction of yet further legislation; the Nationality, Immigration and Asylum Bill 2002. The Bill received its first reading in the House of Commons on 24 April 2002. The changes proposed by the Bill as it stood at this stage are covered in this edition. The changes are both indicated in the text in the relevant places and summarised in tables at the end of those chapters where significant change can be expected. JCWI's views on the Bill are contained in Chapter 2.

As with the earlier JCWI handbooks, this edition contains no footnotes and the final section, concerning information, contains no legislation or similar materials. It is made up of basic, practical information covering visas, fees, country lists for different purposes, the HSMP points system and contact addresses. Similarly, cases and legislation are only cited in the text where it was felt that those references would be of particular help to applicants and their advisers. Wherever possible, tables set out in boxes have been used to give an overview of a particular area and to allow for quick reference. In explaining the requirements of the immigration rules, the format of 'What the rules say' and 'What the rules mean' has been used to enable easy access to the conditions which need to be satisfied on the one hand, and the more detailed explanation of those conditions on the other.

While the above elements of the lay-out of the *Handbook* have all remained the same, in order to keep pace with developments, the *Handbook* has itself inevitably become more detailed. The more complex law and procedure has become in immigration, nationality and asylum, the more a guide such as this has had to adapt to attempt to ensure that the rights of applicants are comprehensively safe-guarded and promoted. The *Handbook* is not, however, intended as an alternative to specialist advice where it is needed. The importance of obtaining sound, early immigration advice has never been higher and a chapter is given over to the availability of advice and its regulation.

JCWI is grateful to the following people, from both inside and outside the organisation, who have contributed to the writing of this edition:

Navita Atreya
Don Flynn
Neil Froom
Belayeth Hussain
Patrick Lewis

Alasdair Mackenzie
Sonali Naik
Tauhid Pasha
David Webb

JCWI also wishes to thank the following people who read and commented on parts of the text, although they are not responsible for the mistakes and omissions: Derek Betts, Barbara Coll, Liz Davies, Fiona Hannan, Peter Jorro, Jonathan Knight, Jennifer Osborne, Nicola Rogers and Raman Ruparell. The present edition is built upon the very strong foundations laid by the work of all the earlier contributors and, in particular, that of the original author, Sue Shutter.

Staff at the Home Office, the Joint Entry Clearance Unit (now 'UK Visas'), UKCOSA, the Office of the Immigration Services Commissioner and the Legal Services Commission have all provided invaluable information and details about various practical matters. Thanks are also due to Andrew Miles for his careful proof-reading and to Boldface Typesetters who generously accommodated the many changes that were made during production. This project has generated an enormous amount of work and would not have been possible without the assistance, guidance and support of all the staff and management at JCWI.

Above all, I wish to acknowledge the contribution of Tauhid Pasha, JCWI's Legal, Policy and Information Director, without whose dedication and hard work on the text, this edition would not have come to fruition.

JCWI values the input of users. The *Handbook* is your resource and your comments, suggestions and experiences will be used to improve it in the future. When sufficient of the changes proposed by the 2002 Bill have been brought into force, it is intended to publish an update to this edition.

Duran Seddon
April 2002

Summary contents

Full contents listing viii

Section 1 IMMIGRATION LAW AND ADVICE
1 Introduction to immigration law 3
2 Proposed changes: The White Paper and the Nationality, Immigration and Asylum Bill 2002 20
3 Seeking and providing immigration advice 39

Section 2 IMMIGRATION CONTROL IN PRACTICE 49
4 Applying to come into the United Kingdom 51
5 Leaving and returning 75
6 Applying to stay in the United Kingdom 90
7 Identifying immigration status 109
8 Problems, emergencies and solutions 130

Section 3 ASYLUM AND HUMAN RIGHTS 145
9 Asylum under the Refugee Convention 147
10 Asylum procedures 173
11 Home Office decisions on asylum 197
12 Family reunion and travel 222
13 Human Rights 231

Section 4 TEMPORARY PURPOSES 273
14 Visitors 275
15 Students 297

Section 5 FAMILY AND DEPENDANTS 321
16 Spouses, unmarried partners, same-sex partners and fiancé(e)s 323
17 Children 365
18 Relatives other than children and spouses 399

Section 6 WORKERS AND BUSINESS PEOPLE 411

19 Workers 413

20 Business purposes 438

Section 7 EUROPEAN RIGHTS OF FREE MOVEMENT 445

21 Background to free movement rights 447

22 Rights of free movement in the European Economic Area 452

23 Association and Co-operation agreements 476

Section 8 DETENTION AND ENFORCEMENT 485

24 Powers of detention 487

25 Getting people out of detention 510

26 Removal, deportation, illegal entry and criminal offences 527

Section 9 BRITISH NATIONALITY 559

27 British nationality 561

28 How to become British 583

Section 10 APPEALS 597

29 Rights of appeal 599

30 Conducting appeals 626

Section 11 WELFARE 657

31 Welfare benefits, housing, health and social services 659

32 Asylum support 689

Section 12 INFORMATION 723

Useful addresses and telephone numbers 725

Visa nationals, fees and overseas posts 737

Work-related applications 743

Commonwealth countries 748

Registering with the police 750

Countries whose adoption decisions are recognised in the UK 751

Abbreviations 752

Further sources of information 755

Glossary 757

CASE LIST 771

INDEX 781

Full contents

SECTION 1
IMMIGRATION LAW AND ADVICE 1

Chapter 1
Introduction to immigration law 3

The development of modern immigration
law 3

The system of immigration control 7
Immigration and nationality law 7
'Leave' and the immigration rules 8
Asylum and human rights 12
Special groups 13

The operation of immigration controls 15
Enforcement 18
Appeals 18

Chapter 2
**Proposed changes: The White Paper and
the Nationality, Immigration and Asylum
Bill 2002** 20

A change for the worse 21

Citizenship and nationality 22

Asylum 25

Detention and enforcement 27

Appeals 29

Criminal offences and powers 33

Border controls 34

Proposals relating to marriage and
relationships 35

Economic migration 37

Chapter 3
**Seeking and providing immigration
advice** 39

Regulation of immigration advisers 40

The Community Legal Service 43

Seeking advice in England and Wales 45

Seeking advice in Scotland and Northern
Ireland 46

SECTION 2
IMMIGRATION CONTROL IN PRACTICE 49

Chapter 4
**Applying to come into the United
Kingdom** 51

Applications made outside the United
Kingdom 52
Entry clearance 52
*Other documents, work permits and
certificates of entitlement* 55
When entry clearance is optional 55
*Entry clearances operating as leave to
enter* 56
Applying for entry clearance 59
Family settlement applications 61
Applications to come to work 63
Entry clearance decisions 63
Revocation of entry clearance 64
*Granting or refusing leave to enter before
arrival* 64

Immigration control on arrival 65

Persons who do not require leave 65

Persons who require leave 66

People who have leave or an entry clearance when they arrive 68

Decisions concerning entry and appeals 71

When the immigration officer cannot make an immediate decision 71

Illegible passport stamps 72

Entry from the Republic of Ireland and through the Channel Tunnel 72

Chapter 5
Leaving and returning 75

General rules 75

People who always qualify to return 77

People with the right of abode and certain British passport holders 77

People with indefinite leave 79

The 'returning residents' rule 80

People with limited leave 83

People whose leave does not lapse when they depart 83

People whose leave lapses when they depart 84

People who left the UK before 30 July 2000 85

People who wish to travel while an application or an appeal are outstanding 86

Those without passports or other travel documents 88

Chapter 6
Applying to stay in the United Kingdom 90

Switching categories 90

The need to apply in time 91

What status does a person have while waiting for a decision? 93

How to make the application 95

The prescribed application forms 95

Applications which do not need to be made on the prescribed forms 100

Home Office decisions 101

Where no application made 103

Notice of decisions 104

Exceptional Leave 104

Long residence concessions 105

Chapter 7
Identifying immigration status 109

Conditions of leave to enter or remain 109

Endorsements by ECOs 109

Endorsements by immigration officers 113

Endorsements by the Home Office 118

Other documents 121

Certificates of Entitlement 121

Work permits 121

Asylum-seekers 122

Refugees and those granted exceptional leave 122

Notice of temporary admission 126

Enforcement notices 127

Chapter 8
Problems, emergencies and solutions 130

Refusal of entry clearance overseas 131

Problems on arrival in the UK 133

Refusal of entry 133

Appeals 135

'Third country' asylum cases 136

Access to welfare and support 138

Arrest, detention and threatened deportation or removal 140

Contacting an MP 141

Using judicial review 142

SECTION 3
ASYLUM AND HUMAN RIGHTS 145

Chapter 9
Asylum under the Refugee Convention
147

The relationship between refugees, human rights and exceptional leave 148
Impact of incorporation of ECHR 149
Non-ECHR exceptional leave 149
Exceptional leave other than after refusal of asylum 150

Legal basis for asylum under the Refugee Convention 150
Changes made under the 1999 Act 151
The Convention as part of UK law 151
The asylum process 152

Refugee status under the 1951 Convention 153
Interpreting the Convention 153
Who is a 'refugee'? 153
Common issues arising under the Convention 161

Ceasing to be a refugee 167

Exclusion from Convention protection 168
The Terrorism Act 2000 170

Chapter 10
Asylum procedures 173

Procedures used when applying 174
Port applicants 177
In-country applicants 179
Asylum Registration Cards (ARC) and fingerprinting 181
The 'Statement of Evidence Form' (SEF) process 181
Asylum interviews 184
One-stop procedure 187
Providing evidence in support 189

Unaccompanied minor asylum-seekers 191

Dependants 192

Permission to work 194

Ways of discouraging asylum-seekers 195

Chapter 11
Home Office decisions on asylum 197
Home Office country information 197

Immigration rules and credibility 198

Certification of decisions 203

'Non-compliance' refusals 205

Third country cases 206
The Dublin Convention 208
The effect of the 1999 Act 209

The Home Office decision 212
Refusal of asylum 213
Decisions to grant refugee status 215

Exceptional leave 216

Delays 219
Backlog clearance 220

Fresh claims for asylum 220

Chapter 12
Family reunion and travel 222

Family reunion 222
Where the sponsor has refugee status 222
Where the sponsor has exceptional leave 227
Other family reunion policies 228
Refusals and appeals 228

Foreign travel 229
People with refugee status 229
People granted exceptional leave 230

Chapter 13
Human Rights 231

The ECHR rights 233
> *Restrictions on the ECHR rights* 236

Using human rights in immigration cases 239
> *Claims for protection* 239
> *Where removal will have a detrimental effect* 251
> *Family or other connections with the UK* 255
> *Making human rights claims* 266

Taking a case to Europe 268

Race discrimination in immigration 270

SECTION 4
TEMPORARY PURPOSES 273

Chapter 14
Visitors 275

Admission as a visitor 275
> *Business visitors* 280
> *Other special classes of visitor* 281

Applying for entry as a visitor 283
> *Entry clearance* 283
> *How long is a visitor admitted for?* 284

Appeals 285

Applying for extensions 287

Visitors applying to change their status 288

Carers 289

Transit visitors 291
> *Direct airside transit* 292

Medical visitors 293

Working holidaymakers 294

Travel outside the UK 296

Chapter 15
Students 297

Students and 'prospective' students 298
> *Entry clearance* 298
> *Entry clearance decisions* 303
> *Arrival in the UK* 304
> *Refusal of entry* 304
> *Family dependants* 305

Extending leave as a student 307
> *How to apply to extend* 309
> *Switching into student status* 309

Permission to work while studying 310

Studies including training 311
> *Nursing, medical and dental students* 311

Other students 312
> *Re-sitting students* 312
> *Writing up a thesis* 313
> *Students' union sabbatical officers* 314

Fees and student grants and loans 314
> *'Home' and 'overseas' student fees* 314
> *Student support* 315
> *Courses for asylum-seekers* 316

EEA students 317

Students who want to change their status 319

Working after studies 320

Travel outside the UK 320

SECTION 5
FAMILY AND DEPENDANTS 321

Chapter 16
Spouses, unmarried partners, same-sex partners and fiancé(e)s 323
> *Circumstances covered by the immigration rules* 324

People coming to the UK as spouses, unmarried partners, same sex partners or fiancé(e)s of people settled in the UK 326

Additional rules for spouses or fiancé(e)s 335

Additional rules for unmarried and same-sex partners 337

The requirement for entry clearance 339

How to apply for entry clearance 339

After entry clearance is issued 342

Refusal of entry clearance 344

People who have been admitted for the 'probationary period' who wish to apply to settle in the UK 345

Claiming benefits during the probationary period 345

Applying for settlement 346

Making the application 346

If the application is refused 347

'Switching' to stay in the UK permanently with spouse or partner 348

How to apply 349

Some problems which may arise 350

Can people switch to being fiancé(e)s? 351

When an application is successful 351

When an application is refused 351

People who cannot satisfy the immigration rules 352

Home Office policy in marriage cases outside the immigration rules 353

Unmarried and same sex partners who are illegal entrants, overstayers or have breached conditions of leave 355

Getting married 356

Making the application 357

Rights of appeal 358

Those who *no longer* have a relationship with a partner 358

Bereaved spouses and unmarried partners 358

Domestic violence concession 358

Marriage or relationship breakdown 361

Accompanying or joining a spouse or partner who is not settled in the UK 363

Workers and business people 363

Students 364

Other temporary categories 364

Chapter 17
Children 365

Children who have reached 18 365

Children who do not have to satisfy the immigration rules 366

Joining both parents settled in the UK 368

Children applying for entry clearance 371

Applying for settlement after one year 373

Joining a lone parent in the UK 373

Joining a person who is not a parent 378

Being joined by parents with whom there is contact 379

People who apply from outside the UK 380

People who apply when they are in the UK 381

Joining parents in the UK who have limited leave 382

Adopted children 384

Children who have already been adopted: applications under the rules 385

*Children who have already been
adopted: applications outside
the rules* 388

Children coming to the UK for adoption
388

Children whose parents may be forced
to leave and children who are in the
UK on their own 391

Unaccompanied children 393

Children born in the UK 396

Before 1 January 1983 396

On or after 1 January 1983 397

Chapter 18
**Relatives other than children and
spouses** 399

Parents and grandparents aged 65
or over 401

Other relatives 406

*Adult sons and daughters: some other
considerations* 407

More distant relatives 409

SECTION 6
WORKERS AND BUSINESS PEOPLE 411

Chapter 19
Workers 413

*Consequences of working
unlawfully* 414

The work permit scheme 416

*Business and commercial work
permits* 417

TWES permits 425

*Sportspeople and entertainers' work
permits* 427

Other work permits 428

Permit free employment under the
immigration rules 429

*Applying for extensions of stay and
indefinite leave* 432

Short-term workers 433

Persons able to work outside the
immigration rules 434

People who work for embassies and high
commissions 436

Chapter 20
Business purposes 438

Business people 438

Investors 439

*Retired persons of independent
means* 440

Writers, composers and artists 440

Innovators 441

Highly Skilled Migrant Programme 441

SECTION 7
**EUROPEAN RIGHTS OF FREE
MOVEMENT** 445

Chapter 21
**Background to free movement
rights** 447

Two systems of law 447

*The European Union and the European
Economic Area* 448

*The way the European Union
works* 448

European institutions 449

European Union legislation 450

*European law reflected in
UK legislation* 451

Chapter 22
Rights of free movement in the
European Economic Area 452

Who qualifies as being an EEA
   national? 452

When can rights of free movement be
   used? 453
   Workers and work seekers 453
   Self-employed people who have
   stopped economic activity 456
   Providers and recipients of services 456

Non-EEA national employees of
   businesses established
   in the EEA 457

Family members of EEA nationals 458
   Who is a 'family member'? 458
   Loss of free-movement rights 460
   UK nationals using EU law?: the
   Surinder Singh case 461
   EEA nationals using the 'ordinary'
   immigration law? 462
   Those admitted under the immigration
   rules later using rights of free
   movement? 464

Evidence of status 464
   Applying for residence permits,
   residence documents and family
   permits 467

Entry procedures 468

Decisions refusing or revoking
   rights 469
   Public policy grounds 469
   Enforcement and detention 470

The effect of claiming public funds 471

Rights of appeal 472

EU rights and obtaining indefinite
   leave 473

Chapter23
Association and Co-operation
Agreements 476

Central and Eastern European Countries
   (CEEC) Association Agreements 476
   Applying 478

Turkish Association Agreement 480
   'Stand-still' provision 481

Co-operation Agreements with Algeria,
   Morocco and Tunisia 482

The future 483

SECTION 8
DETENTION AND
ENFORCEMENT 485

Chapter 24
Powers of detention 487

Background to immigration
   detention 487
   Numbers detained 488
   Length of detention 488
   Places and conditions of detention 489
   Costs of detention 492
   Attitudes of immigration officers to
   detention 492
   Automatic bail hearings 493

Who can be detained? 493
   Detention of 'international
   terrorists' 496

The limits on the power to detain 497
   Court limitations 497
   ECHR limitations 498

Who is likely to be detained? 502
   Detention policy 502
   Oakington Reception Centre 506

Inspection of detention 509

Chapter 25
Getting people out of detention 510

Temporary admission, temporary release and restriction orders 510

Bail from chief immigration officer or police inspector 512

Bail from the adjudicator or IAT 513
Who cannot get bail 513
'Right' to bail from the IAT 516

Bail from Special Immigration Appeals Commission 516

Applying for bail before the Immigration Appellate Authority 517
The application for bail 517
Preparing for the bail hearing 518
Sureties 520
The bail hearing 522
Failure to answer to bail 524

High Court procedures 525
Habeas corpus proceedings 525
Judicial review proceedings 526

Chapter 26
Removal, deportation, illegal entry and criminal offences 527

Port removals 530

Administrative removal 531
Regularisation of over stayers scheme 532
Rights of appeal 533
Overstaying 533
Breach of conditions 534
Obtaining leave to remain by deception 536
Family members of those being administratively removed 536
Deciding whether a person should be administratively removed 537

Deportation 537
Recommendations for deportation 538
Conducive to the public good 540
Family members 541
The deportation process 541

Illegal entry 545
Entry without seeing an immigration officer 546
Entry without obtaining leave from an immigration officer 546
Entry in breach of a deportation order 547
Deception of an immigration officer 547
Removal and return 549

The process of removal 549

How people are traced 551

Powers of arrest and search 552

Criminal offences 553
Proposed changes to criminal offences in the 2002 Bill 556
The prosecution of asylum-seekers 557

SECTION 9
BRITISH NATIONALITY 559

Chapter 27
British nationality 561
Development of British nationality 561
The British Nationality Act 1981 562
Types of British nationality 562
Important changes since 1983 564

Establishing citizenship 564
Passports issued on or after 1 January 1983 565
Passports issued before 1 January 1983 565

British citizens 567

  Checking for British citizenship 567

  People born or adopted in the UK 568

  People born overseas 571

  British citizenship by descent 573

  Citizenship through Crown or designated service 575

British nationals who are not British citizens 576

  Right of readmission 576

  Passing on nationality to children 577

  British nationals with an East African connection 578

  British nationals from Malaysia 579

  British nationals from Hong Kong 579

Chapter 28
How to become British 583

Naturalisation 584

  Requirements 584

  The process of application 587

  Refusals 588

  Crown service 589

Registration 589

  Registration of adults 589

  Registration of children 590

Passports and travel documents 593

Deprivation of citizenship 594

SECTION 10
APPEALS 597

Chapter 29
Rights of appeal 599

The basic appeal system 600

When can people appeal? 601

The one-stop appeal system 606

  Notices under section 75 1999 Act 606

  Notices under section 74 1999 Act 607

  Completing the statement of additional grounds 608

  Preventing grounds being raised in existing appeals and preventing further appeals 609

Notices of decision and appeal 611

Particular appeals 614

  Human rights and discrimination appeals 614

  Asylum appeals where exceptional leave has been granted 617

  Family visitor appeals 618

  Special Immigration Appeals Commission (SIAC) 618

  Certified to prevent appeals to the Tribunal 621

Chapter 30
Conducting appeals 626

Appeal procedures 626

  Before the main hearing 628

  Preparing for hearing 633

  At the full hearing 637

Powers of adjudicators in deciding appeals 642

Appeals and other challenges after the adjudicator has determined the appeal 647

  Home Office personal service of certain determinations 649

  Judicial review 650

The Immigration Appeal Tribunal 651

  Preparing grounds of appeal to the IAT 651

  Before the IAT hearing 654

  At the IAT hearing 655

  After the determination of the IAT 655

SECTION 11
WELFARE 657

Chapter 31
Welfare benefits, housing, health and social services 659

'Subject to immigration control' test 660

Welfare benefits 664

Benefits affected by the 'subject to immigration control' test 665

Benefit rates of income-based JSA/income support and claiming for dependants 668

Refugees and back-dating claims for benefit 669

Additional tests for certain benefits affected by the 'subject to immigration control' test 670

Benefits which are not affected by the 'subject to immigration control' test 672

Links between the Home Office and benefit authorities 673

Further benefit rights for EEA nationals 673

Reciprocal agreements 674

Housing 674

Housing for the homeless 676

Allocation of housing accommodation 678

Social services 678

Immigration status restrictions on community care services 679

What services or assistance can be obtained? 681

Procedures: community care assessments 684

Children Act 1989 685

Provisions 686

Restrictions 686

Health care 687

Chapter 32
Asylum support 689

Who is entitled? 690

Who counts as an 'asylum seeker'? 690

Who counts as the 'dependant' of an asylum-seeker? 694

'Destitute' 694

NASS support or interim support? 695

NASS asylum support 696

Determining destitution 697

What support is provided? 699

Exclusions 703

Procedures 704

Interim asylum support 708

Deciding whether a person qualifies 708

Providing interim support 709

Exclusions 711

Procedures 711

Asylum support appeals 712

Rights of appeal 712

Appeal procedures 713

'Hard cases' support 717

Proposed changes 718

SECTION 12
Information 723

Useful addresses and telephone numbers 725

Home Office 725

Immigration Appeals Offices 726

Immigration Service Enforcement Units 726

Ports of Entry 726

Passport Agency 727

Detention Centres 728

Government Offices 728

Legal help and assistance 729

Law Centres 729

Complaints about advisers 729

British High Commissions and Embassies abroad 730

Immigration, asylum and nationality organisations 732

European and international organisations 736

Visa nationals, fees and overseas posts 737

Visa nationals 737

Selected fees 738

British posts overseas 726

Work-related applications 743

Shortage occupations list 743

Information technology 745

Other occupations 745

Highly Skilled Migrant Programme income band/country list 745

Commonwealth countries 748

Registering with the police 750

Countries whose adoption decisions are recognised in the UK 751

Abbreviations 752

Further sources of information 755

Glossary 757

CASE LIST 771

INDEX 781

Section 1 Immigration law and advice

Chapter 1
Introduction to immigration law   3
The development of modern immigration law   3
The system of immigration control   7
The operation of immigration controls   15

Chapter 2
Proposed changes: The White Paper and the
Nationality, Immigration and Asylum Bill 2002   20
Citizenship and nationality   22
Asylum   25
Detention and enforcement   27
Appeals   29
Criminal offences and powers   33
Border controls   34
Proposals relating to marriage and relationships   35
Economic migration   37

Chapter 3
Seeking and providing immigration advice   39
Regulation of immigration advisers   40
The Community Legal Service   43
Seeking advice in England and Wales   45
Seeking advice in Scotland and Northern Ireland   46

1   Introduction to immigration law

This chapter aims to explain the essential framework of immigration law. We briefly trace the historical development of the modern immigration system during the last century and summarise the Acts of parliament and other rules and regulations which comprise the current immigration law. We then turn to deal with the basic division in immigration law between those who need 'leave' to enter the UK and those who do not. We consider also the position of those people who do not fall neatly on either side of this divide, for example, nationals of other European countries. Similarly, we look at the interplay between a person's 'nationality' and immigration rights. It should also be noted that there is a glossary in Section 12 which helps to explain the various terms used.

In this chapter we also look at how the immigration rules, which are made by the Home Office, operate to regulate immigration control and we summarise the way in which the system of control operates, both in and outside the UK.

The *Handbook* as a whole is separated into both 'Sections' and 'Chapters' and this chapter also aims to indicate where in the book readers will be able to find the information they want. Chapter 2 of this section covers the current proposals for change to immigration law and JCWI's commentary on them. In the final chapter of this section, we look at the availability of immigration advice, give details of how to access that advice and explain how it is regulated so as to prevent bad advice being given.

The development of modern immigration law

About 150 million people worldwide (about 3 per cent of the world's population) live outside the country in which they were born. People emigrate for a variety of reasons: work, family connections and protection from oppression being prominent among them. It is an undeniable fact that those countries with a high proportion of migrants have been enriched by them, both culturally and economically. The National Health Service in the UK, for example, was short of around 17,000 nurses in 2000 with the result that the work permit scheme has been relaxed in an attempt to enable more nurses from overseas to work in the UK.

The increasing ease of transport and development in communications systems during the last century have been among the factors which have led to increased population flows during that time. The UK system of immigration control is indeed a twentieth-century phenomenon. Legislation to control the circumstances in which those who are not British citizens can enter or remain in the UK has, in particular, escalated in the last few decades. As a result, the law relating to immigration, nationality and asylum procedures has become increasingly more complex and detailed over that time. The political interest in immigration and the methods of control, while they have always been close to the current affairs of the day, has never been higher.

Early immigration law

Before 1905, there were no immigration laws in the UK. The entry of people who were not British subjects was technically part of the royal prerogative, and the monarch could also make decisions to expel individuals or groups of people. The Aliens Act 1905 was passed, after two decades of intermittent agitation, in order to prevent refugees, mainly Jewish, poor and fleeing from eastern Europe, from seeking refuge in Britain. The Act only applied to boats carrying more than 20 passengers and to those travelling steerage class who could be excluded if they were 'undesirable', defined mainly as being unable to support themselves and their dependants. The Act applied to 'aliens' which meant people who were not from any part of the British empire. It did, however, set up the first rudimentary machinery for checking entry, which was later expanded and developed.

The post Second World War period

At the end of the Second World War, Britain had to take stock of its role in the world. The effects of the war, and the growing campaign for independence in India, made it clear that the old imperial arrangements had to change. The status of British subject, with its central notion of allegiance to the Crown, was becoming outdated, and from 1949 it was replaced by the new status of Citizen of the United Kingdom and Colonies (CUKC). The term 'British subject' was kept to refer to all the citizens of the Commonwealth. CUKCs had rights to enter and live anywhere in the Crown's dominions, and when Britain looked for labour to rebuild its war-damaged economy, the young men who arrived on the Empire Windrush in June 1948, and those who followed them, arrived as citizens. Indeed, many of the settlers who arrived aboard such ships were ex-servicemen and volunteers who had worked in Britain during the war.

Restrictions set in:
the Commonwealth Immigrants Acts in the 1960s

It was not until the 1960s that racist agitation led the government of the day to consider restrictions on the rights of nationals outside the UK. Two statutes were introduced to bring in controls, the Commonwealth Immigrants Acts of 1962 and 1968. The 1962 Bill was implemented relatively slowly and was opposed by Labour under the leadership of Hugh Gaitskell. However, in their 1964 election manifesto, Labour's approach was to accept the existence of the legislation, at least until new agreements with the Commonwealth governments could be negotiated.

With Labour in power, in March 1968 the second Act was rushed through parliament in three days. The effect was to deny entry to hundreds of thousands of East African Asians settled in Kenya, Uganda and Tanganyika, who were UK passport holders, unless they had a parent or grandparent born, adopted or naturalised in the UK. It constituted a shameful failure to honour assurances previously provided as to the rights of these passport holders. These Acts were followed by the Immigration Appeals Act 1969 which established a system of immigration appeals.

The foundation of current immigration law: the Immigration Act 1971

The structure set up by the above three Acts paved the way for the Immigration Act 1971, passed by the Conservative government, which came into force on 1 January 1973 and still provides the basis of immigration controls in the UK (►see below). It has increasingly been amended in the years since then, firstly by the Immigration Act 1988. The 1971 Act finally ended major, permanent primary migration to the UK from Africa, the Indian sub-continent and the African-Carribean.

By coincidence, the Immigration Act 1971 came into force on the very day that Britain joined what was then known as the 'Common Market', the European Economic Community, which was to open up immigration controls for nationals of all the European member states at precisely the same time as the legislative curtain was being pulled down on non-white migration. The Treaty of Rome, which formed the basis for this European co-operation, had among its central principles the right of free movement of workers and the self-employed.

Asylum and legislation in the 1990s

With rising numbers of people coming to the UK seeking asylum, in the 1990s Conservative governments brought in two major pieces of legislation largely aimed at dealing with the influx of asylum-seekers. In July 1993, the Asylum and Immigration Appeals Act 1993 was introduced. Before that time, asylum was only really mentioned as an afterthought in the immigration rules. The 1993 Act effectively incorporated the 1951 Refugee Convention into the immigration rules and enabled all asylum-seekers to appeal on asylum grounds against negative decisions by the Home Office. It also, however, put the safe 'third country' removal process on to a firm footing, allowed asylum cases to be certified as being 'manifestly unfounded' and it also removed important rights of appeal including those of certain visitors and students.

The Asylum and Immigration Act 1996 extended the certification process to many more categories of asylum-seeker, introduced sanctions on employers who gave work to those unauthorised to take employment and imposed severe restrictions on the welfare entitlements of both those seeking asylum and others.

The Labour government, elected in 1997, set about a major review of immigration and asylum policy. The early abolition of the iniquitous 'primary purpose' test, under which fiancé(e)s and spouses had to demonstrate that the motivating factor of their marriage was *not* to obtain settlement in the UK, proved a false dawn for all those who had for long campaigned for a just immigration system. Although accompanied by new rights of appeal based on the Human Rights Act 1998, the Immigration and Asylum Act 1999 introduced a summary form of removal for those who had gained entry to the UK and would previously have had procedural protection under the 'deportation' process. It re-cast the appeals system with a focus on a single appeal right accompanied by draconian powers to deny appeal rights if grounds to stay in the UK are not raised at the earliest possible stage. It sought also to prevent asylum-seekers from arguing in a court that their removal to a European Union member state may be unsafe because those countries offered less protection; arguments which many asylum-seekers had previously won. It imposed the indignity of vouchers and the isolation and insecurity of dispersal throughout the UK upon those seeking protection but who had no means of financial support.

The 1999 Act also made substantial changes to the very structure of immigration controls. It did this, however, largely by amending the 1971 Act, which remains the cornerstone of the system for control. The 1999 legislation also imposed duties on registrars to report 'suspicious' marriages, strengthened the powers of immigration officers in the enforcement of immigration controls, extended sanctions against those carrying improperly documented passengers into the UK and implemented a system for the regulation of immigration advice.

The current position

Although it was a huge piece of legislation, unfortunately, the 1999 Act did not consolidate all of the existing immigration Acts of Parliament into one. This means that *parts* of all the legislation introduced from 1971 (▶see above) are still in force as well as the 1999 Act. *In addition*, separate Acts of Parliament deal with nationality (the British Nationality Act 1981 – see below) and appeals in national security cases (the Special Immigration Appeals Commission Act 1997). The 2002 Bill (▶see Chapter 2), although it proposes to amend some of the existing law, will also sit alongside the present legislation. Immigration advisers will therefore have to refer to and become familiar with yet another fairly extensive piece of legislation.

It should also be noted that much of the detail of immigration law and procedure are contained in what is called 'secondary' legislation. These are regulations, rules and orders which the government is given a power to make under the main Acts of Parliament, and which apply, for example, to immigration and asylum appeals, the 'one-stop' appeals procedures, the giving of notices of immigration decisions, the requirements to register with the police and the asylum support scheme.

The system of immigration control

Certain people are hardly affected by immigration controls. The 1971 Act defines the class of people who have the 'right of abode' in the UK (British citizens and some Commonwealth nationals ►see Glossary on page 768) and states that they may freely reside in and come and go to and from the UK. Of course, they have to demonstrate that they are entitled to the right of abode when they come into the UK by, for example, producing their British passports and showing them to the immigration officer. The main divide in immigration law is between those who enjoy the right of abode and those who do not. The majority of people who do not have the right of abode require a specific form of permission in order to enter or remain in the UK. The technical term for this permission is 'leave' and we refer to 'leave' throughout the book.

For many years lawyers and Home Office officials have described those who need leave as being people who are 'subject to immigration control'. This is the definition used in the 1996 Act. In this edition, we do not use that phrase to describe this class of people because there is now a new definition of people 'subject to immigration control' contained in section 115 of the 1999 Act. In the 1999 Act, the term is used to describe people who are excluded from various forms of welfare provision. To avoid confusion, we therefore only use 'subject to immigration control' when dealing with welfare entitlements (the provision of welfare and the new system of asylum support is dealt with in Section 11). We describe those who do not have the right of abode, simply as persons who 'need leave' to come to or stay in the UK.

There are, however, certain special groups who do not easily fit the division between those who need leave and those who have the right of abode ►see pages 13-15 below.

A selection of the multitude of different stamps and forms which denote different kinds of immigration status are reproduced in Chapter 7 in order to enable applicants and advisers to identify quickly the status which a person has.

Immigration law and nationality law

'Nationality' is a branch of law in its own right. Questions of nationality or 'citizenship' are closely connected to immigration law because a person's nationality is central in determining what immigration rights they have, but nationality and immigration should nevertheless not be confused. The kind of passport which a person holds depends on their nationality although a passport is only *evidence* of a person's nationality, it is not the ultimate source of it.

Unlike in most countries, nationality and citizenship in UK law are not the same thing. This is because, largely as a result of Britain's colonial past, there are various different kinds of British nationality. It is *not* the case that all British nationals have the right of abode, namely the right to freely enter and live in the UK, free from immigration controls. Only one of the categories of British nationals, known as 'British citizens', carries that right. The link between holding a British passport and being able to come and go freely from the United Kingdom was broken by the Commonwealth Immigrants Acts referred to above.

The main Act of Parliament which now governs nationality is the British Nationality Act 1981. Section 9 of the *Handbook* deals with nationality law. Chapter 27 explains the various different kinds of British national and the different immigration rights which they enjoy. It also explains how to check whether someone is a British citizen and explains the other small category of people who have the 'right of abode'. Chapter 28 explains how people can become British citizens through processes known as 'naturalisation' and 'registration'.

'Leave' and the immigration rules

As to those who need leave in order to enter or stay in the UK, the Acts of Parliament do not set out who should and should not be granted 'leave' nor for how long they should be given it or on what conditions. This is the role of the 'immigration rules' which the Home Office is given the power to make by the 1971 Act. The rules are always entitled 'Statement of Changes in Immigration Rules', and are a convenient way of making law because they can be altered so much more easily than Acts of Parliament. All that is required is that a copy of the proposed new rules is laid before Parliament, where they are subject to what is called the negative resolution procedure. This provides that the new rules may come into force straight away (bigger changes may be postponed to take effect later), and remain in force unless MPs call for a short debate, which may be in committee rather than the whole House of Commons. In that debate it is possible for the rules as a whole to be voted down or accepted, they cannot be amended. A statement of immigration rules has only once been voted down in this way.

As the papers in which the rules are set out all carry the same title, they are known by their numbers. These are prefixed either by HC (for House of Commons paper) if the House is sitting at the time, or, if a change is introduced during a parliamentary recess, by Cmd (for Command paper). Sometimes, rather than amend the rules, the Home Office issues a whole new statement of rules to replace the previous statement. The last time this happened was in 1994 when the present statement known as 'HC395' was laid. It came into force on 1 October 1994 and has been amended since then. The Home Office has indicated that a new consolidated statement of immigration rules is being considered but no time-scale has been disclosed.

Categories of entry under the immigration rules

The rules set out various categories in which people can be granted leave: 'visitor', 'student', 'work permit holder', 'investor', 'spouse', 'unmarried partner', 'au pair', 'refugee' etc. In each category, the rules indicate different requirements which need to be satisfied before a person can be granted leave. For example, a student needs to demonstrate that, among other things, they are able and intend to follow their course of study, and that it is a 'full-time' course.

The vast majority of the categories under the rules require that the applicant can be 'maintained and accommodated' without recourse to public funds. We look at the maintenance and accommodation requirements in detail on pages 328-335. Most of what is explained there applies to these requirements wherever they are to be found in the immigration rules although there are slight variations in the way in which the rules are phrased. For those categories under the rules which are sometimes known as 'temporary purposes' (for example, visitors and students), applicants generally need to show that they intend to leave the UK when the purpose of their stay is over.

The rules also set out the general grounds upon which leave can be refused in any category, other than asylum, even if all of the conditions for the individual category are satisfied.

We deal with the different categories in which people who need leave can enter the UK in separate sections of the *Handbook*.

- Section 4 covers people who are coming to the UK for temporary purposes, including visitors of many different kinds, working holiday-makers and students. The arrangements for finance for students (fees, loans, grants), including EEA students, are also set out in this section.

- Section 5 deals with those who seek to enter or remain as family members. Separate chapters are given to spouses and partners, children (including adopted children) and other relatives. This section deals both with family members who want to join their relatives in the UK permanently and those who are seeking to join their relatives who are here for a limited period. The right to respect for private and family life under Article 8 ECHR is very important to immigration cases involving family members; full details are contained in Chapter 13, pages 255-266.

- Section 6 concerns people who want to come to the UK for work or business purposes. There are many different categories covered here including the work permit scheme, 'permit-free' employment, short-term workers, working outside the immigration rules and the highly-skilled migrants' programme.

In each section, there is a statement of the requirements of the rules which need to be satisfied for the particular category, an explanation of those requirements and practical details about the evidence needed to meet them. There are also details about whether a person can extend their leave in the category, how long an applicant will be able to stay in the UK and information about the rights of any dependants which they have. Details of appeal rights are also included but for comprehensive information about appeals ►see Section 10.

Leave outside the immigration rules

The rules do not, however, cover every circumstance and the immigration authorities always have a discretion to grant leave outside the immigration rules. Some important issues are left as matters of policy outside the rules, and are usually thought of as being 'concessions'. These include the 'long residence concessions', otherwise known as the '10-year rule' and the '14-year rule'. The different 'concessions' are dealt with in the *Handbook* in the part where the concession is most relevant but for a general explanation of the exercise of discretion outside the immigration rules and a list of the most important concessions ►see pages 104-105. The term 'exceptional leave' is also dealt with there.

Limited leave and indefinite leave

The immigration rules also spell out what period of leave is granted to people entering the UK in the various different categories. Leave can either be 'limited' or 'indefinite'. Limited leave is granted to all those who are coming for temporary purposes. Other categories, on the other hand, may lead to the applicant being allowed to stay in the UK permanently under the immigration rules by being granted 'indefinite' leave. Many of these categories first require a person to have been in the UK with limited leave for a particular period. Those categories which are work-related generally require that an applicant has been in the UK for four years with limited leave in that category before they are eligible for indefinite leave. Applicants for indefinite leave as a foreign spouse, however, only have to serve a one-year qualification or 'probationary' year. For unmarried partners, the probationary period is two years.

Some people can be granted indefinite leave straight away, for example, relatives, other than spouses and partners, who qualify to come to the UK permanently. Although the immigration rules state that those recognised as refugees are to be given limited leave, as a matter of practice, since July 1998 they have also been granted indefinite leave straight away.

Another term with a meaning similar to indefinite leave is 'settled', which is used to refer to anyone who normally resides in the UK and who has no limitations or conditions on their right to stay here. Therefore, all those who have indefinite leave or the right of abode in the UK and who ordinarily reside in the UK are referred to as being 'settled'. Those who have indefinite leave are able to leave and return to the UK under a special category under the immigration rules called 'returning residents'. *Anyone* who has indefinite leave, regardless of the basis upon which the indefinite leave was granted, can use the returning residents rule. This category is therefore dealt with separately as part of our general explanation of the practical arrangements of immigration control ▶see pages 79-83.

Conditions of leave

Where a person is granted limited leave, conditions may be imposed on it. The possible conditions are:

- a condition either prohibiting all employment or business activities or restricting a person's employment or business activity to a particular kind;
- a condition requiring the person to maintain and accommodate themselves and their dependants without recourse to public funds (for the meaning of 'public funds' ▶see page 329).
- a condition requiring the person to register with the police (▶see page 535 and page 750 for more details).

In some (but not all) cases, the immigration rules indicate what, if any, conditions should be imposed on the leave. We indicate the usual conditions which are attached to leave in the parts of the book where we deal with the different categories of entrant. However, for a quick reference ▶see the summary on pages 110-111 which sets out the combinations of conditions which are given to people in the different categories. Immigration officials refer to these different combinations of conditions as 'codes'.

Indefinite leave *cannot* be made subject to any conditions.

Where leave is not granted

In most (but not all) circumstances in which a person who needs leave is either refused leave or no immediate decision can be made whether to grant them leave or not, one of two things may happen to them. They can either be granted a form of 'temporary admission' or they may be detained. 'Temporary admission' is a technical term but is also used loosely to describe the various bases upon which the immigration authorities can let a person stay in the UK for the time being while immigration processes are taking place, for example while a decision is being made or arrangements for removal are being put in place. Conditions can be attached to temporary admission and it can be brought to an end at any time. A description of the different forms of temporary admission is on pages 510-511.

The powers of immigration detention under the 1971 Act are an alternative to temporary admission. Other than at Oakington Reception Centre for certain asylum-seekers, it is Home Office policy only to detain people where it is strictly necessary to do so, for example, if there is a risk that they would abscond. Detention is dealt with in Section 8 of this

Handbook. Chapter 24 sets out the powers of detention and includes the various limitations on those powers, including those imposed by Article 5 ECHR (the right to liberty and security). It also contains details of the Detention Centre Rules which regulate the treatment of people while they are detained. Chapter 25 contains information about how to get people out of detention and looks at the practical aspects of making bail applications and of bail hearings.

Asylum and human rights

In the past 10 years asylum law has changed beyond recognition and it continues to be subject to rapid change. The law on asylum stems from the United Nations Convention on the Status of Refugees of 1951, amended by a Protocol in 1967. Before 1993, it was not entirely clear what status this had in UK law and very little was written down about the status of refugees, how their cases should be determined, or what their rights were. The Refugee Convention became part of British law through the Asylum and Immigration Appeals Act 1993 which states that the immigration rules must not be read as allowing the immigration authorities to do anything which contravenes the UK's obligations under the Convention.

The numbers claiming asylum continued to rise in the 1990s and a very large proportion of the case-loads of many solicitors and advisers consists of asylum cases. As indicated above, most of the recent legislative provisions have focussed on asylum-seekers. We deal with asylum in Section 3 in which there are separate chapters covering the definition of 'refugee', the detailed procedures for handling asylum claims and Home Office asylum decision-making (including decisions in 'third-country' cases). The benefits of obtaining asylum are substantial: in particular, refugees can bring family members to the UK without having to satisfy the rules relating to maintenance and accommodation (see Chapter 12).

Human rights

The incorporation of the rights guaranteed by the European Convention of Human Rights (ECHR) by the Human Rights Act 1998 (HRA) has made important changes to all areas of immigration law. Advisers must now always consider whether their case involves any human rights issues. The most important of the rights, as far as immigration lawyers are concerned, are Article 8 (family and private life) and Article 3 (►see below). Although, human rights is a significant topic of itself, this chapter comes within the section dealing with asylum because, in so many asylum cases, applicants raise human rights issues as part of their claim to remain in the UK. Chapter 13 on human rights, however, does contain general details about the way the HRA works, all the different rights which have been brought into UK law and how to interpret them, and the variety of ways in which they may be used in immigration cases.

When we refer to 'asylum' and 'asylum-seekers' in the *Handbook*, we generally use these terms to refer to those who are seeking 'refugee' status under the 1951 Convention. However, the ECHR has had an important impact on asylum law. In particular, Article 3 ECHR, namely freedom from torture or inhuman or degrading treatment or punishment, prevents people from being returned to a country in circumstances where they may be exposed to any of those forms of harm. It has, therefore, added a layer of protection to the asylum system which is important for those who might not satisfy the strict definition of 'refugee' (for the added protection provided by Article 3, in particular ▶see the box on pages 243-244). In some areas of immigration law, for example the system of asylum support, a claim for 'asylum' is now defined as including a claim under Article 3 as well as under the 1951 Convention ▶see page 690.

Exceptional leave following an asylum claim

Anyone who is granted leave outside the immigration rules can be described as having been given leave 'exceptionally'. However, exceptional leave or 'ELR' has also been used by advisers and Home Office officials in a narrower sense to refer to leave which is given to a person who does not qualify for refugee status but who deserves some form of international protection. This form of exceptional leave is also dealt with in Section 3 on pages 216-219.

It should be noted, however, that the Home Office grants exceptional leave to those who have been successful in human rights claims. It is bizarre that the immigration rules themselves do not set out and regulate the leave that should be granted to successful human rights claimants. Leave which is given to them is not given as an act of discretion because the immigration authorities are required to respect applicants' human rights. Paragraph 2 of the immigration rules simply states that the immigration authorities should carry out their duties in accordance with the ECHR but, other than that, the rules are silent on human rights. The granting of 'exceptional leave' to human rights applicants has meant that the policy which sets out the circumstances in which exceptional leave would be granted has become less important because there is a large overlap between the two.

Special groups

Certain groups of people need to be considered separately from the general divide between those who have the right of abode and those who need leave. Included in these groups are those who can benefit from European rights of free movement and various categories of people who are 'exempt' by immigration law from having to obtain leave. The European rights of free-movement for EEA nationals, their family members and the rights provided for in the connected 'Association Agreements' are all dealt with in detail in Section 7. Exemption from immigration control for diplomats is looked at on pages 436-437. We now turn to look briefly at each in turn.

European rights of free-movement

Nationals of the countries of Europe have immigration rights which do not come from UK law but from European law in the form of the EC Treaty and the various directives made under it. The Home Office has had to change its ways of dealing with these cases drastically in the years since 1973, as court cases have gradually shown how far-reaching European free movement rights are. These rights are extended beyond the member states of what is now the European Union (EU) to include three associated states from the old European Free Trade Area, Norway, Iceland and Liechtenstein, which, together with the EU countries, now form the European Economic Area (EEA). EEA nationals can enter the UK without requiring leave to do so, and in this way, even though they do not have the right of abode, they are free from the scheme of immigration control set up by the 1971 Act. Having entered, they are free to take up any employment (with a very few exceptions, mainly in the higher reaches of the civil service and in areas where national security is an issue), or to set themselves up in business or in self-employment.

The immigration rights of nationals of these countries are, however, dependent on them exercising rights of free movement which are recognised by European Community law, namely as workers, self-employed persons, providers or recipients of services, people who are self-sufficient, retired persons or students. They can also be excluded from exercising free movement rights on grounds of public policy, public security or public health. Spouses and other close family members of EEA nationals can also benefit from these free movement rights even if they are not themselves EEA nationals. The government has made regulations (the Immigration (European Economic Area) Regulations 2000) which describe the free movement rights although they are not the source of them.

A number of Eastern European countries, which are not members of the EU, have concluded 'Association Agreements' with the countries of the EU which enable nationals of those countries to migrate in order to establish themselves in business or self-employment. They are sometimes called the 'Europe' Agreements. Again, the source of these immigration rights is not domestic law but the rights they give rise to are also set out in the immigration rules. An older and somewhat different Association Agreement exists in relation to Turkey.

Irish citizens are, of course, EEA nationals, but they already had a special status in British immigration law before the two countries joined the Common Market. There has been no passport control between the two countries ever since the formation of the Irish Republic, and Irish people have always been able to come and work in the UK freely. In effect, they are treated as though they have indefinite leave just by virtue of their nationality. This is not affected by European law, but the rights applying to members of their families who are not themselves Irish are now more clear-cut as a result of European law.

Diplomats and others

The following groups of people can be exempt from immigration controls: diplomats, certain staff and officials of embassies, high commissions and international agencies; employees in the service of foreign governments; members of foreign governments or their representatives in the UK on official business and people attending certain international conferences. Certain family members are also exempt. The exemption from immigration control, which means that they do not need leave, only continues for as long as the person keeps the status for which it was given.

Armed forces

Members of the UK armed forces, a Commonwealth force undergoing training in the UK with UK armed forces and members of visiting armed forces coming to the UK at the invitation of the government, are also exempt from immigration control.

Ship and aircrews

A person who arrives in the UK as the member of a ship or aircraft intending to leave as part of the ship's crew or to leave within seven days of arrival, is also exempt from immigration control.

The operation of immigration controls

Immigration controls operate both overseas and in the UK. Section 2 of the book deals with the general operation of immigration controls and should be referred to on this subject. In particular, Chapter 4 deals with the operation of controls outside the UK for those who wish to travel here and what happens at the port of entry. Chapter 5 covers the situation of those who wish to travel from the UK and return back again and Chapter 6 looks at applying to extend stay in the UK for a limited or indefinite period. The question of 'switching' status from one category of leave to another is covered on pages 90-93. Common problems and emergencies which frequently arise in the practical operation of controls and suggested solutions are dealt with in Chapter 8.

What follows, therefore, is only the briefest overview of the operation of controls, which is dealt with largely in Section 2, and an introduction to some of the concepts and terms used.

In the *Handbook*, we use the term 'immigration authorities' as a shorthand to refer to all those officials who can make decisions about applicants to come to and stay in the UK. They include:

- entry clearance officers (ECOs) who make decisions at British posts abroad about whether people should be permitted to come to the UK ▶see pages 739-742 for a list of posts abroad, the different entry clearance facilities offered by each and the cost of making applications. There is an inter-departmental body which straddles the Home Office and the Foreign and Commonwealth Office called 'UK Visas' (it has recently changed its name from the 'Joint Entry Clearance Unit') which oversees the work of ECOs at the posts abroad;

- immigration officers who are generally responsible for immigration control 'on entry', that is when a person arrives in the UK. They also, however, play an important part in the enforcement of immigration control, namely the detention and removal of those who are not permitted to be in the UK. The immigration service gives their officers different ranks. As well as ordinary immigration officers, there are chief immigration officers and immigration inspectors;

- officials of the Secretary of State for the Home Department who are part of the 'Immigration and Nationality Directorate' (IND) of the Home Office and who are responsible for 'after entry' immigration controls, namely, applications for extensions of stay in the UK. They also have a significant role to play in the enforcement of immigration controls. Until recently, there was a division of responsibility where a person wished to enter or remain in the UK with a work permit. The Department of Work and Pensions (previously the Department of Education and Employment) would decide whether to grant a work permit and the IND would be responsible for the 'immigration' decision to grant or refuse leave. Work Permits (UK), the section which issues work permits, has now been brought within the Home Office and is generally responsible for both decisions. Asylum applications, even if made initially to an immigration officer at port, are always referred to the IND to decide whether the person actually qualifies for asylum, but they may then be referred back for the immigration officer to actually issue the grant or refusal of leave.

Leave to 'enter' and leave to 'remain'

Leave is divided into 'leave to enter' and 'leave to remain'. Naturally enough, a person who arrives in the UK and seeks entry, is given or refused leave to enter. A person who has already entered, whether by having been given leave to enter or having entered illegally, is given or refused leave to remain. Most applications for leave to remain have to be made on prescribed application forms ▶see pages 95-97.

In accordance with the above divisions of responsibility, the traditional operation of controls was always that immigration officers would grant or refuse leave to enter and the Home Office would deal with applications for leave to remain (and see s4(1), 1971 Act). This division of responsibility is, however, becoming somewhat blurred. Officials at the IND are now able to grant or refuse leave to enter to asylum-seekers so as to avoid delays caused by the system whereby the asylum claim is referred by the immigration officer to the IND, which considers the claim and then refers the case back to the port to implement the immigration decision. These powers have not yet been fully implemented. In addition, immigration officers have the power, acting on behalf of the IND, to make decisions to 'vary' (that is to extend or add or remove conditions) leave when a person arrives in the UK who already has leave (see para 31 HC395).

The traditional areas of responsibility are also likely to be broken down in relation to powers of detention. The 2002 Bill proposes changes which will allow a wider group of personnel to authorise detention and/or temporary admission in certain circumstances than is presently the case.

Non-lapsing leave

Changes under the 1999 Act have meant that not all leave 'lapses' when a person leaves the Common Travel Area (CTA) ▶see below. A person may now leave and return to the UK with their leave still fully in force. The way in which this works is explained on page 76.

Entry clearance

'Entry clearance' is the term given in immigration law to documents issued by the immigration authorities which count as evidence that the person is entitled to enter the UK under the immigration rules. Entry clearances must be applied for and obtained from an ECO while the applicant is *outside the UK*. 'Visa national' is the name given to a person who requires an entry clearance for entry to the UK *whatever* the purpose for which they wish to come to the UK, ▶see page 737 for a list of visa national countries. Non-visa nationals will require entry clearance depending on the *purpose* for which they wish to come the UK. For a full explanation of the different terms used to cover entry clearance ▶see pages 52, 55.

Changes made under the 1999 Act have meant that entry clearances can now operate as leave to enter the UK. This has caused much confusion and we explain the way in which these entry clearances operate on pages 56-59. Examples of the new style entry clearances which have this effect are on page 112 in the chapter dealing with identifying immigration status.

The Common Travel Area

The 'Common Travel Area' (CTA) comprises the UK (England, Wales, Scotland, Northern Ireland), the Channel Islands, the Isle of Man and the Republic of Ireland. No immigration control as such operates on journeys within the CTA – passports are not checked. However, because there is no passport control, complicated rules exist to control the situation of people who travel within the CTA who are not EEA nationals. It is still quite possible to enter the UK unlawfully from elsewhere in the CTA even though a passenger had no intention of doing so and came on a commercial flight or ship perfectly openly ▶see pages 73-74.

Enforcement of immigration controls

We use the word 'enforcement' of controls in the book to refer to all the different ways in which people can be required to leave the UK. Enforcement does not have to include detention but often does so and, therefore, we include a chapter on enforcement at the end of the section which also deals with detention. The precise procedure which is operated to force people to leave depends on their immigration status. Chapter 26 therefore describes the separate enforcement procedures which apply in the case of:

- 'port removal' of people who have, arrived, applied for and been refused leave to enter;
- illegal entrants, namely, those who obtained entry to the UK in breach of the immigration law and who are not permitted by the immigration authorities to remain here;
- 'administrative' removal of people who were granted leave but have either breached their conditions of leave, overstayed their leave or who obtained leave to remain by deception;
- deportation, which applies in very few cases following the introduction of administrative removal by the 1999 Act. Administrative removal replaces the powers of enforcement for many people who would previously have been 'deported'. Deportation now only occurs in cases where the Home Office decides that it is 'conducive to the public good', or a criminal court has recommended that a person be deported after convicting them of an offence, or if a person is the 'family member' of a person who is being deported.

The enforcement chapter also looks briefly at other forms of enforcement which are very rarely used. Also covered are the various criminal offences which may be committed which are relevant to immigration control.

Appeals

At present there is a two-tier structure of immigration and asylum appeals. The first appeal is to an adjudicator and thereafter there is an appeal to the Immigration Appeal Tribunal. Together, the adjudicator and Tribunal are known as the 'Immigration Appellate Authority' (IAA). The higher courts (the Administrative Court which is part of the High Court, the Court of Appeal and the House of Lords) can also be accessed in certain cases.

Where rights of appeal exist in relation to different immigration decisions, we flag them up throughout the *Handbook*. In Section 10, however, we deal fully with the rights of appeal which exist under the appeals system and the restrictions and limitations which are placed on them. Among other details, the section contains a summary of the time limits which apply in immigration and asylum appeals ▶see pages 613-614, the powers which the IAA has ▶see pages 642-647, an explanation of the 'one-stop' procedure ►see pages 606-611, the procedure for bringing human rights appeals ►see pages 614-617 and details about appeals concerning national security matters which are heard by the Special Immigration Appeals Commission (SIAC) ►see pages 618-621.

Chapter 30 focuses on practical matters concerning the actual conduct of immigration appeals, in particular the procedures which are operated before the adjudicator and the Tribunal and identifying grounds of appeal to the Tribunal ►see box on pages 652-653.

It should be noted that there are some particular, specialised appeals which we look at in the chapter most relevant to them and not in the section dealing generally with appeals. These are:

- the rights of appeal which are available (or not available) in cases where the immigration authorities are trying to remove an asylum-seeker to a 'safe' third country ►see pages 206-212;

- appeals against decisions in cases involving EEA nationals and their family members ►see pages 472-473;

- appeals and reviews in cases where a person is being detained as a 'suspected international terrorist' under the Anti-terrorism, Crime and Security Act 2001 ►see pages 516-517;

- appeals against decisions of the National Asylum Support Service (NASS) to refuse or to withdraw asylum support ►see pages 712-717.

- bail applications are not 'appeals' as such but for details about making them ►see pages 517-525.

2 Proposed changes

The White Paper and the Nationality, Immigration and Asylum Bill 2002

The Home Office published its White Paper on immigration policy, *Secure Borders, Safe Haven: Integration with Diversity in Modern Britain* on 7 February 2002. The period for consultation was extremely short and only three weeks after the consulting period ended, the government introduced the Nationality, Immigration and Asylum Bill 2002 into the House of Commons. The 2002 Bill sets out the legislative framework for many, although not all, of the changes proposed in the White Paper. Not all of the White Paper proposals need to be contained in primary legislation (a new Act). Some are practical proposals which do not need any legislation at all and have already been introduced. Where this is the case, the changes are incorporated into the *Handbook*. In other cases, the proposals can be effected through amendments to the immigration rules.

This chapter summarises the changes proposed in the 2002 White Paper. In some cases, the proposed changes are set out in more detail in boxes in the relevant chapter in the book. This is the case in particular in relation to the appeals proposals ▶see pages 622-625, the proposed changes in the asylum process and support for asylum-seekers ▶see pages 719-721, the nationality proposals ▶see pages 594-596 and the general asylum proposals ▶see pages 170-172. In addition, in most places where there is likely to be a change, this is 'flagged' up in the text throughout the *Handbook*. Although the government hopes that the new Bill will be passed before the end of 2002, it is not clear when all of the proposals (if they are all proceeded with) will actually become effective and they are likely to be brought into effect at different times. Many of the proposals will also need what is called 'secondary' legislation (regulations or orders) made under the Act. When enough of the changes have been brought in, JCWI plans to update this edition.

The point of this chapter is two-fold:

- to summarise the main proposed changes conveniently in one place;
- to provide JCWI's comments on them.

JCWI has set out its concerns about the 2002 White Paper and Bill through a series of public and parliamentary briefings, all of which are available on JCWI's website (www.jcwi.org.uk) or by contacting JCWI directly.

A change for the worse

In the months preceding the introduction of the White Paper, the Home Secretary spoke about 'managed migration'. He recognised 'the positive contribution of migration to our social well-being and economic prosperity' and called for the need to encourage those resident abroad to come to the UK 'on a sensible and managed basis.' It was hoped that these sentiments might mark a new direction for immigration policy, free of the restrictions of the past and one which truly embraced the diversity of the UK's existing communities and welcomed the strengthening of them. Since the end of large-scale primary migration to the UK in the decades after the Second World War, immigration control has been effective in restricting permanent migration. Permanent migration has generally been confined to those with particular family ties in the UK, EEA Nationals and others who have been able to gain access to the UK employment market through the restrictive work permit system and the 'permit-free' employment categories under the immigration rules, and those accepted as refugees.

There are certain positive proposals contained in the White Paper and the Bill which are to be welcomed. For example, the proposals to end discrimination against 'illegitimate' children for nationality purposes and to make provision in the immigration rules for unmarried partners who *choose* not to marry in addition to those who are legally unable to marry. However, the general thrust of the proposals is to focus immigration policy upon ever more regulation, enforcement, control and punishment. What avenues are opened up are limited to access to the UK for a highly-skilled elite whose migration can always be justified, even to those most sceptical about migration, as serving a particularly narrow, economic self-interest of the UK. Wider humanitarian concerns, the general desirability of increased world-wide integration and the actual demands of a growing economy suffering from skills shortages are not adequately met by the practical proposals contained in the 2002 White Paper or the Bill.

JCWI believes that the proposals will have a profoundly negative impact both on the fairness and effectiveness of the system and also on the public perception of migration to the UK. It is little wonder that public opinion comes to view immigration and asylum as 'problems' which need to be 'solved' when it is fed an official diet which points to the 'need' to segregate asylum-seekers and their children, to detain more of them and enforce their departure. The government is also encouraging the false perception that there are vast numbers of short-term visitors whose only real interest is in contracting non-genuine marriages in order to deceive the immigration authorities and obtain settlement. Further, it tries to characterise those who are making perfectly valid applications and seeking to appeal against negative decisions as people intent on cynically manipulating the system.

There can be no better way of entrenching a 'them and us' mentality than to create a set of rituals around the prize of citizenship which call for public pronouncements of allegiance and classes of instruction to ensure that applicants are sufficiently socialised into 'British' culture. It is tragic that, at the same time that blunt racism has once again gained a toe-hold on political power through local council elections, a Bill is debated which provides material which may be used to fertilise rather than contradict the attitudes which the far right espouse.

Citizenship and nationality

The proposals

The starting point for the discussion in the White Paper around nationality is a sense of failure in race relations arising from the disturbances in the summer of 2001 in Bradford, Oldham and Burnley. The implication is that a proportion of the people who obtain citizenship by naturalisation adhere to cultural values which conflict with those held by the wider British community. The argument continues that competence in the English language and understanding of British values is essential to the effective exercise of rights as a citizen.

The 2002 Bill spells out the following set of measures designed to 'ensure social integration and cohesion in the UK':

- those who apply for naturalisation must have 'sufficient knowledge about life in the UK' and courses will be provided to ensure that this is the case;

- there will be a regulatory framework to ensure that applicants for naturalisation have 'a sufficient knowledge of the English, Welsh or Scottish Gaelic language'. Attendance on courses may be required to ensure that a particular standard is reached. The requirement is to be extended to those applying for naturalisation as the spouses of British citizens who are currently exempted;

- an updated oath of allegiance to be called a 'citizenship oath and pledge'. The suggested pledge is as follows:

  'I will give my loyalty to the United Kingdom and respect its rights and freedoms. I will uphold its democratic values. I will observe its laws faithfully and fulfil my duties and obligations as a British citizen.';

- the citizenship oath and pledge is taken at a 'citizenship ceremony' at local authority facilities such as registrars' offices and community halls;

- extended powers of 'deprivation' of citizenship to enable the Secretary of State to take away British citizenship status from a person who 'has done anything seriously prejudicial to the wider interests of the UK'. In the 2002 White Paper, the government explains that it plans to use its powers of deprivation against those who have concealed material facts such as their past involvement in terrorism or war crimes;

- an appeal against the power of deprivation. The Secretary of State is, however, given wide discretion to deny the right of appeal if he feels the decision was taken on the basis of information which cannot be made public on grounds relating to 'matters of a political kind'.

The 2002 White Paper and Bill also propose the removal of:

- the exemption which permitted race discrimination by a public authority in the exercise of nationality functions;
- the current distinction between legitimate and illegitimate children ▶see pages 567-568, 397;
- the current provision in the British Nationality Act 1981 which states that there is no duty on the government to give reasons for refusing citizenship applications.

The White Paper also makes a commitment to shortening the waiting time for naturalisation applications.

Commentary

Significant progress has been made in recent years in improving naturalisation procedures and the service provided to applicants. JCWI welcomes the commitment to deciding all applications within three months by April 2004.

There are, however, positive reasons to retain the informality of the current procedures for naturalisation. They are attractive and user-friendly to those who would find formidable and threatening the symbolically-charged procedures favoured in continental Europe and Northern America. The British Nationality Act 1981 already requires that applicants for naturalisation (except for those married to British citizens) possess a sufficient knowledge of the English, Welsh or Scottish Gaelic languages. The requirement is only pragmatically enforced. The proposal in the 2002 Bill that a specified level of competence is required will serve as a disincentive to apply. It will also result in the exclusion of that group of people who, for a range of reasons, such as their educational back-ground and childcare demands, may not be able to attend the required courses or pass the required test. The effect of emphasising the importance of English as the 'norm' also has the effect of de-valuing the community languages which are spoken in the UK, rather than encouraging *all* people to expand their language abilities or at least to be sensitive to and accommodating of those with different language skills.

The proposed requirement that applicants for naturalisation attend a specified course to gain 'sufficient knowledge about life in the UK' and take a newly drafted loyalty pledge is based upon the flawed and inherently racist assumption that the discharge of responsibility as a good citizen is conditional upon adherence to core 'British' values. Good citizenship, we suggest, is based upon common objective values such as understanding, integrity, and respect. Those values are universal, they are not peculiar to any particular culture, national tradition or religion. Again, the practical requirement to attend a course and also to pass a test will mean that those unable to do so will be denied their right to acquire the citizenship of the country they are settled in.

The proposed measures attempt a shift in the granting of citizenship from the recognition of a right to the giving of a privilege. Obtaining citizenship should not be made similar to admission to a private club where the applicant has to convince the existing members that their 'face fits the mould' so that the character of the club will remain as it has always been. A policy based on true diversity would recognise that the 'club' is constantly evolving and growing and that there is nothing to fear from the admission of those who bring with them their own traditions and cultures which, properly understood, in fact reflect the same basic principles of decency and respect by which we all hope to live.

Asylum

The proposals

The White Paper treats as a key objective the introduction of a 'managed system of induction, accommodation, reporting and removal centres to secure a seamless asylum process'. The Home Secretary put it more bluntly when he told the media that he wanted an 'end to end system ... to track and deal with asylum-seekers at every stage'. Some of the proposals in the White Paper have been implemented and the other proposals await the implementation of new legislation drafted into the new Bill. The proposals include (▶see pages 170-172 and pages 719-721 for fuller summaries):

- an Application Registration Card (ARC) with the capability of carrying immense amounts of information ranging from biometric data identifying the holder, to conditions of residence ▶see page 122 for an example and ▶see pages 171 and 181 for more details. These are being phased in during early 2002 for new asylum-seekers and existing Standard Acknowledgement Letters (SALs) are expected to be replaced;

- a network of induction, accommodation and reporting centres. Induction centres will house asylum-seekers and their families for a short period of time after their arrival, and from there, if they are destitute, they will be placed in other NASS accommodation which may be an 'accommodation' centre. Four trial accommodation centres will house approximately 3000 people. Each centre will provide in-house health and education facilities. Induction and accommodation centres are not detention facilities although strict residence requirements will be imposed. The Home Office is also in the process of establishing a network of reporting centres at certain police stations and other Home Office facilities;

- no choice as to type of support. NASS will be able to choose what type of support to offer someone, for example, support provided through an accommodation centre. If they refuse to take up such support, NASS may refuse to provide any other types of support;

- cash payments to support asylum-seekers and to replace the much-maligned voucher scheme;

- support will not be provided in the form of a 'cash only' option. It is proposed to remove the option of obtaining support (vouchers or cash) for essential living needs alone; such support will only be provided together with NASS-allocated accommodation;

- conditions of temporary admission will also become conditions on which asylum support is granted. This means that asylum support may be terminated if conditions of temporary admission are breached;

- tightened (but unspecified) procedures in respect of unaccompanied asylum-seeking children (UASCs) to 'sift out adults posing as children at the earliest possible stage', and a reaffirmed commitment on behalf of the Home Office to reach initial decisions in 60 per cent of all UASC cases within two months;

- the creation of 'legitimate gateways for refugees seeking asylum' in co-operation with the UNHCR, Red Cross and other bodies who will assist in identifying refugees abroad who are in need of resettlement.

Commentary

Current asylum policy, while it pays lip service to the UK's fundamental obligations to provide protection to those fleeing from persecution under the Geneva Convention, is essentially based on deterring people from coming to the UK and removing them from the country. The White Paper recognises that the integrity of the current system is in question, but fails to recognise the real reasons for this. Of great concern to everyone are the delays in the system but these are not generally caused by applicants seeking to spin procedures out to maximise their stay in the UK. Applicants and their advisers are forced to comply with ever more restrictive time deadlines to ensure that, for example, asylum statement of evidence forms and 'one-stop' appeal notices are returned within time. If they are not, asylum-seekers are penalised and, indeed, the tight limits operate to the prejudice of their being able to fully present a case and collect all the available evidence.

The false premise of the 2002 White Paper is that integrity will be restored to the system by measures aimed at high levels of monitoring and surveillance of asylum-seekers whose applications are under considera-tion. However, delays and lengthy appeals are caused by matters such as poor decision-making (often based on inaccurate country information), failures to respond to additional grounds raised in one-stop notices, wrongly made decisions that a person has not complied with asylum procedures (►see further on pages 205-206) and endemic delays in implementing decisions following successful appeals to adjudicators which prevent the smooth integration into the community of refugees and those granted exceptional leave. In addition, the dispersal system has made it difficult for very many asylum-seekers to obtain the expert legal advice and representation they need to ensure that their cases are effectively progressed. Leaving aside entirely the question of the fairness and justice of the asylum system, which many applicants believe is lacking, these are all indications of a system which is not operationally sound.

Even faced with immense obstacles in establishing their claims, including the culture of disbelief prevalent in decision-making and often inadequate legal advice, it is well to remember the many asylum-seekers who succeed in establishing their cases. The statistics demonstrate that in 1999, 48 per cent of asylum applicants were granted refugee status or exceptional leave. In 2000, up to 30 per cent of applicants were granted refugee status, exceptional leave to remain or had their appeals allowed. The statistics for 2001 demonstrate that 26 per cent were granted refugee status or exceptional leave, without taking into account the number of successful appeals.

Asylum Support

The government had no choice but to end the voucher system. Through-out its relatively brief existence, the voucher scheme became notorious for its degrading impact on asylum-seekers and its effect in encouraging discrimination against them. However, the proposals for accommodation centres and to double the detention estate will serve only to encourage unfounded fears that asylum-seekers are people from whom the rest of the community needs to be protected. Although they are not detention centres, the restrictive conditions of accommodation centres and their location in isolated areas will impose a significant restraint upon the liberty of the people placed there. As with similar hostels elsewhere in Europe, they could also become targets for racist attacks, with barbed wire and security guards becoming a feature of the centres.

The centres will cater for families with children as well as single people. In-house education facilities for children as well as health services will be provided. The removal of children of asylum-seekers from standard schooling provided by local education authorities and the lack of super-vision by the Department for Education and Skills or OFSTED, establishes a two-tier education system which may be vulnerable to challenge under Article 2 of the First Protocol ECHR (the right not to be denied an education) taken together with Article 14 (prohibition on discrimination). Linked to the separation of asylum-seekers' children from local authority education is the increased facility for the detention of asylum-seeking families. Restrictions upon detaining families with children were removed in October 2001 so that they may now be detained in the same circumstances as childless asylum-seekers.

It is hard to imagine circumstances in which a government would propose the detention of British citizen children who have committed no offence and who are no danger to the community. The approach to children in particular illustrates that, increasingly, asylum policy legitimates standards of treatment of asylum-seekers which would be considered wholly unacceptable if applied to other sections of the community.

The majority of asylum-seekers will continue to be supported by NASS through the dispersal system while the performance of the trial accommodation centres is assessed. Although a cash-based system is being put in place to replace vouchers, asylum-seekers will continue to be expected to live on 70 per cent of basic income support levels. The levels were increased in line with benefit from 8 April 2002 ►see pages 700-701 for the present rates. Unlike people on income support or income-based job-seekers' allowance, however, asylum-seekers, even those with young children, are prevented from accessing benefits such as milk tokens and vitamins. In addition, unlike NASS, local authorities have no rates set down in regulations despite the fact that they will continue to have responsibility for the support of certain asylum-seekers under the 'interim' support scheme which has now been extended to 5 April 2004. The support provided by the different authorities is often inexplicably below the rates at which NASS provides support. Both the British Medical Association, and the Child Poverty Action Group have stated that levels of support provided for asylum-seekers are inadequate and damaging to good health.

The proposed removal of the 'cash only' option will prevent asylum-seekers from receiving any form of support if they choose to live with their friends or family rather than being dispersed into NASS accommodation. It is likely that many asylum-seekers will forgo NASS accommodation, creating even more pressure on already deprived communities. This compulsion to reside in dispersed NASS accommodation or in accommodation centres may give rise to issues under Article 8 ECHR (right to respect for private and family life). Requiring those asylum-seekers who could otherwise provide for their own accommodation needs to accept NASS accommodation also does not appear to be a sensible policy for a government concerned about the allocation of scarce resources and the existing demand upon local housing authorities.

Detention and enforcement

The proposals

The proposals are:

- a 40 per cent increase in detention capacity and the re-designation of existing detention centres as 'removal centres';
- the repeal of most of Part III of the 1999 Act (bail provisions). Part III of the 1999 Act was designed to ensure that detainees are given automatic bail hearings after a set number of days ►see page 493. The justification put forward for this is that these hearings would be:

'inconsistent with the need to ensure that we can streamline the removals process in particular...The significant and continuing expansion of the detention estate since the proposals were first put forward would make the system unworkable in practice';

- the expansion of the power of adjudicators to grant bail to all deportation cases (the White Paper commits the government to finally bringing in this power which is actually contained in the 1999 Act);

- the extension of certain of the immigration powers to detain, grant temporary admission and bail to Home Office officials where those powers had previously been exclusive to immigration officers (in some cases together with police inspectors);

- the removal of 2,500 failed asylum-seekers every month (this target was originally set by the Home Secretary in June 2001) and 30,000 by Spring 2003;

- the power to remove family members of port applicants and illegal entrants. At present, there are powers to enforce the departure of family members of those being deported or subject to administrative removal under section 10 of the 1999 Act. However, family members of those being removed, having been refused leave to enter the UK or as illegal entrants, cannot be removed unless they are liable to be enforced against in their own right. One of the reasons for this proposed change is to ensure that non-British citizen children born in the UK, who would otherwise be irremovable, can be removed with their parents in all circumstances.

Commentary

Detention is now firmly embedded as part of the government's immigration and asylum policy. The number of detention places available has increased threefold, from approximately 900 in 1997 to just under 2,800 by the end of 2001 with the creation of new removal centres at Harmondsworth, Dungavel and Yarl's Wood. Part of the Yarl's Wood complex was destroyed in a fire in February 2002. Although the centre is currently not housing any asylum-seekers, the majority have been detained in alternative accommodation, including prisons (in contravention of the commitment given by the Home Secretary that prisons would no longer be used to detain immigration detainees as of January 2002).

The re-designation of detention centres as 'removal centres' has been described by refugee campaign groups as misleading. At the end of March 1999, 60 per cent of asylum detainees were awaiting an initial decision.

The automatic bail hearings proposed by Part III of the 1999 Act would at least have ensured a minimum level of independent scrutiny of all detentions. Their repeal ends the possibility of this basic procedural safeguard coming into effect. Although it will remain open for those detained to apply for bail, it has been a feature of the current system that many immigration detainees do not know that they have a right to apply and there is a perception among some that applications will not be successful unless sureties offering several thousand pounds are available.

The extension of powers of removal to family members of illegal entrants and those being removed having been refused entry enables this additional group of family members, who have not in their own right contravened immigration controls, to have their departure enforced. One effect of the proposal will be to undermine Article 8 claims where certain family members have leave to be in the UK and would not otherwise be immediately liable to removal. As indicated above, one of the major concerns underlying the proposal is the position of certain British-born children. The proposals represent a further erosion of the rights of children born on British soil, which began with the removal of their automatic right to citizenship by the British Nationality Act 1981. Such children cannot be assumed to have rights to enter and reside in the country or countries of their parents.

Appeals

The proposals

The Immigration and Asylum Act 1999 introduced the 'one-stop appeal' requiring an adjudicator to consider one immigration appeal which would include all other appealable matters including allegations of human rights breaches. The 2002 White Paper observes that there have been delays in the system and that it has caused confusion and states the need to re-structure and simplify the process, in particular so that human rights claims are 'dealt with in a timely fashion and do not frustrate the removals process'.

The 2002 Bill proposes a number of measures (▶see pages 622-625 for a fuller description) including:

- clarification and simplification of the 'one-stop' process;
- defining the specific 'immigration decisions' which can attract appeals. This is particularly intended to ensure that human rights and discrimination appeals cannot be brought against *any* administrative decision, such as the setting of removal directions so as to prevent multiple appeals;
- a right of appeal if the Home Office intends to act on a recommendation for deportation made by a criminal court. In these circumstances the Home Office will issue an initial decision to make a deportation order;
- a new right of appeal against the power to make a decision to 'revoke' indefinite leave which is, in itself, a new proposal;
- denial of 'upgrade' asylum appeals where an applicant is granted exceptional leave for 12 months or less;
- allowing adjudicators to take into account evidence about changes of circumstance after the date of the decision in *all* appeals (i.e. not just asylum

and Article 3 ECHR appeals) *except* appeals against decisions of entry clearance officers. In appeals against ECO decisions, the adjudicator will *not* be allowed to consider any evidence which was not available to the ECO;

- no right of appeal against decisions to refuse applications to enter or remain for a purpose not covered by the immigration rules;
- appeal procedure rules to provide a statutory closure date to prevent multiple adjournments of appeals pending before an adjudicator and to prevent adjournments except in strictly defined circumstances;
- increasing the number of adjudicators by 50 per cent and increasing the processing of appeals from 4,000 cases per month to 6,000 cases per month by November 2002;
- limiting the jurisdiction of the Immigration Appeal Tribunal so that it can only overturn determinations of adjudicators where they are wrong on a point of law;
- preventing judicial review of decisions by the Tribunal to refuse to grant leave to appeal by introducing a separate statutory review procedure;
- ending certification of asylum and human rights appeals which prevents further appeals to the Tribunal.

Commentary

'One-stop' process and human rights appeals

The 'one-stop' appeals process and the system for bringing human rights appeals has confused both applicants and immigration officials. The procedures can be unnecessarily repetitive (►see page 188) and JCWI welcomes clarification of the procedures. However, for the one-stop process to work effectively, it is essential that the additional grounds raised by applicants are properly considered by the Home Office before the appeal, as is intended to be the case under the present system. In practice, this frequently does not occur with the result that many appeals unnecessarily proceed to hearing where they are conceded or allowed on points which should have been considered earlier.

JCWI is also concerned that the definition of appealable 'immigration decisions' excluding matters such as the setting of directions for removal will enable the immigration authorities to prevent applicants appealing on human rights/discrimination grounds by simply not issuing a 'decision' in response. This will happen in those cases where the Home Office is of the view that there is no real need to give consideration to the matters of substance which are being raised. Similar disputes have arisen where applicants have made human rights claims following asylum appeals in which they were not able to raise human rights points ►see pages 615-617 and *Pardeepan*. The likely result is the spending of a great deal of time and energy on legal procedures to determine whether the applicant should be able to appeal which would more productively be spent on dealing with the human rights appeal itself.

Structure of appeal system and judicial review

In addition to the above proposals, the government has also mooted moving towards a one-tier appeals system. It is essential that a two-tier appeals structure is retained. The increasing complexity of the decisions which adjudicators have to make is illustrated by the number of cases in which the Tribunal grants leave to appeal. The frequently changing nature of country conditions in asylum and human rights cases combined with the possibility of further evidence on particular points also make it desirable that the Tribunal retains its broad powers to allow appeals even if there was no error of law by an adjudicator. The alternative is that more 'fresh' applications are made with further appeals.

The government is concerned about the possible abuse of judicial review by applicants and their advisers simply to delay removal. Advisers are required to apply rigorous tests before they obtain public funding for judicial review applications. The judicial review mechanism is a critically important legal safeguard which enables the higher courts to supervise decisions made by the immigration appellate authorities whose determinations are not invariably of such high quality that no such regulation is necessary.

No appeal where application is outside the immigration rules

The proposal to prevent appeals where the application is for a purpose not covered by the rules is a backward step. At present, certain appeals about entry and extensions of leave are denied if particular requirements of the rules are not satisfied (requirements relating to length of stay, age, nationality, citizenship, the possession of an entry clearance or work permit). In addition, the immigration rules prevent adjudicators from re-considering the exercise of *discretion* where the application is outside the immigration rules (see paras 320(1), 322(1), HC395).

However, wrong exercises of discretion and misapplications of the rules are not the only grounds on which people can bring appeals and it is still possible to succeed in appeals where an applicant is arguing that the decision is 'not in accordance with the law', for example, because the immigration authorities have failed to properly apply a concession outside the rules. Denying rights of appeal in these cases will mean that applicants are either forced to try to squeeze their appeal grounds into human rights claims so that they can appeal or resort to judicial review.

Appeals following a recommendation to make a deportation order

The inability to appeal when the Home Office decides to implement a recommendation of a criminal court that a person be deported has always been an anomaly in the system. There were discussions during the passage of the 1999 Act about introducing a right of appeal in these circumstances but, for reasons which were unclear, the proposal was dropped. The inclusion of the right of appeal in the current legislation is welcome. It is to be hoped that this time it will be put into effect, albeit too late to benefit all those who have been deported following recommendations since October 2000.

Changes of circumstance after the date of decision

It is sensible that, in all appeals, the adjudicator or the Tribunal is able to consider the facts at the time of the hearing rather than at the date of the decision. This is only presently the case for asylum appeals and appeals raising Article 3 ECHR.

However, together with this positive proposal, comes a very negative one. The proposal in the Bill is also that in ECO appeals, the appellate authorities will only be able to consider the evidence that was before the ECO. This is a step back from the current position which allows all evidence relevant to the situation at the date of the decision to be considered. The result will be that applicants will have to be absolutely comprehensive, often at great expense and trouble, in producing everything they could conceivably need to rely on to the ECO at the application stage. This is in case their application is refused and they then need to appeal. Where further evidence is available and was not produced in time for the initial decision, applicants may be forced to make a further application in order to have that evidence considered. The result is both unfairness and an unnecessary waste of time and expense for applicants.

'Upgrade' appeals

The denial of appeals to 'upgrade' to asylum status for those who have only been granted exceptional leave for up to 12 months is a proposal to reverse the effect of the decision of the Court of Appeal in *Saad & Diriye* ►see pages 617-618, for this category of applicant. Such applicants who have an arguable legal challenge against the refusal of asylum and who need asylum, for example, because they have close family members abroad with whom they seek reunion, will be forced to bring judicial review proceedings. The proposal therefore contradicts the government's stated aim of reducing the need to resort to judicial review in immigration cases.

Speed and adjournments

The government is obsessed with the speed of the appeals process. This is evident in the proposals to increase the number of adjudicators and the number of cases heard each month, and in the proposal to further limit the circumstances in which adjournments can be granted.

JCWI's view is that, although swift determination is desirable for all, this should not be at the expense of an appeals system which operates fairly and provides high quality decisions. Adjudicators must be sufficiently well trained so as to be able to cope with the complexity of immigration and asylum cases and it must be recognised that adjournments often prevent cases from having to be re-heard or reviewed again at a later stage in the process.

The existing procedure rules prevent adjournments unless refusing the adjournment would prevent the 'just disposal of the appeal'. Any attempt to define the precise circumstances in which appeals can be adjourned will inevitably lead to injustice in cases where there are good reasons but which do not fit the rigid criteria. Many cases are adjourned at present because the adjudicators' lists are over-loaded and there is insufficient time in the day to hear all the cases on the list. Listings should be realistic and it must be recognised that the time of appellants and their representatives is just as valuable as that of the appellate authority. Where their time is wasted, there is also a cost to the public purse.

Criminal offences and powers of the immigration authorities

The proposals

The 2002 Bill proposes the creation of a number of new offences, duties and the expansion of the powers of immigration officials as follows:

- new powers to enter business premises to search for and arrest immigration offenders and to inspect and seize personnel records following the arrest of an immigration offender on those premises;
- increased powers to arrest employers without a warrant for employing those who are not entitled to work and a change in the defence available to employers ▶see pages 415-416;
- a duty upon local authorities, employers and the Inland Revenue to disclose information relevant to a particular person to the immigration authorities;
- the creation of the following new offences:
- assisting another person to breach the immigration laws of any EU member state;
- trafficking of people into or out of the UK for the purpose of prostitution;
- forgery relating to Application Registration Cards;
- failure to comply with a notice requesting information in respect of suspected immigration offences;
- possession of an immigration stamp without a reasonable excuse.

Commentary

Problems relating to fraud, illegal entry and illegal working have emerged from a failure of the current and previous governments to develop policies and strategies for the proper management of all forms of migration. The implementation of a system to effectively tackle fraud and other forms of illegality cannot be disassociated from the need to develop a comprehensive immigration strategy which offers appropriate channels for travel and admission to the UK for everyone with reasonable expectations of entry to visit or join family members, to work or to seek protection under international conventions.

Increasing the prosecution of employers and imposing tougher penalties are measures which are likely to be absorbed as business risks by unscrupulous employers into whose hands those who are not permitted to work will fall resulting in their greater exploitation. Increasing the powers of immigration officers to enter and search only paves the way for driving the employment of such workers further underground. An alternative approach, consistent with the White Paper's aspirations in creating greater opportunities for legal migration, would be a comprehensive programme for the regularisation of those presently working unlawfully.

Border controls

The proposals

The White Paper comments on the numbers of people trying to get across the Channel to the UK from places like the Sangatte centre near Calais in France. It states that the objective of the government should be that those who have no claim to be in the UK are prevented from coming to the UK. The following measures are proposed in the 2002 Bill and White Paper:

- an 'authority to carry' scheme requiring carriers (those who transport people to the UK) to pay a penalty if they bring to the UK someone whom they did not have the authority to carry. The proposal enables the government to make regulations requiring a wide range of carriers to seek prior authority from the Home Office before bringing certain classes of people (possibly based on their nationality) to the UK;
- the continued deployment abroad of immigration officers to carry out 'pre-clearance' checks;
- the continued use of Airline Liaison Officers to advise airlines on passengers who do not carry the right documents for entry to the UK;
- the use of technology such as heartbeat sensors to detect those concealed in vehicles;
- the use of biometric technology to check the identity of people seeking entry.

Commentary

Pre-clearance operations, visa regimes and Airline Liaison Officers have been developed and used in recent years as instruments of government policy to deprive refugees of the opportunity to exercise their rights under international conventions to travel to the UK to seek asylum. In some instances, as the pre-clearance scheme put into operation at Prague airport in the Czech Republic in July 2001 has shown, the work of the immigration authorities in maintaining this form of immigration control has involved probable discrimination on grounds of race and ethnic origin.

A new 'authority to carry' scheme will enable carriers to check the details of passengers against Home Office databases and identify 'potential threats to immigration control and security'. This is a dangerous proposal because it could alert the national authorities of the country where a passenger resides to the whereabouts of that individual with the result that a potential asylum-seeker is then arrested and detained.

The emphasis of the new proposals should be to create routes of entry for migrants, including asylum-seekers, as opposed to restricting the movement of those who may otherwise be entitled to protection. The government does propose a 're-settlement' scheme for refugees possibly based on a quota system. There are, of course, already certain schemes in operation but they offer very limited opportunities ▶see pages 174-177. Any development of these schemes should not be at the expense of preventing people from travelling to seek protection.

Proposals relating to marriage and relationships

The proposals

The 2002 White Paper condemns what it sees as an increasing number of 'bogus' marriages where the applicant may have paid someone else to go through a marriage ceremony or have used a corrupt adviser to arrange such a marriage for them. The same chapter in the White Paper also talks about the government's expectation that the number of arranged marriages between people born in the UK and those living abroad will decline. The following proposals are not incorporated in the 2002 Bill but may instead be implemented through revised immigration rules:

* increasing the probationary period for leave on the basis of marriage from one to two years;

* introduction of a 'no-switching' provision to prevent persons applying to remain on the basis of their marriage if they have been in the UK for six months or less;

* removing the requirement from the immigration rules that unmarried partners must be legally unable to marry before they can obtain leave;

* removal of the probationary period for a couple who have been married or co-habiting for five years or more.

Commentary

Positive proposals

The abolition of the probationary period for those together for five years is of course welcome but likely to benefit only a small number of applicants. Welcome also is the proposal to make provision in the rules for partners who do not choose to marry in addition to those who are legally prohibited from doing so. It probably constitutes discrimination in the enjoyment of their Article 8 rights, for those who do not wish to marry but who are in stable, settled relationships to be denied immigration rights equivalent to married couples or those in same sex relationships.

Increase in probationary period

The probationary period for marriages is proposed to be increased from one to two years on the grounds that 'it will be harder to sustain a relationship for this longer period with a duped partner and it is more likely that, when questioned or interviewed, the lack of a genuine or subsisting relationship will become apparent'. These assumptions are not sustained by evidence. It is common knowledge that people in unhappy marriages are capable of enduring life together for prolonged periods in order to conform with external expectations.

The probationary period itself is known to cause tensions within marriages and relationships. The concession relating to domestic violence had to be implemented in recognition of the fact that, in a few marriages, the male partner may take advantage of his wife's insecure immigration status resulting in abuse. Same sex and unmarried partners currently have a two-year probationary period. It would have been far better to have levelled their rights up rather than the rights of married couples down. The effect on immigration control of course is that applicants will remain in the system for twice as long as they would otherwise have done with the additional administrative expense and inconvenience which that causes.

New 'no switching' rule

The proposal to introduce a 'no-switching' rule to prevent people who have entered the UK for temporary periods of six months or less from applying for leave to remain on the basis of marriage is wholly unwelcome. The White Paper fails to make any sort of argument that the current arrangements present a problem to the administration of immigration control. Instead, it draws the inference that marriages arranged within a short space of time cannot be sustained permanently. It represents an assault upon a cultural norm particular to many ethnic communities for whom marriages may be arranged within a short period of time. The existing immigration rules, under which it must always be shown that the marriage is genuine and that there is an intention to permanently live together, provide a completely adequate safeguard against the problem that the government perceives.

The further comment made in the White Paper is that it is unlikely, given the number of these applicants, that they:

'...would develop permanent relationships within such a short period of time, the indication is that many of these persons had intended to marry all along but had not obtained leave to enter on this basis and had therefore lied about their intentions to the entry clearance officer'.

If this concern really does accurately reflect the situation, it is surely the case that the immigration authorities would declare such people to be illegal entrants (by deception) with the result that they would not then be able to benefit from the marriage or partnership rules.

Arranged marriages

The statement in the White Paper that 'there is a discussion to be had within those communities that continue the practice of arranged marriages as to whether more of these could be undertaken within the settled community here' is an indication that the government intends to become prescriptive about who and where someone from the ethnic communities should marry. In JCWI's view, this is not an appropriate area for the state to intervene. Cultural practices involving marriage and family are matters of choice for the individuals concerned. Attempts at social engineering are unlikely to be effective and are likely to prove counter-productive to building harmonious relations between cultures.

Economic migration

It is recognised in the 2002 White Paper that there is a shortage of workers in certain sectors of the UK economy. The White Paper reviews the current recruitment difficulties faced by employers and acknowledges that they occur at both high and low levels of the skills spectrum to the detriment of productivity and economic growth. The relevant chapter in the White Paper also expands on the concept of managed migration, stating that new routes of entry to the UK for work purposes will counter both illegal working and clandestine entry.

The proposals

The 2002 Bill does not contain any proposals for legislative change in relation to economic migration. The White Paper, however, proposes the following measures, some of which have already been implemented:

- the Highly Skilled Migrant Programme (HSMP) which enables those who can score a requisite number of points based on their previous earnings, qualifications and skill levels, to come to the UK to look for work. This programme is already in operation as a pilot scheme. For a full explanation ▶see pages 441-444 which must be read together with the income bands for the different countries, for which ▶see pages 746-747;

- allowing post-graduate students to switch into work-permit employment. This provision is already in operation as a concession outside the immigration rules ▶see pages 320, 421-422;

- expansion of the seasonal agricultural workers' scheme beyond the agricultural sector to 'meet the demands of short-term casual labour'. It is envisaged that the government will introduce quotas in consultation with businesses and trade unions;

- expansion of the working holidaymakers scheme under the immigration rules to nationals of non-Commonwealth countries, and review of the current restrictions both on the age of applicants and the requirement that employment should only be 'incidental' to the holiday. The latter restriction is currently not being enforced for working holidaymakers in the teaching and health sectors. For further discussion of the scheme and the proposed changes ►see pages 294-295;
- bringing those who advise on work permit applications within the regulatory scheme of the Office of the Immigration Services Commissioner (OISC);
- charging for work permits. Details of how the proposal may work in practice have already been set out in a consultation paper and a new scheme may be introduced during the early part of 2003.

Commentary

The proposals are very specific and facilitate the settlement of workers with very high skill levels only. Despite suggestions that the reform of economic migration policy would be extended to cover workers without formal skill qualifications, this has not materialised. The admission of workers for the purpose of unskilled employment will be restricted under the seasonal workers scheme to short-term, casual workers, who have no rights of family reunion and are expected to return abroad. The possible introduction of quotas would be an unwelcome and unnecessarily in-flexible development. The working holidaymakers scheme is aimed at young people enjoying an extended holiday in the UK and should not be regarded as a main plank in a programme for labour migration.

The HSMP is innovative in that it allows those abroad without a firm offer of employment in the UK to come to *seek* employment or self-employ-ment. The points-based system that regulates the entry of those under the scheme is, however, unduly restrictive and potentially discriminatory. Although an attempt has been made to divide the scales of existing salaries into bands depending on the country from which the applicant comes, they remain weighted in favour of those from developed countries. Comparatively, the wages of highly-skilled public sector workers from mainly black developing countries are very low.

Taken as a whole, the proposals are unlikely to bring about the kind of major change necessary to allow the UK to meet the level of demand for labour migration in the modern world. A process of fundamental review of many of these aspects of immigration policy has been under way at least since 2000 when important changes to the work permit scheme were announced which have made it more accessible to migrant workers with a wider range of skills and experience. However, until the legal avenues of entry are opened up on a far wider scale, the existing proposals will not have the desired effect of both reducing irregular entry to the UK and redressing the existing labour shortage.

3 Seeking and providing immigration advice

The law concerning immigration, nationality and asylum has become ever more complex. The Immigration and Asylum Act 1999 is an enormous piece of legislation but it does not consolidate all of the previous Acts of Parliament concerning immigration into one. There are still important parts of the law contained in earlier legislation, most importantly in the Immigration Act 1971. An understanding of immigration procedures is also not complete without reference to the many pieces of secondary legislation (known as 'Orders', 'Regulations' or 'Rules') which supplement the main legislation, the Human Rights Act 1998, the relevant parts of the Treaty of the European Community (and the immigration-related Regulations and Directives made under it) and the domestic and European decided cases which interpret the law. In addition, a thorough under-standing of both the immigration rules and of Home Office policy outside the rules is needed. The law is also constantly and rapidly changing. Further changes are to be made by the new Nationality, Immigration and Asylum Bill 2002.

Handbooks provide only general information and they quickly become out of date. There are many pitfalls into which people can fall if they do not understand immigration procedures or if they follow incorrect advice. The need for advice in immigration and asylum which is accurate, complete and honest has never been greater. Unfortunately, the provision of immigration advice has been affected by a number of unscrupulous or incompetent immigration advisers (both qualified and unqualified) who have often exploited the vulnerability of those who are in desperate need of help. It is therefore essential for anyone who needs immigration advice to obtain it from a suitably qualified or accredited adviser.

There are now two important control mechanisms which operate to ensure access to proper advice and representation on immigration matters:

- **Regulation of Immigration Advisers.** Part 5 of the Immigration and Asylum Act 1999 imposes restrictions on who is able to give immigration advice and regulates those who do provide advice. The scheme is admini-stered by the Office of the Immigration Services Commissioner (OISC).

39 • **Community Legal Service Quality Mark.** The government set up the

Community Legal Service (CLS) in England and Wales in order to improve access to and the quality of legal services and to base the delivery of services on local needs and priorities. The CLS has established a network of legal services, some of which are funded by the Legal Services Commission (LSC), which replaced the Legal Aid Board. All services funded by the LSC must meet certain minimum standards known as the CLS Quality Mark ▶see, however, page 46 for those seeking advice in Scotland and Northern Ireland.

At the end of this chapter there is a table listing possible sources of immigration advice.

Regulation of immigration advisers

Under the Immigration and Asylum Act 1999, no one may provide immigration 'advice' or 'services' unless they are either 'qualified' to do so or they are exempted from restriction by the new Immigration Services Commissioner ▶see 729 for address. Persons who are 'qualified' are:

- practising solicitors, barristers or legal executives (members of these professions are all regulated by their own professional bodies; the three Law Societies which regulate solicitors throughout the UK, the Bar Council, the Faculty of Advocates in Scotland and the Bar Council of Northern Ireland which regulate barristers; and the Institute of Legal Executives) and those working under their supervision. The definition also applies to similar professionals of other EEA states;

- other advisers who do not fall into the above category but who are *registered* with the Commissioner or who are employed or supervised by a person or body which is registered. All immigration advisers who charge privately for their services must apply for registration. They have to comply with the Commissioner's 'Rules' and 'Code of Standards' (▶see below) and they must pay a registration fee of between £1,800 and £6,000 depending upon the number of individual advisers in the organisation. Registration may be restricted to carrying out particular kinds of immigration work or even to particular groups of clients.

A person who is not 'qualified' to provide the advice may be *exempted* from the restrictions by the Commissioner and therefore able to provide advice and services. Non-qualified advisers in the not-for-profit sector who provide advice free of charge must apply for exemption. In doing so, they must show compliance with the Code of Standards but not the Rules.

Applications for registration or for certificates of exemption are made by completing an OISC application pack. Applications are first considered on the papers and are then followed up by a visit to the premises in order to carry out an audit.

The Commissioner has divided immigration and asylum work into three levels: general (level 1), general casework (level 2), and specialist (level 3).

These levels also reflect the standards set by the CLS Quality Mark scheme. Within each level various categories of advice are identified. The competence that advisers must demonstrate in order to meet the OISC criteria at each level are set out in the OISC's 'Guidance to Advisers'.

Immigration advice and services

The definition of providing immigration advice or services under the 1999 Act is broad. The provision of general information that does not relate to an individual's case is not included. In order to constitute 'advice' it must relate to a particular individual. Providing immigration 'services' to a person means making representations on their behalf to a court (or to the immigration appellate authorities), to the Home Office or any other government department.

The regulatory scheme applies to those who provide immigration advice and/or services to individual clients 'in the course of business, whether or not for profit'. Therefore, those who advise or represent people in a personal capacity only, such as friends and relatives, are not covered by the regulatory scheme. However, those advisory organisations which only provide immigration advice incidental to their core advice duties, for example, welfare advisers, must be aware that the regulatory scheme applies. They should therefore either refer clients who need immigration advice to an alternative provider ('signposting') rather than provide specific advice to an individual, or they should apply to the Commissioner for registration or exemption.

It is a criminal offence for any person to provide immigration advice or services unless they are either qualified or exempted. The maximum penalty for providing advice in contravention of these regulations is imprisonment for two years and a fine (s91 1999 Act).

The OISC Rules and Code of Standards

It is the general duty of the Immigration Services Commissioner to promote good practice by those who provide immigration advice or immigration services. To assist the OISC in its regulatory functions, in October 2000, the Commissioner issued 'The Commissioner's Rules' and the 'Code of Standards'. The Rules relate to the conduct, professional practice and discipline of advisers and make requirements in terms of the fees charged and the accounting and complaints procedures which they operate. The Code of Standards sets a benchmark for the performance of advisers against which the competence and quality of an organisation or adviser may be judged. The Code mirrors many of the CLS Quality Mark requirements.

Complaints against advisers and representatives

An important function of the OISC is to handle and monitor complaints and for this purpose it has set up a complaints scheme. Complaints can be made directly to the OISC against an adviser or representative relating to their competence or fitness, or alleged breaches by them of the Commissioner's Rules or Code (including the level of fees charged). Complaints may also be made to the OISC against solicitors, barristers and legal executives about alleged breaches of their own professional rules. If a similar issue comes to the attention of the OISC, they do not have to wait until a complaint is actually made but may investigate it on their own initiative. However, the OISC does not have the power to consider complaints about those representing government departments such as the Home Office. Such complaints should be made to the relevant section within a government department, and may be made to an MP who can forward the matter to the Parliamentary Ombudsman.

Having decided to uphold a complaint, the Commissioner may:

- if the organisation is registered to advise and the matter is serious enough, require that organisation to apply for continued registration straight away so that their fitness for continued registration can be reassessed or simply indicate that the decision on the complaint should be considered next time that organisation applies for their registration to be continued;
- if the organisation is exempt from registration, consider whether to withdraw the exemption;
- if the adviser is a member of one of the professional bodies (solicitor, barrister, legal executive) or is supervised or employed by such, refer the complaint to their own professional body (Law Society, Bar Council, Institute of Legal Executives). The OISC must also report to the Secretary of State if it considers that one of the professional bodies is failing to provide effective regulation of its members in relation to their provision of immigration advice and services;
- if the person is a registered or exempt adviser, lay a disciplinary charge before the Immigration Services Tribunal which has even greater powers (►see below).

Immigration Services Tribunal

As well as the OISC, the 1999 Act also creates an Immigration Services Tribunal. The Tribunal holds hearings to determine disciplinary charges concerning registered or exempted advisers which are referred to it by the Commissioner. In addition to the powers of the Commissioner, the Tribunal can:

- direct the adviser to re-pay fees where the fee charged was unreasonable;
- fine the adviser;
- restrict the immigration advice or services which the adviser can provide;
- suspend the adviser from providing any immigration advice or services;
- prohibit the adviser from providing immigration advice or services in the future.

The Tribunal also hears appeals against decisions by the OISC to refuse an application for registration or to renew registration by potential advisers and decisions by the OISC to withdraw an exemption from an adviser.

The Community Legal Service (England and Wales only)

Organisations that wish to be part of the CLS network are required to apply to the Legal Services Commission for a Quality Mark at one of the following three levels:

'General Help'. General Help normally constitutes one-off advice for which there is no ongoing case file. Such providers will often refer someone on to a more experienced adviser ('active signposting').

'General Help including Casework'. Straightforward work such as naturalisation applications which require form-filling and other basic correspondence may fall into the 'General Help including Casework' category. Organisations providing immigration advice at this level must possess a Quality Mark specifically in the immigration category. To be certified at this level, they must have at least one person conducting immigration work for at least 12 hours per week. Organisations like Citizens' Advice Bureaux and generalist advice centres are typically funded to carry out this level of work.

More complex work should be referred to a provider who has a contract with the Legal Services Commission to provide 'Specialist Help'.

'Specialist Help'. Organisations that possess the 'Specialist Help' Quality Mark are required by the LSC to extensively train their advisers in various areas of immigration law, ranging from asylum and illegal entry through to leave to remain and Home Office discretionary policies. Such organisations employ in-house trained supervisors who have themselves specialised in immigration law for a minimum period of time. Specialist Help providers also have access to telephone consultancy lines funded by the LSC. JCWI provides such an LSC funded consultancy line. Clarification on complex issues concerning immigration, asylum and nationality law is provided by this service.

Specialist Help organisations typically include solicitors in private practice, law centres, some Citizens' Advice Bureaux and specialist advice agencies. They are all regularly audited by the LSC.

Community Legal Service Funding

CLS funding, which replaced the old legal aid budget is available at the following levels:

- 'Legal Help';
- 'Controlled Legal Representation' for appeals before the immigration adjudicator and Immigration Appeal Tribunal; and

- 'Legal Representation' for cases before the High Court, Court of Appeal and House of Lords.

The Legal Help Scheme

Financial assistance for legal fees in relation to most immigration matters can be provided under the Legal Help Scheme if two basic tests are satisfied. Firstly, eligibility is restricted to those who have little or no income or savings. Financial eligibility levels are set by the LSC and are varied from time to time. Secondly, the adviser has to assess whether or not the client will benefit sufficiently by the provision of legal assistance (the 'sufficient benefit' test). This test is designed to prevent work being carried out in relation to matters which demonstrate no real legal issue. Generally, any query related to bringing someone to the UK, staying in the UK (asylum and non-asylum) and British nationality questions will satisfy this test.

To find out whether or not someone qualifies for Legal Help for a particular immigration problem, the individual should contact the advice provider and may be invited in for a free or fixed-fee initial interview. Where a person does not qualify for Legal Help, they may have to pay privately for assistance.

Controlled Legal Representation (CLR)

Financial assistance under the Legal Help Scheme will not cover the advocacy fees of a barrister or legal representative at a hearing before an immigration adjudicator or the Immigration Appeal Tribunal. CLR may be provided in such proceedings if the financial eligibility levels set by the LSC (the same that apply to the Legal Help Scheme) are met and if two further tests are satisfied.

Firstly, the prospects of the appeal being successful must either be over 50 per cent or if 'unclear or borderline', the case must be of overwhelming importance to the client (asylum cases will usually satisfy this test) or raise significant issues of human rights. If the prospects of appeal are judged to be poor (clearly below 50 per cent), CLR will be refused. However, in some circumstances appropriate 'test cases' which aim to make new law may be funded under this scheme.

Secondly, the 'likely benefits from the proceedings' must justify the legal costs (the costs-benefit test). This is assessed on an estimate of whether or not a private paying client would be prepared to pay for the proceedings, bearing in mind the prospects of success. Again, most asylum cases will satisfy this test, bearing in mind the possible consequences of return to a country of persecution if the Home Office decision is incorrect. Many entry clearance and variation of leave appeals will also satisfy this test, particularly if an appellant is seeking to join family members or is not seeking a short extension of stay.

The prospects of an appeal can only be assessed by a solicitor or a designated supervisor in the organisation that holds the contract with the LSC. If a client is refused CLR, they can seek a formal review of the decision by the LSC. Such a review must be requested within 14 days of the date of refusal.

Legal Representation (previously known as Legal Aid)

Applications for judicial review before the High Court, and appeals to the Court of Appeal and House of Lords may be funded by the LSC under this scheme, which is also known as certificated work. Strict financial eligibility criteria apply and clients will be subject to a much more rigorous set of questions than they would be under the Legal Help or CLR schemes. Financial assessments are conducted by the appropriate LSC regional office and a monthly financial contribution may be payable by the client.

Certificated work is also subject to a merits test. Particular criteria are applicable to judicial review cases, such as the availability of other procedures to challenge the decision of an immigration authority. Furthermore, prospects of the case being successful and the 'costs-benefits test' will be assessed by the regional LSC office. The criteria applicable in both tests is broadly similar to that set out in the CLR scheme.

However, in an emergency, for example when challenging removal directions by way of judicial review, certain solicitors' firms may be able to grant emergency certificates in-house to fund the initial cost of legal proceedings under powers devolved to them by the LSC.

Seeking advice in England and Wales

Those seeking immigration advice should approach organisations approved either by the OISC or the LSC. Details of all not-for-profit, voluntary sector advisers and non-solicitor private advisers, who are approved by the Commissioner to give immigration advice, can be obtained from the OISC ▶see the end of this chapter for details.

Provided that the financial eligibility criteria are met, free immigration advice can also be obtained from not-for-profit advice agencies and solicitors in private practice accredited by the LSC. The advice will only be funded by the LSC if the advice provider has a Quality Mark and a contract with the LSC to provide immigration advice. These solicitors and other agencies are part of the Community Legal Service and are listed in the CLS Directory which is organised into geographical regions across England and Wales and can be accessed via their website. The CLS has also set up a telephone call centre which can provide details of appropriate service providers ▶see details listed at the end of this chapter.

Seeking advice in Scotland and Northern Ireland

The OISC regulatory scheme applies to advisers throughout the UK, including Scotland and Northern Ireland, and details of approved advisers can be obtained from the OISC. However, this list will not include solicitors, barristers (known as advocates in Scotland) or legal executives.

Scotland

Public funding in Scotland is provided not by the LSC but by the Scottish Legal Aid Board under the Legal Aid (Scotland) Act 1986. Provided that the person needing help is financially eligible, assistance towards solicitors' fees for advice and help can be obtained through the 'Advice and Assistance' (also known as the 'Green Form') scheme and representation before an immigration adjudicator and the Immigration Appeal Tribunal can be provided under the 'Assistance By Way of Representation' (ABWOR) scheme. Civil legal aid is available for cases which reach the Scottish Court of Session and the House of Lords. *Any* solicitor in Scotland can provide immigration advice under the above legal aid schemes. However, only a solicitor registered with the Board to provide criminal legal assistance (criminal legal aid or advice and assistance on a criminal matter) can provide legal assistance in connection with any criminal aspect of an immigration problem.

The Law Society of Scotland regulates solicitors providing immigration and asylum advice. The Law Society of Scotland operates a solicitor referral service and can be contacted for the names of solicitors who provide this type of advice ▶see details in the box at the end of this chapter.

Northern Ireland

In Northern Ireland, legal aid funding is managed by the Law Society of Northern Ireland, which is the professional body for solicitors there, under the Legal Aid, Advice and Assistance (Northern Ireland) Order 1981. Provided the person requiring the advice is financially eligible, legal fees are subsidised by the 'Advice and Assistance' scheme. Civil Legal Aid is available for actions in the High Court and above. There is no list of solicitors who provide immigration advice but the Law Society can be contacted for details of solicitors who operate the legal aid scheme ▶see details in the box below.

WHERE TO OBTAIN ADVICE

England and Wales

The CLS Directory contains details of private solicitors' firms and not-for profit sector advice agencies that are approved suppliers of immigration advice. Details can be obtained as follows:

CLS (Community Legal Service) Directory Call Centre on telephone number 0845 608 1122;

CLS 'Just Ask!' website: www.justask.org.uk;

CLS Regional Directories (13 in number) can be found in local libraries, advice centres and solicitors' firms.

The OISC has a list of all not-for-profit sector advice agencies and private advisers (but not solicitors' firms) who are approved by them to give out immigration advice. Details are contained in a useful section in their website called 'Adviser finder' (www.oisc.org.uk/adviser_finder). Alternatively, they can be telephoned on their helpline: 0845 000 0046.

Scotland

The OISC website and helpline (▶see above) can be consulted for non-solicitor agencies.

For solicitors' firms, the Law Society of Scotland provides names of firms who give immigration and asylum advice. Details can be obtained from its website: www.lawscot.org.uk under the 'Firms and Branches' section. Alternatively, it can be telephoned on 0131 226 7411. Ask for the Records Department which will be able to provide a number of solicitors from its list.

It should be noted that the solicitors' firms on the list are not specifically approved by the OISC or the Law Society to give out immigration advice but they will usually be able to apply to the Scottish Legal Aid Board for funding.

Northern Ireland

The OISC website and helpline (▶see above) can be consulted for non-solicitor agencies.

For solicitors' firms, there is no specific list of solicitors who specialise in immigration law, although enquiries can be directed through the Law Society of Northern Ireland for information on solicitors who operate the legal aid scheme.

To contact the Law Society of Northern Ireland's Legal Aid Department, telephone 028 90 23 16 14.

Section 2 **Immigration control in practice**

Chapter 4
Applying to come into the United Kingdom   51
Applications made outside the United Kingdom   52
Immigration control on arrival   65
Entry from the Republic of Ireland and through the
Channel Tunnel   72

Chapter 5
Leaving and returning   75
General rules   75
People who always qualify to return   77
People with indefinite leave   79
People with limited leave   83
People who left the UK before 30 July 2000   85
People who wish to travel while an application
or an appeal are outstanding   86
Those without passports or other travel documents   88

Chapter 6
Applying to stay in the UK   90
What status does a person have while waiting
for a decision?   93
How to make the application   95
Home Office decisions   101
Exceptional Leave   104

Chapter 7
Identifying immigration status   109

Conditions of leave to enter or remain   109
Endorsements by ECOs   109
Endorsements by immigration officers   113
Endorsements by the Home Office   118
Other documents   121

Chapter 8
Problems, emergencies and solutions   130

Refusal of entry clearance overseas   131
Problems on arrival in the UK   133
'Third country' asylum cases   136
Access to welfare and support   138
Arrest, detention and threatened deportation
or removal   140
Contacting an MP   141
Using judicial review   142

4   Applying to come into the United Kingdom

This section looks at the practicalities of immigration control. It covers applying to come and getting admitted to the UK (this chapter), leaving and then returning to the UK (Chapter 5) and applying to extend a stay in the UK for a limited time or indefinitely (Chapter 6). The special arrangements for travel within the 'Common Travel Area' (▶see Glossary) are dealt with on pages 72-74. The Immigration and Asylum Act 1999 has dramatically changed the way in which controls operate. The main changes are set out in the box below.

CHANGES TO IMMIGRATION CONTROL MADE BY THE 1999 ACT

- Entry clearances operate as leave to enter.
- 'Leave' (permission) to be in the UK can remain in place even when a person departs The technical change which permits this prevents a person's leave from 'lapsing' when they depart.
- Leave to enter the UK can be granted to a person before they arrive.
- Leave which a person has when they arrive can be 'cancelled' on their arrival.
- Leave to be in the UK can remain in place when a person is appealing against a refusal to extend their leave provided that the application was made 'in time'.
- Permission to enter the UK can be granted on the telephone or by fax.

  The details of many of these changes are set out in the Immigration (Leave to Enter and Remain) Order 2000. These changes and the circumstances in which they apply are also explained in this section.

Included as part of the description of immigration controls in Chapters 4–6, are explanations of the different immigration status which people are given. Chapter 7 is designed for applicants and advisers to be able to identify immigration status from the documentation which is provided by the immigration authorities in the form of stamps, forms and other documents. Finally, Chapter 8 contains general details of how to deal practically with various common problems and emergencies which arise.

The 2002 White Paper

The government's latest White Paper demonstrates that it is committed to maintaining as tight a grip as possible on border controls. Included in the measures the government is taking are:

- the continued use of Airline Liaison Officers (ALOs) stationed abroad to advise airlines on who is properly documented for travel to the UK. During 2001, over 22,000 people are said to have been prevented from boarding flights to the UK and elsewhere in locations where ALOs are placed;

- 'pre-clearance' of passengers seeking to board flights to travel to the UK by consular officials abroad. A pre-clearance scheme was introduced at Prague airport in the Czech Republic in July 2001;

- the use of 'biometric technology' (iris or facial recognition or fingerprints) to confirm the identity of people who have already been granted entry clearance or leave and to detect those holding documents which have not been properly issued to them;

- the use of X/gamma ray scanners and heartbeat sensors to detect those concealed in vehicles and containers.

Applications made outside the United Kingdom

Entry clearance

An 'entry clearance' is a document which is issued by a British post overseas (British embassy, high commission or consulate), which is evidence that the holder is eligible for entry to the UK. People applying for entry clearance have to satisfy officials at a British post that they qualify under the criteria in the immigration rules for entry in the category in which they are applying or that entry clearance ought to granted exceptionally. If entry clearance is granted, it is normally placed in the applicant's passport. If the applicant is a 'visa national' (▶see below), the legal term for the entry clearance they get is 'visa'. If the applicant is a non-visa national, the legal term for the entry clearance they get is 'entry certificate'. There is little practical difference between the two and therefore we refer to them all as 'entry clearances' throughout the *Handbook*.

Entry clearances have been re-designed as a result of the changes made to the mechanics of immigration control under the Immigration and Asylum Act 1999 which are noted above ▶see page 112 for examples of the new entry clearances. Entry clearances come in two colours. Green entry clearances are used for visitors (including transit visitors) and entry clearances for all other purposes are red. The entry clearances given to visitors are also known as Uniform Format Visas (UFVs). Confusingly, they all bear the name 'visa' even if the holder is a non-visa national. Red entry clearances for all other purposes bear the words 'entry clearance'.

The new style entry clearances have a date on which they become effective and a date of expiry. The date on which the entry clearance becomes effective is given on the entry clearance as the 'valid from' date. Depending upon when the person wishes to travel, the 'valid from' date *may well be later than the date on which the entry clearance is actually issued*. The date on which the entry clearance expires is given as the 'valid until' date. The period between these two dates is the period of the entry clearance's 'validity'. These dates are critical in determining what leave a person will get when they actually arrive in the UK ►see below.

Entry clearances state the conditions which the leave that the person will obtain when they arrive in the UK will be subject to. These conditions are sometimes referred to by immigration officers as 'codes' for shorthand. The codes reflect the various different combinations of conditions which a person can be given. For details of the various codes ►see pages 110-111.

The 'old-style' entry clearances can still be used provided they are still valid. However, no more are being issued so they will soon die out ►see page 113 for an example.

People who need entry clearance

Some people *must* obtain an entry clearance before they come to the UK. For everyone else, getting an entry clearance is optional. Whether a person seeking to enter in a particular category must get an entry clearance is set out in each of the chapters describing the different categories. However, the *general* rules about who *must* get an entry clearance are as follows. The following people must get an entry clearance unless they fall into any of the exceptions listed further below:

- 'visa nationals' must have an entry clearance to come to the UK *whatever* their purpose in coming ►see page 737 for the list of the countries whose nationals are visa nationals. At the current time, there are 111 'visa national' countries;

- 'non-visa nationals' must have an entry clearance where the immigration rules state they need one. Generally, the immigration rules require those who are coming to the UK for settlement *or* for any purpose which may lead to settlement to obtain an entry clearance. For example, people coming to join relatives in the UK to stay permanently or those coming for work, business or self-employment will need entry clearance. Working holidaymakers also need to get an entry clearance. Some people coming for work or training do not obtain an entry clearance as such before their arrival (unless they are also visa nationals) but a 'work permit'. These are issued by Work Permits UK which is now part of the Home Office and fulfil a similar function as an entry clearance ►see below;

- people who hold passports or travel documents issued by the former Soviet Union or the former Socialist Federal Republic of Yugoslavia;

- stateless people and people who do not hold national documentation.

The exceptions

Even if a person is in one of the groups mentioned above, they still do not need an entry clearance if they are any of the following:

- a person returning to the UK within the time of a previous grant of leave given for more than six months provided they are returning for the same purpose as they were previously granted leave (this includes certain leave granted by entry clearances);

- a visitor returning to the UK within the period of validity of the original visit entry clearance;

- a person who qualifies to be admitted to the UK in the category of 'returning resident' (those who were 'settled' in the UK when they last left). They must be returning to the UK within two years in order to be exempt from needing an entry clearance;

- a refugee holding a 1951 Refugee Convention travel document issued by a country which is a signatory of the Council of Europe Agreement of 1959 on the Abolition of Visas for Refugees and who is coming to the UK on a visit of three months or less. The countries which have signed this agreement are: Belgium, Denmark, Finland, France, Germany, Iceland, Ireland, Italy, Liechtenstein, Luxembourg, Malta, Netherlands, Norway, Portugal, Spain, Sweden, Switzerland. Some countries still issue a travel document under the 1946 Refugee Convention and these documents are still accepted by immigration officers;

- Visa national schoolchildren who are resident in an EU member state and who are travelling as part of an organised school group (this exemption is the result of a special agreement between the member states of the European Union).

EEA Nationals and family members

Different considerations relating to entry clearance apply for EEA nationals and their family members. EEA nationals do not require any form of entry clearance in order to travel and be admitted to the UK. However, a non-EEA national coming as a 'family member' of an EEA national must get an EEA 'family permit' before come if they are:

- a visa national, *or*

- coming to the UK to live with the EEA national rather than just for a visit.

The family permit is therefore a form of entry clearance. It can be obtained free of charge from the entry clearance officer at British posts. For more details about EEA nationals and their family members ▶see Chapter 22.

Other documents relating to entry to be obtained before arrival

Work permits and Training and Work Experience Scheme work permits

Work permits and Training and Work Experience Scheme (TWES) permits are *not* technically entry clearances. However, for non-visa nationals they fulfil a similar function because a work permit must have been issued in respect of the person in order for them to obtain entry for work permit employment. However, visa nationals who have a work permit *also* require an entry clearance in order to come to the UK for work permit employment. For details about obtaining work permits ▶see pages 100, 419.

Certificates of entitlement

British citizens and other people with the right of abode in the UK can obtain a certificate of entitlement to the right of abode by applying to the entry clearance officer at a British post overseas. The documents which need to be produced depend on the basis on which the person is entitled to the right of abode ▶see Chapter 27. For instance, a person born in the UK before 1 January 1983 needs to produce their full birth certificate. However, a person born in the UK after that date and claiming entitlement to the right of abode by birth, also needs to produce evidence of either parents' British citizenship or settled status at the time of birth and, if claiming through their father, the parents' marriage certificate. A Commonwealth citizen woman who, before 1 January 1983, married a man with the right of abode should produce evidence of her husband's British citizenship, for example, his passport or certificate of registration or naturalisation as a British citizen, as well as producing their marriage certificate. In all cases, the person applying for the certificate should also provide their own passport. If the application is refused, there is a right of appeal. For an example of a certificate of entitlement ▶see page 121.

When entry clearance is optional

In general, people who are not visa nationals and who are not coming to settle, work or do business in the UK, do not need to get an entry clearance before travelling. They have the choice of applying for entry clearance abroad, or of travelling to the UK without it and seeking entry from the immigration officer at the port of entry.

Although a person does not need an entry clearance in order to obtain admission under the immigration rules, they may still choose to get an entry clearance before travelling so as to be more sure of their eligibility for admission. For example, the immigration rules actually recommend that non-visa national prospective au pairs obtain entry clearance. Among the factors to consider (▶see the box overleaf) in deciding whether to apply for entry clearance when it is not strictly required are the additional cost and delay of getting an entry clearance balanced against the risk of being

---

ADVANTAGES AND DISADVANTAGES OF OBTAINING CLEARANCE WHERE IT IS OPTIONAL

The advantages are:

- people know in advance whether they satisfy the requirements of the immigration rules and therefore they are unlikely to have problems or delays when they arrive in the UK. This may be particularly useful for people who have previously had immigration problems;
- if they are refused entry clearance, they will have spent money only on the entry clearance fee, not also on the ticket to the UK;
- if they get entry clearance but are nevertheless refused entry when they arrive in the UK, they can usually appeal against the refusal and remain in the UK while the appeal is pending, and give evidence at the appeal hearing.

The disadvantages are:

- in some countries, there are delays in considering applications and there may be further delays if the applications are referred to the Home Office;
- there is a fee for entry clearance, which is not returned if the application is refused, and an application may involve more than one long journey to the nearest British post;
- the refusal rates for entry clearance overseas have generally been higher than refusal of entry at ports in the UK;
- if entry clearance is refused, the person's passport will be marked to show this (►see page 113 for an example of these markings) and information about the refusal may be passed on to the authorities in the UK, so that travel to the UK (and to some other countries) will be more difficult in future.

---

refused entry on arrival without one. Even where entry clearance has been obtained, however, admission to the UK on arrival is not guaranteed.

Entry clearances operating as leave to enter

From 28 April 2000, the law changed to allow entry clearances to operate as leave to enter the UK. The way in which entry clearances now operate is not completely clear and the legislation setting the procedures out has been very poorly written. The form of the new style entry clearances is described above on page 52.

Which entry clearances operate as leave to enter?

In order for an entry clearance to operate as leave to enter it must state on it the purpose for which it is given (for example, 'fiancé', 'working holiday-maker', 'visitor') *and* be either:

- endorsed with any conditions on which it has been granted (for example, a condition that there is 'no recourse to public funds'); *or*

- be intended to take effect as *indefinite* leave to enter in which case it must contain a statement to that effect.

The conditions on which the entry clearance is granted then become the conditions of leave. The immigration authorities intend that *all* entry clearances that are granted will operate as leave to enter. However an entry clearance which does not in fact satisfy the above conditions will not operate as leave to enter. Such an entry clearance would probably still be valid but leave would not be given unless the immigration officer granted it on entry.

How do these entry clearances work?

Entry clearances now have an 'effective date' (which may be later than the period on which they are issued) and an 'expiry date'. On the entry clearance itself, the effective date is shown as 'valid from' and the expiry date is shown as 'valid until'. The 'period of validity' of the entry clearance is the period between these two dates. The conditions of the leave which is given are the conditions which are written on the entry clearance.

The applicant must arrive in the UK during the period of the entry clearance's validity. If the holder arrives before the effective date or seeks to enter for a different purpose than that written on the entry clearance, the immigration officer can cancel the *entry clearance itself*. Provided the person arrives within the period of validity and seeks entry in accordance with the entry clearance, they are treated as having *already* been granted leave to enter and they may be examined by the immigration officer only to see whether or not the *leave* (not the entry clearance) should be cancelled. This can only be done on certain narrow grounds ▶see below page 69. If leave is cancelled, then there is generally a right of appeal because the person has been refused entry at a time when they had a valid entry clearance.

Confusingly, although these passengers are treated as though they have already been granted leave before their arrival for *examination* purposes, the Immigration (Leave to Enter and Remain) Order 2000 states that the leave actually 'begins' on the date of their arrival. However, the Home Office has given advice which complicates the position even more. In a letter to Dexter Montague & Partners solicitors in September 2001, it stated that:

'in calculating leave, leave to remain in the United Kingdom begins on the 'valid from' date on the entry clearance and not from the applicant's date of arrival in the UK'.

However, this would mean that a spouse who arrived towards the end of the 12 month period of validity of their entry clearance (intended to be the 12 month probationary period in the UK), would be able to apply for settlement soon after their arrival even though they had not been in the UK with their spouse for anything like the 12 months required. This is unlikely, therefore, to be the correct interpretation. The more likely approach is that leave is calculated from the date of arrival, as the Leave to Enter and Remain Order indicates. For suggestions of how to deal with this issue if, for example, a spouse delays arrival ►see pages 342-343.

How long is leave granted for when an entry clearance operates as leave to enter and can these entry clearances be used more than once?

The length of the leave which is given when an entry clearance operates as leave to enter and the number of times these entry clearances can be used both depend on the purpose for which the entry clearance is given.

Visitor entry clearances. In the case of visitor entry clearances, leave is granted for six months if the period of validity remaining on the entry clearance is six months or more on the date of arrival. If the remaining period of validity is less than six months on the date of arrival, the length of leave given is the remaining period of the validity of the entry clearance.

Take, for example, a person who obtained a visit entry clearance on 15 October 2001 which had an effective date (the 'valid from' date) which was also the 15 October and an expiry date (the 'valid until' date) which was 15 April 2002. If the person arrived in the UK on 2 January 2002, they would only have been given leave until 15 April 2002. They are not given six months leave when they arrive because the remaining period of the validity of the entry clearance is less than six months.

Under the old system, a person could simply arrive within the period during which the entry clearance was valid and be granted six months leave by an immigration officer. Now, however, when the passenger arrives they are simply given a date stamp across the entry clearance to signify their entry. Many people have made the mistake of thinking that they have six months from that date and become overstayers as a result. It is therefore very important for applicants to explain to the entry clearance officer when they are likely to be travelling to the UK. The ECO may then be persuaded to give the entry clearance an effective date close to the departure date so that the passenger gets the maximum benefit from the entry clearance. In fact, ECOs have been given instructions to ask all applicants about their proposed travel plans so that they can ensure as far as possible that the effective date coincides with the applicant's intended date of departure.

The normal period of validity of a visitor entry clearance is six months but it is possible to obtain a long-term entry clearance (with a period of validity of up to five years) if the ECO can be persuaded that the applicant's circumstances justify it.

A visitor entry clearance operates as leave to enter on an unlimited number of occasions during the period of its validity. So, a person may come and go from the UK using the same entry clearance and, provided the immigration rules remain satisfied, it will operate as leave to enter on each occasion. Visit entry clearances can therefore be described as valid for 'multiple entry'.

Other entry clearances. An entry clearance for any purpose other than for a visit can only take effect as leave to enter on *one* occasion. However, one reason for this is that most leave (other than leave given by a visit entry clearance) does not lapse when a person goes out of the UK so that most people will not need their entry clearance to operate as leave to enter on multiple occasions ▶see page 76 for more details about non-lapsing leave.

The period of leave which is given in these cases is to the expiry of the validity of the entry clearance itself. If the entry clearance states that it is to have effect as indefinite leave, then it operates as indefinite leave. As with visit entry clearances, it is important that the applicant indicates to the ECO when it is that they propose to travel so that the effective date of the entry clearance can reflect this.

Delayed departures

Where, for unforeseen reasons, a person delays their departure to the UK so that they enter the UK significantly after the effective ('valid from') date, the Home Office has indicated it will adopt a 'flexible approach' if the person applies for a short extension of stay (▶see letter to Dexter Montague noted above). Such applications will be considered in line with the immigration rules. So, for example, where a visitor arrives significantly after the 'valid from' date they may, if they apply, be granted an extension to allow them to stay for up to six months from their date of arrival.

Applying for entry clearance

A person must be outside the UK in order to make an application for entry clearance. Applications should be made to the designated British post (British embassy, high commission or consulate) in the country in which the person is 'living'. However, applications for visit entry clearances do not need to be made to the post in the country where the applicant is living. The Foreign and Commonwealth Office produces a list of these designated posts ▶see pages 739-742. Most will deal with all types of entry clearance applications but some are restricted to dealing with particular types of applications. Where there is no designated post in their country, applicants can apply to a designated post in any other country which accepts applications in the category in which they wish to enter.

To apply for entry clearance, it is necessary to complete the relevant forms which may be obtained either from the British embassy/high commission or from the Joint Entry Clearance Unit (JECU), which has made the forms available on the internet at http://www.fco.gov.uk/ukvisas/ (JECU has now changed its name to 'UK Visas'). The main form which has to be filled out by everyone is form IM2A. There are other forms which also must be completed if they are applicable to the particular case:

- Form IM2B is for people applying for settlement;
- Form IM2C is for people applying to work in either permit-free or work permit employment, self-employed persons, investors, innovators, or retired persons of independent means;
- Form IM2D is for people claiming the right of abode or persons applying for entry clearance on the basis of UK ancestry;
- Form IM2S is for students;
- Form IM2E is for anyone who has previously applied for entry clearance and been refused or been refused entry on arrival in the UK;
- Form IM2F must be filled in by anyone who has had previous immigration problems in the UK including people who have been removed or deported, or threatened with removal or deportation;
- Form IM2G must be completed by those transitting the UK and remaining airside.

Applicants who have ever 'received social security benefits or been a charge on public funds', or who have criminal convictions must also state these and people who have worked in the UK are asked to 'explain the circumstances' on the form.

A sponsor or relative in the UK may fill in and sign the forms, which may be sent by mail. They may also be handed into the designated post by the applicant. Entry clearance applications are not treated as having been made unless the required fee has been paid although it is possible to ask for the fee to be waived if the applicant is 'destitute'. For the current fees which are payable, quoted in sterling ▶see page 738. These can also be viewed at http://www.fco.gov.ukvisas. Fees should be paid in local currency and are not refundable.

The application is treated as made on the day the British post receives the form and the fee. The date of application is particularly important in settlement applications for children who must be under 18 on the date of application. In all other cases, it is the circumstances on the date on which the application is *decided* which matter, not those on the date of the application (para 27, HC 395). Often the entry clearance officer will interview the applicant and, in some cases, may conduct further investigations such as making enquiries of other agencies or even visiting relatives or neighbours before making a decision.

British posts vary in the time it takes them to deal with an application and there are different queues for different kinds of application. In some countries, the application can be dealt with straight away. In others, for example, the countries of the Indian subcontinent, there have been long delays for people applying for settlement and there may also be delays for visitors. For information as to the expected waiting time, the best course is to contact the post concerned. Many posts have their own websites which provide local visa information. For example, the British High Commission in Dhaka (Bangladesh) currently advises visitors and students to apply at least two months before they plan to travel and that those applying to settle in the UK should allow between four and six months to process the application. Where there has been a previous refusal of entry clearance, applicants are advised that the process can take up to 15 months. According to information released by the Research, Development and Statistics Directorate of the Home Office, in the first half of 2000, waiting times for a first interview for applicants for settlement were up to four months for persons claiming the right of abode, one to eight months for spouses, children and fiances, and one to ten months for those applying after an earlier refusal.

ECOs refer certain cases to the Home Office for advice and instructions. Commonly referred applications are those relating to business, adoption of children and applications which do not qualify under the rules but where there are compelling circumstances which may justify admission. Referrals also sometimes take place where the Home Office holds papers on the person in relation to previous immigration applications. When the case has been referred, representations may be made to the Home Office instead of the overseas post.

Family settlement entry clearance applications

Entry clearance officers at British posts interview almost all people applying to come to the UK for settlement with family members. Children under 10 are not interviewed. Children between 10 and 14 should be interviewed only in the presence of an adult, preferably a parent or guardian, or other adult associated with their family. Questions put to children are normally confined to relatively simple matters and details of the immediate family. All applicants have to satisfy the ECO that they are related as claimed to the person they are applying to join, and that there is adequate maintenance and accommodation for them.

ECOs use interpreters for the interview where this is necessary. Usually the interview will start with a standard initial question to confirm whether the interviewee is tired or unwell and can understand the interpreter. Few people express any worries about this as the likely result would be stopping the interview and a delay in continuing the case. If an interview has already taken place and there have been problems, they should be raised as soon as possible and in as much detail as possible so that they can be investigated and consideration of the case continued quickly.

ECOs make their own notes both in order to make the decision and so as to be able to produce the notes at any appeal against a refusal. Practice concerning interviews varies between the posts. The Home Office has in the past refused to allow applicants to tape-record their interviews but has stated that it has no objection to an applicant taking notes or having another person present at interview or their own interpreter for verification purposes. The Foreign Office wrote to JCWI in September 1996:

'it is still policy to allow requests from MPs, solicitors and other representatives to attend an applicant's interview as an observer. There is no objection to this provided that the applicant concerned has no objections [and] the representative clearly understands that, as an observer, he/she must not intervene while the interview is taking place. But at the end of the interview, the observer may then make comments on the case to the ECO. These ground rules should be spelled out in advance, in writing if necessary, and if the observer fails to abide by them, the interview may be terminated.'

Documents and evidence required in family settlement entry clearance applications

ECOs require some standard information, both about the applicant and about the person he or she is coming to join (the sponsor). This includes:

- the applicant's current passport. If the person has travelled to the UK before, he or she may also be asked for old passports, to show that he or she did leave the UK as required;

- photocopies of the sponsor's passport. If she or he is a British citizen with a maroon British passport, the last page is enough. If the sponsor has an old blue British passport, the first five pages should be submitted. If the sponsor is not a British citizen, copies of all the pages with personal details and all the pages with any immigration officers' stamps on them are required. Because passports should not be sent through the post between countries, British posts will accept photocopies, though it may be advisable to have all the pages certified by a solicitor as genuine copies. In general, the immigration authorities will not accept photocopies of documents, on the grounds that a photocopy might not reveal a forged or altered document;

- the sponsor's birth certificate may be included if he or she was born in the UK although this will be less important if the passport has already been shown;

- evidence of adequate financial support in the UK. If the sponsor in the UK is working, this could be recent pay slips, or a letter from the employer confirming the job and salary, or recent bank statements covering at least the past three months showing money coming in and out. If other friends or relatives will be supporting the applicant, a letter from them will be necessary, confirming that they are able (with evidence as above) and willing to do so. If the sponsor in the UK is running a business, the business accounts or bank statements can be sent.

A spouse from abroad applying to come to join a British or settled spouse in the UK may also provide evidence of his or her own means or plans. If, for example, there is an offer of a job for the spouse when he or she arrives, a letter should be obtained from the prospective employer, indicating the terms of the job, the wages offered and the skill level required. Some evidence of the trading position of the firm could also be included. 'Third party' support from people other than the sponsor, for example, parents-in-law supporting a married couple, is acceptable. This was decided in the High Court case of *Arman Ali*. However, an entry clearance officer may be less inclined to accept that support in these circumstances will in fact be available on a long term basis. For more details about the maintenance and accommodation rules and how they are satisfied ►see pages 328-335.

Applications to come to the UK to work

The British post will need evidence of the work offered. For most types of employment, the employer in the UK has to obtain a work permit for the person from Work Permits UK and the British post will need to see this. Work Permits UK only issues permits when it is satisfied about the pay and conditions offered for the job and so the British post will not normally make further checks on these points. If the employment does not require a permit under the immigration rules, the British post will need a letter of confirmation from the employers about the job and the pay and conditions offered in order to consider whether it meets the requirements of the permit-free employment.

If the application is for business or investment purposes or from a retired person of independent means, full details of their money and business proposals are necessary. ECOs often refer business applications to the Home Office so that it can check on the feasibility of the enterprise. For full details about workers and business people, ►see Section 6 and for details of EEA rights of free movement, ►see Section 7.

Entry clearance decisions

If the ECO is satisfied that the requirements of the rules are met, the person will be given entry clearance. If the ECO is not satisfied that the requirements of the rules relating to the particular category are satisfied, then unless it has been shown that it is appropriate to authorise entry outside the immigration rules, the application will be refused. Like other immigration officials, ECOs must now also consider rights under the European Convention of Human Rights, which have been incorporated into UK law by the Human Rights Act 1998. The immigration rules themselves state that decisions of ECOs and others must comply with human rights (para 2, HC 395).

It should also be noted that the immigration rules relating to each category (other than refugees) only state that leave *may* be granted if the particular requirements of the rules are satisfied. Therefore, even if a person satisfies the rules for the individual category, they may still be refused an entry clearance under the 'general grounds' on which leave can be refused ▶see pages 67-68. The general grounds for refusal are the same for applications for entry clearance as they are for leave to enter when a person arrives at a port.

Decisions are notified in writing and the applicant must be informed of any right to appeal against the refusal and how the appeal may be brought. Not all refusals carry a right of appeal. In particular, people refused entry clearance as visitors (other than for a 'family' visit), or as students who have not yet been accepted onto a course, or who are coming on courses for six months or less, have no right of appeal. It is always, however, possible to bring an appeal on human rights grounds if it is alleged that the decision is in breach of human rights and a human rights appeal can be exercised at the same time as another right of appeal.

Revocation of entry clearance by entry clearance officer

Before a person arrives in the UK, an ECO may revoke an entry clearance after it has been granted. The ECO can do this if:

- s/he believes that the entry clearance was obtained by deception; *or*
- there has been a relevant change of circumstances since it was issued so that the rules are no longer satisfied; *or*
- the person's exclusion is conducive to public good.

Granting or refusing leave to enter before arrival in the United Kingdom

Another change introduced under the Immigration and Asylum Act 1999 Act is that, from 28 April 2000, it is possible for an immigration officer to grant or refuse leave to enter *before* a person has even arrived in the UK. This can happen both before a person has departed from their own country or while they are on their way to the UK. Immigration officers have the power to examine and interview people outside the UK for these purposes. These powers are used to grant leave to enter to groups the Home Office believes are at low risk of abusing immigration controls, for example, school groups and recognised reputable tour groups.

To make this easier still, although the grant and refusal of leave is normally given in a written notice or stamp, immigration officers can now also grant leave to enter by fax or email and, in the case of visitors, it can be given orally over the telephone with a written notice to follow. Decisions can also be notified to a responsible third party, for example, the tour leader of a group. In addition, immigration officers may be sent abroad and make decisions there so as to relieve certain 'pressure points' at ports of entry where there would otherwise be large queues of people waiting to be granted entry.

The reason given by the Home Office both for this change and the introduction of entry clearances operating as leave (▶see above) is to reduce the need for routine questioning at ports of entry and therefore to avoid congestion at the ports. On the Home Office's figures, the amount of passenger traffic has increased by 45 per cent to 84 million people per year over a five-year period from the mid 1990s.

Immigration control on arrival in the United Kingdom

When a person arrives at a port in the UK, immigration officers carry out an examination of them in order to determine whether they:

- have the right of abode in the UK (British Citizens and some Commonwealth nationals);
- may enter the UK without being given leave to enter even if they do not have the right of abode;
- require leave to enter and, if so, whether they should be granted leave to enter the UK and for what period and on what conditions leave should be given;
- already have leave – in these cases the immigration officer can consider whether to cancel the leave;
- require leave and have an entry clearance which operates as leave to enter.

All these different situations are considered below. In order to help immigration officers, non-British citizen passengers over 16 are required to fill out a landing card containing essential information about their circumstances ▶see page 113 for a specimen card. In carrying out their examination, immigration officers are able to search a person, their luggage or vehicle for any documents which help to show the reasons why the person has come to the UK. Documents can be kept for a limited amount of time or copied by the immigration officer.

Persons who do not require leave

'Leave' is a technical term in immigration law for 'permission' to be in the UK. It can be given for a limited or an indefinite period. Limited leave can be made subject to conditions, for example, not to work or have recourse to public funds. Some people, however, do not need leave at all. They are:

- British citizens;
- a small number of other people who have the 'right of abode' in the UK ▶see page 566;
- those who are exempt from immigration control: diplomats and others who work for embassies, members of governments, members of the armed forces including NATO forces, persons attending Commonwealth conferences, employees of some international organisations, certain crews of ships and aircrews; and

- EEA nationals and their family members exercising rights of free movement.

These people are still required to produce to the immigration officer a passport or travel document which demonstrates their identity and nationality together with evidence of their entitlement to enter without leave. Those with the right to abode may demonstrate this by producing their passport or certificate of entitlement. Those exempted from immigration control may have a letter of accreditation or authorisation from the government or international organisation concerned. Diplomats may have been issued, by the Foreign and Commonwealth Office, with either a certificate issued under the Diplomatic Privileges Act 1964 to show their entitlement to immunity or a simple letter of confirmation.

On entry to the UK, a person who is exempt from control will normally be given an open date stamp endorsement on their passport, which is not an endorsement for indefinite leave to enter. If no satisfactory proof of status is available for those claiming exemption but there is no reason to suspect any deception, they will often be granted temporary admission until proof of their entitlement can be shown. A person who is exempt from control can also later obtain a 'notification of exemption' from the Home Office as proof of their immigration status. An example of the open date stamp is shown on page 115.

Persons who require leave

All those not in the above categories require 'leave' in order to come into the UK. Immigration officers at the ports, like ECOs, make their decisions as to whether to grant or refuse leave to these people by applying the immigration rules. Their decisions must also be compatible with the rights under the ECHR. Exceptionally, leave may also be granted outside the rules. For those who require leave and do not already have it or have an entry clearance, if leave to enter is granted, immigration officers stamp the passports showing the date, the time limit (if any) and any conditions on their stay ►see Chapter 7 for examples. The time period for which leave is granted, which is stated on the stamp, runs from the date of the stamp itself. If a person wishes to obtain an extension of stay, it must be applied for before the existing leave runs out. It is worth keeping a record of the date leave expires separate from the passport so that if the passport is lost, the person knows the date until which he or she is allowed to remain and can make any application to stay before the leave runs out. If entry is refused, this is also endorsed on the passport.

The possible conditions which an immigration officer can impose on a limited leave are:

- a restriction *or* a prohibition on employment and business;
- a requirement to register with the police;

GENERAL GROUNDS FOR REFUSAL OF ENTRY CLEARANCE OR LEAVE TO ENTER (paragraph 320 Immigration rules HC 395)

Grounds on which entry clearance or leave to enter 'should normally' be refused:

- not giving all the required information to the immigration officers and, if outside the UK, failing to provide a medical report requested by an immigration officer;
- seeking leave to enter as a returning resident after being away for more than two years (though the specific rules on returning residents say that people may still be admitted, for example, if they have lived here for most of their lives) or where the person does not intend to settle in the UK once more;
- travelling on a passport issued by a state which is not recognised by the British government. In practice, people who otherwise qualify for entry may be admitted on an immigration service form;
- having previously overstayed or broken other conditions of leave;
- having previously entered by deception, or been granted an extension of leave by deception;
- if people cannot show they will be allowed into the country to which they intend to travel after their time-limited stay in the UK (this does not apply to people with entry clearance for settlement or as spouses leading to settlement);
- refusal by a sponsor to sign a maintenance undertaking if requested;
- false information having been given in relation to a work permit application, whether or not the applicant knew about this;
- where children are seeking entry for any reason (except to join their parents or legal guardians) without written consent from the parents or legal guardians. This does not apply to child asylum-seekers;
- refusal of a medical examination when required. This does not apply to people settled in the UK;
- if a person has been convicted of an offence which, if committed in the UK, could be punished with imprisonment for 12 months or more. This can be waived if there are strong compassionate reasons to allow entry;
- if the immigration authorities believe refusal is justified on grounds that the person's admission is not 'conducive to the public good'.

Grounds on which entry clearance or leave to enter 'is to be' refused:

- where 'entry is being sought for a purpose not covered by these rules'. This rule is intended to cover any conceivable reason for coming to the UK by stating that the application must be refused under the rules *unless* it falls within one of the established categories and the rules for that category are satisfied (but ►see page 68);
- if the applicant is subject to a current deportation order;
- where the applicant does not have a valid passport or identity document;
- where a person arrives in the UK with the intention of continuing their journey to the Republic of Ireland, but immigration officers are not satisfied that they will be accepted in that country;
- where the person is a visa national, not having a valid visa for the purpose for which they seek entry;
- where the Home Secretary has directed that the person is excluded on grounds of public good;
- where the medical inspector has confirmed it is undesirable to admit the person. This does not apply to people who are settled in the UK or where the immigration officer is satisfied that there are strong compassionate reasons for admission.

- a condition that the person maintains and accommodates themselves and any dependants without recourse to public funds (the ability to impose these conditions was introduced on 1 November 1996).

Immigration officers may also, if an examination by the port medical officer suggests it is necessary, only allow entry subject to the condition that the person reports for further medical tests or examination by an appointed medical officer. The significance of these conditions is that breach of any of them is a criminal offence and can also lead to a person being removed from the UK.

Each category of entry under the immigration rules, other than part 11 of HC 395 dealing with asylum, sets out a list of requirements which, if satisfied, may result in the grant of leave but which still allow leave to be refused on the basis of one of the 'general grounds' for refusal of leave (see part 9 HC395). These general grounds of refusal apply in exactly the same way to applications for entry clearance. It should be noted that some of them are themselves discretionary although the presumption is leave will be refused where they apply (leave should 'normally' be refused). Others are mandatory (leave 'is' to be refused). These general grounds of refusal are set out in the box above.

Can the general grounds of refusal be waived?

It should be noted that the above general grounds for refusal are contained in the *immigration rules*. The immigration rules themselves can always be waived. Therefore, even where the rules require a refusal, that rule itself can still be waived in an appropriate case. For example, the mandatory rule which states that an application 'is to be refused' if the application is made for a purpose not covered by the rules was introduced for technical reasons concerning appeals. The aim was to make sure that, in all cases, an adjudicator does not have the power to reconsider the exercise of the discretion of the immigration authorities to refuse to grant leave outside the rules. If this rule was always applied, no-one would ever get exceptional leave or entry clearance issued exceptionally. Advisers and representatives must therefore not be discouraged from making representations as to why an exception should be made even where refusal is mandatory under the rules.

People who have leave or an entry clearance when they arrive

If a passenger already has leave when they arrive in the UK, their entry will normally be straightforward. The Joint Entry Clearance Unit (now known as UK Visas) has indicated that:

'it is not envisaged that [immigration officers] will routinely conduct detailed interviews of such persons. Immigration officers will be able to check the validity of the passport and entry clearance and that the person presenting it is the rightful holder.'

However, people may be examined by the immigration officer to determine whether or not that leave should be 'cancelled' (para 2A sch2 1971 Act, and paras 10A–10B, 321A HC 395). This process also applies to people who arrive in the UK with an entry clearance which operates as leave to enter. This is because, for the purposes of examining them, these people are *treated* as having been granted leave to enter *before* their arrival. When they arrive, if they are granted entry, a date stamp is placed across the entry clearance, ▶see page 115 for an example.

After the changes made by the 1999 Act, a person may therefore already have leave when they arrive in the UK in any of the following three circumstances:

1 The passenger still has leave from their previous stay in the UK because it did not lapse when they previously left ▶see page 76 for more details about 'non-lapsing' leave.

2 The passenger has an entry clearance which operates as leave to enter ▶see above page 56-59.

3 Leave to enter was granted by the immigration authorities before the person arrived in the UK ▶see above page 64-65. Where a person was only given leave orally as a visitor, the burden is upon that person to show that they were in fact given it.

In all of these cases, where the immigration officer is carrying out an examination to see whether leave should be cancelled, they may 'suspend' the existing leave. If this is done, a written notice to that effect must be given. Following the examination, the immigration officer may cancel the leave if any of the following conditions apply:

• there has been a change of circumstances such that leave should be cancelled;

• leave was obtained by giving false information or failing to disclose material facts;

• medical reasons make it undesirable to admit the person (unless the person is settled in the UK or there are strong compassionate factors);

• the person's exclusion is conducive to the public good;

Similar criteria are applied by the immigration authorities to cancel any leave which a person has who is *outside* the UK and which did not lapse when they left. A 'change of circumstances' for these purposes means a change since the issue of the entry clearance or leave which undermines the basis for the person's admission under the immigration rules. This would apply, for example, where a child seeking entry as a dependant subsequently marries. The burden of showing the change of circumstances is on the immigration officer. Where leave is cancelled in this way, the passport will be endorsed with a large 'CANCELLED' stamp ▶see page 17, or endorsed in writing on the passport in either red or black ink. This stamp (or written endorsement) is placed over the leave which is being cancelled.

In most cases, examination will be swift, leave will not be cancelled and the passenger will be admitted with their existing leave until its expiry. The period of leave which is given when a person arrives with an entry clearance which operates as leave is slightly more complex ►see above pages 58-59.

It should be noted, however, that a person who has an entry clearance but who arrives in the UK before it becomes effective, or who states that they seek to enter the UK for a purpose other than for which the entry clearance was granted, is not treated as having been granted leave. In these circumstances, the ECO is entitled to simply cancel the entry clearance (see article 6(2) Immigration (Leave to Enter and Remain) Order 2000).

People with entry clearances which do not operate as leave

As stated, all entry clearances are intended to operate as leave. However, if an entry clearance does not satisfy the conditions to qualify for leave, or if it is an 'old style' entry clearance given before the new entry clearances were introduced, the old rules still apply. An immigration officer must decide whether to grant leave or not and what period of leave to give. An immigration officer can refuse entry on a very similar basis to the rules (►see above) for cancelling leave, namely if:

- false representations were made for the purpose of obtaining the entry clearance;
- material facts were not disclosed for the purpose of obtaining the entry clearance;
- there has been a change of circumstances since the entry clearance was issued which removes the grounds for granting admission;
- the refusal is justified on the basis of the person's restricted returnability to another country, on medical grounds, on grounds of their criminal record, a previous deportation order or because their exclusion would be conducive to the public good.

People who have leave and who apply to vary it on entry

Another possibility which may arise for someone who has leave when they arrive is that they may apply to the immigration officer at the port for their leave to be varied (see para 31, HC395). They may ask for it to be extended in time or that the conditions are changed. Where an application of this kind is made at the port then, unlike other applications to vary leave, there is no need for it to be made on a prescribed application form. The immigration officer may (but is not required to) make a decision on this application. If the immigration officer declines to make a decision but does not cancel the existing leave then, after the person has been admitted, they may apply to the Home Office for the same variation.

Decisions concerning entry and appeals

If leave to enter is to be refused or an existing leave cancelled, then the immigration officer must first obtain the authority of either a chief immigration officer or an immigration inspector. If leave is granted, the person will receive the appropriate endorsement on their passport ▶see Chapter 7 for the type of stamps. Written notice must also be given of a negative decision, which must also inform the applicant of any appeal rights. In some cases there is no in-country right of appeal and the only way of challenging the decision is to make further representations or apply for judicial review. If a person has a valid entry clearance, they will generally have an in-country right of appeal. If leave is 'cancelled' as described above, the applicant also has an in-country right of appeal against the decision. This is because people in this position are *treated* as having been refused leave to enter at a time at which they held a valid entry clearance even if they did not actually have one (see para 2A(9) sch 2 1971 Act added by the 1999 Act). So, a person who has leave in the UK, who departs for a trip abroad with leave that does not lapse and returns within their period of leave, now has a right of appeal if denied entry.

Of course, there is always a right of appeal if a person alleges that their removal from the UK will breach their human rights or that they have been subjected to racial discrimination. In such cases they will be able to appeal while in the UK unless the Home Office issues a certificate to prevent the appeal. For full details about appeals ▶see Section 10.

If leave to enter in one category is refused, there is nothing to prevent the person from applying to come in for a different reason before leaving the UK. Those refused entry are routinely asked whether they wish to seek entry for any other reason. Practically speaking, however, it is unlikely that a person will be able to demonstrate that they are genuinely seeking entry in the further category following a refusal on a different basis. Different considerations often apply in the case of asylum-seekers, where there are frequently very good reasons why the person does not immediately declare their intentions. Unless the asylum-seeker can be removed on 'third country' grounds, there will also usually be a right of appeal if an asylum claim is made. After a person has been refused leave to enter the UK and they have unsuccessfully exercised any in-country rights of appeal against the decision, the immigration officer has the power to set directions for the person's removal.

When the immigration officer cannot make an immediate decision

In many cases, in particular where the person is seeking asylum, their examination cannot be concluded straight away. Therefore, while the examination is continuing, the immigration officer has two options. *Either* the person may be detained pending a decision to grant or refuse entry, *or* they may be granted 'temporary admission' to the UK. Temporary admission is not formal 'leave', it is a restricted licence to be in the UK and it can be terminated in favour of detention at any time. Similarly, people who are initially detained under these powers, may later be released on temporary admission by the immigration officer or may be granted bail either by a chief immigration officer or an adjudicator. Temporary admission may be granted subject to conditions (as to residence, employment, reporting to the police or an immigration officer). Those placed in the new 'induction' and accommodation centres are formerly granted temporary admission rather than being detained.

Illegible passport stamps

If the immigration officer does not press hard enough, or does not have enough ink on the inkpad, the stamp may not be fully legible. Before 10 July 1988, if a person was given an illegible stamp, they were deemed to have been granted indefinite leave to enter. This is because the Immigration Act 1971 provides that people must be given notice in writing of the time limit and conditions on which they have been granted entry. When these could not be read, the courts decided that no valid time limit or conditions had been imposed on the person's stay (see *Minton*). Therefore, people who last entered the UK before 10 July 1988 and had no legible time limit placed on their stay, can apply to the Home Office for confirmation that they are settled in the UK. They should obtain specialist advice before approaching the Home Office.

Since July 1988, however, the law has been changed by the Immigration Act 1988 so that people entering since that time who are given illegible stamps are deemed to have been granted leave to enter for only six months with a prohibition on employment.

Entry from the Republic of Ireland and through the Channel Tunnel

The UK and the Republic of Ireland, together with the Isle of Man and the Channel Islands, form what is known as the 'Common Travel Area' (CTA). There are no immigration controls which operate within the CTA. Therefore most people do not require leave to enter when travelling to the UK from the Republic of Ireland (but see below). People's passports are not stamped as they are not examined by immigration officers.

The need for entry clearance

Both the UK and Ireland have their own lists of countries whose nationals require pre-clearance to enter and there is no common entry clearance for both countries. Visa nationals intending to travel to both countries should obtain entry clearances from both the embassies concerned before setting out. This is necessary even though it is unlikely that passports will be checked while travelling between the UK and Ireland. Where a person who requires a visa for the Republic of Ireland arrives in the UK intending to travel on to the Republic of Ireland but does not have such a visa, the immigration officer will contact the Department of Justice in Dublin to determine whether or not the person will be accepted for admission there. If the reply is negative, the person will normally be refused leave to enter the UK.

Travelling to the UK from Ireland

Irish citizens entering the UK automatically become settled on their arrival, as do British citizens entering the Republic of Ireland. Generally for EEA nationals and their family members, EU law rights of free movement apply ▶see Chapter 22.

For many people who are not Irish citizens and who wish to come to the UK, the provisions of the Immigration (Control of Entry through Republic of Ireland) Order 1972 apply. There are, however, exceptions and the circumstances in which this Order does not apply are set out below. Where the Order applies, people who need leave to enter and who travel from outside the CTA and enter the UK from Ireland are treated as having leave to remain in the UK for three months from the date they arrive in the UK. The leave has a prohibition on employment and business. Nothing will be stamped on their passports and there will usually be no evidence of their date of entry other than their travel ticket, if they have kept it. If they wish to remain in the UK for more than three months they should apply to the Home Office for an extension of this stay, with any evidence they have of the date of arrival (so they will not be treated as overstayers) and showing how they fit into the immigration rules to remain longer.

A visa national who has been given an entry clearance endorsed 'short visit' to enter the UK from a British embassy or high commission and who enters through Ireland, is treated as having been given leave for one month from the date of arrival in the UK and is prohibited from entering into employment and business and must register with the police. People with entry clearances for any other purpose are treated as having been given leave for three months.

The order does not, however, give a general means of avoiding immigration controls. Its provisions (▶see above) do *not* apply to:

- visa nationals who do not have entry clearance;
- illegal entrants and overstayers in the UK who cross to the Republic from the UK and then return to the UK;
- people who entered the Republic of Ireland unlawfully from outside the CTA;
- people who have been deported from the UK when the deportation order is still in force;
- people who, on their last attempt to enter the UK, were refused leave to enter;

- people who arrive by air in Ireland and simply transit by air to the UK;
- people whom the Secretary of State has directed should be excluded on the grounds that their presence is not conducive to the public good.

All these people still require leave to enter the UK. If they enter without seeing an immigration officer to grant this leave, they are deemed to have entered in breach of the immigration laws and can be treated as illegal entrants ▶for illegal entry, see pages 545-549. Even if they cross from Ireland, were not examined by an immigration officer, and were unaware that they were doing something wrong, the Court of Appeal decided in the case of *Bouzagou* that people in this situation are illegal entrants. They are liable to removal with no right of appeal until after they have left the UK unless they are asylum-seekers or seek to remain on human rights grounds.

Travelling to Ireland and returning to the UK

People who have limited leave to remain in the UK and who travel between the UK and Ireland and return to the UK within the currency of their leave still have leave. The same applies to people travelling to the UK who were granted leave to enter before their arrival and who travel through Ireland. However, people who are granted leave to enter the UK for a limited period, who travel to Ireland and return again after that leave has already expired, are treated as having been given leave for only seven days and should therefore either leave the UK or make a further application within that time.

Entry through the Channel Tunnel

Immigration law was slightly modified to deal with the situation of immigration control when a person comes to the UK through the Channel Tunnel. Two pieces of legislation, the Channel Tunnel (International Arrangements) Order 1993 and the Channel Tunnel (Miscellaneous Provisions) Order 1994, allow UK immigration officers to carry out the powers described in this chapter both on the trains which run between London, Paris, Lille and Brussels and in 'control zones' in France and Belgium.

5   Leaving and returning

This chapter looks at the position where a person who has already been admitted to the UK wishes to travel and then return. The rules relating to people in this position differ depending on the basis on which they have been admitted and the length of time for which they have been allowed to stay. We look first at the general rules before turning to see how those rules affect different categories of passenger. Then we look at the position of people who want to travel at the same time as they are waiting for a decision on extending their stay.

General rules

Regulations made under the Immigration and Asylum Act 1999, which were introduced in July 2000, have changed the way in which the law operates because now a person may still keep their 'leave' when they depart. 'Leave' is the formal permission which a person is given to be in the UK which is granted by the immigration authorities. The reason for introducing the new system is that it did not seem right that a person who had been in the UK, for example, for three years, might leave for a few days for a trip to the continent and then have to seek leave to enter again on their return and have no right of appeal if refused. Before these changes, almost all leave to enter or remain in the United Kingdom 'lapsed' when a person left the Common Travel Area (the CTA is the UK, Channel Islands, the Isle of Man and the Republic of Ireland). The exceptions to this rule were very narrow and included, for example, Commonwealth nationals who left on day excursions to France, Belgium or Holland.

Immigration officers' powers are much weaker in relation to people who want to leave the UK. They can ask to see passports in order to see whether the person has the right of abode in the UK and in order to establish their identity and nationality if they do not. They can carry out searches and ask to see other documentation. However, this is very rare and, except in exceptional circumstances, they have no powers to prevent a person leaving or to detain them.

Which leave does not lapse?

If a person leaves the UK on or after 30 July 2000, any leave which was given *before or after that date* does *not* lapse when a person goes out of the CTA *if*:

- it is leave which was given by means of an entry clearance (other than a visit entry clearance) which operated as leave to enter *or* it is leave which was given for a period of more than six months; *and*
- the leave has not been 'varied' (changed) by the Home Office so that the leave remaining after the variation was six months or less.

Any leave which does not satisfy the above conditions, still lapses as before when the person goes out of the CTA. Leave which is given by a visit entry clearance *does* still lapse when the holder leaves the CTA. However, this does not matter for visitors who came in with an entry clearance because visit entry clearances can be used on any number of occasions within the period of their validity. Leave which is given automatically by immigration law when a person makes an in-time application to extend their leave or during an appeal ▶see page 93, also lapses when a person leaves the CTA.

How long does 'non-lapsing' leave stay in force for?

If the leave is limited leave and it does not lapse, then it remains in force when the person departs until its natural expiry time. *However*, if the leave is still in force two years after a person has left and the person has not returned within that time, the leave lapses at that point. If the leave was indefinite leave, it will remain in force for a continuous period of two years but will then lapse if the person has not returned to the UK. Where leave remains in force while a person is outside the UK, for obvious reasons, the conditions which are attached to the leave are suspended until the person returns.

Cancellation of leave which has not lapsed

Even if the leave does not lapse when a person departs, it may still be cancelled while the holder is outside the CTA (or when a person returns) if any of the following conditions apply:

- there has been a change of circumstances such that leave should be cancelled;
- leave was obtained by the provision of false information or failing to disclose material facts;
- medical reasons make it undesirable to admit the person (unless the person is settled in the UK or there are strong compassionate factors);
- exclusion is conducive to the public good;
- the person has failed to provide information or documents as requested by the immigration authorities.

Where leave is cancelled in this way when a person arrives in the UK, there is an in-country right of appeal to the adjudicator. The immigration authorities also have the power to 'vary' leave (by adding or removing conditions or altering its length) while the person is outside the UK although this will probably be rare.

People who always qualify to return

People with the right of abode and certain British passport holders

People with the right of abode do not need leave and therefore can enter the UK at any time. This applies to British citizens and some Commonwealth nationals ▶see page 566. Where these passengers have British passports, immigration officers only have to be satisfied that the person travelling is the rightful holder of the passport. Occasionally, they make checks when they suspect that a person is travelling on a forged passport or on a passport issued to someone else and people can be refused entry for this reason. It is up to the immigration officers to prove that a person travelling on a full British passport is not entitled to do so and the person travelling has the right to appeal against refusal and to remain in the UK while the appeal is pending. Certain others travelling on British passports are entitled to very preferential treatment on arrival (▶see below).

Certificates of entitlement to the right of abode

People born in the UK before 1983 are automatically British citizens, as are people born in the UK from 1983 onwards if either parent was a British citizen or was settled in the UK at the time of their birth. They may also be entitled to another nationality by descent from a parent and therefore may be travelling on the passport of the other country. This may be the case when the other country, for example Malaysia or India, does not allow dual nationality or places restrictions on the stay of people using non-national passports. People with the right of abode need to have their passports stamped with a 'certificate of entitlement to the right of abode' ▶see page 121 for an example, as proof of their status in order to qualify to enter the UK. These certificates of entitlement can be obtained either from the Home Office, if the person is in the UK, or from a British post if the person is abroad. There is a fee payable even for people who apply within the UK ▶see page 738 for the amount. Difficulties sometimes arise in countries where the British authorities are suspicious of the documents shown.

Other Commonwealth citizens with the right of abode must obtain certificates of entitlement before travelling to the UK (see s3(9)(b) 1971 Act). They may have the right of abode through the birth of a parent in the UK or through a marriage, before 1 January 1983, to a man with the right of abode. To qualify for the right of abode people must have been

Commonwealth citizens at the time the British Nationality Act 1981 came into force on 1 January 1983. So Camerounians, Mozambicans, Pakistanis, Namibians and South Africans do not qualify as their countries were not then in the Commonwealth. Commonwealth nationals who apply for certificates will need to show original documents to prove their claim to the right of abode. In some countries where there may not be contemporaneous birth or marriage certificates to prove the relationship, people may have difficulties in convincing the British authorities that they qualify, and it may be necessary, for instance, to obtain sworn statements from other people who were present at the time of the marriage or birth.

Certificates of entitlement are valid for the same length of time as the passport on which they are stamped. When people renew their passports they can then apply to the British authorities for a new certificate of entitlement.

Holders of certain British passports

Holders of passports issued before 1 January 1973 in the UK or the Republic of Ireland showing them to be British Dependent Territories Citizens (BDTCs), British Nationals (Overseas), British Overseas Citizens, British Protected Persons or British Subjects (▶see Chapter 27 dealing with these persons), and which are not endorsed showing that the person is subject to immigration control, are freely admitted to the UK even though they are not British citizens. As a result of recent legislation, BDTCs now have full citizenship rights ▶see pages 563-564. British Overseas Citizens who hold a UK passport wherever and whenever it was issued, are granted indefinite leave if they can show that they have been granted indefinite leave at any time since 1st March 1968 (see paras 16 and 17 HC 395).

British Visitors passports

All kinds of British nationals who were resident in the UK used to be able to obtain travel documents through the Post Office. These were called British Visitor's passports and were normally valid for one year and for travel to western European countries, Turkey and Bermuda only. Because the Post Office did not usually demand evidence from people to show that they were British, but issued these documents on request, immigration officers did not necessarily accept a British Visitor's passport as proof that a person was British or was entitled to re-enter the UK.

On 20 December 1994, the Home Secretary stated that British Visitor's passports would be discontinued from 1 January 1996. The reasons the Passport Agency gave included that 'it does not provide definite evidence of national status or identity...it is used in the evasion of immigration controls and...by criminals, terrorists and football hooligans'. Further, the Spanish authorities had stated they would no longer accept them after

October 1995. British Excursion Documents, valid only for short-term visits to France, were discontinued from 1 March 1995.

People with indefinite leave

Under the Immigration and Asylum Act 1999, where a person who has indefinite leave in the UK leaves the CTA, their leave remains in force for two years while they are away and only lapses at that point. Therefore, if a person with indefinite leave travels away and returns within two years, they are entitled to be admitted with their leave treated as continuing unless any of the grounds upon which a person may have their leave cancelled at port applies ▶see page 69. The position before the introduction of these changes was that people who had indefinite leave lost that leave when they left. However, under the immigration rules, it was usually fairly straightforward for them to get indefinite leave again immediately when they returned provided that they returned within two years and certain other conditions were met. These other conditions are known as the 'returning residents' rules and the full requirements of the rules are set out below.

On a first impression, it seems that the introduction of 'non-lapsing' leave means that the returning residents rules are unimportant and that a person returning from abroad with indefinite leave only needs to make sure that their leave cannot be cancelled under the conditions described above. Another problem that some returning residents faced when they returned previously was that they might be granted only limited leave as a visitor rather than indefinite leave again which meant that they lost their ability to benefit from the returning residents rule altogether unless they got indefinite leave again in the future. Again, on first impressions, 'non-lapsing' leave would also eradicate this problem. *However*, the returning residents rules do remain important for the following reasons:

- the returning residents rules have not been withdrawn from the immigration rules;
- it is likely that immigration officers will consider the returning residents rules as a touchstone for deciding whether there has been a 'change of circumstances', which is one of the bases on which leave can be cancelled when a person returns. This is particularly so in relation to the requirement that the person seeks to return 'for the purposes of settlement' (▶see below);
- the rules are still relevant to those cases where leave has lapsed, namely where the person has been outside the UK for over two years.

Entry clearances for returning residents

Provided a person returns within the two years and qualifies for entry under the returning residents' rules, they do not need an entry clearance. However, a visa national who returns after they have been away for over two years does need to obtain an entry clearance. Non-visa nationals returning after two years are not required to get an entry clearance but they may choose to get one so that they can appeal from within the UK if they are refused entry. In addition, people who are unable to return within the two-year period but yet apply for an entry clearance within that time as a means of stating their intentions, are more likely to be admitted. If the application for entry clearance is refused, there is a right of appeal. The entry clearance officer will provide a notice giving brief reasons for the refusal together with information about how to appeal.

The 'returning residents' rule

WHAT THE RULES SAY

The immigration rules require that people must satisfy an immigration officer that:

- they have not been away for longer than two years. However, if a person has been away from the UK for over two years, they may still be admitted as a returning resident if, for example, they have lived in the UK for most of their life;
- they are returning for the purpose of settlement;
- they had indefinite leave when they last left; and
- they did not have assistance from public funds towards the cost of leaving the UK.

As a result of changes introduced by the immigration rules on 2 October 2000, if the person left the UK to accompany abroad a member of the British armed forces or the British diplomatic services or a member of the British Council, then it does not matter if they have been away for over two years or that they had assistance from public funds towards the cost leaving. This does not apply, however, if a spouse goes abroad independently.

WHAT THE RULES MEAN

Not been away for more than two years

Those who had indefinite leave when they left the UK should make every effort to return within two years. The leave of those who have been out of the UK for nearly two years and who are unable to return within this time will lapse after the two year period. They should apply to the British embassy or high commission in the country they are in for entry clearance as returning residents or at least contact the post to express their intention of returning in the future. There is a fee for this ▶see page 738 for the amount. If the application for entry clearance is made before expiry of the two-year period, and the applicant explains the reasons for the delay in travel, it is likely to be granted if the other conditions are satisified.

People who have been away for more than two years before returning or applying for entry clearance to return are in a more difficult position. The rule that an application may still be granted if, 'for example', a person has 'lived here for most of his [or her] life', gives the immigration authorities some discretion, and it is one that can be appealed if necessary. The rules do not give any other examples of the circumstances which would allow people to return to their homes although the Immigration Directorate's Instructions (IDI) state that leave may still be granted where a person:

- has been working abroad for a UK government body, UK company or a United Nations organisation;
- has travelled abroad to work for a particular employer and has returned with that employer;
- has family in the UK but has travelled abroad for prolonged studies;
- has had prolonged medical treatment abroad.

In *all* cases, however, where a person has been away for over two years, the following factors will be taken into account:

- the intentions of the person when they originally left to go abroad;
- the length of the previous residence in the UK;
- the time that the person has been outside the UK;
- the reason for the delay in returning;
- the strength of family ties to the UK (Article 8 ECHR could have an impact here); and
- whether the person has a home in the UK.

The courts have held that being too ill to travel at the relevant time when detailed medical evidence has been provided (*Khokhar*) and having a passport detained by the authorities in connection with legal proceedings (*Armat Ali*) were both strong enough reasons for not returning within the two-year period. People who came to the UK as young children to join their parents and were educated in the UK but who have then spent three or four years abroad without returning home may be able to qualify because of the length of time they have spent in the UK and their family ties.

It is important for people to explain in full, with evidence, the reasons why they have not been able to return to the UK within two years and why they are doing so at the time of the application. People should be prepared to argue their case, particularly if their stay away has been prolonged for reasons outside their control.

Returning for the purpose of settlement

The rules state that a person must be returning for the purposes of settlement. The rules do not require that the person is coming back to stay indefinitely on that occasion but rather that the person intends generally to keep the UK as the place of their ordinary residence. For example, a person who has a fixed-term, five-year contract to work abroad or is engaged in a course of study overseas may only be returning for a few weeks' vacation leave, but still intends to maintain their main home in the UK and to return here permanently later. They should not be refused entry as a returning resident in these circumstances. However, where people do return to the UK for short periods like this, in particular where they have been abroad for a substantial period of time, immigration officers may question them about their future intentions. The questioning has often been personal and intrusive.

Indefinite leave when they last left the country

People must have had indefinite leave when they *last* left. It is not enough to have had indefinite leave but lost it when they last returned and were granted only limited leave. People in that position will not qualify under this rule. Even if they have spent most of their lives in the UK, by being admitted for a limited period any application to settle again is considered at the discretion of the immigration authorities. They might also qualify under some other part of the rules, for example, as the spouse and children of a British citizen if the whole family has returned after some years away.

Not had assistance from public funds to leave

Although this rule refers to 'public funds', it is not intended to mean people who claimed welfare benefits or were housed by a local authority during their previous stay in the UK. Instead it refers to the very small number of people who have been 'repatriated'. Section 29 of the 1971 Act allows for financial help towards travel costs for foreign nationals who wish to return to their countries of origin and s5(6) 1971 Act enables the Secretary of State to make payments to assist persons who are liable to be deported to leave the UK together with their families. The section 29 scheme is administered by the International Social Services of the United Kingdom ▶see page 734 for address details. In order to be eligible for assistance, it has to be shown that it is in the interests of the person to leave and that they lack sufficient means to fund their own departure. The fund is normally only used for those who have indefinite rather than limited leave in the UK.

What happens to returning residents on arrival?

Granted entry

When a person returns within two years of leaving and is re-admitted as a returning resident, their indefinite leave is treated as continuing. Where a person returns to the UK after two years having obtained an entry clearance, the entry clearance operates as leave to enter. The immigration officer will simply place a date stamp over the entry clearance in the passport.

Refused entry

In the case of a person who has returned within the two-year period, if the immigration officer believes that there has been a sufficient change of circumstances so as to deny entry, their leave may be 'cancelled'. Those who return after two years (whose leave has therefore lapsed) and do not qualify for entry under the rule, are simply refused leave to enter the UK.

Returning residents granted limited leave

Sometimes those seeking to return as residents find that they are given only limited leave to enter as visitors even though they were seeking entry as a returning resident. This happens, in particular, where the immigration officer is not sure whether the person satisfies the immigration rules. The immigration officer should prepare a full report where this course is taken. In the past, immigration officers have sometimes granted leave for two months and advised the person to apply in that time for their right to permanent residence to be re-instated by the Home Office. Although there is no specific provision in the immigration rules for being granted indefinite leave as a 'returning resident' after a person has already re-entered, the Home Office will normally re-instate status (see IDI Ch 1, s3, para 3.1) if the person:

- had indefinite leave when they last left the UK, *and*
- in fact qualifies under the returning resident rules, *and*
- makes the application for indefinite leave to remain in time.

Appeals when refused entry as a returning resident

The rules on whether a refused returning resident may appeal are as follows: if a returning resident returns to the UK within the period of two years and their leave is cancelled, there is an in-country right of appeal against the decision provided the cancellation is not accompanied by the grant of limited leave, which is often the case (see *Ishaq*). Those granted limited leave in these circumstances may still contact the Home Office after entry and seek to have their indefinite leave re-instated (►see above). Those returning residents who return having been away for over two years and who are refused entry do not have an in-country right of appeal unless they obtained an entry clearance or unless they allege a breach of their human rights or claim asylum.

People with limited leave

The rules about leaving and seeking to return to the UK for people with limited leave are different depending on whether the person's leave lapses when they depart.

People whose leave does not lapse when they depart

The following two groups of people, who have limited leave in the UK, keep that leave when they exit the CTA:

- people who were given leave by the immigration authorities for more than six months (unless the Home Office has subsequently made a decision to change that leave so that, after that decision, the person only has six months or less remaining);
- people who obtained leave by having an entry clearance that operated as leave to enter (but this does not apply to visit entry clearances).

The leave remains valid while a person is outside the UK until the period for which it was granted comes to an end. *However*, if the leave is still continuing two years after a person has left the UK, it lapses at that point. Provided that the person returns within the period of the leave and there has been no change of circumstances or other reason to justify cancelling the leave, then the person should be re-admitted to the UK.

If any of the grounds for cancelling leave apply, then the leave may be cancelled on arrival by the immigration officer. So, for example, a student who is still following the same full-time course of studies and who still has the financial support available to do this should be readmitted for the same time as he or she had before leaving. However, if that student has actually stopped studying, or has married a settled or British person and intends to stay in the UK permanently with them, then leave may be cancelled on the grounds that entry is now, in reality, being sought for a different purpose. In the case of seeking entry for marriage, of course, that would be entry for which a different entry clearance would be needed. Where leave is cancelled in this way, there is a right of appeal to an adjudicator and the immigration officer should include in the decision information about appealing.

If the leave expires before the passenger returns to the UK, then the person is treated as a fresh arrival and examined accordingly. If the person returns after leave has expired and they are a visa national or otherwise require an entry clearance for the purpose of their entry, they must obtain a fresh entry clearance from a British post. If refused, they will not be able to appeal unless they obtained an entry clearance. As in all cases, however, this does not prevent a person from appealing on asylum or human rights grounds if one of those claims is made.

People whose leave lapses when they depart

After 30 July 2000, the following three categories of people still lose their leave when they depart from the CTA:

- those who obtained leave by a visit entry clearance;
- those granted leave for a period of six months or less *and* who were not given leave by an entry clearance which operated as leave; or
- those whose pre-existing leave has been 'varied' (changed) by the immigration authorities so that it is valid for a period of six months or less from the date of the variation.

Most of these people are visitors but the fact that their leave lapses doesn't harm them *if* they originally came with an entry clearance. This is because visitor entry clearances operate as the grant of leave on an unlimited number of occasions within the period of the validity of the entry clearance. On each occasion that a visitor returns to the UK within the period of the validity of the entry clearance, they are granted leave for a further period of six months if the period of validity of the entry clearance is still six months or more. If it is less when the visitor returns, they are granted leave until the end of the period of the validity of the entry clearance. Visitors, therefore, do not need to obtain a further entry clearance before returning provided that their original entry clearance remains valid. Entry can, of course, still be refused even where a person has a visit entry clearance which acts as leave to enter on the grounds that the leave should be cancelled ►see page 69. In these circumstances, there is a right of appeal.

In addition to visitors who entered with an entry clearance, others whose leave is likely to lapse under the rules above include:

- visitors who did not enter with an entry clearance;
- people granted *extensions* within the rules as visitors;
- students on short courses;
- those coming for short-term work like summer agricultural work who may be given six months leave or less, particularly if they arrive less than six months before 30 November of the year in question.

Also, people are sometimes exceptionally granted a period of six months or less in order for them to fulfill a specific purpose before leaving the UK. The leave of all these people which was not granted by an entry clearance, lapses when they depart. In addition, an automatic extension of leave is given when a person makes an in-time application to stay in the UK and while they are appealing against a refusal of such an application. This type of leave also lapses These people will all need an entry clearance to return to the UK under the ordinary rules.

People who left the UK before 30 July 2000

The new rules about 'non-lapsing' leave apply to leave which has not expired whenever that leave was granted, that is, whether it was granted before or after 30 July 2000. However, the new rules do no not apply to the leave where the holder left the CTA before 30 July 2000. This is because the transitional provisions state that the new rules only apply to leave which was 'in force' at the time that the new rules came into force on 30 July (see article 15(2) of the Immigration (Leave to Enter and Remain) Order 2000). If a person left the CTA before that time, then their leave lapsed at the point they left and was therefore no longer 'in force' on 30 July 2000.

It can be expected that the old rules relating to re-admission *continue* to apply to a person who left the UK before 30 July 2000. In summary , those rules are:

- if the person was granted leave by the immigration authorities for more than six months and they return within that period, they do not need an entry clearance;

- if the person returns within the period of time granted by the original leave which was given for over six months, then although that leave has lapsed, the same time limits and conditions will normally be applied to the leave on re-entry provided that the person returning continues to satisfy the requirements of the rules. Where, however, the person returns at a time when this rule would mean that they would get less than two months, leave will normally granted for a period of two months to give sufficient time for the making of a further application. However, if the same person returns with an entry clearance, then the period and conditions of leave will depend on the entry clearance granted;

- if the person was not previously granted leave for more than six months, or is not returning within the period of the original leave, then they need an entry clearance to return if they would ordinarily need one;

- if they return to the UK after the period of their original leave, they will be treated as fresh arrivals and examined by immigration officers in the ordinary way. If they have an entry clearance which operates as leave, they will generally be granted leave on the basis of that entry clearance. If not, the immigration officer will apply the immigration rules to decide whether they qualify for entry.

People who wish to travel while an application or an appeal is outstanding

Return of passports

While the Home Office is considering an application for an extension of leave or variation of conditions, it is normal for it to keep the applicant's passport. The passport can be requested back at any time if the holder needs it, for example, as proof of identity for a bank, to show to a marriage registrar or to obtain a driving licence. The application will not be treated as withdrawn if return of the passport is requested for purposes like this. Passports take a minimum of two weeks to be returned by post.

It is possible to ask the Home Office to speed up their consideration of the application to extend leave itself so that an applicant can travel outside the UK. The Home Office is only likely to agree to do this if there is an emergency, such as a family illness, which means that the applicant must travel. In such a case, it would be necessary to obtain a letter in English from the medical authorities concerned abroad.

However, if a person simply asks for the return of his or her passport 'for the purpose of travel outside the common travel area', while an application is being considered, then the immigration rules state that the application is treated as withdrawn as soon as the passport is returned (para 34 HC 395). This rule does now seem inconsistent with the changes in the law (see above), which prevent leave from lapsing when people leave the UK, and also the new ability of the Home Office to make decisions on whether to grant or refuse or change a person's leave when they are outside the UK.

Even if the application is treated as withdrawn when a person leaves, if the previous original grant of leave has not yet expired when a person wishes to travel, then that grant of leave is still valid and the rules dealing with a person leaving and returning which are set out above still apply. If the leave would otherwise have expired during the period while the Home Office was considering the application, then, when the Home Office returns the passport, it will normally grant leave to remain for a short period to enable the person to demonstrate in future that they did not actually overstay their leave before leaving. If the person's plans change and he or she does not travel but instead returns the passport and an application form to the Home Office to continue to apply to remain, the Home Office treats this as a new application, made on this date.

It is therefore very important that people who want their passports for any purpose other than travel should make this clear in their request to the Home Office. An application is only withdrawn if the request for the passport is for the purpose of travel. The application remains pending if the passport is taken away from the Home Office for other purposes.

Travelling before an application is decided

If a person only has leave which is granted automatically when they make an in-time application and their original leave has run out, then their leave lapses when they travel outside the CTA.

It is risky for people to travel after their leave has run out and before the Home Office has decided the application, and to expect to be able to return. They will be able to leave the UK without difficulty but when they return, they will have to satisfy immigration officers that they fit into the immigration rules. Until March 1998, it was usual for immigration officers to endorse triangular departure stamps on passports of people leaving, showing the date of departure from the UK. Comparison of the dates of previous permission to stay and the date of departure will usually lead immigration officers to ask questions and then contact the Home Office to check the position. Although passports are no longer stamped on departure, on arrival in the UK immigration officers will often ask about the circumstances of a previous stay.

If the application to the Home Office was straightforward, and if people can satisfy immigration officers that they qualify to enter, they may be granted leave to enter for the period they request provided the rules and any requirements concerning entry clearance are satisfied. If the application appears complicated but it seems likely that it would be granted, people may be admitted for two months and told to apply again to the Home Office within this time. If the application was for a change of status, especially if this was one for which entry clearance is necessary, people may be refused entry. For example, an international student who marries a British citizen in the UK and applies to remain as her husband but travels before the application has been decided and after his leave has expired, will not qualify to re-enter. He does not qualify as a student, because he no longer intends to leave the UK when his studies are completed. He does not qualify for entry as a husband because he does not have an entry clearance for that purpose.

People who need to travel while the Home Office is considering an application sometimes believe it would be easier to obtain emergency travel documents from their own embassies or high commissions and travel on these while the Home Office continues to consider the application. This is not a safe procedure. It is unusual for a travel document to be issued in these circumstances, but if one is, it does not alter the holders' immigration status – that an application for further leave to remain had been made, but not decided, when they left. When they return, immigration officers will probably see that the document was issued from a consular office in London and will wonder what the person's status was in the UK. When they know that an application was pending, they will contact the Home Office about the application and what is happening with it. It is not safe to expect entry to be granted.

Travelling before an application is decided

People who travel out of the country when they have an appeal pending against refusal of leave to remain are unlikely to be allowed back into the country, because the Home Office has already decided they do not qualify to stay. From 1 October 1996, leaving the country while an appeal is pending means that the appeal will be treated as abandoned.

Those without passports or other travel documents

In certain circumstances, the Home Office is prepared to issue travel documents to foreign nationals who cannot obtain or use travel documents from their own national authorities. The different travel documents which may be issued are set out below:

1951 Refugee Convention Travel Documents. These documents are blue in colour and are issued to people who are accepted as refugees under the 1951 Convention.

'Exceptional Leave' travel documents. These are brown in colour. The official name for these documents is 'Certificates of Identity'. They are issued to people who have been given exceptional leave following a failed application for asylum and who do not have a valid passport or other travel document. If the grant of exceptional leave was made before 26 July 1993, the applicant needs to show that they have been formally and unreasonably refused a passport by their own national authorities. This form of travel document can also be issued to people who are settled in the UK and either arrived on a travel document other than a passport but which has since expired or who have been formally and unreasonably refused a passport by their own national authorities.

'Stateless Persons' travel documents. These are red in colour and can be issued to persons who are not nationals of any country.

'Declaration of Identity' documents. These are 'one way' travel documents and can therefore be issued to any foreign national regardless of their status in order to allow them to leave the UK. They are not valid for the person's return.

Further information relating to travel for those recognised as refugees and granted exceptional leave after a failed asylum application, is contained in Chapter 12.

Applying for travel documents

To apply for a travel document, it is necessary to complete form TD112 which can be downloaded from the Home Office website. A fee is payable which is non-refundable even if the application is refused or withdrawn. For details of fees ▶see page 738. The application should be sent by post to the Home Office's Travel Document Section. The Home Office attempts to deal with applications within 10 weeks. Applications can be expedited in urgent cases, for example, if there are pressing medical reasons why the person needs to travel. The travel document is normally valid for the length of leave that a person has. However, where a person has indefinite leave they are valid for a period of 10 years in the case of 1951 Convention or stateless persons travel documents. A person with indefinite leave will normally be given a certificate of identity valid for five years.

6 Applying to stay in the United Kingdom

People who have been allowed to enter or remain in the UK, can apply to the Home Office for permission to extend their stay or to change the conditions on which they have been allowed to remain. It is important, for a number of reasons, to make applications to extend leave before the existing leave has run out. Applications to extend leave are known as applications for leave to *remain* rather than to *enter.* If the application is made 'in time', they may also be referred to as applications to 'vary' leave. Only those with limited leave need to make these applications as those with indefinite leave have no time limit attached to the leave and no other conditions (such as restrictions on work) can be attached to an indefinite leave.

It is possible for people to apply to extend their leave to allow them to remain in the UK in the same category under the immigration rules as they are at present (e.g., a 'writer') or they may apply to 'switch' into a different category under the rules. In order to decide all applications, the Home Office applies the immigration rules and it must also ensure that its decisions are compliant with human rights. While no-one may be treated less favourably than the immigration rules allow, there is always the possibility of asking the Home Office to exercise discretion outside the immigration rules and the Home Office has certain policies which indicate when it will be prepared to act in this way.

This chapter looks at the rules about switching. It also deals with the status a person has while an application to extend leave is being considered and at the practical considerations of applying to extend leave. The chapter also looks at Home Office decisions on applications and at 'curtailment' of (or cutting short) leave. Finally, the chapter looks at exceptional leave and concessions outside the immigration rules.

Switching categories

The table on page 92 explains the circumstances in which people can and cannot 'switch' to another category *under the immigration rules.* In order to understand these rules, it is important to understand the difference between temporary categories of leave under the rules and permanent categories. Generally, temporary categories are ones in which a person is expected to leave the UK after the purpose of their stay has concluded and which are not expected to lead to a person eventually being granted indefinite leave (e.g., visitors and students). Permanent categories are those in which a person does not have to show that they intend to leave the UK at any particular time and which may lead to a person being granted indefinite leave or 'settlement' (e.g., spouse or work permit holder). A person who is allowed to stay in a permanent category does not necessarily get indefinite leave straight away, they may first have to stay in the UK for a period of time with limited leave before becoming eligible to apply for indefinite leave. For example, a foreign spouse is granted a 12-month 'probationary' period under the immigration rules before being able to make an application for indefinite leave. For many people in the UK for work or business purposes, the qualifying period is four years. For the specific rules for all the different categories, the relevant chapter should be consulted.

One general rule is that a person may not usually switch from any category of leave into a permanent category. This is because, in order to obtain admission in permanent categories, it is generally necessary to obtain an entry clearance for that purpose and the applicant must be outside the UK in order to do this. However, there are, of course, exceptions. For example, a person may switch from any category into the category of spouse, unmarried partner or dependant relative of a person settled in the UK. In addition, switching into a temporary category is in some circumstances restricted. For example, visa nationals are unable to switch to remain as students; they must leave and obtain an entry clearance.

The Home Office's February 2002 White Paper, *Secure Borders, Safe Haven*, indicates that a change in the law to prevent certain people switching to remain on the basis of marriage is under consideration.

The box below sets out the rules on switches that are possible in principle under the immigration rules. This does not mean that the Home Office will necessarily grant the application. In all cases, it is necessary to show that the rules of the new category are satisfied *and* that none of the general grounds of refusal apply ▶see page 102. In addition, even where the rules do not permit switching, it is possible to ask the Home Office to make an exception due to the circumstances of the case. It should also be noted that applying to change status *may* cast doubts on the person's original intentions on coming to the UK and may lead to enquiries to determine whether a person is an illegal entrant ▶see Chapter 26.

The need to apply in time

Applications for extensions should always be made to the Home Office in good time *before* the current leave expires. If leave has already expired, then legal advice should be obtained about making a further application without delay.

CHANGES OF STATUS ALLOWED UNDER THE IMMIGRATION RULES

This table lists changes which are specifically allowed under the rules. *This does not mean that an application will automatically be granted; people have to satisfy the Home Office that they qualify.* (See relevant chapter for details.) Other applications may be made, but they are outside the immigration rules, at the discretion of the Home Office ►see pages 104-5 for concessions outside the rules. For example, there is no provision in the rules for a person in the UK to become a fiancé (e), but such applications may be granted when there are strong reasons for delaying the marriage. In addition, certain switching applications to work-permit employment may be granted although not strictly permitted under the rules ►see pages 320, 421-422, as may certain applications to remain as a Highly Skilled Migrant Worker ►see page 444. Applications to remain exceptionally outside the immigration rules are not restricted by the no switching provisions and neither are claims to asylum or to stay based upon an applicant's human rights under the ECHR. It should also be noted that the 2002 White Paper proposes to prevent those who are granted leave for six months or less from swithching to remain in the UK for the purpose of marriage. For switching in 'Association Agreement' cases ►see page 478 and for EU free movement rights more generally ►see Chapter 22.

1 visitor
can change to 8
can change to 2 if *not* a visa national
cannot change to 3, 4, 5, 6, 7, 9

2 student
can change to 8
can change to 1 for short period after end of studies
cannot change to 3, 4, 5, 6, 7, 9

3 work permit holder
permit-free employment*
can change to 8
can change to 9 after four years in this category
can change to 2 if *not* a visa national
can change to 1 for short period after end of work
cannot change to 4, 5, 6, 7

4 working holidaymaker
can change to 8
can change to 2 if *not* a visa national
can change to 1 for short period at end of stay
cannot change to 3, 5, 6, 7, 9

5 business, self-employed, independent means, investor
can change to 9 after four years in this category
can change to 8
can change to 2 if *not* a visa national
can change to 1 for short period at end of stay
cannot change to 3, 4, 6, 7

6 au pair
can change to 8
can change to 2 if *not* a visa national
can change to 1 for short period at end of stay
cannot change to 3, 4, 5, 7, 9

7 fiancé(e)
can change to 8 after marriage
if marriage plans fail, can change to 1
can change to 2 if *not* a visa national
cannot change to 3, 4, 5, 6, 9

8 spouse or unmarried partner with limited leave
can change to 9 after probationary period
if marriage fails, can change to 1
can change to 2 if *not* a visa national
cannot change to 3, 4, 5, 6, 7

9 indefinite leave to remain
no immigration applications necessary
may be able to apply for British citizenship ►see Chapter 28

* Permit-free 'employment' covers the following categories: representatives of overseas newspapers, news agencies or broadcasting organisations; sole reprsentatives of overseas firms; private servants in diplomatic households; overseas government employees; ministers of religion, missionaries and members of religious orders; ground staff of overseas-owned airlines; persons with UK ancestry (Commonwealth nationals only); writers, composers, artists.

The consequences of not applying for further leave in time are serious. People who do not make an in-time application for further leave:

- become liable for administrative removal from the UK as overstayers;
- may have their application for further leave refused under the general grounds for refusal in the immigration rules ▶see page 102. This is particularly important in spouse or unmarried partner applications because the specific immigration rules for those categories require that a person has limited leave at the time that a decision is made on their application and that they have not remained in breach of the immigration laws;
- will, as overstayers, be excluded from most welfare benefits, support from a local authority and local authority housing (if they were not already excluded because of their immigration status);
- become liable to criminal proceedings, although prosecutions are rare.

What status does a person have while waiting for a decision?

'In-time' applications with a delayed decision

In many cases where an in-time application to extend leave is made, it is not possible for the Home Office to make a decision on the application before the leave expires. What is the person's immigration status while they are waiting for a decision and after their leave would otherwise have run out? Are they in the UK unlawfully? Before 1976, applicants who had made applications in time but were still awaiting a decision when their leave ran out became overstayers and lost the right to make an appeal against the refusal because they no longer had leave as required at the time of the appeal. The unfairness of that situation was demonstrated in the cases of *Subramaniam* and *Suthendran* . As a result, the Home Office introduced the Immigration (Variation of Leave) Order 1976 (known as 'VOLO'). The effect of this was to automatically extend leave when an in-time application was made but no decision was made before the applicant's leave expired.

The situation has been modified again from 2 October 2000 following the Immigration and Asylum Act 1999. The circumstances are now slightly different depending on whether the *decision* of the Home Office which is made on the application was taken before or after 2 October 2000. In *both* cases, however, where an in-time application is made, the person *automatically* continues to have leave while they are waiting for a decision.

Decision of Home Office made on or after 2 October 2000

Where the decision of the Home Office is made on or after 2 October 2000, a person continues to have leave if an in-time application was made. It is not important whether the *application* to extend leave was made before or after 2 October. In these cases, if the Home Office refuses the application, leave is treated as continuing until the end of the period which is allowed for appealing against a negative decision from the Home Office (see s3C Immigration Act 1971 added by the 1999 Act).

The time for appealing against a negative decision is 10 working days and the appeal must be made within this time. Working days do not include Saturdays, Sundays, bank holidays, Good Friday, Christmas Day or the period 27 to 31 December. The automatic extension only applies if the decision is made after the leave would otherwise have run out and therefore the Home Office's internal instructions emphasise to case-workers that they should not issue decisions to refuse an application where there is less than 10 days to go before leave expires. In these circumstances, the caseworker should wait until leave has actually expired before issuing the refusal so that the person has 10 working days to appeal without their leave running out.

If an appeal is brought against the decision, then the leave continues for as long as the appeal takes to be 'finally determined', namely until the whole appeal process has been exhausted. This applies to both asylum and non-asylum appeals against decisions refusing to extend leave.

When leave is automatically extended in either of these ways, it is treated as continuing on the same conditions as it was previously granted. So, if there was a condition prohibiting work, this continues during the time of the extended leave. *However*, it should be noted that for benefit and other welfare purposes, a person who has leave *only* as the result of an automatic extension while an appeal is pending is always treated as being a person who is 'subject to immigration control', whatever the pre-existing conditions on their leave, and is therefore excluded from access to most welfare provision (see s115(9)(d) 1999 Act).

Decision of Home Office made before 2 October 2000

If the decision of the Home Office on an in-time application was made before 2 October 2000 but after leave would otherwise have expired, leave is automatically extended until *28 days* after the date of the decision (see VOLO as amended by the Immigration (Variation of Leave) (Amend-ment) Order 2000). Under the old appeals legislation (s14 1971 Act) there was a right of appeal. As with decisions made on or after 2 October 2000 (see above), because the leave is 'extended', the pre-existing other conditions remain the same. However, in contrast to the position where the decision is made on or after 2 October, where an appeal is brought in these cases, there is no automatic extension of leave during the appeals process. So, although people cannot be forced to leave the UK while they are exercising their variation right of appeal, they are still technically overstayers. There are no direct restrictions on these people to prevent them from working: if they do not have leave, the conditions (such as working restrictions) of the leave also do not continue. Since 1996, however, conditions preventing people from working have only been one obstacle to being able to legally obtain work. In most cases, it is a criminal offence for an employer to give work to overstayers and so working is still prevented ▶see pages 415-416 for more details about who can work.

Successive applications

In all cases, the law only allows for *one* automatic extension of leave before the immigration authorities again grant leave. Where a further application is made during the period of automatically extended leave while an application is already outstanding, the Home Office will treat the application as a variation of the existing application. This is the case even if it raises entirely new grounds for staying in the UK, for example, if a person who originally sought to extend their leave as a visitor subsequently makes an application to remain as a spouse. The Home Office will then issue only one decision on the application as varied which will result in one right of appeal. Although it is a single decision, it will cover both grounds on which the application was based unless, in the second application, the person clearly indicates that they are withdrawing the grounds for the original application in favour of the second one.

Evidence of automatic extensions

Passports are not endorsed and returned showing that an automatic extension of leave has come into operation. It is therefore important that evidence of an in-time application to extend leave is kept in the form of copies of the application form, the acknowledgement received from the Home Office and the decision itself so that it can be shown that the person did not become an overstayer.

How to make the application

Before November 1996, there were no special rules as to what counted as an application for an extension of leave. Any clear request to the Home Office, either in person or by letter accompanied by a passport or travel document, was acceptable. Since then, however, applications to the Home Office for leave to remain must be made on the appropriate Home Office prescribed application form. This is the case whether the person is making an in-time or out-of-time application. Certain applications can still be made without using a prescribed form ▶see below, page 100.

The prescribed application forms

The application forms can be obtained by telephoning the Application Forms Unit at the Home Office (telephone no: 0870 241 0645) or they can be downloaded from the Immigration and Nationality Directorate website (http://www.ind.homeoffice.gov.uk). Eight prescribed application forms were issued in April 2002. The forms change regularly and new forms will be issued for applications made on or after 15 November 2002. Using the correct, up-to-date, application form for the purpose for which further leave is being requested is vital. The forms issued in April 2002 are as follows:

Form FLR (M). This form should be used to apply for further leave to remain in the UK as the spouse or unmarried partner of a person present and settled in the UK.

Form FLR(O). This form should be used to apply for further leave to remain as an au pair, doctor/dentist in post graduate training, domestic worker, ship/aircraft crew, permit-free employment, visitor, private medical visitor, seasonal agricultural worker, person of UK ancestry, working holidaymaker, writer/artist/composer or on any other basis. Those applying under the Highly Skilled Migrant Programme (HSMP) have to submit form FLR(0) together with the HSMP form.

Form FLR (S). This form should be used to apply for further leave to remain as a student or a student nurse.

Form SET (M). This form should be used by a person seeking *indefinite* leave to remain (settlement) as the spouse or unmarried partner of a person present and settled in the UK.

Form SET (F). This form should be used to apply for indefinite leave to remain in the UK as a family member (not husband, wife or unmarried partner) of a person present and settled in the UK.

Form SET (O). This form should be used to apply for *indefinite* leave to remain as a person who has been in the UK for four years as a domestic worker, in any work permit free category, as a person of UK ancestry, in work permit employment, as a writer/composer/artist or on any other basis.

Form BUS. This form should be used to apply for further leave *or* indefinite leave as a business person, sole representative, retired person of independent means, investor or innovator (the form has been made available interactively on the Home Office website).

Form ELR. This form should be used to apply for further leave *or* indefinite leave as a person who was granted exceptional leave after a refusal of asylum.

If a person applying to remain has dependants who seek to remain with them, there is a place on the forms for them to be included. If the application is being made for alternative purposes, then more than one form should be submitted.

The Home Office requires *original* documents and insists that if photocopies are provided that they must be certified by the issuing authority for example, building society passbooks which can be certified as genuine by the building society branch office. When evidence relating to the maintenance and accomodation rules has to be submitted, documents relating to financial resources, for example, wage slips or bank statements, should cover a period of at least three months.

Applicants should keep copies of the application form and the documents sent so that it can be proved that an application has been made.If the application is being sent by post, it should be sent by recorded delivery to the Home Office's 'Initial Consideration Unit' at the Integrated Casework Directorate at Lunar House ▶see page 725 for the address.

The Nationality, Immigration and Asylum Bill 2002 proposes to allow the Home Office to obtain from applicants data about their physical characteristics (including features of the iris and any other part of the eye). These proposals also apply to entry clearance and leave to enter applications.

Ensuring that the application is valid

The application must be made on the correct form and the form must be properly completed and sent to the Home Office along with all the documents requested on the form or an explanation of why those documents have not been supplied and when they will be sent. Although further information can be added in covering letters, *every* question asked on the form must be answered on the form itself. If these procedures are not followed, the application is treated as not valid.

The Initial Consideration Unit decides whether or not applications are valid. When an application is invalid, the parts which are not satisfactory are marked in red pen and the entire form and documents returned to the applicant.

If the application is returned as invalid, no application is treated as having been made. If the person later corrects or amplifies the form and returns it to the Home Office, it is the date of return which counts as the date of the application. There is therefore a serious possibility that applications originally sent in time will not be counted and that they will be returned after the person's leave to remain has run out. This means that the applicant loses rights of appeal against refusal and it may be that leave runs out before the person is able to re-submit a valid application ▶see above page 93 for the consequences of failing to apply in time.

Applications should be made well within time so that, if rejected as invalid, there is still further time to submit a valid application before time expires. However, applications will not usually be dealt with until there is less than four weeks of leave remaining and the Home Office discourages people from making applications before this time. Unfortunately, although the Home Office states that the Initial Consideration Unit will return invalid applications by return of post, it can take up to a month or sometimes even longer to decide whether an application is actually valid. The old Tribunal case of *Lubetkin* probably still applies, so that an application is treated as made on the day on which it is sent rather than the date of its receipt.

If the Home Office returns an application for amendment, and in the meantime the form used has been replaced by a new version, the new form must be used to re-apply. In these cases, applicants should attach the old form, with its red markings to the new one when it is sent in.

If the Home Office has rejected as a valid application a form which was submitted in time, so that a later refusal did not attract a right of appeal, consideration should be given as to whether to challenge the decision refusing to accept the first application as validly made. This can be done by submitting a notice of appeal against the decision and asking for the question of whether there is a right of appeal to be decided by the adjudicator as a preliminary issue. In the Tribunal case of *Deroiche*, the Tribunal found that the wording of one form was unclear and misleading and that the rejection of the form for a minor non-compliance was unreasonable in the circumstances.

The '24-hour' and '48-hour' priority services

The '24-hour' and '48-hour' priority services are both procedures operated by the Home Office for applications made by immigration representatives on behalf of their clients who are registered with the Home Office as able to use the service. The Home Office calls these applicants 'Third Party Applicants' (TPAs). TPAs must be regulated by one of the professional bodies (e.g., solicitors) or registered with or exempted from registration with the Office of the Immigration Services Commissioner (OISC). As of January 2002, the services were being used by over 230 organisations. The services guarantee to TPAs a 24 or 48-hour turnaround of urgent 'straightforward' applications, which they make by post on a nominated day of the week.

Until September 2001, TPAs would have a certain number of case slots allocated to them in order to make these applications under the 24-hour service. As a result of the increasing numbers of applicants attending in person with applications, slots were reduced to one case per TPA. Instead, a 48-hour service was introduced and TPAs now have one case slot under the 24-hour service and however many slots they had taken away in September 2001 transferred to the 48-hour service. The services are to be kept under review and may well change again.

Only 'straightforward' applications are dealt with under these services. A straightforward application is any application *other than* the following (guidelines issues by the Public Enquiy Office on 31 January 2002.):

- an application relating to asylum except for applications for further exceptional leave to remain (ELR) or for settlement where the applicant is a recognised refugee and has completed four years of residence as such in the UK;
- further ELR applications where the applicant has applied for an upgrade to full refugee status;
- long-residence concession cases;
- any case where the applicant has been refused an extension of leave in the last two years;

- all indefinite leave applications (not including spouses) where the dependant/s did not enter the UK with the correct entry clearance including all applications made on form SET(F) (see above);
- all applications under European law and Association Agreement cases;
- applications for further leave to remain in business, as an investor, or as a sole representative of an overseas firm;
- indefinite leave applications for a person established in business, as an investor, as a retired person of independent means, as a sole representative of an overseas firm or as a representative of an overseas newspaper or news agency;
- all applications from people who are dependants of anyone in the above categories.

Applications made in person by applicants

If the application is urgent, it is also possible for it to be taken in person to the Home Office's Public Enquiry Unit (PEO) at Lunar House in Croydon (which has changed its name back to the PEO after a period when it was known as the Public Caller Unit) or to the regional Public Enquiry Offices in Belfast, Birmingham, Glasgow or Liverpool. The Home Office states that, if possible and if the application is straightforward, the PEO will deal with the application on the day, but if not, it will be taken in for completion by post.

This service is only for applicants themselves and is not available where a representative is making the application on behalf of the applicant. It is intended as an equivalent service to the urgent postal services described above but for unrepresented applicants. Only the applicants themselves and their dependants are allowed into the PEO. Representatives have not been received since November 1997. Interpreters should be available inside. There are long queues at the PEO in Croydon and people can wait all day to be seen. The queues at the other, regional, PEOs are shorter. The person applying still needs to fill in the form completely and take all original documents with them.

Delays in decisions

There have been very serious delays in dealing with applications by the Home Office over the past few years. According to information released by the Home Office in January 2002, 'straightforward' postal applications (i.e., *not* those in the list above) were then being dealt with within six to eight weeks. The stated aim is to reduce the waiting time to three weeks.

Applications made from outside the UK

It should also be noted that applications to extend leave can now be made from outside the UK. So a person who has left the UK and whose leave has not lapsed, can submit an in-time application while abroad. The prescribed application forms do not have to be used when such an application is made. The drawback to this is that the immigration rules state that the Home Office is not obliged to consider such an application (see para 33A, HC 395).

Applications which do not need to be made on the prescribed forms

The following applications do not need to be made on the prescribed forms described above in order to be valid.

Asylum applications

The immigration authorities are under a duty to treat an asylum application as having been made whenever a person indicates either in writing or orally that they will be in some sort of danger if they are returned to their country of origin. For further details about what constitutes a claim for asylum ►see pages 690-691.

Work permit related applications

Until June 2001, applications for further leave to remain for work permit employment were sent to a section of the then Department of Education and Employment rather than to the Home Office. Following the re-organisation of government departments after the election in June 2001, the Home Office has itself taken over the section of the previous DfEE (now the Department for Education and Skills) which processed work permits, 'Work Permits (UK)'. Work Permits (UK) was itself previously called the 'Overseas Labour Service' (OLS). In practical terms, it is the *employer* who applies for an extension of the work permit by filling in form WP1X, which can be obtained from Work Permits (UK) or downloaded from their web-site: http://www.workpermits.gov.uk/. Applications can also be made by email using a similar form available on the same site.

From 4 February 2002, Work Permits (UK) also deals with the actual in-country immigration application for leave as well as issuing work permits. It has its own dedicated team of 20-30 people to deal with the immigration part of the applications. Only in exceptional cases are the applications referred to Croydon, for example, where security checks need to be carried out or where further guidance is necessary. Work Permits (UK) has stated that, in 2001, it was dealing with 95 per cent of applications for work permits within five days. The February 2002 White Paper states that 90 per cent of complete applications are decided within a day of receipt. The Home Office has stated that it wants to introduce legislation to enable Work Permits (UK) to charge for its services. Charging is likely to be introduced in early 2003.

The passports and/or police registration certificates of the applicant and any dependants must always be included with the application to Work Permits (UK) (or if the application is made by email, they should be received within five working days of the application). If the application is successful, the passport will be returned endorsed with the further leave and any conditions of leave and the work period will be extended.

EEA applications

EEA nationals and their family members who are in the UK may apply for residence permits (for EEA nationals) or for residence documents (for non-EEA national 'family members' of EEA nationals). Neither EEA nationals with the right to live in the UK nor their family members *need* to have a residence permit or document. Their right to be in the UK exists independently of documentation but these documents can be obtained as evidence of their status in the UK.

Residence permits are normally valid for five years but they can be issued for less if the EEA national is working in the UK for a shorter period. If a residence document is given to a family member, it will be issued for the same period as the permit given to the EEA national. It should be noted that a non-EEA national family member who has a valid residence document does not need a new EEA family permit each time they return to the UK after travelling abroad. There is no charge for the issue of these permits/documents. Applications can be made on Form EEC1 which can also be downloaded from the Home Office website.

Applications for further leave to remain under the Association Agreements between the EU and certain other countries also do not need to be made on a prescribed form. They can be made with a covering letter enclosing the relevant documents.

For more details about obtaining residence permits and documents ▶see pages 464-468, and for details about Association Agreement applications ▶see Chapter 34.

Applications made outside the UK or on entry

Applications to vary leave made when the applicant is outside the UK or applications made to the immigration officer on arrival to the UK by someone who already has leave (e.g., because they previously had leave which did not lapse) also do not need to be made on a prescribed form (see para 32, HC395).

Home Office decisions

The Home Office makes decisions by applying the requirements contained in the relevant immigration rules. In addition, decisions of the Home Office must always comply with an applicant's human rights under the ECHR. The immigration rules themselves do not set out the rights which are protected and the effect which they have on applications, they simply require the immigration authorities to 'carry out their duties... in compliance with the provisions of the Human Rights Act 1998' (para 2 HC 395). The rules for

GENERAL GROUNDS FOR REFUSAL OF LEAVE TO REMAIN

Paragraph 322, HC 395

Grounds on which applications for leave to remain 'should normally be refused':

- making false representations or failing to disclose a material fact when applying for leave to enter or remain in the past;
- breaking a condition imposed on previous leave to enter or remain, for example, overstaying or working without permission;
- if people have not been able to support themselves or family members without recourse to public funds;
- if a person's character, conduct or associations make it undesirable to allow him or her to remain, or if they are a threat to national security;
- if a sponsor refuses to give an undertaking of support, or has not complied with such an undertaking in the past;
- if people have not complied with any undertaking or declaration about the length or purpose of their stay;
- if people cannot show that they will be allowed into another country at the end of their stay (except those who qualify for settlement, or spouses of settled people);
- if people do not produce documents or information required by the Home Office within a 'reasonable time';
- if people fail to attend an immigration interview without a reasonable explanation;
- if a child is applying to remain not in conjunction with his or her parents or legal guardians and does not have the written consent of a parent or guardian to do so. This does not apply to child asylum-seekers.

Grounds on which applications for leave to remain 'are to be refused':

- where the application for further leave is being made for a purpose not covered by the immigration rules.

If any of these factors might apply to a person, it is important to explain in any application why they should not be used as a ground of refusal and how the person otherwise qualifies for leave to remain.

the different categories in which leave can be granted are set out in the relevant chapters of this book. However there are also general grounds upon which leave to remain can be refused.

The immigration rules list 10 grounds on which an extension of stay 'should normally be refused' (►see box above). There is also one circumstance in which the rules state that leave 'is to be refused'. This is where the application is being made for a purpose not covered by the immigration rules. This rule suggests that applications made outside the rules, asking the Home Office to use its discretion, will never be successful. In fact, there is *always* a discretion to waive *any* immigration rule.

Decisions made by the Home Office where no application has been made

Curtailment

In certain circumstances, the Home Office may 'curtail' an existing limited leave ▶see box below. This means bringing the leave to an end before it is due to expire. The Home Office can do this of its own accord if certain matters come to its attention and without any application having been made. When leave is curtailed, the person becomes an overstayer which means they can be 'administratively removed' from the UK (▶see pages 533-534 for an explanation of this form of removal). Curtailment also has welfare benefit implications as the person then becomes 'subject to immigration control' even if they were not before.

However, there is a right of appeal against a decision to curtail leave if the leave is cut short so that there are less than 28 days left. If an *appeal* is made against the decision, then the decision itself does not take effect during the time that it takes to finally determine the appeal and so arguably the person is not 'subject to immigration control' (unless they were already) for welfare purposes during the period of the appeal. Officers at the Benefits Agency may not appreciate this and it may be necessary to quote the relevant parts of the legislation (para 16 sch 4 1999 Act; and in relation to old appeals, s14(1) 1971 Act, para 7 sch 2 1993 Act, both preserved by paras 2(5) and 3(4) sch 2 Immigration and Asylum Act 1999 (Commencement No 6 and Consequential Provisions) Order 2000. It should be noted that SIIS 1999 Act treats as subject to control those who have leave 'only' because a variation appeal is pending

---

CIRCUMSTANCES IN WHICH LEAVE MAY BE CURTAILED

Paragraphs 322-323, HC 395

The circumstances in which leave can be curtailed are as follows:

- false representations are made or there is a failure to disclose a material fact for the purpose of obtaining a previous leave;

- failure to comply with any conditions attached to the grant of leave to enter or remain;

- failure to continue to meet the requirements of the rules under which leave was granted;

- failure of the person to maintain or accommodate themselves and any dependants without recourse to public funds;

- it is undesirable to allow the person to remain in the UK in the light of their character, conduct, associations or the fact that they represent a threat to national security.

whereas those whose leave is curtailed still keep their original leave pending the appeal).

Changing conditions of leave

In addition to curtailment, the Home Office may, acting of its own accord, add, vary or take away *conditions* (working, recourse to public funds etc) which are attached to leave without any application having been made. There are no specific rules as to when this can be done but people cannot be treated less favourably in terms of conditions than the immigration rules for their particular category provide. The 1999 Act took away the right of appeal against a decision to vary conditions. Only curtailment decisions (see above) carry with them the right of appeal.

Notice of decisions

If the application to the Home Office to extend leave is successful, the Home Office will endorse the further leave and conditions in the passport or travel document, for examples of stamps ▶see pages 118-121, and may also inform the person in writing of the decision.

If however, the application is unsuccessful or the Home Office has itself changed the leave without an application having been made (see above), then this will also be notified in writing together with information about any right of appeal which exists against the decision. In most cases, provided the application was made in time, there is a right of appeal against the decision. There are no rights of appeal, however, if the Home Office grants further leave, although not for the length of time or on the conditions that the applicant wanted. Rights of appeal are also denied if, for example, the application was not made in time or the application was to 'switch' into a category which the immigration rules do not allow without the applicant having been admitted with the relevant entry clearance. Except in 'third country' asylum cases or certain other certified cases, there will always be an in country right of appeal on asylum, human rights or discrimination grounds if the relevant application has been made. The rules about appeals are complex.

Exceptional Leave

If an applicant cannot satisfy the immigration rules, the Home Office always has the power to make favourable decisions outside the rules if they are satisfied that there is sufficient reason to do so. When a person has strong compassionate or other reasons for needing to remain in the UK, but does not fit into the immigration rules, an application outside the rules should be considered. It should also be considered whether these grounds amount to a human rights claim to remain in the UK, perhaps on the basis that the effect of separation from family members will be unduly harsh upon them or because they are ill or vulnerable in some way such that the effect of requiring them to leave would interfere with their human rights. Full details should be given of the reasons why the person needs to remain together with any available evidence to support this.

Form FLR(O) (for limited leave) or SET (O) (for indefinite leave) should be used for these exceptional applications. Often, if the exceptional application is being made after an asylum claim has failed, advisers simply make further representations including a human rights claim which, in practice, the Home Office will consider. Form ELR is only used to apply for further leave for a person who has *already* had a period of exceptional leave after a refusal of asylum.

Any application which does not meet the requirements of the rules is an 'exceptional' application and any resulting leave is 'exceptional' leave because it is given as an exception to the rules. Often the term 'exceptional leave' is used in a much narrower sense, to mean leave which is given on a humanitarian basis to those who have applied for, but have been refused, asylum. This kind of exceptional leave is dealt with in the section dealing with asylum ▶see pages 216-219. Sometimes exceptional leave is given as a 'one off' because of the particular circumstances of the case. In other cases, leave is granted exceptionally on the basis of an established policy or concession which the Home Office has outside the rules. These concessions are therefore covered in the section to which they are most relevant. The most important relate to:

- 'carers' ▶see pages 289-291;
- those with HIV/AIDS ▶see pages 253-254;
- domestic violence ▶see pages 358-361;
- domestic workers ▶see pages 434-435;
- enforcement against people with settled spouses ▶see pages 353-355;
- enforcement against people with children with long residence in the UK ▶see pages 392-393
- 'under 12' concession ▶see pages 377-378;
- inter-country adoptions ▶see page 338;
- family reunion for those refused asylum but granted exceptional leave ▶see pages 227-228;
- recommendations made by adjudicators ▶see pages 646-647.

In addition, the Home Office has concessions outside the rules covering people who have lived in the UK for a long time (see below).

The long residence concessions

The Home Office operates concessions outside the rules under which people may be granted indefinite leave to remain on the basis of their long residence in the UK. The details of the concessions are currently in Chapter 18 of the Immigration Directorate's Instructions (IDI). The concessions are based on the principles of the European Convention on Establishment, which the UK ratified in October 1969. This Convention states that nationals of countries which are a party to the Convention should not be required to leave the host country they are in if they have lawfully resided there for over 10 years unless there are particularly compelling reasons why they should be required to leave, for example, relating to national security, public order, public health or morality. However, the Home Office concessions cover the nationals of *any* country. In addition, those whose residence in the UK has been partly or wholly unlawful can also benefit depending on the circumstances. Applications under the concessions should be made on form SET (O).

Lawful residence: the '10-year concession'

If people remain in the UK legally for more than 10 continuous years, they will normally be allowed to stay permanently. They will be granted indefinite leave to remain in the UK and become settled. If a person was late in applying for permission, even if that permission was subsequently granted, the person was an overstayer for a period and therefore may not fit into the concession. However, the Home Office has stated that a *short* delay in submitting an application will not stop the 10-year period running.

If an in-time application is made but there is a delay in determining the application, that period counts towards the period of lawful residence because a person is automatically granted leave during the period it takes to make a decision. The concession also states that time spent waiting for an appeal against a Home Office refusal will count towards the 10-year period if the appeal is subsequently successful. So, if a person is waiting for an appeal at the end of the 10-year period, he or she will not be granted settlement then, but will have to wait for the outcome of the appeal and only if it is successful will indefinite leave be granted. The concession further states that time waiting for an appeal may also count towards the 10-year period, even if the appeal is unsuccessful, but leave is subsequently granted either on the recommendation of the adjudicator, or before the appeal is determined, or where a further successful application is submitted shortly after the appeal. After the 1999 Act, however, it may now be possible to argue that, if an in-time application is made, time spent appealing against a refusal of the Home Office to vary leave *always* counts as lawful residence because leave is treated as continuing while a variation appeal is pending (see para 17 sch 4 1999 Act).

Time spent exempt from immigration control, for example, as a diplomat or other work at an embassy, counts towards the 10-year period. However, the applicant would have to leave their job and cease to be exempt from control before the Home Office would consider any application for indefinite leave.

The people most commonly able to benefit from this concession are students. However, as the immigration rules provide that students must intend to leave the UK at the end of their studies, and as this concession became more widely known, it became more difficult for people who have been students for eight or nine years to obtain extensions of their stay. If officers ask detailed questions about the student's plans and intentions after their studies and if the responses suggest that they might in the future apply to settle under this concession, further student extensions are often refused. It should be noted that students whose studies in the UK have been sponsored by their home governments or another international agency may make an application under the concession without the need for a letter consenting to their being granted settlement from their sponsoring body. The lack of such a letter of consent should not affect the application.

Where a person has completed less than 10 years' continuous lawful residence, indefinite leave may still be granted on the basis of substantial residence but only if there are 'very strong compelling circumstances'.

Unlawful residence: the '14-year concession'

Where a person has remained in the UK for over 14 continuous years, whether legally or illegally, this will also normally qualify them for settlement. Time spent exempt from immigration control also counts towards the 14-year period. In general, when a deportation decision or order or notice of illegal entry has been made against the person earlier, this 'stops the clock' and the Home Office is entitled to disregard any residence after this time for the purposes of counting the 14 years. The Home Office was held to be entitled to do this in the case of *Ofori*, but only if the person concerned has become aware of the notice (*Popatia*). Now that 'administrative removal' (▶see Chapter 30), has taken over much of what was previously deportation, it is unclear whether directions for administrative removal also stop the clock, but it is likely that they do. However, the current Home Office policy contained in the IDI suggests that the period after the enforcement decision should not be ignored *altogether*:

'each case should be considered on its merits and the length and quality of the overall period of residence should still be taken into account, together with all other relevant factors and balanced against the need to maintain an effective control'.

Between 10 and 14 years

Where a person has remained in the UK for between 10 and 14 years but cannot, because some of the residence was unlawful, qualify under the 10-year concession, there is a possibility that an application will be allowed. The factors which the Home Office take into account in deciding whether to grant leave in these circumstances are the length of continuous residence, the proportion of it which was lawful and the strength of ties with the UK. Family ties, in particular, are important in this context.

Continuity of residence

It will be seen that, under both concessions, there is a requirement that the period of residence is 'continuous'. Continuity of residence will generally not be broken by a small number of short absences of up to six months abroad. This is because absences of this length are generally not taken as disrupting or cutting off ties with the UK. However, if the absences are 'frequent' it will be necessary to explain why the person needs to leave the UK so often. It may be, for example, that there have been business related trips or visits abroad made in order to maintain family ties. In some cases, even absences of longer than six months may be taken as not breaking ties with the UK. Again, the reason for such absences should be carefully explained in the application. Continuity of residence will, however, be broken if a person was previously removed or deported from the UK or if they left the UK previously with no intention of returning or in circumstances where there was nothing to indicate that there were strong ties to the UK.

Refusing applications: 'strong countervailing factors'

If the above requirements are met for either the 10-year or 14-year concession, indefinite leave will normally be granted. It will not be granted, however, if the Home Office decides that there are 'strong countervailing factors' against the applicant. This will be the case if the person has an existing criminal record (namely, where the offences are not yet 'spent' under the Rehabilitation of Offenders Act, or took place during the last five years). Minor and non-custodial offences do not count. 'Deliberate and blatant attempts to evade or circumvent' immigration control also constitute strong countervailing factors. Examples of conduct which fall into this last category are:

- using forged documents;
- absconding from conditions of temporary admission;
- contracting a marriage of convenience for immigration purposes.

The concession states that, in particular where the applicant would otherwise benefit from the 14-year concession, the countervailing factors need to be 'exceptionally serious'.

British Overseas Citizens

A further long-residence concession outside the immigration rules seems to exist to benefit British Overseas Citizens (BOCs) (for a description of BOCs, ▶see page 576). According to a letter written by the Home Office to JCWI, and which was referred to in the case of ex parte *Patel*, BOCs who have been in the UK with limited exceptional leave for four years, may be granted indefinite leave.

7   Identifying immigration status

The stamps which entry clearance officers (ECOs), immigration officers and officials at the Home Office put in a person's passport or travel document denote the immigration status of that person. This chapter gives examples of common passport stamps and documents used by the immigration authorities. It is intended for reference, to help advisers identify endorsements so as to determine a person's status. The immigration authorities may also mark passports when entry clearance or leave is refused. These endorsements are also covered in this chapter. For a full description of how the system of immigration control operates, see the earlier chapters of this section.

Conditions of leave to enter or remain

One of the most important aspects of immigration status is the conditions which can be attached to limited leave (indefinite leave cannot have conditions attached). The conditions which are likely to be imposed depend on the category under the immigration rules in which a person is admitted or granted further leave. The box below summarises the conditions imposed on people in the different categories. The immigration authorities refer to the different combinations of conditions as 'codes', although this term is not used in the immigration legislation or the rules. They are referred to instead in guidance and instructions issued to immigration officials, and sometimes immigration officials will refer to conditions of leave by a particular code number in their reports and other documents. It should be noted that, where a person arrives with entry clearance, the conditions which their leave will be subject to, are endorsed on the entry clearance. Exceptional leave is generally not made subject to any conditions although it can be limited or indefinite.

Endorsements by entry clearance officers

British embassies, high commissions and consulates endorse passports when they deal with entry clearance applications from people wanting to come to the UK. The entry clearance document is a sticker ('vignette') placed into the passport and is often known as a visa or an entry certificate

SUMMARY OF CONDITIONS

The text to the right of each code sets out the conditions that will be contained in the passport endorsement, followed by the different categories of people under the rules who will receive that endorsement. So, for example, the only condition imposed on a person who is granted leave as a spouse or unmarried partner during the probationary period will be a prohibition on public funds (code 1). He or she will be permitted to take any employment.

Code **Conditions and categories of people under the rules**

code 1 **No recourse to public funds**
Issued to:
dependants of students who are granted leave for 12 months or more;
dependants of work permit holders;
persons with UK ancestry seeking employment;
postgraduate doctors and dentists;
spouses and unmarried partners during their probationary period;
those exercising rights of access to children.

code 1A **No conditions**
Issued to:
those coming for family reunion with sponsors who have limited exceptional leave;
those with limited exceptional leave and their dependants.

code 2 **No recourse to public funds**
Work and any changes must be authorised
Issued to:
business people and investors;
students on courses of longer than six months;
student nurses;
innovators;
those seeking to establish themselves under EC Association Agreements;
work permit (including TWES) holders;
writers, artists and composers.

code 3 **No work or recourse to public funds**
Issued to:
dependants of students who are granted less than 12 months' leave (or may be issued with code 5N to same effect);
fiance(e)s;
retired persons of independent means;
students on short courses (of six months or less);
visitors (or may be issued with code 5N to same effect).

Code	Conditions and categories of people under the rules

code 4 **No recourse to public funds. To work as [nature of work] with [employer]. Changes must be authorised.**

Issued to:

au pairs;

domestic workers;

ministers of religion;

overseas government employees;

private servants in diplomatic households;

seasonal workers;

sole representatives of overseas firms;

working holidaymakers.

code 5N Leave to enter for six months. Employment and recourse to public funds prohibited.

Issued to:

students on courses of six months or less (may also be issued with code 3)

visitors (may also be issued with code 3)

code 8 **Existing limited leave and conditions endorsed on new passport/travel document.**

The holder has leave to enter or remain that was granted on [date] and expires on [date].

Issued to:

Those who already have leave and wish to have it confirmed in a new passport. The pre-existing leave is stated on the new endorsement as a code number.

ILE/R **Indefinite leave to enter/remain**

Issued to:

those joining or staying with relatives settled in UK;

spouses/unmarried partners after probationary period;

those who have been in the UK for four years in most of the categories leading to settlement;

returning residents;

refugees;

those who have been in the UK for four years with exceptional leave granted following refusal of asylum;

family reunion where sponsor has refugee status or indefinite leave granted after four years exceptional leave.

Notes

1. Leave granted under codes 1 to 4 can also be supplemented with a condition that the holder registers with the police (▶see page 535 and the list on page 750 for those who may be required to register with the police).

2. The stamps for the above forms of leave were re-designed and new stamps were issued on 30 July 2000. The old stamps for codes 1A and 5N were retained. Examples of the stamps are set out later in this chapter.

3. Set out above are the conditions imposed on leave in the main categories under the immigration rules; the table is *not* exhaustive.

(▶see pages 52-64 for a full discussion of entry clearances and who needs to apply for them).

Two new-style entry clearances have been in use from 2 October 2000 replacing the old entry clearance stickers. They operate as 'leave to enter' provided they contain the requisite information ▶see page 56. The entry clearance only becomes effective from the 'valid from' date and expires on the 'valid to' date. These dates are critical to establishing the length of leave a person has when they actually arrive in the UK.

Visit entry clearances

The green Uniform Format Visa (UFV) is issued to visitors only (including transit visitors). The conditions attached to the grant of leave to enter are printed in the 'REMARKS' section beneath the holder's name, date of birth and nationality.

Other entry clearances

The red entry clearance is issued to all those who are not entering as visitors. The conditions attached to the grant of leave to enter are printed in the 'Obsrv.' section of the red entry clearance. The conditions which are appropriate for the different purposes for which entry clearance can be granted are summarised in the box above.

Old style entry clearances

Old-style entry clearances may still be valid. Their expiry date and whether they allow single or multiple entry should be checked.

Refusal of entry clearance

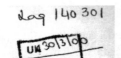

When an application for entry clearance has been refused, the post may indicate this in the passport by stamping a small box (see left) containing the name of the post, date and reference number of the application, and the stamp will have a line drawn through it. If no line is drawn through it, this indicates that the application is still pending. In some instances, instead of stamping a box into the passport, the ECO may write the words 'entry clearance applied for' in the passport, followed by the date of application and name of the post. If the application has been refused, these words may be underlined.

Endorsements by immigration officers

On arrival in the UK, immigration officers may subject all passengers to an examination to determine whether or not they are British citizens or otherwise have the right of abode. If the passenger needs leave, and does not already have it, it is the immigration officer's job to apply the immigration rules to decide whether to grant or refuse leave and, if it is granted, on what conditions.

Landing cards

Non-British national passengers can be required to fill out a landing card prior to their arrival in the UK in order to assist immigration officers. The landing card is kept as a record and the immigration authorities may later refer to the information given on it.

Those arriving without entry clearance or pre-existing leave

Leave to enter the United Kingdom is
hereby given for/until ....

....

CODE 1A

Leave to enter for/until
No recourse to public funds

CODE 1

Leave to enter for/until
No recourse to public funds Work (and any changes) must be authorised

CODE 2

Leave to enter for/until
No work or recourse to public funds

CODE 3

Leave to enter for/until
To work as/with
Changes must be authorised No work or recourse to public funds

CODE 4

LEAVE TO ENTER FOR SIX MONTHS:
EMPLOYMENT AND RECOURSE TO
PUBLIC FUNDS PROHIBITED

IMMIGRATION OFFICER

* (114) *

- 8 NOV 2000
HEATHROW (1)

CODE 5N

The above are examples of endorsements made to indicate a grant of
leave to enter when someone arrives in the UK without leave or an entry
clearance. The endorsement shows the time period for which leave is
granted and any conditions of leave. The conditions attached to the leave
granted by an immigration officer depend on the category in which leave
is granted (►see 'summary of conditions' box on pages 110-111).

Each of the above endorsements will be accompanied by a date stamp containing details of the date of endorsement and at which port and by which immigration officer it was issued. If the immigration officer has made a computer or written record of the grant, a special number will be issued in the uppermost box of the endorsement which indicates the grant of leave.

Those arriving with entry clearance

If a passenger arrives with entry clearance (which operates as leave to enter), and is being admitted to the UK, then the immigration officer will not stamp their passport on arrival with the length of stay allowed or the conditions of stay. Instead, the officer will simply endorse the entry clearance vignette with a date stamp showing the date of entry as in the example given.

Normally, these entry clearances will be stamped on first arrival only. However, if the person has a visit entry clearance which is valid for longer than six months, in which case it is envisaged that they will enter the UK as a visitor on a multiple number of occasions, the passport may then be endorsed with a code 5N square date stamp with conditions attached (▶see page 114 for the code 5N stamp). Of course, all visit entry clearances can be used for any number of entries within their period of validity.

Open date stamps

A date stamp (see left) on its own which is not stamped across an entry clearance or has no conditions attached to it is called an 'open date stamp'. These may be issued to the following categories of people: returning residents, diplomatic officials and others who are 'exempt' from control, ▶see page 15 for a list of those who may be exempt, and EEA family permit holders.

Variation of leave on entry

If a person arrives with an entry clearance which operates as leave or already has leave which has not lapsed (▶see page 76 for non-lapsing leave), they can apply to an immigration officer to vary or extend that leave or to rectify an error made by the ECO. The words 'Leave varied to' will then be placed above one of the code stamps.

Leave varied to:

Leave to enter for/until
No recourse to public funds

Registration with police

If immigration officers impose a requirement that the passenger registers with the police on entry (▶see pages 535 and the list on page 50 for who may be required to register with the police), this will be endorsed as shown.

Register with the Police
within seven days

The immigration officer may use the endorsement shown to remove a condition to register.

The holder is no longer required to
register with the Police

Indefinite leave to enter

There are few circumstances in which people entering the UK for the first time without entry clearance are granted indefinite leave immediately. One example is those who apply for asylum on arrival and are ultimately recognised as refugees. They are given an open date stamp and an endorsement stating that they have indefinite leave (for an example of these endorsements on a letter recognising a person as a refugee ▶see page 123).

Those who already had indefinite leave when they last left the UK and are granted entry as returning residents will have their passports endorsed with an open date stamp.

When a person is travelling for the first time on a new passport, it is sensible to carry the old passport as well, so that the immigration officer can immediately see what the

Given indefinite leave to
enter the United Kingdom

person's status is. The immigration officer will then endorse the passport with the indefinite leave stamp shown. When this has been done, there is no need to continue to carry the old passport as well as the new one when travelling.

Refusals

When people are refused leave to enter the UK, their passports are still stamped with the square date stamp but an ink cross is put through this to show the refusal of leave to enter.

If a refusal is withdrawn following a successful appeal, the word 'WITHDRAWN' will be written diagonally across the previously marked square date stamp.

When people are refused leave to enter or their leave is cancelled, they will also be given a notice in writing or a form stating in brief the reasons for the decision and informing them of any appeal rights which they may have.

Cancellation of leave

On a person's arrival, the immigration officer has the power to cancel the leave otherwise given by an entry clearance or which the passenger has

because their leave did not lapse when they last left the Common Travel Area or were given by an immigration officer before their arrival in the UK (►see pages 69-70 for a description of this process). When an immigration officer cancels leave in this way, the passport will be endorsed with a large 'CANCELLED' stamp placed over the leave which is being cancelled. If the passport is not stamped in this way, it may instead be endorsed in writing in red or black ink.

While an immigration officer is examining a passenger after their arrival to decide whether to cancel their leave, they may 'suspend' their leave. A notice indicating such a suspension should be issued to the passenger.

Confirmation of existing limited leave in a new passport

	Code
The holder has leave to enter/remain that was granted on	
by .... and expires on	

CODE 8

If a person has limited leave with the conditions of the leave contained in their existing passport and a new passport is obtained to replace it, a code 8 stamp can be issued to 'transfer' that person's existing leave to the new passport. This stamp came into effect on 30 July 2000 and differs from previous practice because the new code 8 stamp acts as confirmation that leave exists in another document. The immigration ser-vice states that this is to avoid the creation of a situation where someone could end up with two periods of non-lapsing leave running concurrently.

Leaving the UK

Prior to March 1998, it was the practice of immigration officers to stamp people's passports with a triangular stamp when they left the UK. The stamp showed the date, port of exit and the number of the immigration officer. These exit stamps are no longer used.

Endorsements by the Home Office

When the Home Office has any dealings with a person, the person is given a Home Office reference number. This happens, for example, when a person who has already entered the UK makes an application to vary their leave (for example, to extend it). This is a unique personal reference; it is normally the first letter of the person's surname followed by six or seven numbers. For Arabic or Chinese names, the Home Office uses the first letter of the first name. This reference should always be used in any correspondence and will help the Home Office to find any file.

Although it is still the practice of the Home Office to write the Home Office reference number inside the back cover of the passport when processing applications for variation of leave, this is not done as consistently as previously due to organisational changes.

The following are examples of endorsements made after entry by the Home Office when further leave to remain is granted. ▶See the 'summary of conditions' box on pages 110-111 for the type of conditions which will be attached to leave granted in the various different categories.

Leave to remain in the United Kingdom is hereby given

Until..........`...

....
on behalf of the Secretary of State
Home Office

Date...

CODE 1A

Leave to remain in the United Kingdom on Condition that the holder maintains and Accommodates himself and any dependants Without recourse to public funds is hereby Given

Until...

....
on behalf of the Secretary of State
Home Office

Date ....

CODE 1

Despite the wording of the Code 2 stamp, responsibility for authorisation of all work has now formally transferred to the Home Office.

Leave to remain in the United Kingdom, on Condition that the holder maintains and accommodates himself and any dependants without recourse to public funds, does not enter or change employment paid or unpaid without the consent of the Secretary of State for Employment and does not engage In any business or profession without the consent of the Secretary of State for the Home Department is hereby given

Until...

....

Date ....

CODE 2

Leave to remain in the United Kingdom on condition that the holder maintains and accommodates himself and any dependants without recourse to public funds is hereby given

Until..

....

on behalf of the Secretary of State
Home Office

Date ....

CODE 3

Leave to remain in the United Kingdom on Condition that the holder maintains and accommodates himself and any dependants without recourse to public funds is hereby given

Until..

The holder is not engaged in employment paid or unpaid other than with.........................

....

and is not to engage in any business or profession without the consent of the

....

Secretary of State for the Home Department

....

on behalf of the Secretary of State
Home Office

CODE 4

When the Home Office grants leave, the endorsement will be signed by the official who has granted the leave and then stamped with a pentagonal date stamp containing the date of issue and the number of the official in brackets.

Indefinite leave to remain

When the Home Office grants indefinite leave, it sticks into the passport a green vignette (see below) showing that there is no time limit or conditions on the person's stay. Until 1992, indefinite leave to remain was shown by a stamp rather than a vignette, the design of which was changed periodically (see below right for the last version of the stamp).

When indefinite leave has been granted, but the passport on which it was endorsed has expired, and the person obtains a new passport, the new passport may be stamped by the Home Office with the 'no time limit' stamp (see right).

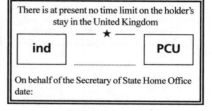

Refusals

When the Home Office refuses further leave to enter or remain, it underlines the most recent leave to enter or remain in the passport. This may not be noticed by the person but shows any other immigration official that there has been a refusal. The person will also be notified in writing and must be given notice in writing of any appeal rights.

If the passport is a new one, with no leave to enter or remain stamped in it, the Home Office may underline the person's Home Office reference number, written on the inside back cover of the passport.

The Home Office used to write 'EMB' by the side of the last leave to enter or remain granted, or on the inside back cover of the passport. This practice has now been discontinued.

Other documents

Certificates of Entitlement

People who have the right of abode in the UK but who are not travelling on British passports need to get this right confirmed by the British embassy or high commission before travelling. They will be given a certificate of entitlement to the right of abode, which is a vignette (like the entry clearance vignette) embossed into the passport. This can also be issued by the Home Office following an application made within the UK.

Work permits

Visa nationals travelling to the UK for work permit employment are required to apply for an entry clearance before they travel. They should produce to the ECO the work permit (an example is shown here) which is obtained on application by the employer from Work Permits (UK) (Work Permits (UK) is now part of the Home Office rather than the old DofEE or the Department of Work and Pensions). Those who are not visa nationals are not required to obtain prior entry clearance, but they must show the work permit to the immigration officer on arrival. Leave to enter will usually be granted with code 2 conditions endorsed in the entry clearance or a code 2 stamp endorsed by the immigration officer.

WORK PERMIT

IMMIGRATION ACT 1971   PERMIT NUMBER E   700546

DEPARTMENT FOR EDUCATION AND EMPLOYMENT
WORK PERMITS (UK)
MOORFOOT, SHEFFIELD, S1 4PQ

WORKER REFERENCE No.   0165680   PERIOD COVERED BY PERMIT
DATE OF ISSUE   20Sep2001   18 months from date of entry to UK

PARTICULARS OF PERMIT HOLDER

SURNAME
XXXXXXX   XXXXXXXXXXXXXXXX
OTHER NAMES

XXXXXXXXXXXXXXXX

DATE OF BIRTH   XXXXXXXXXX   SEX   Male
PASSPORT NUMBER   XXXXXXXXX
ISSUING GOVERNMENT   UNITED STATES OF AMERICA

PARTICULARS OF EMPLOYMENT

EMPLOYER'S NAME   XXXXXXXXXXXXXX XXXXX XXXXXXX   EMPLOYER'S ADDRESS
      LIMITED   XXXXXXX XXXXXXX XXXXXXX
OCCUPATION   XXXXXXXXX XXXXXXXX   LONDON
SALARY REMUNERATION   XXXXXXX PER ANNUM

OFFICIAL STAMP   PHONE NUMBER   XXXX XXX XXXX

E700546   PLEASE READ CONDITIONS PRINTED ON THE BACK

WP(UK) 1
Crown Copyright April 2001

Asylum-seekers

Application Registration Card

Application Registration Cards (ARCs) have been issued from early 2002 to asylum-seekers, ▶see page 181 for further information about ARCs. They are a replacement for Standard Acknowledgement Letters (SALs).

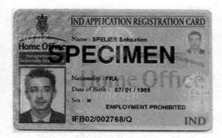

Standard Acknowledgement Letter

Standard Acknowledgement Letters (SALs) may have been issued to asylum-seekers who have not had an initial decision on their application. They will bear the applicant's and any dependants' photographs and will indicate whether or not the applicant has permission to work. There are two types of SAL. Those who applied for asylum at port on arrival may be issued with a SAL1 and in-country applicants with a SAL2. As stated above, the SALS are being phased out in favour of ARCs.

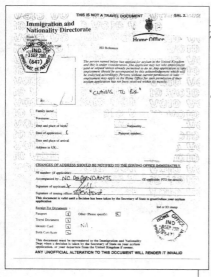

Refugees and those granted exceptional leave

Refugees

Refugees' national passports are not stamped, because they cannot use them without forfeiting their refugee status. They will be given a letter from the Home Office which explains their position as refugees and some of their rights in the UK and which states that they have been given indefinite leave. The letter will be endorsed with the indefinite leave stamp and an open date stamp.

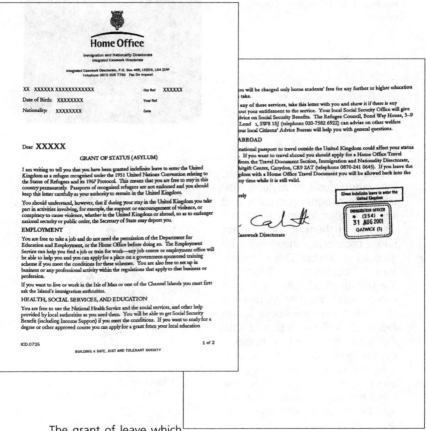

The grant of leave which is endorsed on the letter is issued by the Home Office. If the application was considered as one for leave to enter, until recently, the endorsement was always issued by an immigration officer. However, the Home Office now have the power to issue the leave endorsement themselves in asylum cases, although the person claimed asylum at port.

Refugees may be given refugee travel documents, issued by the Home Office under the United Nations Convention relating to the Status of Refugees, and the indefinite leave to remain will be endorsed in them on a vignette, ▶see page 120 for an example of this vignette. The travel documents are valid for all countries except the refugee's country of origin.

Exceptional leave

People granted exceptional leave, following refusal of asylum, may use their national passports and will have leave to enter or remain stamped in them. If they do not have passports, they may be granted a Home Office brown travel document called a 'Certificate of Identity'. If limited exceptional leave is being given, a code 1A stamp (see above for an example), will be endorsed into the travel document or passport by the Home Office or the port granting limited leave without other conditions. If indefinite leave has been granted, this will also be endorsed into the travel document.

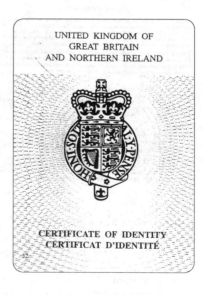

These travel documents are also not valid for the country of the holder's origin. For more details ▶see pages 88-89.

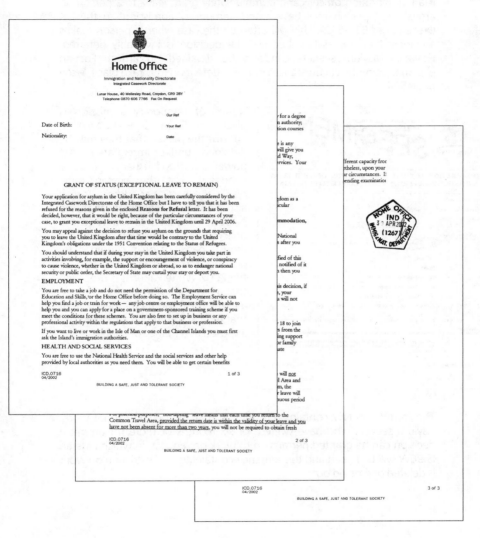

A letter will also be issued to those granted exceptional leave following refusal of asylum. An example of this letter is shown below.

Home Office

Immigration and Nationality Directorate
Integrated Casework Directorate

Lunar House, 40 Wellesley Road, Croydon, CR9 2BY
Telephone 0870 606 7766 Fax On Request

Our Ref

Date of Birth: Your Ref

Nationality: Date

GRANT OF STATUS (EXCEPTIONAL LEAVE TO REMAIN)

Your application for asylum in the United Kingdom has been carefully considered by the Integrated Casework Directorate of the Home Office but I have to tell you that it has been refused for the reasons given in the enclosed **Reasons for Refusal** letter. It has been decided, however, that it would be right, because of the particular circumstances of your case, to grant you exceptional leave to remain in the United Kingdom until 29 April 2006.

You may appeal against the decision to refuse you asylum on the grounds that requiring you to leave the United Kingdom after that time would be contrary to the United Kingdom's obligations under the 1951 Convention relating to the Status of Refugees.

You should understand that if during your stay in the United Kingdom you take part in activities involving, for example, the support or encouragement of violence, or conspiracy to cause violence, whether in the United Kingdom or abroad, so as to endanger national security or public order, the Secretary of State may curtail your stay or deport you.

EMPLOYMENT

You are free to take a job and do not need the permission of the Department for Education and Skills, or the Home Office before doing so. The Employment Service can help you find a job or train for work — any job centre or employment office will be able to help you and you can apply for a place on a government-sponsored training scheme if you meet the conditions for these schemes. You are also free to set up in business or any professional activity within the regulations that apply to that business or profession.

If you want to live or work in the Isle of Man or one of the Channel Islands you must first ask the Island's immigration authorities.

HEALTH AND SOCIAL SERVICES

You are free to use the National Health Service and the social services and other help provided by local authorities as you need them. You will be able to get certain benefits

ICD.0716
04/2002

1 of 3

BUILDING A SAFE, JUST AND TOLERANT SOCIETY

For practical purposes, "non-lapsing" leave means that each time you return to the Common Travel Area, **provided the return date is within the validity of your leave and you have not been absent for more than two years**, you will not be required to obtain fresh

ICD.0716
04/2002

2 of 3

BUILDING A SAFE, JUST AND TOLERANT SOCIETY

ICD.0716
04/2002

3 of 3

BUILDING A SAFE, JUST AND TOLERANT SOCIETY

Notice of temporary admission

If an immigration officer cannot immediately grant leave to a person on arrival, that person may be granted 'temporary admission' to the UK (►see pages 510-512). This will often be the case when a person makes an application for asylum because the decision is invariably deferred. However, asylum seekers can also be detained on arrival. For an explanation of the circumstances in which detention may take place, ►see page 504.

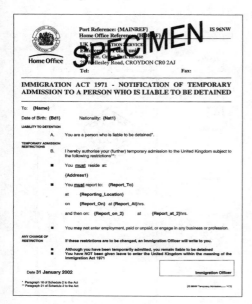

Notice of temporary admission is given on Form IS 96(W/NW). It informs the person that they may be detained under Immigration Act powers, and will usually contain a condition that the person must reside at a particular address. It may also contain a condition that the person is required to report to the police or an immigration office on a regular basis, or on a certain date, possibly for a further interview. In the 2002 White Paper, it is proposed that a network of 'reporting centres' are set up throughout the UK and that regular reporting restrictions are imposed as a matter of course.

The form IS 96 NW contains a restriction that the person cannot work. Asylum seekers who have waited for six months or more for an initial decision can be granted permission to work on request, in which case an IS 96W will be issued and the sentence containing the restriction on work is deleted or crossed out.

Enforcement notices

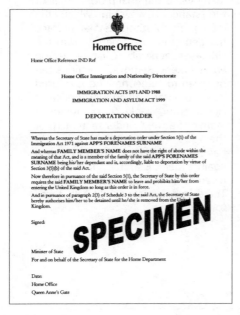

Deportation order

The circumstances under which people can be deported have been narrowed by the 1999 Act ▶see pages 537-538. A notice of intention to deport is issued in the first instance except to those being deported following a recommendation by a criminal court (but this is likely to change under proposals in the 2002 Bill). Following the conclusion of any appeals against the notice of intention, a deportation order can be made. Notice of intention to deport may be issued on Form APP104. Deportation orders are in the form shown.

Notice of illegal entry/ Notice to someone subject to administrative removal

An illegal entrant is someone who enters the UK in breach of the immigration laws. This may occur in a number of ways ▶see pages 545-549. When the immigration authorities decide that someone is an illegal entrant, they will issue them with an IS 151A informing them of their liability to removal and to be detained. The same form is used to notify a person that they are subject to 'administrative removal' (for example, as an over-stayer) under section 10 of the 1999 Act. For an explanation of the circumstances in which someone may be subject to administrative removal ▶see pages 531-537.

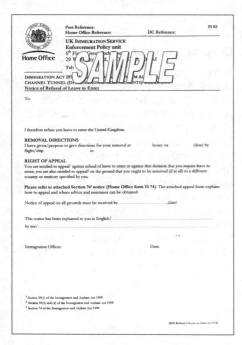

Removal directions

'Removal' is the final process in all of the standard ways in which the immigration authorities may enforce the departure of someone from the UK ▶see generally Chapter 26 on enforcement. Removal directions can be given to someone who is refused leave to enter; served with notice of illegal entry; liable to be removed 'administratively' under section 10 of the 1999 Act; or a person who has had a deportation order signed against them. Examples of the forms given to all these people are shown. There are variations of all these forms.

Removal directions for those refused leave to enter (IS 82)

Removal directions for illegal entrants and those subject to administrative removal (IS 151B)

Removal directions for those who have had a deportation order signed against them (IS118)

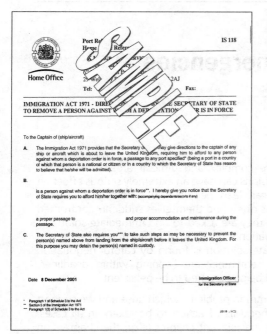

Port Reference
Home Reference

IS 118

Home Office

2AJ

Tel: Fax:

IMMIGRATION ACT 1971 - DIRECTIONS BY THE SECRETARY OF STATE TO REMOVE A PERSON AGAINST WHOM A DEPORTATION ORDER IS IN FORCE

To the Captain of (ship/aircraft)

A.   The Immigration Act 1971 provides that the Secretary of State may give directions to the captain of any ship or aircraft which is about to leave the United Kingdom, requiring him to afford to any person against whom a deportation order is in force, a passage to any port specified* (being a port in a country of which that person is a national or citizen or in a country to which the Secretary of State has reason to believe that he/she will be admitted).

B.

is a person against whom a deportation order is in force**. I hereby give you notice that the Secretary of State requires you to afford him/her together with: (accompanying dependants/escorts if any)

a proper passage to   and proper accommodation and maintenance during the passage.

C.   The Secretary of State also requires you*** to take such steps as may be necessary to prevent the person(s) named above from landing from the ship/aircraft before it leaves the United Kingdom. For this purpose you may detain the person(s) named in custody.

Date   8 December 2001   **Immigration Officer**
                                          for the Secretary of State

*   Paragraph 1 of Schedule 3 to the Act
**   Section 5 of the Immigration Act 1971
*** Paragraph 1(3) of Schedule 3 to the Act

IS118 - (VC)

8 Problems, emergencies and solutions

Immigration and asylum are complex and difficult areas. The consequences of Home Office decisions can have an extremely serious effect on people's lives. Bad advice can lead people into problems that were otherwise avoidable. Advisers often find themselves suddenly confronted with emergencies for which they are asked to find immediate solutions. The Home Office and immigration service can often act unpredictably and frequently the best immediate solution is found by careful negotiation with them. Key things to remember are keeping within deadlines, knowing who to contact and being prepared to be persistent.

Below, we look at certain common problems which arise and we suggest practical approaches with checklists of action to be taken. In all cases, advisers should also consult the relevant chapter (e.g., the chapters on appeals, detention and welfare) for the detailed background to the problem.

The importance of getting representation

Obtaining representation in immigration and asylum cases has become more and more vital over the last few years. It is important to remember that the Home Office Immigration and Nationality Directorate exists to carry out and enforce the immigration law, not to give advice, either to advisers or individuals. If people want further information they should get in touch with an independent specialist source such as JCWI, IAS, the Refugee Legal Centre, or a solicitor/adviser/local law centre/CAB that is part of the Community Legal Service with a specialist quality mark in immigration and asylum law and/or is regulated by the Office of the Immigration Services Commissioner. For details of who is available to provide representation, how to contact them and about public funding for advice and representation ►see Chapter 3. Unlike the immigration authorities, an independent adviser will not record information which may later be used against the person.

If the Home Office or immigration officers have given some advice or information in a case, it should not be assumed that everything that has been said is correct. Advisers are likely to know just as much about the law as many Home Office staff do. Home Office threats are not always carried out. People should not give up just because the Home Office has refused an application, or has sent out threatening letters. Even when people have been told to leave the country without delay, under threat of administrative removal or deportation, decisions can sometimes still be altered by further detailed representations about the case or even by contacting the client's MP.

Refusal of entry clearance overseas

A relative or friend may seek advice on behalf of someone who has been refused entry clearance overseas.

The following points should be taken into account in obtaining further information and providing advice.

1 Find out what the person was applying for (e.g. visit, family settlement).

2 People refused abroad should be given a written notice explaining the reasons for refusal and whether there is a right of appeal against refusal. Ask whether the person in the UK has copies of the decision and appeal forms and also the documents which were given to the entry clearance officer at the time of the application. If not, ask him or her to get copies and return with them.

3 Most people have a right of appeal against refusals of entry clearance unless they are:

- visitors who are not 'family' visitors;
- prospective students;
- students coming for courses of six months or less;
- refused on grounds that their exclusion is conducive to the public good;
- those who do not qualify under the immigration rules in the category for which they are applying because of their age, nationality, lack of passport or work permit or who are seeking to enter for a longer period than the rules allow in that category (six months in the case of visitors).

Examples of people prevented from appealing under the last category are: people who wanted to enter as an au pair but are not aged between 17 and 27, non-Commonwealth nationals seeking to enter as working holidaymakers and people who want to come to take up a course of work training without having been issued with a TWES permit.

4 A person may obtain a right of appeal on human rights or discrimination grounds if they make an allegation that these rights have been infringed.

5 The time limit for bringing the appeal is 28 days after the decision is received by the appellant. The decision may have been given by hand, in which case time starts running straight away but if it was sent through the post to the applicant outside the UK, it is not deemed to have been received until 28 days after it was sent and the appellant has 28 days from that time to appeal (see regs 6, 48 Immigration Appeals (Procedure)

Rules 2000 and reg 8 Immigration and Asylum Appeals (Notices) Regulations 2000).

6 The appeal is lodged by returning it to the British embassy, high commission or consulate which has made the decision (the address is stated on the notice of decision). People with a right of appeal will be given forms to fill in to lodge the appeal.

7 When there is a right of appeal, the notice of refusal will state (very briefly) the reason why the person has been refused. This may be too vague to be very helpful and it may therefore be necessary to wait until all the papers are to hand and instructions can be taken on them before setting out a detailed case. Advisers often state as grounds of appeal that

'the decision was not in accordance with the immigration rules, the law and/or discretion should have been exercised differently'

and make an allegation that the decision is in breach of the person's human rights if that is appropriate. However, in certain cases it may be appropriate to submit further evidence and representations at this stage where it is thought that the grounds of refusal can easily be overcome. This is because decisions are reviewed after grounds of appeal are submitted.

8 If there are no rights of appeal, ECOs can sometimes be persuaded to change their mind and review the case if representations are made. If they will not but there is a change of circumstances which means that the applicant is now likely to be granted an entry clearance, it may be worth making a fresh application. The alternative where there is no right of appeal is to challenge the decision by judicial review if there are proper grounds for doing so ▶see pages 142-144 below.

9 Even before the removal of the right of appeal for visitors in 1993, some British embassies and high commissions had been discouraging people from applying for visit entry clearances. Where entry clearance was optional, people were often told that it was not necessary and that they should travel and apply for leave to enter at the airport in the UK. Where people were visa nationals, and the ECO thought on a superficial inspection that they were likely to be refused, they were often told that if they withdrew their applications they would not have to pay the entry clearance fee and there would be no record of any refusal. This, of course, also meant that they had no chance of appealing.

10 If the person abroad has not been given a written notice of refusal, he or she has not legally been refused. Unless the person wants to withdraw, or not to pursue, the application, he or she should go back to the British embassy or high commission and insist that the application be formally considered and decided.

11 If an appeal is brought, full details of the reasons for refusal along with copies of any other documents submitted in support of the application, and,

possibly, a record of the interview at the British post, will be sent to the appellant and their representative in time for the appeal. At this stage, if the person has not already arranged for someone to represent them at appeal, this should be done. ▶See section 10 for further information on appeals.

Problems on arrival in the UK

Advisers may need to respond urgently when they are asked to assist someone in difficulties at an air or sea port on arrival. Problems may arise in both asylum and immigration cases. In urgent cases it will be necessary to deal directly with the immigration officers in charge of the case, usually by telephone.

It is important not to be intimidated by immigration officers. They are ordinary people who are not all-powerful. A 'chief immigration officer' may sound important but he or she is only the second tier of official with more senior 'inspectors' above them. Be firm but courteous with immigration officers and assume that negotiation is possible. If they do not alter their decision or are obstructive, it is possible to ask to speak to a chief immigration officer or an inspector to continue the negotiations. Applicants *cannot* be refused leave to enter nor can the leave which they have on arrival be cancelled by an immigration officer acting alone. Immigration officers must always obtain the authority of a chief immigration officer or an inspector (see para 10A, HC 395) before taking these steps.

The procedures which apply on arrival to the UK have become more complex under the Immigration and Asylum Act 1999. For full details of the different possibilities ▶see pages 65-72.

Refusal of entry

People coming for settlement, or for employment, generally require an entry clearance and provided they have one, problems in these cases are rare. Similarly, people returning to the UK within a period of leave which they already have are unlikely to encounter difficulties. These people are only likely to have problems if:

- there has been a change of circumstances which undermines the basis for admission agreed by the ECO or previously granted in the UK;
- there has been deception;
- refusal is justified on medical grounds or on the basis that the person's presence is deemed not 'conducive to the pubic good'.

In addition, a person may have their entry clearance 'cancelled' if they arrive before its 'effective date' (the 'valid from' date stated on the entry clearance), or if they seek entry for a purpose other than that stated on the entry clearance.

Problems on arrival are most likely to arise where someone is coming for a temporary purpose, does not have an entry clearance and is unable to prove to the immigration officers that they satisfy the immigration rules. As the number of countries whose nationals need entry clearances to come to the UK for any purpose continues to increase, this kind of emergency becomes less frequent.

If an adviser is contacted about a problem of this sort, they should as soon as possible try to find out the following details about the person and the circumstances of the case:

- name (preferably as on his or her passport);
- nationality;
- date of birth;
- port of entry (including which terminal at airports, or which dock at Dover) and approximate time of arrival;
- purpose of travel, and what period of entry they are likely to have asked for;
- whether he or she was travelling alone and, if not, the details of any person accompanying them;
- if possible, the port reference number (this will be on any papers that he or she has been given by immigration officers);
- from which country and port or airport the person travelled (with flight details);
- does the person have entry clearance?
- what did the person say to the immigration officers?
- what evidence to support his or her statements was shown to them?
- what information have the immigration officers given about why they are not satisfied?
- has the person been in the UK, or attempted to come to the UK, before? If so, when, and what happened?
- what is the person's marital status? If married, what are the nationality, whereabouts and intentions of their spouse and any children?
- what does the person want to do now?

Find out whether the person has been refused leave to enter or whether he or she is still being questioned before a decision is made. If the person is still at the air or sea port, this can be found out by contacting the immigration service there. Give the port reference number if you know it, or alternatively, details of where the person arrived from and when, his or her name and nationality and date of birth. Immigration officers usually refer to the person as the 'passenger' or 'pax' for short.

In all cases ask the immigration officer for details of how far the case has got, what action the immigration service have actually taken and what they plan to do next. Copies of all documents that have been served on the applicant should be requested. The applicant may be kept at the airport while being questioned or they may have been released on temporary admission (TA). The documents themselves should indicate what has happened on the case. If the reference number includes 'RLE', the person has probably been refused leave to enter. If not, there may still be no decision on the case.

Note that, under the 1999 Act, it is now possible for the 'leave' that a person had when they arrived (because it did not lapse when they last left or because they have an entry clearance which has operated as leave) to be suspended while further examination of the person's circumstances takes place. This does *not* mean that a decision has been made to actually cancel the leave so that they are refused entry. If the person has not yet been refused entry, it may be possible to convince the immigration officers to grant entry. Getting them to reverse a refusal decision already made will be much harder.

Get as much information as possible from immigration officers about why they are suspicious and check this with the person him or herself or with their friends or relatives in the UK. If there are any obvious mis-understandings or errors which can be corrected, the immigration officers may be satisfied and grant entry. It may be that there is certain evidence available which has not yet been brought to the officer's attention. For example, the most frequent ground upon which those seeking entry for temporary purposes are refused is that they do not intend to leave at the end of their stay. It may be that it is possible to produce further evidence to the port about the circumstances of the person in their own country which shows that they are settled with ongoing interests there to which they will return, for example, evidence of their work or study. In cases where it is not accepted that the person can financially be supported, it may be that there is a sponsor who is willing to go to the port or telephone the immigration officers to confirm how they know the passenger and provide details of their means.

Appeals

Advisers should identify at an early stage whether the person who has been refused on arrival will be able to appeal against the decision. *Aside from asylum and human rights cases*, on entry appeal rights are restricted as follows:

1 People travelling with entry clearance have the opportunity to appeal against the decision and to remain in the UK for the hearing, no matter what the purpose or period of entry they were seeking. The exceptions to this are:

- where the entry clearance itself is cancelled by the immigration officer either because a person arrives before it is actually valid, or they state that they want to enter for a purpose other than that stated on the entry clearance;

- where the applicant is denied entry because they do not qualify under the immigration rules in the category for which they are applying because of their age, nationality, lack of passport or work permit or are seeking to enter for a longer period than the rules allow in that category;

- where they are refused on the ground that their presence is not conducive to the public good.

2 People travelling without an entry clearance or a work permit cannot appeal in the UK, they must return home in order to appeal. In addition, they have no right of appeal at all if:

- they are denied entry because they do not qualify under the immigration rules in the category for which they are applying because of their age, nationality, lack of passport or work permit or are seeking to enter for a period longer than the rules allow in that category;

- they are refused on the grounds that their presence is not conducive to the public good;

- they are seeking entry as a visitor, a prospective student or a student enrolled on a course of six months or less.

The notice of the decision should explain any rights of appeal. If the appeal is from within the UK, notice of appeal must be given within 10 working days. If the appeal is from outside the UK, the person has 28 days to appeal starting from the date of their departure from the UK. For more details on appeals ►see Section 10. Where there is no right of appeal at all, the only remedies are negotiating with the immigration officers or (rarely) judicial review.

'Third country' asylum cases

'Third country' asylum cases are those in which a person makes a claim for asylum in the UK, usually after having passed through another country, and the immigration authorities want to return the person to that 'third' country in order for the asylum claim to be dealt with there. For full details about these complex procedures ►see pages 206-212.

The legislation passed since 1993, including the Immigration and Asylum Act 1999, has made it increasingly difficult to avoid these removals. The legislation prevents appeals to the adjudicator in many cases and often the only alternative is judicial review.

If advisers are contacted on behalf of an asylum-seeker who is likely to be removed on a 'third country' basis, the basic *information* which needs to be obtained is:

1 The name, age, nationality of, and port reference number of the asylum-seeker; the date of their arrival and the essential reasons why they are claiming asylum.

2 How has the asylum-seeker arrived in the UK and through which countries have they travelled? If the asylum-seeker and the immigration officers disagree about the countries which the asylum-seeker has travelled

through, what evidence is there that the asylum-seeker has been in the country the immigration officer believes they have been in?

3   What are the particular reasons why the person does not want to return to the third country?

4   Does the person have any dependants or other family members in the UK? What other connections do they have with the UK? Have they been to the UK before?

5   Is the asylum-seeker in good health, are they particularly traumatised by their travel or other experiences?

6   Have the immigration authorities actually made a decision as to what should happen to them? Has a third country certificate been issued in the case?

7   Is the case being treated under the Dublin Convention and if so, has the other 'Dublin' (third) country agreed to accept responsibility for the asylum-seeker? For details about the Dublin Convention ▶see pages 209-211.

8   If the case is not being dealt with under the Dublin Convention, what evidence is there that the third country is prepared to accept the person back?

The *legal* questions which advisers need to ask themselves based on the above information are:

1   Is it likely that the person will simply be returned to the UK from the country to which it is proposed to send them so that any attempt to remove them will be ineffective? If so, judicial review may be appropriate.

2   If the person is not being removed to an EU member state or to Canada, US, Norway or Switzerland, are there grounds for saying that the third country may send the person on to their country of origin even though they have a valid asylum or human rights claim that may succeed if it were considered in the UK? If so, an in-country appeal can be brought.

3   If the person is being removed to an EU member state or to Canada, US, Norway or Switzerland but not under the Dublin Convention, are there grounds for saying that the third country may send the person on to their country of origin even though they have a valid asylum claim or human rights claim? If so, a human rights claim/appeal and/or judicial review may be appropriate.

4   If the person is being removed under the Dublin Convention and there are grounds for saying that the third country may send the person on to their country of origin even though they have a valid asylum or human rights claim, it may still be very difficult to challenge the decision.Specialist advice should be taken.

5   In any case, are there separate grounds for saying that the removal of the person to the third country is in breach of their human rights or are

there strong other compassionate factors which could be used to persuade the immigration authorities to allow the claim to be dealt with here? This may be the case if:

- the asylum-seeker has family and friends or strong connections or long residence in the UK;
- the asylum-seeker is unwell, very young, vulnerable and the effect of being removed could have a serious effect on their health or well-being;
- the reception arrangements for the person in the third country itself are inadequate and likely to have a severe detrimental effect upon the person.

In these cases, it may be appropriate to bring a human rights appeal against the decision.

Access to welfare and support

Legislation and regulations over the last few years have increasingly restricted access to social security benefits and many forms of community care services for those who are not British Citizens or do not have indefinite leave. The Immigration and Asylum Act 1999 created a very broad class of people defined as 'subject to immigration control' who are excluded from these forms of welfare support. For full details of access to welfare and support ▶see Section 11.

Relevant questions for advisers to ask themselves are:

1 Is the person 'subject to immigration control'? A person will *not* be subject to control and will not be excluded from welfare provision if:

- they do not need leave to be in the UK, that is, they have the right of abode as British citizens or they are exempt from immigration control or they are exercising EU rights of free movement;
- they are an EEA national;
- they have leave which is not subject to a condition that they will not have recourse to public funds or was given on the basis of a maintenance undertaking (advisers should check the passport stamps to see what the conditions are). If a maintenance undertaking was given, advisers should check it was given in the proper form so that it has effect ▶see page 663.

2 Is the person exempt from the 'subject to immigration control test' for certain benefits? For example, are they nationals of a country which has ratified the European Convention on Social and Medical Assistance or the Social Charter and can be said to be 'lawfully present' in the UK; or were they given leave under a maintenance undertaking over five years ago or signed by a sponsor who has now died (for full details of the exemptions, ▶see pages 665-667 and 676-677)?

3 Is the person an 'asylum-seeker' for asylum support purposes so that they can get access to asylum support from the National Asylum Support Service or a local authority? A person will be an asylum-seeker if:

- they have made a claim to be a refugee under the 1951 Convention; or
- they have made a claim for protection under Article 3 ECHR (prohibition on torture and inhuman degrading treatment or punishment).

A person continues to be an 'asylum-seeker' for these purposes if they are appealing against a negative decision *or*, even if the appeals process has been concluded, while they remain in the UK if they have a child dependant living as part of their household. It should be noted that a person who has had an asylum appeal dismissed may have subsequently made an Article 3 ECHR claim which entitles them to asylum support.

4   If the person previously had asylum support which was terminated before it was otherwise due to end, for example, because of the person's conduct, is it now worth making a re-application for asylum support on the basis of a change in circumstance or are there 'exceptional circumstances' justifying a reconsideration? (See reg. 21, Asylum Support 2000 Regulations). Can the termination of the asylum support be challenged?

5   Is the reason why the person is 'subject to immigration control' because they have not yet been provided with the immigration status which they should have received? For example, they may have succeeded in their appeal or the Home Office may have agreed to grant the person asylum or exceptional leave but there has been a long delay in actually issuing the papers so that the person can then access the welfare support which they need. In these cases, the remedy is often to demand that the papers be issued without delay or even to bring judicial review proceedings in order to obtain the relevant papers from the Home Office.

6   Is the person eligible for support under the Home Office's policy on providing support in 'hard cases'? ►see pages 717-718. It should be noted that, even where a person does not fit the criteria, the Home Office must still exercise discretion on the basis of the individual case as to whether to provide support or not. In principle, the fund is open to anyone who has been granted temporary admission, released from detention or granted bail.

7   Is the person disabled, aged or sick so that it can be said that their needs are made more acute by the lack of support than an ordinary fit, able-bodied person? If so, they may be entitled to support from social services under their community care responsibilities ►see pages 679-684.

8   Is the person a child or part of a family with a child or children? If so, they may be able to get support under section 17 Children Act ►see pages 685-687.

It should be noted that the law is still not entirely certain in relation to some of the above questions. In particular there are ongoing cases concerning 2, 7, and 8.

The above check list is not fully comprehensive, for full details of access to the above forms of provision, and for access to housing from a local authority ▶see Chapter 31.

Arrest, detention and threatened deportation or removal

Advisers are often contacted on behalf of people who are being held by police or immigration officers on the grounds that they are unlawfully in the UK having entered illegally or having overstayed or breached their conditions of leave. In these cases, the person is usually being threatened with removal from the UK. Those who are regularly advising people at police stations should consult the second edition of the Law Society's book *Immigration Advice at the Police Station*.

Speak to the officer dealing with the case at the Home Office or the immigration service office to register your interest in the case and ensure that you will be informed of any decision or action that is taken.

As soon as possible, find out the following information:

- the detainee's name, date of birth and nationality;
- the Home Office or immigration service reference number;
- where the person is detained;
- under what authority the person is detained, for example, as an alleged illegal entrant or as someone who has overstayed;
- whether the person is being detained only for immigration reasons or they are also being detained for criminal reasons;
- if the person is detained for criminal reasons, whether they have been charged with any offence and what type of investigation is ongoing;
- has the person been given any papers, and if so, what?
- are there any plans to remove the person from the UK, and if so, when?
- what the detainee wants – for example, to contest the situation in every possible way, to return to the country of origin as quickly as possible, to be released for a short period to make arrangements to leave?

1 If it seems that the person is being investigated for a criminal offence (including an 'immigration' criminal offence such as breach of conditions), it is important that the person sees a solicitor specialising in criminal cases. Such solicitors must now be contracted to the Criminal Defence Service which is managed by the Legal Services Commission. Duty solicitor schemes are available for advice and assistance at police stations and magistrates courts.

2 Try to negotiate temporary release or bail. The factors which the immigration service will consider include:

- does the person have a stable home? For example, how long has he or she lived at their address; is this with family or close friends with whom he or she would want to keep in touch?

- is the person in employment, and for how long?
- has the person abided by any immigration or bail conditions in the past?
- what incentive does the person have to keep in contact with the immigration service?
- how strong is the person's case for remaining in the UK?
- is the person particularly vulnerable in some way?

It is less likely that a woman or child will be detained, but probable that a young man without close family ties, who has not lived at the same address for long and who does not have a strong immigration case, will be. If the person is not immediately released, visit as soon as possible to find out exactly what he or she wants to do and to take full instructions. For full details about detention ▶see Chapters 24-25.

3   If there are plans to remove the person very quickly, and he or she wants to contest removal, speak to the chief immigration officer or the Home Office official dealing with the case. If there is new information or arguments which have not been considered before, for example, marriage, a long-standing relationship, or an asylum claim, the authorities should delay the person's removal while representations are considered, which may take some time. In particular, consider whether there are any human rights claims which can be made on behalf of the person. Both asylum and human rights claims will lead to appeal rights, except in certain narrow circumstances, and people cannot be removed until those appeals have been dealt with.

Contacting an MP

If the person has already been through the formal processes of dealing with the immigration authorities without success – making an application, appealing against a refusal, losing the appeal – it may be worth contacting the local Member of Parliament. If MPs try to intervene while an appeal is pending, they are usually told that their representations will not be considered until after the appeal has been decided. Use the constituency MP of one of the friends or relatives the person is coming to be with unless the applicant has been living in the UK, in which case use their own MP. Be aware, however, that some MPs refuse to take on such cases at all, or need a great deal of persuading to do so.

It is important to telephone or write to the MP with full details of the case and ask him or her to forward any representations with a further covering letter to the Member of Parliament Correspondence Section (MPCS) at the Immigration and Nationality Directorate or to contact the Home Office Minister's office directly. The intervention of an MP can also sometimes help to get an imminent removal deferred, particularly if matters are raised through an MP which have not been considered before.

MPs can be contacted at the House of Commons, which may also be able to give the number of the MP's secretary or constituency office. The House of Commons Information Office should be able to provide the name of the constituency, and of the MP, if details of the applicant's or sponsor's address can be provided.

Using judicial review

Judicial review is a High Court procedure that can be used to challenge decisions which are made by public authorities including the immigration authorities. The branch of the High Court which deals with judicial review cases is now called the 'Administrative Court' (it used to be called the 'Crown Office'). It can *only* be used:

- where there is no other available way of overturning the decision, for example, a right of appeal; *and*
- where there are grounds for challenging the decision as being *unlawful*.

Judicial review will only be available in a minority of cases. It cannot be used in the same way as an immigration appeal to an adjudicator, where appellants are able to ask an adjudicator to make new findings of fact different to those accepted by the immigration authorities. Judicial review can also not be used simply because there are compassionate features about a case but the Home Office still will not grant leave outside the immigration rules. There are two stages to the procedure for judicial review. The first is called the 'permission' stage. In order to be granted permission to apply for judicial review, it is necessary to show the judge that it is arguable that the decision was unlawful.

The first stage normally takes place without a hearing with a judge considering the papers prepared by the claimant's lawyers. If the judge rejects the claim after looking at the case papers, the claimant can try to get past the first stage again at a court hearing. If the first stage is successful, then the second stage is the full hearing of the claim for judicial review in which the court finally decides whether the decision was unlawful. The average waiting time for the first stage in 2001 was eight weeks and the average waiting time for reaching the second stage was 20 weeks. If the claimant is successful at the second stage, it doesn't necessarily mean that they get to stay in the UK but that the immigration authorities or the immigration appellate authorities have to reconsider their original decision in a lawful way.

Judicial review is a complex procedure. It can only be applied for on a particular form called 'N461'. For claims made after 4 March 2002, there is a special 'protocol' which must have been complied with before the claim is made. In order to bring a claim for judicial review, a specialist solicitor in immigration or asylum work should be contacted for advice. For details of how to contact such a solicitor and the availability of any public funding ▶see Chapter 3. If the claim is to proceed, the solicitor will almost certainly instruct a barrister to help bring the claim.

The most common circumstances in which judicial review is used in immigration and asylum cases is to challenge:

- a determination of an immigration adjudicator who has dismissed an asylum or human rights appeal *and* upheld a Home Office certificate, so that there is no further right of appeal to the Immigration Appeal Tribunal (IAT);

- a determination of the IAT not to grant leave (permission) to appeal to the IAT against a decision of an adjudicator. There is no other right of appeal in these cases; the 2002 Bill proposes, however, to prevent judicial review of these decisions and to have a separate 'statutory' review procedure where the case papers are looked at without the possibility of a further hearing. Under this procedure, there are also proposals to financially penalise advisors who bring claims which have no chance of success;

- a certificate issued by the Home Office that an asylum-seeker can be removed to a 'safe third country' (see s11, 12 1999 Act). Before the 1999 Act, there were many judicial reviews against these decisions. However, the 1999 Act tries to limit the circumstances in which challenges can be brought, preventing the courts from considering whether removals to EU member states under the 'Dublin Convention' procedures are 'safe'. There remains an in-country right of appeal against third country asylum removals which are not to an EU member state or to Canada, the USA, Norway or Switzerland. Therefore, judicial review is not available in those cases;

- a decision by the immigration authorities to proceed to enforce the departure of a person where they have made a human rights claim and are trying to bring an appeal (s65 1999 Act) against a decision not to allow them to stay in the UK but the Home Office are seeking to remove the person on the grounds that they have no right of appeal;

- a certificate issued by the Home Office that an asylum-seeker is not entitled to bring a human rights or discrimination appeal to an adjudicator against a decision that they should be removed to a safe 'third' country because their human rights/discrimination claim is 'manifestly unfounded' (see s72(2)(a) 1999 Act);

- a certificate issued by the Home Office that a person who makes a late claim for asylum or a late human rights/discrimination claim rather than in the course of another in-country appeal, has no legitimate reason to claim asylum and should not therefore be permitted to bring an asylum appeal (see s73 and s76(5) 1999 Act);

- a decision by the National Asylum Support Service to disperse an asylum-seeker, in circumstances where they have no right of appeal to the Asylum Support Adjudicator because there has been no decision to actually stop providing support, or to refuse to provide it;

- a decision by the National Asylum Support Service not to provide 'hard cases' support (s4 1999 Act).

Urgent judicial review cases

The Administrative Court also has the power to hear urgent cases and to give urgent orders called 'injunctions' or 'interim orders' to prevent the immigration authorities, for example, from removing a person from the UK until the judicial review can be dealt with. From February 2002, there is a new procedure for making urgent applications to the Administrative Court which requires the claimant's lawyers to fill in an additional form explaining the need for urgency and the timescale within which the first stage needs to be considered. The papers must also be faxed to the defendant. The new urgent procedures are set out in a 'Practice Statement' issued by the court which is published in the All England Law Reports ([2002] 1 All ER 633). There are however penalties for abuse of the system. In most cases claimants' lawyers are able to persuade the Home Office that whatever action it is threatening to take should be delayed so that the urgent procedure does not need to be used. Again, it is vital that people seek specialist advice from an experienced solicitor in relation to these procedures.

Section 3 **Asylum and human rights**

Chapter 9
Asylum under the Refugee Convention 147

The relationship between refugees, human rights
and exceptional leave 148

Legal basis for asylum under the Refugee
Convention 150

Refugee status under the 1951 Convention 153

Ceasing to be a refugee 167

Exclusion from Convention protection 168

Chapter 10
Asylum procedures 173

Procedures used when applying 174

Unaccompanied minor asylum-seekers 191

Dependants 192

Permission to work 194

Ways of discouraging asylum-seekers 195

Chapter 11
Home Office decisions on asylum 197

Immigration rules and credibility 198

Certification of decisions 203

'Non-compliance' refusals 205

Third country cases 206

The Home Office decision 212

Exceptional leave 216

Delays   219
Fresh claims for asylum   220

Chapter 12
Family reunion and travel   222
Family reunion   222
Foreign travel   229

Chapter 13
Human Rights   231
The ECHR rights   233
Using human rights in immigration cases   239
Taking a case to Europe   268
Race discrimination in immigration   270

9 Asylum under the Refugee Convention

At the time that the Immigration Act 1971 was introduced, Home Office figures indicate that there were only 200 or so people who claimed asylum every year. Over 80,000 people (excluding dependants) claimed asylum in 2000 and over 52,000 applications were made between January and September 2001. Refugee flows depend upon political conditions abroad but the main nation states of applicants for asylum at present are: Afghanistan, China, the Czech Republic, the Democratic Republic of Congo, Pakistan, India, Iran, Iraq, Sierra Leone, Somalia, Sri Lanka, Turkey, the former Yugoslav Republics and Zimbabwe.

Over recent years, asylum has become the single most important and controversial issue in immigration and nationality. It has also become an issue of substantial political importance and the subject of intense public debate both during and between national elections. It is unfortunate that the debate has become so coloured by misunderstandings, mis-information, political expediency and, often, blatant prejudice. JCWI believes that the overwhelming majority of people fleeing to these shores are in genuine need of humanitarian protection as a result of widespread oppression around the world. The organisation will continue to lobby for a system which delivers fairness and justice to asylum-seekers and one in which their personal dignity is respected.

The incorporation into UK law of most of the protections and guarantees of the 1950 European Convention of Human Rights (ECHR) has had a significant impact on the asylum system. Taken altogether, this section covers rights to asylum under the 1951 Refugee Convention, rights under the ECHR and the granting of exceptional leave. In this chapter, we look at who legally qualifies for asylum as a refugee within the meaning of the 1951 Convention. In ▶Chapter 10 we deal with the procedures which people have to go through in order to claim asylum, including how people are asked to give details of their claims, the documents they are given, including 'one-stop' notices and how unaccompanied minor asylum-seekers are dealt with. ▶Chapter 11 covers how the Home Office reaches decisions on asylum applications, the 'certificates' that are issued in certain cases and the issue of returns to safe 'third' countries. ▶Chapter 11 also covers the giving of decisions in asylum cases and the grant of exceptional leave to remain. Rights under the ECHR are dealt with in

▶Chapter 13. That chapter does not just look at the effect of the ECHR in claims for 'protection' (ie on grounds similar to asylum) but at the effect of the ECHR in immigration cases more generally. Chapter 12 considers the rights of all the people considered in this section to bring family members to the UK and also their rights to obtain travel documents and to leave and return to the UK. Asylum and human rights appeals against negative decisions generally are covered with other appeals in ▶Section 10.

All the major changes to the asylum system made by the Immigration and Asylum Act 1999 are covered in this section. In February 2002, the government issued a White Paper, *Secure Borders, Safe Haven,* which proposes further important changes to the system. The proposals in the White Paper and 2002 Bill are summarised in the box ▶see pages 170-172. The welfare and support arrangements proposed by the 2002 Bill are dealt with in more detail in Section 11 ▶see pages 719-721.

The relationship between refugees, human rights and exceptional leave

Refugees and exceptional leave

'Refugees' are people who come within the definition set out in the 1951 Refugee Convention as being people who that Convention is designed to protect ▶see definition on page 153. The immigration rules state that these people are to be granted 'asylum' and this chapter is concerned solely with them.

As well as granting asylum under the Refugee Convention, the Home Office has also for a long time recognised that there are many people who, although they do not fit the definition of 'refugee', are in need of protection. Therefore, in deciding whether to grant humanitarian protection, the Home Office took into account the UK's international obligations other than under the Refugee Convention, for example, under the ECHR, the UN Convention Against Torture and Other Cruel, Inhuman or Degrading Treatment or Punishment 1984 and the International Covenant on Civil and Political Rights 1996. As a result, the Home Office developed a practice of granting 'exceptional leave' to people who would benefit from those conventions or where there otherwise appeared to be strong humanitarian reasons for granting protection. Formally, in-country applicants are granted exceptional leave to remain (ELR) and port applicants are granted exceptional leave to enter (ELE), although they are both often referred to as 'ELR'. For ease, we will refer simply to ELR. If an asylum-seeker was being refused asylum under the Refugee Convention, the Home Office would automatically consider granting exceptional leave and that is still the case. Now, however, the incorporation of the ECHR means that ECHR rights must be considered as part of the decision-making process.

Impact of incorporation of ECHR

From 2 October 2000, rights under the ECHR have been incorporated into domestic law by the Human Rights Act 1998 (HRA). The HRA requires public bodies, such as the Home Office, to act in accordance with the ECHR. This has had an important impact on the system for protection. In many cases, the reasons why a person wishes to remain in the UK are relevant both to a claim for asylum under the Refugee Convention and to rights under the ECHR. Establishing a claim to remain as a refugee is preferable because it gives greater rights. For example, successful applicants get indefinite leave straight away, have rights to family reunion within the immigration rules and can obtain a Refugee Convention travel document. However, claims and appeals under both conventions are often made together because there are certain circumstances in which it may be decided that, although a person does not qualify as a refugee, they do qualify for protection under, for example, Article 3 ECHR (prohibition against torture or inhuman or degrading treatment or punishment). For details of the differences between the two ▶see pages 243-244.

In some cases, of course, the grounds for a human rights claim may be completely different from any asylum question under the Refugee Convention. For example, a person may allege that removing them from the UK would separate them from family members with the right to remain here and therefore is in breach of Article 8 ECHR (family life).

Many of those to whom the Home Office may previously have granted ELR now have a *right* to be admitted to or remain in the UK under the ECHR. The Home Office treats those who establish rights under the ECHR in the same way as it has always treated those falling into the ELR category and in fact grants them ELR (see para 4.90, 2002 White Paper and para 4.3 ch5, s4 Asylum Policy Instructions (API)). It is odd that those with such important rights should still be described as being treated 'exceptionally' when the grant of their status does not depend at all on an exercise of discretion. This is even more odd when it is remembered that a claim under Article 3 is considered to be an 'asylum' claim for the purposes of asylum support. It is to be hoped that the immigration rules will in future clearly set out the rights to be granted leave of those who succeed in human rights claims. At present, the rules simply state that immigration officials must carry out their duties 'in compliance with the Human Rights Act 1998' (see para 2, HC 395).

Those allowed to stay in the UK as a result of ECHR rights are therefore usually given a period of four years' ELR and are able to apply for indefinite leave subsequently.

Non-ECHR exceptional leave

There remains a wide discretion to grant ELR to people who apply for asylum and who do not qualify under either the Refugee Convention or the ECHR. For details of the Home Office ELR policy ►see pages 216-219. The number of people who fall into this category since the incorporation of the ECHR is less than previously.

Exceptional leave other than after refusal of asylum

In this section we have referred to ELR granted following an asylum claim and human rights claim. There are, however, many other circumstances, unrelated to asylum in which people can be granted leave 'exceptionally' where this simply means treating them more generously than the immigration rules strictly allow. Where the Home Office has a policy to treat people in different circumstances exceptionally, this is dealt with in the appropriate chapter. However, for a general explanation of this wide meaning of exceptional leave and for a list of the most important concessions under which it is often granted ►see pages 104-105.

Legal basis for asylum under the refugee convention

The basis of the law on refugees is the 1951 UN Convention relating to the Status of Refugees and its 1967 Protocol (the 'Refugee Convention'). The Refugee Convention is one of a group of international instruments which are basic to international human rights law and which were constructed following the Universal Declaration of Human Rights of 1948 (UDHR). Article 14(1) of the UDHR guarantees the right of all individuals to seek asylum from persecution in other countries.

The Refugee Convention was prepared and debated in the aftermath of the Second World War, to address the problem of mass displacement of people in Europe. In 1967 a Protocol was added to the Convention, which extended the definition of refugees to people forced to seek refuge because of events that took place after 1950.

The most important right which is guaranteed by the Refugee Convention is the right of a person who is a refugee not to be returned to a country or territory where they will face persecution (Article 33 of the Refugee Convention). The prohibition against a contracting state returning a person in this manner is also sometimes known by its equivalent in French, 'non-refoulement'.

The UK is one of the 141 states which are bound by the Refugee Convention. However, before 1993, the UK had no specific asylum law and asylum was mentioned almost as an afterthought in the immigration rules, after all other ways in which people might qualify to come to the UK had been listed. Since 1993, three major Acts have been passed dealing with asylum. They are the Asylum and Immigration Appeals Act 1993, the Asylum and Immigration Act 1996 and the Immigration and Asylum Act 1999. The last Act followed the government's White Paper *Fairer, Faster and Firmer – A Modern Approach to Immigration and Asylum* published in July 1998, which promised a comprehensive, integrated strategy to replace the piecemeal approach of the past. Three further Acts have also affected the asylum process in certain cases: the Special Immigration Appeals Commission Act 1997, Terrorism Act 2000 and the Anti-terrorism, Crime and Security Act 2001.

Changes made under the Immigration and Asylum Act 1999

Although the 1999 Act repealed much of the previous immigration and asylum legislation, some parts of the previous Acts were left intact and must still be referred to. The 1999 Act and other procedural reforms modified asylum law and procedures in the following ways:

- a strengthening of measures to refuse to consider asylum cases substantively on third country grounds;
- a broadening of carriers' liability legislation;
- an asylum support scheme designed as a disincentive to would-be, non-genuine asylum-seekers;
- quicker and more streamlined decision-making including greater use of 'non-compliance' refusals;
- an overhaul of appeal rights including the new 'one-stop' appeal;
- increased powers to arrest, search and fingerprint and an increase in the use of detention.

The Acts are supplemented by the immigration rules explaining the procedures and listing the factors which the Immigration and Nationality Directorate at the Home Office must take into account when considering asylum applications. The Home Office also publishes its Asylum Policy Instructions (API), which give guidance on how decisions are taken in practice.

The Convention as part of UK law

The fact that the UK is a signatory to the 1951 Convention does not automatically make it a part of the UK's own law. Signing a treaty only creates obligations between states in international law not domestic law. However, the most important obligation under the Convention – not to send a refugee to a country where they fear persecution – has been incorporated into UK law as follows:

- an asylum claim is defined by section 1 of the Asylum and Immigration Appeals Act 1993 as:

  'a claim made by a person...that it would be contrary to the United Kingdom's obligations under the [1951 Refugee] Convention for him to be removed from, or required to leave, the United Kingdom'.

- section 2 of the 1993 Act states that the immigration rules must not be interpreted as allowing the immigration authorities to do anything which would be contrary to the Refugee Convention;

- the immigration rules confirm that the asylum claim will be determined in accordance with the UK's obligations under the Convention and asylum will be granted if the applicant has arrived in the UK, satisfies the definition of refugee and their removal would be contrary to the Convention. In all other cases, asylum will be refused (para 327–335 HC 395);

- if an adjudicator or the Immigration Appeal Tribunal (IAT) hearing an asylum appeal finds that the decision of the immigration authorities to return the appellant to their country of origin would be in breach of the Convention, the appeal must be allowed (s69 1999 Act).

Although they are not specifically incorporated into UK law, the UK does seek to observe other obligations under the Convention, for example, the provision of Convention travel documents to refugees (Article 28) and giving refugees equal rights with UK citizens in the provision of welfare support such as social security and housing (Articles 21–24).

Although advice is given in the *UNHCR Handbook* about the procedures to be operated in determining who is a refugee, these are only advisory. The Home Office is not prevented, therefore, from making far-reaching administrative changes in how it deals with applications. It has, for example, frequently tightened time limits within which asylum-seekers must lodge their evidence. The Home Office has also set out in the immigration rules the factors which it will take into account in the course of deciding whether people satisfy the legal conditions to be a refugee ►see pages 190-202.

The asylum process

The Home Office considers each person's application for asylum in detail. If it is satisfied that they meet the criteria of the Convention, they will be granted refugee status or 'asylum'. If the Home Office does not accept that an applicant meets the criteria for being granted refugee status, it will go on and consider whether the asylum-seeker should be allowed to stay either under the ECHR or on any other exceptional basis.

In certain cases, the Home Office may consider that it can swiftly return the asylum-seeker to a safe 'third country' for that country to deal with their claim to asylum ►see pages 206-212. In these cases, appeal rights are much more restricted.

Because the administrative and legal systems are so rapidly changing, it is particularly important that all asylum applicants get good advice and representation.

Refugee status under the 1951 convention

Interpreting the Convention

In the case of *Adan & Aitseguer*, the House of Lords decided that there is only one true legal definition of a refugee within the meaning of the Convention. In theory, therefore, the definition of refugee is an international one which is applicable to all the signatory states. In practice, signatory states have their own systems of law and have interpreted the Convention in different ways, which has been an issue of particular concern where the Home Office has wanted to remove people to safe third countries. Despite continued differences of interpretation and procedure, as the process of harmonisation of laws within the European Union continues, general decisions regarding refugee protection are increasingly being made in European ministerial meetings and committees and then implemented nationally. In a speech in April 2001 to the Foreign Press Association, the then Home Secretary, Jack Straw, confirmed the government's aim to harmonise across the EU both asylum procedures and the interpretation of the Convention. This sentiment is repeated in the 2002 White Paper.

Assistance in the proper interpretation of the Convention is provided by the United Nations High Commissioner for Refugees (UNHCR), which is the UN agency set up and invested with responsibility for overseeing the concerns of refugees internationally. Its *Handbook on procedures and criteria for determining refugee status* was prepared as a guide to signatory countries on the interpretation of the Convention. This is very helpful in preparing an asylum case, as its principles are generally accepted by the Home Office. It has been approved as a useful tool of interpretation many times by the courts, most enthusiastically by the Court of Appeal in the case of *Robinson.*

Who is a 'refugee'?

Article 1A(2) of the Convention, as amended by the 1967 Protocol, defines a 'refugee' as any person who:

'owing to a well-founded fear of being persecuted for reasons of race, religion, nationality, membership of a particular social group or political opinion, is outside the country of his nationality and is unable or, owing to such fear, is unwilling to avail himself of the protection of that country; or who, not having a nationality and being outside the country of his former habitual residence is unable or, owing to such fear, is unwilling to return to it'.

Below, we look at the individual elements of the definition separately and at some of the case law which interprets them. We then look at some issues which regularly arise in applying the definition to particular cases.

The most important obligation under the Refugee Convention is not to return ('refouler') a refugee to the place where they are at risk. Article 33(1) of the Convention states:

'no Contracting State shall expel or return ('refouler') a refugee in any manner whatsoever to the frontiers of territories where his life or freedom would be threatened on account of his race, religion, nationality, membership of a particular social group or political opinion'.

The definition of refugee in Article 1A (2) and the prohibition on return in Article 33 are repeated in the immigration rules (see para 334 HC 395 – 'grant of asylum'). On reading those two Articles, it might at first appear that a person who is a 'refugee' (has a 'well-founded fear' of persecution for a Convention reason) has to jump *another* hurdle by showing that their 'life or freedom' would be threatened if they are returned before they are entitled to be granted asylum. However, the courts have decided that there is only one hurdle. If a person has a fear of 'persecution' within the meaning of Article 1A(2) in the country to which they are to be sent, then that is sufficient to show that their 'life or freedom' will be threatened there as well (see *Sivakumaran* in the House of Lords and *Adan v SSHD* in the Court of Appeal).

Outside country of nationality or former habitual residence

The definition makes it clear that a person cannot be a refugee while they are still in their country of origin. The aim of the Convention is to help people who have sought protection abroad. This is one of the reasons why it is not possible, under the immigration rules, to apply for asylum from the country of origin. Only very exceptionally are any applications from oveseas at all considered ▶see pages 174-177. The reference in the definition to a person 'not having a country of nationality and being outside the country of his former habitual residence' means that the protection of the Convention is extended to stateless persons, provided that they meet the other criteria in the definition.

Well-founded fear

The *UNHCR Handbook* suggests that persecution can be seen in both subjective and objective terms. Whether there is a subjective fear depends upon the person's state of mind as to whether they actually believe that they will suffer harm if returned to their country. It is usually this real mental fear of the claimant which triggers their flight from the country. Psychological trauma and post-traumatic stress experienced by the claimant constitute important evidence to be put forward in support of the claim.

However, in the landmark case of *Sivakumaran*, the House of Lords established that, in order to qualify as a refugee, it is necessary to establish not only a subjectively-held fear, but also that there is an *objective* fear of persecution as well. This means that the claimant not only fears a certain outcome but that there is an actual risk of that outcome occurring if they were to be returned. So, if a person, for whatever reason, genuinely fears a particular event but there is no risk of that event actually occurring, they will not be a refugee. In other words, the objective element of the test can override the subjective. The court decided that this interpretation was justified by the inclusion in the definition of the requirement that the fear of persecution be 'well-founded'. In practice, asylum decision-making largely focuses on the objective aspect of the fear since, if there is in fact a risk, it can generally be assumed that a person who has claimed asylum on the basis of it does indeed hold a fear in their own mind.

Persecution

There must be a *current* fear of persecution in order for a person to be a refugee. In *Adan*, the House of Lords had to decide whether a Somali, who had left his country because of a well-founded fear of persecution and was *now* 'unable to avail' himself of the protection of the state because the state had collapsed, was a refugee. The House of Lords held that it was not enough that the applicant left because of a fear of persecution which existed in the past nor that there was currently no functioning state in Somalia. It was necessary to have a continued well-founded fear of persecution for a Convention reason.

The *UNHCR Handbook* states that while threats to life or freedom will always amount to persecution, other serious violations of human rights can also qualify (para 51). So, for example, long-term discrimination and harassment, particularly in the context of an atmosphere of general insecurity, might also be considered as persecution, in addition to overt physical threats. While the *UNHCR Handbook* notes that the various attempts to formulate a general definition of persecution have met with little success, one general approach that has been greeted by the courts in the UK with some approval is that set out by Professor James Hathaway in his book *The Law of Refugee Status* (1991). He regards the Refugee Convention as being part of a family of human rights laws which are interlinked and internationally accepted. He therefore sees the failure of a state's responsibilities under these human rights laws as constituting the kind of serious harm which amounts to 'persecution'.

Hathaway constructs a hierarchy of human rights and fundamental freedoms and defines persecution by reference to them. This hierarchy is reflected in the following four categories.

First category. At the top of the hierarchy are rights such as the freedom from arbitrary loss of life, protection against torture or cruel, inhuman or degrading punishment or treatment, freedom from slavery and freedom of thought, conscience and religion. These rights should always be observed and protected by the state even in times of acute crisis or emergency. Failure to observe them amounts to persecution.

Second category. In the second category are those rights which states may exceptionally not observe in times of crisis or emergency: freedom from arbitrary arrest and detention; rights to a fair trial, personal integrity and internal movement; freedom of speech and association, and other basic democratic rights. Persecution will arise where a state fails to observe these rights unless it can show that it was necessary, having regard to the circumstances of the emergency, for those rights to be overridden.

Third category. Into the third category come social and economic rights: to work and to decent working conditions; housing; medical care; social welfare; education and the right to cultural expression. If a state ignores these rights altogether or upholds them but only in a discriminatory way, then the result may be persecution.

Fourth category. The final category of rights are those which are not seen as 'core' entitlements in human rights law: the right to own and be free from deprivation of property and to be protected against unemployment. Failure to observe these rights will not generally amount to persecution.

Professor Hathaway's general principles were approved in the Immigration Appeal Tribunal (IAT) case of *Gashi* and were also commented upon favourably by the Court of Appeal in *Ravichandran*. In that case the Court of Appeal held that the arbitrary round-up and detention of young Tamils immediately following terrorist atrocities did not amount to persecution but that persecution had to be viewed 'in the round' with all circumstances taken into account including the reasons motivating the particular treatment. The round-ups had taken place in the context of terrorist attacks. The court indicated that, had the detention been long-term, accompanied by physical ill-treatment or motivated by the Sri Lankan authorities out of malice to Tamils, it would probably have constituted persecution.

The Court of Appeal has also, however, adopted another more straight-forward approach. In *Kagema*, a case concerning the displacement of Kikuyus from the Rift Valley in Kenya, the Court of Appeal suggested that the correct approach was to view 'persecution' as an ordinary English word which had simply to be applied to the facts of each and every case. Technical or general definitions would not help the decision-maker in that task. The problem of an approach which operates without any real framework is that the task of assessing persecution becomes far more arbitrary, and inconsistent decisions are more likely. It may also produce surprising and often unfavourable results. The appellants in *Kagema*, for example, were unsuccessful in their claims even though they had repeatedly been displaced from their homeland.

Convention reason for fear of persecution

Refugees have to show that the persecution they face is for one or more of the reasons listed in the definition in Article 1A(2): race, religion, nationality, political opinion or membership of a particular social group. It is generally up to the people seeking asylum to satisfy the Home Office about their situation and the danger in which this would place them if they had to return. However, refugees may well not be able to identify or analyse Convention reasons themselves and the *UNHCR Handbook* confirms that there is no duty on them to do so.

The focus for deciding whether there is a Convention reason for the persecution is upon the acts of the persecutors rather than the understanding of the persons affected. So, for example, a mistaken belief on the part of the persecutor that a person holds a particular political opinion is enough to bring any resulting persecution within the Convention. In addition the persecutor may interpret certain acts, which others might view as being quite innocent and innocuous, as signifying a political stance and react disproportionately. In both situations, it is common for lawyers to talk of a political opinion that is 'imputed'. This concept was accepted at an early stage by the IAT (see eg. *Asante*) and has subsequently been accepted by the higher courts and applied by the Home Office.

Race, religion and nationality are reasonably straightforward grounds. Claims based on race have to take into account the UN Convention on the Elimination of All Forms of Racial Discrimination. 'Religion' can also mean freedom of 'thought, conscience, and religion', as stipulated in the International Covenant of Civil and Political Rights. Religious belief arguably covers the right not to hold a theistic religious belief. However, in the Court of Appeal in *Omoruyi* it was held that the Ogboni secret cult in Nigeria, which practised certain rites and rituals, was an intrinsically criminal organisation rather than a religion. 'Nationality' includes both ethnic and linguistic groups and any national minorities within a country.

Clearly, the various different reasons can overlap in relation to the same fear. For example, a person from a particular tribe or ethnic background may be persecuted as a result of their race but the state may also associate them with a particular political stance as well. The two Convention reasons which have caused more debate have been 'political opinion' and 'membership of a particular social group'.

Political opinion or belief

Political rights such as freedom of expression and association are obviously fundamental values in democratic societies and the term 'political opinion' has to be understood within this context. Although there has been a heavy emphasis by decision-makers on the individual's own opinion and active participation in political activity, as seen above, political opinion includes both directly held and attributed opinions. Although most 'political' refugees will have given some outward expression of their views, a person may still fall within the Convention even though they have had no opportunities to express their political opinions.

As with all of the criteria set out as defining a refugee, the meaning of political opinions and beliefs must be read broadly in favour of protection by the Convention. In his book, *The Refugee in International Law* (1996), Professor Guy Goodwin-Gill comments that the notion of a 'political refugee' is of a person:

'...pursued by the government of a state or other entity on account of his or her opinions which are an actual or perceived threat to that government or its institutions, or to the political agenda and aspirations of the entity in question'.

As was made clear in the IAT case of *Gomez*, 'political opinion' cannot be limited' to party politics. So, for example, trade union activists have often been found to be persecuted on grounds of political opinion.

In assessing whether an attitude amounts to a political opinion, it is important to look to the context of the particular country and apply a flexible meaning. So, for example, the API recognise that 'if a woman resists gender oppression, her resistance is political'. In some cases, Commonwealth courts have found that violations of the dress code in certain Muslim states or the exercise of human rights, such as a breach of China's one-child policy, can be sufficient to found a political opinion.

Membership of a particular social group

The category of persecution over which there is most debate, and which is often the most difficult to establish, is membership of a particular social group. The *UNHCR Handbook* defines this as 'persons of similar background, habits or social status' and states that fear of persecution on these grounds may often overlap with others. This Convention reason has been argued with success in some gender-based claims and cases where persecution is experienced as a result of sexual orientation. In certain circumstances, a family has been accepted as constituting a particular social group (see *Hernandez* (IAT) but compare *Quijano* in the Court of Appeal).

The question of whether particular groups constitute a 'particular social group' within the Convention depends upon the social conditions existing in the relevant country. This is an area in which state practice in recognising refugees has varied. Canada has granted asylum to a Saudi Arabian woman on the grounds of her activities challenging sex discrimination and to a woman from Trinidad who had suffered physical abuse from her husband on the grounds that there was no network of support for women in her position in Trinidad. The United States has granted asylum to women facing genital mutilation, to a gay man from Mexico and more recently, to women facing forced marriage and domestic violence.

The Home Office has not yet accepted all of these arguments but has occasionally granted ELR to gay men from countries such as Iran. In an older case in the High Court, a man from the Turkish Republic of Northern Cyprus was unsuccessful because it was not accepted that if he returned he had to 'practice' his homosexuality although it was assumed in his favour that homosexuals could constitute a particular social group *(Binbasi)*. More recently, in the House of Lords in *Shah and Islam*, it was stated that homosexuals could constitute a particular social group if they suffered discrimination as that group. More recently still, it was agreed on all sides in the Court of Appeal in *Jain* that homosexuals in India are a social group because of the adverse impact of Indian law. IAT decisions have not been consistent. In the case of *Golchin,* it was held homosexuals are not a 'social group', but in *Vraciu*, in Romania, they are. There have been some recent successes in persuading immigration adjudicators that homosexuals from Jamaica constitute a particular social group and are subject to persecution from elements within society against which the state has been unwilling and unable to protect the gay community.

Shah and Islam is now the leading case on 'social group'. In that case, the following principles were laid down by the House of Lords in order to identify members of a particular social group:

- members of a social group must have in common an immutable characteristic which it is either beyond their power to change or which is so fundamental to their identity or conscience that they cannot be required to change it;
- the social group must exist independently of, and not be defined by, the persecution. If it were otherwise, anyone who was persecuted would be a member of a social group. This was the central finding by the Court of Appeal in *Savchenkov*, which concerned alleged persecution by the Russian mafia. It was decided that persecution of a group comprising law-abiding citizens for refusing to co-operate with the mafia was not a group which existed independently of the persecution;
- counteracting discrimination is a fundamental purpose of the Convention. Therefore, if there is discrimination against members of a group, that is a relevant factor in identifying whether that group is a 'particular social group';
- the cohesiveness of the group is another factor which is relevant in determining whether it is a group within the meaning of the Convention but there is no *requirement* that the group be cohesive.

In the actual cases of *Shah and Islam*, women from Pakistan were held to be a particular social group because they were identifiable by gender, they were discriminated against and the state did not protect them. Since then the IAT has upheld a number of gender-based claims, such as those of a Ukrainian woman forced into prostitution *(Dzhygun)* and an Iranian woman who left her violent husband and feared prosecution for adultery *(Fatemeh)*.

The meaning of 'immutable characteristic' (►see above) has caused considerable debate. In the Court of Appeal in *Ouanes*, an Algerian midwife, whose work involved giving contraceptive advice, was held not to be a member of a particular social group as her work did not have sufficient impact upon her individual identity or conscience so as to make it 'immutable'. However, the court indicated that other types of employment might be sufficiently connected to a person's identity, for example, work as part of a religious order. Similarly, conscientiously fulfiling a civic duty by seeking legal redress against illegal actions of police officers has been held not to make someone a member of a social group *(Storozhenko)*.

Standard of proof

In principle, the burden (or onus) of showing that the criteria for coming within the definition of refugee are established, rests with the asylum-seeker. However, the 'standard' of proof is a different legal concept from the 'burden'. The burden of proof concerns whose job it is to prove the relevant facts. The standard of proof specifies the *degree* of certainty to which a matter has to be proved before it is taken into account for legal purposes.

In criminal cases, the burden of proof is on the prosecution to prove the case against an accused to the standard of 'no reasonable doubt'. In most civil cases, the burden lies upon whoever is asserting a relevant fact to prove it to the standard of 'balance of probabilities', which means anything above 50 per cent. In asylum cases, although the investigative process often centres largely on what has happened in the past to a particular person, the actual question to be answered is what will happen in the future if the person is required to return. Inevitably, this question involves a degree of speculation and prediction and is not as amenable to traditional concepts of 'proof'.

The approach which has been laid down by the courts is as follows. In *Sivakumaran*, the House of Lords decided that the standard of proof that had to be reached in showing that a fear was 'well-founded' was that there had to be a 'serious possibility' or 'reasonable degree of likelihood' or 'real risk' of it occurring. The standard of proof is therefore at the lowest end of the scale and is less onerous than the ordinary civil standard of balance of probabilities. One indication given in *Sivakumaran* was that the standard was similar to showing a 'one-in-ten' chance.

Whether there is a 'real risk' of a person being persecuted if returned is a simple enough question. However, over recent years, the courts have had to consider the approach that should be taken to determine what happened to an applicant in the past as part of the process of deciding what may happen to them in the future. Although the ultimate question is always whether there is a risk on return, in many cases whether the applicant is telling the truth about what has happened in the past is extremely important in determining the claim. The correct approach to the assessment of past events was confirmed by the Court of Appeal in *Karanakaran*. The court directed decision-makers to weigh all the evidence in assessing the risk of persecution. The decision-maker must *not* exclude anything from consideration unless they are in no doubt that it did *not* occur. Asylum-seekers are therefore to be given the benefit of any doubts the decision-maker has about the history they have given.

There are two reasons for the low standard of proof. First, it recognises that people should be protected from serious harm if there is a significant risk of it occurring, not only if there is over a 50 per cent chance of it happening. Secondly, it recognises that most asylum-seekers will not be able to produce documentary evidence or witnesses in order to back up their claims but that this alone should not mean that their claims do not succeed. The lower standard must be applied by the Home Office in making the decision in the first place and by adjudicators and the IAT on any appeal.

Common issues arising under the Convention

The definition of refugee has led to a great number of court decisions, both in the UK and in the legal jurisdictions of the other signatory states, which explain the meaning that is to be given to the definition. The interpretation of the basic elements of the definition is set out above. Below we look at some frequently re-occurring situations in asylum cases and the way in which the courts have applied the Convention in those circumstances.

Non-state agents

In most cases, the applicant fears harm directly from the state or its agents, for example, police or security officials. In some cases, however, the offensive acts which an applicant fears are carried out by members of the public with no connection to the state.

In *Horvath*, the House of Lords examined the meaning of persecution where the source of potential harm derived from 'non-state agents'. The case involved a Roma from Slovakia who had suffered extreme racially-motivated violence from skinheads and claimed that the national authorities were not protecting him. The majority in the House of Lords decided that the word 'persecution' in the refugee definition does not simply mean sufficiently serious ill-treatment but must also involve a failure of the state to afford protection against the ill-treatment. If the state is not failing in its obligations, then a person will not be a refugee *even if* their fears are well-founded. In deciding whether the state could protect, the central considerations were whether there was a discernible system of criminal justice operated by the state *and* a reasonable willingness to use that system so that there was a ready disincentive for those who might otherwise commit acts of serious harm against others. If a state tolerates or condones acts of serious harm by others, then its role in failing to provide protection enables that harm to qualify as 'persecution'.

The perhaps surprising conclusion reached in *Horvath* can be traced to the principle that the obligation to grant refugee status only arises if the person's own state is 'unwilling or unable' to discharge its own duty to protect its own nationals. The reason underlying the decision was the view that the general purpose of the Convention was to enable a person who no longer had the benefit of protection of their own state to turn to the international community for 'surrogate' protection.

From a further decision of the Court of Appeal, *Vallaj and Canaj*, it seems that this protection may also come from agencies which are not, in fact, state authorities, such as international peace-keeping forces and a UN interim administration. In that case, the Court of Appeal rejected an argument that an ethnic Albanian from the Serbian province of Kosovo could not be excluded from refugee status on the basis of protection available from those other agencies.

Civil war and 'singling out'

In certain cases, it may be that state control in the country of origin has broken down completely so that no one authority can be said to be in control of the relevant country or territory. Frequently, in these cases, there will be internal conflict between the different groups who are competing for power. This was the case in *Adan* where the House of Lords decided that what the claimants actually feared was death, injury or loss of freedom as a consequence of the civil war in Somalia and which applied to all Somalis. The civil war was being waged between different clans with non-combatants of one clan being at risk of attack as a result of their perceived association with the interests of an opposing clan. The House of Lords held that an applicant would have to show a risk 'over and above' the risks which were inherent in the civil war in order to be successful in an asylum claim.

This was another surprising result given that earlier case law had made it clear that there is no need for a person to show that they will be 'singled out' for ill-treatment in order to show that they are at risk of persecution and that ill-treatment as part of a group is sufficient. In *Jeyakumaran*, Taylor J had held that it did not matter that a Tamil family had not been targeted individually but that they were part of a wide class of Tamils being similarly treated. The judge commented:

'Whilst I am conscious of the administrative problem of numbers seeking asylum, it cannot be right to adopt artificial and inhuman criteria in an attempt to solve it'.

It appears that a major concern in *Adan* was the likely number of people who might benefit from a decision which suggested that all Somalis were potential refugees. *Adan* will only apply in very extreme cases where there is a general state of chaos such that no one authority can be said to be in the ascendant, controlling territory and providing a minimum level of organisation so that it may be recognised as the state authority. It will not, therefore, apply to countries such as Algeria where, although there is armed unrest, there is a clear, functioning state authority.

Past or future persecution

As we have seen, there must always be a currently held fear of persecution. This does not mean, however, that evidence of past persecution is irrelevant. It is usually of central importance and often constitutes the best evidence that a person is likely to be persecuted in the future. If it can be shown that a person has been persecuted in the past, then, unless there has been a dramatic change in circumstances in the country the effect of which is to remove that risk in the future (e.g. a change of government or a complete and effective overhaul of the internal system for protection against human rights abuses), a risk of continued persecution in the future can often be assumed (see para 45 *UNHCR Handbook*).

The question of whether a person is at risk is judged according to the political and social conditions prevailing in the country at the date of the decision, as opposed to the date of the asylum claim. Similarly, an adjudicator must consider the evidence as of the date of the hearing rather than simply at the date when the Secretary of State made the decision (in contrast to other immigration appeals except those involving Article 3 ECHR, although the appeals provisions in the 2002 Bill are likely to change this ►see page 623). This principle can work harshly against people who claim asylum and then have to wait a long time before a decision is made by the Home Office, by which time the prevailing conditions in their country may have improved. This was the case, for example, in *Ravichandran* (►see above).

Just as the existence of past persecution is not conclusive evidence that a person is a refugee, nor is it necessary to have suffered persecution in the past to establish that there is a risk in the future. It may be that the asylum claimant managed to escape the country before they were actually subjected to ill-treatment. In other cases, it may be that the asylum-seeker did not actually *leave* their country because of a fear of persecution but that the fear has arisen due to events taking place after the person has left. Such a person can still qualify as being 'outside' their country owing to a fear of persecution as they are claiming asylum on the basis that they are remaining outside their country because of their fear of return. Persons in this position are known as refugees *sur place*.

It may also be that the fear arises not as a result of a change in country conditions since departure but rather as a result of the activities overseas of the asylum-seeker, for example, if they have taken part in demonstrations or if they have written public material critical of their own state after arrival in the host state. In these cases, however, the Home Office often consider these activities to be self-serving and therefore damaging to the person's credibility (▶see below).

Persecution or prosecution

Persecution is distinct from prosecution, though the two can be connected. People who fear returning to their country because they may face criminal charges, even when these are connected with political activity, are not usually considered to be at risk of persecution. This was confirmed by the Court of Appeal in *O v IAT*. However, few if any regimes will admit to persecuting their political opponents and prosecution is often simply a mask for what is in fact persecution. It is therefore important to look to the particular circumstances to see whether either the existence of a particular offence in the law of the relevant country or indeed the way in which the law is being applied means that the law is being used as an instrument of oppression. Good indicators of this may be any of the following:

- the criminal penalties for a certain action in a particular country are disproportionate to those in most other countries;
- a fair trial against the charge is denied or is unlikely;
- there is evidence to show that the law is being applied in a discriminatory way, for example, against persons of a particular faith or political persuasion;
- the circumstances suggest that there are ulterior reasons for pursuing a prosecution against the individual in question.

Conscientious objection to military service

Generally, unwillingness to perform military service or desertion from the armed forces is not a ground for refugee status. According to paragraph 168 *UNHCR Handbook*, dislike of military duty or fear of combat on their own are not sufficient to constitute a well-founded fear of persecution. However, the requirement to perform military service may engage Convention protection in certain limited circumstances. These circumstances were fully explored in the IAT case of *Foughali* and were also dealt with by the Court of Appeal in *Zaitz*. In both cases, the right of an individual to object to military service on genuine grounds of conscience was given some recognition.

However, the law is now contained in the decision of the Court of Appeal in *Sepet and Bulbul*. In that case, two Alevi Kurds objected to performing military service in Turkey on the basis that they were opposed to the policy of the government and supported the right of self-determination for Kurdish people. By a majority, the Court of Appeal held that there was no settled rule of international law which requires states to allow conscientious objectors to avoid military service. This meant that the requirement to perform military service and reasonable punishment as a sanction for failing to perform could not amount to persecution. *Sepet and Bulbul* therefore narrows the categories of people who might qualify for asylum on military service grounds. However, in November 2001, the House of Lords granted the Kurds leave to appeal and so the law may well change. The appeal is likely to be heard sometime in the second half of 2002. Until the outcome of that appeal, the law is that only the following persons may qualify for refugee status on the basis of a requirement to perform military service:

- those who can show that they will be punished disproportionately for a Convention reason for failing to perform the service;
- those whose service would involve their being associated with repugnant acts which are contrary to the basic rules of human conduct (e.g. conducting a military campaign contrary to the laws of war) and who do not wish to take part in the service for those reasons;
- those who can show that the conditions and regime of their military service will be so severe that it amounts to persecution and that those conditions will be discriminately applied to them for Convention reasons. Certain asylum-seekers have alleged that this is the case, for example, in relation to service in the irregular Popular Defence Force in Sudan.

Women asylum-seekers

Shah and Islam ▶see above page 159, is clearly an extremely important development. Research had estimated that, while more than 60 per cent of the world's refugees are women, only about 15 per cent reach Europe to seek asylum. The particular difficulties faced by women in claiming asylum led to the development of gender guidelines, published by the Refugee Women's Legal Group (RWLG) in July 1998, for use by both advisers and decision-makers. The principal argument that the guidelines put forward is that women's cases should be dealt with under the main framework of the Convention, as are men's, rather than demanding special treatment which might not afford women asylum-seekers the full protection of refugee status. They further argue that the history of the application and interpretation of the Convention to date betrays a lack of understanding of how women participate in political, religious and other struggles. As a result, the Home Office has marginalised and undervalued women's experiences of persecution. This, in turn, has reinforced a prejudice that women's cases are, in general, less meritorious.

The RWLG guidelines set out to establish legal and procedural principles to avoid these pitfalls so that both advisers and decision-makers can better listen to women asylum-seekers. For example, one of the issues raised by the guidelines is the question of what is meant by 'political activity'. This is usually interpreted as such things as membership of political parties, speaking at or arranging meetings, producing and distributing leaflets and recruiting new members. These activities are more often carried out by male than female activists. Women's roles do not easily fit into these perceptions. Despite the heavy risks they run, women are very often considered to have had only marginal involvement, which is not sufficient to attract the attention of the authorities. The Home Office API now state that:

'It should be remembered that political acts can also include less direct actions such as hiding people, passing messages or providing community services, food, clothing and medical care'.

The guidelines also deal with situations of persecution where women have transgressed existing cultural, religious or social norms which results in a backlash from the state, family or religious institutions. The guidelines define these activities as serious political acts. They also address certain procedural issues relating to the collection and assessment of evidence, and the questioning of asylum-seekers. Since the publication of the guidelines, the Home Office has begun to develop its own gender guidelines for caseworkers.

Internal flight alternative

It has been argued by receiving states that there is no obligation to grant refugee status to an applicant from a country where, for example, there is a localised civil conflict. In those cases, the question has arisen as to whether it is reasonable to expect the applicant to seek protection in a separate safe area of the country rather than obtaining protection abroad. This has become known as the 'internal flight' or 'internal protection' alternative. It is reflected in the immigration rules, which state that a person may be refused asylum if there is a part of the country from which they come in which they do not have a well-founded fear of persecution, and to which it would be 'reasonable' to expect them to relocate.

Examples of internal safe areas which the Home Office and adjudicators have found in individual cases have been Colombo for certain Tamils from Jaffna and Islamabad for Ahmadis from Karachi. Further, the Home Office has increasingly sought safe areas to which to return asylum-seekers, for example, the Kurdish Autonomous Region of Northern Iraq for Kurdish Iraqi asylum-seekers. The difficulty in Kurdish Iraqi cases is that the Home Office had not (as of early 2002) been able to identify a safe *route* of return to the safe area.

In the main case on internal flight, **Robinson**, the Court of Appeal considered the circumstances in which it might be appropriate to require asylum-seekers to relocate internally. The court held that all the relevant circumstances had to be considered, such as: whether the safe area was accessible, whether the applicant would have to undergo great danger or hardship to travel there, and whether a new life would be viable there. They approved a test of whether it would be 'unduly harsh' to expect a person to relocate.

Ceasing to be a refugee

Under Article 1C of the Refugee Convention, a person who is a refugee may cease to qualify if any of the following circumstances apply:

- if the refugee voluntarily re-avails themselves of the protection of the country of nationality or voluntarily re-acquires his or her old nationality;
- if the refugee voluntarily acquires a new nationality;
- if the refugee voluntarily re-establishes him or herself in their country of nationality;
- if there is a change in the circumstances which gave rise to recognition as a refugee, so that the person no longer satisfies the criteria for recognition.

Typical circumstances leading to cessation, therefore, are the acquisition by the refugee of a new passport from their country of nationality or a visit to that country. Since 1998, it has been the policy of the Home Office, when granting asylum to refugees, to given them indefinite leave. The standard Home Office letter granting indefinite leave to remain as a refugee contains a warning that use of the passport of nationality could affect refugee status. However, the Home Office has also acknowledged that not all visits back will cause status to be lost on return to the UK. In a letter from the Asylum Appeals Policy Directorate to Tyndallwoods solicitors dated 26 August 1999, the Home Office stated:

'A refugee who is settled here may travel to their country of origin at any time provided they can secure a national passport on which to do so. Travel to their country of origin in itself does not automatically bring a refugee within the provisions of Article 1C (the cessation clauses) of the 1951 UN Convention Relating to the Status of Refugees. However, if a refugee applies for and obtains a national passport it will be assumed, in the absence of proof to the contrary, he intends to avail himself of the protection of his own authorities. We do accept that there are circumstances where a refugee will feel compelled to travel to their country of origin and will therefore obtain a passport on which to do so. If such circumstances are considered to be sufficiently compassionate, then it will not be appropriate to revoke the person's refugee status. The revocation of a person's refugee status does not involve the loss of their ILR'.

As the letter acknowledges, a person accepted as a refugee in the UK is *both* recognised as a refugee *and* given indefinite leave. Although recognition leads to indefinite leave, the two are separate and one does not necessarily disappear with the other. For example, where, after recognition and grant of indefinite leave, there is a change of circumstances in a refugee's country of origin which removes their fear of persecution, the person still retains their indefinite leave. Where a person has been recognised as a refugee, the burden of showing that a change of circumstances in the country of nationality is sufficiently fundamental to deny refugee status, is on the state. It should also be noted that, where the state takes a long time to determine the status of someone who it is accepted was a refugee at some earlier point and it is alleged that the circumstances giving rise to the fear have materially changed, the state needs to demonstrate that there has been such a change (see *Demrikaya, Arif*).

The 2002 Bill proposes new powers for the Home Office to 'revoke' a person's indefinite leave if they cease to be a refugee because they have voluntarily availed themselves of their own country's protection, re-acquired a lost nationality or re-established themselves in their own country, or obtained the nationality of another country. The Home Office approach to these cases, therefore, may become less flexible.

Any refugee who is considering travelling back to their own country, *even* in the circumstances described in the letter above, should therefore first obtain careful advice. In addition to the proposals in the 2002 Bill, the immigration authorities have powers under existing legislation to take action if they believe leave was obtained by deception (deportation on grounds that a person's presence is not 'conducive' to the public good) or 'administrative' removal for obtaining leave by deception. Further, although the powers under the 1999 Act are not yet completely clear, it is also possible that an indefinite leave could be cancelled on arrival on the ground that there has been a change in circumstances since the leave was given (see para 2A sch 2 1971 Act).

Exclusion from convention protection

A small number of people who are 'refugees' can be excluded from the protection of the Convention. Exclusion applies to the following people:

- those who are not deserving of international protection (▶see below);
- those who are a danger to the security of the host country (▶see below);
- those who do not require any further protection from the host country because they can obtain protection from another United Nations agency or organisation.

The effect of denying protection to certain refugees is to potentially expose them to persecution. These exclusions do not apply, however, to the protection which is given by Article 3 ECHR (torture and inhuman or degrading treatment or punishment). The absolute nature of Article 3 protection was confirmed by the European Court of Human Rights (ECtHR) in the case of *Chahal v UK*.

There is little UK case law interpreting the grounds for exclusion. Before the recent Anti-terrorism, Crime and Security Act 2001, it was possible to argue that the seriousness or extent of the persecution feared had to be considered in deciding whether a person should be excluded. However, section 34 of the 2001 Act aims to prevent any such considerations from being taken into account.

In exclusion cases where the Secretary of State has specified that the applicant falls to be excluded from the UK on grounds of national security or other similar political reasons, the right of appeal is to the Special Immigration Appeals Commission (SIAC) rather than to the ordinary immigration appellate authorities. Where a case is referred to the SIAC, under changes made by the Anti-terrorism and Security Act 2001, it is possible for the Secretary of State to ensure that SIAC first considers whether the person should be excluded without considering whether they are, in fact, a refugee. For more details about SIAC and these procedures ▶see pages 618-621. For details about the detention of those suspected of being 'international terrorists' and the role of the SIAC in relation to them ▶see pages 496-497, 516-517.

Refugees who do not deserve international protection

Those who are undeserving of international protection are people who have committed any of the following (see Article 1F of the Convention):

- a crime against peace, a war crime or a crime against humanity;
- a serious non-political crime outside the country of refuge before recognition as a refugee;
- acts contrary to the purposes and principles of the United Nations.

These exclusions are to be interpreted narrowly and the burden of proving that an exclusion clause applies rests on the state. A 'serious non-political crime' is not closely defined because of the differences between countries' criminal laws, but would have to be a crime for which a very serious penalty could be imposed. There is a growing trend for governments to use this category to exclude political activists who have a connection with armed groups.

In the case of *T*, the House of Lords decided that an Algerian who claimed to be a member of the Front Islamique du Salut (FIS) and to have been involved in bomb attacks on civilian targets was excluded, even though there was a 'political' motivation for the crime. The court ruled that a crime is a political one for these purposes only if it is *both* committed for a political purpose (such as overthrowing the government or bringing about a change in state policy) *and* there is a sufficiently close link between the crime and the political purpose. Where the act is out of all proportion to the political aim, the crime is to be treated as a non-political one.

Similarly, there is little case law on the 'purposes and principles' of the United Nations, but the SIAC has held that terrorist acts fall within this definition (*Singh & Singh*).

Refugees who are a danger to the host country

Articles 32(1) and 33(2) of the Convention exclude from protection those who are a danger to the security of the host country. The letter granting refugee status contains a warning against activities involving violence so as to endanger national security or public order. So far, cases of refugees being excluded on these grounds have been rare.

The Terrorism Act 2000

Although the Home Office has indicated that the purpose of the Act is not to affect asylum-seekers, it does have potentially serious consequences for some asylum-seekers who are, or have been, supporters or members of 'proscribed' organisations. The Terrorism Act brought together previous terrorist legislation and placed it on a permanent footing. It widens the definition of 'terrorism' to actions or threats of action involving serious violence against persons or property, for the purpose of influencing the government or intimidating the public, and which are carried out for political, religious or ideological causes. The Home Secretary is given power to proscribe organisations by order and, to date, 21 organisations have been proscribed.

A series of criminal offences has been created, including belonging to a proscribed organisation, or inviting support for it by, for example, arranging meetings. An offence is also committed where there is reasonable cause to suspect that funds raised may be used for terrorism. Finally, it is an offence to fail to disclose information that a person has been involved with fund-raising or money laundering for terrorist purposes when such information is obtained in the course of a trade, profession, business or employment. This could impact on people advising asylum-seekers who are not protected by professional legal privilege.

The Act creates a dilemma for some asylum-seekers fleeing persecution on account of a well-founded fear of persecution for reasons of political opinion who, by demonstrating membership or support for a proscribed organisation, may expose themselves to the risk of prosecution in the UK. The initial list of organisations included, for example, the PKK and the LTTE, which potentially affects large numbers of Turkish Kurd and Sri Lankan Tamil asylum-seekers.

CHANGES TO ASYLUM AND HUMAN RIGHTS PROPOSED BY THE 2002 WHITE PAPER AND BILL

The government's White Paper, *Secure Borders, Safe Haven: Integration with diversity in Modern Britain* (February 2002), proposes further changes to the asylum system. These changes have not yet all been brought into effect although some of them have been introduced. The Nationality, Immigration and Asylum Bill 2002 also proposes certain changes.

- **'New' Dublin Convention.** The Dublin Convention came into force in September 1997 to provide criteria about which EU member state is responsible for dealing with the claim of any asylum-seeker who claims asylum in any of their territories. For details of the working of the Dublin Convention ▶see pages 209-211. The government now wants to negotiate a revised Dublin Convention mechanism to more clearly define the member state responsible and to enable quicker third country transfers of asylum-seekers to the responsible state.

- **Resettlement programme.** The government envisages a programme whereby those claiming to be in need of protection can have their claim considered before they reach the UK. Such people would then be able to travel lawfully to the UK without the use of agents and false documentation and without arriving here clandestinely. It is likely that the UK would work closely with the UNHCR to identify candidates for resettlement and may well set an annual quota of people who may be accepted.

- **The 'Application Registration Card' (ARC).** ARCs are replacement forms of identification for Standard Acknowledgement Letters (SALs). The Home Office Asylum Screening Unit in Croydon has been issuing them to new asylum applicants from 31 January 2002. They are biometric smart cards with personal details including a photograph, fingerprints and employment status. The ARC contains the date on which the holder must next report and is to be used as a means of identity for obtaining NASS support. ARCs are intended to be much less susceptible to forgery and counterfeiting than SALs. All existing SAL holders should eventually be given an ARC to replace their SAL.

The government intends to link the process of replacing SALs with ARCs for existing cases with an audit of the asylum-seeker's position, which may include an interview to see whether there are any significant new developments in their case and to conduct a check on their status. Some cases may be resolved by granting the person leave. In other cases, requirements for regular reporting are likely to be imposed.

- **Induction and accommodation centres.** These centres are intended to provide a 'holistic' approach to asylum- seekers from arrival to either integration or removal. People will be given a basic introduction to the system and its procedures at an 'induction centre' and, if they need asylum support, may then be housed at an 'accommodation' centre. It is intended that the date for an asylum interview will be booked while the person is at the induction centre. A person may be required to reside at an induction centre for a period of 14 days even if they have alternative accommodation available to them. The 'residence restriction' which requires a person to remain at the induction centre is imposed as a condition of temporary admission, but the 2002 Bill also proposes that these restrictions can be imposed on asylum-seekers who have existing leave when they claim asylum.

In neither of these centres are asylum-seekers actually detained. They are not, however, a replacement for detaining asylum-seekers; the government remains fully committed to the use of detention powers. For more details about these centres and other changes affecting asylum support, ▶see pages 719-721.

- **Increased reporting.** Asylum-seekers housed in accommodation centres may be required to report daily. However, those who are dispersed or not supported by NASS will be required to report at the NASS address, police stations or 'reporting centres'. Requiring asylum-seekers to report is not a new departure but the government intends to increase the use of reporting and link it to the service of asylum decisions and appeal determinations in some cases. Changes to the rules about appeal determinations were made in January 2002 to give Home Office staff the responsibility of serving them in some cases ▶see pages 649-650.

- **Increased removal.** In June 2001, the Home Office set a target of removing 2,500 asylum-seekers a month leading to the removal of 30, 000 by Spring 2003.

In order to try and achieve this, the Home Office is intent on working increasingly with the police and using specially chartered flights (in particular for Kosovan Albanians). The government intends to set up an immigration 'hotline' for members of the public to report people to the Home Office.

- **Removal centres.** Existing detention centres, other than Oakington Reception Centre, are to be re-designated as 'removal centres'. The Home Office intends to increase the number of detention places to 4,000 in order to assist with an increased rate of removals.

- **Changes for unaccompanied minor asylum-seekers.** A number of changes are expected in relation to unaccompanied children seeking asylum:

- children who do not qualify for asylum or exceptional leave but who cannot be removed because proper facilities for their reception and care in their own countries have not been identified, will be given leave to remain in the UK only until they are 18 (the Home Office have already implemented this change);

- children will more often be interviewed by the immigration authorities about their claims for asylum. Previously the Home Office would try to consider these claims by considering the written information and only interview children where absolutely necessary.

- **Appeals system.** Several changes are proposed to the appeals system affecting asylum-seekers including increased personal service by the Home Office of negative appeal determinations and ending judicial review of decisions of the Immigration Appeal Tribunal refusing leave to appeal. Further details are set out in the chapter dealing with appeals ▶see pages 622-625.

- **Voluntary assisted returns programme.** This programme is operated for the Home Office by the International Organisation for Migration (IOM) and Refugee Action. The purpose of the programme is to assist asylum-seekers who choose to return to their country of origin. The government intends to increase the capacity of the programme and to give early access to it by informing asylum-seekers about it while they are at the new induction and accommodation centres. The 2002 Bill enables the Home Office to fund the IOM and Refugee Action for this programme. The Bill also allows the Home Office to make direct payments to 'voluntary leavers' to allow them to travel back to their country of origin and re-establish there. Visits back to 'explore and prepare' for the possibility of return can also be funded.

- **Refugee integration.** The government wants to see improvements in the transition of those granted refugee status or given exceptional leave from being supported to integration and independence. A 'National Refugee Integration Forum' has been set up for this purpose with the intention that it works together with local authorities, other government departments and both the voluntary and private sectors on issues such as accommodation, community development, education of children, employment and training (including English language skills) and positive images. A report of the Forum's work is due in April 2002.

The government sees many refugees as, in reality, economic migrants and states that it is keen to open up further avenues for legal economic migration in order to address skills shortages in the UK. The asylum proposals must therefore be understood together with changes such as the Highly Skilled Migrant Programme, the ability of some to 'switch' into work permit employment while in the UK, and career opportunities in the UK for international students.

For a summary of all the proposals in the 2002 White Paper and the Bill, and JCWI's views on them, ▶see Chapter 2.

10   Asylum procedures

The Refugee Convention does not itself lay down any procedures for the determination of refugee status and therefore the governments which have signed the Convention and Protocol choose the procedure which they will adopt to decide whether people qualify. This chapter looks at the practical procedures for claiming asylum in the UK, at some special classes of applicant and at the procedures carried out by the Home Office to investigate and determine their claims. We look also at the technical decisions which are served upon asylum applicants, whether they are successful or not, and at the 'one-stop' appeal notices which are also given to them. This chapter also looks at how the Home Office deals with people who are applying as the dependants of a principal asylum-seeker and also at unaccompanied minors. It also looks at the possibility of asylum-seekers taking paid or voluntary work.

The most important principle which the UK courts have declared in relation to asylum procedures is that cases must be considered with the most 'anxious scrutiny' to ensure that the decisions are 'in no way flawed' (*Musisi*). This is because asylum determination procedures concern the life and liberty of the individual and therefore only the highest standards of consideration and fairness are acceptable in order for the process to be lawful (*Thirukumar*).

The basic procedure is that all asylum decisions are made by the Home Office Integrated Casework Directorate (ICD). If people apply for asylum at a port of entry, immigration officers will take some details but will refer the case to the Home Office for a decision. People already admitted to the UK for some other purpose may apply direct to the Home Office for asylum, whatever their status under immigration law. The proposals in the 2002 White Paper to introduce 'induction', 'accommodation' and 'removal' centres, together with increased reporting and the introduction of 'ARCs' instead of SALs, will all have a major impact on the asylum process.

Guidance from UNHCR

173   The *UNHCR Handbook* does provide some guidance on procedures. For instance, it recommends a particularly sensitive approach to both mentally

disturbed applicants and unaccompanied minors. It states that consideration of claims from those groups requires special care, often involving the obtaining of medical reports and seeking evidence as far as possible from objective sources. Also, in a letter from its UK office written in relation to a case in the Court of Appeal about the nature of asylum appeals (*Massaquoi*), the UNHCR indicated that it views appeals procedures to be 'integral' to refugee status determination and that asylum procedures must be 'fair and effective'.

Generally, the burden of demonstrating that a person comes within the definition of 'refugee' rests with the asylum-seeker. However, as the *UNHCR Handbook* points out, often a person will not possess individual evidence and all the means to demonstrate that they have a well-founded fear of persecution. Therefore, at least at the stage of initial examination of the claim, there is a shared responsibility on both the asylum-seeker and the Home Office to obtain the evidence necessary to investigate all of the circumstances. In practice, the Home Office cannot be relied upon to conduct all the necessary investigations into a claim and it is very much left to the asylum-seeker or their representatives to search for and collect evidence. This will particularly be the case where the asylum-seeker's history concerns matters about which little is generally known.

Procedures used when people apply for asylum

The procedures operated by the immigration authorities when people claim asylum have been and continue to be the subject of constant change. Often the Home Office introduces pilot projects to assess the benefits of a new procedure and so different procedures are adopted for different people. People reading this section therefore need to be aware that it is not always possible to predict how the Home Office will act in any individual case and that further changes are always likely. For the different procedures which are operated for asylum-seekers who are assessed as suitable to have their claims dealt with at Oakington Reception Centre while they are detained there ▶see pages 506-509.

Applying for protection from overseas

Under the Refugee Convention, people cannot be 'refugees' while still in the country in which they fear persecution. The first part of the definition of refugee is that a person must be 'outside' their country of nationality. They must therefore normally leave that country before claiming asylum in a safe country. The UK will also generally not accept responsibility for a.person who is no longer in their own country but is outside the UK because the obligation under Article 33 of the Convention is not to send people *to* persecution. There is no obligation to admit refugees from other parts of the world. The presumption is that the application for asylum should be made to the authorities of the country where the person is. *In rare cases*, however, people do succeed in making applications from abroad for protection in the UK. *There is no provision in the immigration rules* for these applications which are, therefore, considered only exceptionally. In addition to the conditions set out below, for these kinds of applications, it should be remembered that some of them may raise issues under Article 8 ECHR (private and family life).

The intention of the Home Office, as set out in the 2002 White Paper, *Secure Borders, Safe Haven*, is to expand the circumstances in which asylum-seekers can be pre-screened abroad for admission to the UK with the help of the UNCHR.

Mandate refugees

'Mandate refugees' are those who are in their own country *or* in a third country and who have been recognised as refugees by UNHCR. Usually the UK will admit mandate refugees where the UNHCR has put them forward for re-settlement and the administration of the referral is then carried out on behalf of the UNHCR by the British Red Cross (BRC). It is advisable therefore to obtain the involvement of these agencies if any approach to the Home Office is to be made. However, mandate refugees may also make direct applications for entry clearance to come to the UK which may be considered exceptionally. They should present evidence that the UNHCR has recognised them as refugees.

Factors taken into consideration in deciding whether to admit a mandate refugee outside the immigration rules are (API, Ch2, s3 paras 3–5):

- whether there is some threat to the safety or well-being of the refugee in their present country of refuge;
- whether there are compassionate circumstances involved in the case;
- whether the UK is the most appropriate country of refuge.

In deciding whether the UK is the most appropriate country of refuge, the Home Office will consider whether the applicant has close ties with the UK, for example, close family members who are settled in the UK or who are in the UK for a purpose which may lead to settlement. Close family members are spouses, minor children and parents or grandparents over the age of 65. Other family members may exceptionally be considered as 'close'. The applicant may also have close ties with the UK if they have resided in the UK previously.

If the referral is made through the BRC, then no formal notice of decision needs to be given and there is no right of appeal. If a formal entry clearance application has actually been lodged then there will be a right of appeal.

'10 or more' plan

This is a further scheme which was established by the UNHCR and is run by the BRC. The aim is to enable the host country to admit 10 or more disabled people who have been accepted by the UNHCR as refugees to be re-settled. Referrals must be made to the Home Office through the BRC. Applications are assessed both by the UNHCR and by the Home Office. Factors taken into account include the severity of the disability, the availability of treatment in the country of refuge, the applicant's other circumstances in the country of refuge and whether the UK is the 'most appropriate country of refuge' (see API, Ch2, s4, paras 2, 4).

Group refugees

There have been limited government programmes for refugees from particular countries; for example, Chileans in the 1970s and Vietnamese during the 1980s. These programmes are based on a government decision to accept a quota of people who are already recognised as refugees. Such groups have usually been given permission to enter for four years and granted settlement at the end of that time. People who have come in this way may be referred to as 'programme refugees'.

Temporary protection

In 1992 the government announced that up to 1,000 Bosnian ex-detainees and their families would be allowed to come to the UK. They were allowed in very gradually. Only a small proportion actually arrived and they were not formally recognised as refugees. On arrival, they were given an unusual status, called 'temporary refuge,' usually for six-month periods, and were told not to expect to be allowed to stay longer. In fact, they have been granted extensions of exceptional leave and, subsequently, granted settlement. Those granted exceptional leave were told that they could return for short trips to Bosnia in order to 'test the water' and, crucially, be re-admitted within their period of leave if they decided not to re-settle in Bosnia.

The UK also participated in the Humanitarian Evacuation Programme in response to the crisis in Kosovo in 1998–1999. Over 4,000 people were permitted to come here and, after a period of temporary protection, were offered an assistance grant to return home to 'explore and prepare', that is, to see whether they could return. The vast majority have not had their exceptional leave extended but have been returned on the basis that it is now safe for them.

Transfer of refugee status

There are certain circumstances in which the UK will accept responsibility for people who have been recognised as refugees by another country (see API, Ch2, s2). In accordance with the European Agreement on the Transfer of Responsibility for Refugees (EATRR), the Home Office will accept responsibility for the transfer of and grant indefinite leave to a person who:

• is lawfully resident in the UK; and

- has been recognised as a refugee under the Refugee Convention by one of the countries which has ratified the EATRR (Denmark, Finland, Germany, Italy, Netherlands, Norway, Portugal, Spain, Sweden, Switzerland); and either:
- has been allowed to stay in the UK for two continuous years (not including periods spent studying, training, receiving medical treatment, in prison or pending an immigration appeal which is dismissed); or
- has been granted indefinite leave in the UK; or
- has been allowed to stay in the UK beyond the period of validity of the travel document granted by the other country, provided that the reason for the extension beyond that period was not studying. It must also be the case that the UK cannot obtain the re-admission of the person to the original country under the EATRR, for example, by requesting that they be re-admitted within the six months of the expiry of the travel document.

If the application does not come within the EATRR (above), then the Home Office may still exceptionally grant the transfer. Transfers are only granted in these cases where the UK is 'clearly the most appropriate country of refuge'. Factors taken into account are: length of time in the first country of refuge, strength of ties in the first country compared to ties in the UK and any compelling compassionate circumstances.

Applications for asylum made abroad

The above categories all concern people who have already been accepted as qualifying for some sort of protection and who are applying for re-settlement to the UK for short or long-term purposes. In very rare cases, the Home Office (on referrals from entry clearance officers) will agree to the admission of people who have not yet been recognised where they have made an application for entry clearance to come to the UK on asylum grounds from a third country. The following conditions must be met (API Ch2, s1):

- the applicant is a refugee within the meaning of the Refugee Convention; and
- the applicant has close ties with the UK; and
- the UK is the most appropriate country of refuge.

▶See above under 'Mandate refugees' for the meaning of 'close ties' and 'most appropriate country of refuge'.

Applying on entry to the UK: 'port applicants'

People seeking asylum at an airport, sea port or international train terminal should apply to an immigration officer for asylum, explaining the danger they would be in if they had to return. Often people are afraid to approach an immigration officer, having previously been persecuted by officials. People also may not know the correct procedure for applying for asylum and may believe it would be safer to gain entry to the UK in some other category, for example, as a visitor, and later apply for asylum. It will be clear that failing to claim on arrival can have a negative effect on the credibility of the claim and can also lead to its 'certification' ▶see pages 203-205 for the meaning of this.

When people apply for asylum at a port of entry, a decision on the application is not made immediately. The immigration rules state that all decisions on asylum have to be referred to the Home Office. Usually immigration officers carry out a short 'pro-forma' screening interview to establish basic details about the person's identity and their route to the UK as well as checking to see whether they meet the conditions for referral to Oakington Reception Centre to have their claim dealt with there. Asylum-seekers who are to be referred to Oakington will be detained and transferred there. Questions are also asked to determine whether the applicant is returnable to a safe third country without full consideration of the claim.

Until recently, the applicant would be given an on-entry Standard Acknow-ledgement Letter (SAL1), which the asylum-seeker may use as proof of identity. In early 2002, these forms of identity were being replaced with Application Registration Cards (ARCs). While the application is under consideration, the applicant cannot be removed from the UK. The applicant can either be given temporary admission or they may be detained. If they are granted temporary admission, it will normally be granted on conditions that they report to an immigration officer at a particular time, that they remain at a fixed address and that they are prohibited from working. The document granting temporary admission is called an 'IS96' ▶see page 126 for an example. As a result of new developments, the applicant may be required to stay at an 'induction centre' as a condition of temporary admission.

In most cases, the asylum-seeker will be issued with a Statement of Evidence Form (SEF) and also a 'one-stop' notice under section 75 of the 1999 Act, which must be completed and returned to the 'Asylum Co-ordination Unit' at the Home Office. After the SEF has been considered, the Home Office is likely to invite the asylum-seeker to a further 'substantive' interview in order to ask them to give more details of the claim before a decision is taken. For full details of the SEF process, which also applies to in-country claims ▶see pages 181-184 below.

In some cases, however, it is possible that an asylum-seeker will not be given a SEF but will instead be interviewed at the port on the substance of their claim very shortly after their arrival in the UK. It is unsafe for asylum-seekers to be interviewed in this way before they have had access to legal advice and assistance. Unfortunately, immigration officers at ports of entry tend to act unpredictably and advisers have been unable to tell when a port will do this rather than issuing a SEF.

If the immigration officer believes that s/he is dealing with a case in which the person can be returned to a safe third country, it is possible that the asylum-seeker will be detained at this stage and, in a 'Dublin Convention' case, the immigration authorities will begin the process of making a transfer request to the other country. For full details about third-country cases, the Dublin Convention and appeal rights in these situations ▶see pages 206-212.

Applying after entry to the UK: 'in-country' applicants

People may apply for asylum after being allowed into the country for any other purpose, for example, as visitors or students. More than half of asylum applicants apply 'in-country'. They must apply to the Home Office for leave to remain in the UK as refugees rather than making an application to the port that they originally arrived at. The application should be made with as little delay as possible. No prescribed application form is needed. As with applications made at port, in most cases, the asylum-seeker will be issued with a SEF Form and a 'one-stop' notice under section 75 of the 1999 Act.

Applications by people who have entered the UK illegally or who have overstayed should also be made to the Home Office rather than at the port. Even those applicants who pass through immigration controls and are granted entry and then attempt to seek asylum at the port, unaware that they could have claimed at the control desk, are generally then directed by the immigration officers or police to make a claim at the Home Office. This is despite the fact that the port immigration officers have a power to bring the person back within their jurisdiction and to register the asylum claim. This can be done by cancelling the giving of leave to enter within 24 hours and then examining the person again at the port as though they had just arrived (see para 6(2), sch2 Immigration Act 1971). This power is very rarely used.

Postal applications

Under present Home Office practice, applicants who live in London cannot make a postal application for asylum. If they do, they will be sent a letter inviting them to attend at the Home Office Asylum Screening Unit in Croydon where their applications will be processed. The Home Office will not 'record' the asylum claim as having been made for the purposes of accessing support from NASS until the asylum-seeker attends at the ASU. Postal applications for those living outside London are, at present, acceptable (although this may change). Full names, dates of birth and nationality of all applicants and dependants should be given.

Applying in person at the Asylum Screening Unit (ASU)

At the Asylum Screening Unit (ASU), an applicant will be asked basic questions in order to determine their identity, nationality and to determine whether it is a third country case. A checklist is also completed to determine whether the person may be referred to Oakington Reception Centre. Persons who are to be referred to Oakington are detained and then taken there.

In early 2002, it came to light that at two of the 24 desks at the Croydon ASU a new screening questionnaire had been introduced with four 'levels' of scrutiny. It has also been introduced at ports. At the first level, asylum-seekers are asked basic screening questions and at level two they are asked brief questions about the basis of their claim to asylum. At the close of level two, normally, the SEF would be issued. However, if the immigration officer is not satisfied about the applicant's identity or nationality, the procedure progresses to the 'assertive' interview stage at level three, which takes place in a separate interview room with an immigration officer who is not constrained in the questions that can be asked. If there are suspicions that the asylum-seeker has committed deception offences, for example, made multiple applications for asylum and for benefit or support, level four interviewing will take place at a police station after the asylum-seeker has been cautioned by the police that they are being investigated for criminal matters.

Representatives have been very concerned about the level two questions because they delve into the details of the claim usually in the absence of a representative. Although representatives are allowed into the ASU, they may not be able to obtain funding from the Legal Services Commission to attend with asylum-seekers during the screening process, except in cases where the claimant is a minor.

There are ongoing negotiations between the LSC, representatives and the Home Office about the nature of screening processes and the need for representation in certain cases.

'SEF-less' procedure

In most cases a SEF will be issued and, after it has been completed, the asylum-seeker will be invited to an interview. The Home Office has, however, for some time been experimenting with a procedure without the use of SEFs. It is not possible to predict which asylum-seekers will be processed without a SEF. If no SEF is issued on the day of screening, the asylum-seeker will instead be given a date for interview within approximately two weeks. In these SEF-less cases, the asylum-seeker is given a standard period of five days after the substantive interview in which to make further representations or provide further evidence (parliamentary written answer of Barbara Roche MP, 16 March 2000).

Liability for detention

As with asylum-seekers at port, in-country applicants can be detained while their claims are being decided. However, in-country applicants are not immediately liable to detention while awaiting a decision from the Home Office if they claim asylum within the period of an existing leave to be in the UK.

Application Registration Cards (ARCs) and fingerprinting

ARCs are replacement forms of identification for Standard Acknowledgement Letters (SALs). ARCs are issued to both asylum-seekers and each dependant ▶see page 122 for an example. The Home Office Asylum Screening Unit in Croydon has been issuing them to new asylum applicants from 31 January 2002. They contain the following information about asylum-seekers: name, date of birth, gender, nationality, place of issue (ASU or the port), date of issue, a photograph of the applicant, whether they are with dependants (or, if they are a dependant, the name of their principal), the language(s) they speak and whether there is a prohibition on them taking employment. Fingerprint details are also contained on the ARC.

The 1993 Act provides for fingerprinting of all people who have made asylum claims and their dependants. It also gives immigration and police officers the power to arrest without warrant anyone who does not comply with the fingerprinting requirement and states that fingerprints are to be destroyed either within a month of the person being granted settlement or after ten years. Fingerprinting normally takes place early in the asylum application process either at the port, the Asylum Screening Unit or other Home Office Public Enquiry Offices. When a child is fingerprinted, another adult, either the parent or guardian or another responsible person, must be present. The Home Office has not stated any lower age limit for fingerprinting children, although in practice children under 16 are not normally fingerprinted.

For the purposes of fingerprinting, the 'dependants' of an asylum-seeker are defined as:

- a spouse, *and*
- children under 18 of an asylum-seeker who are
- – not British citizens, *and*
- – do not have indefinite leave to remain in the UK.

This is intended to ensure that only people whose stay in the UK depends on an asylum claim are covered by these provisions.

The 'Statement of Evidence Form' (SEF) process

The Statement of Evidence Form (SEF) is currently issued to most asylum-seekers after they have claimed asylum at the port or at the Home Office (▶see above). It must be completed in English and returned within 10 working days of issue. This time-limit is strictly applied. If it is not kept to, the asylum-seeker is likely to be refused on the ground of failure to comply with the requirement to provide information about the claim ▶see pages

205-206. As to granting extensions of time for submitting the SEF, the Home Office has stated in a letter to ILPA dated 29 January 2001:

'A decision to grant an extension will only be made in exceptional cases where there is a reasonable explanation for an applicant's inability to make a prompt and full disclosure of material facts'.

The SEF is divided into different sections. It first asks the asylum-seeker to tick a box stating the basis of their claim, namely, whether it is based on race, religion, political opinion or other reasons including membership of a particular social group. It is, of course, possible to tick more than one of these boxes as the claim may have more than one aspect to it. The different sections of the SEF then ask the applicant to set out what has happened to them, who was responsible for any ill-treatment, whether family members have suffered difficulties, whether there is a safe area to which they could go, whether there are outstanding charges against them and what event caused them to leave. There is also a section dealing with military service. Asylum-seekers and representatives often find it easier to give the details in their own way by stating 'see attached' under many of the sections and then appending to the form a full statement setting out the basis of the claim including all the details which they would otherwise put in the different sections.

There have been serious problems with applications being refused on grounds of 'non compliance' for alleged failure to return the form in time when, in fact, the form has been submitted within the deadline.

SEF interviews

After the SEF has been considered, asylum-seekers are normally asked to attend an interview with the Home Office in order to clarify and expand upon the details they have given. In 2000, as part of the drive to speed up decision-making, the Home Office started using offices in Leeds and Liverpool, as well as Croydon, to conduct these interviews. In reality, the interviews are often used as an opportunity to obtain material in order to challenge the credibility of the applicant. At the outset of a SEF interview, the asylum-seeker is read a statement explaining that it is not necessary to repeat all of the details which have already been set out in the SEF. However, very unfairly, asylum-seekers are often penalised in Home Office refusal letters for failing to repeat information which they have already given and which they believed had been taken into account. In rare cases, applicants may be called back for further interviews, usually because of previous misunderstandings or in cases where new evidence has come to light. For more details about asylum interviews generally ▶see pages 184-187 below.

Submitting further evidence after the SEF interview

The Home Office intention is to make decisions 'immediately' after SEF interviews and so, if there is any further information or evidence which needs to be put forward before the decision, the asylum-seeker or their representative needs to act extremely quickly. If it is clear at the interview stage that it is intended to provide further evidence, this should be made known to the interviewing officer and the asylum-seeker should try to provide any evidence of the steps made to obtain the further information and when it will be provided. In the case of reports from the Medical Foundation for the Care of Victims of Torture, the Home Office position is that (API Ch17, s3, para 2.1):

'Special arrangements have been agreed to allow requests for an extension... for post-interview representations for the Medical Foundation to prepare and submit a medical report. Such requests should be carefully considered and only refused in exceptional circumstances. In all cases, the representatives or applicant should provide written confirmation from the Medical Foundation (for example, an appointment card) that the Medical Foundation has agreed to provide a report'.

However, this appears to apply not just to Medical Foundation report cases. In a letter to ILPA of 10 October 2001, the Home Office stated simply:

'Where evidence has been provided that a medical statement is to follow, for example, we have received an appointment card or letter confirming consideration of the applicant's case, a decision will be delayed for a reasonable time until the report is available'.

Practical problems

SEFs and the tight time-limits that have accompanied them have further eroded the fairness of the investigation procedure. The *UNHCR Handbook* reminds the state of the particular difficulties faced by those fleeing persecution and the likely lack of documentary evidence to support a claim.

The imposition of a rigid and very optimistic timetable for the submission of evidence works unfairly against applicants. It is no co-incidence that the measures introduced following the White Paper, *Fairer, Faster and Firmer,* in 1998 to speed up decision-making, coincided with an increase in initial refusals.

Ten days is rarely sufficient for a newly arrived asylum-seeker, who may not speak any English, to be able to complete the SEF form, which undeniably requires a degree of expertise, if it is to be completed adequately. There is no doubt that an experienced adviser can improve an applicant's chances of recognition enormously by assisting to complete the written application, preparing a written statement and suggesting supporting documentary evidence to accompany it. The introduction of compulsory contracting by the Legal Services Commission from 1 January 2000, led to a reduction in the number of quality immigration solicitors available to do publicly-funded work. The combination of a fall in the supply of legal advice and the telescoping of procedures has led to a crisis whereby applicants are simply unable to find representation. The number of new applicants has not dropped significantly over the same period.

Added to this has been the introduction of the dispersal policy. Many applicants have found it difficult to find suitable representation in areas of the country where there is a lack of expertise in asylum. The system has also made it extremely difficult for many asylum-seekers to stay in contact with their advisers, particularly if they have been dispersed hundreds of miles away from them.

Asylum interviews

Asylum interviews are regularly criticised by representatives and asylum-seekers. Interviewing officers can be aggressive, dismissive or ask questions which indicate that they do not really understand the basis of the claim or the basic country conditions which the asylum-seeker has fled.

Often the way that an interview is handled can have a very important impact on a case and it is critical therefore that difficulties at interview are addressed immediately or, if not, shortly afterwards by letter. Criticisms of the interview process should not be left until an appeal by which time the claim will have been refused and complaints may be seen as self-serving. Asylum interviews which take place at ports have been particularly criticised (see *Breaking down the barriers*, ILPA April 2000).

Certain aspects of the SEF interview process are covered above, but the following general points should be noted about all asylum interviews.

- Representatives attending interviews should have a general knowledge of the relevant legal issues which is sufficient to enable them to help their client at the interview. They should have been briefed in advance of the interview and they should take a full, accurate note of the interview as it progresses (see Legal Services Commission, General Civil Contract Specification Rules at s12.4 concerning representatives attending immigration interviews).

- There is no absolute right to have a legal representative at an interview *but* any decision of the immigration authorities to exclude a representative has to be a decision taken on proper and relevant grounds (see the High Court decision of **Lawson**). The same approach applies to interpreters attending on behalf of the asylum-seeker (see **Bostanci**). Any representative or interpreter who is excluded from an interview should ask for a statement of reasons for the decision so that its legality can be judged.

- Where asylum-seekers have suffered particular experiences, for example a sexual assault, or if they have certain strongly held beliefs, they may request an interpreter and interviewing officer of the same gender. The Home Office has stated that 'such requests will be complied with as far as is operationally possible' (Home Office letter to ILPA, 27 March 2000).

- The Home Office has issued guidance to interviewing officers about viewing scars in interviews on the following lines (see letter to ILPA dated

21 September 2000). It is acceptable for an asylum-seeker to show an interviewing officer scars during an interview and the interviewing officer must make no judgment or comment on the scars but will make a factual record in the interview notes of what has been shown. If the injury is alleged to have been caused by a recent incident but looks so old as to cast doubt upon the account, the interviewing officer may ask questions to try to verify the claim. If viewing scars would require the removal of significant clothing, the officer may decline and the asylum-seeker may be asked to attend the medical centre after the interview for a note to be taken. Unwillingness to show evidence of scars during the interview itself will not be used to discredit the applicant.

Preparing for interview

The Home Office relies on the detailed information given by the asylum-seeker as the basis for the claim to asylum. It is necessary to explain in detail exactly what has happened to the person, what activities he or she has engaged in which could result in persecution and what has happened to members of the family or the particular group to which the asylum-seeker belongs. Advisers should go through these details with the asylum-seeker in date order, before any interview. If a clear and detailed statement has been provided of the claim and the sequence of relevant events is either on the SEF form or sent to the Home Office before the interview, then it is likely that the interview will proceed much more smoothly as the interviewer will be more likely to understand the basis of the claim. In addition, if the applicant has a copy of their own statement to read, then that will help them to prepare for the interview.

Being 'fit and well' for the interview

Asylum-seekers should be warned that asylum interviews can be very stressful, particularly at ports. Although applicants are asked whether they are fit and well to be interviewed, many feel too intimidated to say if they are feeling tired or unwell. In *Clavijo-Hoyos*, the IAT criticised reliance on an interview record, which although signed by the applicant as a correct and true statement, had been obtained when the applicant was clearly extremely tired after a long journey without sleep.

Role of representatives

In November 1996, the Home Office issued draft guidance for representatives at asylum interviews, making clear its view that:

'representatives and their interpreters may attend interviews as observers at the discretion of the interviewing officer...observers must refrain from interrupting during the interview, they will be permitted to add their comments at the end of the interview'.

The warning which is now read out to representatives at interview is:

'I would ask your representative not to interrupt during the course of the interview. If he or she wishes to make any comments they will have the opportunity to do so at the end of the interview'.

Experienced representatives have been able to contest the restrictive nature of this guidance in order to ensure that their clients are fairly treated. In many cases the mere presence of a representative will at least ensure that the applicant is treated courteously so that they feel more comfortable in presenting their story.

Home Office interpreters

Many asylum-seekers do not speak English and their interviews will therefore be carried out through an interpreter, normally employed by the Home Office or immigration service on a sessional basis. If the representative or clerk at the interview is not fluent in both languages, an independent interpreter should also be present at the interview, to note any difficulties in interpretation. The standard of interpreting provided through the Home Office's interpreters is variable and, unless someone is there to check what is interpreted, misunderstandings can easily arise. These misunderstandings can be fatal to claims for asylum. As indicated above, the Home Office has agreed that it is permissible to have an independent interpreter present. It has stated:

'minor discrepancies in translation should be noted throughout the interview and brought to the attention of the interviewing officer at the end of the interview. The interviewing officer should be made aware immediately of any major difficulties over interpretation'.

If the asylum-seeker does not understand the official interpreter, it is important that he or she makes this clear to the interviewing officer, and a new interview with an interpreter in the correct language or dialect should be arranged.

Declaration

At the end of asylum interviews, applicants are invited to sign a declaration that they have understood the questions put to them and that they were given an opportunity at the end of the interview to make further comments. Previously, there was a practice of reading over the entire interview to check its accuracy and the applicant would have the opportunity to make any corrections and then sign each page. The change of practice makes no sense as it means that the asylum decision may be affected by a misunderstanding during the course of the interview and that the notes of interview are a less authoritative record of the applicant's evidence if the matter goes on appeal to an adjudicator. Applicants should be given a copy of the interview record if they request it. If there are important mistakes in the record of interview which have not been ironed out during the interview itself, advisers should make representations about the mistakes as soon as possible.

One-stop procedure

The 'one-stop' procedure was introduced by the 1999 Act and came into effect in October 2000. The purpose of the procedure is to ensure that *all* the reasons any individual might have for staying in the UK are considered together by the Home Office and, if refused, at the same appeal. This is done by giving applicants 'one-stop' notices which require them to disclose any additional grounds which they have not previously given for staying in the UK. There are two kinds of 'one-stop' notice which are very similar in their effect although they are served on people in different circumstances.

For further details about the effect on appeal rights if the one-stop procedure is not complied with ►see pages 609-611. It should be noted that the 2002 White Paper proposes to 're-structure the legislation to simplify the one-stop appeal provisions' so changes can be expected in this area.

'One-stop' notices under section 75 of the 1999 Act

A one-stop notice is issued under section 75 of the 1999 Act to any of the following categories of people *who claim asylum or claim to be allowed to stay in the UK on human rights grounds:*

- people who arrive in the UK without leave to enter, an entry clearance or a work permit;
- illegal entrants;
- people who have overstayed their leave in the UK;
- people who have breached their conditions of leave, or who obtained leave to remain by deception;
- a 'family member' of any of the above people, meaning their spouse, their child (or the child of their spouse), their unmarried partner who has been living with the claimant for two of the last three years and a person who is 'dependent' on the claimant or upon whom the claimant is 'dependent'.

The notice is issued at the same time as the SEF and states that the applicant must disclose any additional grounds (apart from asylum and/or human rights grounds already given) which they have not previously disclosed for staying in the UK. The notice is accompanied by a statement of additional grounds which should be completed with any further human rights or compassionate grounds for remaining. The form must be completed and returned within 10 working days together with the SEF. The notice also states that the consequence of failure to raise additional grounds might be the loss of the opportunity to appeal against refusal on those grounds.

If a person given a section 75 notice has their application refused then, with the notice of refusal, they are served with one of the second kind of one-stop notices ►see below. Although they are therefore given similar forms at the time of refusal, it is obviously beneficial for applicants to raise all their reasons for wanting to stay in the UK on the first occasion so that they can be considered. The Home Office has often failed to give consideration to matters which are only raised at the time of the notice of appeal although the relevant notice states that the decision will be reviewed in the light of the statement of additional grounds and that further reasons will be given if the decision is to be maintained.

'One-stop' notices under section 74 of the 1999 Act

These notices are issued to those who have, for any reason, had *any* of the following negative immigration decisions made against them in respect of which they have a right of appeal:

* refusal of leave to enter;
* decision to refuse to allow them to remain in the UK;
* decision to make a deportation order;

These notices are also issued to any 'family members' (▶see above for definition) of any of the above people who are themselves in a similar position.

Because these people already have in-country rights of appeal, they are given appeal forms at the same time that they are given their section 74 notice. Examples of people who fall into this category (i.e., those who have in-country appeal rights) are those refused entry at a time when they hold a valid entry clearance or whose leave is cancelled when they arrive in the UK and those who apply to extend their leave shortly before it expires. Section 74 notices are also given to those to whom the Secretary of State has issued a notice of intention to deport who also may appeal against the decision.

Notices under section 74 also include a statement of additional grounds for the person to complete. The notice specifies that a person must now state *any human rights claim, claim for asylum or claim to have been racially discriminated against* in the decision that has been made and it warns the applicant that failure to raise additional grounds in time may mean that an adjudicator is unable to deal with them. As with statements returned in response to section 75 notices, statements under section 74 must be returned within 10 working days. If the case involves issues of national security, the time-limit for returning a section 74 statement is five days.

Potential problems with section 74 and 75 notices

There are similar difficulties which attach to the completion and return of one-stop forms within the time-limit as there are with SEFs. The Home Office has maintained that no legal assistance should be required as all the applicant has to do is set out simple factual grounds. However, it is unlikely that applicants themselves will know which facts might be relevant given the complexity of human rights law. Even the notices themselves state: 'If you have not yet taken advice on your position,

I strongly advise you to do so now'. Applicants should always seek advice about filling in the statement of additional grounds. They may be returned by hand, fax or post to the address/fax number which is given on the notice itself. They must be signed by the applicant or their representative.

Providing evidence in support of an asylum application

Because the events which an asylum-seeker describes have happened in a different country and often some of the incidents occurred a long time ago, it is often very difficult or impossible to provide evidence of them. Most claims depend very much on the asylum-seeker's own evidence of their circumstances which is why credibility plays such an important role in the process. Even though there are difficulties, asylum-seekers should do their best to produce what evidence they can to support their claims. Often asylum-seekers are penalised for not producing evidence which they could have been expected to obtain. Evidence can be given to the Home Office by hand at interviews or when the claim is made or sent in by post. Just because an asylum-seeker has not actually brought the evidence with them does not mean that efforts should not be made to produce it. If the asylum-seeker claimed asylum at a time when they didn't have representation, advisers should always check with them what evidence they have already handed in as such evidence can sometimes be buried in a Home Office file and never properly taken into account.

Examples of evidence which an asylum-seeker might produce are as follows.

Medical reports. Medical reports are often submitted in order to support a claim by an asylum-seeker that they have been tortured. They are useful in showing both the physical scars or conditions left after mistreatment and in demonstrating that the asylum-seeker suffers from psychological or psychiatric conditions resulting from torture. They are rarely conclusive and the extent to which they can help depends upon the level and experience of the medical expert and the care taken in the preparation of the report. The most experienced provider of reports is the Medical Foundation for the Care of Victims of Torture ▶see address on page 735. The Home Office states that their reports 'should not be dismissed unless any concerns have been raised with the Foundation first', that specific reasons must be given in the refusal letter if the report is dismissed and, where a report is submitted after an application has been refused, 'the case should be reviewed before any appeal'.

Sometimes a person may have been tortured but there are no signs remaining. In these cases, the Home Office should be reminded of their own internal guidance:

'Interviewing officers and caseworkers should note that not all forms of torture result in physical scars or injuries that are identifiable during a medical examination or visible to an interviewing officer. Therefore the

lack of scars or the lack of a medical report does not indicate that the applicant has not been tortured'
(see API Ch17, s3, para 2.4–2.5).

Expert reports. Advisers regularly commission expert reports, often from academics who are particularly knowledgeable about the situation in the country concerned, to support asylum claims. Expert reports are normally used at the appeal stage rather than at the stage of the application. The IAT has become increasingly concerned that experts' credentials and the basis and the sources of their knowledge are made clear. Experts should also approach the case from an independent standpoint, not as the supporter of the asylum-seeker (*Slimani*, IAT).

Arrest warrants/court documents. Documents issued by the state authorities that the asylum-seeker claims to fear can often win cases. Great care should be taken, however, when advising clients about these documents as both the Home Office and adjudicators are frequently very sceptical of them. The Home Office is often able to make checks to verify the documents to see whether they are false. Care should be taken to see if the dates and place names on the documents fit with the applicant's account. Asylum-seekers must also be able to explain how they managed to obtain the documents in the first place. Often it is advisable to ask a country expert to comment on the documents.

Statements and letters from witnesses. Often asylum-seekers are able to produce supporting statements from other people in the UK or letters from those overseas who themselves know something about the applicant's circumstances. This kind of evidence is not usually taken seriously by the Home Office as it considers that it can be easily manufactured. Where such evidence is put forward, the witness should state how they know about the evidence they are giving, for example, did they see it themselves? Letters from abroad should be accompanied by a copy of the envelopes in which they arrived.

Evidence from political organisations. Where asylum-seekers have continued their political activity in the UK, it is often useful to obtain confirmation from the branch of the political organisation based here. It may be that a letter can be written or photographs produced of certain activities. It may be that the organisation is able to provide details of the aims, ideas, structure and operation of the organisation which will also help the claim.

In addition to the above, it is also useful to refer the Home Office to evidence about the general conditions in the country in question which support the claims made by the asylum-seeker. Advisers usually produce large amounts of country material for appeals but it can also be useful to refer to at least some limited country material at the application stage, especially if the material covers ground which is relevant to the case and which is not covered in the Home Office's Country Information Policy Unit

(CIPU) report. For more details about CIPU reports ▶see pages 197-198 and for more details about the availability of country evidence generally ▶see pages 635-637.

Unaccompanied minor asylum-seekers

In 2000, 2,735 unaccompanied children applied for asylum in the UK. The immigration rules make specific provision for unaccompanied child asylum-seekers, recognising their particular vulnerability. The rules suggest that more consideration should be given to the objective risks in their country of origin rather than the child's understanding of them. They state that children will not be interviewed about their claims, 'if it is possible to obtain by written enquiries or from other sources sufficient information to properly determine the claim' (para 352, HC 395). Where an interview is considered necessary, a 'parent, guardian, representative or another adult who for the time being takes responsibility for the child' must be present. The officers who conduct the interview have received training in dealing with children.

The 2002 White Paper proposes to change the rules so that children will more often be interviewed by the immigration authorities about their claims for asylum. In some cases the Home Office have begun to do this *before* the rules have been changed. Advisers should be quick to remind the Home Office of the wording of the existing immigration rules until such time as they are actually amended.

Speed of decisions

The Home Office also intends to deal with these applications more speedily than other cases. It has an 'Unaccompanied Children's Module' which deals with all questions about unaccompanied children and makes enquiries to substantiate their cases.

In practice, many young people have been affected by the same delays as adults. If they reach 18 before any decision has been made, the Home Office may treat them in the same way as adult asylum-seekers. If the application is refused, the appeal should also be expedited.

Policy on exceptional leave where no reception facilities are available

The Home Office has stated that it:

'will not seek to remove an unaccompanied child under the age of 18 from the UK unless it is possible to put in place acceptable reception and care arrangements in their country of origin. If this does not prove possible the child will be granted exceptional leave to enter or remain.'

The Home Office have already implemented a new policy, referred to in the 2002 White Paper, to give exceptional leave on this basis to minors who do not otherwise qualify for asylum or exceptional leave on general grounds *only* until they are 18 years old.

Age dispute cases

From 14 September 2000, if an asylum-seeker claims to be a minor but the Home Office believes that their appearance 'strongly' suggests that they are over 18, they will be treated as an adult until such time as credible documentary evidence is produced which demonstrates that they are of the age claimed. In borderline cases, the Home Office has stated that it will continue to give applicants the benefit of the doubt and deal with the applicant as a minor. Where there is an age dispute, the Refugee Council's panel of advisers (below) will still be informed of the case.

Refugee Council Panel of Advisers for Unaccompanied Refugee Children

In conjunction with the Refugee Council, the government has set up a panel of advisers to provide unaccompanied children with an individual adviser. The adviser then helps the child to deal with the authorities such as social services departments, schools and the immigration service. Their role is also to find interpreters and legal advisers and to offer support and other help. When a child applies for asylum after entry, it is essential that the Refugee Council adviser goes to the Asylum Screening Unit with the child, otherwise staff may refuse to process the claim. A responsible adult has to be present when a child is to be fingerprinted.

If a child already has a legal representative, the representative should ensure that the Refugee Council's panel of advisers are aware of their involvement and that the panel has full details of the child ▶see page 735 for their contact details.

Dependants

An asylum-seeker's spouse and their children who are under 18 at the time of the application are normally treated as the applicant's dependants. Children born to the asylum-seeker while a claim is pending can also be added to the claim by submitting the birth certificate to the Home Office. Children who become 18 before the claim has been decided remain as dependants for the purposes of the claim. Family members other than the spouse and minor children can exceptionally be treated as dependants, particularly if actual dependency can be established. This category would include elderly parents or siblings and also unmarried partners. The right to family life under Article 8 ECHR must also be taken into account in deciding who is to be considered as a dependant.

No guidelines are set out in the immigration rules as to what additional factors are to be taken into account in determining whether a person can qualify to be treated as a dependant but the API direct officers to consider (Ch 6, s1, para 3.1):

- whether the dependant is related as claimed to the principal;
- whether they are dependent on the principal;
- whether they were part of the family unit before the principal fled to the UK.

When a decision is made whether to grant refugee status or exceptional leave to remain to the main applicant, similar leave or 'leave in line' will be granted to the dependant. Dependants also cannot be removed unless and until the principal applicant's asylum claim is finally resolved against them after any appeals (but see below for what happens in circumstances where the Home Office considers that this rule is being abused).

Does a 'dependant' need to have arrived with the principal applicant?

The immigration rules (para 349, HC 395) state that the dependants should be 'accompanying' the principal. However, provided the family members arrive and apply to be treated as dependants before an initial decision is made on the asylum claim, they are normally treated as such. If they apply after a decision on the claim, they will not usually be treated as dependants but they will not be removed while the principal is appealing against the decision. If refugee status or exceptional leave is eventually granted to the principal, the application is then considered as an application for family reunion (API, Ch 6, s1, paras 2, 4). For details about family reunion applications ▶see Chapter 12.

'Abuse' of the dependants rule

The Home Office amended the immigration rules to address what it viewed as being an abuse in the system where refused principal applicants later tried to become dependants. For example, a husband claims asylum with his wife as a dependant and the claim is refused. After a negative appeal on the husband's case, the wife then claims asylum with her husband as dependant. As a result of the change in the rules, the husband, because he has previously been refused in his own right, can be removed from the UK as soon as his wife receives a negative decision on her application from the Home Office even if she appeals against that decision (para 349, HC 395). Of course, the husband might now wish to raise Article 8 ECHR in a case such as this.

Dependants claiming in their own right

Dependants have the choice of whether to make an asylum claim in their own right. This is advisable where they have their own separate grounds for claiming, in which case they should make that claim at the earliest opportunity. Adult children are normally expected to make a claim in their own right. If a dependant delays making a claim for asylum, then the immigration rules state that this can be taken into account in assessing their credibility if no reasonable explanation for the delay is provided.

Permission to work

If an asylum-seeker is granted temporary admission rather than being detained, one of the conditions normally attached to the temporary admission is that they are not permitted to work. Under section 8 of the 1996 Act, employers are liable to be prosecuted for employing persons who are unauthorised to work. However, the Home Office has a discretion to lift working restrictions from the temporary admission and therefore to give 'permission' to work. Where the Home Office grants this permission to an asylum-seeker, then it is not a criminal offence for an employer to employ them (see Immigration (Restrictions on Employment) Order 1996). Whether the asylum-seeker is permitted to work is indicated on the new Application Registration Card. Otherwise it will be stated on the form of temporary admission and/or the SAL.

The Home Office is willing to grant an asylum-seeker permission to work if it has not issued a decision on the asylum application within six months of it being made. Permission is not automatic, asylum-seekers must ask for it and it may be withheld if an asylum-seeker has failed to complete a SEF. Once permission has been granted it will not normally be withdrawn until any appeal against a negative asylum decision has been dealt with. When asylum is refused within six months and people appeal, they will not usually be allowed to work during the appeal period however long this takes. Dependants are not usually granted permission to work 'unless there are wholly exceptional or compassionate circumstances, for example, long term physical or mental disability of the main applicant' (API, Ch8, s3, para 1).

If the asylum-seeker has previously been in the UK in a capacity which entitled them to work and then they applied for asylum in-country, their entitlement to work continues under the previous conditions of leave.

Asylum-seekers and voluntary work

On 12 February 2001, the Home Office announced that it was 'keen to see asylum-seekers and recognised refugees take an active interest in the welfare of their own communities and the local community by undertaking voluntary activity in the UK'. It was stressed that such activity should not lead asylum-seekers to believe that it will mean that they can remain in the UK. On the same day, the Home Office issued guidance to organisations who are considering offering voluntary work to asylum-seekers to ensure that the activity does not in fact amount to employment or job substitution. The guidance also enables organisations to reimburse asylum-seekers for their food and travel costs in the course of their volunteering.

Ways of discouraging asylum-seekers

In common with other European countries, the UK has developed policies with the aim of discouraging potential asylum-seekers. While paying lip-service to their international commitments, successive governments have introduced a range of administrative measures, the aims of which have been to reduce the number of persons arriving in the UK and claiming asylum. As the political debate about asylum has become increasingly intense, these measures have been introduced against a backdrop of widespread stigmatising of asylum-seekers by sections of the press and media as well as some leading politicians. The most frequently presented negative image is of asylum-seekers being mainly economic migrants abusing the asylum system. One important supposed deterrent is the asylum support system which is examined in ▶Chapter 32.

Asylum-seekers are, by definition, often unable to approach the authorities of their own country in order to obtain passports or exit visas. Even to approach the embassy of another country to apply for a visa could place them in great danger. Also, except in the rarest cases, asylum-seekers are unable to obtain a visa in order to seek asylum. As a result, asylum-seekers are forced to resort to agents, forged documents or clandestine entry in order to seek asylum. Under Article 31 of the Refugee Convention, refugees should not however be prosecuted on account of their illegal entry if they have travelled directly from the country where they fear persecution and claim asylum within a short time of their arrival. The High Court has decided that the UK is bound to honour this obligation (*Adimi*). In the same case, the court commented that states which have signed the Refugee Convention seem to be 'increasingly striving' to prevent the arrival of asylum-seekers and that the combined effect of visa requirements and carriers' liability made it 'well-nigh impossible' for refugees to travel to countries of refuge without the use of false documents.

Measures such as visa regimes and carrier sanctions do not result in fewer asylum-seekers but rather in the increased use of illegal and, very often, dangerous means of securing entry. As certain recent cases both in the UK and in the Republic of Ireland have shown, the need to resort to these illegal means can result in tragedy with asylum-seekers discovered dead in the containers in which they have hidden. The various means of discouraging asylum-seekers are set out in the box below. The 2002 White Paper looks at further ways to strengthen border controls and to prevent illegal entry.

DISCOURAGING ASYLUM-SEEKERS

Visa regimes. The imposition of a visa restriction means that a national of any one of the list of so-called 'visa national' countries cannot travel to the UK without first obtaining an entry clearance or 'visa'. The immigration rules do not allow applicants to apply for entry clearance to come to the UK to seek asylum. People can only apply for protection from abroad in very restricted circumstances. As economic or political instability affects particular countries, they are added to the list. For example, Colombia and Ecuador were added in 1997 and Slovakia in 1998. For a complete list of visa national countries ►see page 737.

Carriers' liability legislation. People without entry clearances still manage to travel to the UK and claim asylum. For this reason the Home office enlisted the airlines to assist in immigration control through the Immigration (Carriers' Liability) Act 1987. This provided for fines on airlines of £2,000 for each passenger they bring to the UK without correct documentation. This means that the airlines will check people's documentation and refuse to let them board unless they have valid documentation. The 1987 Act was repealed and replaced by Part II of the Immigration and Asylum Act 1999 which extended liability to the carriage of clandestine entrants in any vehicle, ship or aircraft. The measure was particularly aimed at cross-Channel traffic but has not proved effective. It has been much criticised by the powerful road hauliers' lobby, which claims that it is physically impossible to maintain sufficient vigilance to prevent stowaways entering their vehicles. The government has rejected demands for a waiver of fines when the clandestine entrant proves to be a genuine refugee. In December 2001, the High Court decided that the imposition of these civil penalties on hauliers was unlawful and this was upheld by the Court of Appeal.

Checks abroad. Increasingly, immigration officials are being stationed abroad to advise airlines whether passports and entry clearances are genuine. This may be very dangerous for those who wish to flee but who are banned from travelling by their national authorities as those authorities may be alerted to their attempts to leave. In 2001, immigration officers stationed at Prague airport in order to screen passengers boarding flights to the UK were withdrawn after protests from Czech nationals.

For a period in 2000, the British Embassy in Khartoum began asking some entry clearance applicants to sign a declaration that they did not fear persecution in Sudan and would not claim asylum on arrival in the UK. The implication was that anyone who refused to sign would not be believed as to the true purpose of their entry clearance application or their intention to leave the UK at the end of their visit. Of course, this device can have no value in assessing the credibility of a subsequent asylum claim of someone who signed such a declaration in order to escape from persecution.

Preventing asylum-seekers as transit passengers. The 1993 Act extended carriers' liability to transit passengers. It also created powers for the Home Office to decide which transit passengers are required to have entry. The intention was to put an obstacle in the way of those who would otherwise seek to claim asylum in the UK while in transit. For details about the entry clearance requirements for transit passengers ►see page 292.

Detention. Large numbers of asylum-seekers are detained during the course of their asylum applications and the numbers are set to increase as the government is intent on increasing its detention estate. The use of detention can have a very negative effect on already traumatised asylum-seekers. The use of detention and the criteria for detaining asylum-seekers generally and at Oakington Reception Centre is covered in detail in Chapter 24.

For details about further developments relating to border controls in the 2002 White Paper and Bill ►see pages 34-35.

11   Home Office decisions on asylum

The legal conditions which need to be satisfied in order to qualify for asylum as a refugee under the Refugee Convention are set out in ▶Chapter 9. This chapter looks at Home Office decision-making in practice, to see what is taken into account in deciding whether a person qualifies. A central question in many cases is the credibility of what the applicant has said about their circumstances. We also consider the circumstances in which the Home Office can 'certify' an appeal to try to prevent the asylum-seeker from appealing beyond the level of the adjudicator ▶see pages 203-205.

This chapter also looks at the circumstances in which the Home Office makes a decision to refuse asylum *without* actually considering whether the person is a refugee on the ground that they can be returned to a 'safe' third country for their claim to be considered ▶see pages 206-212. We also look at the policy of the Home Office to grant exceptional leave in certain cases where it has refused to recognise a person as a refugee ▶see pages 216-219. The actual giving of the Home Office decision is also covered ▶see page 212-216, as well as delays in the Home Office making decisions and issuing papers ▶see pages 219-220. Finally, we look at the possibility of making 'fresh' claims for asylum after an earlier claim and any appeal has been decided negatively ▶see pages 220-221.

Home Office country information

The Home Office considers applications in the light of the detailed information it has about the situation in different countries and how the person's history fits in with this. Its Country and Information Policy Unit (CIPU) produces country information on the following countries which are then published on the Home Office website (www.ind.homeoffice.gov. UK):

Afghanistan, Albania, Algeria, Angola, Bangladesh, Burundi, Cameroon, China, Colombia, Czech Republic, Democratic Republic of Congo, Ecuador, Eritrea, Ethiopia, Ghana, India, Iran, Iraq, Kenya, Lebanon, Lithuania, Nigeria, Pakistan, Poland, Romania, Russia, Rwanda, Sierra Leone, Somalia, Sri Lanka, Sudan, Turkey, Uganda, Ukraine, Federal Republic of Yugoslavia and Zimbabwe.

The CIPU assessments are also supplemented by advice notes and bulletins which are frequently published. Where the case raises questions about particular events, Home Office case-workers deciding a claim are able to contact CIPU for specific advice and sometimes CIPU, in turn, may contact the Foreign and Commonwealth Office for more information.

Each country assessment gives a brief summary of the country's history, geography, political and human rights situation by drawing together information from a wide range of sources. They are updated twice yearly (in April and October) but they are summaries and cannot be relied upon to completely accurately reflect the position in each country. The sources for the country conditions described in the body of each assessment are contained in footnotes towards the end and the source material of any particularly contentious statement should be checked. CIPU itself keeps a copy of all the original source material which is referred to in the assessments. The Home Office very often selects the most optimistic reports of prevailing conditions. Immigration lawyers also frequently find that reasons for refusing asylum are in conflict with parts of the country assessment. Because the assessment attempts to summarise lots of sources, which may themselves be conflicting, they are often themselves contradictory. Applicants and their advisers should therefore conduct their own research about the relevant country conditions.

Because often there is no individual proof or evidence to substantiate a fear of persecution, the decision will depend on the Home Office's assessment of the person's truthfulness. Background evidence is important to the question of credibility because if an asylum-seeker gives an account which fits in with what is generally known about the country, this supports their credibility. The courts have consistently emphasised that a credibility assessment should be made in the light of the objective country conditions.

Immigration rules and credibility

The success of the application often depends on whether the person's account is believed. There is a widespread perception that adverse credibility findings are far too easily reached. The UNHCR has stated that:

'It is not advisable to list the factors which should be given special consideration in assessing an asylum-seeker's credibility. Evaluation of credibility is a process which involves the consideration of many complex factors, both objective and subjective, which are impossible to enumerate. Since all these may be equally important, singling out any of these factors will, by necessity, be incomplete and arbitrary.'

The immigration rules list 'matters which may damage an asylum applicant's credibility' and we look at these in turn. Several of these factors were discussed in meetings of European interior ministers in 1992 and 1993, which passed a resolution on 'manifestly unfounded' asylum cases. In all cases, these factors should not automatically undermine the credibility of the claim but must be considered together with all the circumstances of the case. If any of the factors are present, it is important that the asylum-seeker should try to explain why they should not be taken as adverse to credibility in their case. Some of the factors may also lead to the Home Office not only refusing the claim for asylum but also 'certifying' it so as to prevent an appeal beyond the level of the adjudicator.

Claiming asylum after entering the UK

'The applicant has failed without reasonable explanation to apply forthwith upon arrival in the UK, unless the application is founded on events which have taken place since his arrival in the UK.'
(para 341(i) HC 395)

This rule is aimed at people who enter (or try to enter) the UK in some other capacity, for example, as visitors or students, and only later apply for asylum. Many applicants will be unable or unwilling to apply immediately on arrival in the UK. People who have been tortured or brutally treated by officials may be traumatised and will not be able to tell their story to the first official they meet. Organisations dealing with torture victims know that it can take a long time to build sufficient trust to talk freely about such experiences. The requirement is contrary to the spirit of paragraph 198 of the *UNHCR Handbook* which states that people may well be afraid to give full and accurate accounts of their cases because of their past experiences. The case of *Ejon* is helpful as it confirms that victims of torture can be expected to be reluctant to talk about their experiences without this necessarily affecting their credibility.

In many cases, people may legitimately hesitate before making an asylum application once they have escaped from immediate danger. Applying for asylum is a drastic step, it means cutting off the possibility of returning to one's home country and may put relatives and friends in danger. People are often reluctant to do this and need time to think through the consequences with advisers or with others from the same community.

For others, a failure to claim asylum immediately may only be a reflection of their lack of knowledge of asylum procedures or they may have been instructed by an agent, keen to avoid detection and to retrieve false travel documents after passage through controls, not to claim at the port of entry.

An asylum applicant who bases their claim upon events that took place since their arrival in the UK, for example, a change of circumstances in their country of origin, cannot be criticised for not claiming on arrival. Refugees in this position are called by a French description: refugees 'sur place'. A delay in claiming after the relevant events have taken place may be held against applicants even in these circumstances. Those delays may also be explained by the person not wanting to cut off ties, hoping that the situation would improve, or even a delay in realising what was actually happening on the ground in their country.

Claiming after a negative immigration decision has been made

'The application is made after the applicant has been refused leave to enter...Or has been recommended for deportation...Or has been notified of the Home Office's decision to make a deportation order against him or has been notified of his liability of removal.'
(para 341(ii) HC395)

This rule is intended to apply to 'last minute' applications for asylum which are perceived as attempts to prevent being removed from the UK at all costs. However, a late claim is not necessarily without merit and there may be good reasons for the delay. For example, it may be that the applicant had every expectation of being able to remain in the UK on other grounds with no need to rely on asylum and therefore only claimed asylum where, due to unforeseen events, they were suddenly faced with the prospect of removal.

False evidence or claims

'The applicant has adduced manifestly false evidence in support of his application, or has otherwise made false representations, either orally or in writing.'
(para 341(iii) HC395)

Often people, not just in asylum cases, who have a good case are tempted to make their claims more elaborate in order to try to strengthen them yet further because they are afraid of refusal. Making sure that this does not happen depends on getting good, early advice. If a person has already embroidered their claim with additional information which is clearly not true, then careful advice should be obtained about how this can be explained. Depending on how this factor is applied, it may contravene Article 31 of the Refugee Convention, which accepts that refugees may need to disguise their initial intentions or their identity in order to flee to safety. For more details about the effect of Article 31 ▶see pages 557-558.

False passports

'On his arrival in the UK the applicant was required to produce a passport...and either failed to do so without providing a reasonable explanation, or, produced a passport which was not in fact valid and failed to inform the immigration officer of that fact.'
(para 341(iv) HC395)

For all the reasons discussed above, asylum-seekers may not feel secure enough on arrival to reveal all the details of their case, and this may well include details of the documents on which they are travelling. The applicant may have thought that, if they revealed that they were using false documents, they would face immediate refusal and return to the country of danger.

Applicant had destroyed or disposed of travel documents

'That the applicant has otherwise, without reasonable explanation, destroyed, damaged or disposed of any passport, other document, or ticket relevant to his claim.'
(para 341(v) HC395)

The Home Office has stated that almost two-thirds of people applying for asylum at the ports have no travel documents when they arrive. It believes that people have destroyed documents or returned them to agents who will use them again, or that they may have travelled through another country to which they would be returnable but that they are attempting to hide this so that their application will be considered in the UK. It may also be more difficult for the Home Office to establish people's identity if they have no travel document.

Inconsistent activities

'That the applicant has undertaken any activities in the UK before or after lodging his application which are inconsistent with his previous beliefs and behaviour and calculated to create or substantially enhance his claim to refugee status.'
(para 341(vi) HC395)

A person who has been in clandestine opposition in his or her home country may be able to act more openly once in the relative safety of the UK, and, therefore, they may have difficulty in showing that their views expressed in the UK are a continuation of long-held beliefs. Equally, public involvement in the UK may make it more dangerous to return to the country from which asylum is sought.

The case of *Senga* held that, depending on the circumstances of the case, the fact that an application for asylum had been made at all could put a person in danger from the authorities of his or her country. While recognising this point in principle, the Court of Appeal in *Mbanza* indicated that this was only likely to be so in very few cases. It stated that a fraudulent claim to asylum was itself likely to undermine the credibility of the claim that the person has any real fear as a result of making the claim. However, as the Court of Appeal made clear in *Danian*, the ultimate question is whether the claimant has a well-founded fear of being persecuted for a Convention reason and *not* whether he or she is to blame for creating that fear. It was also recognised in *Danian* that any applicant who was at risk would, in any case, be able to raise Article 3 ECHR.

Application for asylum made in another country

'That the applicant has lodged concurrent applications for asylum in the UK or in another country.'
(para 341(vii) HC395)

If applications are made in more than one country, the Home Office will wonder whether the asylum-seeker is 'shopping' to see which will accept the claim or using asylum as a basis for foreign travel for reasons other than a need for protection. It would also be possible for the Home Office to request details of the application from the other country and then compare them with those given in the application made in the UK, to see if there were any discrepancies. If a claim has been made in another country, rather than considering whether the person is a refugee or not, the Home Office may seek to return the asylum-seeker to that country on 'third country' grounds.

Actions of agents

The rules (para 342 HC395) also specifically state that the actions of anyone acting as an 'agent' of the asylum applicant may be taken into account in considering the above factors. No definition of agent is given. An asylum application may therefore be adversely affected by the actions of corrupt agents in the country of origin, incompetent advisers, or any friends who try to assist or advise. If relevant, these actions should be carefully explained. It is essential for advisers to make sure that any information put forward in connection with a claim is complete and correct and that it is first agreed with the applicant. Statements or the contents of letters of representations should always be translated back to the applicant so that they can confirm the information which is being provided to the Home Office.

Applicant as part of a group of other asylum-seekers

The immigration rules (para 344 HC395) also provide for an applicant who is part of a group whose claims are 'clearly not related to the criteria for refugee status' to be refused asylum without examination of their individual circumstances. The Home Office is still required to have regard to 'any evidence produced by the individual to show that his claim should be distinguished'. This is a further provision which allows for accelerated and unsafe decision-making and is against the spirit of the Convention which requires that each case be assessed individually. It begs the questions of what is a group, and what or who is 'clearly' outside the Convention? It allows for the kind of stereotyped, cursory decision-making which in the past has allowed Tamils and Kurds, later granted full refugee status, to be labelled initially as 'bogus' by ministers and officials.

Certification of decisions

If asylum (and exceptional leave) is refused, the applicant will receive a letter setting out the reasons for refusal of asylum. In some cases, the Home Office will include within the reasons for refusal a 'certificate' issued under paragraph 4 of schedule 9 to the 1999 Act (which will be stated). Claims under both the Refugee Convention and the ECHR can be certified. These certificates should not be confused with either third country certificates (►see below) or other certificates which prevent people from appealing at all ►see pages 509-611. The effect of certificates given under this provision is more limited; the asylum-seeker may appeal to the adjudicator. However, if the adjudicator dismisses the appeal *and* upholds the certificate, then there is no further right of appeal to the Immigration Appeal Tribunal (IAT). In these cases, the only way of challenging the determination of the adjudicator is to apply for judicial review.

From 7 January 2002, changes have been made to the procedure for issuing the determination of the adjudicator to asylum-seekers in these cases (see the Immigration and Asylum Appeals (Procedure) (Amendment) Rules 2001). Under the new procedure, the determinations in dismissed certified appeals are sent to the Home Office, which may then arrange to send the determination to the appellant or to give it to them in person. Handing an appeal determination to the failed asylum-seeker in person gives the Home Office an opportunity to detain them in readiness for removal.

The adjudicator can dismiss an appeal but not uphold the certificate, in which case there is a right of appeal. If the adjudicator allows the appeal, then the Home Office has a right of appeal to the IAT regardless of whether the adjudicator upholds the certificate.

Problems have arisen with these certificates due to the fact that the Home Office 'reasons for refusal' letter will now deal with both asylum and human rights claims. In *Zenovics*, the IAT held that the effect of a certificate being upheld on either claim was to prevent a further appeal to the IAT on both asylum and human rights matters. This creates obvious anomalies, for example, where an asylum claim is certified because there is no Refugee Convention reason which in no way affects the human rights claim. The Home Office therefore stated that it would only certify a claim if both the asylum and the human rights elements merit a certificate. However, the Court of Appeal subsequently overturned *Zenovics* and so it is possible to appeal to the IAT if the adjudicator agrees with a certificate which only, in truth, applies to *either* the asylum *or* the human rights appeal. The 'uncertified' appeal can be taken further to the IAT.

The Home Office always has discretion as to whether to certify, even if the conditions for certification are established. It has also confirmed that it will not certify in complex cases or where exceptional leave is granted or where the refusal is based on 'non-compliance' grounds ►see below.

There are several alternative bases on which a claim can be certified. The category of countries designated as generally safe (the 'white list'), which used to form a basis for certificates and which was contained in the 1996 Act, was abolished by the 1999 Act. The government's 2002 White Paper goes further and states the government's intention to abolish these kinds of certificate altogether on the grounds that they complicate the appeals process.

Grounds for issuing a certificate

Under the 1999 Act, in order for a claim under the Refugee Convention or the ECHR to be certified, the Home Office must first state that 'the evidence does not establish a reasonable degree of likelihood that the appellant has been tortured in the country to which they are to be sent'. In *addition*, the Home Office must certify that any of the conditions set out below apply.

It should be noted that the Home Office certificate, in order to be valid, must be correct at the time of the decision which is being appealed (*Ziar*). If the certificate is defective, because, for example, the Home Office has certified one of the following conditions but forgotten to certify that there is no evidence of torture, the certificate cannot later be amended. In such a case, the appeal must proceed as an uncertified case.

- 'The applicant failed to produce a valid passport on request, without reasonable explanation, or produced an invalid passport without saying so.'

Often asylum-seekers have destroyed their passports or they are using forged or counterfeit documents because they simply had no choice. This should be regarded as a reasonable explanation. Certification on this basis can be very unfair as there is no logical link between the failure to produce a document and the merits of the asylum claim or any abuse of the system. It is important that any disputes as to what happened on arrival are resolved as soon as possible so that the immigration officer's records are correct.

- 'The claim was made after the refusal of leave to enter, a decision to deport or recommendation for deportation, or notification of removal as an illegal entrant.'

This is intended to prevent 'abuse' of the system by last-minute asylum or human rights claims designed to hold up removal. It is a question of fact whether the claim was made after any of the above immigration decisions was made. However, if a decision had been taken but not given to the asylum-seeker, it is arguable that the case should not be certified.

- 'The claim under the Refugee Convention does not show a fear of persecution for a Convention reason, or the fear it shows is manifestly unfounded or the circumstances giving rise to it no longer exist.'

- 'The claim under the Human Rights Convention does not disclose a right under the Convention or is manifestly unfounded.'

There has been a disturbing tendency for decision-makers to add on a 'manifestly unfounded' certificate at the end of decision letters when it is inappropriate to do so. Often, it is added on after negative findings on credibility. The category is intended for situations where there is clearly no need for protection, for example, because the country concerned is clearly now safe or the reason for the fear is not one of the Convention reasons, for example, if solely economic reasons are given. The current Asylum Policy Instructions (API) confirm that, if there is any doubt as to whether a claim should be certified, it should not be. In *Vallaj*, the High Court held that a claim is 'manifestly unfounded' if it can be seen, on a quick appraisal of the case, that it is 'plainly and obviously' without foundation. A claim cannot be manifestly unfounded if the answer only becomes plain after lengthy and detailed consideration.

In *Gavira*, the High Court held that the question of whether the asylum-seeker's claim 'shows' a fear of persecution for a Convention reason should be determined on the basis that the account presented is true. Certification on that basis is not intended to involve questions of the applicant's credibility.

- 'The claim is manifestly fraudulent or any of the evidence adduced in support is manifestly false.'

A manifestly fraudulent claim is one that has been wholly fabricated or where an identity has been created or borrowed, or other important evidence has been manufactured.

- 'The claim is frivolous or vexatious.'

This category overlaps with others and is little used. When the 1993 Act, which first introduced this phrase into asylum law, was passed, it was suggested by the government that it was intended to deal with situations where a claim was based on matters such as a dislike of the weather or the applicant's in-laws. It might also apply to repeat claims after leaving and then returning to the UK where there is no significant change of circumstances.

'Non-compliance' refusals

A controversial method of disposing of asylum applications is to refuse them on 'non-compliance' grounds. The immigration rules state as follows:

'A failure, without reasonable explanation, to make a prompt and full disclosure of material factors, either orally or in writing, or otherwise to assist the Secretary of State in establishing the facts of the case may lead to the refusal of an asylum application. This includes failure to comply with a notice issued by the Secretary of State or an immigration officer requiring the applicant to report to a designated place to be finger-printed, or failure to complete an asylum questionnaire, or failure to comply with a request to attend an interview concerning the application, or failure to comply with a requirement to report to an immigration officer for examination'.

In 2000, the Home Office started refusing a large number of claims on the basis that the applicants had not submitted their asylum questionnaires (SEFs) within the 10-day time-limit set. It soon became apparent that there was a systematic failure at the Home Office to link the forms to applicants' files and, in the vast majority of cases, applicants had in fact lodged the SEF in time. This placed many asylum-seekers in considerable difficulties as the negative decision affected their entitlements to benefits, made them liable to be dispersed under the National Asylum Support Service (NASS) scheme and affected their ability to obtain permission to work. Even when the asylum-seeker demonstrated that the form had been sent in in time, the Home Office initially refused to withdraw the decision to refuse asylum.

The problem came to court in the cases of *Karoaglan, Hadavi and Bashiri*. At this point, in May 2001, the Home Office agreed to change its policy and to withdraw decisions where, within three months of the decision, evidence was produced to the Home Office that the asylum-seeker had complied with the 10-day limit and a request was made that the erroneous decision be withdrawn. Approximately 7,000 cases were affected. The Home Office has attempted to resolve the problem by having a dedicated address for the return of SEFs.

The IAT ruled in the case of *Ali Haddad* that, even if an asylum-seeker has not complied with requirements made by the Home Office, cases should not be decided either by the Home Office or adjudicators on that basis alone. The decision-maker must always consider the actual evidence before them which goes to show that the person is a refugee. If a non-compliance case does go to appeal, representatives should therefore ensure that they fully prepare the case with all of the evidence necessary to show that removing the appellant would be in breach of the Refugee Convention.

Third country cases

There are some cases in which, although a person makes a claim to asylum, the Home Office does not have to decide whether or not they do have a well-founded fear of persecution before requiring them to leave the UK. This applies in cases where the asylum-seeker may be returned to a 'safe third country' for that country to decide whether the applicant actually is a refugee. The immigration authorities can deal with the asylum claim in this way when either:

- the asylum-seeker did not arrive in the UK directly from the country where they claim to fear persecution but from another country in which they had an opportunity to claim asylum; or

- there is 'clear evidence' that the asylum-seeker will be admitted to the proposed safe third country.

By removing a person to a safe third country, the Home Office is able to say that its own obligations under Article 33 of the Convention are not breached because, even if the person is a refugee, they are not being returned to a place where they face a risk of persecution. The third country concept is based on the belief among states that an asylum-seeker who crosses into the territory of one state is that state's responsibility if there is a claim to international protection and on the assumption that a genuine asylum-seeker will seek asylum in the first safe haven they find. The concept is not set out in the Refugee Convention but it has increasingly been relied upon, particularly by agreement among European states. Most importantly, they have negotiated the Dublin Convention (▶see below), which allocates responsibility between European states for dealing with asylum applicants.

The 1993 Act: third country appeals

The practice of third country returns was first made formal in UK law under the Asylum and Immigration Appeals Act 1993. That Act created the system under which the Home Office could certify applications as being 'without foundation' if the claim should be dealt with by another country. It also created a right of appeal against the certificate. To the government's embarrassment, there was then a period in which appeals against proposed third country returns to other European states were very often successful. Often it was shown that there had been breaches of procedures and other failings which indicated that people would not have their claims properly considered and may be removed to their country of origin even though they were at risk of persecution there.

The 1996 Act: judicial review in third country cases

The government responded with the Asylum and Immigration Act 1996 which withdrew the in-country right of appeal in respect of cases where the third country was an EU state or a 'designated country', namely Canada, the USA, Norway or Switzerland. The Home Office immediately resumed third country removals to EU states and applicants had to resort to the High Court procedure of judicial review in order to challenge their removal.

In the cases which followed, the courts decided that the Home Office was required to take reasonable steps to make sure that it was aware of the circumstances and procedures in the country to which the person would be removed and ensure that there was no risk that the person would be sent on by the third country in breach of the Convention. Applying these principles, a decision to remove two Albanian Kosovars to Germany was quashed (*Gashi*). In *Adan and Aitseguer*, the House of Lords held that, where the third country interpreted the criteria under the Convention for satisfying the definition of 'refugee' wrongly, the UK could not remove applicants to those countries. The court decided that there was no margin for different interpretations of the Convention by the different signatory states because the Convention has only one international meaning. In those cases, Germany and France were found to be lacking by not recognising persecution by 'non-state' agents. For the circumstances in which a person can be a refugee on the basis of fears from 'non-state' agents ►see pages 161-162.

These cases prompted the government to take yet further measures under the 1999 Act to prevent asylum-seekers from challenging third-country removals in the courts (►see below).

The Dublin Convention

The Dublin Convention was signed by EU governments in June 1990 and came into force on 1 September 1997. The purpose was to set criteria under which responsibility among the member states for dealing with asylum applicants could be allocated. It should be noted that a revised agreement is likely to replace the Dublin Convention; the 2002 White Paper indicates the government's aim to negotiate another international agreement. Under the Dublin Convention, the state which is responsible for dealing with an applicant is a state which meets any of the following criteria. The criteria are listed in the order in which they apply, so for example, a state in which the asylum-seeker has a family member who has been recognised as a refugee is the responsible state even if there are other states which meet any of the later criteria:

1 A state in which the claimant has a family member recognised as a refugee under the Refugee Convention (family member here means spouse, unmarried child under 18 years or parents if the asylum-seeker is an unmarried minor).

2 A state which has issued a valid residence permit or visa to the asylum-seeker.

3 A state into which the asylum-seeker illegally crossed from outside the EU, provided the asylum-seeker has not remained living in another state for six months or more after making an asylum application in that second state.

4 A state into which an asylum-seeker lawfully entered without needing a visa.

5 A state in which the asylum application was lodged.

Since September 1997, asylum-seekers have been given a 'screening' interview to establish which country is responsible. Decisions are made by a specialist 'Third Country Unit' at the Home Office. If the Home Office believes the person can be returned, it will try to obtain the agreement of the third country before removing the applicant. The Convention sets out a timetable for the negotiations to take place between states as to which has responsibility. Prior to the Dublin Convention, the procedure was different. Refused asylum-seekers were sent to the last safe EU country through which they travelled before coming to the UK, rather than being sent directly to the first safe country they arrived at in the EU, or whichever other country was appropriate under the above criteria. The earlier procedure involved the receiving country sending the asylum-seeker on again if it believed there was another country that should accept responsibility.

An asylum-seeker for whom the UK is not responsible under the Dublin Convention can still make representations to the Home Office to suggest why, exceptionally, their claim should still be considered here. The immigration rules only state that the Home Office will 'normally' return a person to the third country where the relevant conditions are satisfied (para 345 HC 395). There may be family or other connections in the UK or other special reasons why the normal course should not be followed.

The effect of the 1999 Act on third country cases

Before 2 October 2000, the Dublin Convention had no direct effect in UK law. However, the Immigration and Asylum Act 1999 incorporated the Dublin Convention by its reference to 'standing arrangements with member States'.

Third country removals under the Dublin Convention

Section 11 of the 1999 Act covers removals to EU member states under 'standing arrangements' (i.e., the Dublin Convention and any further agreements replacing that Convention). The procedure is that the Home Office can certify (the 'certificate' will be in the form of a letter) that:

- the EU member state has accepted that it is the responsible state under the Dublin Convention (normally, the Home Office will provide its correspondence with the immigration authorities of the other state to show this); and

- the asylum-seeker is not a national of the EU member state to which they will be sent.

A person can appeal against the certificate on the grounds that the conditions are not satisfied, namely, that the other member state has not accepted responsibility or that they are a national of that member state. However, this appeal can only be brought from abroad (see ss 71, 72(2)(b) 1999 Act). These appeals are very rarely brought. An in-country appeal is possible on human rights grounds under section 65 1999 Act if an allegation is made that removal is contrary to the asylum-seeker's human rights or that they have been discriminated against. This appeal can be exercised from the UK and removal cannot take place while the appeal is pending (see s11(3) 1999 Act).

However, the Home Office can deny the asylum-seeker an in-country right of appeal by issuing a (further) certificate stating that the human rights or discrimination allegation is 'manifestly unfounded' (s72(2)(b) 1999 Act). If the Home Office issues such a certificate, it can remove the person even though a human rights allegation is made. Asylum-seekers may then consider whether to challenge the 'manifestly unfounded' certificate by judicial review and ask the Home Office not to act in the meantime or ask the High Court for an injunction to prevent removal while the judicial review is outstanding. In order for a claim to be properly certified as being 'manifestly unfounded', the courts have held that the Home Office must be able to show that an appeal to the adjudicator against the decision would have 'no chance whatsover of succeeding' (Collins J in *Thangarasa*) or, put another way, that there is 'plainly nothing of substance in the case' (Laws LJ in the same case in the Court of Appeal).

Section 11 certificates are much more powerful that those issued previously because the 1999 Act also states that, where a person is being removed under the Dublin Convention, the third country 'is to be regarded as' a safe country for the purposes of the Refugee Convention. In other words, the Act *presumes* that the third country will not either persecute the asylum-seeker or send them to a country where they are at risk of persecution. The intention is to prevent the courts from being able to decide that returns to these countries cannot take place on the basis that the third country is not safe. In *Ibrahim* in the Court of Appeal, the Home Office successfully relied on this presumption in a case involving the return of a Sudanese national to France, in which the applicant alleged a fear of persecution under the Refugee Convention from non-state agents in Sudan. This position was followed by the High Court in *Mohammed*.

The presumption in section 11 refers to the Refugee Convention, not the ECHR. It is possible, therefore, for an asylum-seeker to raise human rights objections to being removed on third country grounds. Possible grounds may be:

- the asylum-seeker has close family members or connections in the UK giving rise to family or private life under Article 8;
- the physical or mental state of the asylum-seeker is such that the effect upon them of enforcing their departure to yet further unfamiliar surroundings would infringe their human rights under Articles 3 or 8.

As indicated previously, the Home Office may try to prevent a human rights appeal by issuing a 'manifestly unfounded' certificate where a human rights allegation is made. In principle, Article 3 ECHR, like the Refugee Convention, also allows a person to argue that their removal to a third country breaches human rights if the third country may send them to their country of origin where they are at risk of mistreatment (see *TI v UK*). In *Yogathas & Thangarasa*, two Tamils were trying to avoid return to Germany as a safe third country. Both feared persecution at the hands of the Sri Lankan authorities and non-state agents in the form of the LTTE. The court decided that return to Germany was not in breach of Article 3

ECHR because, even if Germany's interpretation of the Refugee Convention and the ECHR was not correct, German law and procedures under its Aliens Act would not in practice result in the asylum-seekers being removed to Sri Lanka in breach of either Convention. The Court of Appeal also relied on the ability of the asylum-seekers to apply to the European Court itself while in Germany if the need arose.

Advisers should be aware that in the area of third-country cases in particular, the law is still developing, and further decisions of the courts may change the position. The cases of *Yogathas & Thangarasa* (see above) are to be heard by the House of Lords. For a problem-solving approach to current third country cases ▶see pages 136-138.

Non-Dublin Convention third country removals

Section 12 of the 1999 Act covers all other third country removals, namely:

1 To EU member states other than under the Dublin Convention (or similar agreements).

2 To 'designated' countries, currently Canada, Norway, Switzerland, USA.

3 To all other countries.

In *all* of these cases, the Home Office can seek to remove the person to the third country only after it has certified that:

• the asylum-seeker is not a national or citizen of the country to which they are to be sent;

• the asylum-seeker will not face a risk of persecution in the third country;

• the third country will not send the asylum-seeker to their country of origin if they risk persecution there.

In *all* of these cases, there is no presumption that the third country is safe. The Home Office must directly consider the question of safety in each case and the Home Office's decision on this issue can, if there are proper grounds, be challenged on appeal and in the courts.

In the *first two cases* (removals to EU member states or designated countries), an appeal can only be brought by the asylum-seeker after he or she has left the UK (see ss71 and 72(2)(b) 1999 Act). In those cases, if there is a question of safety, it is likely therefore to be raised on judicial review before the asylum-seeker is removed. This is how similar cases under the 1996 Act proceeded because, if a person waits and then appeals from abroad, the damage is likely to be irretrievable. In the *third* category of case (removals to non-EU and non-designated states), there is an in-country right of appeal just as there was for EU member state removals when the 1993 Act was in force.

In all three cases, human rights or discrimination claims objecting to the third country removal can be made which give rise to a right of appeal (see s65 1999 Act). However, as in Dublin Convention removals, the Home

Office can certify these claims as 'manifestly unfounded' so as to deny an in-country right of appeal.

Other third country cases

Most third country cases follow established patterns: they are 'Dublin Convention' returns or the person has passed through an identified safe country. Occasionally, however, a third country case arises which is out of the ordinary, for example, where the Home Office has actively tried to find an alternative destination for an asylum-seeker. The following are examples:

Dr Al Masari. Dr Masari is a well known Saudi dissident who claimed asylum in the UK and who the immigration authorities tried to send to the Dominican Republic. He succeeded in showing that he would not be safe from the Saudi authorities there.

Afghan hijacked aircraft case. In February 2000 an Ariana hijacked airliner landed at Stansted having been diverted during an internal flight in Afghanistan. Many of the passengers claimed asylum and ministers announced that they were seeking alternative countries of reception for them. In particular, it was suggested that they may be returned to safe 'neighbouring' countries.

Close connection with another country. If an asylum-seeker has close connections with another country as well as the one from which he or she is claiming asylum, the Home Office may suggest that asylum is not necessary because there is another country to which they could go. People who are dual nationals are always expected to go to their safe country of nationality. This has also been used, for example, for people of Jewish origin, who have been told that they could go to Israel. The Court of Appeal agreed with this view in the case of *Miller*.

In the above cases, as with all other third country cases, it must be the case that the asylum-seeker has either passed through the third country and had an opportunity to claim *or* that there is 'clear evidence' that the asylum-seeker will be accepted into the third country. In these kinds of cases the Home Office will usually be relying on 'clear evidence' of admissibility which applies after it has negotiated with the country in question. These cases will generally fall under section 12 rather than section 11 of the 1999 Act (▶see above). There will therefore be an in-country right of appeal on the question of the safety of the third country together with any human rights grounds the applicant may bring.

The Home Office decision

After the Home Office has made a decision, it must be communicated to the asylum-seeker. If refugee status is being refused, the Home Office will also consider whether the reasons put forward in the asylum claim mean that exceptional leave should be given. For the procedures if exceptional leave is granted ▶see below pages 216-219.

Invitations to withdraw asylum applications

Often where asylum-seekers have also made some other immigration application, such as a marriage application, they are invited by the Home Office to withdraw their asylum application so that there is no asylum decision. Asylum-seekers should take careful advice before doing this. Firstly, a person could be left without any permission to be in the UK at all if the other application is refused. Even if leave as a spouse is granted, it might be legitimate to continue to pursue the asylum claim. For example, marriage leave is initially only granted for one year and renewal depends on satisfying the immigration rules. As stated above, refugees are entitled to immediate settlement and Refugee Convention travel documentation.

Decisions to refuse refugee status and exceptional leave

Refusals are now sent by post to the applicant and his or her representative. Obviously, it is important that any changes of address or of representative are registered so that appeal rights are not lost. The requirement to serve port decisions personally has been abolished. In port cases, the letter is sent from the immigration service to the applicant and his representative. Decisions made following in-country claims for asylum are usually sent out by the Home Office. However, from July 2001, the Home Office is also able to send out its own notices giving or refusing leave in port cases rather than notifying the port and expecting it to issue the decision (see Immigration (Leave to Enter) Order 2001). The intention is to save time and administration. The extent to which this will be implemented and the effect it will have on saving time remains to be seen.

Refusal of asylum

Reasons for refusal letter

Refused applicants will receive a 'reasons for refusal' letter which sets out a summary of the claim to asylum followed by the reasons for refusal. These reasons often consist of a series of paragraphs referring to the conditions in the relevant country and also raising matters concerning the applicant's credibility. There is usually a brief paragraph dismissing the possibility that refusal would lead to a breach of the applicant's human rights. Finally, if the refusal is to be certified so as to attempt to deny an appeal to the Immigration Appeal Tribunal, the certificate is added at the end of the letter.

The refusal letter is important as it puts the applicant on notice of the main issues she or he will have to deal with at the appeal. Advisers have become frustrated by apparently 'systematic' refusal letters which contain standard paragraphs, sometimes bearing little or no particular relation to the claim itself. Inadequate refusal letters should be challenged immediately with representations as it is sometimes possible to get the decision reversed after it has been looked at by a different officer.

The quality of the reasons given for refusal is often extremely poor. Asylum Aid has commissioned two reports, *No reason at all* (1995) and *Still no reason at all* (1999), both of which illustrate that Home Office reasons for refusal letters frequently involve legal mistakes, reliance on defective country information taken from the Home Office's own country assessments and inadequate treatment of medical evidence.

Documents sent with reasons for refusal letters and appeals

Together with the refusal letter, the applicant will receive the following:

1 A notice of refusal containing details of an 'immigration decision' made as the consequence of the asylum refusal and the relevant rights of appeal.

2 A 'one-stop' notice and statement of additional grounds (issued under s74 1999 Act).

3 Appeal forms together with explanatory notes.

It is the notice of the immigration decision (1 above) which actually triggers the right of appeal to an adjudicator under section 69 1999 Act (►see box below). The rights of appeal themselves and the procedure for appealing are described in ►Section 10.

IMMIGRATION DECISION GIVING RIGHT OF APPEAL

The type of immigration decision which is issued and which gives rise to the right of appeal depends upon the immigration status of the asylum-seeker at the time of the claim to asylum. The decision may be any of the following:

- refusal of leave to enter – this is issued in port cases where the claim to asylum was made before the person passed through immigration controls;

- removal directions following a decision that the asylum-seeker is an 'illegal entrant';

- removal directions to an asylum-seeker who is an 'overstayer' or in breach of their conditions of leave or who has obtained leave to remain by deception;

- a refusal to vary existing leave so as to allow the person to remain in the UK as a refugee – this is issued where the claimant already has some (other) form of leave at the time as their application for asylum;

- a notice of intention to deport a person because the Secretary of State has decided their presence is not conducive to the public good or as the family member of a person who is to be deported;

- a deportation order – this is issued where the person claims asylum after notice of intention to deport has been issued or a court has recommended their deportation as part of a criminal sentence (the 2002 Bill proposes to bring deportation following court recommendations into line with other types of deportation so that a notice of intention to deport, as above, will be issued in these cases as well);

- a refusal to revoke a deportation order – this is issued where the person claims asylum after a deportation order has already been made.

For more details about removal, illegal entry and deportation ►see Chapter 26.

In all cases, the right of appeal arises on the basis that the consequence of the person having to leave the UK would be a breach of the Refugee Convention.

The statement of additional grounds under section 74 of the 1999 Act (number 2 above) requires the refused asylum-seeker to raise any further grounds for wishing to stay in the UK. Most asylum-seekers will have already been given a 'one-stop' notice at the time of their claim for asylum (under s75 1999 Act). It is vital that advisers take detailed instructions from their clients to ensure that the statement of additional grounds is fully completed. It is likely that there are human rights grounds which can and should be raised arising out of the details of the claim. The Home Office has stated that it only expects applicants to mention the basic facts which underpin any application and, therefore, they can be completed without expert advice. However, adjudicators are now making it clear that they expect a fully-reasoned argument as to why the appellant has a human rights claim so that the Home Office can, if necessary, prepare a supplementary decision letter to deal with it. For further details about the 'one-stop' procedure ▶see pages 187-189, 606-611.

Decisions to grant refugee status

The Refugee Convention does not require states to grant permanent residence to refugees or to give them any particular immigration status. The immigration rules state that those who are recognised as refugees will be given limited leave. In *Adan*, the Court of Appeal suggested that it would be open to the Secretary of State to grant limited leave and then seek to return persons previously recognised as refugees if the situation improved so that they were no longer in fear of persecution in their own country. Until the government White Paper *Fairer, Faster, Fairer* was issued in July 1998, refugees were granted leave for four years and would usually be given indefinite leave after that. From 27 July 1998, the policy has been to grant indefinite when recognising someone as a refugee. Refugees granted four years' leave prior to 27 July 1998 can now apply for indefinite leave immediately. Dependants of the refugee will also be granted indefinite leave in line with the refugee.

Strictly speaking, the Home Office does not 'grant' refugee status but recognises someone as a refugee. This is because, applying the Refugee Convention definition, the applicant has been a refugee since they met the criteria under the Convention even though they had not been declared to be one (see para 28 *UNHCR Handbook*).

The letter recognising refugee status and indefinite leave

As with refusals of status, recognition of status and the grant of indefinite leave will be sent by post. The standard letter granting refugee status (ICD0725 ▶see page 123 for an example) reflects the Refugee Convention which provides for refugees to have the same civil rights and duties as UK nationals. The letter explains:

- that the refugee can stay permanently in the UK provided they do not engage in violence such as to endanger national security;
- that they can work freely without needing to obtain permission to work;
- that they are eligible to apply for welfare benefits or social housing;
- that they can access the NHS, social services and obtain funding as a 'home student' for further or higher education;
- that they can travel abroad. The letter suggests that travel might affect refugee status. This is because a voluntary return to the home country may trigger the cessation clauses and lead to a loss of refugee status. For more details about this ▶see pages 167-168.

The letter also informs the refugee that any NASS support will cease. This is because the refugee is no longer an 'asylum-seeker' and is entitled to apply for social security benefits instead. It also gives information on organisations which give advice on the above entitlements.

How many people are granted refugee status or exceptional leave?

The 1993 Act was accompanied by a change in Home Office policy. The proportion of refusals of asylum rose steeply after the Act, from 15 per cent in the 18 months before July 1993 to 75 per cent in the following 15 months and up to 80 per cent by late 1996. By mid 1998, this had changed and the proportion of favourable decisions began to rise. However, the figures for 2000 showed a fall again in the percentage granted refugee status or exceptional leave to remain down to 22 per cent. In 2001, a record 118,195 decisions were made. According to Home Office statistics these were as follows:

Recognised as a refugee	10,960	
Granted exceptional leave to remain	19,510	
Total	30,470	(26%)

Refused after substantive consideration	65,540	
Refused on third country grounds	705	
Refused on non-compliance grounds	21,480	
Total	87,725	(74%)

Exceptional leave

If the Home Office decides that the applicant does not qualify for refugee status, it will go on to consider whether there are compassionate or humanitarian reasons for allowing the applicant to stay in the UK. If there are, the Home Office may grant a lesser status called 'exceptional leave to remain' or 'ELR' (for those applying at port, this is strictly 'exceptional leave to enter' but we will refer to both as ELR). This status is granted at the discretion of the Home Office. There is no provision for it in the immigration rules. However, the circumstances in which it is granted

(►see below) are very similar to the circumstances in which the Home Office must now allow people to stay in the UK on the basis of their human rights under the ECHR (in particular Articles 3 and 8). Therefore, the incorporation of the ECHR has taken over a lot of what was previously the Home Office's ELR policy. Even though the general law and the immigration rules (para 2 HC 395) mean that the Home Office *must* make its decisions in accordance with the the the ECHR, confusingly the Home Office still calls leave granted as a result of ECHR rights 'exceptional leave' (API Ch5, s4, para 4.3 and 2002 White Paper para 4.90).

The last version of the published criteria of the Home Office (in early 2002, the API were being updated on this issue) stated that ELR would be granted following a failed asylum application (API, Ch5, s1):

1 if return to the country of origin would result in the applicant being tortured or subjected to cruel, inhuman or degrading treatment; or the removal would result in an unjustifiable break-up of family life; for example,

- where there are substantial grounds for believing that the applicant would suffer a serious and wholly disproportionate punishment for a criminal offence;

- where there is credible medical evidence that return, due to the medical facilities in the country, would reduce the applicant's life expectancy and subject him or her to acute physical and mental suffering, in circumstances where the UK can be regarded as having assumed responsibility for his or her care;

2 where the applicant does not satisfy the Refugee Convention criteria but there are compassionate or humanitarian reasons for not requiring him or her to return;

3 where ministers have agreed that, for humanitarian reasons, a general country policy will apply.

ELR granted in	1992	1993	1994	1995	1996	1997	before 27/7/98
Years before ILR can be considered	7	7	7	6	6	5	4
ILR	1999	2000	2001	2001	2002	by 27/7/02	by 27/7/02

Period of leave granted when exceptional leave given

Before 1998, ELR was usually given for an initial year followed by two further periods of three years. After a total of seven years, indefinite leave was granted. From 27 July 1998, the Home Office announced that ELR would initially be granted for four years. Furthermore, people can now apply for indefinite leave after four years' ELR, rather than the previous seven. This new policy applies to decisions made on claims after the policy came into effect. For people who had already been granted ELR, the policy has been phased in over a period of years. The application form which must be used to extend ELR or apply for settlement after a period of ELR (the form is called 'ELR') has been drafted to include a table of qualifying dates (▶see above).

People granted ELR will be sent a standard letter (ICD0716) informing them that their asylum claim has been refused but that ELR is to be granted. It does not set out the reasons for the asylum refusal. Like the refugee status letter, this letter also contains similar information about entitlements, although there are important differences as to family reunion and travel documents ▶see Chapter 12.

The letter granting ELR says that applications for extensions of leave will be carefully considered. The absence of the security of knowing that their leave will be extended leaves people feeling concerned about what will happen when their leave expires. Although it remains a possibility that the Home Office may decide that exceptional leave is only a temporary offer of protection, its usual practice is to grant indefinite leave upon request where the applicant was initially granted four years' exceptional leave after 27 July 1998, even in cases where, arguably, the need for protection has disappeared. However, the Home Office is moving towards increased use of temporary protection and has indicated that this may be used more where it is, currently, not possible to arrange for the person to travel back. For example, in cases from Afghanistan, Somalia and Kurds from Northern Iraq, advisers may find that applicants are granted 12 months' leave with no expectation of renewal. The spouse and minor children dependants of people who are already in the UK and granted exceptional leave, are normally granted leave in line.

Right of appeal

In a case decided under the 1993 Act, the Court of Appeal has made it clear that there is a right of appeal where ELR is granted and that the right of appeal is an effective one (see *Saad, Diriye & Osario*). Applicants are, therefore, entitled to challenge the asylum decision on appeal even if, in fact, they are not going to be removed anywhere by the Home Office. For more details about these rights of appeal, ▶see pages 617-618. Achieving refugee status can be of fundamental importance to those who wish to bring their family members into the UK. However, in line with the indication that temporary protection may be used more frequently, the 2002 Bill proposes to reverse the effect of *Saad* for those granted leave of 12 months or less. This will mean that those people would not be entitled to bring asylum appeals until the Home Office was in a position to remove them. They could still seek judicial review of asylum refusals as did many asylum-seekers in the days before the 1993 Act introduced comprehensive rights of appeal for those refused asylum.

Delays in making decisions and issuing documents

A considerable practical problem has arisen in that the Home Office has taken a very long time, in some case many years, to decide individual cases. The problem of the backlog of cases was exacerbated by the operational reorganisation caused by the Home Office's physical relocation in 1998 to 1999 and 2001. People affected by the delays can complain directly to the ICD Complaints Unit. If no satisfactory reply is received, then an MP can be asked to refer the matter to the Parliamentary Ombudsman. Alternatively, the MP could be asked to enquire about the progress of the case directly with the ICD or the Home Secretary. The Home Office's aim is to decide an asylum claim within two months and for appeals to be resolved in the following four months.

There have been cases of asylum-seekers applying for judicial review on the basis that they were being caused real prejudice or hardship. In *Deniz Mersin*, the High Court considered an asylum-seeker who had won his appeal against refusal but who had not received a grant of refugee status after seven and a half months. The judge said that the Home Office had a duty to accept the adjudicator's decision, given that it did not appeal against it, and grant the applicant leave within a reasonable time, having regard to the prejudice caused to him. If there is no longer an appeal pending at present, those who have succeeded in their appeals and are waiting for papers will have difficulty claiming any form of welfare support. They cannot receive benefits as they are 'subject to immigration control' because they have no leave, and they can no longer get asylum support because they are no longer 'asylum-seekers' following the disposal of the appeal. As a result of these delays, from 8 April 2002, asylum-seekers continue to be entitled to asylum support for 28 days following a decision of the Home Office to grant asylum or ELR, or after an adjudicator or the Tribunal has found them to be a refugee (the previous period of grace was only 14 days).

Further irritation is caused as status letters very often contain mistakes as to the person's name and date of birth. This can lead to delays in establishing entitlements and needs to be remedied immediately by sending the document back to the Home Office for correction.

Backlog clearance

The Home Office recognises the problem of claims being outstanding for many years and it has a general policy to grant exceptional leave where the claim has been undecided for seven years without a decision from the Home Office. A special backlog clearance policy was announced in the *Fairer, Faster, Firmer* White Paper of July 1998. The main features of this policy were as follows.

1 Asylum-seekers with asylum claims outstanding since before 1 July 1993 would normally be granted indefinite leave unless their presence was not conducive to the public good (e.g., because of their conviction for a serious criminal offence) or the claim had been made after the commencement of deportation or removal proceedings.

2 For applications made between 1 July 1993 and 31 December 1995, compassionate or exceptional factors would be weighed up to consider the grant of exceptional leave. People in this category were sent special questionnaires asking them about their family, their record of working, or doing voluntary or community work, and their health.

3 All applications made after 31 December 1995 would be decided in the normal way.

In the majority of cases in categories 1 and 2 above, exceptional leave of four years was normally granted.

The backlog, which once stood at over 100,000 cases, had been reduced to 24,000 as at June 2001.

Fresh claims for asylum

Where an asylum application has gone through the process of decision and appeal and has still been unsuccessful, it is always possible to make further representations to the Home Office to try to overturn the decision. The Home Office must consider all further representations which are made. However, in relation to some second applications, the Home Office is required to go further and to acknowledge that the asylum-seeker has made a 'fresh' claim to asylum with the result that, if the further representations are refused, a formal notice of decision must be issued against which there is a further right of appeal. A 'fresh' claim to asylum therefore re-triggers the whole asylum decision-making process as though it was a first claim.

The principles concerning fresh claims were established by the Court of Appeal in *Onibiyo* in which a young Nigerian asylum-seeker whose father, one of the first failed asylum-seekers to be returned by the UK to Nigeria following the execution of Ken Saro-Wiwa, disappeared after his return. On the facts of the case, the court did not overturn the decision of the Home Office that the case did not amount to a fresh claim, but the court set out a test for determining whether a fresh claim had been made. This test subsequently became part of the immigration rules:

'Where an asylum applicant has previously been refused asylum during his stay in the UK, the Secretary of State will determine whether any further representations should be treated as a fresh application for asylum. The Secretary of State will treat representations as a fresh application for asylum if the claim advanced in the representations is sufficiently different from the earlier claim that there is a realistic prospect that [asylum will be granted]. In considering whether to treat the representations as a fresh claim, the Secretary of State will disregard any material which: (i) is not significant; or (ii) is not credible; or (iii) was available to the applicant at the time when the previous application was refused or when any appeal was determined'.
(para 346, HC 395).

The test is often difficult to pass. If an asylum-seeker's account of events has been comprehensively disbelieved, significant evidence which could make a difference to the claim will be required. In many cases, people try to rely upon material which could and should have been put forward at the time of the earlier application or appeal. Although that evidence can be used to try to persuade the Home Office that the person is, in fact, a refugee, it is discounted in deciding whether there is a fresh claim to asylum which gives rise to further appeal rights. However, it has been recognised that asylum-seekers who are traumatised through unspeakable experiences may only relate those events at a later stage in an environment in which they feel able to do so. Where this is the case, the evidence should not be discounted (see *Ejon*).

In cases where the decision of the Home Office refusing asylum which gave rise to the appeal was before 2 October 2000, asylum-seekers who cannot pass the fresh claim test may still obtain a human rights appeal after the dismissal of their asylum appeals. This was the result of the undertaking given by the Home Office before the IAT in the case of *Pardeepan*, to the effect that those unable to raise human rights during the course of their asylum appeals would be given time to raise them subsequently and to appeal if necessary. However, even in those cases, the IAT has issued guidelines that the second adjudicator will always take the decision of the earlier adjudicator as the starting point in determining the second appeal (see *Devaseelan*).

12 Family reunion and travel

This chapter deals with two of the most important considerations for asylum-seekers after they have been allowed to remain in the UK: their ability to be reunited with their family members abroad and their ability to travel out of the UK and return. The position is different depending upon whether a person has been granted asylum as a refugee or granted exceptional leave to remain in the UK on human rights or other grounds. In both cases, refugee status is the more beneficial status. Under 'family reunion' we look at the situation of family members wanting to come and join people who have already been granted leave in the UK. For the position of family members who arrive with the asylum-seeker, or who arrive before a decision is made on the principal's asylum claim and who wish to be considered as dependants of the asylum-seeker, see under 'dependants' ▶ pages 192-194.

In all cases concerning family reunion, advisers should consider not just the immigration rules and Home Office policy but also the effect of Article 8 ECHR ▶ see pages 255-266. In some cases, family members may be able to rely upon the presence of a sponsor and other family members in the UK in an application for transfer of refugee status or in an application for asylum from abroad. These cases are rare but for more details of them ▶ see pages 174-177.

Family reunion

Where the sponsor has refugee status

The Final Act of the Conference which adopted the 1951 Refugee Convention recommended that governments ensure the refugee's family unity. In response, the Home Office has, for many years, maintained a policy of allowing the spouse and minor children of the refugee to join them in the UK. In October 2000, this long-standing policy was finally incorporated into the immigration rules (paras 352A–352F HC 395).

In order to be admitted as the spouse of a refugee:

- the applicant must be married to a person who has been granted leave in the UK as a refugee;
- the marriage must have taken place before the refugee left their country in order to seek asylum;
- the applicant must not be a person who would be excluded from the protection of the Refugee Convention under Article 1F if they applied in their own right for asylum.

In order to be admitted as the child of a refugee, the applicant must:

- be the child of a person who has been granted leave in the UK as a refugee;
- be under 18;
- not be leading an independent life, be unmarried and not have formed an independent family unit;
- have been part of the pre-existing family unit at the time the refugee left their country in order to seek asylum;
- not be a person who would be excluded under Article 1F of the Refugee Convention if they were to seek asylum in their own right.

Significantly, the rules for family reunion do not require the family members to be maintained and accommodated in the UK without recourse to public funds. If the family members cannot, however, satisfy the above rules, they may still be able to make an application under the ordinary rules relating to family members, under which they will generally have to satisfy the maintenance and accommodation requirements. The immigration authorities are prepared to be flexible to some extent in applying the immigration rules to family members of refugees ▶see below pages 225-226.

If the application is accepted, the rules provide for limited leave to enter or remain to be granted. In practice, however, as with refugees, indefinite leave is normally given.

The need for entry clearance

If the family member is applying from overseas, then the rules state that they must obtain an entry clearance. If, however, the family member is applying for leave to remain, for example, where the family member is already in the UK for some other purpose under the immigration rules, then the rules do not require them to have an entry clearance. Often, family members applying from abroad do not have and are unable to obtain travel documents in order to come to the UK from their national authorities. Part of the reason for this may be that the family members are afraid to approach those authorities because their sponsor is wanted by them and they may make it difficult for the family members to leave. Entry clearance posts are able to issue a one-way identity document called 'GV3', valid for travel to the UK together with the entry clearance.

Entry clearance fees

The fees which are payable for obtaining entry clearances (for the amounts ▶see page 738), are often waived in family reunion cases where the sponsor is a refugee or has exceptional leave. In the High Court case of *Jama*, a decision of the embassy in Addis Ababa to refuse to waive fees was challenged in circumstances where the sponsor had exceptional leave and was claiming income support and the children family members were in a refugee camp with no resources. Before the final hearing of the case, the embassy agreed to waive the fees. On 14 January 2002, the Joint Entry Clearance Unit (now 'UK Visas') issued guidance in *draft* to ECOs which states:

- fees for entry clearances can be waived in the case of 'destitute persons'. This most commonly occurs in family reunion cases and only rarely in other cases;
- *Jama* (above) does not 'bind future policy' but it indicates that a judge would find in favour of applicants in cases where the circumstances are similar;
- it is for the applicants to show that they are destitute;
- in deciding whether an applicant is destitute, the ECO is entitled to consider what support the applicant could reasonably expect to receive from the sponsor. The receipt of income support and other allowances by the sponsor 'are not conclusive proof of financial incapacity' although 'they may be taken as pointing to financial incapacity and should be given due weight'. ECOs should also seek details of the savings held by the sponsor;
- if the applicant's travel to the UK is being met by the sponsor, the ECO can assume that there is an ability to pay the entry clearance fee. If the cost is being met by a charity or non-governmental organisation, this strengthens the claim of destitution.

WHAT THE RULES MEAN

Person granted leave as a refugee

The family reunion rules are for those who have sponsors who have actually been recognised as refugees. Entry clearance will not be granted under the rules in order for a family member to come to the UK to join an asylum-seeker.

Pre-existing family

The rules allow the admission of family members who were part of the pre-existing family. For spouses, the marriage must have taken place before the person granted asylum had left the country of origin. Child applicants must also have formed part of the family unit at that time.

Before the family reunion policy was made part of the immigration rules, it was possible to succeed with family reunion where the marriage had taken place after the grant of refugee status, for example, where the couple had been engaged but were prevented from marrying because of the refugee's flight. The Immigration Appeal Tribunal (IAT) had held in the case of *Gamelsid* that these circumstances came within the policy. The rules do not allow for these circumstances but advisers have noted that some posts continue to be more generous than others where the marriage takes place after the refugee has left. It is certainly worth raising Article 8 ECHR in these cases.

Children leading an independent life

The additional rule that requires the children of a refugee to be unmarried, not leading an independent life and not to have formed an independent family unit, is the same as that which applies under the general rules relating to the admission of children ►see page 370.

Exclusion under Article 1F Refugee Convention

It will be very rare for family members to be excluded from family reunion because they would have been excluded under Article 1F if they had applied for asylum. This will occur only if the family member:

- has committed a crime against peace, a war crime or a crime against humanity;
- has committed a serious 'non-political' crime outside the UK;
- is guilty of acts 'contrary to the purposes and principles of the United Nations'.

For more details about when these circumstances apply to refugees generally ►see pages 168-169.

Other family members

The rules for family reunion for refugees cover only 'spouses' and minor children. The rules do not cover other family members such as common law or same-sex partners or over-age children. Where the family members are not spouses or minor children, as well as considering the use of Article 8 ECHR , applicants might also benefit from any of the following:

- as a concession outside the rules, the Home Office states that it may 'exceptionally allow other family members (e.g. elderly parents) to come to the UK if there are "compelling, compassionate circumstances"' (API, Ch6, s2, para 2). This might, therefore, include minor siblings or children over the age of 18 who are still dependent and have not formed independent families of their own;

- the *UNHCR Handbook* which states that the *'minimum'* requirement is that spouse and minor children are admitted (paragraph 185) and:

'In practice other dependants, such as aged parents of refugees, are normally considered if they are living in the same household...the principle of family unity operates in favour of dependants not against them';

- according to a letter written by the then immigration minister, Barbara Roche MP, on 30 June 2000, the Home Office will also admit to the UK both the parents of a child who has been granted refugee status and the other minor dependent children of those parents:

'Under the family reunion concession, a minor who has been recognised as a refugee can immediately apply for his parents and any of their other minor dependent children to join them in the United Kingdom';

- one of the recommendations made by the Council of Europe Committee of Ministers concerning family reunion for refugees and others on 15 December 1999 was:

'Member states should pay particular attention to applications for family reunion concerning persons who are in a vulnerable position. In particular, with regard to unaccompanied minors, member states should, with a view to family reunion, co-operate with children or their representatives in order to trace the members of the family of the unaccompanied minor'.

Where the pre-existing family member arrives without entry clearance

Family members who arrive in the UK and seek family reunion with a person who has been granted refugee status, but who do not have an entry clearance, are asking for discretion to be exercised outside the immigration rules in order for them to be admitted. The same is true of family members who arrive in the UK after a negative decision has been made on the principal applicant's asylum claim but where the principal is later successful in their appeal. The Home Office may not accept these latter applicants as 'dependants' on the asylum claim but will not remove them until the outcome of the asylum appeal (see API, Ch6, s1, para 2). Those who arrive before an initial decision has been made are usually treated as dependants and automatically treated in line with the asylum-seekers.

Whether discretion will be exercised will largely depend on whether the other requirements of the rules are satisfied for family reunion, in particular, whether the applicants are pre-existing members of the refugee's family. In cases where the immigration authorities refuse to exercise discretion or to defer decisions to remove family members until the outcome of the principal application, the family member should consider whether they wish to apply for asylum in their own right, even if the danger they would face is mainly because of their connection with the relative they are coming to join. An Article 8 claim should also be considered in these circumstances.

Where the family member is not part of the pre-existing family

Where a spouse is applying to stay with a refugee and the marriage took place after the refugee left their country of origin, the general marriage rules will normally apply. However, the Home Office has stated (see API Ch6, s3, para 3):

'If the sponsor is a recognised refugee in the United Kingdom, case-workers should be flexible about the application of the maintenance and accommodation requirements. This is because it might be unreasonable to expect someone who has fled persecution to be able to be self-sufficient here immediately.'

These situations will most commonly arise when a refugee meets and marries a person, who themselves need leave to be in the UK, after their arrival in the UK. If the relationship (although not the marriage itself) was in existence before the refugee came to the UK, the immigration authorities may still be persuaded to treat the case as one of family reunion. If not, then at least this more flexible approach to the rules will apply.

Where the sponsor has exceptional leave

As their status letter informs them, those with exceptional leave granted following a refusal of asylum, have no 'right' to be joined by any family members. There is nothing in the immigration rules about them and they have to rely on Home Office policy. Under this policy, as with family reunion for refugees, the 'pre-existing' spouse and minor children (and other family members, as a matter of discretion) may be considered for admission. The Home Office has stated that family reunion will not normally be considered until the sponsor with ELR has completed four years in this category (see API Ch6, s2, para 3.2). After four years, the requirement in the immigration rules that the sponsor has indefinite leave will be waived. In practice, however, since July 1998, most people with ELR will be granted indefinite leave after four years anyway. Applications may be granted before the four-year point but only if there are 'compelling, compassionate circumstances' (see API above).

The four-year rule operates very harshly in many cases. For example, in one case, the Home Office did not consider that the case of a Kurdish child who had cerebral palsy was compelling enough, nor was his death considered enough to allow his brothers and sisters to join their parents afterwards until the family's solicitors had begun a judicial review application. Refugee community groups and others have been campaigning against the four-year rule and it has now become somewhat easier for children to join parents when both are in the UK with ELR.

Maintenance and accommodation

The current API states that 'in all cases, the applicant will be expected to satisfy the maintenance and accommodation rules', but these can, of course also be waived exceptionally.

Interestingly, in the section dealing with marriage applications where the marriage post-dates the sponsor coming to the UK, the API indicates that leave will not be refused on maintenance and accommodation grounds alone (see API, Ch6, s3, para 3).

Other family reunion policies

In addition to the immigration rules and the general concessions made to the immigration rules in family reunion cases, the Home Office sometimes operates concessions which relate to families of a particular nationality. From 1988 until January 1994, the Home Office operated a concession for Somali family members in Somalia or in refugee camps in Ethiopia or Djibouti, who were unable to travel to a British embassy to apply for entry clearance. Their sponsors in the UK were able to apply to the Home Office for entry clearance on their behalf and provide the documents in support so that the Home Office could then inform the British post that entry clearance should be granted. This made the process easier for displaced families but the concession was withdrawn when the Home Office believed it had become safe for people to travel again. There was no substantive appeal against the 'preliminary assessment' letters. A similar arrangement for the families of Vietnamese refugees was also withdrawn on 1 November 1999.

Between 1988 and 17 January 1996, the Home Office operated the Somali Family Reunion Policy. In addition to the procedural concession mentioned above, it provided for a more flexible approach to the family members who could qualify. It enabled family members who were dependent members of the refugee's immediate family unit to be admitted. This was largely in recognition of the extended and inter-dependent nature of Somali families. The most beneficial aspects of the policy only applied to refugee sponsors, not to those with ELR. The policy remains important for those who made applications before 17 January 1996.

Refusals and appeals

If entry clearance is refused, then there is a right of appeal to an adjudicator. It may be that the family member wishes to argue that they have been refused under the immigration rules when, in fact, they satisfy them. However, appellants are also able to argue on appeals that a particular published policy has not been taken into account or properly applied and that a decision is 'not in accordance with the law'. The Court of Appeal decision in *D S Abdi* confirmed that it is possible to succeed at an appeal on this basis. Even where the policy is set in vague terms, for example, where there is a concession which relates to showing 'exceptional compassionate circumstances', these arguments can still be raised. In its ruling in *Onen*, the IAT stated that an appellant can ask for the appeal to be allowed on the grounds that the immigration authorities failed to take relevant matters into account in deciding whether those circumstances exist.

It is also important that the right to respect for private and family life under Article 8 ECHR of the family members is raised and considered in these appeals. Although it does not create a right of entry, all immigration decisions must be taken in accordance with the ECHR. Much of the Article 8 case law concerns marriage cases where couples might be able to enjoy their family life in another country. This will usually not be the case where the sponsor has been granted leave to remain in recognition that they cannot return to their country. However, the question which will arise is whether the interference which occurs as a result of the refusal of entry is 'proportionate' to the interests of immigration control.

Foreign travel

People with refugee status

A person recognised as a refugee is entitled to a travel document known as a 'Convention travel document' or CTD. A fee is payable with the application which, from 14 January 2002, is £30.00. Since 19 August 1996, the Home Office has issued machine-readable dark blue documents ▶see page 124 for an example. Previously, they were pale blue cardboard-covered ones. The documents are valid for all countries except the one from which the person needed asylum. CTDs are normally valid for a period of 10 years. For general details about travel documents issued by the Home Office and about making applications for them ▶see pages 88-89.

Because refugees are generally granted indefinite leave, their leave does not lapse when they travel abroad unless they remain outside the country for 2 years. However, a refugee should be re-admitted to the UK at any time during the validity of the travel document so that remaining outside the UK for more than two years will not disqualify the refugee as it will other returning residents (see *Shirreh*).

The refugee should continue to use the CTD, even after obtaining settlement, until he or she obtains either British nationality or the nationality of another country. Under no circumstances should a refugee attempt to return to their own country on a CTD. Refugees should not attempt to return to their own countries at all without taking very careful advice ▶see pages 167-168 for further details.

Some countries which have not signed the Refugee Convention do not recognise CTDs. Under the Council of Europe Agreement on the Abolition of Visas for Refugees 1959, a refugee travelling on a CTD can travel to any EU country, except France, without obtaining a visa for that country, provided that the trip is for less than three months. Once a refugee has naturalised as a British citizen they are of course entitled to a British passport and can travel using that ▶see Chapter 28 for the naturalisation requirements.

People granted exceptional leave

People with ELR are told that they are expected to use the passport of their original country. If they travel to any other country they should be readmitted to the UK. They will normally be given four years' leave and so they will not need an entry clearance in order to return. However, if they return to their country of origin, they may be refused re-entry on the grounds that they no longer need exceptional treatment and protection from the UK. If that happens, they may need to make a new application to re-enter on asylum grounds. This will be considered by the Home Office on the basis of their current circumstances.

Even if they are re-admitted at port, it may still be more difficult for those with ELR who returned to their country of origin, to gain an extension of their stay in the future. It may be clear that they have travelled back to the country to which they said they could not return, and the Home Office may ask more questions to determine whether it is now safe for them to return permanently. If the country is one for which there is a blanket policy, and if there was an emergency reason for travel there, such as the serious illness or death of a close relative, further leave may be granted but this cannot be assumed.

Some people may not wish or be able to obtain travel documentation from their national authorities. Those people will be granted an inferior type of travel document to that issued to people with refugee status. It is called a certificate of identity and is brown in colour ▶see page 124 for an example. It is valid for all countries except the country of nationality or former habitual residence. The document is less useful than a CTD (▶see above) as some European countries refuse to recognise it. In addition, the Home Office may refuse to grant travel documents to those who were first granted ELR before 26 July 1993, unless they can produce evidence that they have been formally and unreasonably refused a passport by the authorities of the country of their nationality. For both these reasons, many people with ELR are keen to naturalise as British Citizens so that they can use British passports.

13   Human Rights

On 2 October 2000, the Human Rights Act 1998 (HRA) came into force. The importance of this was that most of the rights contained in the European Convention on Human Rights (ECHR) were incorporated into UK law. The immigration rules (para 2, HC 395) reflect this incorporation by requiring entry clearance officers, immigration officers and all the staff at the Home Office's Immigration and Nationality Directorate to make sure that their decisions comply with the ECHR. Before the HRA, in order to enforce the ECHR rights, a person would have to apply to the European Court of Human Rights (ECtHR) itself which is a long and complex process. Prior to 2 October, the most the UK courts could do was to ensure that the government took the ECHR rights into account when making decisions which affected peoples lives.

This chapter looks at the ECHR rights themselves and how they work ▶pages 233-238. It then looks at three particular areas in which the rights have a substantial impact in immigration cases:

1   claims for 'protection' from harm in the person's country of origin ▶see pages 239-251;

2   cases where forcing someone to leave the UK will have a particular detrimental effect upon them ▶see pages 251-255;

3   cases where the applicant has a family or other connection with the UK ▶see pages 255-266.

In 1 in particular, we look at the greater protection which the ECHR may give compared to the Refugee Convention. The most important ECHR rights for immigration cases are covered by Article 3 (prohibition on torture and inhuman and degrading treatment or punishment) and article 8 (right to respect for private and family life). Article 5 ECHR is also important as it sets out the circumstances in which people can be detained for immigration reasons. We look at Article 5 separately in Chapter 24 ▶see pages 498-502.

At the same time as the HRA came into force, the parts of the Immigration and Asylum Act 1999 which gave a right of appeal on human rights grounds also came into force (section 65). For human rights appeals ▶see pages 614-617. The one-stop appeals system was partly designed to ensure human rights are considered at the same time as other grounds. For details about this system ▶see pages 606-611, but there is a check-list of the different ways in which human rights can be raised below ▶see pages 266-267.

With effect from 2 April 2001, the government amended the Race Relations Act 1976 to prohibit race discrimination in immigration and asylum. However, the prohibition on discrimination is not absolute, there are circumstances where discrimination is permitted. Race discrimination appeals are triggered in the same way as human rights appeals. We look at race discrimination on pages 270-272.

European Convention on Human Rights (ECHR)

The European Convention for the Protection of Human Rights and Fundamental Freedoms (ECHR) is an international treaty of the Council of Europe that the UK ratified in 1951. The Council of Europe is an intergovernmental organisation which was formed at the end of the Second World War by the European countries who were keen, in the aftermath of the battle against fascism, to encourage respect for the rule of law, to protect fundamental freedoms and to protect social and economic development. The purpose of the ECHR was to ensure a 'fair balance' between the various fundamental rights of the individual against the interests of the wider community. The intention was to enable people to enforce their rights against the state where it breached those rights and, in some cases, to allow them to obtain compensation.

European Court of Human Rights (ECtHR)

The European Court of Human Rights is based in Strasbourg, France. The court has jurisdiction on all matters concerning the implementation and application of the ECHR and the protocols to the ECHR, both in cases of disputes between two states and in cases of an individual taking an action against a state. Each member state nominates one judge to the ECtHR. Before November 1998, if a complaint about human rights was to be taken to Europe, it first had to be made to the European Commission which would decide whether the complaint was admissible. The matter could then progress to the ECtHR itself. There is now one single court which makes decisions about whether the complaint is admissible and also makes the final ruling on the case.

People can raise the issue of whether their human rights have been violated by applying to the ECtHR. However, they must go through all the court procedures in the UK before they can make a complaint to the ECtHR. For details about how procedures before the ECtHR work ▶see pages 268-270. In practice, few cases will have to go that court because of the right to bring appeals in the UK.

The Human Rights Act 1998

The Human Rights Act 1998 (HRA) is the mechanism for incorporating rights granted by the ECHR into UK law. There are a number of 'protocols' to the ECHR which contain rights some of which are also incorporated. The way in which the HRA incorporates the rights is set out in the box.

THE HUMAN RIGHTS ACT 1998

The key points about the HRA are that it:

- states which rights under the ECHR are made part of UK law ▶see below;
- makes it unlawful for a 'public authority' (including the immigration authorities and the adjudicator or Immigration Appeal Tribunal) to act in a way that is incompatible with an incorporated ECHR right (s6 HRA);
- allows the 'victim' of the breach of human rights to bring claims in the appropriate court against the 'public authority' for actions that are in breach of the ECHR. In immigration cases this will usually be by bringing a human rights appeal;
- requires UK courts and tribunals (this includes adjudicators and the Immigration Appeal Tribunal) to take into account the judgments made on cases decided by the ECtHR (but ECtHR decisions are *not* binding on the UK courts and tribunals);
- requires that legislation which is made by Parliament and also regulations and rules which are made by the government (including the immigration rules) are interpreted in a way which 'so far as possible' is compatible with the ECHR incorporated rights;
- allows certain courts to make declarations of incompatibility where the legislation passed by Parliament is incompatible with the ECHR;
- allows people to claim compensation for breaches of their human rights.

The rights

Rights contained in the ECHR which have been incorporated

The following rights were incorporated into UK law by the HRA on 2 October 2000:

- the right to life (Article 2);
- prohibition on torture and inhuman or degrading treatment or punishment (Article 3);
- prohibition on slavery and forced labour (Article 4);
- right to liberty and security (Article 5);
- right to a fair trial (Article 6);
- protection from punishment for acts which were not offences at the time they were committed (Article 7);
- respect for private and family life, home and correspondence (Article 8);

- freedom of thought, conscience and religion (Article 9);
- freedom of expression (Article 10);
- freedom of assembly and association (Article 11);
- right to marry and found a family (Article 12);
- prohibition on discrimination (Article 14).

Protocol 1

- right to property (Article 1);
- right to education (Article 2);
- free and fair elections (Article 3).

Protocol 6

- abolition of the death penalty (Article 1);
- allowance for death penalty in time of war (Article 2).

The HRA does *not* incorporate the following two obligations on the state: to ensure that everyone within its jurisdiction has their rights safeguarded (Article 1); to ensure that there is a way of enforcing the rights in the state's own courts or institutions (Article 13). The government says that the reason for not specifically incorporating these rights is because they are already secured by bringing in the HRA itself.

The prohibition on discrimination

Article 14 is different from the other incorporated rights because it cannot be used on its own; there is no general right to be free from discrimination. Article 14 states that:

'The enjoyment of the rights and freedoms set forth in this Convention shall be secured without discrimination on any ground such as sex, race, colour, language, religion, political or other opinion, national or social origin, association with a national minority, property, birth or other status'.

Article 14 provides a right not to be discriminated against in 'enjoying' the other ECHR rights and so it can only be used together with those other rights. *However*, it is not actually necessary to establish a *breach* of the other ECHR rights in order to show that there has been discrimination. In order to show a breach of Article 14, it is necessary for an applicant to show:

- they have suffered less favourable treatment on one of the grounds mentioned or an equivalent ground; *and*
- the treatment *affects* their other rights under the ECHR.

However, there will be no breach of Article 14 if the state can show that there is a legitimate purpose for the discrimination and that the detriment to those discriminated against is outweighed by the interests of the community.

An example of how Article 14 might be used in immigration cases is the case of *Arman Ali*. In that case, the High Court stated that if the maintenance and accommodation requirements in the immigration rules did not allow a couple to be supported by others, they would not be compatible with Articles 8 and 14. This is because the rules would discriminate against people's ability to enjoy family life if they were less able to support *themselves* (such as the ill or the disabled) even though there would be no real justification for the less favourable treatment because there would be no increased demand on public funds. In the many circumstances in which the immigration laws do discriminate against different groups, the government's response would be that differentiation is justified in the interests of maintaining a proper immigration control.

In *Abdulaziz*, the ECtHR found unjustifiable gender discrimination in the different way in which the then immigration rules treated husbands and wives. However, in the same case the court accepted the government's justification for certain immigration rules relating to marriage (to exclude entry based on marriages which have been entered into for immigration reasons) which had a greater negative impact upon marriages between people from the Indian sub-continent. The court therefore rejected the claims based on race discrimination.

Derogations and reservations

There are certain circumstances in which a state is entitled to not observe the rights in the ECHR and protocols:

- A state can 'derogate' from the ECHR in times of 'war or other public emergency threatening the life of the nation' (Article 15). The state can only do this to the extent that the situation it faces 'strictly requires' the suspension of the rights. Some rights, however, cannot be derogated from under any circumstances (►see below). Under the ECHR as well as the HRA, the UK has to go through a specific process in order to derogate and specify the public emergency which applies. In contrast, when the state is relying upon the interests of the community in order to restrict other rights in *individual* cases, it can simply state that it is applying the restriction on the right which is already contained in the ECHR. The derogation of particular relevance to UK immigration law is the one made by the UK in relation to Article 5 and suspected 'international terrorists' ►see pages 496-497.

- A state can enter 'reservations' about any Convention rights when it signs up to them. The UK has entered a reservation about the requirement in Article 2 of the First Protocol to respect the right of parents to ensure that education and teaching are in conformity with the parents' religious and philosophical beliefs. The UK intends to comply with this right under its national laws 'only insofar as it is compatible with the provision of efficient instruction... and the avoidance of unreasonable public expenditure'.

Restrictions on the rights contained in the ECHR

Although the incorporated rights listed above read very grandly, in most cases they are subject to restrictions. The first means of restricting them (derogation and reservation) is dealt with above. We classify the rights into four groups depending upon the ways in which they can be limited or restricted as follows. For details ▶see the box below.

1 Rights which are absolute with no derogation permitted.

2 Rights which can be restricted but only in specifically defined circumstances.

3 Rights which can be restricted in more generally stated circumstances in the interests of society.

4 Rights which appear to be absolute but into which restrictions can be implied.

THE RESTRICTIONS UPON ECHR RIGHTS

The rights can be classified into four groups according to the different ways in which they are limited. The classifications are not precise but are useful in understanding the way in which the ECHR works.

1. Absolute rights which cannot be derogated from

For the ability of a state to 'derogate' from a right ▶see page 235. Rights which are absolute and 'non-derogable' are:

The right to life (Article 2). This right cannot be derogated from except where the death is the result of 'lawful acts of war'. Even though we have listed this right as 'absolute' in requiring the state to protect a person's life and to prevent it from being intentionally taken away, there are certain circumstances where the taking of a life is not regarded as breaching the right (▶see page 241 where the right is set out in full).

Prohibition on torture and inhuman and degrading treatment and punishment (Article 3). The fact that no derogation can be made from Article 3 is very important in immigration cases because it means that, whatever the emergency, a person cannot be sent to a country where they will be exposed to the prohibited treatment (▶see further below). *However*, as a result of the 11 September 2001 attacks, the UK has derogated from Article 5 (right to liberty) to enable suspected 'international terrorists' to be detained indefinitely even though they cannot, for example, under Article 3, be removed from the UK.

Prohibition of slavery (Article 4 paragraph 1). The prohibition against holding people in slavery or 'servitude' is an absolute, non-derogable right. However, the right not to be required to perform forced labour can be derogated from.

Prohibition on punishment for an act which was not a crime when it was committed (Article 7). Freedom from punishment for something that was not a crime when it was done, is another absolute, non-derogable right. However, this does not prevent criminal offences and penalties being imposed for acts which at the time when they were committed, were recognised by 'civilised nations' as being crimes.

2. Rights which can be restricted but only in specifically defined circumstances

The following rights are all subject to certain specific restrictions which are set out in the Convention itself. They can also be derogated from by the state in times of war or public emergency.

Right to liberty (Article 5). A person may be detained provided that domestic law authorises it for any of the following reasons: if they have been convicted of an offence; have failed to comply with an order of a Court; if they are suspected of committing an offence (or to prevent them from committing one); if they are of unsound mind, an alcoholic, drug addict or vagrant. Detention is also lawful under Article 5 in order to prevent the spread of infectious diseases or to prevent a person making an 'unauthorised entry' into the UK or for the purpose of deporting or extraditing them. For more details ▶see pages 498-502.

Right to marry (Article 12). The right to marry and to found a family can be restricted only by the 'national laws governing the exercise of the right'. There is no specific restriction on what laws the state is permitted to have but they must not undermine the essence of the right to marry.

Requirement to perform forced labour (Article 4). Requirements to perform labour are permitted where a person is lawfully detained under Article 5 or where the work is military service (or alternative civilian service), or there is an emergency which threatens the well-being of the community or it is work which is part of 'normal civic obligations'.

3. Rights which can be restricted by more generally stated circumstances, in the interests of society

The following rights are subject to more generally defined restrictions which can be applied by the state to individual cases. These rights can also be derogated from by the state in times of war or public emergency:

- respect for private and family life, home and correspondence (Article 8);
- freedom for a person to manifest their religion or beliefs (Article 9);
- freedom of expression (Article 10);
- freedom of assembly and association (Article 11).

In the case of these rights, the ECHR provides a positive right in the first paragraph of the relevant article, followed by the circumstances in which the right can legitimately be interfered with in the second paragraph. In each case, it is for the applicant to show that the protected right is being interfered with. If the applicant can show an interference, the state must then demonstrate that the interference was:

- 'in accordance with the law' or 'prescribed by law'; and
- carried out for one of the purposes referred to in the relevant article (the permitted reasons given in the different articles vary slightly but the following are

examples: the interests of public safety, the rights and freedoms of others, the prevention of disorder and crime, the economic well-being of the country, national security); and

- 'necessary' in the interests of a democratic society. This is generally taken to mean that the interference in the person's human rights must be 'proportionate' to, or in a fair balance against, the interest of the community which the state is seeking to uphold.

These elements are looked at more closely under Article 8 ▶see pages 255-266. It should be noted that the exercise of freedom of expression, assembly and association of 'aliens' can be interfered with by the state without regard to the above rights (Article 16 ECHR) but the meaning of this restriction has rarely been considered by the ECtHR.

4. Rights which appear to be absolute but into which restrictions can be implied

The following rights may appear to be absolute but have actually been interpreted with implied restrictions. Another way of looking at them is to say that the actual content of a particular right itself is more limited than it might at first appear. These rights can also be derogated from by the state in times of war or public emergency.

Right to a fair trial (Article 6). The ECHR states that there is a right to a fair trial in deciding a person's 'civil rights and obligations' and in deciding any charge against them. Article 6 then goes on to state some basic minimum rights in criminal cases; for example that everyone shall be presumed innocent until proved guilty and that those accused are entitled to time to prepare a defence and to interpretation facilities. However, Article 6 does not define the actual meaning of 'fair trial'. Because the words are open to interpretation, the ECtHR has held that there is room for implying limitations where necessary (*Golder*, ECtHR).

Right to possessions, education, free elections (rights under the First Protocol). These rights are also limited by implication. For example, a state does not 'deny' a person an education provided that it grants equal access to the educational facilities which exist and allows people to gain benefit from their education. Within those limits, the state is not required to set up particular types or levels of education (*Belgian Linguistics* case, ECtHR). States may reasonably regulate access to education, for example, a person who has not passed their qualifying examinations may be denied access to a university or a further education place.

It should also be noted that Article 17 ECHR (which is also incorporated) tries to prevent extremists, for example, fascists, from taking advantage of the rights in the Convention in order to destroy others' ECHR rights:

'Nothing in this Convention may be interpreted as implying for any state, group or person any right to engage in any activity or perform any act aimed at the destruction of any of the rights and freedoms set forth herein or at their limitation to a greater extent than is provided for in the Convention.'

Using human rights in immigration cases

In this part we look at three types of situation arising in immigration cases where rights under the ECHR are very important.

Claims for protection. In many cases, people claim protection in the UK as a result of a fear of a particular harm that will be inflicted on them if they return to their country of origin. These are cases where the person is likely to have claimed asylum. In some circumstances, it may be possible to succeed by relying on ECHR rights, although a claim could not succeed under the Refugee Convention. Potentially, many of the different ECHR rights are relevant in these cases, although Article 3 ECHR is the most important.

Detrimental effect of return. There are some cases where a person claims that they cannot return to their country of origin because of the physical, mental or other detrimental effect that return would have upon them. Often, these cases are about the standard of medical or other facilities available to a person in the country to which they are to be sent. These cases are sometimes, but not always, also brought under the Refugee Convention ▶see pages 251-255. These cases will usually raise issues under Articles 3 and 8 ECHR.

Family or other connections. In some cases, people can argue that removing them from, or refusing to admit them to, the UK is a breach of their rights under Article 8 ECHR (private and family life) because of their need to be together with family members or because of the other connections they have developed with the UK ▶see pages 255-266.

Below, we look at these three categories in turn.

Claims for protection

Some asylum-seekers who do not qualify for protection under the 1951 Convention, may still qualify for protection under the ECHR. Getting refugee status is, for most people, better than succeeding in a human rights claim. This is because success under the 1951 Convention results in an immediate grant of indefinite leave instead of limited exceptional leave and because of the other benefits of refugee status such as access to 1951 Convention travel documents and rights to family reunion ▶see Chapter 12. These additional rights of refugee status have repeatedly been stressed in the higher courts (see e.g., *Karanakaran*, Court of Appeal). Human rights claims should not therefore be brought *instead of* refugee status claims, if a refugee claim can be made. Advisers should, however, be prepared to emphasise the human rights aspects of an asylum claim where there are reasons to think that the claimant may obtain protection under the ECHR *even if* they cannot demonstrate that they are a refugee.

Below, we look at the different rights in turn and how they may be used in these cases. First, it is necessary to consider whether the ECHR can be used in a claim for protection at all where it is claimed that a person will suffer harm when removed to another country – this has become known as the argument about the 'extra-territorial' effect of the ECHR.

Extra-territorial effect of ECHR

The Home Office has taken the position that, where an applicant fears some form of ill-treatment in their country of origin, Article 3 is the only right under the ECHR which can protect them. The Home Office argues that this is because it is only Article 3 which has 'extra-territorial' effect. It says that Article 3 can be used in these circumstances because it is such an important, fundamental right that a state must not only not directly inflict the harm, but must also not expose a person to that harm by sending them somewhere else where they may receive it. The ECtHR has, in many cases, prevented states from sending a person to another country where they will face Article 3 treatment (see *Soering* and *Chahal*, both ECtHR).

The IAT considered this question in the starred decision of *Kacaj* and held that:

- there is no real reason to use the term 'extra-territorial' effect because if a person will face a violation of their human rights in the country to which they are sent, the 'sending' country commits a breach of the ECHR in its own territory by the act of expulsion;
- all the articles of the ECHR (with, for special reasons, the possible exception of Article 2) have what has been called 'extra-territorial' effect;
- where the claim is for protection, it will be rare that a breach of one of the rights which are restricted by generally stated conditions (such as Article 8, ▶see above pages 237–238) can be established if Article 3 is not breached. This is because, in those cases, the state will usually be able to justify the return on the grounds that it is in the interests of immigration control.

The IAT refused to follow the decision of the Court of Appeal in *Holub* concerning the right not to be denied an education ▶see further below page 255. In that case the court had not decided the question of extra-territorial effect 'authoritatively' because it found that there would be no breach in returning the applicants anyway. What little European case law there is on the topic suggests that the ECHR should not be limited as the Home Office argues. In *Soering*, the court suggested that a 'flagrant' breach of the right to a fair trial under Article 6 in the country of destination may amount to a breach of the sending country's obligations. In *Devaseelan*, the IAT applied this approach to Articles 5 and 6. It stated:

'The reason why flagrant denial or gross violation is to be taken into account is that it is only in such a case – where the right will be completely denied or nullified in the destination country – that it can be said that removal will breach the treaty obligations of the signatory state however those obligations might be interpreted or whatever might be said by or behalf of the destination state'.

In *Bensaid*, the ECtHR appeared to accept that an Algerian who complained of being returned in circumstances where he might not be able to access proper health care could, in principle, rely on Article 8 (private life).

Kacaj was appealed to the Court of Appeal who sent the case back to the IAT for reconsideration but on different grounds to the points covered above. It is likely that there will be further legal developments in this area.

The right to life (Article 2)

'1 Everyone's right to life shall be protected by law. No one shall be deprived of his life intentionally save in the execution of a sentence of a court following his conviction of a crime for which this penalty is provided by law.

2 Deprivation of life shall not be regarded as inflicted in contravention of this article when it results from the use of force which is not more than absolutely necessary:

a) in defence of any person from unlawful violence;

b) in order to effect a lawful arrest or to prevent the escape of a person lawfully detained;

c) in action lawfully taken for the purpose of quelling a riot or insurrection.'

Although Article 2 allows the death penalty, there is a further 'optional' protocol to the ECHR (number 6), which the UK has signed up to, and which states that the death penalty is to be abolished except in times of war.

Article 2 requires a state not to take life (except in the lawful situations described) and also to act positively to protect it. Article 2 can be used in cases where there is a risk of extra-judicial or judicial killing by agents of the state, or where there is a risk of fatal violence from others against which the state cannot offer the required standard of protection (*Osman*, ECtHR). However, Article 2 has been held not to protect a serving soldier whose occupation is a hazardous one (*Fadli*).

In *Cicek* and in *Tas*, the ECtHR found that the Turkish authorities were responsible for the disappearances and deaths of individuals following their detention by the Turkish authorities. Of particular concern to the court was Turkey's failure to investigate, explain or justify the deaths in custody of these persons. In the court's view, this was a breach of the state's procedural obligation to protect the right to life under Article 2. The unacknowledged detention was also found to be a grave violation of Article 5. In *Tas*, the court also found that the family members of the deceased had suffered a violation of their Article 3 rights because of the state's attitude and reaction to them when they attempted to obtain information about the circumstances of the death of their family member.

In *Kacaj*, the IAT queried whether Article 2 would have 'extra-territorial effect'. However, in practice, most breaches of Article 2 will also be breaches of Article 3.

Prohibition on torture or inhuman or degrading treatment or punishment (Article 3)

'No one shall be subjected to torture or to inhuman or degrading treatment or punishment.'

Article 3 has the greatest impact for asylum-seekers. There is no doubt about it having 'extra-territorial' effect. It is also not restricted in the protection which it provides by qualifications or exceptions.

In *Kacaj*, the IAT considered the standard of proof in Article 3 cases. It concluded that there was nothing to suggest that the standard should be any different from the Refugee Convention standard. The question is whether the applicant has established that there is a 'real risk' that, if returned, he or she will be exposed to the prohibited treatment.

Article 3 can be divided into three separate categories of ill treatment:

1 Torture.
2 Inhuman treatment or punishment.
3 Degrading treatment or punishment.

It is necessary to show that the ill-treatment feared is of sufficient severity to meet that protected by any of these three forms of harm. Torture is the most severe. Inhuman and degrading treatment are less severe. In deciding whether the treatment is severe enough, it is necessary to take into account both the likely duration of the treatment and factors relating to the victim, such as their sex, age and health and the corresponding effect upon them (*Ireland v UK*, ECtHR). Harm which is inhuman or degrading may be inflicted by way of 'treatment' or 'punishment' and there is a large area of overlap between the two.

Torture. Torture is the most serious form of harm. It is deliberate, inhuman treatment which causes very serious suffering (*Selmouni*, ECtHR). Torture is not defined in the ECHR but it is given a definition in other international human rights instruments such as the UN Convention Against Torture and Other Cruel Inhuman or Degrading Treatment or Punishment. In international law, torture is usually considered to:

- cause severe pain or suffering, either physical or mental;
- be intentionally inflicted to obtain a confession or information or to intimidate or coerce;
- be inflicted by a public official.

However, torture under Article 3 is not necessarily so limited. A single act which causes sufficiently severe suffering will constitute torture. So in *Aydin*, in which a woman had been stripped, beaten, sprayed with cold water and raped, the ECtHR considered that the sexual violation itself would have been sufficient to meet the definition.

CIRCUMSTANCES IN WHICH ARTICLE 3 ECHR MAY PROVIDE PROTECTION WHEN THE REFUGEE CONVENTION DOES NOT

1. **No exclusions from protection**. The right to be protected under Article 3 is absolute and unqualified. A person excluded from protection under the 1951 Convention because of their conduct or because they are a threat to national security may not be removed if, as a result, they will be exposed to a risk of treatment contrary to Article 3. In *Chahal*, the applicant had been involved in political activities in the UK in support of the struggle for freedom in Punjab. The Home Secretary made a decision to deport him on the grounds of national security. He was detained and eventually lost his case for protection under the 1951 Convention. The UK resisted Mr Chahal's claim that a return to India would expose him to a risk of torture on the basis that there was a balance to be struck between the right and the person's conduct. This was rejected by the ECtHR which stated:

   '…whenever substantial grounds have been shown for believing that an individual would face a real risk of being subjected to treatment contrary to Article 3 if removed to another State, the responsibility of the contracting state to safeguard him or her against such treatment is engaged in the event of expulsion. In these circumstances, the activities of the individual in question, however undesirable or dangerous, cannot be a material consideration. The protection afforded by Article 3 is thus wider than that provided by Articles 32 and 33 of the United Nations 1951 Convention on the status of refugees'.

2. **No 'Convention reason' needed**. Under the Refugee Convention, asylum-seekers have to show that they risk harm as a result of one of the reasons listed (race, religion, nationality, political opinion, membership of a particular social group). No such 'reason' for the harm has to be shown under Article 3. The purpose of Article 3 is to protect individuals from serious harm regardless of why it is caused. So, for example, those whose fears of returning to their country result from family pressure, or danger from criminal (e.g., mafia) attacks, may be protected by Article 3.

3. **Protection in civil war situations**. Exposure to the 'ordinary' effects of a civil war will not amount to persecution for a 1951 Convention reason, unless the risk to the particular individual is 'over and above' the risk to the general population as part of the 'ordinary' consequences of civil war ▶see *Adan* on pages 162-163. However, Article 3 can give protection in these circumstances even though the risk to the applicant is the same as the risk to others (see *Ahmed*, ECtHR, where the asylum-seekers feared being returned to Somalia).

4. **No need to show a risk of 'persecution'**. Although it is becoming more accepted that human rights has a large part to play in deciding whether what a person fears amounts to 'persecution', this is not always accepted. In *Kagema*, the Court of Appeal held that persecution was an uncomplicated factual question which gave the decision-maker a wide margin to decide whether the treatment does in fact qualify. In *Ravichandran*, the short judgement of Lord Justice Staughton is often quoted to the effect that persecution must be at least serious and persistent (indicating repeated events). Article 3 may therefore provide greater protection because:

   - Article 3 does not carry with it a requirement of continuation or persistence;
   - the lower intensity forms of harm (inhuman and degrading treatment and punishment) may provide protection where the harm is not severe enough to amount to 'persecution'.

In *Kacaj*, the IAT recognised that Article 3 could be violated by actions which did not have a 'sufficiently systematic character to amount to persecution' but doubted whether there would be many instances in which treatment that breached Article 3 would not also amount to 'persecution'.

5. **'Non-state agents' cases.** An essential element of persecution under the Refugee Convention is that there must be a failure on the part of the state in the country of origin to provide a 'sufficiency of protection'. Following *Horvath*, if the 'failure' on the state's part is absent, it appeared to be the case that a person is not a refugee *even if the protection does not actually eradicate the risk of serious harm*. Like the Refugee Convention, the ECtHR has held that Article 3 can apply where the danger emanates from persons who are not public officials (*HLR*, ECtHR). Unlike the Refugee Convention, however, the wording of Article 3 does *not* indicate that there has to be some state involvement or responsibility for the risk of harm. It appears, therefore, that Article 3 protects against any real risk of harm from non-state agents which exists, regardless of whether there is a sufficiency of protection. However, in *Kacaj*, the IAT held that the 'sufficiency of protection' test also applies to claims under Article 3. In both *Kacaj* and the High Court case of *Dhima*, the courts seem to have interpreted *Horvath* more favourably to asylum-seekers. Those cases seem to indicate that the protection must be 'sufficient' to eliminate the 'reality' of the risk of harm. This would seem to close the gap opened up by *Horvath*. There may be more developments in this area.

6. **No need for 'ill-treatment'.** Article 3 does not require ill-treatment by the receiving state, any person or group of people. It could be breached simply by the effect of removal on the individual in question or the effect on them of the withdrawal of facilities presently provided in the sending state. We look at this under the category of case 'detrimental effect of return' ►see below pages 251-255.

7. **British citizen relatives.** Article 3 does not require that a person is outside his own country. The 1951 Convention requires that a person is outside his country of origin or habitual residence. Article 3 applies to anyone within the territory of a contracting state. This means that Article 3 could apply, for example, to cases where a British citizen child will effectively be forced to leave with a non-British parent where the conditions which they would face in the place to which they are removed amount to inhuman and degrading treatment.

8. **Third country cases.** Article 3 may make a difference in 'safe third country' cases where removal is to be to a European Union member state under 'standing arrangements' (such as the Dublin Convention). In these cases, the government has passed legislation which declares those countries to be safe (see s11 1999 Act). The difficulty that asylum-seekers now have in challenging decisions on 'safety' grounds are made clear by the Court of Appeal case of *Ibrahim* and the High Court case of *Mohammed & Others*. In principle it is a breach of a country's obligations under Article 3 to send a person to another country from where they will be removed in breach of Article 3 (see *TI v UK*, ECtHR). Even in those cases, the Home Office relies on the ability to bring a human rights claim in the country to which the person is to be sent after their removal or to apply to the ECtHR from that country (see *Mohammed & Others*, High Court; *Yogathas & Thangarasa*, Court of Appeal). *Yogathas & Thangarasa* are due to be heard by the House of Lords.

Many of the differences in protection provided by Article 3 and the 1951 Convention listed above, also apply to the protections provided by the other rights under the ECHR.

Inhuman treatment. For there to be 'inhuman treatment' the degree of suffering does not need to be as serious as for torture and it does not need to be deliberately inflicted (*Ireland v UK*, ECtHR). In that case, the 'five techniques' of wall standing, hooding, subjection to noise, sleep deprivation and food and drink deprivation amounted to inhuman treatment. The threat of torture may also amount to inhuman treatment (*Campbell*) as may poor conditions of detention, if they are sufficiently severe, such as overcrowding, deprivation of contact with the outside world and the withholding of food and medical treatment.

Degrading treatment. 'Degrading treatment' also causes less suffering than torture. The distinctive quality of degrading treatment is that it 'grossly humiliates'. Race discrimination is capable of amounting to degrading treatment (*East African Asians* case, EComHR) as is some corporal punishment.

The critical question is: what protection does Article 3 provide which is not already provided by the Refugee Convention? In the box above we set out the circumstances in which Article 3 either will or may potentially provide protection when the Refugee Convention does not.

Prohibition against slavery and forced labour (Article 4)

'1 No-one shall be held in slavery or servitude;

2 No-one shall be required to perform forced or compulsory labour;

For the purposes of this article the term "forced or compulsory labour" shall not include:

a) any work required to be done in the ordinary course of detention imposed according to the provisions of Article 5 of this Convention or during conditional release from such detention;

b) any service of a military character or, in the case of conscientious objectors in countries where they are recognised, service exacted instead of compulsory military service;

c) any service exacted in case of an emergency or calamity threatening the life or well being of the community;

d) any work or service which forms part of normal civic obligations.'

This article absolutely prohibits slavery. It has been little used but may be relevant where returning someone would expose them to gangs trafficking in women or children for prostitution. The article also prohibits forced or compulsory labour but allows exceptions such as work required in the ordinary course of detention or military service. Abductions by militias of forced recruits in military struggles would, however, be likely to contravene the right.

The right to liberty (Article 5)

'1 Everyone has the right to liberty and security of person. No one shall be deprived of his liberty save in the following cases and in accordance with a procedure prescribed by law:

a) the lawful detention of a person after conviction by a competent court;

b) the lawful arrest or detention of a person for non-compliance with the lawful order of a court or in order to secure fulfilment of any obligation prescribed by law;

c) the lawful arrest or detention of a person effected for the purpose of bringing him before the competent legal authority on reasonable suspicion of having committed an offence, or when it is reasonably considered necessary to prevent his committing an offence or fleeing after having done so;

d) the detention of a minor by lawful order for the purpose of educational supervision or his lawful detention for the purpose of bringing him before the competent legal authority;

e) the lawful detention of persons for the prevention of the spreading of infectious diseases, of persons of unsound mind, alcoholics or drug addicts or vagrants;

f) the lawful arrest or detention of a person to prevent his effecting an unauthorised entry into the country or of a person against whom action is being taken with a view to deportation or extradition.

2 Everyone who is arrested shall be informed promptly, in a language which he understands, of the reasons for the arrest and of any charge against him.

3 Everyone arrested or detained in accordance with the provisions of paragraph 1(c) of this article shall be brought promptly before a judge or other officer authorised by law to exercise judicial power and shall be entitled to trial within a reasonable time or to release pending trial. Release may be conditioned by guarantees to appear for trial.

4 Everyone who is deprived of liberty by arrest or detention shall be entitled to take proceedings by which the lawfulness of his detention shall be decided speedily by a court and his release ordered if the detention is not lawful.

5 Everyone who has been the victim of arrest or detention in contravention of the provisions of this article shall have an enforceable right to compensation.'

Article 5 states that everyone shall have the right to liberty except in certain limited circumstances set out in the article, such as normal criminal or legal processes which must also be clearly provided for in the law of the country concerned. The main purpose of Article 5 is to protect people from arbitrary detention. Article 5 also provides certain procedural safeguards for those people who are lawfully detained, such as the right to be informed of the reason for their arrest and any charge against them, the overseeing of detention by a court, a trial within a reasonable time and a right to compensation for unlawful detention. Where a person is to be returned to their country in circumstances where they face detention in breach of these conditions, there may be a breach of Article 5. Article 5 may offer greater protection than the Refugee Convention, for example, where:

- it is found that the person faces detention contrary to Article 5 but for only a brief period of time and without the risk of ill-treatment such that they are not at risk of treatment severe enough to amount to 'persecution';

- detention, although arbitrary, is carried out for a legitimate purpose without risk of ill-treatment and cannot be said to amount to 'persecution' (e.g., the 'round ups' of young Tamils in Columbo to counter a threat of violence, was found not to amount to persecution in *Ravichandran*).

In both cases, it should be remembered that the IAT has found that only 'flagrant' or 'gross' breaches of Article 5 in the country of return will mean that the sending state is in breach of the right ▶see above page 240.

Article 5(1)(f) allows detention in the UK in certain circumstances for immigration reasons. For details about when detention by the immigration authorities themselves may be in breach of Article 5 ▶see pages 498-502.

The right to a fair trial (Article 6)

1 'In the determination of his civil rights and obligations or of any criminal charge against him, everyone is entitled to a fair and public hearing within a reasonable time by an independent and impartial tribunal established by law. Judgement shall be pronounced publicly but the press and public may be excluded from all or part of the trial in the interests of morals, public order or national security in a democratic society, where the interests of juveniles or the protection of the private life of the parties so require, or to the extent strictly necessary in the opinion of the court in special circumstances where publicity would prejudice the interests of justice.

2 Everyone charged with a criminal offence shall be presumed innocent until proved guilty according to law.

3 Everyone charged with a criminal offence has the following minimum rights:

a) to be informed promptly, in a language which he understands and in detail, of the nature and cause of the accusation against him;

b) to have adequate time and facilities for the preparation of his defence;

c) to defend himself in person or through legal assistance of his own choosing or, if he has not sufficient means to pay for legal assistance, to be given it free where the interests of justice so require;

d) to examine or have examined witnesses against him and to obtain the attendance and examination of witnesses on his behalf under the same conditions as witnesses against him;

e) to have the free assistance of an interpreter if he cannot understand or speak the language used in court.'

In general terms, this is the most commonly invoked of all the ECHR rights. The ECtHR has itself indicated that a 'flagrant' breach of Article 6 in the receiving state could amount to a breach of the right (*Soering*).

Immigration rights themselves have been held not to constitute 'civil rights' within Article 6 (*Maaouia*, ECtHR).

Prohibition on punishment for an act which was not a crime when it was committed (Article 7)

'1 No one shall be held guilty of any criminal offence on account of any act or omission which did not constitute a criminal offence under national or international law at the time when it was committed. Nor shall a heavier penalty be imposed than the one that was applicable at the time the criminal offence was committed.

2 This article shall not prejudice the trial and punishment of any person for any act or omission which, at the time when it was committed, was criminal according to the general principles of law recognised by civilised nations.'

Article 7 ECHR can be raised if a person faces prosecution and trial on return for an offence which was not an offence when the person carried out the act in question. Where a person is at risk of unfair prosecution and trial proceedings, the circumstances may well come within the 1951 Convention.

Right to respect for private life, family, home, correspondence (Article 8)

'1 Everyone has the right to respect for his private and family life, his home and correspondence.

2 There shall be no interference by a public authority with the exercise of this right except such as is in accordance with the law and is necessary in a democratic society in the interests of national security, public safety or the economic well-being of the country, for the prevention of disorder or crime, for the protection of health or morals, or for the protection of the rights and freedoms of others.'

The rights under Articles 8, 9, 10 and 11 are all set out similarly. They all provide rights which can be interfered with if the interests of the community in preventing, for example, disorder or the economic well-being of the country, justify the interference. In order to see whether an interference can be justified in any case, the harm to the individual caused by the interference is balanced against the interest of the community.

The right to respect for 'private life' in Article 8 has a role in 'claim for protection' cases. Treatment which is less severe than Article 3 treatment may still infringe a person's private life where there are 'sufficiently adverse effects on physical and moral integrity' (*Bensaid*, ECtHR). One example is the effect upon a person's private life of the treatment of them by the state and the community as a result of their sexuality.

In *Jain*, the Court of Appeal agreed that there was a broad international consensus that everyone has a right to respect for their private life which includes their sexual life. It noted that criminalisation of homosexual activity between consenting adults in private was not regarded by the international community at large as being acceptable. The court had regard to the decision of the ECtHR in *Modinos* in which a breach of Article 8 was found in circumstances where, although the law criminalised homosexual activity, the Attorney General in Cyprus had a policy of not actually prosecuting people. The Court of Appeal appreciated that:

'the very existence of a legal prohibition can continuously and directly affect a person's private life'.

This approach was followed by the IAT in *Z*. However, in *Ashley*, the IAT found that there was no breach of private life if the applicant was removed to Zimbabwe, partly because he had given evidence that he would be faithful to his partner who would remain in the UK and therefore he would not wish to be sexually active in Zimbabwe. These cases are likely to be the subject of a further decision by the Court of Appeal.

In *Kacaj*, the IAT indicated that it was unlikely that there would be an unjustifiable breach of restricted rights (such as Article 8) if Article 3 was not also breached. The above cases provide an example of circumstances in which Article 8 may be breached even though there is not necessarily a breach of Article 3 or of the Refugee Convention.

Advisers should not, however, abandon the Refugee Convention in this kind of case. *Jain* (see above) was a case brought under the Refugee Convention before the incorporation of the ECHR. The court stated that there was a spectrum of conditions in different states, ranging from the enforcement of a criminal law against same sex activity to countries where a person is as free to take part in such activity as he or she 'is to breathe'. The question was 'when [on the spectrum] to ascribe the word "persecution" to those pressures'. In *Jain*, the court found that there was no persecution because the applicant's only fears were that he would have difficulty in finding a homosexual partner, that there would be disapproval from sections of the community if he did and that he would be expected to enter into a heterosexual marriage. Importantly, the court stated that it could well be the case that on facts 'not greatly dissimilar' from those in *Jain*, a fear of persecution would be justified.

Freedom of thought, conscience and religion (Article 9)

'1 Everyone has the right to freedom of thought, conscience and religion; this right includes freedom to change his religion or belief and freedom, either alone or in community with others and in public or private, to manifest his religion or belief in worship, teaching, practice and observance.

2 Freedom to manifest one's religion and beliefs shall be subject only to such limitations as are prescribed by law and are necessary in a democratic society in the interests of public safety, for the protection of public order, health or morals, or for the protection of the rights and freedoms of others.'

Freedom of thought, conscience and religion are absolute rights. It is only the 'manifestation' of religion or beliefs which can be restricted by the limitations in Article 9(2). So, if a person can show that their right to actually *hold* their belief will be infringed if they are returned, the Home Office may not be able to rely upon the requirements of immigration control to justify returning them, nor on any justification which the receiving state may have for interfering with the right. However, where a person has relied on Article 9, the ECtHR has tended to treat claims as raising issues under Articles 10 and 11 (in which restrictions apply in all circumstances) rather than Article 9. For example, in *Young* a personal conviction against joining a trade union was dealt with under Article 11 (►see below) rather than 9.

It has been suggested that Article 9 could be relied on by conscientious objectors together with Article 4 but this view was rejected by the Court of Appeal in *Sepet* and *Bulbul*.

Freedom of expression (Article 10)

'1 Everyone has the right to freedom of expression. This right shall include freedom to hold opinions and to receive and impart information and ideas without interference by public authority and regardless of frontiers. This article shall not prevent states from requiring the licensing of broadcasting, television or cinema enterprises.

2 The exercise of these freedoms, since it carries with it duties and responsibilities, may be subject to such formalities, conditions, restrictions or penalties as are prescribed by law and are necessary in a democratic society, in the interests of national security, territorial integrity or public safety, for the prevention of disorder or crime, for the protection of health or morals, for the protection of the reputation or rights of others, for preventing the disclosure of information received in confidence or for maintaining the authority and impartiality of the judiciary.'

Article 10 guarantees the right to hold opinions and impart information and ideas without interference by a public authority. The article goes on to set out limitations as prescribed by law and necessary in a democratic society. Cases usually involve issues of press freedom but could also involve forms of political or cultural expression. The ECtHR found in the case of **Ozgur Gundem** that the state had unjustifiably interfered with a newspaper's right to express views about what was happening in the South East of Turkey. It had arrested journalists and forced the closure of the newspaper. The court found that there was a violation of Article 10.

Freedom of assembly and association (Article 11)

'1 Everyone has the right to freedom of assembly and freedom of association with others, including the right to form and to join trade unions for the protection of his interests.

2 No restriction shall be placed on the exercise of these rights other than such as are prescribed by law and are necessary in a democratic society in the interests of national security or public safety, for the prevention of disorder or crime, for the protection of health or morals or for the protection of the rights and freedoms of others. This article shall not prevent the imposition of lawful restrictions on the exercise of these rights by members of the armed forces, of the police or of the administration of the state.'

Article 11 specifically includes the right to form or join trade unions. Again, the right is not absolute and it is qualified in certain circumstances as prescribed by law. Those who have been or will be prevented from forming or joining a political party or organisation might rely on Article 11.

Cases where removal will have a detrimental effect on the individual

There are situations where the effect of a person's removal may have such a detrimental effect on them that it amounts to inhuman and degrading treatment (Article 3) or an unjustifiable interference with their private life (Article 8 ECHR). Cases so far have concerned the effect of removal in withdrawing medical and social facilities which a person is currently receiving. A person cannot stay in the UK to receive treatment from the NHS under the rules relating to visitors. Those rules allow for the admission of a person to obtain private medical treatment for a 'finite' period and the applicant must intend to leave the UK after the completion of the treatment. They must also be able to maintain and accommodate themselves without recourse to public funds. Therefore, in cases where these rules cannot be met, the patient will be relying on the ECHR rights and/or the Home Office's general discretion outside the rules. For Home Office policy in this area ▶see below.

In the well known case of **D v UK**, the applicant, who was suffering from AIDS, was to be removed to St Kitts in the Carribean. The abrupt withdrawal of the medical and welfare facilities provided to him in the UK, which had assumed responsibility for his care, and the absence of proper facilities in St Kitts would hasten his death and expose him to acute mental and physical suffering were he to be removed. In those circumstances, the ECtHR held that removal would amount to inhuman treatment. This was the case *even though* the conditions in St Kitts did not themselves breach Article 3.

Another case which came before the ECtHR, *Bensaid*, concerned an Algerian national who developed schizophrenia and began receiving treatment from the NHS. He claimed that returning him to Algeria would be a breach of Articles 3 and 8 because he would be likely to suffer a relapse if he was returned, his health would also be undermined as it was 75 kilometres to the nearest hospital from his family home (the family did not have a car) and medication would not be provided for free. The court accepted in principle that:

- Article 3 can be used to protect a person from removal where the source of the harm is not the direct or indirect responsibility of the authorities in the receiving country;
- the suffering associated with relapse into hallucinations and psychotic delusions which involved self-harm, harm to others and a lowered ability to function socially, is harm which could be within Article 3;
- mental health was a crucial part of 'private life' within Article 8 because it is a necessary part of a person's personal identity and is required in order for them to develop relationships with others.

On the facts of the case, the court decided that there was no sufficient real risk established that the applicant would suffer the harm feared as a result of the removal. This was because: the applicant could have suffered relapse even if he remained in the UK, medical treatment was available in Algeria (although not free) and there was no evidence that he could not travel to obtain the medical treatment even without a family car. The court therefore dismissed the risk of deterioration in health as speculative and said that any interference with private life was justified under Article 8 (2).

It may also be that a breach of Articles 3 or 8 could be established where a person will be exposed to abject destitution and the intense suffering which would result. In *Fadele*, a complaint was considered admissible under those articles where children were to be forced to live in Nigeria in deprived circumstances detrimental to their health and education. There was then a friendly settlement between the applicant and the UK government without the case having to go to a full hearing before the court.

Home Office policy relating to HIV/AIDS and other serious illnesses

Home Office policy relating to those with HIV/AIDS or other serious illnesses is contained in the IDI at Chapter 1 section 8 and was updated in 2001. 'Serious illness' means any condition which is 'seriously debilitating, terminal or life threatening', for example, cancer. The policy states that being a person who has HIV/AIDS or other serious illness is not a reason in itself for refusal under the immigration rules. However, it also states that a 'port medical inspector [may] decide that the particular circumstances of an individual merit exclusion on medical grounds'. For entry clearance and people applying for leave to enter, the immigration rules state that the application can be refused if, in the view of the medical inspector, 'for medical reasons, it is undesirable to admit a person'.

The policy does little more than allow people to remain in the UK where the Home Office considers that to remove them would be in breach of the ECHR. It is for this reason that the only really beneficial part of the policy relates to 'after entry' cases, namely, circumstances in which the UK may be considered to have assumed responsibility for the person's care (see *D* above).

Entry clearance applications. Where an application for entry clearance is made and it comes to the ECO's attention that the person has AIDS/HIV or other serious illness, the application will normally be referred to the Home Office. The policy states that the applicant should 'fully meet the requirements of the immigration rules' for the category in which they wish to enter. Account is to be taken of whether the person has sufficient funds to be able to pay for any necessary treatment as well as sufficient funds for their maintenance and accommodation. A person with these illnesses who wishes to come to the UK specifically for medical treatment should meet the usual requirements of the immigration rules relating to medical visitors ▶see page 293.

'On entry' cases. If, on arrival, a person is noted to be suffering from AIDS/HIV or other serious illness, the port medical inspector will provide an estimate of the likely costs of treatment so that the immigration officer can consider the application for entry under the rules taking account of the applicant's means. If the case involves 'particularly compelling or compassionate circumstances', discretion may be exercised to grant exceptional leave.

'After entry' cases. The policy states that applications from people who have already entered the UK and have AIDS/HIV or other serious illness are given 'careful individual consideration' on their particular merits. The Home Office will normally ask for evidence from the applicant's consultant confirming:

- the nature of the medical condition;
- the treatment that the person has been receiving, the duration of the treatment and the consequences of the treatment being withdrawn;
- the applicant's life expectancy;
- the applicant's fitness to travel.

Leave will be granted to enable the person to carry on being treated by the NHS where the UK's obligations under the ECHR would be breached if they were to be returned. The Home Office's understanding of Article 3 is that it requires people to be allowed to remain if:

- the UK can be regarded as having assumed responsibility for the person's care; and
- there is credible medical evidence that return, due to a complete absence of medical treatment in the country concerned, would significantly reduce the applicant's life expectancy; and
- the applicant would face acute physical and mental suffering if returned.

The policy also states, however, that Home Office case-workers must consider whether, after the time taken by exercising appeals and other delays, the medical picture might be different at the stage of removal. If there is no realistic prospect of removal, then the case-worker must consider granting leave on compassionate grounds.

EEA nationals and family members. The policy applies equally to EEA nationals and their family members. However, EEA nationals will generally be admitted to the UK under the European rights of free movement ▶see Chapter 22. Although EEA nationals can be refused entry on grounds of public health, the Home Office has accepted that those with AIDS or who are HIV positive should not be refused entry on this basis and that those EEA nationals coming to the UK specifically for NHS treatment cannot be refused entry on those grounds under Community law (see para 3.6 of the policy above).

Carers. Those who wish to care for a relative with AIDS/HIV or other serious illness may be admitted as a visitor under the immigration rules. The maximum permitted period for visitors is six months but extensions may be granted if the circumstances are exceptional. During the period of time that they are caring, the carer is expected to make long-term care arrangements for the person. Enforcement action taken against carers who enable disabled or ill patients to live an independent and dignified life at home may violate the private life rights of the person cared for (*Camenzind*, ECtHR). For full details about Home Office policy relating to carers ▶see pagess 289-291.

Mental Health Act cases

Where a person who has leave to be in the UK is suffering from a very severe mental illness such that they are detained as an in-patient under the Mental Health Act 1983, there is a specific procedure for their removal from the UK (see s86 1983 Act). The initiative for removing such people is not with the Home Office but with the hospital where they are receiving care. The patient cannot be removed under this procedure unless (see, in addition to the 1983 Act, IDI Ch1, s8, para 4):

- specific arrangements have been made for the person's care and treatment in their own country;
- the doctor in charge of the case considers that it is in the interests of the patient to be removed;

- the patient is fit to travel;
- a medical escort is provided to accompany the person to their destination; and
- the patient has a valid passport and any necessary transit visas.

A person only has a right of appeal against removal under this procedure on human rights grounds but the Home Office must obtain the approval of the Mental Health Review Tribunal before proceeding.

Right not to be denied an education

In a number of cases, the ECtHR and the European Commission have declared inadmissible claims that expulsion which would result in an inferior education for young children, breaches the right not to be denied an education under Article 2(1) First Protocol ECHR (see *Jaramillo*, *Sorabjee* and *Ajayi*).

In *Holub*, the Court of Appeal considered the case of a Polish girl who claimed she had missed too much of the Polish syllabus while in the UK. She claimed, in particular, that the Polish educational system was so inflexible and rigid as to the factual knowledge which is required to progress through the system that she would be unable to catch up and would not be able to advance into higher education. In essence, therefore, it was the dislocation in her education which would be detrimental to her were she required to leave education in the UK and try to re-integrate into the Polish system. The court decided that, given her abilities and the fact that she had kept up her Polish, she would be able to manage and the extent of any educational prejudice with which she faced was therefore not severe enough to breach the Convention. The Court of Appeal also stated their view that the right not to be denied an education could not have 'extra-territorial' effect (for the meaning of 'extra-territorial effect, ▶see pages 240-241 above). However, this latter view was stated to be not 'authoritative' and the IAT in *Kacaj* later refused to follow it. Therefore, it is still possible to raise education cases under this right but the prejudice will have to be extremely strong before a court is likely to find any breach of the Convention.

Family or other connections with the UK

The third general situation in which the rights under the ECHR have a major impact in immigration cases, is where a person has family or other substantial connections with the UK.

Article 8(1) protects individuals against state interference with their private or family life, home and correspondence (for the text of Article 8 ▶see page 248 above). Article 12 (right to marry and to found a family) is unlikely to arise as the result of an immigration decision unless Article 8 is also breached. It might be relevant separately if an immigration decision prevents a person from marrying. However, nearly all the cases have been argued and dealt with under Article 8.

Article 8 does not give an automatic right of residence wherever a person has strong family ties in the UK. It is a restricted right and it recognises the general right of the state to control the admission of non-nationals into its territory by its own immigration laws. Therefore, in immigration cases where the applicant does not qualify under the immigration rules, Article 8 is really about striking the balance between these two conflicting interests: the family life of the applicant/s and the immigration law of the state.

An immigration decision affecting the family will be in breach of Article 8 if:

1 the relationship is covered by the meaning of 'family life'; and

2 the decision 'interferes' with the 'right to respect' for family life; and

either

3 the decision is not 'in accordance with the law'; *or*

4 the decision is not made in order to further one of the legitimate aims (national security, public safety, economic well-being of the country, prevention of disorder and crime, protection of health, protection of the rights and freedoms of others); *or*

5 the extent of the interference cannot be justified as 'necessary in the interests of a democratic society' in order to fulfil a legitimate aim (this is also referred to as whether the decision is 'proportionate').

The burden of showing 1 and 2 is on the applicant. If the applicant shows that the decision interferes with the right to respect for family life, then the onus is on the state to show that none of the conditions in 3, 4 or 5 apply. If the state cannot do this, then there is a breach of Article 8. In the case of **Mahmood**, the Court of Appeal summarised the effect of Article 8 in immigration decisions affecting the family ▶see box on page 265. Below, we look at each of the above elements in turn.

Family life

Whether the case involves family life between the different parties does not just depend upon formal ties, for example, whether a couple are married. It depends largely on the strength of ties which exist between the family members. Unlike the definition of, for example, 'family visitor' in visitor appeals ▶see page 286, there is no simple definition in the ECHR or its case law of when family life exists. For the principles which can be derived from the case law ▶see the box below. The ECtHR has held that *intended* family life can be protected by Article 8, for example, that between fiancé(e)s who have not yet begun living together (**Abdulaziz**).

Same-sex relationships do not come within family life (**Kerkhoven**, EComHR). However, same-sex relationships can be protected as part of the parties' 'private life' under Article 8 (**X and Y v UK**). It is possible, therefore, to apply the same general approach to same-sex partners as heterosexual couples. The factors taken into account to judge the

DOES THE RELATIONSHIP AMOUNT TO FAMILY LIFE ?

Particular relationships

Although there is no definition of 'family life', the following principles can be taken from the decisions of the courts relating to particular relationships. They must also be read with the general factors set out below.

- **Husband and wife**. The relationship between husband and wife is central to family life although marriage alone will not given rise to family life if, for example, the marriage is found to be a sham (*Moustaquim*, ECtHR). The fact that a marriage takes place but is not valid does not exclude family life (*Cabales*, ECtHR).

- **Unmarried partners**. The relationship between unmarried partners can amount to family life (*Keegan, Johnston*, both ECtHR). The particular factors to be taken into account are the length and stability of the relationship, the future intentions of the parties, whether they live together and whether they have had children.

- **Children and parents**. The relationship between child and natural parent is also fundamental to family life and family life will generally be assumed in these cases (*Keegan*). Family life is not prevented where a child is 'illegitimate' (*Boughanemi*, ECtHR). Later events will only break family life in 'exceptional circumstances' (*Berrehab*, ECtHR). For example, in the case of *Gul* before the ECtHR, a separation of seven years between the applicant and his son did not exclude family life as the applicant had continued to ask the Swiss authorities to admit his son from Turkey and he had also continued to visit him. In *Berrehab*, divorce between the parents did not break the ties between father and child who had maintained regular contact visits. In *Boughanemi*, the father-child relationship involved family life even though the father only recognised the child 10 months after birth and had made no provision for the child.

- **Adoptive children and parents**. The relationship between adoptive parents and children amounts to family life (*X v France*, EComHR).

- **Foster children**. The relationship between foster parents and children probably amounts to family life (*Gaskin*, ECtHR) but this has not been as clearly established as it has for adoptive children and their adoptive parents.

- **Adult children and parents, adult siblings.** In some cases, the Strasbourg case law has stressed the need for evidence of continuing, particularly close links, for example, financial dependency, in order to show family life between adult children and parents. In some cases, relationships between adult children and their parents and between adult siblings will not amount to family life (*Advic*, EComHR) and strong evidence will be needed to show otherwise. However, in *Boughanemi*, the ECtHR presumed that family life continued to exist between an adult son (of 33 years) who was to be deported and his parents and seven brothers and sisters.

- **Grandparents and grandchildren**. In *Marckx*, the ECtHR stated its view that family life included 'at least the ties between near relatives, for instance, those between grandparents and grandchildren'.

- **Aunts, uncles, nieces, nephews**. A relationship between uncle and nephew was held by the Commision to amount to family life in *Boyle* where the uncle had played the part of father to his nephew. In *Nhundu & Chiwera*, the IAT found that family life continued to exist between a minor, orphaned nephew and his aunt. The child had grown up regarding his aunt as his mother. However, in the same case, family life had ceased to exist between the aunt and an adult, non-dependent nephew who was in good health and had experience in the employment field.

- **Polygamous marriages**. Relationships between the parties of polygamous marriages, even if they are formally invalid, may amount to family life (*A v Netherlands*). However, a country like the UK, which does not permit polygamy, will generally be able to justify denying entry to more than one spouse under Article 8 (2) (*Bibi*, EComHR).

- **Transsexuals**. Relations between a transsexual and their opposite sex partner can amount to family life. In *X, Y and Z v UK*, the ECtHR found that there was family life between the parties and their child by artificial insemination.

General factors to be taken into account:

- the frequency of contact between the family members;
- the length of the relationship;
- whether the family members live or have lived together;
- the level of the emotional dependency between the family members;
- the level of any financial dependency between the parties;
- the level of any practical dependency between the parties.

strength of the ties between same-sex partners will also be the same as those for unmarried heterosexual partners (▶see box above). Although the language of the ECHR does not change, its interpretation develops to keep pace with modern day conditions. It is therefore possible that, eventually, same-sex relationships will be recognised as amounting to family life.

Interference with the right to respect for family life

If the relationship/s involve 'family life', it next has to be shown that the immigration decision excluding a person from the UK or removing them will result in an 'interference with the right to respect' for that family life.

The case law in this area can be confusing. *Sometimes the factors relevant to this issue are considered as part of the question of whether the interference in family life was 'necessary' in the interests of the community* ▶see below pages 261-266. If an applicant manages to show an interference with family life on the basis of the factors set out in this section, the state will have a hard task in showing that the interference is justified. However, if less stringent criteria are applied to determine an interference with family life, the applicant may face greater difficulties at the final stage.

The relevant questions are (*Abdulaziz*, ECtHR):

1 Are there 'obstacles' or 'special reasons' why family life cannot be established elsewhere ?

2 Did the parties to the relationship know that they would not necessarily be able to maintain their family life in the country in which they wish to live at the time family life was established (e.g., when they began the relationship or got married)?

It is often very difficult to successfully argue that there are obstacles to establishing family life elsewhere. The following are examples of cases where the ECtHR has *rejected* the argument that there are obstacles:

- closeness of settled partner to family in the UK and sickness of settled partner's father in the UK (*Abdulaziz*);
- risk of social rejection in the non-settled partner's country of origin (*Balkandali*, ECtHR);
- a Turkish couple of Kurdish origin who had been granted the equivalent of exceptional leave in Switzerland, where the woman was also receiving specialist health treatment, were not able to be reunited with their two sons who remained in Turkey – the decision is best understood on the basis that the couple had been able to return to Turkey for visits (*Gul*, ECtHR).

The following are examples of circumstances which may lead to a finding that there are obstacles preventing family life being established elsewhere:

- it is not possible to obtain legal rights of residence for both family members in another country (*Beldjoudi*, ECtHR);
- the family will suffer an interference with other human rights if they try to establish family life in another country – this might particularly benefit those who have been granted refugee status or exceptional leave on the basis that they cannot be expected to return to the country in which the non-resident partner is living or will be expected to return to. Further, in *Nhundu*, the IAT stated:

  'We would accept that in principle an appellant whose private and family ties in the UK were not on their own strong enough to give rise to a violation of article 8, could nevertheless succeed under that article if removal would expose him or her to a real risk of significant harms or serious obstacles, *albeit harms falling below the Article 3 threshold.*' (emphasis added)

  However, on the facts of that case, the IAT still found that the low-level form of harassment that the appellants faced was not enough to mean that Article 8 was breached;

- the person who is expected to leave has a child by a relationship which has now broken down so that their previous partner cannot be expected to relocate abroad with them. In *Berrehab*, a Moroccan national complained that he would not be able to continue to exercise his rights of access to his four year-old daughter from whose mother he was separated. In finding for him, the ECtHR had regard to the distance between the Netherlands and Morocco, the financial difficulties he would have if returned, the age of the child and the frequency of the pre-existing contact between father and child. The Home Office introduced changes to the immigration rules specifically to allow contact with children from parents abroad ▶see pages 379-382;

- there are wider family relationships which will be ruptured if one family unit is required to go to live in the other country. For example, the settled spouse may have living with them a child from an earlier relationship who has frequent and regular access to their other natural parent, who cannot reasonably be expected to relocate to another country. The Court of Appeal ruled in *Iskio*, however, that this will not be conclusive of a breach of Article 8;

- severe health difficulties for any of the family members if forced to live abroad (see *Fadele* (EComHR) in which the children had actually suffered severe health difficulties on going to live in Nigeria);

It may be that 'obstacles' can be shown from a number of factors which together make it unreasonable to expect the family to relocate. Further factors of relevance are whether:

- the settled family member has long residence in the UK or other ties to the UK (e.g., property or employment);

- the settled family member has links with the proposed country of re-location (e.g., past residence there);

- the adaptability of family members to living elsewhere (factors relating to language, culture, religion, social practices, health and the ages of any children are all relevant);

- the existence of other family ties in the alternative destination and the other social, educational and economic prospects of the family there.

The above must also be read together with a recent useful case decided in August 2001, *Boultif*. In that case, the ECtHR held that there would be a breach of Article 8 if the applicant, an Algerian national, was prevented from living in Switzerland. The important background to the case was as follows:

- the applicant entered Switzerland where he met and married a Swiss citizen and they lived together for about four years. They had no children;

- the applicant was then imprisoned for two years for a particularly 'ruthless and brutal' robbery and damage to property. He was also convicted for unlawful possession of firearms;

- the Swiss authorities refused to allow the applicant to remain in Switzerland;

- the applicant raised the fact that, in Algeria, people live in fear of fundamentalism and he also pointed out that he had worked successfully both before and after serving his sentence;

- although the applicant had lived in Italy before going to Switzerland and had returned there, he was staying there irregularly and it could not be shown that both he and his wife would be permitted to live lawfully in Italy.

The court held that it was 'practically impossible' for the applicant and his family to live outside Switzerland. It stated:

'The court has considered, first, whether the applicant and his wife could live together in Algeria. The applicant's wife is a Swiss national. It is true that the applicant's wife can speak French and has had contacts with her mother-in-law in Algeria. However, the applicant's wife has never lived in Algeria, she has no other ties with that country and indeed she does not speak Arabic. In these circumstances she cannot, in the court's opinion, be expected to follow her husband, the applicant, to Algeria.'

In accordance with the law

The state must show that any decision is 'in accordance with the law'. This means that the immigration decision must be based upon a clear law so that the decision does not arbitrarily interfere with family life. A decision based on the immigration legislation and rules will generally satisfy this condition.

In pursuance of a legitimate aim

The immigration decision must be made in the interests of society generally for one of the reasons set out in Article 8(2) (▶see page 248 for text). Immigration control, in accordance with immigration law, has consistently been held both by the ECtHR and the UK courts to be justified in order to prevent disorder or crime. Immigration decisions may also be made in order for the protection of the rights and freedoms of others or to preserve the economic well-being of the country.

Extent of the interference 'necessary' in the interests of society

The more difficult job for the state is to show that the immigration decision is 'necessary' in order to protect the interests of the community. In order to do this, the interest of the state in pursuing immigration control has to be balanced against the interference with family life caused by the decision. Another way of describing this balance is to say that the immigration decision must be 'proportionate' to the interference with family life.

Two negative decisions of the Court of Appeal upheld the balance that the Home Office had struck between these two interests: *Mahmood* and *Isiko*.

In *Mahmood*, the appellant was a national of Pakistan who had entered the country unlawfully and subsequently claimed asylum. The asylum application was refused but he married shortly before the decision. The Home Office decision was upheld in concluding that it was reasonable to expect the applicant's wife to return to Pakistan. She was a British citizen but she originated from Pakistan where she had lived until she was about 13 years of age and could re-adjust to life there. Weighed against the interests of the applicant was the interest of the community in maintaining immigration control where the immigration law had not been complied with. The applicant had argued that, although he had not obtained an entry clearance, there was no 'legitimate purpose' in requiring him to return to Pakistan as he in fact satisfied the requirements of the immigration rules such as maintenance and accommodation and intention to live together as spouses. It was only a procedural requirement that he had not complied with. However, the court held:

'Firm immigration control requires consistency of treatment between one aspiring immigrant and another. If the established rule is…that a person seeking rights of residence here on grounds of marriage (not being someone who already enjoys a leave, albeit limited, to remain in the UK) must obtain an entry clearance in his country of origin, then a waiver of that requirement in the case of someone who has found his way here without an entry clearance and then seeks to remain on marriage grounds, having no other legitimate claim to enter, would in the absence of exceptional circumstances to justify the waiver, disrupt and undermine immigration control because it would be manifestly unfair to other would-be entrants who are content to take their place in the entry clearance queue in their country of origin'.

In *Mahmood*, the court also set out general principles relating to Article 8 in immigration cases ▶see page 265.

In *Isiko* there were a number of family relationships which would be disrupted by the removal of the two applicants who were both citizens of Uganda who had married, then divorced after which other family ties had been established. However, the immigration history of both applicants was described as 'deplorable'. One of the applicants had then been convicted of rape and had made a 'baseless' claim to asylum to try to prevent removal.

In both *Isiko* and *Mahmood*, the Home Office had applied its policy, DP/3/96, which is intended to reflect the requirements of Article 8 in marriage cases. For full details of this policy ▶see pages 353-355. While the court considered the policy to be lawful (although badly drafted), it stated in *Isiko* that this did not mean that 'every act of implementation of the policy is inevitably lawful'. Cases could arise where 'deportation would be a disproportionate response to the breach of immigration control'. It is clear, therefore, that the circumstances of each case need to be looked at individually in order to see whether, in fact, the decision of the immigration authorities complies with Article 8.

Therefore, in building a good Article 8 case, advisers need to consider the following:

- What is the strength of family ties ? What are the nature of the difficulties which would be faced by the family in the receiving state if family life was required to be pursued overseas (►see above under 'family life' and 'interference with right to respect for family life')? These are the considerations which are placed on the applicant's side of the weighing scales.

  Advisers might also consider whether the applicant would be likely to be re-admitted to the UK if immigration control has been breached (►see page 67). What would be the length of the delay in making any further application and what would be the particular effect on the family members of that delay ? What are the chances of maintaining family life by contact visits from abroad?

- How strong is the public interest in enforcing controls in the individual case? A poor immigration record, reliance on public funds or a criminal record might weigh heavily against the rights of an applicant. On the other hand, the applicant may only have breached controls in order to make an asylum or human rights claim which did have *some* basis, although it was not found to be sufficient to qualify the applicant for protection. There may have been long delays in the decision-making process (not the fault of the applicant) during which time family life was established. Should applicants be penalised for not putting their emotional lives on hold during such delays? The applicant may have a good working record and may be supporting dependants who would otherwise be reliant on public funds so that removing the applicant would, in that sense, be contrary to the interest of the community.

  Even if the applicant has committed serious criminal offences, there have been cases where removal has been held not to be justified where the applicant has long residence in the country in question. For example, in *Moustaquim*, the applicant was Moroccan but he had lived in Belgium since the age of one. He committed a substantial number of criminal offences as a juvenile and was deported. The ECtHR held that the interference with his family life of some 20 years standing (with his parents and siblings) was not justified. The same conclusion was reached in the case of *Beldjoudi*. In that case, the applicant had been born in France, but lost his French nationality when his family moved. He later married a French woman but committed a string of serious offences.

  Advisers must therefore look for all the positive aspects of their individual cases. They should also consider whether there are any aspects of *private* life which, combined with family life considerations, mean that the decision to exclude the applicant is disproportionate ►see further below page 266.

  The following recent cases are given as further examples to illustrate the way the balance between the family interests of the individuals concerned and the interests of immigration control has been struck and to illustrate further relevant factors for advisers to look out for:

Sen v the Netherlands (December 2001, ECtHR). In *Sen* the ECtHR found that there was a violation of Article 8 in a case where the Dutch authorities had denied a residence permit to the eldest child of two parents legally resident and settled in the Netherlands with their two younger children, both of whom were born in the Netherlands. The court noted that the child had spent her whole life in Turkey and had strong links with the linguistic and cultural environment of her country. Against this there was the fact that there was a major obstacle to the rest of the family's return to Turkey in that the parents had settled as a couple in the Netherlands many years ago. The court concluded that the Netherlands had failed to strike a fair balance between the applicants' interest and the state's interest in controlling immigration.

Boultif v Switzerland (August 2001, ECtHR). The circumstances of this case are set out above (▶see pages 260-261) as it is relevant to when a partner can be expected to relocate. The ECtHR also gave some 'guiding principles' on whether an immigration decision excluding a person is 'necessary' in the interests of the community in particular in a case where offences have been committed, stating that:

'...the Court will consider the nature and seriousness of the offence committed by the applicant; the length of the applicant's stay in the country from which he is going to be expelled; the time elapsed since the offence was committed as well as the applicant's conduct in that period; the nationalities of the various persons concerned; the applicant's family situation, such as the length of the marriage, and other factors expressing the effectiveness of a couple's family life; whether the spouse knew about the offence at the time when he or she entered into a family relationship; and whether there are children in the marriage, and if so, their age'.

Sukhjit Gill (December 2001, IAT). An Indian national claimed his removal to India would violate his Article 8 rights because he acted as a carer for his father who was settled in the UK and was suffering from diabetes. The adjudicator accepted that there was a close relationship between father and son and that the son cared for his father in the UK and that, consequently, his removal from the UK would be disproportionate. On the Home Office's appeal, the IAT agreed that the son's removal was disproportionate. Among the factors considered relevant in determining whether the decision was 'necessary' were the considerable delay on the part of the Home Office leading to the development of close ties in the UK and the fact that the father's health might deteriorate if the son was removed with the possible need for increased public provision for him.

Romuald Andela Mindoukna (November 2001, IAT). The appellant was a national of Cameroon and a failed asylum-seeker who stated that removing him to Cameroon would violate his Article 8 rights with his partner and child. The IAT accepted that there were serious grounds for thinking that the applicant would not succeed in an application for settlement from Cameroon or indeed in an application to come to the UK in order to visit his family. During the course of the proceedings, the IAT stated that a welfare report concerning the child should be produced from the local authority in whose area the child was living in order for the court to have a better understanding of the effect of removal of the father. The IAT encouraged representatives in similar cases to invite adjudicators to request such reports. The IAT indicated that permanent separation as the result of an applicant's immigration history preventing their re-admission may violate Article 8. The case was sent back to the adjucator for re-hearing.

Dilaver Cobo (October 2001, IAT). The IAT followed the reasoning in *Mahmood* in dismissing an Article 8 appeal on the basis that it was not disproportionate to require an applicant to leave the UK and to apply for entry clearance in the ordinary way. It was stated that any 'consequent, even temporary, interference with his right to family life comes within Article 8(2)'. In that case, however, there were many omissions in the evidence available at the appeal which were relevant to the 'strength of

---

THE ARTICLE 8 PRINCIPLES SET OUT BY THE COURT OF APPEAL IN MAHMOOD

1　A state has a right, under international law, to control the entry of non-nationals into its territory, subject always to its treaty obligations.

2　Article 8 does not impose on a state any general obligations to respect the choice of residence of a married couple.

3　Removal or exclusion of one family member from a state where other members of the family are lawfully resident will not necessarily infringe Article 8, provided that there are no insurmountable obstacles to the family living together in the country of origin of the family member excluded, even where this involves a degree of hardship for some or all members of the family.

4　Article 8 is likely to be violated by the expulsion of a member of a family that has been long established in a state if the circumstances are such that it is not reasonable to expect the other members of the family to follow the member expelled.

5　Knowledge on the part of the resident spouse at the time of marriage that rights of residence of the other party to the marriage were precarious, leans against a finding that an order excluding the applicant spouse violates Article 8.

6　Whether interference with family rights is justified in the interests of controlling immigration will depend on:

(i) the facts of the particular case; and

(ii) the circumstances existing in the state whose action is impugned.

the family life said to be under threat of interference'. The IAT stated that the applicant would have the opportunity to mend the gaps in the evidence on the application for entry clearance.

AHR Soloot (August 2001, IAT). The IAT found that there was a breach of Article 8 partly on the basis that, if the applicant was required to return to apply for entry clearance, he would be unable to do so in Iran, where he was to be sent, as there were no facilities for doing so there. In addition, the applicant might be unable to exit Iran to make an entry clearance application as he had previously left that country in violation of the exit regulations. At the very least his exit would be delayed.

Other connections in the UK

A person may have connections in the UK, other than family ties, which are relevant to a human rights claim. The right to respect for private life under Article 8 includes the right of a person to develop their own personality and their relationships with other people (*Botta*). Particularly in cases involving long residence, there may be significant elements of private life which need to be taken into account. This may be the result of close friendships or derive from school, study or working life. It is possible to *add* these elements of private life to any family connections to determine whether, taken together, there is a breach of Article 8. In *Nhundhu* and *Chiwera*, the IAT, after considering certain decisions of the ECtHR, stated:

'In the context of immigration and asylum cases, the court has come to view the right to respect for private and family life as a composite right. This approach requires the decision-maker to avoid restricting himself to looking at the circumstances of 'family life' and to take into account also significant elements of the much wider sphere of 'private life'...One consequence of this approach is that a person may be able to establish a protected right under Article 8 either by reference to significant elements of family life or significant elements of private life or a mixture of both.'

Exceptionally, there may be other human rights at stake arising from a person's connections to the UK. For example, in *Quaquah*, the High Court held, in circumstances where deportation would seriously interfere with the applicant's ability to prepare his civil action against the Home Office for malicious prosecution, that the decision interfered with the 'equality of arms' principle in Article 6 (right to a fair trial).

Making human rights claims

Human rights may be raised with the immigration authorities or the adjudicator and Immigration Appeal Tribunal in any of the following ways.

Independent application. A human rights claim can be made as an independent application if the applicant has no other basis for coming to or staying in the UK. The Home Office distinguishes between human rights 'applications' and 'allegations', stating that 'applications' do not give rise to a right of appeal if they are refused. This, however, is a technicality – if there is no other right of appeal within which the applicant can raise human rights, they simply need to make an 'allegation' (▶see below) that the negative decision was in breach of their human rights, in order to establish a right of appeal. Although strictly an in-country human rights application should be made on Form FLR(O) (see para 32, HC 395), in practice, the immigration authorities consider human rights grounds which are raised with them without use of the form.

Part of asylum or other application. In many cases, Refugee Convention claims overlap with human rights grounds. If a Refugee Convention claim is to be refused, the Home Office should always consider the ECHR in addition. The Home Office will consider Article 3 in particular but, where the circumstances alleged by the applicant indicate that one of the other rights is directly relevant, those rights should also be considered. This is the case even if the ECHR is not raised by the applicant. If leave on human rights grounds is also to be refused, the 'reasons for refusal' letter should cover the ECHR (see API Ch5, s4, paras 4.2 and 4.3). However, applicants should not rely on the immigration authorities to work out the human rights grounds that may be relevant but should state them as part of the application.

One-stop notices. One of the purposes of the 'one-stop' procedure is to allow human rights grounds to be considered by the Home Office together with any claim to asylum and for the Home Office and the adjudicator to consider ECHR grounds at the same time as an appeal is being brought on other grounds against a negative immigration decision. For full details about the one-stop procedure ▶see pages 606-611.

Human rights appeals following an allegation against a particular decision. A person can appeal on human rights grounds by making an allegation that any decision made which relates to his or her immigration rights to enter or remain in the UK was in breach of their human rights (s65(1) 1999 Act). The allegation can be made simply by writing to the decision-maker and stating that the decision is in breach of rights under the ECHR. For details about human rights appeals and the circumstances in which the immigration authorities can deny appeal rights, ▶see pages 609-611, 614-617.

As part of another appeal. Even if no allegation has been made, or if a one-stop notice has not been filled out, it is still possible to raise human rights before an adjudicator or the IAT during the course of an appeal which is being brought on different grounds. This is because section 65(3)(4) of the 1999 Act states that the adjudicator and IAT have power to deal with human rights grounds where a 'question arises' as to human rights during the course of an appeal. Applicants should, however, always try to raise human rights as early as possible.

Taking a case to Europe

After the Human Rights Act, people can still make complaints to the ECtHR in Strasbourg. They must first, however, try to overturn the decision which they claim breaches their human rights by all other means in the UK. Normally in immigration cases this will involve bringing a human rights appeal under s65 of the 1999 Act and using the court system. Applicants should seek advice if they think that they have a case to take to the ECtHR.

Applications to the ECtHR proceed in two stages. There is first a decision as to whether the complaint is 'admissible'. If the application passes this stage, it proceeds to a decision on the 'merits'. If an application is declared to be admissible, the court may try to get the parties to agree to a friendly settlement. Legal decision-making used to be divided between the European Commission and the European Court of Human Rights but, from November 1998, there has been a single court. The court does, however, sit in the following divisions:

- plenary court. This does not hear cases but deals with administrative matters, including adopting rules of procedure;
- 'committees' of three judges;
- 'chambers' of seven judges;
- 'grand chambers' of 17 judges.

A committee can decide that an application is inadmissible if it is unanimous. Otherwise, the decision on both 'admissibility' and 'merits' is heard by a chamber. Cases involving very serious matters, which affect the interpretation of the ECHR, are heard by the grand chamber.

Procedure for making an application

Applications should be made using the application form provided by the court. The application must be made within six months of the final decision of the domestic court (see Article 35 ECHR). The time limit is very strictly applied by the court. Failure to observe it, even by a day, will result in the case being declared inadmissible. In urgent cases, the application can be made by letter provided the form is sent without undue delay to the secretary of the court later. If an application is made by letter, the court registry will acknowledge receipt and will send a form warning the applicant to complete the form within a reasonable time.

The form sets out clearly what information is needed by the court. The form or letter can be lodged by post or fax. Failure to include the relevant information can lead to the application not being registered. Legal representatives must provide a letter of authority signed by the applicant.

In the application, applicants are required to provide the following information:

- their name, age, address and occupation;
- the name, address and occupation of anyone acting as their representative;
- the respondent country;
- a statement of the facts;
- the relevant domestic law;
- the articles of the Convention which the applicant is relying on together with any relevant case law;
- the object of the application;
- the details of the orders the applicant wants the court to make;
- judgments, decisions and any other documents relating to the application.

Filling in the application form is the most important part of the application procedure. Legal advisers must set out the complaint fully when returning the form. Failure to properly raise an issue at the initial stage of the procedure will mean that the court will not entertain arguments about the issue subsequently.

Procedure before the court

The usual procedure followed before the ECtHR can be summarised as follows:

- lodging the application: this must be done within six months of the last domestic decision. The time limit can only be waived if there is a continuing breach of the applicant's human rights;
- the application is registered;
- a judge is appointed as 'rapporteur'. The rapporteur may contact a party for more information about the complaint;
- examination by a committee of three judges. The majority of cases are declared inadmissible at this stage. There is no appeal if a case is declared inadmissible. The admissibility criteria under Article 35 ECHR includes a 'manifestly ill-founded' test. This is why it is so important to properly substantiate the claim at the initial stages;
- if the case is likely to be admissible, the committee will communicate notice of the application to the government concerned;
- observations on the application are filed by the parties;
- admissibility decision made by chambers of seven judges. There is the possibility of an oral hearing although most admissibility decisions are made without a hearing;
- possibility of friendly settlement negotiations;
- judgment by the chamber on the merits;
- exceptional cases are referred to a grand chamber of 17 judges which may receive oral and written evidence.

Interim measures

If the state is acting or is shortly going to act in a way that is alleged to be in breach of a person's human rights, occasionally the chamber or its president may suggest to the state any 'interim measures' it considers appropriate (rule 39 of the Rules of the ECtHR). This can be done at the request of the parties or by the court acting on its own. Requests by parties should be made in writing and, if urgent, faxed with advance notice being given to the court that faxes and any supporting documentation are being sent.

Requests for interim remedies are most common in deportation and extradition cases but may also be made in any case where there is an 'apparent real and imminent risk of irreparable harm'. Rule 39 indications are not often made and they are not binding on the state.

Legal funding

Financial assistance from the UK's Community Legal Service Fund is not available for proceedings before the ECtHR. An applicant can request financial assistance from the court. The registry will send a declaration of means form for the applicant to complete. Assistance may be granted from the time that observations in writing are received from the respondent. However, the financial assistance rates are extremely low.

Race discrimination in immigration

As a result of the Race Relations (Amendment) Act 2000, the Race Relations Act 1976 has been extended so that race discrimination is prohibited in areas which were not previously covered. The immigration authorities are not permitted to discriminate on grounds of 'race or colour' (see new s19B–19F, 1976 Act). However, the immigration authorities are permitted to discriminate on the grounds of 'ethnic or national origin' or 'nationality' under specific 'authorisations' which have been made by the Home Secretary. The two authorisations are: the Race Relations (Immigration and Asylum) Authorisation 2001 ('the first authorisation') and the Race Relations (Immigration and Asylum) (No 2) Authorisation 2001 ('the second authorisation').

The first authorisation

The first authorisation allows discrimination on grounds of nationality where there is statistical evidence showing a pattern of breaches of the immigration laws by persons of that nationality or where there is evidence that significant numbers of people of a particular nationality have breached or will breach immigration laws. The authorisation does not name the national groups likely to be discriminated against. Discrimination permitted by this authorisation could violate Article 14 ECHR if the discrimination cannot be objectively justified. It is difficult to understand what type of evidence of patterns of breaches will be needed.

The second authorisation

The second authorisation permits discrimination by reason of a person's ethnic or national origin where that person:

1 is of Chinese ethnic origin and who presents a Malaysian or Japanese passport or another travel document issued by Malaysia or Japan; or

2 is a member of one of the following ethnic or national groups: Kurd, Roma, Albanian, Tamil, Somali, Afghan.

On 11 June 2002, the Home Office announced that it was revoking this second authorisation.

Appeal rights

The 2000 Act also creates a right of appeal to an adjudicator from a decision about entitlement to enter or remain in the UK on grounds that the Race Relations Act 1976 has been breached. The appeal is under section 65 of the Immigration and Asylum Act 1999 (as amended) and is triggered by making a race discrimination allegation in the same way as human rights allegations trigger human rights appeals ▶see above page 267. A discrimination allegation can also be raised during the course of another immigration appeal. If an adjudicator or the IAT allows an immigration appeal on race discrimination grounds, they can also refer the matter to the county court to determine a claim for compensation (see s57A(3) Race Relations Act 1976).

Reviews

The government is committed to undertaking reviews of the authorisations made under section 19D of the Race Relations Act 1976. Pontic Greeks were removed from the second authorisation on 8 November 2001 on the grounds that they did not represent an immediate threat to the United Kingdom's immigration control sufficient to justify their continued inclusion. As indicated, the second authorisation itself is being revoked. The statistical evidence initially relied on by the government to seek to justify the authorisations included:

• there were 1,756 inadequately documented Afghan arrivals during 2001, including 90 with forged documents;

• there were 65 Albanians who were served with illegal entry papers in December 2001;

• there were 205 inadequately documented Chinese arrivals in December 2001. In addition, 100 Chinese people were detected travelling on falsified Japanese passports during 2001;

• there are large numbers of undocumented arrivals, clandestine entries and refused asylum applications from nationals of countries where Kurds represent the greatest risk to immigration control (in 2001, there were 603 undocumented arrivals from Iran, 891 from Iraq and 2,337 from Turkey);

- large numbers of passengers from Poland (904) and the Czech Republic (182) from where Roma represent a threat to immigration control, were refused leave to enter at UK ports in December 2001;
- there is evidence of immigration abuse by Somalis. In December 2001, 40 cases of forged documents, 44 cases of inadequate documentation and 238 cases of non-clandestine illegal entry were detected;
- there is evidence of immigration abuse by Tamils, including 2,813 undocumented arrivals in 2001 and over 3,900 cases of illegal entry.

Section 4 **Temporary purposes**

Chapter 14
Visitors   275
Admission as a visitor   275
Applying for entry as a visitor   283
Appeals   285
Applying for extensions   287
Visitors applying to change their status   288
Carers   289
Transit visitors   291
Medical visitors   293
Working holidaymakers   294
Travel outside the UK   296

Chapter 15
Students   297
Students and 'prospective' students   298
Extending leave as a student   307
Permission to work while studying   310
Studies including training   311
Other students   312
Fees and student grants and loans   314
EEA students   317
Students who want to change their status   319
Working after studies   320
Travel outside the UK   320

14 Visitors

This section deals with people who are coming to the UK for temporary reasons, in particular for visits and for studies. Those who wish to come to the UK for a short period for a particular reason, such as to see family or friends, or for a holiday, are generally looked at under the immigration rules as 'visitors'. People who wish to come to the UK for a brief period to conduct business have to satisfy the same rules. For details about business visitors ►see pages 280-281. In addition, the Home Office has provided examples of 'special classes' of visitors who are treated under the same rules ►see pages 281-283.

However, there are three kinds of visitor who are treated differently. Firstly, since 1994 there have been separate rules for those coming to the UK for the purpose of private medical treatment ►see page 293. Secondly, separate rules apply to 'transit' visitors, namely, those who are simply passing through the UK en route to another country ►see pages 291-292. Thirdly, there are separate rules for Commonwealth nationals who wish to come to the UK for an extended holiday and to work for some of the time that they are here in order to support themselves ('working holidaymakers') ►see pages 294-295. The government's 2002 White Paper proposes extensive changes to the working holidaymaker category, including its extension to non-Commonwealth nationals. All of the above categories of people are covered in this chapter. In ►Chapter 15, we look at people who want to come to or stay in the UK for the purposes of study.

Admission as a visitor

Visa nationals and entry clearance

Visitors who are visa nationals (►see page 737 for a list of visa national countries) must obtain an entry clearance (often known as a 'visa') from a British embassy, high commission or consulate before travelling to the UK. The applicant for entry clearance must be outside the UK at the time that they apply. The application can be made to any post which is designated to accept visit entry clearance applications ►see pages 739-742 for a list of posts, and ►see pages 283-284 below for more details about entry clearance.

Visitors who are not visa nationals do not need to obtain entry clearance but may do so if they wish or, alternatively, may apply for permission at a British port or airport. There are always advantages and disadvantages in applying for entry clearance where it is optional ▶see page 56. Often the best course depends on the particular circumstances of the case but the formal requirements of the immigration rules are the same.

WHAT THE RULES SAY

The immigration rules on visitors state that people must:

- be genuinely seeking entry for a period stated by them which is for not more than six months;
- intend to leave at the end of their visit;
- not intend to take employment, paid or unpaid, or to produce goods or provide services, including selling goods or services direct to the public, during the visit;
- not intend to study at a state school;
- maintain and accommodate themselves and any dependants from resources available to them, without working or recourse to public funds; or be maintained and accommodated by relatives or friends;
- be able to meet the cost of their onward journey.

It should be noted that even if a visitor fulfils the above requirements of the rules, they may be refused entry under the general grounds of refusal which can be applied to all non-asylum cases ▶see page 67. The period of leave which is given is normally six months. In all cases, the leave which is given will normally be granted on conditions prohibiting employment and recourse to public funds. Under the immigration rules, extensions of stay can only be granted to allow the visitor to spend a maximum of six months in the UK altogether. This rule is occasionally waived (see below).

There is no separate provision in the rules for the dependants of visitors. Family members travelling together will themselves need to fit into the visitor rules.

WHAT THE RULES MEAN

Although the rules are the same for most visitors, whatever the purpose of the visit, unfortunately, the way they are often interpreted for people from different countries and economic backgrounds, is very different.

Genuinely seeking entry for a visit for a limited period

The immigration authorities have to be satisfied that the person is a genuine visitor. This means that their purpose in coming to the UK is to undertake a visit and not some other purpose such as taking employment or study. There are, however, some special classes of visitor where elements of the visit include business or research ▶see below. If the visitor is vague about the purpose of their visit or the officer takes the view that the reason for which the visit is sought is not believable, given the applicant's circumstances, then entry will be refused. The immigration authorities frequently treat the applicant's social and economic background as relevant in making such assessments.

The visitor must also specify the period for which they wish to stay. This must not exceed six months and it should be consistent with the purpose of the visit. If the visitor is vague about the period they wish to stay, then the officer may not be satisfied that the person in fact intends to only stay for the period which is finally stated and admission may be refused.

The Immigration Directorate Instructions (IDI) point out that there is no restriction on the number of visits a person may make within any given time but people are not normally expected to stay in the UK for more than six months in any 12-month period. If a person appears to be spending a great deal of time (in particular, if it is more than 50 per cent of their time) in the UK, suspicions may be raised that the person is not a genuine visitor. Immigration officers are particularly likely to consider information about past visits where people stay almost for the six-month visit limit and then return after a very short absence. The immigration officer may suspect that the person is attempting to get round the six-month visit period and may have other reasons for seeking to remain in the UK. This may be particularly difficult for people with close family members living in the UK.

It is also not necessarily safe to stay in the UK for the full six-month period given if the visitor originally stated that they intended to stay for a more limited period. For example, if a person stays for five months having said they intended a two-week visit for a relative's wedding, this could be taken into account in assessing their reliability when they make applications in the future.

Intention to leave

This is the most difficult part of the rules to satisfy because it relates to the applicant's state of mind (their 'intentions'), which is very difficult to prove. However, because the burden of proving that the requirements of the rules are satisfied rests on the visitor, if there is any ambiguity, the officer may simply refuse on the grounds that they could not be satisfied that this requirement is met.

In assessing this requirement, the officer may go into details about a person's life and background, demanding evidence of financial status and family circumstances, to see if they believe the person's story. They may ask a lot of questions: why will you need to go back after only two weeks? Who will look after your children/farm/business while you are away? Surely you can't afford to spend this amount of money on so short a visit? Surely it will be cheaper and more convenient for your relative to come to see you? If you found a place to study would you do so?

Immigration officers will often search luggage and read any correspondence, including personal letters, making whatever inferences they see fit. The IDI state:

'All documents produced by the passenger should be assessed in conjunction with any other evidence, *however circumstantial*, which may be relevant to the case' (emphasis added).

An important factor in assessing the intention to return is the existence of an incentive to return. If there are definite reasons why visitors have to return, they should state what they are and try to produce evidence. For example, a person in employment could have a letter from their employer, confirming the length of their holiday and when they are expected back at work. A person who is a student in their own country could have a letter from the college, confirming when the next term will begin. For someone without such a structured life it can be more difficult and immigration officers admit to using something they call 'nose', their claimed sixth sense, telling them when someone is not genuine. Officers are also encouraged to think 'would I do that?' in connection with information that they are given. They may, however, not appreciate the differences in cultures which place greater importance on particular events. By the same token, the officer may make assumptions about the norms of particular cultures in order to support their reasoning. Again, because it is up to the visitor to prove their intention, not up to the officer to disprove them, it is easy for officers to refuse applications without an objective basis for doing so. The Immigration Appeal Tribunal has made it clear on many occasions that, while officers are allowed to draw appropriate inferences, those inferences should be based on something more concrete than 'mere suspicion'.

Some groups are more likely to be refused because assumptions are made about their intentions. For example, negative assumptions are often made about people from poorer countries, people who are relatively poor by the standards of the country from which they come and people with relatives settled in the UK, particularly if they are young and single or if they are elderly with no family members to look after them. Also, people with a family history of migration, those who are unemployed, those that are in the middle of, or have just finished, their studies and those with an 'adverse' immigration history are targets for refusal.

A sponsor may sometimes be called to answer questions by an immigration officer when an applicant arrives in the UK. Suspicions about the applicant's intentions may arise in certain circumstances. The IDI state:

'If a passenger or his sponsor is shown to have attempted to deceive the immigration officer or some other person in some material respect or where there are material discrepancies between what the passenger and his sponsor say, when the sponsor can reasonably have been expected to know the facts, these are again grounds for doubting the passenger's credibility and not therefore being satisfied as to their intentions'.

Special care needs to be taken in advising those with an adverse immigration history, which could include previous periods of overstaying, a previous refusal of a visitor's entry clearance or those who have simply stayed on for longer than they originally intended. If a refusal is likely on those grounds, then evidence should be given to explain why there was a longer period of stay or overstaying. Evidence of changes of circumstances or priorities will often be important. Special attention needs to be given where a refusal is partly based on a previous visit refusal. In 1993, the right of appeal against refusals of entry clearance to those applying as visitors was removed by the Asylum and Immigration Appeals Act 1993 (it has been restored under the 1999 Act for 'family visitors' only). Therefore, if the earlier refusal took place after July 1993, reliance upon it by the officer is self-serving since that refusal could not be challenged on appeal.

The maintenance and accommodation test

This requirement allows officers to enquire about the financial resources available to visitors and/or their friends and relatives who may have to support them. Officers will also want to know how the visitor will be accommodated in the UK. They may be staying in a hotel or guest house, in which case they need to show sufficient funds to be able to pay for this, or they may be accommodated by family and friends.

If visitors are bringing their own money, evidence such as their bank statements or a letter from their employer confirming their salary should be produced. If friends or relatives in the UK are supporting them, a letter of invitation confirming willingness to support the visitor is necessary, together with the sponsor's bank statements or other supporting evidence of resources. There is no advantage in having such letters attested by solicitors; it is the evidence itself that is important.

Officers may decide that a person has insufficient means and therefore is unable to support themselves. Lack of financial resources of the applicant is also often taken by officers as a sign that the applicant really intends to work in the UK and to stay for longer than the period stated. However, if a person arrives with a substantial amount of money, this is sometimes also taken as an indication that a person intends to stay for longer than they are stating. These calculations often depend on the circumstances; for example, what might be considered too much money for a Guyanese citizen could be thought to be perfectly adequate for a visitor from North America. Officers can also make suggestions to applicants; for example, 'would you work if you find a job?' and use the answer, if in the affirmative, as a basis for refusal.

When visitors who are coming to spend time with family or friends arrive in the UK without entry clearance, it may be useful for the sponsor to come to the airport to meet them, with evidence of the financial support that is available. If the sponsor does not go to the airport, it is useful if the visitor has a telephone number for the sponsor with them, so that the immigration officer can make contact without delay, should they wish to do so.

The maintenance and accommodation requirements apply to most categories under the immigration rules. For more general details about satisfying these requirements ▶see pages 328-335.

Meeting the cost of the return journey

This usually means that the visitor should have a return or onward ticket, or be able to show that they have the means to buy one. However, officials will not automatically assume that the possession of a return ticket means that a person is a genuine visitor who plans to return. They may say that the return half of the ticket can be refunded if a person decides not to leave.

Business visitors

The purpose of some visits strains the requirements of the immigration rules and the conditions upon which admission as a visitor is normally given. This applies to some business visitors and some of the 'special classes' of visitor ▶see below. Nevertheless, the IDI have identified the circumstances in which the Home Office is prepared to grant entry to these groups as visitors.

According to the IDI, business visitors are admissible if they are coming to the UK in order to 'transact business'. This includes: attending meetings and briefings, fact finding, negotiating or making contracts with UK businesses to buy or sell goods or services, although they must not be involved in selling goods or services directly to members of the public in the UK. Business visitors may also come for training in techniques and work practices used in the UK, provided that the training is confined to observation, familiarisation and classroom instruction. These visitors must have their main place of business and home outside the UK and not engage directly in business while here.

The Home Office has also stated (IDI Ch2, s1, annex B para 4.2) that it is prepared to admit the following persons as visitors, even though strictly they fall outside the immigration rules because they are in fact supplying a service in the United Kingdom:

- those delivering goods and passengers from abroad, such as lorry drivers and coach drivers, provided they are genuinely working an international route;
- tour group couriers contracted to a firm outside the UK, who are seeking entry to accompany a tour group and who intend to leave with that tour group;
- those coming as speakers in a conference where this is not run as a concern and the conference is a 'one off';

- advisers, consultants, trainers, trouble-shooters etc, provided they are employed abroad by the company to which the client firm in the UK belongs;
- representatives of computer software companies coming to install, debug or enhance their products;
- representatives of foreign machine manufacturers coming to repair their company's products within the guarantee period;
- representatives of foreign machine manufacturers coming to erect, dismantle and install machinery which is too heavy to be delivered in one piece;
- 'monteurs' who are workers coming for up to six months to erect, dismantle, install, service, repair or advise on the development of foreign machinery.

Other special classes of visitor

The IDI also give further details of certain 'special classes' of visitors (IDI Ch2, s1 annex B). They are really no more than examples of persons who are coming to the UK for a short period for a specific purpose other than the 'traditional' reasons for a visit (to see relatives or holidaying) and who intend to leave when that purpose is completed. However, unlike visitors generally, some of these groups do intend to do some kind of work (even if they are not paid for it) and some of them are able to obtain admission for longer than six months in total.

Academic visitors. They may be admitted for more than six months but not more than 12 months. Such visitors can be postgraduate researchers sponsored by the Royal Society or the British Council, a charitable educational or research organisation, a university or similar institution. Alternatively, they may be privately financed and coming to carry out research for their own purposes while on sabbatical leave from overseas institutions. In addition, they may be academics (including doctors) who are taking part in formal exchange arrangements with UK counterparts, eminent doctors or dentists coming to take part in research, teaching or clinical practice, or visiting lecturers who are coming to give a single lecture or series of lectures.

Appellants seeking re-admission to attend appeal hearings. They have to show that they will leave the UK regardless of the outcome of their appeal. When granting leave, due regard is taken of the likely duration of the appeal.

Archaeological excavations. Visitors may come to take part in archaeological excavations if they are doing unpaid work as volunteers, or are paid only subsistence and travelling expenses. They may stay for up to a maximum of 12 months.

Child minders for relatives. Visitors may act as temporary child minders for relatives where the visitor is a close relative of the parent. Distant relatives are only acceptable if they have formed part of the family unit or are the closest surviving relatives of the parents. It has to be shown that neither parent is able to supervise the daytime care of the child, that the arrangement is not simply to enable both parents to take gainful employment or to study, that neither parent is in a category which may lead to settlement and that the visitor will not receive a salary. If it is suspected that the arrangement amounts to employment (paid or unpaid), the application will be refused.

Doctors coming for PLAB tests. A person coming to sit for his or her PLAB test has to satisfy the requirements of the rules relating to visitors, except that it is acceptable for them to intend to stay on for postgraduate training if successful in the test. However, they have to show that they will leave if they fail to pass the test. They may be admitted for six months with a possibility of an extension for up to 12 months.

Amateur entertainers and sportspersons. An amateur entertainer or sportsperson who receives no more than board and lodging and reasonable expenses arising from his or her activity, may be admitted as a visitor provided they satisfy the requirements relating to visitors. However, professional entertainers and sportspersons may also be admitted provided that they are not employed. They may come for such things as personal appearances, promotions, television chat shows, the publication of a book, negotiating contracts and discussing sponsorship deals etc. They may be admitted for up to six months.

Marriage visits. Passengers coming to the UK for the sole purpose of getting married and then intending to return may be admitted as visitors. They may be admitted for up to six months. Any extension of their leave may be considered exceptionally. If good cause can be shown for the delay in getting married and evidence is produced that the marriage will shortly take place, they may be given another extension of six months.

Persons coming for job interviews. Interviewees may be admitted for six months if they can show that, if successful, they will return to their country to await the issue of a work permit or entry clearance for that purpose.

Visitors seeking visas for other countries. These visitors may be admitted, provided that they can show that they are genuinely seeking entry in order to obtain a visa and that the duration of their visit will not exceed six months. Similarly, a person seeking a settlement visa for a third country may be admitted as a visitor, provided that they can show that their visa application will be decided in a short and clearly defined period and that they are returnable to another country after their stay in the UK.

Carers. A person may be admitted to the UK to provide short-term care for a sick relative or friend or to make long-term arrangements for their care. However, they may only be admitted for up to six months, although it may be possible to extend their stay. For more details about carers ▶see below pages 289-291.

Parents of children under 12 years. ▶See pages 395-396 for more details about the immigration rules relating to these parents.

Applying for entry as a visitor

Entry clearance

Since the summer of 1992, entry clearance officers (ECOs) in some British high commissions and embassies have operated an unofficial 'pre-assessment sift' process in relation to people applying for entry clearance for a visit. ECOs make an initial assessment of applications to decide which are likely to succeed. They then tell some people that they may apply but they are likely to be refused and invite them to withdraw the application and not have to pay the non-refundable fee. Negative 'pre-assessment advice' may be given to the following types of applicants: those with inadequate documentation in support of their application, those recently refused by other posts, those with plainly unrealistic plans for their visit, for example, those with no friends or relatives and who have made no arrangements for their stay. The only redress people have when their applications have been 'sifted' is to pursue a formal application, which is likely to be prejudiced by an ECO's initial views. Because this takes place abroad and people often do not understand the bureaucratic procedures at the embassy or high commission, there is little knowledge of or protest against this practice. The pre-assessment process has no basis in law.

As stated above, entry clearance is compulsory for visa nationals but non-visa nationals have a choice as to whether to get one. For general details about the procedures for applying for entry clearance ▶see Chapter 4. There is now a further incentive to obtain an entry clearance. Procedures under the 1999 Act mean that an entry clearance is to be treated as leave to enter. People arriving with entry clearances are admitted with leave when they arrive, unless one of a number of narrow conditions, such as a change of circumstance or deception, applies. In addition, visit entry clearances operate as leave on an *unlimited* number of occasions during the period over which they are valid. So, although the leave which is granted to a visitor lapses when the person leaves, if they return within the period of the validity of an entry clearance it has effect as leave to enter on each occasion.

The holder of an entry clearance must arrive in the UK during the period of the validity of the entry clearance (shown as 'valid from' and 'valid until' on the entry clearance sticker itself ▶see page 112 for an example of an entry clearance). The period of validity for visit entry clearances will normally be six months although they can be given for up to five years in appropriate cases where frequent visits are likely and the immigration authorities are confident that they will not be abused.

Which visit entry clearances operate as leave to enter?

It is intended that *all* entry clearances which are granted will now operate as leave to enter. However, in order to have this effect, the law says that the entry clearance must satisfy two conditions. It must:

- state that it is for the purpose of entry as a visitor;
- state the conditions to which the leave is subject (these conditions will normally be a prohibition on both employment and recourse to public funds).

For general details about entry clearances operating as leave to enter the UK and the practicalities of leaving and returning to the UK ▶see Chapters 4 and 5.

How long is a visitor admitted for?

Visitors who arrive with an entry clearance

When the holder arrives in the UK with an entry clearance which operates as leave, they are treated as having been admitted for six months beginning on the date of arrival provided that, at that time, there are six months or more remaining of the validity of the entry clearance. If, at the time of entry, the remaining period of validity of the entry clearance is less then six months, the person will be admitted until the end of the period of the entry clearance's validity. If the remaining period of validity is more than six months, the visitor is still only granted leave for six months from the date of arrival.

When a person is admitted at the port with an entry clearance, a date stamp will be placed over or by the side of the entry clearance. It is important for people to remember that this does *not* signify a grant of leave for six months from that date. The period of leave is limited to the period of validity of the entry clearance if that is less than six months away. It is very important, therefore, for people to explain to ECOs when it is that they plan to travel so that the 'valid from' date on the entry clearance, which is the beginning of its period of validity, is given as close as possible to the departure date. Precisely for this purpose, ECOs have been given instructions to ask all applicants when it is they will travel. The 'valid from' date can be after the date on which the entry clearance is actually issued. In this way, visitors can get the maximum benefit from their entry clearance.

Visitors who arrive without an entry clearance

A non-visa national who arrives at the port and who qualifies under the immigration rules as a visitor will be granted leave by the immigration officer for up to six months. From February 1988, the immigration rules stated that in most cases visitors should automatically be admitted for six months even when they intend to stay for a few days. From 1 October 1994, the rules have been less clear, stating only that people may be admitted for a period 'not exceeding' six months, subject to a condition prohibiting employment, so there is more scope for immigration officers to admit people for less than six months if they are not entirely satisfied about their intentions. Most visitors are, however, admitted for the full period of six months.

There have been reports of certain ports granting periods of 'temporary admission' to certain visitors who wish to stay for a short period. This is unlawful; if a visitor satisfies the rules, they should be granted leave. Temporary admission may be granted to people pending a decision as to whether they satisfy the rules.

Visitors should keep a note of the period of the validity of the entry clearance separately, so that, even if the passport is lost, they will know the length of the period they have been admitted for and therefore the date by which they need to apply for any extension of stay if that is necessary.

Appeals

There are restrictions (set out below) on appeals both for those who have been refused entry clearance and for those refused leave to enter at the port. In neither case can a person appeal if they have asked for entry to the UK for longer than six months or if the Home Office has decided that the person's presence in the UK would not be conducive to the public good. Where there is no right of appeal, representations can be made to the ECO or the immigration officer as to why they have made the wrong decision. In addition, if there are human rights reasons why the person ought to be able to come or to stay or the person has been discriminated against and these matters are raised in representations, there will generally be a right of appeal on human rights grounds. The only other remedy against the refusal in these cases is judicial review. Those refused at the port who then claim asylum have a right of appeal on asylum grounds. For full details about appeals ▶see Section 10.

When the government originally abolished rights of appeal against visitor entry clearances, it also appointed an independent monitor to report on entry clearance refusals. The first such monitor was Lady Elizabeth Anson, who was previously an adjudicator. Rabinder Singh QC has now succeeded her. The monitor's role is to review a random sample of visitor refusals, and to assess whether they are in accordance with the law. Lady Elizabeth, in all her annual reports, criticised the 'pre-sift' practice (see above) and urged that applicants should be clearly informed of their right to pursue the application. Rabinder Singh's first report was issued in November 2001. He also considered the pre-sift process and recommended that the procedure be the subject of a formal study.

Appeals against entry clearance decisions

If entry clearance is refused, the applicant will be given a notice to this effect which explains any appeal rights. The right of appeal against refusals of entry clearance for visitors was removed in 1993. The 1997 Labour election manifesto promised 'a streamlined system of appeals for visitors denied a visa'. This promise was kept, but only in part. From 2 October 2000, there is a right of appeal against refusals of visit entry clearances but only if the applicant is a 'family visitor' (see s60(5) 1999 Act). Under regulation 2(2) of the Immigration Appeals (Family Visitor) (No 2) Regulations 2000, a 'family visitor' is a person who applies for entry clearance to visit any of the following relatives:

- spouse, father, mother, son, daughter, grandfather, grandmother, grandchild, brother, sister, uncle, aunt, nephew, niece or first cousin (first cousin means the son or daughter of the applicant's uncle or aunt); *or*

- the father, mother, brother or sister of his or her spouse; *or*

- the spouse of his or her son or daughter; *or*

- his or her step-father, step-mother, step-son, step-brother or step-sister; *or*

- his or her unmarried partner with whom he or she has lived for two of the last three years before the date when the application for entry clearance is made.

The time limit for appealing is 28 days (although if the notice of refusal is given by sending it to the applicant overseas by post, then they are not treated as having received it until 28 days after it was sent and the 28-day appeal time limit runs from that point). The notice of appeal must be lodged with the British post which made the decision. There was a fee payable to exercise the appeal right and the notice of appeal had to be accompanied by the relevant fee payable in local currency. The fees were £125 for an oral hearing and £50 for an appeal without a hearing. The fees were abolished on 15 May 2002.

Those advising in relation to these appeals should note that after they have been lodged, they are listed and dealt with quickly (►see page 618 for the likely time-scales). The present practice of ECOs is to rely on the notice of refusal as their reasons for the decision. Advisers should therefore, immediately upon receipt of such a notice, begin the process of preparing the appeal. Where an appeal is dismissed, any application to the Immigration Appeal Tribunal (IAT) for leave should be prepared in detail, particularly if the appeal is to be heard in writing only. In such cases, the president of the IAT has recently indicated that once a chairman of the IAT has decided to grant leave, he/she will then immediately proceed to deciding the appeal itself.

Appeals against refusals of entry at port

There is a right of appeal for visitors who are refused entry at port, provided that they have a current entry clearance. They are entitled to remain in the UK while the appeal is being considered. The time limit for appealing is 10 working days. However, if a passenger arrives in the UK with an entry clearance but the immigration officer cancels the entry clearance because the person has arrived before the entry clearance has become valid, or because the person asks for entry other than as a visitor, the passenger will not have a right of appeal.

Applying for extensions

There is no provision in the immigration rules for extending a visit beyond a total stay as a visitor of six months. Most visitors are admitted for six months initially but those who are admitted for less may apply for extensions to take them up to the six-month limit. If people do wish to stay longer than planned, they should show good reasons for their change of plans, otherwise it may be refused on the grounds of a failure to 'honour any declaration or undertaking given orally or in writing as to the intended duration and/or purpose' of their visit (see para 322(7), HC 395).

Those already with leave in the UK under other categories, for example, as a student, may apply for an extension of stay as a visitor up to a maximum period of six months. However, if a person who has been admitted to the UK as a seasonal agricultural worker applies to stay for a visit, the time already spent in the UK as a seasonal agricultural worker counts towards this six months.

If leave is granted for less than six months and an application to extend stay up to the six-month limit is made and it is refused, there is a right of appeal. If a person was originally given less than six months and seeks an extension for a period which, if granted, would mean that the *total* period would be in excess of six months, the Home Office should still consider granting leave for a period to bring the total period up to six months. It should be remembered that, by the time an appeal is processed for hearing, the person is likely to have fulfilled any desire to remain in the UK up to the six-month maximum.

Where a person has already been given six months in the UK as a visitor and an application is made to remain as a visitor beyond the six-month time limit, it is an application made outside the immigration rules and is therefore dealt with at the discretion of the Home Office. The immigration rules state that an extension of stay 'is to be refused' in these circumstances. The Home Office has stated that such applications will only be granted in exceptional compassionate circumstances.

Some of the categories of 'special classes of visitor' listed above are examples of situations where an extension beyond six months may be granted. Another example is where a visitor seeks an extension because s/he has been unable to obtain a flight. An extension beyond the six-month limit may be granted in these circumstances provided the application is made before the leave runs out and a ticket with a confirmed flight is produced. Exceptional applications for extensions for carers are considered below.

A person's passport will be marked to show if they have been refused an extension ▶see page 120 for an example. This may make it difficult for them to return to the UK, or to travel to other countries, in the future. Even if the visitor leaves the UK when the Home Office replies, they will be on record as having been refused the extension. If they apply again in the future, officials may not be satisfied that they intend to leave the UK at the end of the next visit. Visitors should therefore be told about the possible long-term consequences of applying for extensions. It is important only to apply to extend a visit if it is really necessary.

Making the application

People must use the official Home Office form FLR(O) and send it to the Home Office, together with all the documents requested or an explanation of why the documents are not available and when they will be sent. The application must be sent in before the leave runs out. It is important to set out the reasons for wishing to stay longer, that is, why the visitor's plans have changed since the time they were admitted, and to state the further length of time required; for example, 'I want to remain as a visitor for another three months in order to look after my sister whose baby is expected next week'.

If there is any evidence to support the reasons for staying longer and to demonstrate that the person will in fact leave the UK at the end of the further time, this should also be sent to the Home Office. The passport must be sent to the Home Office with the application. The other requirements of the rules, about maintenance and accommodation and about the visitor's intention to leave at the end of the visit, must all still be satisfied.

Visitors applying to change their status

The immigration rules provide for some changes of status for people who have come to visit the UK and prohibit others. The rules currently allow visitors:

- to apply to stay and settle with some close relatives, for example, parents coming to visit their children settled in the UK may apply to stay permanently with them;
- to marry and to apply to stay with their spouses or unmarried partners

(however, the 2002 White Paper contains proposals to prevent people in the UK in temporary categories from switching to stay with a spouse or partner and so this situation may change in the future);

- to apply for asylum or to remain on human rights grounds;
- if they are not visa nationals, to apply to stay as students.

For further details about switching status ▶see pages 90-92. Even if the rules do not allow the person to switch, this does not mean that they cannot apply for such changes, but that any application is likely to be refused. The Home Office would need to be satisfied that there were very exceptional reasons to consider granting changes of status outside the rules.

People should make applications to the Home Office before the time limit in their passport runs out on the appropriate official Home Office form ▶see pages 95-101, asking for a change of status and showing how they fit into the relevant parts of the immigration rules concerning their new status. It is important to explain why their plans have changed since they came in for the visit and what has made them decide to remain for a different purpose. If the Home Office suspects that the person concealed their true reasons for wishing to be in the UK when they arrived, they may ask detailed questions to see whether the person is an illegal entrant by deception.

Carers

There is no specific provision in the immigration rules for carers. Where a person wants to come to the UK in order to care for a friend or relative for a short period of time or in order to make practical arrangements for that person's long-term care, they will be able to so if they can satisfy the ordinary rules relating to visitors (see above).

The Home Office does, however, have a concession outside the immigration rules for people who are in the UK for a temporary purpose to extend their stay in order to care for a sick relative or friend who is suffering from a serious illness, such as cancer or AIDS, or who are mentally or physically disabled (see IDI Ch17, s2). All cases are considered on their individual merits, depending on the nature of the compassionate circumstances involved. The purpose of the concession is not to allow carers to remain indefinitely but only for a temporary period until alternative arrangements for the patient's care have been put in place. The application is being made for further limited leave and should be made on form FLR(O).

The first application for an extension

The concession states that applications for extensions from carers who are *friends* of the patient should normally be refused. Applications can, however, be granted in these cases if there is an emergency, for example, where the patient has suddenly become ill and there is no time to arrange alternative care and there is no one else in the UK to whom the patient can turn. Applications will be more readily granted where the carer is a *relative* of the patient. In both circumstances, in addition to the compassionate features of the case, the factors which are taken into consideration are:

- the nature of the illness or the condition;
- the kind of care which is needed;
- the care which is available from other sources, such as social services or other relatives and friends;
- the patient's prognosis.

Advisers should therefore obtain evidence about the above matters. It will be essential to have a letter from a doctor to explain the nature of the condition, the care needs which it gives rise to and the prognosis. If leave is granted, it is likely to be for a period of three months with a prohibition on work and recourse to public funds. The Home Office will make clear to the applicant by letter that leave is being given on the understanding that alternative arrangements will be made for the future care of the patient.

Further applications

Applications for *further* leave by a carer who is a friend or relative of the patient should be supported by the following:

- a letter from an NHS consultant with full details of the illness or condition and its prognosis;
- *if* the local social services department have been involved in the case, a letter from them setting out the benefit of the continued presence in the UK of the carer and explaining why suitable alternative care cannot be arranged;
- evidence that alternative arrangements have been or are being explored;
- details of the patient's family in the UK, how the patient was previously cared for and why those arrangements are no longer suitable or available;
- details of the applicant's circumstances in their own country, including whether he or she has dependants, their employment (the Home Office will not generally grant leave on a longer-term basis if the carer is married or has dependants);
- evidence to show that the applicant can be maintained and accommodated without working or recourse to public funds. It should be noted that a patient may be entitled to obtain attendance allowance in order to pay a person to care for them. The Home Office has confirmed that:

'The allowance is paid to the patient rather than the carer and therefore the carer would not be considered to be in receipt of public funds. If the patient is claiming other benefits and is using these to support and accommodate the carer, provided that the patient is not claiming any extra benefit for the carer then again this should not be considered as recourse to public funds unless the carer was to claim benefits in his own right' (IDI, Ch17, s2, para 6).

The central issue in many cases will be whether the circumstances justify the applicant, who is close to the patient, being able to stay to care for them as opposed to their being provided with what can be offered by social services. It may be that there is a case to be made under Article 8 ECHR (right to respect for private and family life) for the relative or friend being allowed to stay. Representatives might also want to consider the extra cost to the public of care being provided by social services instead of the carer. In deciding whether any interference in private or family life, which wold be caused by refusing to allow the carer to remain, is justified under Article 8, the additional cost of care needs to be considered as well as the interests of immigration control.

A Home Office refusal to grant further leave was successfully challenged in the High Court in *Zakrocki* because of strong evidence that the best care plan for an elderly, severely disabled man was for his Polish relatives to carry on looking after him in his home. This was consistent with the government's policy of care in the community, and the local authority regarded it as more appropriate and less costly than residential care. The immigration issues had to be balanced with the rights of the disabled man, a British citizen, to remain in the UK and be looked after in accordance with the policies and duties that apply to citizens of this country. A further similar case, *Green*, was unsuccessful in the High Court. The IDI (Ch17, s2, para 4.2) relies upon the decision of the High Court in *Green* and therefore officers are likely to quote it in their decision letters. However, the IDI does not recognise that the Court of Appeal subsequently granted Ms Green permission to appeal and the Home Office conceded her case and granted exceptional leave before that appeal could be heard.

In cases where there are sufficient compassionate circumstances to grant *further* extensions, the Home Office may grant leave for up to 12 months at a time. Carers will not normally qualify for settlement unless they can benefit from the long residence concession ▶see pages 105-108.

Transit visitors

There are separate provisions for the admission of transit passengers. They have to show that:

- they are in transit to another country outside the Common Travel Area ▶see Glossary, and are assured entry there;
- they have the means and intention of travelling there straightaway;
- they are assured of entry to their country of destination; *and*

- they intend and are able to leave the UK within 48 hours.

These rules are for people who wish to actually *enter* the UK for a short period either because they need to get to another port to continue their onward journey or because they want to spend time outside the transit area before continuing. Transit visitors are admitted to the UK for a maximum of 48 hours and any application for an extension beyond that time is to be refused under the immigration rules. A person who wants to spend a few days, for example, visiting friends and family before continuing their journey, has to satisfy the ordinary rules as a visitor.

Entry clearance requirements for transit visitors

Visa nationals normally require an entry clearance to come to the UK. However, the requirements for visa nationals who are transit passengers to obtain entry clearance can be waived for some passengers (see IDI, Ch2, s2, annex D). This waiver applies where:

- the passenger is arriving by air and has a confirmed booking on an onward flight which departs within 24 hours to their country of destination; and

- the passenger has any necessary documentation to be admitted to their country of destination and transit visas for any other countries it will be necessary to transit through; and

- the passenger's name does not appear on the Home Office's 'Warnings Index'.

The waiver can still apply where the passenger will travel between two airports in the UK to get the connecting flight. *However*, the waiver *does not* apply if the person is a national of any of the following countries: Afghanistan, Colombia, Democratic Republic of Congo, Ecuador, Eritrea, Ethiopia, Federal Republic of Yugoslavia, Ghana, Iran, Iraq, Libya, Nigeria, People's Republic of China, Republic of Croatia, Slovak Republic, Somalia, Sri Lanka, Turkey and Uganda. The same applies to any person who holds a travel document issued by the 'Turkish Republic of Northern Cyprus' or the 'Former Socialist Federal Republic of Yugoslavia', neither of which are recognised by the UK authorities. If a transit passenger arrives with an entry clearance and is refused entry, they are entitled to appeal.

Direct airside transit

People who are intending to pass directly in transit through the UK *without* actually entering the UK need a 'Direct Airside Transit' entry clearance only if they are a national of any of the countries listed above. They will only exceptionally be admitted to the UK, for example, if they have missed flight connections or because of the re-routing of aircraft. The immigration officer will still need to be satisfied that they are genuinely seeking entry in transit. Entry may be granted for up to 48 hours.

Medical visitors

Some of the requirements for entry as a medical visitor are the same as for an ordinary visitor (see above). Medical visitors have to show that they do not intend to take employment, produce or provide goods and services in the UK or to study at a maintained school. They must also be able to demonstrate that they and their dependants will be maintained and accommodated without recourse to public funds and that they are able to meet the cost of their onward journey. *However*, they also have to meet the following additional requirements:

- the course of medical treatment is of finite duration (not open-ended in length) and they intend to leave the UK at the end of it;
- they can provide evidence of the medical condition requiring consultation or treatment in the UK, the arrangements that have been made for private medical treatment, the estimated cost and duration of the treatment and of the funds available to pay for it.

If the person is suffering from a communicable disease, the medical inspector (at the port of arrival) must be satisfied that there is no danger to public health. There is nothing in the rules to state that immigration officials should take into account the availability of treatment in the person's country. Medical visitors can be admitted for up to six months initially. However, there is *no maximum time limit* for medical visits and so it is possible to obtain an extension under the immigration rules to stay for longer than six months. In order to get an extension, applicants have to produce evidence in the form of a letter from a registered practitioner who holds an NHS consultant post or who appears in the Special Register of the Medical Council (registrars) providing full details of the following:

- the nature of the illness, the proposed treatment and the frequency of consultations;
- the likely length of the treatment;
- details of the cost of the treatment and confirmation that all expenses are being met; and
- where treatment amounts to private visits to a consultant for what appears to be a relatively minor ailment, details of the progress made.

Applicants also need to produce evidence that they have paid their costs of treatment to date and that they are able to meet the future costs of treatment and of their maintenance in the UK. If the application is refused, as long as it was made in time, the person will have the right to appeal (because no maximum time limit is laid down for medical visits) and may remain lawfully in the UK during the time it takes to make a decision and to appeal.

Working holidaymakers

The immigration rules allow Commonwealth citizens (▶see page 748 for a list of Commonwealth countries) between the ages of 17 and 27 (inclusive) to come to the UK for a working holiday of up to two years. Provided that an applicant was in this age group at the time of their first entry to the UK as a working holidaymaker, they may extend their leave so that they have remained in the UK for a total of not more than two years even if they are over 27 when they are seeking to extend their leave. In addition, the IDI indicate that there is some flexibility in the age requirement. If a person is one or two weeks over the age of 27 at the time that they seek entry, they may still be admitted. They may also be admitted if they are up to six months too old provided that their arrival has been delayed by exceptionally compelling or compassionate circumstances.

All working holidaymakers are required to obtain an entry clearance regardless of their nationality. Applicants must be unmarried unless they are travelling with their spouse and both intend to take a working holiday together. Working holidaymakers must not have dependent children who are either five or over or who will reach that age before the end of the working holiday and they must not have any other commitments which require a regular income (for example, the need to provide for other dependent relatives). They must have the means to pay for their onward journey and be able to support and accommodate themselves without recourse to public funds. They must intend to leave at the end of their holiday.

Working holidaymakers must also intend to take employment, which is only *incidental* to their holiday, and not engage in business or provide services as a professional sportsperson or entertainer or pursue a career in the UK. The basic rule is that working holidaymakers must not intend to work for the majority of their time in the UK and their employment must not be the dominant purpose for coming here. The rule of thumb set out in the IDI is that applicants may take periods of full-time employment provided they do so for less than 50 per cent of the holiday. Part-time work extending beyond 50 per cent of the holiday is permissible, provided it is clear that the applicant will also be having a holiday. Similar guidance is given relating to the extent of any part- or full-time study that the working holidaymaker may wish to do while here.

Although the IDI state that a professional career must not be pursued, a degree of flexibility is allowed for those who wish to teach in the UK as supply teachers or work as nurses through agencies. Certain other medical disciplines are also mentioned, such as being employed as a radiographer (IDI Ch4, s2 annex c). This is presumably in response to the shortage of labour in these particular areas. Work Permits (UK) also operates with a degree of discretion outside the immigration rules by allowing holidaymakers to switch into work permit employment without having to apply for entry clearance from outside the UK. This discretion is not restricted to the above disciplines, however, and switching may be allowed for all types of work permit employment so long as the application for the work permit itself has been approved.

Children of the working holidaymaker aged under five years may be admitted, provided that they can be supported and accommodated without recourse to public funds and provided it is intended that the child will leave (usually with their parent) before reaching the age of five. Where only one of the parents is being admitted, that parent must either be the sole surviving parent or they must have had 'sole responsibility' for the child's upbringing or there must be serious and compelling family or other considerations which make the exclusion of the child from the UK undesirable, and there must be suitable arrangements in the UK for the child's care. These requirements are similar to those which apply where a child seeks to be admitted for settlement to join only one parent in the UK ▶see pages 374-377.

Proposed changes to the working holidaymaker rules

Although the working holidaymaker category is intended to benefit all young Commonwealth nationals, it is predominantly the 'white' Commonwealth which has been able to take advantage of this rule. For example, according to figures released by the Foreign and Commonwealth Office in 2000, during 1999, 18,800 Australians, 8,080 New Zealand nationals and 3,730 Canadians were admitted as working holidaymakers. Over the same period, 50 Indian nationals, 40 Pakistani nationals, 20 Sri Lankans, 120 Ghanaians and five or less nationals of Barbados, Sierra Leone and Uganda were admitted.

The 2002 White Paper recognises this discrepancy between 'black' and 'white' Commonwealth countries and proposes a comprehensive review of the scheme to make it 'as inclusive as possible'. A revised version of the scheme is also envisaged to form part of the government's new economic migration policy to provide 'an additional, temporary, flexible workforce'. The proposed changes include:

- extending the scheme to a range of non-Commonwealth countries;
- reviewing the current age restrictions;
- relaxing the requirement that employment must be incidental to a holiday;
- formally allowing working holidaymakers to switch into work permit employment.

People who wish to come to the UK as au pairs or to do seasonal work at agricultural camps are covered in Chapter 19.

Travel outside the UK

Each time a person visits the UK, they have to satisfy the immigration officer that they fit into the immigration rules. Visit entry clearances which count as leave to enter have that effect on an *unlimited* number of occasions within the period of the validity of the entry clearance. So, although the leave which is granted to a visitor lapses on their leaving the UK, if they return within the period of the validity of the entry clearance, it has effect as leave to enter on each occasion. Visa nationals do not need to apply for a further entry clearance when they return within the period of validity of such an entry clearance.

This should help people who are considering travelling and returning to the UK, for example, those planning to go to other European countries as well as the UK, or, for example, those who want to go on Hajj with relatives living in this country and visit them before and afterwards.

Those who are planning to return to the UK successively over a long period of time should try to persuade the ECO to grant an entry clearance with a long period of validity. Guidance notes issued by JECU (now UK Visas) indicate that they may be issued with a period of validity of up to five years.

Those with entry clearance can still be refused entry, however, if there has been a relevant change in circumstances so that they do not satisfy the visitor rules, or it is discovered that false representations were made in order to obtain the entry clearance, or if refusal of entry is justified on medical grounds or on the grounds of the person's criminal record.

15 Students

For a long time, the immigration rules have allowed people to come to the UK in order to study. The expectation is that, like visitors, those coming to study will stay in the UK only temporarily. Therefore, although it is possible for students to extend their stay to do further study, most students have to show that they intend to leave the UK at the end of their proposed studies. However, as a result of a recent Home Office concession, certain students, for example, those wishing to take courses at degree level or higher, no longer need to demonstrate an intention to leave.

Most students arriving in the UK have already chosen and been accepted on to a particular course of study. It is also possible, however, to come to the UK as a 'prospective' student, provided the person will take up their course of study within six months. As well as 'ordinary' students, the immigration rules also provide for the following people:

- student nurses;
- postgraduate doctors and dentists;
- students who are re-sitting exams;
- students who are writing up their thesis;
- students' union sabbatical officers.

This chapter covers all the above categories of student. The last three categories were only added to the immigration rules from 2 October 2000. The rules allow postgraduate doctors and dentists to be in the UK partly in order to be trained in their professions. The rules also provide for the family members of students to be admitted to and stay in the UK. Training and work experience more generally form part of the work permit scheme and are therefore covered in Chapter 19. Separate considerations apply for students who are nationals of the EEA. These students are covered in this chapter. For more details about free movement in the EEA ▶see Chapter 22.

An important change in immigration law relating to most students is that they no longer have to specifically ask for permission to do part-time work. From 21 June 1999, most have been automatically allowed to do at least *some* work while studying ▶see below page 310.

Students and 'prospective' students

Entry clearance

Students and prospective students who are visa nationals ▶see page 737, have to obtain entry clearance from a British embassy, high commission or consulate before travelling to the UK. Those who are not visa nationals do not need to obtain entry clearance but may do so if they wish, or they may apply for permission when they arrive at a British port or airport ▶see page 56 on the advantages and disadvantages of applying for optional entry clearance.

WHAT THE RULES SAY

People coming to the UK as students must show:

- that they have been accepted for a course of study at a publicly-funded institution of further or higher education, *or* at a *bona fide* private education institution which maintains satisfactory records of enrolment and attendance, *or* an independent fee-paying school outside the maintained sector;
- that they are able and intend to follow either a recognised full-time degree course at a publicly-funded institution of further or higher education, *or* a weekday full-time course involving attendance at a single institution for a minimum of at least 15 hours organised daytime study per week of a single subject or directly-related subjects, *or* a full-time course of study at an independent fee-paying school;
- if under the age of 16 years, that they are enrolled at an independent fee-paying school on a full-time course of studies which meets the requirements of the Education Act 1944;
- that they intend to leave the UK at the end of their studies;
- that they do not intend to engage in business or take employment, except part-time or vacation work with the agreement of the Secretary of State ▶see below page 310; and
- that they are able to meet the costs of the course and to maintain and accommodate themselves and any dependants without engaging in business, working or having recourse to public funds.

People who intend to study in the UK but who have not yet been accepted, for a full-time course may be admitted as 'prospective students', for up to six months.

Prospective students have to show that:

- they have a genuine and realistic intention of undertaking, within six months of entry, a course of study which would meet the requirements of the rules;
- they intend to leave the UK on completion of their studies, or on

completion of their time as prospective students if they are not accepted as students; and

- they can maintain and accommodate themselves and any dependants without working and without recourse to public funds.

WHAT THE RULES MEAN

Publicly-funded institutions of further or higher education

The expression 'publicly-funded institution of further or higher education' is not defined in the immigration rules. Such institutions are, however, intended to be those which are referred to in the Education Act 1996:

- further education and sixth form colleges funded by the further education funding councils throughout the UK;
- universities and other institutions of higher education funded by the higher education funding councils.

Bona fide private education institutions

Bona fide private education institutions which maintain satisfactory records of enrolment and attendance are also not defined in the immigration rules. The words bona fide mean that the institution must be genuinely providing education. Private educational institutions, often attended by international students, include secretarial colleges and language schools. They may incidentally be institutions of further or higher education but are not publicly-funded. They also include American universities with campuses in the UK offering American degrees and qualifications. Because these institutions are not publicly accountable, the immigration authorities are given wide latitude to check that they are bona fide and that they keep satisfactory records of enrolment and attendance.

The IDI (Ch3, s1, annex C) give further guidance on bona fide private institutions including information on accreditation of such institutions by organisations such as the British Accreditation Council for Independent Further and Higher Education. A college does not have to be accredited to be regarded as bona fide but accreditation is an indication that a college is likely to be regarded as such.

Independent fee paying schools

Like the previous two institutions, independent fee-paying schools outside the maintained sector are not defined in the immigration rules. They include preparatory ('prep') schools and public schools. According to education law, an independent school is a school at which full-time education is provided for five or more pupils of school age and which is not maintained by a local education authority. City Technology Colleges and City Colleges for the Technology of the Arts are not actually defined as 'maintained' but, according to the Home Office, are publicly-funded and so they are not independent for the purpose of the rules.

The IDI (Ch3, s1, annex C) state that the maintained sector includes all publicly-funded schools including grant-maintained schools, voluntary-aided schools, sixth form colleges attached to maintained schools, special schools and nursery schools. None of these schools, therefore, are 'independent' schools. Independent schools must be registered with the Department of Education and Skills and an unregistered school will not be regarded as an independent school for the purpose of the rules. The expression 'fee-paying' describes the school rather than the parent, so that a pupil on a scholarship could presumably qualify for admission as a student under the immigration rules.

Full-time studies

Students will normally need a letter from the institution at which they intend to study, confirming that they have been accepted on a particular full-time course. Depending on the college and the level of studies, the immigration authorities may also ask for details of the precise number of hours per week the student will be studying. They also need to know the level of fees and whether the whole fee, or a deposit towards this, has been paid. It is not a requirement of the rules that a deposit or fees have been paid in advance to the educational institution, but if any money has been paid, confirmation of this is likely to help an application.

'Full-time' for immigration purposes is defined as at least 15 hours organised daytime, weekday classes per week. The study must be at a single institution, but can include two or more related part-time courses. Evening classes that commence after 6pm, (or before 6pm if the majority of the class takes place after 6pm) and weekend classes will not be counted towards the 15 hours. It is generally accepted by the immigration authorities that English language courses for non-English speakers can be combined with another course to meet the 15-hours requirement. Where two part-time courses are not apparently related, the student or the institution may need to explain why a particular study combination is desirable or helps a student in their career.

If the full-time course is at first or higher degree level at a publicly-funded institution, it is sufficient that the institution designates the course as 'full time'. Even though there may not be formal classes for this number of hours, it is assumed that the 15 hours requirement is met.

Maintenance and accommodation

Students must show that they have the money to pay their fees and to live in the UK without needing to work and without recourse to public funds. Overseas students usually have to pay full-cost fees for their courses, often amounting to several thousand pounds. Although they are allowed to work part-time, any earnings from employment they may obtain will not necessarily be taken into consideration by the Home Office in assessing their financial viability although any savings they have built up through working here can be taken into account. Earnings from guaranteed part-time work at a publicly-funded institution of further or higher education or full-time employment for sandwich course students arranged by the institution may be taken into account however.

If a student's spouse has been permitted to stay in the UK and has permission to work, his or her actual (rather than potential) earnings may be taken into account. Dependants of students are permitted to work where the student has been granted leave for at least 12 months ▶see page 306.

Students may provide evidence of financial support in several ways. If they are supported by a government or other scholarship, a letter from the scholarship-giving agency will probably be sufficient, confirming the amount of money and arrangements about fees. If students are being privately supported, a letter from the sponsor confirming their willingness and ability to support the student is necessary. The sponsor should produce evidence of their means covering about three months, which may be recent original bank statements or pay-slips. When a friend is supporting the student, or anyone else who has no immediately obvious interest in doing so, the immigration authorities may ask more questions about their and the student's motives.

Most other categories under the immigration rules contain a requirement that the applicant can be maintained and accommodated without recourse to public funds. For further details of these requirements ▶see pages 328-335.

Ability to follow the course

Immigration officials also have to be satisfied that the student is academically able to follow the course. In dealing with entry clearance applications, ECOs are encouraged to check with the local British Council office if they have doubts about any foreign qualifications or certificates shown to them. The immigration authorities should not normally attempt to second-guess enrolment decisions by colleges as to the student's ability to follow a course. The IDI (Ch3, s1, annex A) indicate that where an officer is doubtful about a student's ability to follow the course, the college principal should be contacted and asked to make an assessment of the student. Immigration officials themselves have no qualifications with which to make an assessment as to the ability of a particular student to follow a particular course and often they will base their decisions on their own appraisal of the student's proficiency in English when answering questions in interview.

The Immigration Appeal Tribunal (IAT) decided in the case of *Pattu-wearachchi* that it was valid for a student coming to do a vocational course to decide, at entry, to follow an English language course first, and this change of plan did not invalidate the entry clearance granted. Many institutions include an English language test as part of their application process. If this has been done, and the college finds the student's English acceptable, this should be explained to the immigration authorities.

Intention to leave the UK and the Home Office concession

Under the immigration rules, students have to show that they intend to leave the UK at the end of their course of studies. In many cases, it is impossible to prove at the outset of a course what a person will do at the end of it, and immigration officials therefore may make subjective decisions. Because official scholarships or sponsoring agencies often stipulate that a student must return, this part of the rules is rarely a problem for officially-sponsored students, since they are not, without the consent of their sponsor, able to switch to privately-funded studies if their sponsorship ends. However, privately-funded students may encounter more difficulties. The immigration authorities may ask what benefit the course will be to the person after returning home and about the student's future career plans, and whether the course is available in his or her home country. It may be helpful to have evidence of job advertisements from the country of origin which specify the qualification the student hopes to obtain, or even evidence of a job offer on return. It is certainly important to relate the qualifications to be obtained to employment prospects in the home country. Other evidence of commitments in the country of origin, for example, having a spouse and children there, could also be helpful.

In a concession outside the rules announced by the Home Secretary on 17 October 2001, students applying for courses at degree-level or higher, student nurses, and postgraduate doctors and dentists no longer need to satisfy the immigration authorities that they intend to leave the UK at the end of their studies. This concession also applies to students undertaking foundation or language courses on which their degree places are conditional. The concession is in line with the current policy of the Home Office to allow students falling into these categories to transfer into work permit employment even though the immigration rules would otherwise prevent them from switching status. Although it is too early to give full details about how this concession is operating in practice; such students are advised to make it clear to the immigration authorities if they plan to transfer into work permit employment at the end of their studies.

The immigration rules require that a student intends to leave the UK at the end of their 'studies', not necessarily at the end of the first course on which they enrol. If students wish to continue to follow higher-level courses after the one for which they are seeking entry, they should explain this. The immigration authorities can decide whether these plans appear to them to be realistic, either academically or financially. In the case of *Kharrazi,* concerning a 12-year-old boy's plan to progress to university from school, the Court of Appeal held that such an intention could fall within the immigration rules if it formed part of a 'coherent and definite whole which was reasonably capable of being carried out by him'. If a student has any other relatives who have become settled in the UK, particularly if they entered as students in the past, immigration officials may be particularly suspicious about the applicant's longer-term intentions.

In the absence of direct evidence of intentions, much will rest on drawing of inferences from the particular circumstances of the student, including the student's academic record. The IAT has been careful to warn that inferences must be drawn only from *evidence* and that mere suspicion that a person will not return is not enough.

Additional rules for prospective students

People hoping to study in the UK may not have made definite arrangements to do so before travelling. They may be travelling or intending to travel to the UK to look for a suitable course, or to come for an interview at a particular institution. In these circumstances, it is important that they explain their intentions to study to the immigration official and seek entry clearance or entry to the UK as a 'prospective student' and then later apply to extend their stay in the UK if they are accepted. Prospective students have to satisfy the immigration authorities that they have the money to support themselves for the period during which they are arranging their studies as well as during any course. Students from countries which have strict foreign exchange control regulations may have problems in showing financial support to undertake a course before they have been accepted on it. Prospective students must also satisfy immigration officials, that if they are not successful in obtaining a place, they will leave the UK by the end of the period of leave granted.

Students, or those seeking advice on their behalf may feel that, as they have no specific study plans, they should seek entry as visitors. This is not advisable. It is important that students make their intentions clear on arrival. The dangers of entering as visitors and seeking to change status once studies have been arranged are twofold:

- people could be treated as illegal entrants because they did not reveal their true intentions, or the period for which they wished to remain, on arrival (e.g., see the *case* of *Durojaiye*);
- as stated above, visa nationals cannot change their status while in the UK to become students.

Entry clearance decisions

If entry clearance is granted, it will operate as leave to enter provided it specifies the purpose for which it has been issued and the conditions to which the leave will be subject. Unlike a visit entry clearance, a student entry clearance will act as leave to enter on one occasion during the period of validity, but due to the non-lapsing of leave when a person departs from the Common Travel Area (CTA), will not have to be renewed upon re-entry during its existence if the leave granted was for more than six months. The period of validity of the entry clearance and therefore the leave which it gives, will generally depend on the length of the course (see below).

Students applying for courses which will last for six months or less, and prospective students, do not have a right of appeal against a refusal of entry clearance as a student. This has been the case since appeal rights were cut back by the 1993 Act and which was confirmed in the 1999 Act (see s60(4)(5)). Their only appeal is on human rights or discrimination grounds. Students who have already been accepted on to a course of over six months' length do have a right of appeal against the refusal of entry clearance and will be given appeal forms to fill in when they are notified of the decision. These should be completed and returned to the entry clearance post.

Arrival in the United Kingdom

Normally, students should be granted leave to enter until 31 October following the *end* of their course in accordance with the IDI (Ch3, s1), or for courses that do not follow the standard academic year, for an additional two months following the end of the course. In practice, however, for courses that last more than a year, students are frequently only allowed in for one year at a time. Higher-level degree students may be admitted for the full length of their course, particularly if they have evidence of financial sponsorship for the whole period. The length of time allowed and the conditions will be indicated on the students' passports both in the entry clearance sticker and stamps showing any extensions which have been granted. For full details about calculating the leave granted by an entry clearance ►see pages 58-59.

Students will either be given a prohibition on working or a restriction on working. Those on short courses admitted for six months or less will often be prohibited from working. Such students may still request permission to work, in which case their passports may be endorsed with a requirement that any employment must be authorised. Students enrolled on a course for six months or more will also have their passports endorsed with a requirement that employment must be authorised. These students are now automatically authorised to take part-time and vacation work, and sandwich placements ►see below.

Refusal of entry

Students with an entry clearance

Students and prospective students who arrive with entry clearance have the right to appeal against any refusal of entry and are able to remain in the UK while the appeal is pending.

Students without an entry clearance

Students who are not visa nationals do not need to obtain entry clearance before travelling but if they do not, and if they are unable to satisfy an immigration officer on arrival that they qualify to enter, they may be refused entry and can be sent straight back. If they are seeking entry as prospective students having not yet enrolled on a course, or if their course would last for less than six months, they will have no right of appeal at all (other than on human rights/discrimination grounds). Students accepted on to longer courses can appeal against a refusal under the rules relating to studies but only after they have left the UK.

Where a person has been refused entry, and does not have an appeal right from within the UK, representations may be made on their behalf to immigration officers as to why they should be admitted. However, unless there is important new evidence or exceptional and compelling compassionate reasons, it would be unusual for immigration officers to change their mind once a decision to refuse has been made. If they are not satisfied that a student is able to follow the course that he or she intends to take, further evidence from the academic institution may be helpful to show that the student does meet its admission criteria. If the reason for the refusal is related to the intention to leave at the end of studies, it is very difficult to alter the decision, unless concrete evidence is produced showing that the person does have an incentive to return.

Family dependants

The immigration rules allow spouses and children (under the age of 18) of students and prospective students to be admitted to and to stay in the UK. The same rules apply to family members of student nurses, those re-sitting exams, writing up theses, and postgraduate doctors and dentists, all of whom are described below. The status of family members is dependent on the student. They will be given the same time limit on their stay as the student him or herself and cannot be given a longer period.

The rules require spouses of students and prospective students to show that:

- they are married to a person admitted to, or allowed to remain in, the UK as a student;
- the couple intend to live together as husband and wife while the student is studying, and the marriage is still subsisting;
- there will be adequate maintenance and accommodation for them, and any dependants, without recourse to public funds;
- they do not intend to work unless permitted to do so;
- they intend to leave the UK at the end of any leave granted.

The only other family members allowed are children aged under 18 on first arrival in the UK. The requirements are that they:

- are coming to join a student or prospective student already admitted to or allowed to remain in the UK;
- are unmarried, and must not have formed an independent family unit, nor be leading an independent life;
- will be maintained and accommodated adequately without recourse to public funds;
- will leave the UK after any period of leave granted to the parent.

No provision is made in the rules for leave to be given to unmarried and same sex partners of students.

If a dependant accompanies or joins a student who has leave for 12 months or more, the dependant will be free to work. Dependants will be prohibited from working where less than 12 months' leave is granted to the student unless the dependant was already free to work and the leave is being granted as an extension of existing status. However, immigration officers are instructed to exercise discretion and to allow the dependant to work if the student was granted less than 12 months due to Home Office administrative delays and would have been granted 12 months or more if the application for an extension had been dealt with on the date that it was made. If students' dependants are allowed to work, and do so, this work does not give them any independent claim to remain in the UK in their own right. They are still expected to leave with the student.

Although the rules stipulate that family members may only come to join a student 'admitted to or allowed to remain in the UK', the Home Office confirmed in a letter to UKCOSA (the Council for International Education), dated 12 October 1994:

'Where a student wishes to bring his family to the UK with him, he can apply for entry clearance or, where appropriate, leave to enter for the whole family, at the same time. He does not need to gain entry himself first'.

Welfare entitlements

Dependent children of students are not required to attend independent fee-paying schools unless seeking entry as students in their own right. They are able to receive state education. However, they will be required to leave with their parents on completion of their parents' studies. Those children who would be required to leave shortly before the completion of their own studies or an important exam, may, however, be granted an extension outside the rules to allow them to complete the school year or to sit the exam.

Students and their families will normally be subject to a 'no recourse to public funds' condition usually barring them from obtaining the core social security benefits, including income-based jobseeker's allowance, income support, housing benefit, council tax benefit, and most disability benefits. Students will generally be unable to obtain child benefit for their children unless the claim has continued since before 8 October 1996. Although the Housing Accommodation and Homelessness (persons subject to immigration control) Order 1996 provides that hard-to-let council accommodation leased by education institutions to students is not counted as recourse to public funds, they cannot generally be considered for accommodation as homeless persons, nor allocated accommodation from the local authority housing register ►see Chapter 31 for more details about access to welfare provision. There are certain exemptions which enable access to welfare provision. One which is particularly relevant to students is where their source of funding from overseas has been temporarily disrupted.

Extending leave as a student or 'switching' into student status

Applying to extend stay in the UK as a student

WHAT THE RULES SAY

In order to extend their leave, students must show:

- they are enrolled on a full-time course and, if the course has begun, must produce satisfactory evidence of regular attendance on it, or on any other course they have attended in the past;
- evidence of satisfactory progress on the course, including the taking and passing of any relevant examinations;
- they would not, if this extension was granted, have spent more than four years on courses of less than two years' duration (or longer courses if broken off before completion);
- they have not come to the end of a period of a scholarship from a government or an international scholarship agency, or they have the written consent of their sponsor for further studies, and can show sufficient sponsorship funding.

WHAT THE RULES MEAN

Full-time studies, maintenance and accommodation, intention to leave

The Home Office requires evidence that students are still enrolled for a full-time course of study, that the money for maintenance and accommodation is still available and that they intend to leave at the end of their studies. These requirements can be satisfied in the same way as when the student first applied to stay (see above).

Regular attendance

Students have to prove that they have been in regular attendance on the course they have been following. The Home Office can check attendance records with their colleges. The student application form (FLR (S)) includes a section for completion by the college about the student's studies and attendance. The institution may also provide a letter confirming the student's satisfactory attendance. If students have not attended regularly for good reason, for example, illness, this should be explained to the Home Office and supporting evidence sent in, such as medical certificates for the period that they were unfit to attend.

The requirement that private education institutions '*maintain satisfactory records of enrolment and attendance*' suggests that the Home Office also expects colleges to maintain written records, though it does not give details of what standard of records is expected.

Satisfactory progress

This was a new requirement in the present statement of immigration rules, HC 395. In the past, the Home Office had refused to grant extensions to students who had failed examinations on several occasions, on the grounds that they did not appear to be able to follow their course. They also refused students who had not sat the examinations for which they were preparing, on the grounds that they did not appear to be attempting to bring their studies to an end, or did not intend to leave the UK at the end of their studies. Therefore, if students applying for extensions are unable to take examinations for any reason, it will be important for the institution to confirm the explanation to the Home Office.

Short courses

The rules state that extensions of stay should also not be granted to students who would be spending more than four years on short courses. Short courses are defined as courses of less than two-years' duration, but include longer courses which were abandoned before completion. This is unnecessarily restrictive for some students whose planned courses are short or who may change their minds during courses. The Home Office has stated that it may be flexible about this in individual cases (IDI, Ch3 annex A para 10). It is important to explain in the application the reasons for abandoning a particular course, or why the student is continuing on short courses, if possible with supporting letters from the course tutors or lecturers, to show that this is part of a regular and co-ordinated plan of studies.

The Home Office prefers students who follow obvious study paths to an academic goal and is suspicious of those it believes may be 'perpetual students'. This rule may also be used against students starting a new course after they have already been studying for many years because the

Home Office may suspect that they are hoping to bring themselves within the '10-year' long residence concession to be able to stay permanently. In a case like this, the Home Office is also likely to doubt the student's intention to leave the UK at the end of their studies.

How to apply to extend

Students who wish to remain in the UK longer than the initial time they have been given, need to apply to the Home Office for permission, before the time given runs out. As long as the application is made in time, the person applying will still be lawfully in the country while the Home Office is considering it and during the period of any appeal.

The application must be made on the appropriate form (FLR(S)) and be accompanied by all the documents specified on that form (or acceptable explanations as to why they are not included and an indication of when they will be). If the application is refused, there is a right of appeal against the refusal. If the application is made late, or it has been rejected as invalid and there is no time to correct it before the initial time expires, the student will be in the UK without authority. If that application is then refused, there is no right of appeal. Applications can be made by post or in person at the addresses specified on the form. Applications are normally decided within two to three months, although can sometimes take over six months.

Switching into student status

People who are not visa nationals

People who are not visa nationals and who have entered the UK for another purpose, for example, as visitors, can apply to the Home Office to change their status to become students using form FLR(S), the same form as for students who want to extend their stay. If people apply to become students shortly after gaining entry in some other way, the Home Office may wish to ascertain that there has been a genuine change of mind to become a student, and that this decision took place after they entered. If at the time of their entry people had already considered studying, or had definite plans to do so, the Home Office could treat them as illegal entrants on the ground that they had deceived the immigration officers when they arrived in the UK, so it is important for a person who plans to study to enter as a prospective student.

Visa nationals

Visa nationals who entered for any purpose other than studies will, under the immigration rules, be refused permission to change their status to become students. It is probable that they will have to leave the UK and apply at the British post where they are living for a student entry clearance. This does not apply to postgraduate doctors and dentists who may apply to stay in the UK without having to obtain an entry clearance.

Permission to work while studying

If students want to obtain part-time or holiday employment, unrelated to their course, this may be possible. If students' passports are endorsed with a prohibition on working, they need first to apply to the Home Office for this to be varied to a restriction on working. This will normally be done if the Home Office is satisfied that the students do not need to work in order to be able to continue to pay for their studies.

All students on courses of longer than six months will be issued with a 'restriction' on working, requiring employment to be authorised. Permission to work used to have to be obtained from job centres. However, this is no longer necessary. From 21 June 1999, to reduce administration and act as an incentive to potential overseas students, students with working restrictions (*not* a prohibition) are automatically authorised to take employment subject to the following restrictions:

- they must not work for more than 20 hours per week during term time except where the placement is a necessary part of their studies and with the agreement of the education institution. Those on work placements during sandwich courses and internships can work for longer than 20 hours per week without having to apply for permission (but see below);
- they must not engage in business, self-employment or the provision of a service as a professional sportsperson or entertainer;
- they must not pursue a career by filling a permanent, full-time vacancy.

Work placements on sandwich courses must be 'clearly-defined' and:

- the course must lead to a degree or qualification awarded by a nationally recognised body; and
- the placement must be undertaken with the approval of the institution.

The permission to work also covers short internships under certain conditions. The Department for Education and Skills (DfES) produces a leaflet '*International students working in the UK: what you need to know*' which gives further details of student permission to work including internships and sandwich placements.

As mentioned above, guaranteed part-time work at a publicly-funded institution of further or higher education in the U.K. at which the student is enrolled is taken into account when assessing a student's financial means.

Any position taken can only be temporary in nature. It is important to note that if a student is caught working when not permitted, or it is established that they have exceeded their hours of permitted work, then the immigration authorities may treat them as breaching their conditions of leave. Working in breach of conditions is a criminal offence and has serious consequences. It can lead to prosecution under the 1971 Act (see s10 1999 Act).

Studies including training

Some studies normally include a large amount of practical work, for example, nursing or accountancy. Such students are not treated consistently under the immigration rules. Nursing students are counted as students for immigration purposes, even if they are paid by health authorities, or receive training bursaries. There are specific provisions in the rules for them, and for doctors and dentists engaging in postgraduate training. However, accountancy students, architects and lawyers, and others who obtain a professional qualification while working as a trainee at a firm, require work permits, which the employer has to obtain from Work Permits (UK) under its Training and Work Experience Scheme ▶see pages 425-427.

Nursing, medical and dental students

WHAT THE RULES SAY

Nursing students have to show:

- they have been accepted for training as a student nurse or midwife, leading to a recognised British qualification, or are already qualified abroad and are enrolled for an adaptation course leading to registration in the UK under the Central Council for Nursing, Midwifery and Health Visiting, and did not gain this acceptance by misrepresentation;
- they are able and intend to follow the course of training;
- they do not intend to work or engage in business other than their nursing training; and
- they have sufficient funds for accommodation and maintenance in the UK without recourse to public funds. This can include funding from a Department of Health bursary.

People wishing to train as nurses may also enter as prospective students, in order to come for interviews at hospitals, and to finalise arrangements for their training. Visa nationals are not able to change status within the UK to become student nurses; they must have entered with a student or prospective student entry clearance. The spouses and children of student nurses are admissible on the same terms as those of other students.

Postgraduate doctors and dentists who want to study and gain experience in the UK have to satisfy the following rules:

- applicants must either be graduates of UK medical schools intending to do their pre-registration house officer jobs for up to 12 months, *or* be eligible for provisional or limited registration with the General Medical Council or General Dental Council and intend to undergo postgraduate training in a hospital or the Community Health Services;

- applicants cannot spend more than one year as pre-registration house officers nor more than four years, in aggregate, in posts at Senior House Officer or equivalent level, and they must intend to leave the UK at the end of their training period. They will normally be admitted for 12 months initially, and may be granted yearly extensions up to a maximum of four years; and

- they must show that they can maintain and accommodate themselves and any dependants without recourse to public funds.

Their spouses and children are eligible for entry on the same terms as those of other students.

It must be noted that, although the immigration rules specify that both student nurses and postgraduate doctors and dentists must intend to leave the UK at the end of their course or period of training, a concession outside the immigration rules, announced on 17 October 2001, waives this requirement for them.

Student nurses, postgraduate doctors and dentists wishing to switch into employment after qualification can obtain work permits without having to leave the UK ▶see page 320.

Other students

A number of other specific categories of student were added to the immigration rules in 2000. Students may wish to remain in the UK or return after their formal studies are over to continue to write up a PhD thesis after the formal period of study has ended, or to re-sit an exam without attending classes. Leave was previously granted to such students under concessions which have now been incorporated into the immigration rules. There is also now provision in the rules for students' union sabbatical officers.

Re-sitting students

WHAT THE RULES SAY

Students who wish to enter to re-sit examinations have to:

- meet all the requirements for admission as students ▶see above, or *alternatively*, if they are no longer actually enrolled full-time on a course and attending classes, that they met all the requirements for admission as students in the previous academic year and they continue to meet the following requirements:
  - they intend to leave the UK at the end of their studies,
  - they do not intend to engage in business or take employment except authorised part-time or vacation work,
  - they are able to meet the costs of their course, and to maintain and accommodate themselves and any dependants without recourse to public funds;

- produce written confirmation from the education institution or independent fee-paying school that they attend, or have attended in the previous academic year, and that they are required to re-sit the examination;
- provide satisfactory evidence of regular attendance during any course which has already begun, or any course which they attended in the past;
- *if* they have been studying with a government or international scholarship agency sponsorship which has come to an end, obtain the written consent of their official sponsor for a further period of study and provide evidence that sufficient sponsorship funding is available; and
- show that they have not previously been granted leave to re-sit their examination.

People who seek leave to remain to re-sit examinations are required to show that they were admitted on student entry clearances, if they are visa nationals. The spouses and children of those re-sitting examinations are admissible on the same terms as those of other students. Leave will be granted to cover the period of the first available re-sit.

Writing up a thesis

WHAT THE RULES SAY

Students who wish to enter to write up a thesis have to:

- meet all the requirements for admission as students, or *alternatively,* if they are no longer actually enrolled full-time on a course and attending classes (note that most research students don't 'attend classes'), show that they met all the requirements for admission as students in the previous academic year *and* continue to meet the following requirements:
  - they intend to leave the UK at the end of their studies,
  - they do not intend to engage in business or take employment except authorised part-time or vacation work,
  - they are able to meet the costs of their course, and to maintain and accommodate themselves and any dependants without recourse to public funds;
- demonstrate that they are a postgraduate student enrolled in an educational institution as either a full-time, part-time, or writing up student, and can demonstrate that their application is supported by the educational institution;
- *if* they have been studying with a government or international scholarship agency sponsorship which has come to an end, obtain the written consent of their official sponsor for a further period of study and provide evidence that sufficient sponsorship funding is available; and

- have not previously have been granted leave to write up the same thesis.

Leave will normally be granted for a period of 12 months. A further 12-month period may be granted if the institution can explain why a student could not complete the thesis, for example, due to prolonged illness or where the thesis submitted needs to be rewritten because it has not reached the required standard. A letter from the university will be required.

If a student is already in the UK and seeks to extend their leave to write up a thesis, then they have to additionally demonstrate that they were originally admitted on a valid student entry clearance if they are a visa national.

The spouses and children of those re-sitting examinations or writing up theses are admissible on the same terms as those of other students.

Students' union sabbatical officers

Sabbatical officers are elected by their unions normally for one year, and are paid, full-time workers. The requirements for entry or an extension of leave are similar to those who are seeking to re-sit their examinations or write up theses in that they currently are or were students in the previous academic year, can maintain and accommodate themselves and intend to leave the UK on completion of studies which may be resumed. Leave will normally be granted for a period of 12 months up to a maximum of two years. Unlike other students, there is no provision in the immigration rules for the admission of the dependants of students' union sabbatical officers.

Fees and student grants and loans

'Home' and 'overseas' student fees

Overseas students normally have to meet the full cost of their courses of study in the UK. The Education (Fees and Awards) Regulations 1997 allow institutions to charge higher fees to overseas students, and these can be several times higher than home student fees. In order to qualify as home students, students must satisfy their educational institution that:

- they have been 'ordinarily resident' (▶see Glossary) in the UK and Islands (the Channel Islands and Isle of Man) throughout the three-year period preceding the 'relevant date', which will be 1 January, 1 April or 1 September closest to the beginning of the first term of their course; and

- at no time during this period were they in the UK and Islands 'wholly or mainly for the purpose of receiving full-time education'; and

- they are 'settled' (ordinarily resident with no restrictions on the time that they are permitted to remain) in the UK (not including 'the Islands') on the 'relevant date' (see above).

There are exceptions to these rules for refugees, those granted exceptional leave (see below) and for family members of these groups. Allowances are also made, in relation to the residence period, for those who have worked temporarily outside the UK and Islands for all or part of the three-year period. Separate rules also apply to students who are EEA nationals ►see below.

It is for the various educational institutions to apply these rules and make decisions about who qualifies as a home student. The guidance on fees issued to them by the Department for Education and Skills suggests that the above criteria should be strictly applied.

For example, to qualify for home student fees for a degree course which begins in October 2002, a person will need to show that they are 'settled' in the UK on 1 September 2002 (the 'relevant date') and that they have been ordinarily resident since 1 September 1999. They cannot have been here for any of that time wholly or mainly for the purpose of full-time studies. An institution is likely to conclude that someone who was in the UK with leave as a student at any point in the relevant three years cannot qualify. However, a dependant who attended school in the UK and who wishes to enter higher education may satisfy the requirements because they were not necessarily here for the purpose of receiving full-time education themselves, but were simply here accompanying their parents. Those who have been granted leave under various other categories of the rules may also qualify.

The following groups do not have to satisfy the above requirements in order to qualify for home fees:

- those granted asylum as refugees who are ordinarily resident in the UK;
- those granted exceptional leave following rejection of an asylum application and who are ordinarily resident in the UK;
- spouses and children of those in the above two groups.

These exceptions apply immediately upon grant of refugee status or exceptional leave, so that, even if the students have already started on a course, they will only have to pay home student fees on the next occasion that fees are due.

Student support

Student support is generally available for home students in higher education and can take the form of:

- a grant towards tuition fees, depending upon the student's parents' income;
- a student loan to help towards living costs;
- grants for family dependants and various other grants to help towards childcare, travel, books and equipment etc;

- disabled students', allowances.

For the 2002/03 academic year, the most a home student will have to pay towards undergraduate tuition fees is £1,100. It is worth checking, therefore, whether or not a student is eligible for home status.

Student support is available for the following courses of higher education:
- a first degree, such as a BA, BSc or BEd;
- a Foundation Degree;
- a Diploma of Higher Education (DipHE);
- a Higher National Diploma (HND);
- a Higher National Certificate (HNC);
- a Postgraduate Certificate of Education (PGCE) or other postgraduate course of initial teacher training leading to the award of qualified teacher status or a specified equivalent qualification;
- certain courses that prepare students for professional examinations.

Those required to pay home fees rather than overseas student fees are generally eligible for the above forms of student support ►see above pages 314-315 for those eligible to pay home fees. *However*, those who have been granted exceptional leave following the refusal of an asylum application *additionally* need to demonstrate that they have been ordinarily resident in the UK for three years not wholly or mainly for the purpose of full-time education in order to qualify for student support.

In order to get student support, it is necessary for the student to apply to the local education authority where they live in England and Wales, the Students Awards Agency in Scotland or the appropriate Education and Library Board in Northern Ireland.

Eligibility for home fees and student support can be complex. UKCOSA (the Council for International Education) is able to advise in more detail on this. A useful guide is also available from the Department for Education and Skills on their website (www.dfes.gov.uk/student support).

Courses for asylum-seekers

Asylum-seekers will not qualify for home fees as they are not 'settled'. Asylum-seekers in higher education are also not eligible for student support. Special provisions are, however, made for asylum-seekers on courses of *further* education in England, ensuring that only home fees or no fees at all are payable. In order to qualify, the asylum-seeker must be:
- attending courses funded by the Learning and Skills Council of England; and
- in receipt of assistance from the National Asylum Support Service (NASS), means-tested benefits, assistance from Social Services, or the asylum-

seeker must be an unaccompanied minor between 16 and 18 years of age in the care of a local authority social services department.

In Scotland, courses funded by the Scottish Further Education Council are available to asylum-seekers enrolled on English language classes or on a low income.

Non asylum-seekers who have been living in England for three years but are not settled may also be eligible for Learning and Skills Council-funded further education courses at colleges in England unless they have been given leave as students and their leave expires before the end of the course they plan to take.

EEA students

Most EEA nationals are not subject to UK immigration law and rules but to European Community legislation ▶see Chapter 22 for more details. This means that they do not require leave to enter the UK and are free to travel between EEA countries to exercise their free movement rights. They may move in order to work, to seek work, to do business, be self-employed or to provide or receive services. Similarly, EEA nationals who are non-economically active can move between EEA countries subject to them having sufficient funds to maintain and accommodate themselves. EEA nationals are able to obtain 'residence permits', which confirm their right to live in a particular EEA country.

There are two categories of EEA nationals who may have rights as students in the UK. The first category are those who qualify under the specific directive on students. The second category are those who have established, and can retain, status as workers under the terms of the European treaties.

First category

As to the first category of EEA students, their rights are contained in EC Directive 93/96. This provides for free movement for students:

- enrolled at recognised educational establishments for the principal purpose of following vocational training courses; and
- who have declared that they have sufficient resources to avoid becoming a charge on public funds; and
- who are covered by all-risk sickness insurance.

These students have a right of residence for the period of their studies, and are entitled to residence permits for that duration if they apply for them. Their spouses and children, of whatever nationality, can also stay for this period, and will be issued with residence documents, on request. The directive refers to 'vocational' courses, but in practice this probably means all courses. EEA students' earnings or potential earnings can be considered to show that they will be able to support themselves. As EEA nationals, they are also free to work without needing separate permission.

Second category

As to the second category of students, that is those EEA nationals who have worked here before studying, their rights are contained within EC Regulation 1612/68, relating to the free movement of workers. They may retain the more extensive right of residence which goes with that status. This has advantages for family members, who will benefit from the usual five-year residence permits and who will be able to work without restriction.

Students who are no longer actually working will retain their status as workers if they:

- have been in employment since last entering the UK (but not simply in order to qualify for a grant); and
- were engaged in economic activity which was not marginal or ancillary but 'genuine and effective'; and
- intend to study on a vocational course related to their previous employment in the UK or, in the case of involuntary unemployment, intend to transfer to a new employment sector.

Students who work part-time whilst studying, provided the work is not marginal or ancillary, may argue that they are exercising their right to work and will fall within this category as workers anyway.

EEA students' rights to pay home fees and receive grants and loans

The following EEA students will be entitled to pay home fees and are eligible to receive some student support:

- EU nationals (and their children of any nationality but not their spouses) who have been ordinarily resident in the EEA for the three years leading up to the 'relevant date' (►see pages 314-315) provided their residence was at no point in the three years mainly or wholly for the purposes of receiving full-time education. It should be noted that this category does not include nationals of Iceland, Liechtenstein or Norway, which are member states of the EEA but not the EU;
- EEA workers (and their spouses and children of any nationality) who have been ordinarily resident in the EEA for the three years leading up to the relevant date, provided their residence was at no point in the three years mainly or wholly for the purposes of receiving full-time education. This group is the same as the 'second category' of EEA students identified above.

Students in either of the above two groups pay home fees and can obtain means-tested *grants* towards their fees. However, currently only those who are EEA workers and their families are eligible for *loans* towards living costs. There is an outstanding test case (***Bidar***), about whether EU nationals who have been resident in the UK for the relevant three years, but have not obtained indefinite leave and do not qualify as 'workers', should be eligible for loans for living costs. In early March 2002, the High Court agreed to refer this question to the European Court Justice (ECJ) for a ruling.

Spouses of EEA workers, whether or not they are EEA nationals themselves, are eligible for both grants and loans on the same basis as the worker spouse, provided that they are installed together in the UK and the spouse has three years' ordinary residence in the EEA, not wholly or mainly for the purposes of education.

Students who want to change their status

The immigration rules allow for certain people to 'switch' from being a student into another category. The rules allow students:

- to apply and settle with some close relatives. For example, children studying in the UK whose parents later gain settlement may apply to stay and settle with them;
- to marry and apply to stay with their spouse or partner ▶see Chapter 16 (the 2002 White Paper proposes to prevent this form of switching for those admitted to the UK for short periods; this could affect students studying on short courses);
- to apply for asylum or to remain on human rights grounds ▶see Section 3.

It is also possible to obtain a short extension as a visitor, for example, to attend a graduation ceremony. Applications to change status should be made to the Home Office before the time limit on the student's current leave runs out ▶see Chapter 6 for more details about making applications.

The rules do not allow students, other than EEA nationals, to stay:

- in order to work or to be self-employed;
- in order to set up a business;
- as working holidaymakers;

This does not mean that students cannot apply for such changes, but that any application is likely to be refused, with no right of appeal. The Home Office would need to be satisfied that there were very exceptional reasons for considering an application, without making the person leave the UK to obtain entry clearance first. People should be referred for specialist advice about the consequences of such applications. However, see below for work permit concessions relating to certain students. For general details about switching ▶see pages 90-92.

An application to extend stay in a different category may be refused if a student who is sponsored by their government or an international sponsorship agency does not obtain written consent to the proposed variation.

Working after studies

The 2002 White Paper recognises that students with degree-level qualifications 'have the potential to produce valuable benefits for the UK through joining the workforce at the end of their studies'. Current Immigration Directorate Instructions incorporate a concession for graduates, student nurses and postgraduate doctors and dentists to be able to obtain work permits without having to first leave the country. Leave will normally be granted to people in these categories if:

- the student holds a valid work permit issued by Work Permits (UK) (the grant of leave is now usually issued by Work Permits (UK) as well as the actual work permit itself);
- the applicant does not have an adverse immigration history; and
- if the person was sponsored by their government or an international scholarship agency as a student, has obtained their consent.

The 2002 White Paper promises the introduction of new immigration rules explicitly permitting degree-level graduates, student nurses and postgraduate doctors and dentists to switch into work permit employment. Under an existing concession these students also do not have to demonstrate an intention to leave the UK when applying for entry as students. All other students will be expected to leave the UK and apply for entry after their prospective employer has obtained a work permit through Work Permits (UK).

If people (including students) have lived legally in the UK for more than 10 years, the Home Office has stated that it will consider making an exception to the immigration rules to grant them indefinite leave to remain because of the length of time they have spent in the UK ▶see pages 105-108 for more details of this '10-year' concession.

Travel outside the UK

Most students will be granted leave to enter the UK for a period of over six months. In that case, under changes introduced by the Immigration and Asylum Act 1999, their leave to be in the UK does *not* lapse when they depart from the Common Travel Area and travel abroad. This is also the case where a student obtained entry clearance before coming to the UK because entry clearances generally operate as leave to enter and that leave does not lapse when the person departs. Provided none of the limited exceptions apply (eg. a material change of circumstances), and the student returns within the period of their leave, the student should be re-admitted when they return. A student who returns in these circumstances has a right of appeal if they are refused entry as a student.

Section 5 **Family and dependants**

Chapter 16
Spouses, unmarried partners, same-sex partners and fiancé(e)s 323

People coming to the UK as spouses, unmarried partners, same sex partners or fiancé(e)s of people settled in the UK 326

People who have been admitted for the 'probationary period' who wish to apply to settle in the UK 345

'Switching' to stay in the UK permanently with spouse or partner 348

People who cannot satisfy the immigration rules 352

Those who no longer have a relationship with a partner 352

People who wish to accompany or join a spouse or partner in the UK who is not settled but who is in the UK for the time being 363

Chapter 17
Children 365

Children joining or staying with both parents settled in the UK 368

Children joining a lone parent in the UK 373

Children joining a person who is not a parent 378

Children being joined by parents with whom they have contact 379

Children accompanying or joining parents in the UK who have limited leave 382

Adopted children 384

Children whose parents may be forced to leave and
children who are in the UK on their own 391

Children born in the UK 396

Chapter 18
Relatives other than children and spouses 399

Parents and grandparents aged 65 or over 401

Other relatives 406

16 Spouses, unmarried partners, same-sex partners and fiancé(e)s,

This section looks at the rights of members of the family to accompany, join and stay in the United Kingdom with a person who has a right to be in the UK. The present chapter covers partners, both married, unmarried and same sex, and fiancé(e)s. In Chapter 17 we look at the rights of children. The admission and stay of all other relatives is dealt with in Chapter 18. For details about family reunion with refugees and people with exceptional leave to remain ▶see Chapter 12. For details about applications of *dependants* of those seeking asylum ▶see pages 192-194.

The 2002 White Paper, *Secure Borders, Safe Haven*, makes various proposals which will affect those in relationships (▶see the box below).

The rights of family members looked at in this section are largely set out in detail in the immigration rules. However, there are also certain policies operated by the Home Office outside the immigration rules which are also taken account of here, for example, the concession relating to domestic violence in marriages. In considering the position of family members, it is also important to remember that some people may benefit from parts of the law *other than* the immigration rules and the Home Office policies. In particular, this applies to family members of EEA nationals, those who can benefit from Article 8 ECHR (right to respect for private and family life) and some Commonwealth citizen women. We look first at these groups.

Family members of EEA nationals. Family members of EEA nationals and others exercising European Community rights of free movement have independent rights. Ireland is also an EEA country, so foreign spouses of Irish nationals who have come to the UK can generally be admitted. Some family members may make use of the decision in the case of **Surinder Singh**. This establishes that British citizens who have exercised their right of free movement within the EEA, that is, who have lived in another EEA country with their spouse and who later wish to return to the UK, are entitled to do so under European rights of free movement, rather than under ordinary UK immigration law. For further details about the rights of EEA family members ▶see pages 458-464.

Article 8 ECHR. Even if a person cannot satisfy the immigration rules, they may be able to establish a right to come to or to stay in the UK under

Article 8 ECHR which contains the 'right to respect for private and family life'. Article 8 does not give all couples or other family members a right to live in the UK on the basis that one partner has a right to be in the UK. One of the most important principles under Article 8 is that it does not guarantee to a couple a choice of which country they wish to live in. However, in some cases it does benefit applicants who cannot satisfy the immigration rules, in particular if it is not possible for them to establish their family life elsewhere. Article 8 is covered on pages 255-266.

Commonwealth citizen women. Some Commonwealth citizen women who married British citizen men have the 'right of abode' and do *not* have to meet the requirements of the immigration rules. They are women who were Commonwealth citizens on 31 December 1982 (the day before the British Nationality Act 1981 came into force) and who were married on or before that date to British citizen men, or men with the right of abode. These women should apply to the British post before they travel for a 'certificate of entitlement to the right of abode' for which a fee is payable.

What circumstances are covered by the immigration rules?

The immigration rules concerning marriage and relationships and the purposes of those rules are often very difficult to explain. It is widely believed that being married to a British citizen or to a person with indefinite leave to remain in the UK gives a person a 'right' to enter or remain in the UK with his or her spouse. *This is not correct.* British

---

PROPOSALS IN THE WHITE PAPER

Secure Borders, Safe Haven (February 2002) makes the following proposals for changes that will affect those in relationships:

- a 'switching' proposal to forbid switching *into* marriage or partnership from people in the UK in a temporary capacity, such as visitors. The proposal is aimed primarily at marriages arranged in the UK;
- an increase in the initial probationary period of leave granted to spouses for one year to two years. This equalises the marriage rules between spouses and unmarried partners. It is stated to be aimed at 'sham' or bogus marriages;
- the introduction of a provision in the rules for those heterosexuals in 'firmly committed' relationships who do not *wish* to marry, as well as those who are *unable* to do so;
- the White Paper also includes criticism of arranged marriages with spouses from abroad, rather than from the UK, and links this to forced marriages. This suggests that the government may be considering a return to a 'primary purpose' type rule in which it has to be shown that the primary purpose of the marriage is not admission to the UK;

For more details about these and other proposals in the White Paper, and the 2002 Bill and JCWI's comments on them ▶see Chapter 2.

immigration law gives no automatic rights to non-British citizen family members. The immigration rules contain provisions allowing spouses, fiancé(e)s, unmarried and same-sex partners of those who are settled in the UK, or who are coming to the UK for settlement, to be admitted to the UK and to remain here permanently. They also contain provisions which enable partners to accompany those who are not settled but are coming for a limited period whether or not the person may eventually settle.

The term 'settlement' is used a lot in this section. The formal definition of settled is 'ordinarily resident' with no limitation on the length of time for which a person is allowed to stay. 'Ordinarily resident' generally means lawful presence for a settled purpose. People with limited leave cannot be settled as they have a limitation on the period of their stay. People with indefinite leave are almost always accepted as settled as are those with the right of abode (usually British citizens).

The introduction of a provision in the immigration rules for unmarried partners, including same sex partners, who are not able to marry is a welcome development. They can now be admitted and allowed to stay on the basis of their relationships. These applications may be made where the partner is either settled here or has been admitted for a limited period in certain categories. A further welcome amendment to the immigration rules allows bereaved spouses and partners to obtain settlement.

These changes have not, however, gone at all far enough. As will be seen below, the immigration rules are, at present, harder to satisfy for those in unmarried and same-sex relationships than they are for those in hetero-sexual, marital relationships. In addition, no provision is currently made in the immigration rules for those in firmly committed relationships which are similar to marriage, who are able to marry but who have no intention of doing so. The 2002 White Paper makes certain proposals which address these issues (▶see box above). The changes are likely to be effected by amendments to the immigration rules rather than by new legislation.

The different circumstances covered in this chapter

The different circumstances of people in relationships which are covered in this chapter are divided into the following six groups:

1   people who wish to *enter* the UK who are either accompanying or joining their settled partners and who intend to settle permanently in the UK. They need to make applications for entry clearance before travelling ▶see pages 326-345.

2   people who have been admitted as in (1) for an initial probationary period and who then wish to apply for settlement in the UK ▶see pages 345-348.

3   people in the UK for reasons unconnected with their partners, for example, as visitors or students, and who wish to remain permanently in the UK with them ▶see pages 348-352.

4 people as in 3 above, but who cannot satisfy the immigration rules because they are illegal entrants, overstayers or have only temporary admission to the UK, for example, as asylum-seekers ▶see pages 352-358.

5 People who entered (or remained in) the UK as the partners of those settled here, and who wish to remain in the UK permanently, but whose relationships have broken down as a result, for example, of domestic violence, or because their partners have died ▶see pages 358-363.

6 People who are accompanying, or coming to join partners who are not settled in the UK but who are in the UK at least for the time being, for example, as students, work permit holders or business people. They sometimes need to get entry clearance before they travel and sometimes can apply when they arrive ▶see pages 363-364.

These six categories are looked at in turn below.

People coming to the UK as spouses, unmarried partners, same sex partners or fiancé(e)s of people settled in the UK

WHAT THE RULES SAY

The rules state that the requirements to be met by people seeking *entry* to the UK as spouses/unmarried partners or fiancé(e)s are that:

- they are seeking entry on account of their relationship to a person who is present and settled in the UK or who is on the same occasion being admitted for settlement;
- they and their spouse/partner/fiancé(e) intend to live together permanently as husband and wife (or in a relationship akin to marriage for unmarried partners); and
- they will be able to maintain and accommodate themselves adequately, together with any dependants, in accommodation they own or occupy exclusively, without recourse to public funds.

All applicants must obtain an entry clearance. Applicants may also be refused admission if any of the general grounds on which entry can be refused apply to them ▶see page 67.

The rules for spouses and fiancé(e)s also require that they have met the other party to the marriage and, in the case of spouses, that they are seeking entry as the husband or wife and that the marriage is subsisting.

The rules for fiancé(e)s require that instead of seeking admission as a married person, they must show that they are seeking entry *for* marriage. In addition it must be shown that the fiancé(e) will be adequately maintained and accommodated until the date of the marriage and that, after the marriage, the couple will be able to maintain and accommodate themselves. The difference in the wording reflects the fact that the couple may not be living together until after they are married.

The rules for unmarried partners and same-sex partners are the same *except* that they do not have to show that they are seeking entry for *marriage*, but *in addition* to the above rules, they must show:

- they have been living together in a relationship 'akin to marriage' which has lasted for two years or more;

- they are legally unable to marry under UK law *other than* on grounds of age or that they are related; and

- any previous marriage (or similar relationship) by either partner has permanently broken down.

Note that these rules refer to 'unmarried partners'. This includes same-sex partners as well as heterosexual couples who are not able to marry.

WHAT THE RULES MEAN

Present and settled in the United Kingdom

One partner (or spouse/fiancé(e)) must be 'present and settled' in the UK or 'on the same occasion be admitted for settlement'. In order to be 'settled' a person must have the right of permanent residence in the UK without any restrictions or conditions on their stay. In practice, this means the spouse should have the right of abode in the UK (British citizens and a few Commonwealth nationals ▶see pages 566-567), or 'indefinite leave to remain' and the UK should be their normal place of residence. So, the settled person must be in the UK at the time the application is made, or must be travelling to the UK, for settlement, with their partner from abroad.

Intention to stay together permanently

The couple have to satisfy the official that they intend to stay together permanently as husband and wife or (for unmarried partners) in a relationship 'akin to marriage'. In practice and in particular in relation to applications from spouses from abroad, since the removal of the reviled primary purpose rule (in June 1997), the numbers of applicants refused under this head has increased, despite earlier assurances to the contrary from the Foreign and Commonwealth Office.

Questions may be asked about how the marriage or relationship came about and concerning where the couple intend to live after marriage as well as information about their respective families. The couple must show they are committed to each other whether or not they reside in the UK. Plausible reasons should be given by the settled spouse if they are unwilling to live in any country other than the UK with their partner.

Certain marriages or relationships may be scrutinised more closely than others, for example, relationships between couples who have had a 'whirlwind romance', are of strikingly different cultures, have a wide age difference or who do not speak the same language. Again in practice, subjective conclusions about age differences and appearance have been made by ECOs in reaching their decision. Previous cohabitation for temporary periods abroad or the birth of a child should be sufficient to satisfy the rule. However, it should be noted that unlike under the old primary purpose rule, there is no automatic concession of the issue where there is a child born of the relationship.

There is a continuing practice for immigration officials to consider marriage applications from citizens of developing countries as economically motivated. Even where this is a factor, it should not itself undermine the intention to live together on the part of the couple. If a couple have been married or in a relationship for some time, but have not been together for much of it, this can also be a problem. Where there is inadequate accommodation in the UK, this could also be used to argue that the couple will not be staying together. In *Khan*, the IAT emphasised that the relevant question, where a couple had been living apart after the marriage, was their intention to cohabit in the future.

It should be noted that, in the 2002 White Paper, the government has stated that it wants to promote a discussion on arranged marriages and has suggested that one consideration should be that the marriage is arranged within the UK. Any changes to the immigration rules to reflect such a proposal should be viewed with concern and may lead to the effective re-introduction of a 'primary purpose' test.

Maintenance and accommodation

Under the immigration rules, most people applying for leave to enter or remain in the UK must show that they do not need to claim 'public funds' in order to support and accommodate themselves and their dependants before leave can be a granted. The meaning of public funds is set out in the box below. These requirements do not apply to:

- refugees and their dependants;
- people applying for exceptional leave (but does apply to their dependants who are seeking family reunion with them);
- returning residents (although they should not have caused a charge on public funds when they left the UK);
- special voucher holders (though this scheme has now been withdrawn with effect from 5 March 2002);
- transit visitors.

The details set out below relating to maintenance and accommodation are therefore relevant to many other categories in which people can seek to enter or stay in the UK.

PUBLIC FUNDS ARE:

Income Support/Income-based Jobseekers' Allowance (JSA)
Accommodation from a local authority as a homeless person;
Allocation of accommodation from the housing register of a local authority;
Housing Benefit and Council Tax Benefit;
Working Families' Tax Credit;
Disabled Person's Tax Credit;
Child Benefit;
Attendance Allowance;
Severe Disablement Allowance;
Invalid Care Allowance;
Disability Living Allowance.

Public funds do not include NHS treatment, state education or community care services, but ▶see Chapter 31 for access to these services

'Additional' recourse to public funds. The immigration rules say that the couple must be able to maintain and accommodate themselves and any dependants without recourse to public funds. In October 2000 the immigration rules were amended (para 6 HC395) to incorporate the long-standing Home Office policy that this means that no *additional* public funds must be necessary for the support of the applicant who is coming into or applying to remain in the UK. This has therefore removed the doubts created by the courts' previous interpretation of the rules and the policy. The Home Office's general policy objective is not to prevent a British citizen or settled sponsor from receiving any public funds to which they are entitled in their own right. The Home Office has stated that the settled partner may claim working families' tax credit and child benefit to which they are entitled under the social security legislation in respect of their spouse/partner and children (see IDI, Ch8, annex H, para 2). However, as an exception, the Home Office has also stated that, where a foreign wife claims working families tax credit on behalf of her husband *who is present and settled in the UK*, this should not be considered as recourse to public funds (IDI, Ch, s4, annex W, para 2.4).

Child benefit counts as public funds. However, in *marriage cases* where one of the partners is a British citizen or is settled, the British or settled spouse can claim, and the Home Office will not refuse on the grounds of recourse to public funds 'if the only extra benefit' being claimed is child benefit (IDI, Ch1, s4, annex W, para 2.5).

Adequate maintenance. In determining whether the couple can support themselves and any dependants, the immigration authorities will take into account the UK sponsor's earnings or savings. However, good evidence of this is required and applications are often refused because of inadequate pay slips or bank statements. Often sponsors are paid in cash and their earnings are difficult to prove. Since the introduction of the national minimum wage it is arguable that any person in full-time employment and being paid at or above that rate would have to be regarded as in receipt of a sufficient amount, depending of course on the needs of any dependants. If the partner in the UK is on benefit, but the partner abroad has the offer of a job in the UK for when he or she arrives, this may be taken into consideration.

Although the Immigration and Asylum Act 1999 prevents people from claiming public funds if they have a condition prohibiting them from getting public funds attached to their leave, it is insufficient to satisfy the rules to say that there *could not be any* additional recourse to public funds. It cannot be argued that two people can live on one person's benefit without any additional income to support the applicant. This is becaues the rules require the person to be 'adequately' maintained. The Home Office view is that the level set by income support (or income-based job-seeker's allowance) is the minimum standard of support considered to be acceptable or adequate to meet the rules. The IAT upheld this view in **Begum (Momotaz)**. In addition, in **Uvovo**, it held that to meet the requirements of the rules, the support must be of a level to include the equivalent of free school meals and prescription charges that would be available to a person on income support or income-based JSA.

Spouses and partners seeking to enter or remain in the UK are entitled to work during the probationary period and to rely on their proposed earnings to meet the maintenance requirement of the rules. Fiancé(e)s may not work until they have been given leave to remain as spouses. Applicants in other categories who are prohibited from working cannot meet the requirements of the rules in this way. The spouses (and children) of students may work, where they have been admitted for 12 months or more. However, the Home Office will only take into account their actual earnings when they are applying to remain in the UK (IDI Ch3, annex M), rather than their potential earnings when seeking entry, in determining whether there is sufficient maintenance.

In the case of **Azam**, the IAT held that, in considering maintenance, the ECO had a duty to take into account the possibility of an applicant finding work on arrival. A letter making a job offer ought to explain why the job offer is made, perhaps because of a family relationship or because the applicant is a friend of the employee. It should also, so far as possible, be supported by some evidence of the business's operation and viability to take on another employee. In **Khan**, it was accepted that people may prefer to employ relatives in order to assist them to come to the UK and that this did not necessarily undermine the genuine nature of the job offer made.

The Home Office IDI (Ch8, s1 annex H) state that jobs that are unrealistic in the light of the applicant's skills (which includes language) or job offers that appear to have been manufactured and are unlikely to be long-term, will be rejected. However, the guidance states that 'care must be taken not to make assumptions' and the fact that unemployment is high in a particular area should not on its own be a good enough reason to reject the proposal of a job for the applicant.

The maintenance proposed does not have to be available at the date of decision but only when the person arrives in the UK. So a woman with the right to return to work after maternity leave, for example, may rely on her future employment and earnings. The same applies to the availability of a job offer for a spouse or partner on their arrival in the UK. This also applies to the rules relating to accommodation (►see below). The maintenance and accommodation requirements extend only to those who are dependants at the time of the decision. The Home Office has stated that it would not be appropriate to base a refusal on the grounds that the couple would not be able support and accommodate any children they may have in the future and that questions about whether the couple intend to start a family should not be asked.

Accommodation. If the settled or British spouse or partner is living in local authority accommodation, this does not prohibit a partner from abroad from coming to the UK because no *additional* accommodation is necessarily required. However, advisers should check the accommodation is big enough and that the landlord or local authority have no objections to any dependants residing there. People can often tell this by looking at the conditions of the tenancy agreement.

The rules state that accommodation must be owned or occupied 'exclusively' by the sponsor for the use of the family, not merely that there must be accommodation 'of their own'. However, the Home Office IDI (Ch8, s1, annex H) state that:

'Accommodation can be shared with other members of a family provided that at least part of the accommodation is for the exclusive use of the sponsor and his dependants. The unit of accommodation may be as small as a separate bedroom but must be owned or legally occupied by the sponsor and its occupation must not contravene public health regulations and must not cause overcrowding as defined in the Housing Act, 1985'.

Therefore, exclusive occupation of a bedroom for a married couple should be sufficient (*Zia (Raja)* and *Kasuji*).

Accommodation will not be adequate if it is overcrowded. The Housing Act 1985 contains statutory definitions of overcrowding which cover both privately owned houses and those owned by local authorities. A house is overcrowded if two persons of 10 years old or more, of opposite sexes (other than partners) have to sleep in the same room (this is the 'room standard'), *or* if the number sleeping in the house exceeds that permitted in the Act (this is the 'space standard').

The Act sets out two tests for measuring the space standard. In practice, however, the Home Office uses only the following test for measuring the space standard (IDI, Ch8, annex H, para 6.3). The number of persons permitted to stay in the accommodation is dependent upon the number of rooms available, as set out in the table below. It should be noted that a room only counts if it:

- has a floor area larger than 50 square feet; and
- is of a type normally used as a bedroom or a living room. Kitchens and bathrooms do not count.

It should also be noted that children under the age of one do not count and that children aged between 1 and 10 years only count as half a person.

Number of rooms	Permitted number of persons
1	2
2	3
3	5
4	7.5
5	10
with an additional two persons for each room in excess of 5	

However, there are separate overcrowding provisions for a house in multiple occupation (HMO), which is defined as a 'house which is occupied by persons who do not form a single household'. This is a very wide definition and the Home Office view is that it does not cover only hotels and hostels but could also cover houses lived in by two or more couples of different generations where they do not share common facilities. The most common occurrence of this is likely to be where a couple are intending to live independently in a house also occupied by the settled partner's family. The definition can include a house lived in by two or more couples even if they are related.

There are no hard and fast rules to determine overcrowding in the case of HMOs. A local authority can serve a notice stating that an HMO is overcrowded or further residents should not be permitted. If the accommodation available is an HMO, the local authority may simply be asked to provide confirmation that they do not object to the additional person/s residing there.

As noted above, accommodation does not have to be owned. Council or privately rented accommodation is quite satisfactory. If the accommodation is subjct to a mortgage, a letter from the building society or other mortgage provider, confirming the ownership of the property and the number of rooms, should be sufficient. If it is council accommodation, a letter from the council confirming the tenancy, the size of the accommodation and that there is room for the extra person(s) to live there, will be necessary. Such letters can be difficult to obtain from local authority housing departments as they are often not regarded as urgent or a matter of priority.

If the accommodation is privately rented, a letter from the landlord confirming the size and the tenancy and that he or she has no objection to the extra person coming should be submitted. The immigration authorities may want to see the terms of the lease or tenancy agreement for rented accommodation, to be sure that the letting or sub-letting is allowed and that the numbers of people permitted to live in the property is not exceeded. This is particularly important where the landlord is a relative and formal evidence, for example, a rent-book, may be important to show that the accommodation is actually occupied in a legal sense by the sponsor, rather than simply being provided by the relative. Although, in our view, simple occupancy can come within the rules, it may be more difficult to show availability in the long term without a formal tenancy agreement and the Home Office view is that 'third party' support can only be taken into account for a short period (see below).

When landlords are unwilling to write letters confirming the position or, when the property is owned or is council accommodation, the local authority cannot be persuaded to write to confirm that a particular property is adequate and that the applicant/s will be permitted to live there, or where there is doubt, it may be advisable to pay for a private report from an independent surveyor to confirm that the accommodation is suitable and would not be statutorily overcrowded were the person and any dependants to be admitted. Otherwise, advisers should be careful to identify the space available in the accommodation for the proposed number of people who will live there and be able to explain how it falls within the above criteria.

It may be difficult for large extended families sharing the occupation of a property to satisfactorily establish to the immigration authorities how many people actually live in the accommodation, although in local authority housing this should be easier to determine.

It is often more difficult for women in the UK than men to show that their partners from abroad can be maintained and accommodated in the UK. A woman looking after young children may not be able to work and therefore may rely on benefits. If she is living with other members of her family, for example her own parents, in their accommodation, she will have to show, either that this will be an adequate long-term arrangement and that the couple will be paying their own way, or that they have realistic plans and expectations of having their own home soon. An IAT decision in August 1991, *Kausar*, suggested that it was easier to satisfy this requirement when a couple live in a separate family unit, rather than in joint family living arrangements.

The accommodation does not have to be available at the date of the decision of the ECO but only when the person(s) arrives in the UK. However the courts may not admit evidence of available accommodation at a later appeal if the arrangement was not in existence or at least discussed as a proposal for the family at the date of the decision, (see the

IAT decisions in *Kazmi* and *Azad*). The 2002 Bill may restrict the position on appeals even further by preventing an adjudicator from having regard to *any* evidence unless it was available to the ECO.

Third party support. It may be possible for other family members, or friends, to show that they will support the couple. The immigration authorities require a letter to confirm the support as well as evidence such as recent pay slips or bank statements to prove ability to support. The important thing is to show that, when the spouse or fiancé(e) from abroad comes to the UK, the family will not need to have recourse to public funds. However, the Home Office view as set out in the IDI (Ch8, s1, annex H) is that third-party support can only be for a short time exceptionally outside the rules. In our view, the rules do not require a couple to support themselves from their own resources and to insist on this may be unlawful and incompatible with the right to respect for private and family life under Article 8 of the ECHR, especially where, for example, the sponsor is aged or disabled and cannot work and there are obstacles to the couple living abroad permanently. The High Court upheld this view in *Arman Ali* though the Home Office has not changed its guidance or practice even where there is the offer of a maintenance undertaking. There are earlier conflicting IAT decisions which are sometimes still relied upon by the Home Office. Some IAT cases rejecting long-term support such as **Ahmed (Ishaque)** and *Begum* (*Zabeda*) were settled by the Home Office when they were appealed to the Court of Appeal. There are, however, earlier IAT decisions which are more favourable in terms of third-party support such as *Balwinder Kaur* and *Modi*.

In practice, it is likely to be a question of proving that there is sufficient third-party support available in the long term (*Yousaf*). Indeed, the Tribunal accepted in *Begum (Hasna)* and *Bibi (Sonor)* that the earnings of a dependent child could be taken into account when assessing whether there would be sufficient money to maintain the family in the UK.

It should be noted, however, that the wording of the rules in this respect for admission of spouses and partners (including their dependants) is different to that for fiancé(e)s (before marriage), children and other relatives. These groups are required *to be* maintained and accommodated, not to maintain themselves. In practice, however, it can be argued that the overall intention and purpose of these rules, when read with Article 8, is to enable family life while at the same time avoiding an increased demand on public funds, and to ensure that in fact there will be sufficient maintenance and accommodation available.

Maintenance undertakings

Maintenance undertakings are not generally taken from spouses, fiancé(e)s or partners. This is for two reasons. First, people in this category will normally, initially be given limited leave with a condition preventing them from having recourse to public funds, which prevents access to benefits anyway. Second, the Home Office view that couples should not rely on third-party support, means that it will rarely be appropriate for them to ask a third party for an undertaking. The Home Office has stated that undertakings will only 'exceptionally' be accepted in cases of marriage and partnerships, namely,

'if it is clear that it would only be in effect for a limited period and the couple have a realistic prospect of supporting themselves thereafter'. (see IDI, Ch8, annex H, para 5.1)

Undertakings are more frequently taken from sponsors in other dependent relative cases (►see page 405) where indefinite leave will be granted which would, without an undertaking, permit the applicant to obtain benefits under the legislation.

Additional rules for spouses or fiancé(e)s

Spouse or fiancé(e)

A spouse means someone who is legally married in a way recognised by UK law. The term does not cover common-law spouses or same-sex relationships. A fiancé(e) must be someone who is legally able to marry under UK law. This excludes people under 16 even if they have legally married, or are legally free to marry, in the country from which they come. It also excludes people who are not yet divorced, even if divorce proceedings are under way.

Polygamous wives can be included, as long as they were validly married in a country which permits polygamy and as long as they are the *only* wife among the polygamous wives, who has ever entered the UK as a spouse. Since section 2 of the Immigration Act 1988 came into force on 1 August 1988, it has not been possible for a woman who is a wife in a polygamous marriage and whose husband has previously brought another woman to the UK as his wife, to come here on this basis. This applies irrespective of the legality of the marriage or whether the wife concerned is the first wife of the marriage.

The same rules also apply to Commonwealth women who have gained the right of abode through marriage. A woman who has the right of abode because of a polygamous marriage cannot exercise that right if another wife has already come to the UK on that basis.

Therefore, if one wife has ever been admitted in the past to join the husband in the UK either as a spouse under the dependency rules or exercising her right of abode, another wife can only qualify to enter if the marriage of the wife who is or has been in the UK has ended by divorce or if she has died. This can lead to a conflict of interest where advice is being given to more than one family member. The ECtHR has found that the rules relating to the admission of polygamous wives are not in breach of the ECHR.

Marriages and divorces in other countries

There is often cause for confusion in countries with very different marriage laws. Many people believe that, for example, a Ghanaian customary marriage is 'not recognised' in the UK, or that after seven years' separation a marriage in the Philippines is 'automatically' ended. Couples may then marry, in the UK or abroad, in good faith, but then the Home Office may investigate past statements and allege that the marriage is bigamous and therefore not valid. The police may be asked to investigate with a view to prosecution for bigamy. The whole subject is very complicated as it involves the relationship between different countries' laws which may be constructed on entirely different bases. It is not proposed to go into all the details here. Broadly, however, if a marriage is legally recognised and valid in the country in which it took place, it will be recognised as a valid marriage under UK marriage law. The validity of certain forms of marriage may depend on the country in which they took place and the domicile (which means more than simple residence in a country ►see Glossary) of parties to the marriage. For example, a Nigerian customary marriage, where there is no documentation and the ceremony is an exchange of gifts between the families, will be valid if it takes place in Nigeria and both parties were domiciled in Nigeria at the time of the marriage. It will not be valid if it takes place in Britain or any other country which does not recognise this form of marriage.

Similarly, a customary divorce will also be valid if it took place in the prescribed forms in a country which recognises customary divorce and in which both parties were domiciled. Therefore when a person living in the UK performs a customary divorce abroad, and then marries again, the Home Office may argue that a divorce should take place in the UK before the person is free to marry again in the UK.

Immigration status, nationality and the country where the marriage took place do not affect people's ability to divorce in the UK. There may be extra delays in that papers may have to be sent to a spouse abroad, who may be difficult to contact and unwilling to co-operate, particularly when divorce is more difficult, or impossible, in that country. There is no need for specialist information about the divorce laws of the country in which the marriage took place if the divorce is taking place in the UK.

If a person has gained entry to the UK on the basis of a marriage which is later found to be invalid, the person can be treated as an illegal entrant. For example, a Filipino woman married a British man in Hong Kong when they were both working there. She had believed that because she had been separated from her husband in the Philippines (where divorce did not exist) for more than seven years, she was free to marry again, and later came to Britain. She was treated as an illegal entrant when she later tried to bring her children from her first marriage from the Philippines to join her, and it was discovered that there had been no divorce. She was able to obtain a divorce in the UK and then marry her British husband again in order to secure her status.

The couple have met each other

The meeting does not have to take place before an application for entry clearance is made but the couple must have met before the applicant spouse or fiancé(e) is interviewed about his or her application. This requirement was intended to place an extra hurdle in the way of some arranged marriages, where the couple may not meet before the wedding day, or where the wedding is by proxy. It is only likely to be a problem for fiancé(e)s, as a married couple will almost certainly have met at the wedding. In some cases, however, it involves the extra cost of a journey abroad or to the UK before the marriage.

The IAT found, in the case of *Meharban*, that a meeting does not have to take place in the context of a marriage. It is acceptable if the couple met each other as children, as long as they both have clear recollections of the meeting and know each other as individuals. The fact of meeting can be proved by photographs of the couple together, by the recollections of both parties, by passport stamps showing that both were in the same country at the same time and by supporting statements from relatives or friends who know of the meeting.

Additional rules for unmarried and same-sex partners

Prior to 2 October 2000 there had been in operation a concession outside the immigration rules to provide for the entry and stay of unmarried and same sex partners. This was introduced on 13 October 1997 with a four-year living together requirement which was reduced to two years on 16 June 1999.

Living together in a relationship 'akin to marriage'

The couple must have been living together in a relationship 'akin to marriage' for two years or more. Both heterosexual and homosexual partners will be required to show their relationship is in the model of a marriage. Proving that a couple are living together in a relationship 'akin to marriage' will be determined by evidence in support of such a claim, for example, statements from friends, domestic bills, letters. Permanent intention may be demonstrated by mutually-beneficial wills, guardianship of children and shared property and bank accounts.

The two year requirement

The couple will need to show that they have lived together for all or part of the two years prior to the application. Up to six months spent living apart for good reason, for example, to work or take care of a relative, is permitted provided the relationship subsists. Where a relationship has existed for less than two years, consideration may be given to the application if there are the most compelling compassionate circumstances. However, the circumstances would need to be exceptionally strong with cogent proof to have a chance of making a successful application.

Showing that the relationship is subsisting during periods of separation will be easier for couples who have the financial resources to keep up their relationship for two years, for example, by visits.

The Home Office have stated in a letter to Cameron McKenna dated 31 August 1999 (reported in *Legal Action* November 1999) that it is not necessary for all of the two-year period to have been spent in the UK and that time spent here as a 'visitor' can be included in calculating the two-year period. So a person may be able to obtain entry for a visit for six months or in order to study and at the same time be accruing time with their partner in the UK in order to make a subsequent application for settlement. Unless the non-settled partner intends to make the settlement application from abroad, there may be difficulties in demonstrating an intention to leave in these circumstances for the purposes of the visitor or student rules. The Home Office seems to contemplate that this is possible. Although people should be advised of the strict position under the rules when seeking entry to visit their partner or while they are here studying, and also in a relationship, they therefore also need to be aware that the rules may well be relaxed in practice.

The rules unfairly discriminate against those who are unable to marry as opposed to those who are married. Married couples do not have to provide long-term evidence of their relationship. Only under the very strict Home Office instructions for married couples making a marriage application outside of the immigration rules (DP/3/96) are married couples required to show that they have lived together for two years prior to enforcement action ▶see page 353.

Unable to marry

The parties must be *legally* unable to marry. This means that there currently is no provision in the immigration rules for heterosexual couples who do not wish to marry, only for those who cannot do so. This may change if the 2002 White Paper proposals become law ▶see page 324. The change would be made by amendments to the immigration rules.

The couple must be legally unable to marry under UK law *other than* because they are related by blood or aged under 16. These new rules are specifically for those people who are unable to marry, because they are the same sex, transsexual or because there is some other bar to marriage, such as an existing marriage of one of the partners. The rules also include those who do not wish to divorce their previous partners, for example, for religious reasons. The rules exclude those seeking entry for marriage who are legally unable to do so because they are under 16.

Previous marriage or similar relationship has permanently broken down

Each of the parties to the unmarried partnership is required to provide information regarding any previous marital or other relationship akin to marriage they have had. They will be asked to specify how long ago the previous relationship was terminated, either by divorce or by separation (IDI, Ch8, s7, annex AA)

The requirement for entry clearance

All spouses, partners and fiancé(e)s must obtain entry clearance before travelling to the UK if they are planning to remain permanently. Spouses, partners and fiancé(e)s who are visa nationals (see Glossary) must obtain entry clearance even if they are only planning to stay for a short time. It is possible, for example, for a spouse to plan to come simply to visit the partner in the UK, or for a fiancé(e) to come simply for the marriage ceremony, after which the couple plan to live permanently elsewhere. However, it can sometimes be difficult to persuade immigration and entry clearance officers of this. They may suspect that the applicant is trying to avoid either the queues abroad or the detailed interview they would face if they were to apply from there. They also later risk being declared illegal entrants if the immigration authorities believed that they had concealed their real intention. For in-country applications for a spouse or partner ▶see pages 348-352 below. Fiancé(e)s cannot make such applications from the UK under the immigration rules and may only apply where there are exceptional compassionate circumstances. The inconvenience or the expense of having to travel home to obtain an entry clearance is not sufficient reason to grant leave to remain outside the Rules (IDI, Ch8, s2).

Where circumstances change after admission, there should be no difficulty in making an application to remain. The IAT in *Corte* (*Dela Vina*) held that a Filipino woman with a visit entry clearance, whose British fiancé's divorce had been finalised since the visa was issued, still qualified to enter:

'Approaching it on a commonsense view we do not think that because the couple decided to get married during their visit to this country the basis of the appellant's admission was removed. All that she was then seeking was limited leave to enter'.

How to apply for entry clearance

For general details about entry clearance and entry clearance applications ▶see pages 52-64. Applicants will almost certainly be interviewed by an official at the British post. It is very important that couples should understand the reasoning behind the questioning at the British high commission or embassy and be prepared in advance for the kind of questions they may be asked. The above rules should therefore be explained to them before they apply or attend the interview. Often, people feel that they have been tricked or pressurised into giving answers to immigration officials which do not actually reflect their true feelings or intentions.

In some countries, particularly those of the Indian subcontinent, the Philippines, Thailand and Jamaica, there are substantial delays before applications will be considered. Often, inadequate numbers of staff have been sent to the posts and they carry out long interviews and checks on people, which are time consuming. For example, in 2001 the waiting times at the British high commission in Bangladesh for applications for entry clearances for spouses was 20 weeks (and 26 weeks for re-applicants). It is possible to get waiting times from the websites of the individual embassies and high commissions. Alternatively, they can be contacted directly. It is very difficult to bring forward an interview date unless there are exceptional compassionate circumstances, for example, the severe illness of either partner. The fact that a couple want to be together for the birth of a child is not normally considered a strong enough reason.

Because of these delays, it is sensible to advise people to make applications well in advance of the time they hope to travel. For example, if a man in the UK seeks advice about his proposed marriage in India and is planning to travel for the wedding in several months' time, it is sensible for his fiancée to apply straight away to the British high commission, explaining when her wedding is planned and when her fiancé will be in India and to ask that an interview is fixed after the wedding while they are in India. The more notice that is given, the higher the chance that the post will be able to arrange this. If a couple marry while one is waiting in the queue for interview for a fiancé(e) entry clearance, they should inform the post but they will not have to start the application again.

It is helpful for the British or settled spouse/partner/fiancé(e) to be present at the interview, so that he or she is available if the ECO wants to check anything about the situation in the UK. Foreign Office policy is to allow requests from representatives to attend an applicant's interview as observers provided that the representative clearly understands that, as an observer, he or she must not intervene while the interview is taking place. At the end of the interview, the observer may then make comments on the case to the ECO.

At the interview, the official will need evidence relating to the marriage or relationship and of the support and accommodation available.

Information needed from spouses

Proof of the marriage. If the original copy of the marriage certificate is in the UK, it should be sent to the spouse abroad to take to the British high commission or embassy at the time of the interview, with a certified photocopy being kept by the partner in the UK. If there is no such certificate in existence, the spouse abroad should explain this. In India, for example, if there is no marriage certificate, there may be a declaration under the Hindu Marriage Act that the wedding has taken place. If it is a customary marriage, for example, in West Africa, the British post may require statutory declarations from members of the family of both sides to confirm that the correct procedures took place.

Proof that the couple were or are free to marry. If either party has been married before, the British post will need to see evidence that the previous marriage(s) has ended, by death, divorce or annulment. The evidence could be original divorce certificates or statutory declarations to prove a customary divorce, or the original death certificate of a previous spouse who has died.

Proof that the couple are over 16. The parties' passports containing their dates of birth are normally adequate proof of this.

Information needed from unmarried partners

Unmarried partners need to be able to show that any previous marriage (or similar relationship) of either partner has permanently broken down. Each couple should therefore include in a letter, details of any previous marital or similar relationship that has irretrievably broken down stating how long ago that relationship has ended. Any divorce certificate (decree absolute) should be provided.

These applicants also need proof that they are unable to marry. A same-sex partner will satisfy this requirement. Couples who are not of the same sex must prove they are legally unable to marry. A copy of their marriage certificate(s) should be produced. Where a divorce is in the process of being obtained, proof of the divorce proceedings should be provided.

Proof that the relationship has lasted for two years or more could include:

- joint tenancies or mortgage, bank or building society accounts, investments, insurance policies (eg. car, health, home or life), or bills;
- letters addressed to both or either of the couple at the same address to show they have been living together, with the date stamped envelopes if available;
- Department of Social Security correspondence, national insurance records, health (doctor's, dentist's, hospital) records also confirming the address of the parties;
- birth certificate(s) of any children of the relationship;
- photographs of the couple together;
- letters exchanged between the couple, itemised telephone statements, a record of email or fax transmissions, that show a continuing relationship when the couple had to live apart.

If the couple are together at the time of interview, they should go together to the British post. The couple will be interviewed separately.

After entry clearance is issued

Law and practice about the operation of entry clearance was changed by the 1999 Act. For further details about the procedures when an entry clearance has been granted, about refusing entry to those in possession of an entry clearance and about travelling in and out of the UK ▶see pages 56-59, 68-72, 83-86.

Spouses and partners

If the application is successful, the spouse or partner will be granted an entry clearance. This will now actually operate as leave to enter beginning on the date when the person arrives in the UK. The purpose of the entry clearance is to enable the applicant to be admitted to the UK for an initial probationary period of 12 months (spouse) or 24 months (unmarried partner) after which they can apply to settle.

The entry clearance will have an 'effective date' (shown as 'valid from') and an 'expiry date' (shown as 'valid until'). It is 'valid' between these two dates. The 'valid from' date may be *after* the date on which the entry clearance was issued and entry clearance officers have been instructed to ask applicants when they propose to travel so that the 'valid from' date can be as near as possible to this time. A person must arrive in the UK during the period of validity of the entry clearance. The entry clearance then has effect as leave beginning on the date of entry and lasting until the 'valid until' date. This may well be less than the 12-month probationary period for spouses and less than the two-year period for unmarried partners. It should be noted therefore that people do *not* automatically get 12 months or 24 months leave to enter given by the immigration officer from the date of their arrival in the UK.

Confusingly, however, the Home Office, in a letter to Dexter Montague solicitors dated 13 September 2001, suggests that the period of leave to enter is calculated from the date of validity of the entry clearance. This might mean that a person arriving in the UK 11 months after the date their entry clearance was 'valid from' would be regarded as having had leave for 11 months prior to arrival, allowing him or her to apply for settlement after one month of presence in the UK. This does not seem to be a sensible interpretation of the process and does not correspond with the Immigration (Leave to Enter and Remain) Order 2000 which states that leave 'begins' on entry to the UK. We suggest:

- if possible, people should travel as soon as possible after the 'valid from' date and negotiate the 'valid from' date with the ECO at the time of issue or ask them to change it afterwards if there has been some unforeseen delay;
- if there has been a delay between the date of validity and travel, on arrival a person can ask the immigration officer for their leave to enter to be varied up to the maximum period permitted in this situation (which is 12

months as a spouse, 24 months as an unmarried partner). This can be done on arrival although it is unlikely that many people will be aware of this opportunity or will be advised of it by the immigration officer. This application can be made orally and without any prescribed form (see the new immigration rule 31A, HC395);

- if the immigration officer declines to deal with that application (which s/he is entitled to do), or if the person has not tried to vary their leave to enter on arrival, they may apply on form FLR(M) to the Home Office for an extension of their leave in the capacity of a spouse or partner to complete the required probationary period in the UK before they are eligible under the rules to qualify for settlement.

- if there is only a short delay in meeting the qualifying period, applicants can wait until near the end of the initial period of leave and make the relevant settlement application. Given the usual delays in processing such applications on the part of the Home Office, by the time the decision is actually taken, the applicant is likely to have met the qualifying probationary period and the application sought should not be refused for this reason.

The entry clearance placed in an applicants' passports by the entry clearance officer will normally include a condition requiring them to maintain and accommodate themselves and any dependants without recourse to public funds. There is normally no other restriction, which means that they are free to take employment or run a business ▶see page 112 for an example of an entry clearance with conditions endorsed. Applicants are not normally given any further information about their rights and status by the immigration officers on arrival.

The above procedure is very different from the previous position when spouses with a prior entry clearance were admitted for a period of 12 months which ran from the date of arrival and lasted for 12 months regardless of the date of the issue of the entry clearance (provided the applicant arrived within the period of its validity which was usually six months). If people do not understand the new rules, there is a danger that they will overstay their leave and then, when they wish to apply to settle as a spouse or partner, they will not be making an application within the rules.

Fiancé(e)s

Fiancé(e)s will usually be given an entry clearance valid for six months which operates as leave to enter from the date of arrival in the UK and ending on the expiry date in the same way as described above. They are normally subject to a prohibition on employment and business activity as well as a condition prohibiting them from having recourse to public funds.

Fiancé(e)s are expected to get married within the initial period of their leave which will normally be six months, provided they arrive in the UK at around the time of the 'valid from' date on their entry clearance. They should apply to the Home Office, on the official application form FLR(O), for further permission to remain if they cannot marry within the initial period of leave, explaining why the marriage has not yet taken place and showing satisfactory evidence that it will take place at an early date. However, if by that time the couple have married, then an application for variation of their leave on form FLR(M) as a spouse should be made. This would normally be granted for one year initially. While the application is under consideration, the prohibition on work and business continues.

When an application for entry clearance is refused

If an application for entry clearance is refused, the British post has to give the spouse, partner or fiancé(e) a formal notice stating that the application has been refused, with brief reasons for the refusal and information about the right to appeal, and a form to fill in to appeal against the refusal. Any appeal has to reach the British high commission or embassy within 28 (actual not working) days of receipt of the date of refusal, which is deemed to have been received 28 days after it was sent if it was only sent by post to the applicant overseas. Time starts straight away if it was handed to the applicant.

At the time of lodging the appeal, it may be worth making representations to the ECO to persuade them that the rules are met or requesting the exercise of discretion and asking for a waiver of certain aspects of the rules where there are compassionate circumstances. It is important at this stage, if not earlier, to include any human rights grounds to be argued at the appeal. Article 8 ECHR is likely to be the most important.

When a spouse, fiancé(e) or partner is refused entry clearance and appeals against the refusal, it is the practice of officials at the British post to give a full question-and-answer record of the interview as part of their statement of their reasons for refusal. However, it will usually not be provided until the appeal has been lodged. This sometimes makes it difficult to submit detailed grounds of appeal as the full case against the person refused may be not known. It is sometimes better to put in general grounds of appeal and then supplement them later or prepare written grounds for the appeal hearing once the person refused can comment on the full details of the refusal.

If the appeal is lost, the couple can make representations to the Home Office to reconsider the case. Unless there is new information which was not available at the appeal, it is unlikely that representations will be successful. If there was new information available at the appeal upon which the adjudicator makes a recommendation to the ECO/Home Office because of the compassionate circumstances of the case, the decision may be reconsidered on this basis. Failing any of these options, the person abroad may make a fresh application to come to the UK. If later in time the couple have married or the relationship has endured for a longer period or there is a child, depending on the basis of the refusal, these developments may make a material difference to the outcome.

It may be that an application that was refused before the Human Rights Act 1998 came into force on 2 October 2000, might have a stronger prospect of success were it to be made again later. However, advice should be sought before any re-application is made to avoid wasting time and money and risking prolonged separation.

People who have been admitted for the 'probationary period' who wish to apply to settle in the UK

People who are admitted to the UK as a spouse or a partner must complete a 'probationary' period of leave to enter or remain before they can apply for settlement in the UK. This is 12 months for spouses and two years for unmarried partners. This also applies to couples who apply in-country, having entered in some other capacity, to remain as a spouse or partner ▶see below. As noted above, calculating when the probationary period runs from is now more difficult and where a person has been admitted for a period one or two months short of the required period it may be advisable simply to submit a settlement application on the basis that, by the time the Home Office has determined their application, they will have accumulated the necessary period of leave.

The 2002 White Paper suggests that the probationary period for spouses should be increased from one year to two years. This would equalise the position as between married and unmarried partners but only by 'levelling down' so that all are treated less favourably. The stated reasoning of the Home Office for this change is to try to deal with 'sham' marriages.

Claiming benefits during the probationary period

It is expected that the couple will not have any 'recourse to public funds'. There is, however, no objection to other residents in the same household receiving public funds to which they are entitled in their own right. The question is whether there is *additional* recourse to public funds as a result of the applicant's presence in the UK. Furthermore, the Home Office policy stated in the IDI (Ch8, s1 annex H, para 8) is that if a couple need to claim public funds for a short period during the probationary period, through no fault of their own, but are mainly able to support themselves, this will not lead to a refusal. In most cases, the partner from abroad will be prevented from accessing public funds because they will have a condition attached to their leave which prohibits them from obtaining public funds. The effect of the condition is to make the person 'subject to immigration control' which denies access to most welfare entitlements.

A couple asking about entitlements to benefit during their probationary period should therefore be informed if either of them has an entitlement to claim. However, it is important that they know about the possible immigration consequences should they need to claim for a prolonged period, or should they still be claiming at the time of the settlement application. For details, in particular about claiming Working Families' Tax Credit and child benefit ▶see page 329

If a refusal is made solely on the grounds that a couple cannot show that they can support themselves, there is a right of appeal provided the application is made in time. During the appeal period, the spouse or partner from abroad is allowed to work, so if one of them could then find work and they no longer needed to claim benefits, a fresh application to the Home Office could be made, which should then be granted.

Applying for settlement (indefinite leave to remain)

WHAT THE RULES SAY

The immigration rules state that the requirements for indefinite leave to remain are:

- the person was admitted, or was given an extension of stay, for 12 months as a spouse, or two years as the unmarried partner of a settled person and has completed that period;
- the person is still the spouse or partner of the same person and the marriage or relationship is subsisting;
- the couple intend to live together permanently as husband and wife, or as unmarried or same-sex partners in a relationship akin to marriage; and
- the couple can maintain and accommodate themselves and any dependants without recourse to public funds.

Making the application

Before the spouse or partner has completed the requisite period of leave to enter or remain in that capacity, they should apply to the Home Office for settlement (indefinite leave to remain) on form SET(M). The spouse or partner who is British or settled should be in the UK at the time the application is made and must confirm the marriage or relationship is still subsisting. If he or she is temporarily abroad, this should be explained to the Home Office and it should be informed when he or she returns.

Documents required for the application

The documents generally required for the application are:

- the applicant's passport;
- the spouse or partner's passport or, if a British citizen without a passport, other evidence of settlement such as the full birth certificate and evidence of the person's residence in the UK for the past three years, such as a driving licence, income tax coding, building society or bank statement or national insurance or NHS number. The application form requests evidence for three years but there is no legal justification for this period. However,

the request must still be complied with otherwise the Home Office may (as they are entitled under the rules to do) treat the application as not valid;

- the original marriage certificate;
- passport-sized photographs of both spouses or partners;
- proof that the couple have lived together during the probationary period. The forms request 'five items of correspondence addressed to you during the past year from the following sources if they clearly show that you and your spouse live at the same address'. The sources include the local authority; British Telecom; a gas, electricity or water company; a bank; building society or a credit card company. For couples living in rented accommodation, or in joint family accommodation where the bills and official documents come to another family member, this can cause serious difficulties;
- evidence of financial support, for example, bank statements for the past six months or pay slips for the past three months, to show that the couple can be supported without recourse to public funds.

It is usual for these applications to be granted routinely if the Home Office has no reason to suspect any problems. If the Home Office has been informed, either by the couple or anyone else, that they have separated or that there have been marital problems, or if they have claimed public funds during the year, it is likely that the Home Office will ask more detailed questions. They may want to interview the couple to be sure that the immigration rules are met.

The Home Office also states, in their IDI (Ch 8, annex C), that where there is reason to doubt the lasting nature of a marriage, or where the marriage seems to have broken down but there is a real prospect of the marriage being reconciled, it may grant a further 12-month probationary period instead of refusing the application outright.

If the application is refused

It is possible to appeal against the refusal to grant settlement. Where a person is refused, an adjudicator will be able to allow the appeal where there is evidence to dispute the Home Office conclusions in rejecting the application, for example, that the couple were not living together, or could not demonstrate that they could adequately maintain and accommodate themselves. An adjudicator can also allow an appeal if the Home Office has failed to apply its concessions relating to family and marriage (see below). Where the couple's intention to live together is in dispute, then the couple's own evidence in court will be crucial in addressing that as a reason for refusal.

If no appeal is lodged, then the person will become an overstayer who is liable to administrative removal without an effective in-country right of appeal. Previously, people in this position would have had to be considered by the Home Office for deportation in relation to which there were appeal rights. Now this procedure has been removed (except for those people who applied to regularise themselves prior to 2 October 2000). Unless a human rights or asylum claim is made, there is no opportunity for a person's circumstances to be examined by an independent adjudicator.

People in the United Kingdom for other purposes who wish to 'switch' to stay in the UK permanently with their spouse or partner

People who are already in the UK and who meet or marry their spouse or partner in the UK (in addition to those who entered as fiancé(e)s), can apply to 'switch' their status to remain permanently with them. For example, visitors or students may apply to the Home Office to remain because they have married a British citizen or a person settled in the UK. They do not need to leave the UK in order to get an entry clearance for that purpose. However, it must be clear that there has been a genuine change of circumstances since the original leave was granted. The initial application is for a period of limited probationary leave as with 'on entry' spouse or partner applications.

The 2002 White Paper suggests that changes may be made to the rules to prevent those here in temporary capacities for six months or less, from switching to stay with spouses or partners.

WHAT THE RULES SAY

The immigration rules state that (*in addition* to the requirements – ▶see pages 326-327 above – in relation to spouses or partners seeking entry to the UK), the Secretary of State must be satisfied that:

- the applicant has limited leave in the UK;
- the applicant has not remained in the UK in breach of the immigration laws; *and*
- the marriage has not taken place after a decision has been made to deport the applicant 'or after he or she has been recommended for deportation' or has been given notice (under s6(2) of the Immigration Act 1971) that such a recommendation is under consideration following conviction for a criminal offence.

WHAT THE RULES MEAN

Any application from a spouse or partner who has overstayed their leave, or has otherwise breached immigration laws, for example, by entering the UK illegally or breaching their conditions of leave, will be refused under the immigration rules. Similarly, where a decision to deport a person has been made, the application will be refused under the rules. A decision to deport could have been made, for example, on 'conducive to the public good' grounds, without the person having become an overstayer or otherwise breached immigration law. These people may, however, still succeed in persuading the Home Office to exercise discretion in their favour (▶see below pages 352-358).

How to apply

Applications may be made in writing or in person at the Home Office, before the person's leave to remain runs out, on the prescribed application form FLR(M). The applicant is legally in the UK while the application is being considered, provided the application was made in time (and has been accepted by the Home Office as valid). The conditions attached to the original leave to remain, for example, a prohibition on working, are still valid until the application is decided. The application may take some time to process. Despite this, however, the Home Office has confirmed in a letter to Camden Law Centre dated 30 March 2001, that they will apply the rules which require the applicant to have completed the full term of their leave to remain in the probationary capacity before settlement can be granted. This applies even where it would mean that, by the time the initial application is decided, the couple had actually been living together for longer than the probationary period.

The Home Office often does not subject couples making these applications to the detailed questioning as at some posts abroad. The application form asks the couple a list of questions about their relationship: when and how they met, when and why they decided to marry and their plans for the future. For same-sex or unmarried partners, the requirement that the couple have been living together in a relationship akin to marriage for two years is more difficult to establish. If the relationship was conducted in the UK, the non-UK partner would have to have been in the UK in another capacity under the immigration rules for two years. Formally, there needs to be a change of intention to remain as an unmarried partner after the qualifying period. However, at present, at least in practice, where an unmarried couple have been living together and the applicant in the UK is in a temporary capacity, there is not usually an issue raised by the Home Office, even where the relationship was in existence at the time, for example, entry clearance was issued for a seperate purpose.

The application form also requests a list of documents. The documents specifically required for marriage applications are the civil marriage certificate and, if either person had been married before or has been in a long-term same-sex or unmarried relationship, evidence of how that marriage or relationship ended, such as a divorce or death certificate. The application form also requests evidence to show that the settled spouse has lived in the UK for the past three years. The purpose of this is to help to show that the person is 'settled'.

Both the person applying and the settled spouse or partner have to sign declarations to confirm that the marriage or relationship has not been terminated, that they are still living together and plan to do so permanently. If the person is legally in the UK at the time of the marriage or relationship and at the time of application, and if the couple are able to maintain and accommodate themselves without recourse to public funds, there is a good chance that the application to remain will be granted unless there are doubts about the relationship itself.

Some problems which may arise

Marrying shortly after arrival

The Home Office may be suspicious of people who marry soon after gaining entry for another purpose. For example, if an applicant gained an entry clearance as a visitor stating that they would be going back to their job in their country after three weeks and then gets married after being in Britain for a fortnight and applies to stay as a spouse, the Home Office may suspect that this was their intention from the beginning. They may suspect that the applicant wanted to avoid the problems and delay involved in applying for a fiancé(e) entry clearance. The Home Office may therefore treat the person as an illegal entrant who entered the UK by deception. For further details of illegal entry ▶see pages 545-549. It is therefore important to explain how and why the person's plans changed after arrival in the UK, as well as showing how the applicant fits into the rest of the immigration rules on marriage.

Marrying towards the end of period of leave

The Home Office may also be suspicious of people who marry very shortly before their leave to remain runs out, and may believe that the marriage was entered into so that the person could stay in the UK and that the couple have no intention of living together permanently or even that the marriage was a 'sham'. Evidence of the length of relationship and of the reasons why the marriage was planned for that particular date may be helpful in this situation.

Duty on Registrars to report 'sham' marriages

Under the 1999 Act, there is a duty on marriage registrars to report to the Home Office any suspicions they have about possible 'sham' marriage. These are defined as being marriages between any person who is not a British citizen or an EEA national and any other person (whether or not that person is a British citizen or EEA national) that have been entered into for the purposes of avoiding the effect of immigration law. The purpose of this innovation must be to try to identify those people who do not genuinely intend to live together. If it were to be interpreted more widely, it would amount to the re-introduction of the old 'primary purpose' rule which was abolished in June 1997.

Can people switch to being fiancé(e)s?

There are no provisions in the immigration rules for people who have been allowed into the country on some other basis to apply to remain as fiancé(e)s. A person who is in the UK for a temporary purpose may have plans to marry which cannot be achieved while his or her leave to remain is still current, for example, because the British or settled partner is awaiting a divorce. It may be worth making an application as a fiancé(e) outside the rules, at the discretion of the Home Office, using the prescribed form FLR(O). The application should explain the reasons for the delay in marrying.

The couple may well be able to marry while waiting for the Home Office to respond. After the marriage, they should continue the application for leave to remain to the Home Office, by submitting form FLR(M) together with the evidence requested on it, and asking for leave to remain as a spouse. If the original application was undecided at the time of the new application, then the further application will be decided at the same time as the earlier one (which effectively means instead of the earlier one). However, if the original application has already been refused, then, although leave is regarded as continuing for the purpose of lodging an appeal, a further application as a spouse cannot strictly be considered until any appeal has been dealt with.

When an application is successful

If an application is successful, a spouse or partner will be given leave to remain for a probationary period initially (12 months for spouses, two years for unmarried partners), without any restrictions on employment and the passport stamp will usually include a condition that the person is maintained and accommodated without recourse to public funds in the same way as those given leave to *enter* as a spouse. Shortly before the end of the probationary period, the person should apply to the Home Office for settlement ▶see above pages 345-348 for the procedure. During that period the non-settled spouse or partner may travel abroad with or without their spouse or partner and be readmitted. However, if there have been long absences abroad there may be difficulties in satisfying the 'intention to live together' requirement later. If there have been, for example, marital difficulties, a further probationary period may be granted instead of settlement.

When an application is refused

If the application was made while the spouse or partner from abroad had leave to remain, there is the right to appeal against a refusal. The Home Office must give the person a letter explaining the reason for refusal and the right to appeal, and forms to fill in to appeal. The forms must be returned to the Home Office within 10 (working) days. The spouse may remain legally in the UK while the appeal is outstanding. The person may also wish to raise human rights arguments referring to Article 8 ECHR, especially where there are children involved.

People who want to stay in the UK with their spouses or partners but who cannot satisfy the immigration rules

People who are in the UK and who wish to stay permanently with their spouse or partner but who cannot satisfy the immigration rules to do so, can be divided into two main groups.

1 People who applied for entry at port other than on the basis of their marriage/partnership and have been granted temporary admission or have been detained ('on entry' cases). These people may be awaiting a decision (eg. on an asylum application) or they may have already been refused entry.

2 People who have entered the UK but who never had, or no longer have, leave or who have breached immigration control in some other way. They include overstayers and illegal entrants ('after entry' cases).

'On Entry' cases

In 'on entry' cases, the rules cannot be satisfied if the applicant has arrived without an entry clearance for marriage or partnership. Article 8 is relevant in these cases. The Home Office will often refuse to accept that Article 8 is breached on the grounds that family life can be carried on elsewhere, or that the interests of immigration control require that the applicant applies for entry clearance like other applicants (see the Court of Appeal in *Mahmood*). There may be good reasons why applying for an entry clearance abroad is not practicable, for example, where there is no functioning post in the person's country or origin. There may also be other circumstances which make it unreasonable to expect an applicant to return with a British child even temporarily. For example, it may be unreasonable to expect nursing mothers to return to countries where there is a danger to the child's health or risks from land mines or to return to other unsafe areas. It may be that the applicant has no means of support abroad. For more details about how Article 8 ECHR may be used ▶see pages 255-266.

'After Entry' cases

People who have overstayed their leave or breached their conditions of leave or who entered the UK illegally will not fall within the terms of the rules. The rules state that people applying to stay for marriage or partnership must not have 'remained in breach of the immigration laws' and they must have leave at the time that they are applying. These people are therefore also making an application outside the rules. Where any of these people make an application on the basis of marriage, it is considered (under the Home Office published policy) outside the rules concerning marriage (▶see below). Similarly, it may be possible to challenge refusals on human rights grounds under Article 8.

Home Office policy in marriage cases outside the immigration rules

The following policy applies to illegal entrants, overstayers and those who have breached conditions of their leave. It does not apply to the 'on entry' category of people described above. The policy became much stricter from 13 March 1996, when the Home Office published new internal instructions on marriage called 'DP/3/96'. It applies to marriages which 'came to the notice' of the Home Office after that date. For marriages which came to the attention of the Home Office before that date, the much more generous DP/2/93 policy applies. DP/2/93 also covered unmarried partners; *DP/3/96 does not*.

It is important to note that, even though DP/3/96 has been accepted as being, in general, a lawful policy for the Home Office to operate, this does *not* mean that its application in all cases will be compliant with Article 8. This was made clear by the Court of Appeal in the case of *Iskio*.

DP3/96 states that action to force a foreign spouse to leave should not normally be started:

'**where the subject has a genuine and subsisting marriage with someone settled here and the couple have lived together in this country continuously since their marriage for at least two years before the commencement of enforcement action *and* it is unreasonable to expect the settled spouse to accompany his/her spouse on removal.**'

This 'enforcement action' is defined as:

- a specific instruction to leave with a warning of liability to deportation if the person fails to do so (the standard letter that people receive after an appeal has been dismissed, or an out-of-time application has been refused). Since the introduction of administrative removal under section 10 of the 1999 Act, service of such a notice under this provision will also amount to enforcement action although the policy has not been formally revised or updated; or

- service of a notice of intention to deport or of illegal entry papers; or

- a court recommendation for deportation.

If any of these actions have started, they 'stop the clock' and the person does not gain any more time by making representations or appealing.

Even if the marriage has subsisted for two years before enforcement action started, the Home Office must *also* believe that it is 'unreasonable' to expect the settled spouse to live abroad. It is up to the couple to make sure that the Home Office has all the information on which to make a decision; the Home Office will not necessarily ask for it. In deciding whether it is reasonable to expect the family to live abroad, the Home Office will consider whether the applicant:

- has very strong and close family ties with the UK, such as older children from a previous relationship who form part of the family unit; *or*

- has been settled and living in the UK for at least seven years; *or*
- has medical reasons for remaining and medical evidence which conclusively shows that his or her life would be significantly impaired or endangered if he or she had to leave.

Any other matters which are put to the Home Office can also be considered. The instructions stress that 'each case is to be decided on its individual merits and, for instance, a particularly poor immigration history may warrant the offender's enforced departure from the UK notwithstanding the factors referred to above'. Therefore, it is important that all the background and history of the couple's relationship should be explained to the Home Office at the time of application, rather than waiting for any further questionnaire. People should not rely on the application form alone, as it does not provide space for all the exceptional or compassionate factors. It should be accompanied by a further covering letter of explanation.

Where there are children of the marriage (even those with the right of abode), this is not enough in itself. The Home Office believes that 'a child of seven years or younger could reasonably be expected to adapt to life abroad'. However if the child suffers from 'serious ill-health for which treatment is not available in the country to which the family is going', this may be enough to enable the family to stay. The Home Office used to be of the view that a child of under *10 years* could adapt but that approach was amended by a policy statement on 24 February 1999 (DP/6/99).

People who have committed criminal offences

People who would otherwise benefit from DP/3/96 (see above) but who have committed offences may be refused. The policy states: 'Serious crimes which are punishable with imprisonment, or a series of lesser crimes which show a propensity to re-offend, would normally outweigh the family ties.

People who marry after enforcement action begins

The instructions further state that 'where a person marries after the commencement of enforcement action, removal should normally be enforced' and that 'detailed enquiries in order to ascertain whether the marriage is genuine and subsisting should not normally be undertaken'. Therefore, people who marry after they have had immigration problems cannot expect to be allowed to remain'.

A failure to consider the nature and strength of the relationship and all the compassionate circumstances of the case and to weigh them against the interests of immigration control, may be contrary to Article 8 ECHR. However, it will still be much harder to win these cases under Article 8 than cases where the marriage took place before enforcement began.

Some people may wish to try to persuade the Home Office that their situation is so exceptional as to warrant being granted leave to remain. Others may leave the country and apply for entry clearance to return, but no guarantee can be given that this will be granted. People can be refused under rule 320(11) for a 'failure to observe the time limit or conditions attached to any grant of leave to enter or remain in the UK' or, more generally, if 'it seems right' to the immigration officer that, considering a person's character, conduct or association, their exclusion from the UK was 'conducive to the public good'. People can also be refused if they previously entered the UK by deception (para 320(12), HC395).

There are likely to be delays in the application being considered, as the British high commission or embassy may well refer such cases to the Home Office for instructions. The couple may therefore be separated for months while the case is considered.

People who marry before enforcement action but who have been married for less than two years

People who marry *before* any enforcement action is taken but have not been married and living together for two years before the date of the enforcement action, are not directly provided for by DP/3/96. In a Scottish Court of Sessions case, *Abdadou,* the court decided that, in these cases, the Home Office should consider the compassionate circumstances relating to the family life without any presumption, either that the application be refused or allowed. The Court of Appeal in *Mahmood* recommended that the terms of the policy be reconsidered to deal with this gap.

DP/2/93 – Cases where the marriage or relationship came to the attention of the Home Office before 14 March 1996

Cases where the marriage or relationship was made known to the Home Office before 14 March 1996 are still considered under the more beneficial policy DP/2/93. In these cases, the marriage or relationship has to have subsisted for two years but the two years do *not* have to have pre-dated enforcement action. This policy also applies to common law relationships 'akin to marriage'.

Unmarried and same sex partners who are illegal entrants, overstayers or have breached conditions of leave

Unmarried and same sex partners who are not lawfully in the UK may apply to remain outside the rules relating to same-sex partners. Such applicantions will be considered on a discretionary basis by the Home Office. Under the rules, the application can be refused solely on the grounds that a person was in the UK without leave. There are no disclosed Home Office guidelines regarding enforcement action in cases concerning these applicants. However, it is possible to ask that discretion should be exercised for an unmarried couple, by stressing the length of the relationship, the difficulties there would be for the couple in living in the other person's country, or the particular reasons why it is necessary for the settled partner to remain in the UK. In some cases, the Home Office has treated the application as one for settlement with a close relative, and it has been refused because the settled partner is not a 'relative'. The IAT held in two cases in 1994, *Lizarzaburu* and *Livingstone*, that the Home Office should instead consider these applications on a similar basis to applications on the grounds of marriage. However, these cases were prior to the implementation of the unmarried partners' concession and the subsequent changes in the immigration rules. In *Hashim*, the High Court held that there would be hardship for the gay partner of a British citizen to return to Malaysia to seek an entry clearance because of the negative attitude towards same-sex relationships there. However, the fact that same-sex and unmarried partners are now covered within the immigration rules may in practice make it harder for applicants outside those rules who do not meet the requirements. The failure to establish a defined policy like DP/3/96 for unmarried and same sex partners may result in decisions made which can be challenged on human rights grounds. It must be remembered that non-marital relationships can amount to 'family life' and that same-sex relationships, while not necessarily amounting to family life, do involve the parties' 'private' life.

Community legislation may be helpful to common-law, gay and lesbian couples in the light of *Reed v Netherlands*. Unmarried relationships are recognised in the immigration regulations of Denmark, Finland, the Netherlands, Norway and Sweden. British citizens may therefore travel to these EEA countries and be joined there by an unmarried partner. For example, a British and Ghanaian gay couple might travel to Denmark, marry and live together there (if the British partner is exercising European free movement rights there). Some couples have been able to do this successfully in the Netherlands.

Getting married

When people have lost their passports, or do not wish to show them, they may have difficulty in arranging a wedding. The marriage registrar must, by law, be satisfied as to the identity, age and freedom to marry of couples requesting marriage. If the registrar is satisfied by what couples say, no further evidence need be produced. If not, instructions to registrars from the General Register Office state that the best evidence from a person from abroad is a passport. Birth certificates may be acceptable, but will not show whether people have been married, or whether they still hold their nationality of birth. Registrars state that a passport issued more recently and which has a photograph of its holder, is more useful. Passports issued by many countries state whether the holder is married or single. Other evidence, such as driving licences, may be acceptable at the discretion of the registrar.

Under the 1999 Act registrars have a duty to report to the Home Office any suspicions they have about 'sham' marriages. Reports of people being unable to book a wedding because the registrar has not accepted other evidence of their identity are therefore likely to continue. There have also been cases where a registrar, suspicious about a particular person has alerted the immigration authorities to the date fixed for a wedding, or the immigration authorities have requested information from the registrar and people have been arrested as overstayers before they are able to marry. It is important to remember that even in detention people are able to marry and that under the ECHR there is a 'right to marry and found a family' (Article 12).

Making the application

The application should be made on form FLR(M). The important factors to bring out in making these applications are:

- how long the person has been in the UK. If there are no substantial ties in the UK, human rights applications are less likely to be successful. It is important to note that the old right of appeal against deportation for those who had remained in the UK for over seven years has been removed by the 1999 Act;

- how long the relationship has subsisted before enforcement action. Evidence should be produced to show this, for example, that there are children of the relationship, there has been joint purchase or renting of property, or evidence that the couple have been together for a long time. When there is a child or children involved, particularly if they are nearly seven years old, it is worth reminding the Home Office of the internal instructions relating to them (▶see above). In addition, where there is a child not of the relationship but who is resident in the UK with their other parent and who has contact with either the applicant or his or her spouse or partner, this may be an additional factor to raise in the application as it is relevant to the human rights of the parent and child;

- whether it is practicable to establish family life abroad. It is important to address what possibilities there are of establishing family life abroad and what difficulties or obstacles there might be in doing this;

- other parts of the immigration rules. Are all the other parts of the rules satisfied? For example, can the couple maintain and accommodate themselves without recourse to public funds?;

- the person's previous immigration history and any problems the applicant has had with the Home Office in the past are also relevant factors. They should therefore be explained. When a marriage takes place at the end of a long series of applications, previous marriages or relationships or other immigration problems, the Home Office will be particularly suspicious of the intentions of the applicant.

The Home Office may send out a further questionnaire. Any applicant and their spouse or partner may be asked to go to the Home Office or to an immigration office, where they may be interviewed separately, but both may be asked the same questions about their meeting and relationship to see if they give the same answers. Sometimes the immigration service come to a couple's home, unannounced, in order to see whether they are living together and whether there is any evidence that a couple live at that address.

Rights of appeal

If the application was made when the spouse/partner or fiancé(e) from abroad did not have leave to remain and is liable to removal, there is no right of appeal against the refusal under the immigration rules. However, a human rights appeal against a negative decision can be lodged under section 65 of the 1999 Act if the applicant alleges that the decision is in breach of their human rights. Previously the only option at this stage of refusal was to lodge a High Court judicial review application to prevent removal.

If the application is successful, the person will usually be given 12 months' leave to remain (or two years in the case of an unmarried partner), with no restrictions on taking employment, but with a prohibition on public funds.

People who want to stay in the UK although they *no longer* have a relationship with a partner

Bereaved Spouses and Unmarried Partners

Since 2 October 2000, there has been provision in the immigration rules for the settlement of spouses or unmarried partners who are in the UK with limited leave as a spouse or partner and whose British or settled spouse or partner dies within the probationary period. The rules require that the applicant can show that the relationship was still subsisting at the time of death and that the parties intended to continue to live together. In practice, this may be difficult to prove. However, there would have to be clear evidence that the relationship had broken down for the Home Office to conclude that there was no such intention. Bereaved spouses and unmarried partners do *not* have to satisfy the maintenance and accommodation requirements when they make their application to stay under the immigration rules.

Domestic Violence Concession

Following a vigorous campaign fought by Southall Black Sisters and others, on 27 July 1998 the Home Office announced a concession to the one-year rule for women who have been victims of domestic violence. The concession is contained in the IDI (Ch8, s1, annexes C and C2).

WHAT THE DOMESTIC VIOLENCE CONCESSION SAYS

Where a person has been granted 12 months' leave on the basis of marriage and the marriage breaks down *because of* domestic violence during that 12 months, the person will be granted indefinite leave to remain, provided that the domestic violence can be proved by any of the following pieces of evidence:

- a court injunction, non-molestation order or other protection order (other than an *ex parte* or 'interim' order); *or*
- a criminal conviction against the abusive spouse; *or*
- a police caution issued to the abusive spouse.

WHAT THE DOMESTIC VIOLENCE CONCESSION MEANS

The wording of the concession restricts those who can benefit from it to those whose marriages broke down *within the initial one year period on account of domestic violence*. However, the reality for many women in such circumstances is that they do not seek to regularise their immigration position as they are more concerned about protecting themselves and often their children from an abusive husband.

In recognition of this, if the Home Office has indicated (IDI Ch 8, s1 annex C2) that it will not reject an application solely because it is made after the wife's leave has expired. This is because it is acknowledged that, due to the circumstances of the violence, the settlement application may not be made in time. However, the Home Office will usually reject applications from 'long-term overstayers'. Women who stay with abusive partners and then fail to regularise their immigration position and whose marriages then break down are unfairly excluded from the terms of the concession.

The requirements relating to the evidence needed to show that violence occurred are also unfair and exclude many women for whom seeking the evidence might expose them to even greater risk. It is simply not an option for many women to go to the police and to have to go to court and give evidence against their abusive partner in order to try and secure a conviction in a criminal court or hope that their husband will admit the offence so that the police will then issue a caution. It is arguable that this is too high a standard of proof for immigration cases. In addition, pursuing matters in the family courts and seeking final injunctions or non-molestation orders, may expose women to contested applications for contact orders with children of the marriage or for residence orders which they might otherwise have avoided.

So, in reality, many women are unable to gain any benefit from the concession as it is and may have to seek to rely on other immigration or human rights claims, for example, in relation to their children or their length of residence here or risks on returning to their country of origin. Where women do want to make these applications and they do not have any of the items of evidence that are required under the concession, they should still forward whatever evidence they do have of the violence, for example doctors' or hospital reports or statements from friends, relatives or social workers.

Until a woman's status in the UK is finally resolved, she is likely to be either an overstayer or a person who continues to have a condition on her probationary leave prohibiting her from having recourse to public funds. Therefore, she will usually have no access to benefit and may only be given support through the local authority if she is determined as having needs that arise other than just through her destitution ▶see pages 679-681 for more details. In addition, she may be able to access support under the Children Act 1989, if she has the care of a child. *However*, if she claims asylum (which includes an Article 3 ECHR claim for support purposes), then she may be accommodated by the National Asylum Support Service (NASS). NASS may, however, disperse her away from her network of support. Advice about the practical consequences of making a human rights or asylum claim should be obtained in advance, as well as advice about the strength of the case. Advisers should be quick to stress the need for women in such a vulnerable position to remain within their support structures and also to emphasise their length of residence in the area and the effect of dispersal on the education of any children.

How to make an application

The application should be made on the SET(O) form with a detailed covering letter addressing the requirements of the concession. Reference to human rights arguments, where they are relied upon, should be included in the letter. The application should also enclose the appropriate proof, where possible. It was indicated in a Parliamentary reply by a Home Office minister on 16 June 1999 that, where a prosecution is pending and none of the other required pieces of evidence is available, they will only grant further periods of six-months' leave until the outcome of the criminal proceedings. It was further stated that where proceedings are pending for an injunction, non-molestation order or other protection order, a decision on the application will be delayed.

What if the application is refused?

If an application is refused under the concession and the person had leave at the time of applying, then an appeal can be brought. On the appeal, the applicant can argue that the decision was 'not in accordance with the law', where it can be argued that the Home Office did not apply their policy correctly or if they decided it without establishing the correct facts. In addition, or alternatively, an appeal raising human rights grounds can be made. Where there are no children involved, the woman's right to respect for private life should be emphasised. There may also be risks of human rights abuses on return to their country of origin following the breakdown of a marriage for domestic violence or other reasons. Therefore, it may also be appropriate to refer to Article 3 (inhuman or degrading treatment) and in some cases to make an asylum claim under the Refugee Convention (see the House of Lords case of *Shah* and *Islam*).

Circumstances where the domestic violence concession does not apply

It should be noted that the concession does not apply to the spouse or partner of a sponsor who themselves only has limited leave to remain. Nor does it apply to fiancé(e)s. In both cases, the Home Office would argue that the applicants were not in the UK for the purposes of settlement. However, if a domestic violence issue arose and there are reasons why the individual cannot return home, an application should be made to the Home Office using the SET(O) form with a covering letter requesting the exercise of discretion by the Home Office, again raising any relevant human rights arguments.

The concession also does not apply to the spouse or partner of an EEA national here exercising European free movement rights. Again, if a relationship broke down on account of domestic violence, especially towards the end of the four-year qualifying period (▶see pages 473-475) for applying for settlement, then an application could be made under SET(O) in the same way. It should be remembered, however, that for EEA nationals, as long as the EEA spouse is exercising treaty rights, his/her partner can still remain as their dependant unless they are actually divorced.

Marriage or relationship breakdown after settlement has been granted

If a marriage or relationship breaks down *after* the person has been granted settlement, this does not affect his or her immigration position. The person remains settled even if she or he is divorced or separated from his or her partner. When the separation has been difficult, it is not uncommon for the spouse who is British or was settled first to threaten the other partner with deportation. This is an idle threat if settlement has already been granted. The only exception to this is when the Home Office believes, and can prove, that settlement was granted through deception. This will be the case if a couple had already separated at the time settlement was granted but had agreed at that stage not to inform the Home Office, or if the couple had never intended to remain together. It is then possible for the Home Office to begin enforcement proceedings on the grounds of that person's deception. This is rare. It is, however, a criminal offence for a person 'if, by means which include deception by him, he obtains or seeks to obtain leave to enter or remain in the UK'.

Marriage and relationship breakdown in other cases

The one-year probationary rule for marriage has been in force since 1 August 1988. The two-year rule for unmarried and same-sex partners was brought into the rules on 2 October 2000. The 2002 White Paper proposes to increase the probationary period for married couples to two years. If marriages or relationships break down during that probationary period, for reasons other than domestic violence or bereavement, and couples are no longer living together at the end of it, the partners from abroad no longer have any claim under the immigration rules to remain because of the marriage or relationship. Either they will have to show that they fit into some other part of the immigration rules, or that there are strong exceptional compassionate reasons, or human rights reasons, to permit them to stay.

In the past, the presence of children of the marriage was considered significant, but the Home Office current policy is that 'the general presumption is that a child who has spent less than seven years in the UK would be able to adapt to life abroad'. When the marriage has ended, the person cannot use application form SET(M) but should use SET(O).

In respect of women whose relationships have broken down, the Home Office has stated that it will consider 'the respective strength of a woman's ties with the UK and her own country and whether she would suffer any hardship if she was to return to her own country.' Its guidance also indicates that:

'leave to remain is not normally granted unless there are the most exceptional compelling or compassionate circumstances. The factors to be considered would include: the length of time the applicant was married before the breakdown; the length of time the applicant has been resident in the UK; the applicant's age and the proportion of time spent abroad before entering the UK; whether there are children of the marriage and the applicant's close family and other ties both in the UK and abroad'.

Applying to stay for access to children

For people whose relationships have broken down and who have children who are resident with the UK resident parent, the other parent may apply under the immigration rules to remain in the UK for the purpose of having contact with their child(ren), for more details ▶see pages 379–382. However, where the non-settled parent and the non-settled child are both living together and the child has contact with his/her other parent who is settled in the UK but is not residing with the child, then both the child and parent from abroad will have to seek leave to remain in the UK outside the immigration rules, relying on the right to family life.

People who wish to accompany or join a spouse or partner in the UK who is not settled but who is in the UK for the time being

Workers and business people

The immigration rules relating to this category have been amended so that the unmarried or same-sex partners, as well as spouses, of these people can be admitted to the UK. Spouses or partners of people coming for work may eventually obtain settlement in line with the worker or business person themselves. The rules cover sponsors and partners of people in the following groups: workers with work permits; workers in permit-free employment; business people; investors; and retired persons of independent means.

The common requirements are:

- the applicant must intend to live together in the UK with their spouse or partner;
- if the applicant is the unmarried or same sex partner of the worker, that they have been living together in a relationship akin to marriage which has subsisted for two years or more and they are legally unable to marry;
- there will be adequate maintenance and accommodation for them without recourse to public funds; and
- they must not intend to stay in the UK beyond their spouse's period of leave.

Applicants need an entry clearance to come to the UK for this purpose and they can be refused if any of the general grounds of refusal apply.

People *who are already in the UK* and who wish to 'switch' to remain with their spouse or partner are not entitled to do so under the immigration rules. However, even where no entry clearance has been obtained, Home Office case-workers may grant the application *if* all the other requirements of the rules are satisfied and there are exceptional compassionate circumstances. If the person is the spouse or partner of a person in the UK as a 'person with UK ancestry' (▶see page 432), switching may be permitted even if there are no exceptional circumstances (see IDI, Ch5, s9, para 2.2).

The form that should be used for these limited extensions of leave is FLR(O), which does not have a specific part for spouses or partners, but they can qualify under the 'other' category. The form assumes that the worker and his or her spouse or partner are applying together for an extension of stay, rather than that the spouse or partner might be applying independently when, for example, he or she had permission to remain on a different basis before the marriage. It is, however, quite acceptable for the application to be made independently.

If the application is successful, leave to enter or remain will be granted for the same length of time as the spouse or partner who is a worker, business person etc. The rules state that the spouses or partners of retired persons of independent means will not be allowed to work, but nothing is said about any employment conditions to be imposed on others. Home Office practice is not to restrict employment, so spouses or partners of workers and business people are normally free to work. Where limited leave is being given, the person will normally have a public funds prohibition as a condition of their leave endorsed on their passports.

Students

The spouse and children of students can be admitted to the UK in line with the student. Although there are rules relating to the admission of unmarried partners for others with limited leave (►see above), there is no provision under the immigration rules or published Home Office policies making similar provision for students. An application could be made outside the rules stating that the person met the other requirements (►see above) of the rules for the admission of spouses and partners seeking entry in a temporary capacity. Arguably, human rights discrimination grounds could also be raised as there is no apparent justification for their omission from the rules.

Spouses of students seeking entry have to show that they can be maintained and accommodated without recourse to public funds and that they intend to leave the UK at the end of any period granted. If the period they are granted is less than 12 months, the spouse will be prohibited from working. If it is 12 months or over, nothing is stated about working but Home Office practice is not to restrict the spouse from working and, in practice, students are often only able to fund their studies with the additional income that their spouse or partner is earning. For full details about the admission of the various different types of student and their spouses ►see Chapter 15. Students' spouses should use application form FLR(O) if they are applying separately from the student, and FLR(S) if the student and spouse are applying together, in-country for an extension of leave.

Other temporary categories

The immigration rules also permit the spouses of teachers and language assistants (under approved exchange schemes) and those in approved training or work experience to be admitted. The normal rules relating to intention to stay together while in the UK and support without recourse to public funds apply. However, as with students, unmarried partners of those in these categories are not admissable under the immigration rules. No provision is made in the immigration rules for either spouses or partners of visitors, of au pairs, seasonal workers at agricultural camps or working holidaymakers. Spouses or partners of people in those categories (ie. as visitors, working holidaymakers etc.) have to qualify in their own right. They may qualify under the same rules.

17 Children

This chapter covers the rights of children to come to and stay in the UK with their parents or guardians. It also covers the rights of children to be joined in the UK by their parents, where the parents do not otherwise have the right to be in the UK.

The chapter therefore covers the immigration rights of children in the following circumstances:

- children joining or staying with parents who are settled in the UK, or accompanying parents coming for settlement ▶see pages 368-373;
- children coming to join a lone parent in the UK, or accompanying a lone parent or relative for settlement ▶see pages 373-378;
- children joining or staying with a person in the UK who is not their parent ▶see pages 378-379;
- the rights of children to have a parent, with whom they have contact, join them in the UK and remain with them ▶see pages 379-382;
- children accompanying or joining parents who are in the UK with limited leave ▶see pages 382-384;
- the rights of adopted children ▶see pages 384-391;
- children whose parents may be forced to leave the UK and children who are in the UK on their own ▶see pages 391-396;
- children born in the UK ▶see pages 396-398.

For details about unaccompanied minors seeking asylum in the UK ▶see pages 191-192. Children applying as the dependants of asylum-seekers are covered on pages 192-194. For the rights of family reunion for children of parents in the UK who have been recognised as refugees or granted exceptional leave ▶see Chapter 12.

Children who have reached 18

This chapter generally concerns children who are below the age of 18. However, some children who reach 18 can still benefit from the rules set out in this chapter because:

1 The age of a child seeking to come to, or stay in, the UK for the purposes of settlement is determined as of the date of the application rather than the

date of the decision. So a child may have turned 18 by the date of the decision but still be granted leave under the immigration rules ▶see page 370 below for when an application is treated as having been made.

2 Children who come to the UK with a view to being settled with a parent, or parents, who are settled in the UK and who are given limited leave, may subsequently be granted indefinite leave even if they reach 18 by the time they come to apply for indefinite leave. The same applies to those children who are admitted with limited leave to join a parent or parents who have limited leave in a category under the immigration rules which may lead to settlement (e.g., work or business-related purposes ▶see pages 382-383). Provided that they apply while they still have *leave* as a child dependant, it doesn't matter that they have subsequently become 18. They may still be granted extensions or indefinite leave in line with their parent(s).

Other children who have reached the age of 18 have to satisfy additional requirements in order to be admitted under the rules ▶see pages 406-409.

Children who do not have to satisfy the immigration rules

Some children have immigration rights which do not derive from the immigration rules. They are as follows.

Children who are British citizens. People born in the UK before 1 January 1983 are British citizens and have the right of abode in the UK. Those born abroad before 1983 to British citizen fathers are automatically British citizens and are also, therefore, free to enter and remain in the UK. Children born in the UK from 1 January 1983 onwards are automatically British citizens if either parent was a British citizen or was settled here at the time of the child's birth. Most children born abroad from 1 January 1983 onwards are automatically British citizens if, at the time of the birth, either parent was a British citizen who was born, adopted, registered or naturalised in the UK. In all cases, the father's status counts only if the parents were married at the time of the birth or subsequently marries. To check on the nationality status of children born in the UK or children with British parents ▶see pages 396-398 and Chapter 27.

The Nationality, Immigration and Asylum Bill 2002 proposes changes to nationality law which will allow the husband of the child's mother at the time of birth to pass on his nationality. If she was not married, the natural father may pass on his nationality. Also under the proposals, there are more complex rules about passing on nationality where the pregnancy came about by artificial insemination.

Others with the right of abode. A person who is a Commonwealth citizen and who was born before 1 January 1983 to a parent who was born in the UK has the right of abode in the UK and does not have to prove anything more than these facts to obtain a certificate of entitlement to the right of abode. If the parent relied on is the father, the parents have to have married.

People claiming these rights need to have their position confirmed abroad before travelling, by applying to a British post overseas. If they are British citizens, they may obtain British passports. If they are Commonwealth citizens with the right of abode, they have to obtain a certificate of entitlement to the right of abode. They will need the birth certificate of the parent born in the UK, the marriage certificate of their parents if the parent concerned is their father, and their own birth certificate to show who their parents are. If these certificates are not available, or not accepted as genuine, it may be difficult to satisfy the British authorities about the relationship.

Children of EEA nationals. Nationals of an EEA country other than the UK who are exercising European rights of free movement in the UK are entitled to be joined here by their dependants. Normally included as dependants are children and grandchildren up to the age of 21 and beyond that age if the children are still dependent. For full details about dependants of EEA nationals ▶see pages 458-464.

Children of diplomats. Children of diplomats and others who work in embassies and high commissions and who form part of the household of the diplomat are exempt from immigration controls for as long as they continue to satisfy those conditions ▶see pages 436-437.

Human rights and other considerations

In addition to the immigration rules and the Home Office policies outside the rules which are considered in this chapter, Article 8 ECHR (right to respect for private and family life ▶see pages 255-266 for full details) may also be relevant in some cases involving children. However, although the relationship between parents and their minor children will almost always amount to 'family life', in *Isiko* the Court of Appeal maintained the principle that immigration decisions which separate them can be justified especially where the parents' immigration history is very poor and/or criminal offences have been committed by the parent who is facing removal.

The Home Office interprets the immigration rules on children without direct reference to other childcare legislation such as the Children Act 1989. The 1989 Act states that when a court determines any question concerning a child, the child's welfare must be the paramount consideration. The court proceeds on the basis that children should remain with their families wherever possible. Immigration law, even read together with Article 8, does not contain any such assumptions. In *Ahmed and Patel* and in *Gangadeen*, the Court of Appeal treated the best interests of the child as a factor in immigration decisions involving family life but not as paramount. That case also confirmed that the United Nations Convention on the Rights of the Child (ratified by the UK in 1991) is not directly applicable in immigration cases.

Children joining or staying with both parents settled in the UK

WHAT THE RULES SAY

The rules for children coming to join settled parents state that they must:

- be the child of parents settled or being admitted for settlement to the UK;
- be under 18;
- be unmarried, not have formed an independent family unit and not be leading an independent life; and
- be maintained and accommodated, in accommodation owned or occupied exclusively by their parent(s) without recourse to public funds.

The child must obtain an entry clearance to come to the UK. If both parents are alive but one parent is not living in the UK and does not intend to live here, more tests must be satisfied. If one of the parents is dead, however, there are no additional rules to satisfy ▶see pages 373-378 for circumstances where a child wishes to join a lone parent in the UK. The following two points should be noted as applying to children in this and the other categories under the immigration rules relating to the admission of children.

1 As with most applications under the rules, children can still be refused leave if any of the general grounds for refusal apply ▶see page 67.

2 A child will be refused under the rules if their mother is a party to a polygamous marriage who would be refused admission for settlement under the rules denying admission to polygamously married women (this is generally the case where one living wife has already been admitted, ▶see page 335 for further details and; paragraphs 278 and HC 395).

The rules are similar for a child who is accompanying, coming to join or staying with parents in the UK where one parent has limited leave and the other is settled. In those circumstances, the child will be admitted for one year 'with a view to settlement' and will be able to apply for indefinite leave at the end of the year if they continue to satisfy the same conditions.

The rules also now provide for the children of fiancé(e)s to come to the UK with the fiancé(e) and to be granted limited leave of up to six months (paras 303A-F, HC 395). Extensions may be granted if the fiancé(e) (their parent) is also granted an extension because the marriage has not yet taken place. The child can also obtain indefinite leave in line with the rules set out above, when their parent alsoseeks indefinite leave. However, children coming with fiancé(e)s also have to show that there are serious and compelling family orother considerations which would make their exclusion from the UK undesirable, that there is no other person outside the UK who could reasonably be expected to care for them and that suitable arrangements have been made for their care in the UK.

WHAT THE RULES MEAN

Parents

In the immigration rules relating to the settlement of children (and for the admission of children for other purposes), the word 'parent' *includes* (para 6, HC 395):

- the stepfather of a child whose father is dead;
- the stepmother of a child whose mother is dead;
- the father as well as the mother of a non-marital child;
- in the case of a child born in the UK who is not a British citizen, a person to whom there has been a genuine transfer of parental responsibility on the ground of the original parent(s)' inability to care for the child (eg. be a foster parent or another relative).

However, 'parent' does not include an adoptive parent where the application is for the purposes of settlement. For the rules about applications for settlement for adopted children ▶see pages 384-391. Where the application is not for the settlement of the child, however, the definition of parent includes an adoptive parent but *only* where the child was adopted in accordance with a decision taken by the competent administrative authority or court in a country whose adoption orders are recognised by the UK ▶see page 751 for the list of these countries.

Parents settled in the UK

The actual requirements are that either both parents are settled in the UK or they are coming to the UK for settlement at the same time as the child or one parent is settled/being admitted for settlement and the other is being admitted 'with a view' to settlement. In the last case, one parent will be applying for leave 'with a view' to settlement and is likely to be given 12 months limited leave (usually the probationary period for married couples). In order to be 'settled' a person must be a British citizen or have the right of abode in the UK or have indefinite leave to enter or remain in the UK. The UK must also be their normal place of residence. The parents must also either be in the UK or accompanying the child when they travel to the UK.

If both parents are settled, the child should be given indefinite leave. If one parent is granted limited leave with a view to settlement, the child is likely to be given 12 months' leave in line with them if the application is successful.

Under 18

Children must be under 18 on the date of application to come to or remain in the UK (see para 27, HC 395). In all other cases, applications are decided on the circumstances existing on the date of the decision. This rule is to ensure that a child's application is not refused because delay in determining it means that the child no longer satisfies the age requirement. An application from abroad is considered to be made on the day the application forms and the fee are received by the British post. An application in the UK is made on the date it is posted (see *Lubetkin*) but proof of posting must be obtained. To be valid, in-country extension applications have to be made on the correct Home Office application form and be accompanied by all the documents specified on the form, or an explanation of why any documents are not available and when they will be sent. It is therefore important that an in-country application is made correctly before a child reaches 18.

However, these concerns do not apply to a child who is admitted in the first place with a view to settlement with their parents, and who later applies for indefinite leave on the same basis. Such a child should be be granted indefinite leave if they satisfy all the other rules, even if the child has, by the date of application for settlement, reached the age of 18 (see para 298(ii)(b), HC 395).

Refusals based simply on age where continued dependency can be shown may raise an issue under Article 8 ECHR.

Unmarried/not leading an independent life/ not formed an independent family unit

A child who is married is not eligible to be admitted under the immigration rules, even if he or she is still under 18. Marriage means that the child has formed a closer family link with his or her spouse and no longer qualifies to join his or her parents. Children who are not married but who are coming up to adulthood can be refused if immigration officials believe they have formed an independent family unit, or are leading an independent life. These circumstances are not defined further. They possibly exclude from admission a child who has dependants of their own, even if they are not married to or living with the other parent, and children who have become self-sufficient or dependent upon someone else.

Maintenance and accommodation

The 'maintenance and accommodation without recourse to public funds' requirements apply to the vast majority of categories for admission under the immigration rules. It should be noted that the rules relating to children state that they should be maintained and accommodated 'by the parent' or parents. If third-party support is available, however, and the application is refused for this reason, this may be contrary to Articles 8 and 14 ECHR. For full details of the maintenance and accommodation requirements ▶see pages 328-335.

Children applying for entry clearance

Children have to satisfy entry clearance officers (ECOs) at the British embassy or high commission that they qualify. The evidence that may be required is as follows:

- proof of the child's relationship to the parents. If the child has a birth certificate showing the names of both the parents, this is very helpful. However registration of births is not universal or compulsory in some countries and a birth certificate may not exist. Also British officials are often suspicious of documents that are produced by governments in poorer countries of the world and often refuse to accept them. If the document does not exist, this should be explained and alternative evidence produced instead; for example:

  - records from the school the child is attending to show what that institution has been told about the child's age and parentage,
  - records from the hospital where the child was born,
  - information from the midwife or anyone else who knows about the birth,
  - affidavits from people, preferably not related to the child and parents, confirming their knowledge of the birth and relationship;

- proof of the parents' status in the UK, for example, certified photocopies of his, her or their passports;

- the parents' birth certificates if either of them was born in the UK;

- evidence of financial support available to the children;

- evidence of accommodation available to the children.

Interviews and investigations

Children may well be interviewed (unless they are under 10) and the person who has been caring for them abroad is also likely to be interviewed. Questions should be confined to relatively simple matters and details of immediate family. Older children may be questioned on their own (not in the presence of a responsible adult) and in more depth. All children will need to show evidence about their relationship to their parent(s) and of maintenance and accommodation available in the UK. Parents and children should be aware that in certain cases, for example, where no satisfactory documentary evidence, to establish age, that the child is related as claimed, 'sole responsibility' for lone parent applications, or if there is a question over whether a child has established an independent family unit, then the Foreign Office staff may conduct a 'village visit'. This means that they may go to the place where the child resides and ask questions of persons in the local community. The evidence obtained may later be produced in an appeal and may require a further independent village visit report to counter any negative conclusions. This is both time-consuming, expensive and the independence of any such report is likely to be called into question.

For further details about entry clearance applications generally ▶see pages 52-64.

DNA testing

DNA profiling can prove conclusively that children are related to their parents. The test involves taking a small blood sample from the child and the parents and testing this for the DNA in the blood to see that the child's DNA corresponds to that of the claimed parents. It is a much more certain way of determining relationships than by asking family members detailed questions. However, it can also show, for example, that a father is not the father of a child whom he has always accepted and believed to be his.

DNA tests will be provided for families applying to come to the UK for the first time 'where the relevant relationships cannot be demonstrated easily by other means' to the ECO, who would otherwise be likely to refuse the application. If families agree to take the test, arrangements will be made by the British post, at no extra cost to the family (the level of entry clearances fees takes account of the likely costs of these procedures). If the family refuse, this should not be a reason in itself for refusal of the application.

The scheme does not, however, generally apply to re-applicants, namely, people who have been refused once and who are applying again. Families not included in the scheme may still have tests carried out on their own initiative. They must get in touch with one of the companies which the Home Office has approved to carry out DNA testing and follow the company's procedures. If the application has been refused and there is an immigration appeal pending, and the family qualifies for legal funding from the Legal Services Commission (LSC), it is possible in limited circumstances for the expenses of the test to be met. The LSC has laid down specific criteria setting out when the costs of DNA tests will be met by them. If the family want the test done before a decision, or if LSC funding is not available, the family can pay privately.

If the application is successful

If the ECO is satisfied that the rules are met, entry clearance will be granted to the child. Entry clearances now operate as leave to enter the UK. If the child is being admitted for settlement, the entry clearance will be endorsed with a statement that it is to have effect as indefinite leave. Otherwise, the entry clearance will be valid for a particular period (probably 12 months) and will operate as leave to enter until the expiry date of the entry clearance. After being admitted, the child is immediately entitled to state education and National Health Service medical treatment.

If the application overseas is refused

The British post will issue a notice explaining why the application was refused, stating the child's right to appeal against the refusal, and sending forms to fill in to appeal. It does not matter if a child becomes 18 while the appeal is pending; the important date is the date of application. If the appeal is successful two years later, when a child is 19 or 20, he or she should be granted entry clearance. However, if an appeal fails, but a child later produces fresh evidence, for example, a DNA test result, and applies again, the application is considered to be made on the date of the second application. Advice should be taken in these cases and where possible, therefore, care should be taken not to withdraw an initial application that was made while the applicant was under 18.

Applying for settlement after one year

If the child has been granted leave only for a limited period, it is important that an application is made to the Home Office, before the leave expires, on the official application form SET(F). If a parent is applying for settlement at the same time, this should be done on form SET(M) and the child should be included on this form. The Home Office will need the passports of the parents and the child, a photograph of any child over the age of 16, the child's birth certificate and evidence that the family is able to be maintained and accommodated without recourse to public funds, before settlement is granted. It is rare for a child to be refused at this stage, unless the parent he or she accompanied or came to join has been refused.

Children joining a lone parent in the UK

WHAT THE RULES SAY

If one parent is *dead*, a child can join or be allowed to remain with the other parent provided that parent is present and settled in the UK, or is being admitted for settlement at the same time as the child. The same rules as for children joining both parents (see above) apply and there are no other specific requirements the child has to meet apart from proving the death of the deceased parent. The child will be given leave in line with their parent.

However, if an application is being made for a child to join a lone parent where the other parent is still alive, there are further rules which must be satisfied. It must be shown that the lone parent is present and settled in the UK, has been admitted with a view to settlement or is being admitted for settlement/with a view to settlement at the same time as the child; and

- the parent has had 'sole responsibility' for the child's upbringing; *or*
- there are serious and compelling family or other considerations in the child's own country which make the child's exclusion undesirable and suitable arrangements have been made for the child's care in the UK.

The rules relating to maintenance and accommodation, age and being unmarried/not leading an independent life, which apply where both parents are being joined, must also be satisfied. Children applying to come to the UK to join a lone parent must also obtain entry clearance.

Where the child seeking to join the sole parent is under 12 years old, the immigration authorities operate a discretion outside the rules to allow the child to come to the UK ▶see pages 377-378.

WHAT THE RULES MEAN

A substantial amount of case law has grown up around these require-ments of the rules. A parent will never literally have had 'sole responsi-bility' when they have been living in a different country from the child and so allowances are made. The alternative 'exclusion undesirable' require-ment is notoriously difficult to satisfy.

The 'sole responsibility' rule

The sole responsibility rule was first introduced in 1969. The government's stated intention was to prevent the growth of all-male Pakistani families, where men who had come to work in the UK were sending for their sons, but not their wives and daughters, and it was felt that this was not in the best interests of the children. The result was that families applied to come to the UK.

The communities which continue to suffer most from the sole respon-sibility rule are people from the Caribbean and from West Africa. Many women from these regions migrated in search of work, leaving young children in the care of an older relative, commonly a grandmother, for what was intended to be a short period until they could make a home for them in the UK. Money was sent for their support and close contact was maintained, but it was often not possible to say that sole responsibility for the child was with the mother. In such cases, ECOs have been known to ask many questions about contact with the child's father, who may well have remained abroad but was separated from the mother and child. It is clearly hard for children or grandparents to admit that the child has been abandoned; but if the father's contact had been kept up, even sporad-ically or at a very low level, this could be a reason for refusing the child entry clearance.

Sole responsibility does not simply apply between parents as to who has that responsibility but relates to other relatives or carers who may have assumed that role in the absence of one or both parents.

In *Rudolph*, the Immigration Appeal Tribunal considered what should be proved in order for a child to qualify under this rule. In that case, the parents were separated and the child had been brought up in a convent in Sri Lanka while her mother was in the UK. The IAT stated:

'we need therefore to be satisfied not only that essential financial support was provided by Mrs Rudolph but also that she was regularly consulted about and expressed a continuing and positive concern for [the child]. We agree...we should not necessarily rule out 'sole responsibility' if for a limited time during childhood it cannot be proved. It is a matter of looking at the childhood as a whole and all the actions of the mother'.

Another case, *Ramos*, gave further guidance on sole responsibility. A Filipino mother abandoned by her husband, had left her daughter with her own mother when she came to the UK to work to support them; the child's aunt and uncle lived nearby. The girl was not allowed to come to join her mother. It was stated:

'Obviously there are matters of day-to-day decision making in the upbringing of a child which are bound to be decided on the spot by whoever is looking after the child in the absence of the parents settled here, such as getting the child to school safely and on time, or putting the child to bed...and so forth. In the present case it is not in doubt that money was provided by the mother here to support the child, and indeed the grandmother, but that again is not per se conclusive of sole responsibility...The suggestion is of course not that the father has had any responsibility or that the mother has abandoned all responsibility, but that the true conclusion on the facts is that responsibility has been shared between the mother and the grandmother and possibly also the uncle and aunt'.

The Home Office sets out the following factors as relevant to sole responsibility (IDI, Ch8, annex M):

- the period the parent in the UK has been separated from the child;
- the previous arrangements for the care of the child prior to the parent coming to the UK;
- who has (or has had) the day-to-day care and control of the child since the sponsor came to the UK;
- who supports the child financially;
- who takes decisions about the child's upbringing;
- the degree of contact between parent and child;
- what role the other parent and relatives outside the UK have played in the child's care and upbringing (if any).

In general terms, the well-established principles of sole responsibility are (and see *Williams*):

- it is not necessary for the sole responsibility to be throughout life;
- financial support is a factor but not conclusive;
- the decision maker should look at the role played by the parents but also at the part played in the upbringing by others;
- it is not fatal that others played a part in day-to-day care;
- each case depends on its own facts but the evidence must be such that it can be fairly said that the sponsor remained in sole control of the child's

upbringing and responsible for the important decisions relating to the child's upbringing, such as where s/he lives, goes to school and any religious instruction.

Importantly, in the recent case of *Nmaju,* the Court of Appeal held that the rules allowed for circumstances where the sponsor could have had sole responsibility for a short time. In that case, the period of responsibility was for only a few months after the death of the other carer. This is important in cases where, for example, grandparents have become incapable of continuing their caring role and the parent returns to the country of origin for a short time to take charge of the child before applying to bring them to the UK.

Exclusion undesirable

Exclusion undesirable is an alternative to the sole responsibility rule. It can also be used where a 'relative' rather than a lone parent is seeking to bring a child to the UK. If a 'sole responsibility' case reaches appeal, an adjudicator is bound also to consider the exclusion undesirable alternative. However, in the case of *Tiongson* the IAT determined that where sole responsibility is satisfied, it was not incumbent upon an adjudicator to proceed to consider whether exclusion is undesirable.

Proving that a child qualifies under this rule can often be very hard. For example, in one case where it was accepted that a father in Trinidad had sexually abused his daughter, but there was no evidence he had done anything other than beat his twin sons, the girl's appeal was allowed but her brothers' appeals were dismissed.

In deciding whether the rules are met, the conditions in the country in which the child is living are the main focus. It is incorrect, however, to weigh those conditions against the conditions available in the UK. In *Rudolph*, the IAT stated:

'We are of the opinion that such [family and other] considerations must be applied to the country in which the appellant lives and not to those pertaining in the UK...The specific example of when the general requirements will be met [is] the inability of the parent in the foreign country to look after the child. It is strongly arguable that once we have found as a fact that Mr Rudolph is incapable of looking after [her child] the appellant's case is made'.

Some cases have stressed the need for incapacity rather than just unwillingness to look after a child. A parent may be physically or mentally incapable of caring for a child. The failure of the other parent to actually look after a child can be a strong indication of their incapacity to do so (*Awuko*, IAT). Where the other parent actually abandons the child, this should be sufficient (*Haughton*, IAT).

In *Saluguo*, a child was living in comfort with her aunt and siblings in the Philippines. However, she was able to come to the UK where her mother, a domestic worker in the UK, had worked for years under very poor conditions so as to provide her children with support and an education and desperately wanted to be joined in the UK by her youngest child.

In *Ali (Iqbal)*, the High Court required a case to be reconsidered where a child had applied to accompany his mother to join his 'father' in the UK but DNA testing showed that the man, who he had always believed was his father, was not and the application was refused. However, Iqbal had always been accepted as a child of the family and had never been involved in any deception. The court accepted that these circumstances and the presence in the UK of both people who had acted as parents amounted to serious family considerations making the child's exclusion undesirable.

This rule has also been used in inter-family adoption cases where the adoption is either not formalised or where it is not recognised by the UK ▶see pages 378-379, 388. Indeed the Home Office instructions (IDI Ch8, s5, annexes R and Q) state that any such family adoptions should also be considered under this rule as well as under the rules on coming to the UK for adoption. This is particularly relevant to inter-family adoptions from the Indian subcontinent, where there is no recognition of formal adoptions by the UK and where adoptions outside the family are very rare. Again the particular facts of any such *de facto* adoption situation will determine the likelihood of success. The strength of the relationship that the adoptive child has with his or her natural parents, despite the claimed adoption, will be a relevant factor. Of course, culturally in such circumstances, there would not be a western-style breaking of ties with natural parents, who would remain part of the child's extended family with whom they would retain close contact.

The rules must now be read so far as possible as complying with ECHR rights (see s3(1) Human Rights Act 1998 (HRA)) which means that these rules must be applied so as to be consistent wth the right to respect for family life under Article 8 ECHR.

The 'under-12' concession

If children are under 12 at the time of application, they may be permitted to come to the UK even if they do not satisfy the above rules relating to joining one parent. Because of the very great difficulty of satisfying the sole responsibility rule (and because of the complaints and campaigning against it), the Home Office does not apply the full rigours of the rules against children who are under 12 when they make their application. They would 'fairly freely' be allowed to join a parent settled in the UK 'provided there is suitable accommodation'. This is an old policy which was originally made public in 1995.

The policy has now been incorporated into the Home Office instructions (IDI Ch8, annex M, para 12). The Home Office has refused to write the concession into the immigration rules and has made little attempt to publicise it. Officials at British posts overseas do not always have regard to this concession unless they are reminded about it. The previous gender discriminatory requirement that, where the lone parent is the father, 'there is a female relative resident in the household who is willing to look after the child and is capable of doing so', has been dropped . This was presumably to make the concession compatible with the Human Rights Act. However, it may be still be advisable to address who other than the father (where he has had little contact with the child or where he is unable to care for them) is also be available to look after the child on a day-to-day basis as this is still an application that is made outside the rules and therefore at the discretion of the Home Office.

Where there is a mixed group of siblings, some of whom are older and do not qualify under the rules, and do not fall within this concession as well as younger children under 12, the relevant considerations as to whether the children can be admitted are: the consequences of splitting the group, whether the children have been living together as a group, the arrangements for the care of the children in the UK, how many children there are either side of the 12-years dividing line and the degree of hardship involved if they were all to remain abroad. Where a child does not come within the rules because they are the child of a polygamous marriage (►see pages 335, 368), they cannot benefit from the concession.

The maintenance requirement is not strictly applied to children admitted under the under-12 concession, provided that there is adequate accommodation available for them (see IDI, Ch8, annex H, para10.1).

Children joining a person who is not a parent

It must be remembered that, in all of the immigration rules, a 'parent' does not necessarily have to be the natural parent. It may be a step-parent replacing a parent who is dead or, in some circumstances, someone to whom there has been a transfer of parental responsibility ►see page 369 for the definition of parent under the rules. The rules referred to above may therefore be used, in those circumstances, where the parents are not the natural parents.

However, even where the sponsor does not satisfy the definition of a parent in the immigration rules, a child can still join a 'relative' who is present and settled (or being admitted for settlement) in the UK if they can satisfy the 'exclusion undesirable' requirement of the rules (see para 297(i)(f), HC 395). 'Other relative' for these purposes, is not defined and should, in the light of Article 8 ECHR, be read broadly. The child must, of course, satisfy the other requirements of age, be unmarried/not leading an independent life and be able to be supported without recourse to public funds.

Children may therefore qualify to join another relative if they are living in extremely difficult circumstances overseas. This is usually only possible if the child's parents are dead and if there are no other relatives in the country of the child's origin who could look after him or her instead. An adult sibling, for example, married and settled in the UK, might be the only relative to care for a child after their parents have died. Grandparents settled in the UK might wish to care for a grandchild abandoned by his or her parents. Any application for a child to join a relative other than a parent should be made in great detail, explaining the exceptional circumstances why the child needs to come to, or remain in, the UK and why no other arrangements could be made in the country of origin. Again, depending on the particular circumstances and family relationships involved, arguments relating to the right to respect for family life may assist in such applications and at any appeal.

Children being joined by parents with whom they have contact

When immigration rules were introduced to provide for persons exercising rights of access to children resident in the UK, the rules were very restrictive and were essentially only for short-term access visits. From 2 October 2000, the rules have been amended to enable parents to eventually settle in the UK if they have children to whom they have rights of access here. Entry clearance is still is required for a parent coming to the UK. However, a parent who is in the UK and who has leave when, for example, the marriage or relationship breaks down and who wishes to make an application to remain, can do so from within the UK. Previously, applications such as this were all made outside the rules and were often only granted after long battles with the Home Office.

The definition of 'parent' for the purposes of the immigration rules should, in particular, be remembered in 'access' applications ▶see page 369. Most notably, there is no requirement that the parents of the child were ever married.

The purpose of these rules is to attempt to comply with the ECtHR ruling in the case of *Berrehab*. This concerned a Moroccan man who was deported away from his Dutch ex-wife and their young child, with whom he had maintained very close contact. The difficulty involved in maintaining such frequent contact from abroad was held to be an infringement of the right to respect for family life under Article 8.

However, more recently, the case of *Poku* found that there was no violation of Article 8 when a couple, both of whom had a child from a previous relationship as well as two children of their own, had married when the wife was already threatened with deportation. The

European Commission held that the couple 'must be taken to be aware of [the wife's] precarious immigration status and the probable consequential effects' when they got married. The inevitable loss of contact between the children of the previous relationships and one of their parents was, in that case, found not to be a breach of the Convention.

Parents who reside abroad with their children and who wish to bring their children to the UK to visit the partner from whom they are separated, are not specifically provided for in the rules. They, or the child on his or her own, could apply for entry as a visitor for this purpose

People who apply from outside the UK

WHAT THE RULES SAY

A parent from abroad who is seeking to enter the UK in order to exercise their rights of access to their child in the UK must satisfy the following rules:

- the applicant must be the parent of a child who is resident in the UK;
- the parent or carer with whom the child lives permanently is resident the UK;
- the parent from abroad has evidence that he or she has rights of access to the child;
- the parent intends to continue to take an active part in the child's upbringing;
- the child is under 18; and
- the parent can maintain and accommodate him or herself without recourse to public funds.

Applications can also be refused on the basis of the general grounds for refusal. The parent must obtain an entry clearance before coming to the UK for this purpose.

WHAT THE RULES MEAN

The evidence of access rights which is required is either a residence or contact order, made by a court in the UK which grants rights of access to the child who is living here. Alternatively, it is sufficient if the parent can produce a certificate from a district judge confirming the parent's intention to maintain contact with the child. The provision in the rules for a certificate in the alternative is in line with the non-interventionist approach of the family courts not to make orders (such as for contact) where such matters can be agreed between the parents.

The Home Office acknowledged in a letter to Bates Wells & Braithwaite solicitors of 21 December 2000 that, as the rules currently stand, a parental responsibility agreement registered in the High Court and signed by both parents would not be sufficient to meet the strict requirements of the immigration rules. The Home Office is therefore intending to review these provisions relating to rights of access to children in the UK and to amend them as appropriate. In the meantime, such applications will be considered exceptionally outside the immigration rules where there is such an agreement.

The parent from abroad will have to confirm their intention to take an active role in the child's upbringing, which means playing a part and taking an interest in the child's schooling, health, social and other activities. Parents admitted under these rules are usually given leave for 12 months and they are also able to work to support themselves which is a welcome change from the old rules relating to access 'visits'.

People who apply when they are in the UK

WHAT THE RULES SAY

Parents can apply under these rules if they are already in the UK without having to leave to obtain entry clearance. The same rules as above apply but with the following modifications:

- the child visits and stays with the applicant on a frequent and regular basis and the applicant intends this to continue;
- the applicant takes and intends to continue to take an active role in the child's upbringing;
- the applicant has limited leave to remain in the UK as the spouse or unmarried partner of a person present and settled in the UK who is the other parent of the child;
- the applicant has not remained in breach of immigration laws; and
- as an alternative to producing evidence of a court order, the parent can provide a statement from the child's other parent (or from a supervisor where access is supervised) confirming that the applicant is maintaining contact with the child.

WHAT THE RULES MEAN

These rules are clearly aimed at the situation where the applicant's relationship with the child's other parent has broken down at a time when the applicant had limited leave and they wish to remain in the UK where they have access to their child. The application should be made on form FLR(O). It will be noted that the nature of the contact is looked at more closely between parent and child compared to out-of-country applications, largely because there is an opportunity to examine the nature of the ongoing contact and role played by the parent in the child's upbringing. In the first instance, leave will be granted for 12 months and the parent is permitted to work during that time.

Applications for settlement on the basis of access to a child

After a person has completed a period of 12 months, either granted on entry or in-country, as a parent exercising rights of access, he or she is eligible to apply for indefinite leave. When the initial period of 12 months is about to expire an application should be made on form SET(F). The child must still be under 18 years for the parent to obtain indefinite leave.

Children accompanying or joining parents in the UK who have limited leave

The situations described earlier in this chapter are generally where a child's parents are settled in the UK or are British citizens, or where the child is resident in the UK and hoping to be joined by parents. Children may also be given leave to accompany, join or stay in the UK where their parents are in the UK (or are being admitted to the UK) with *limited* leave for one of the particular purposes under the rules. If the child is allowed to come, they will be given leave for the same length of time as their parent(s). Usually, if the parent is prohibited from working (as, for example, persons of independent means are prohibited), the child will also be prohibited from working. If the parent has a restriction on working, that is, may work only with the consent of the immigration authorities, the child will usually be given no restrictions on working. Children coming for a visit with their parents are admitted as visitors in their own right rather than as 'children of visitors'.

For all the categories looked at below, 'parent' includes all those set out in the general definition of parent contained in the rules ▶see page 369 and it includes adoptive parents where the adoption decision was in accordance with the relevant country's procedures whose adoption decisions are recognised in the UK ▶see page 751 for list of countries. This list of countries may expand when the relevant parts of the Adoption (Intercountry Aspects) Act 1999 are brought into force. These children do not have to meet the additional requirements for adopted children who are coming for settlement ▶see below.

Children of workers and business people

The rules state that the unmarried children under 18 of people admitted as work permit holders; for permit-free employment; as business people/self-employed people; investors; writers, composers and artists; and retired persons of independent means, must apply for entry clearance abroad in order to come to join them. They have to show that they have not formed an independent family unit or led an independent life and that there will be adequate maintenance and accommodation for them in accommodation exclusively occupied by their parents (however ▶see page 331 for the meaning of exclusive occupation), without recourse to public funds, that they will not remain in the UK for longer than the leave given to their parents and that none of the general grounds for refusal apply to them. If only one parent is in the UK and the other is still alive, the more restrictive rules about children joining lone parents (►see pages 373-378) must be satisfied.

There is a concession which is operated for children over the age of 18 (and dependent parents) of sponsors who are work permit holders as 'intra company transferees' and have been posted to the UK by their employer. Such dependants may be admitted provided that they are genuinely dependent on the work permit holder, intend to remain part of the family unit and will not seek to remain in the UK beyond the period of leave granted to the work permit holder (see IDI, Ch5, s9, para1.1).

When the parents apply to extend their leave to remain, their children should apply on the same form. If the parent(s) is applying for *further leave* as a work permit holder, children need only be included in the Work Permits (UK) form WP1X. If the parent(s) is applying for *further leave* as a business person, sole representative, retired person of independent means, investor or innovator, the children should be included in form BUS. Parents in other employment categories, including those in permit-free employment and highly skilled migrants, should include their children in form FLR(O). If the children are not formally mentioned in the application to the Home Office they may become overstayers while the parents' application is under consideration.

When the parent(s) is applying for *indefinite* leave as a business person, sole representative, retired person of independent means, investor or innovator, they should also apply for their children using form BUS. Those applying for *indefinite* leave in any of the other categories, including work permit holders, should include their children on form SET(O). It does not matter if the children have become 18 during the time they have been living here, they will still be granted further leave or settlement in line with their parent(s) if they currently have leave on this basis.

Children of students

Students are permitted to bring their children with them. If they are visa nationals, they must obtain entry clearance from the British post overseas. If they are not, they do not need entry clearance and can apply for leave to enter at an air or sea port. In most other respects, the rules are similar to those for the children of workers. Children of students also have to show that they will not remain in the UK after any period of leave granted to their parent(s). The rules relating to accommodation for them do not, however, state that it must be exclusively owned or occupied by the family. The Home Office has recognised that students are likely to live in shared or college accommodation. They will be admitted for the same length of time as the student. If this is for less than a year, they will be prohibited from working.

The immigration rules allow children to join one parent in the UK without having to satisfy the 'sole responsibility' or 'exclusion undesirable' requirements.

Children of teachers and language assistants and of people in approved training or work experience

Children of teachers and language assistants and of people in approved training or work experience can obtain leave to be in the UK with their parents. They must be under 18, unmarried and be supported in the UK without recourse to public funds. They must not intend to stay in the UK for longer than their parent(s). They can only be admitted to join a lone parent if their other parent is dead or if they satisfy either the 'sole responsibility' or 'exclusion undesirable' rule. They must obtain entry clearance to come to the UK.

Children of working holidaymakers

Working holidaymakers are permitted to bring their children to the UK. However, only children who are under five and who will leave the UK before reaching that age can come. This is intended to be consistent with the principle that underlies the working holidaymaker rules, which is that essentially they are for young (under 27) people who have not yet settled down. The maintenance and accommodation requirements must be satisfied. If only one parent is in the UK and the other is still alive, the more restrictive rules about children joining lone parents must be satisfied. These children also require an entry clearance to come to the UK.

Adopted children

As has been seen above ▶see page 369, in certain cases, the general definition of 'parent' allows adopted children to be admitted under the immigration rules, provided the adoption was in accordance with the relevant country's procedures whose adoption decisions are recognised in the UK. However, this definition of parent does not apply to the immigration rules concerning children coming to the UK with or to join their parent(s) *for the purpose of settlement*. The immigration rules (▶see below) make separate provision for children in this category.

In one way the rules are wider: although the adoption must have taken place in accordance with the foreign country's procedures ('in accordance with a decision taken by the competent administrative authority or court' in the country in question), the adoption does not have to be legally recognised in the UK. In particular, it does not matter which country the adoption took place in. However, in another way, the rules are more restrictive because there are additional requirements which relate to the *reasons for the adoption* which must be satisfied.

Children who have already been adopted: applications under the rules

In some cases, the immigration rules do not need to be satisfied at all. An adoption which takes place in the UK, when either adoptive parent is a British citizen, automatically gives the child British citizenship. Children adopted before 1 January 1983 only became British citizens if the adoptive father was British but ▶see pages 590-593 for further information about applying to register children to become British citizens.

At present, an adoption which takes place outside the UK does not automatically affect the nationality of the adopted child. However, when section 7 of the Adoption (Intercountry Aspects) Act 1999 comes into force, this will have the effect of providing for the recognition of overseas adoptions in Hague Convention countries by British parents and will also make such an adopted child a British citizen. The Hague Convention concerns international co-operation on inter-country adoptions.

The immigration rules dealing with the situation where an adoption takes place outside the UK and the child therefore needs leave to enter the UK to join their adoptive parents are as follows.

WHAT THE RULES SAY

The child must meet the general rules for children seeking to enter the UK for the purposes of settlement (▶see pages 368-369). If only one adoptive parent is seeking to bring the child to the UK and the other parent is living, either the 'sole responsibility' or 'exclusion un-desirable' rule must be satisfied.

The additional rules which must be satisfied are that:

- an adoption 'in accordance with a decision taken by the competent administrative authority or court of [the child's] country of origin or the country in which [the child] is resident' has taken place;

- the adoption took place either when both adoptive parents were living together abroad or when either or both of them were settled in the UK;

- the child has 'the same rights and obligations as any other child of the marriage';

- the adoption took place because of the inability of the birth parents or current carers to care for the child and there has been a genuine transfer of parental responsibility;

- the child has lost or broken ties with the family of origin; and

- the adoption was not one of convenience arranged to facilitate the child's admission to or remaining in the UK.

The IDI (Ch8, annexes R and Q) explain in detail the practicalities and procedures involved for a couple wanting to bring an adopted child, or a child they want to adopt, into the UK. It includes guidance about providing detailed medical and social reports about both the child and the adoptive parents and states the need for certain documents which are not mentioned in the rules but are required in practice (▶see below). It should be noted that Annex Q is rather misleading in its suggestion that the Adoption (Intercountry Aspects) Act 1999 is in force when, in fact, only certain sections have so far been implemented and in particular the nationality provisions have not been.

The application can be refused if any of the general grounds for refusal apply. A child applying to be admitted to the UK must obtain an entry clearance whether or not they are a visa national. Applications may also be made after a child has entered in another capacity without the need for entry clearance.

If the application is granted, and the parent(s) are settled in the UK, the child will be granted indefinite leave. If the parent(s) only have limited leave which was given with a view to settlement, the child will normally be given 12 months in the first instance and may subsequently apply for indefinite leave. If entry clearance is refused, the child may appeal against the decision. The child may also appeal against a decision to refuse leave to enter if they arrive with an entry clearance and against a decision to refuse to allow them to remain in the UK if they applied to remain at a time when they had leave. Article 8 ECHR may be important in any appeals.

WHAT THE RULES MEAN

Adoption by competent authority or court

The adoption decision must have been taken under the proper procedures for adoption in the child's country of origin, or the country where the child is living. This does not mean that the adoption has to be legally recognised in the UK, so it does *not* have to have taken place in one of the countries whose adoption decisions are recognised in the UK (▶see page 751 for a list of the relevant countries) or fit with other more complex legal rules about recognising overseas adoptions. The immigration rules only state that the adoption decision must have been taken by the competent administrative authority or court in the relevant country. The IDI (Ch8, annex R) are incorrect in not recognising that this is the case; they indicate that adoptions which do not take place in one of the countries whose adoption decisions are legally recognised are outside the rules.

Informal adoptions which do not take place before a court or similar authority are therefore not covered by the rules. These adoptions are sometimes called *de facto* adoptions. Both this rule and that which requires the adoptive child to have the 'the same rights and obligations as any other child of the marriage' were introduced in 1994 and appear to be aimed against adoptions of Muslim children. A series of court cases about a Pakistani child called *Tohur Ali* had previously established that an informal adoption could qualify a child for admission. There is no official adoption procedure under Islamic law and, although it is comparatively common for a child to be brought up by another close relative, such as an uncle, there will often be no formal legal process and the child may not be considered a full child of the marriage for inheritance purposes. The rules also operate against adoptions which have taken place in countries where adoption is not recognised as a legal change of status so as to provide adopted children with the same rights as others.

Reasons for adoption

The rules state that the adoption must have come about as a result of the inability of the original parent(s) or current carer(s) to look after the child and there must be a 'genuine transfer' of parental responsibility for the adopted child. The adoption must not be 'one of convenience' arranged to 'facilitate' the child's entry to the UK. The child must also have 'lost or broken' their ties with their original family.

When an adoption takes place mainly because a couple in the UK are unable to have children, or where it reflects a family or cultural practice or tradition, for example, in cases concerning families from the Indian sub-continent, the adoption will often not qualify the child for admission under the rules.

The adopted child needs to apply for entry clearance to come to join the adoptive parents. If at that stage the child is living with its birth parents, the rules will not be met as the ties will still be existing. The British post requires a social report about the child's current circumstances abroad and the reasons for the adoption, as well as the child's and adoptive parents' passports, the adoption order, and a photograph of the child. If the adoption is by relatives, poverty of the family abroad is not normally accepted as an adequate reason for adoption, as ECOs may allege that family in the UK could send financial support. ECOs may also claim that arrangements have been made within a family to send a child to the UK for educational or other purposes, rather than for a genuine adoption and may refuse entry clearance.

If it is the case that the parents cannot continue to care for the child because they are physically or mentally ill, medical evidence should be obtained to show that they cannot take responsibility. If a child has been adopted from an orphanage or other agency caring for children, ECOs will require evidence that the child was genuinely available for adoption. The IAT has held that incapacity to care can include unwillingness to do so (*Kauser*).

It may now be possible to put forward human rights arguments, in particular raising the discrimination relating to the right to family life, to challenge cases where these rules have been applied where the adoption is a genuine one but the rules fail to respect the practice in different cultures. One such case, awaiting a decision before the ECtHR is **Singh** (**Pawandeep**) **v UK**, in which the adoptive parents are infertile. The family courts in the UK considering adoption applications have been quite forthright in their criticism of the immigration rules, even where the child had been brought into the UK as a visitor when the adoptive parents had intended to keep the child in the UK permanently (**Re J**, Court of Appeal).

Children who have already been adopted: applications outside the rules

If the adoption took place informally, not in accordance with valid procedures in the child's country, it is possible to make an application outside the immigration rules. The IDI (Ch8, annex R) state that a child may be admitted to the UK under a *de facto* adoption where:

- the adoptive parents have been living or working abroad for a substantial period of time; *and*
- they have been caring for the child for a substantial period and have decided to treat the child as their own permanently; *and*
- the child regards the adoptive parents as his or her parents rather than their natural parents.

Aside from the requirement that the adoption took place in accordance with valid procedures, the other requirements of the adoption rules (▶see above) must, of course, also be met. Even though these applications are outside the rules, a child who is refused admission may still appeal on the ground that the policy has not been properly applied to their case as well as raising any possible Article 8 grounds.

Alternatively, if the adoption is informal, there are two ways of still making an application under the rules:

- an application could be made for the child to join a relative 'other than a parent' under the ordinary rules relative to the admission of children. It must be shown that the child's 'exclusion is undesirable' ▶see pages 376-377, 378-379;
- an application can be made to bring the child to the UK *for* adoption (see below).

Children coming to the UK for adoption

From 2 October 2000, the Home Office introduced new rules to allow for the entry to the UK of children who have not yet been adopted but who will be adopted in the UK. This reflected a previous practice outside the immigration rules. The rules are similar to those seeking entry as a child who has already been adopted but the child does not have to have already broken ties with their original family. They must intend to do so, however. An entry clearance must be obtained.

Procedure for bringing a child to the UK for adoption

The Home Office has a long and complicated process (outlined in the previous RON 117 form used for applications outside the rules) which must be followed in order that detailed checks can be made on the child's and the prospective adoptive parents' circumstances to see whether it is likely that the proposed adoption would be approved by a British court. This procedure does not appear to have changed even though these applications are now within the rules.

The Home Office sends a detailed standard letter to those enquiring about the process which gives full information about the procedure. Detailed medical and social reports must be obtained on the child and on the prospective adoptive parents from official sources such as the Department of Health in the UK and the social services authorities where the child is living. This should give details of the child's parentage, the circumstances of the birth parents and the current carers, the degree of contact with the birth parents, the reasons for adoption, the date and reason for the child's entry to an institution, or going to live with foster carers, and how this was arranged.

Written consent to adoption from the child's birth parents, or those legally responsible for the child, done 'freely' after the child is at least six weeks old, is required. This needs to be done before starting the entry clearance application. Both adoptive parents must have visited the child before applying for entry clearance. It is likely that the application will be referred to the Home Office by the ECO. The Home Office states this should 'normally' take not more than three weeks, but in practice it takes longer. The Home Office, if satisfied, refers the case to the Department of Health to check that health requirements are met. Some local social services departments refuse to co-operate because of their own policies discouraging inter-country adoption.

After the application is decided

As with other children applying to come to the UK, if the application for entry clearance is refused, there is a right of appeal and the post applied to should notify the applicant of their appeal rights. If the application is successful, the child is admitted for 12 months initially. During the year, the parents can begin the process of adoption under British law. They should keep the Home Office informed of its progress. If progress is slow, the Home Office may grant a further extension of stay. When the adoption is granted, this gives the child the right to settle in the UK and British citizenship if either adoptive parent is a British citizen.

Because of the delays and complications of this procedure, British or settled parents have sometimes circumvented it by travelling abroad and bringing babies or young children back with them, without entry clearance for this purpose. The Home Office and adoption agencies discourage this practice, because it is effectively impossible to refuse entry to young children and to return them abroad on their own and because the detailed checks necessary to ensure the suitability of the adoption have not taken place.

The Immigration and Asylum Act 1999 provides for further penalties for those facilitating the illegal entry of any person (including children) to the UK. The Adoption (Intercountry Aspects) Act 1999 (which is not yet fully in force) makes it a new criminal offence for anyone other than a child's parent to bring a child in for adoption without prior authorisation from the Department of Health or an adoption agency. The penalty for non-compliance is a fine of up to £5000 and/or up to three months' imprisonment. The Adoption of Children from Overseas Regulations 2001 also aim to deter people from bringing children into the UK for the purpose of adoption, unless they have been first assessed and approved by the local authority or a voluntary adoption agency and had their suitability endorsed by the Secretary of State.

The Home Office also may seek to make people who bring in a child without entry clearance liable for costs if the local authority has to take the child into care. However, in some inter-family adoptions, adoptive parents may see this as the only way of being able to bring in a child. Visa-national children cannot normally enter in this way, as most airlines will not carry them without an entry clearance.

Adoption proceedings in the UK

It is not only parents of children who entered the UK for the purpose of adoption who apply to adopt children here, as the adoption cases of *Re J* (see above) and *Re B* show. Sometimes applications are made to adopt children who have entered the UK for other reasons. The family courts have been fairly sympathetic in these cases, attaching prime importance to whether there has been a genuine transfer of parental responsibility or whether the adoption was motivated only by the wish to help the child obtain the right of abode and whether the adoption would be of real benefit to the child.

Internal instructions to immigration officials (DP4/96) confirm the Home Office's views about adoptions for immigration purposes and its intention to combat them. They state:

'The Family Court will generally attach much more weight to the child's welfare than to irregularities surrounding the immigration status of the child or a parent. Where however it is clear that the court proceedings are designed purely to enable the child or the parent to evade immigration control, consideration may be given to instructing the Treasury Solicitor with a view to intervention in the proceedings. There must be evidence, not just a suspicion, that there has been a serious attempt to circumvent the immigration control and decisions to intervene must be taken at not less than SEO [Senior Executive Officer] level. Where intervention has been agreed, the papers should be copied to the Treasury Solicitor's office as soon as possible. Their normal practice is then to apply for the Secretary of State to be joined as a respondent, and to file an affidavit setting out the child's and/or the parents' immigration history and the Secretary of State's objections'.

So, when it is proposed to adopt a child who needs leave to be in the UK, the court will inform the Home Office who will then decide whether to attempt to intervene in the adoption proceedings. It is therefore important that social services departments and solicitors dealing with adoption are aware of this possibility.

Children whose parents may be forced to leave and children who are in the UK on their own

Children whose parents may be forced to leave the UK

Where a child is in the UK as part of a family and his or her parents have no right to be in the UK, the Home Office will usually try to ensure that the child leaves with them. Where a child is under 18 years and has a parent who is being either deported from the UK or who is being removed under Section 10 of the 1999 Act (known as 'administrative' removal), the child may be deported or removed as part of the parent's 'family' (together with any spouse). Children and spouses can be required to leave in these cases even if they are lawfully in the UK for some other reason. The immigration rules (▶see below) set out the factors which need to be taken into account in deciding whether family members should also be required to leave in these circumstances (paras 362–368, 395A–395D, HC 395).

At present, if the parent is being removed under other enforcement powers (illegal entry, or having been refused entry at port), the immigration authorities can only remove the child if there are grounds for removing the child in its own right, for example, the child is an illegal entrant, an overstayer etc. However, the 2002 Bill proposes to give the immigration authorities power to remove family members in these cases as well. The Home Office is particularly concerned about non-British citizen children who are born in the UK. Although these children are subject to immigration control, they cannot be removed other than as the family member of someone whose departure is being enforced.

In addition to the immigration rules, the Home Office also has policy on the approach to cases where it is considering enforcing the departure of a family in the UK. The guidance is known as DP/069/99, DP/4/95 and DP/4/96. The position of unaccompanied children is also referred to in this guidance ▶see page 393.

Although the criteria in the rules only apply to certain cases (administrative removal and deportation) and the policy is intended for 'after entry' cases, rather than those who have been refused entry, similar factors can be relied on by representatives in all cases.

Also, in all cases, Article 8 ECHR may be relevant. Full details about Article 8 are contained in Chapter 3 and it is also looked at in relation to parents having rights of access to children above ▶see pages 379-380. Where the circumstances of a child returning to their or their parents' country of origin will result in severe hardship for the child, Article 3 may also be relevant.

The immigration rules

Where one parent is being deported or administratively removed, in deciding whether the child or other parent should be required to leave as well, the immigration authorities must always take into account all the normal matters relating to the person affected which are contained in the immigration rules. These factors are age, length of residence in the UK, strength of connections with the UK, personal history (including character, conduct, employment record), domestic circumstances, any criminal record, compassionate circumstances and representations made on the person's behalf. The following additional factors must be taken into account when considering enforcement against spouse and children:

- the ability of spouses to maintain themselves and any children in the UK or to be maintained by relatives and friends without being a charge on public funds for the foreseeable future;
- in the case of a child of school age, the effect of removal on their education; and
- the practicability of any plans for the child's care and maintenance in the UK if one or both parents were deported or removed.

In addition, the Home Office will normally not deport or remove a child as the family member of a person being required to leave if:

- the child and their other parent are living apart from the person who is being deported or removed; or
- the child has left home and established him or herself on an independent basis; or
- the child married before a decision was made to deport or remove their parent.

In addition, the Home Office will normally not deport or remove a spouse as a family member of a person being required to leave if:

- he or she has qualified for settlement in their own right; or
- he or she has been living apart from the deportee.

Home Office policy

Home Office policy (DP/069/99) relates to cases where enforcement action is being taken against the parents of a child with long residence in the UK. The policy is that enforcement action will not usually proceed against the family as a whole where the children were born in the UK and have lived here continuously until the age of seven years. The same applies to children who came to the UK at an early age and have lived in the UK for seven or more continuous years.

However, although this is the usual policy, the family's departure may still be enforced if the individual circumstances of the case justify it. The Home Office will take into account the following factors:

- the age of the children;
- length of the parents' residence in the UK without leave;
- whether the parents have evaded immigration control and delayed removal;
- whether the parents children were conceived at a time when the parents had leave;
- whether removal has been delayed by repetitive representations;
- whether the parents have a history of criminal behaviour or deception;
- whether return to the country of origin would result in hardship for the children;
- whether the children's health would seriously be put at risk by return.

For details about Home Office policy concerning couples who are married ►see pages 353-355.

Unaccompanied children in the UK

Children who are on their own and who are under 16 years of age and whose departure from the UK can be enforced (because they arrive without leave, are illegal entrants, can be 'administratively removed' or deported), should only have their departure enforced if their voluntary departure cannot be arranged. It must be clear that the child will be met on arrival and that they will be properly cared for afterwards. Home Office caseworkers may contact the welfare section of the foreign embassy or high commission to try to confirm this. If there is evidence that the care arrangements are seriously below the standard normally available in the country concerned, or they are so inadequate that the child would face a serious risk of harm, enforcement will generally not proceed (see DP/4/96, paras 2-3 and IDI Ch8, annex M para 7). For details about unaccompanied minors seeking asylum ►see pages 191-192.

Local authority care

If a child is unaccompanied and in need of care or, for any other reason, the standard of care available to them is inadequate, the local social services department of a local authority has a statutory responsibility to provide for their welfare. It is therefore possible for a child who is not settled in the UK to be taken into the care of the local authority. The local authority will then have to make arrangements for the child. This may be attempting to trace the parents in order to return the child to them abroad, or it may be applying to the Home Office for permission for the child to remain here exceptionally.

For a child who is not a British citizen, being taken into care does not in itself alter the child's immigration status. Local authorities will, therefore, themselves need to take legal advice before assisting the child to make applications to the Home Office. If it appears clear that there will not be further contact with the family and that the child's long-term future will be in the UK, then if the authority applies to the Home Office for settlement on behalf of the child with full details of the circumstances, it is likely that the application will be granted. It is extremely important that any such application should be made to the Home Office before the child is 18, on form SET(O) with a covering letter setting out the legal and human rights arguments relied on.

Home Office policy is generally to grant indefinite leave to children (IDI Ch8, s4, annex P para 8) where the parental rights and duties (or 'parental responsibility') have been vested solely in the local authority. However, before such a grant is made, parental responsibility is likely to be with the local authority on a permanent basis. If not, then it may consider granting only limited leave. The overall Home Office position is set out in the IDI, (Ch8, s3 annex M, para 6.1):

'**Our aim will normally be that the child should return to his parents and/or their country of origin, however it is important to take account of welfare considerations which may take precedence over the immigration implications of allowing a child to remain here'.**

The guidance also confirms that, even where a parent may abuse immigration control by leaving a child in the UK, the child cannot always be held responsible for this predicament. However, the fact that the child may be 'better off' in the UK is not, of itself, sufficient for the Home Office to grant leave to remain and they will seek to establish whether there are parents and or relatives who can care for the child in his or her own country. The Home Office may also seek to return a child into the care of the welfare authorities of their own country, even where the care would fall below the standards that the child could expect to receive in the UK.

Fostering arrangements

Families from abroad may want to make arrangements for their children's care in the UK, even if they themselves are unable to stay. A comparatively common situation is for a couple to come to the UK to study and decide they are unable adequately to concentrate on their studies while caring for the children. They therefore make private fostering arrangements. The children of overseas students are able to be with them in the UK under the immigration rules so there is often no reason to inform the Home Office about these arrangements while the whole family is still in the UK.

There are no provisions in the immigration rules for the children to stay if the parents leave and want the child to remain with the foster parents, so as not to disrupt the children's education, for example. If an application is made to the Home Office for the child to remain exceptionally, it should be done with great care and explanation of the plans for the child to rejoin his or her parents abroad in the future. In some cases, the foster parents are unaware of any immigration implications and the children may inadvertently become overstayers. Specialist advice should be obtained.

Other family court procedures

It is possible that relatives or friends of children may take certain legal steps to safeguard children's welfare, such as custodianship, wardship, contact orders and residence orders. While adoption in the UK gives a child definite immigration and nationality rights, these other orders do not affect a child's immigration status but merely mean that the leave of a court must be obtained before a child can be removed from the UK. When making an order, for example, that a child should reside with a relative, the family courts attach much more weight to the child's welfare than to irregularities surrounding the immigration status of the child or their parents. The implication is that Home Office officials should proceed with great care when court orders of this kind have been obtained. If one of these orders is applied for (or if an adoption order in the UK is applied for), the Home Office may ask to make its own representations to the family court if 'it is clear that the court proceedings are designed purely to enable the child or the parent to evade immigration control' (see DP/4/96, para 10).

Children at school

A child at school may be able to remain in the UK in their own right. This means that the child must be going to a private, fee-paying school and support must be available to pay the school fees and for the child to live here. If the school is not a boarding school, there should be adequate arrangements for looking after the child. The Home Office must also be satisfied that the intention is for the child to leave at the end of the studies. The immigration rules do not permit visa nationals to change their status to become students, so if the child is applying from within the UK and is a visa national, the application would be outside the rules.

There is no provision in the rules for a child to stay in the UK in order to attend, or to continue to attend, a state school. This can create problems when the child has been in the UK with the family for a short-term purpose, for example, if the parents are students, or diplomats or other workers posted to the UK for a term of duty, who then have to take up another post when the child is at a critical stage of education. An application to the Home Office may be made, exceptionally, for permission to continue with studies in these circumstances.

There is now provision within the immigration rules for leave to be granted to parents of children under 12 who are attending an independent fee-paying school and who satisfy the student rules. A sole parent can remain with the child without having to satisfy the 'sole responsibility' or 'exclusion undesirable' rules. The parent must be able to maintain and accommodate themselves, not seek to make the UK their main home and they must be able to show evidence of a second home abroad. Only visa nationals require entry clearance and parents who make successful applications may be granted successive periods of 12 months' leave. The parent is not permitted to work. Clearly this provision is only intended to benefit the wealthy and even then there is a restriction on the age of the child, presumably because it is thought that over that age a child does not need his/her parents to be living in the same country as them while they attend school.

Children born in the UK

People born in the UK before 1 January 1983

Except for the children of diplomats, any person born in the UK before 1983 is automatically a British citizen by birth. This gives the child full rights to remain in the UK and to return at any time as an adult, even if he or she was taken abroad as a baby. There have been instances of people, mainly of West African origin, who have had difficulty convincing the British high commissions abroad that they were born in the UK. Others who have travelled on British passports have had difficulty in satisfying immigration officers that they are in fact British citizens on arrival. A third group are those who have been arrested in the UK as illegal entrants and claim to have been born here before 1 January 1983. Often the problem is one of establishing the person's identity.

Applicants should produce their full birth certificate (the one which has details of both parents so that it can be confirmed that the father was not a diplomat). Further evidence may be needed to establish that the person applying is the child who was born in the UK and left at a very young age. DNA blood testing can establish that they are the child of their parent or parents who were in the UK at the time of their birth but it may not always be sufficient to show that the applicant is a child of that relationship, as they could be another child born abroad, in which case they *may* not be British. If there are close family friends or relatives living in the UK who have remained in contact with the person throughout, they may be able to make statements to confirm their continuous knowledge of the person applying. If the person had been registered with a general practitioner or there are records of childhood immunisations or other medical treatment, this might also be helpful. If he or she had lived here long enough to go to a childminder, nursery or school and records can be found, these may also be of use.

For details about obtaining passports and certificates of entitlement to the right of abode ▶see pages 55 and 593.

People born in the UK on or after 1 January 1983

Since 1 January 1983, not all children born in the UK have been born British citizens. Only a child with a British or a settled parent is automatically born British in the UK. At present when the parents are not married, only the mother's status counts. Other children born in the UK have no claim to British nationality by birth and require leave to be in the UK. Therefore, some children born in the UK whose fathers are British are not themselves British. This is because of the special meaning given to 'parent' in nationality law (the definition of 'parent' in the immigration rules is wider). However, the 2002 Bill proposes to allow a man who was married to the mother of the child at the time of the birth to pass on his nationality to the child even if he is not the natural father. If the woman was not married, then the natural father's nationality may be passed on under the proposals.

A child born in the UK and not born British, does not have any leave to be in the UK although they need leave. However, these children are not illegal entrants because they have not entered unlawfully. They are not overstayers or in breach of their other conditions of leave because they have not had leave. They cannot be refused leave to enter the UK and then removed because they have not arrived at a port and applied for leave to enter. In principle, therefore, they could remain in the UK indefinitely, but if they left the UK, they would have to satisfy the immigration rules in order to return. However, non-British citizen children born in the UK, can be required to leave the UK if:

- their parent is being removed under the Home Office 'administrative' powers of removal; *or*
- their parent is being deported from the UK.

This is because these powers to require a family member to leave do not depend on the immigration status of the family member but rather on the immigration status of their principal. The 2002 Bill proposes to allow the removal of family members (including children) of a principal who is being removed as an illegal entrant, or having being refused leave to enter.

The immigration rules (see above) set out the factors which need to be considered in deciding whether to require the child to leave the UK. If children born in the UK live here until they are 10 years old, they gain the right to register as British citizens ▶see page 590.

The 2002 Bill proposes to remove the current minimum age for registration (which is 10) for a child who is stateless and born in the UK.

Applications under the rules for children born in the UK

There is a special section in the immigration rules to cover children born in the UK who are not British (para 304–309, HC 395). If parents wish to obtain leave to remain for such a child, the Home Office will grant this if one parent has leave to enter or remain or if one of them has the right of abode or is a British citizen. Following the proposed changes to nationality law (►see above) most children with a British citizen mother or father will themselves be British citizens and it will not be necessary to rely on these rules. The child will be given the same leave as the parents. If the parents' leave differs, the child will be given the longer. However, if the parents are living separately, the child will be given leave in line with that parent with day-to-day care.

If one parent is settled, or has British citizenship, the child can be given indefinite leave. This would apply, for example, to a child whose parents were not married and whose mother was an overseas student with limited leave so that the child would not be born British. If the child's father was a refugee with indefinite leave or a British citizen, the child, at present, would obtain indefinite leave in line with his or her father. If the child born in Britain is in the care of the local authority which has sole parental responsibility for the child, he or she should be given indefinite leave.

If neither parent has leave, the Home Office may grant successive periods of three months' leave to a child born in the UK if the following conditions are satisfied (see para 307, HC 395):

- both parents of the child are in the UK;
- it appears unlikely that the parents will be removed in the immediate future; and
- there is no other person outside the UK who could reasonably be expected to care for the child.

These circumstances might arise, for example, in the case of an asylum-seeking couple whose application is at its early stages or which is taking some time to determine.

For these applications, the Home Office will only require evidence that the child is the child of the parent(s) and of the parents' immigration status. Importantly, it does not have to be shown that the child can be maintained and accommodated in the UK without recourse to public funds. Children making applications under these rules to remain with a sole parent do not have to satisfy the 'sole responsibility' or 'exclusion undesirable' rules.

If children travel overseas at a time when they have not yet been granted leave to remain in the UK, they may be admitted back into the UK under these rules provided that they have been away from the UK for less than two years and they satisfy the above requirements – importantly they will need to still be under 18 and have a parent with leave in the UK, or who is travelling with them and is being admitted. An entry clearance will be required for children who are visa nationals in these circumstances.

18 Relatives other than children and spouses

Apart from children and spouses, there are many other relatives who may need or want to come to stay permanently with family members settled in the UK. This chapter looks at those other relatives which include sons and daughters who are 18 and over. It should be noted that the rules are to enable dependent relatives to come to the UK for *settlement* with relatives settled in the UK. Successful applicants are given indefinite leave. There is no provision in the immigration rules for relatives other than spouses, unmarried partners and children, to come to the UK with their family members and be granted leave in line with them while they are here, for example, as a work permit holder. They could come, however, for a short period to *visit* the relative.

The immigration rules concerning these other relatives are very restrictive. The relatives provided for in the rules can be divided into two groups. First, the rules provide for parents and grandparents aged 65 and over. Secondly, the rules provide, more restrictively still, for adult sons and daughters, aunts, uncles, sisters, brothers and also parents/grandparents who are under 65. More distant relatives are not mentioned at all but may of course be admitted at the discretion of the Home Office outside the immigration rules.

Other distant relatives may also benefit from Article 8 ECHR depending on the strength of the family ties. For who can come within Article 8 ►see pages 257-258, and for how Article 8 works ►see pages 255-256. Article 8 may also benefit applications where, in principle, the relationship is covered by the rules (e.g., a grandparent over the age of 65) but where the applicant cannot in practice satisfy the rules yet it would still be an unjustifiable interference with family life to refuse the application.

Does the applicant need to use the dependent relative rules?

Because of the restrictive nature of the rules, it is worth checking first of all that the relative actually needs to rely on the rules for the settlement of dependent relatives.

Relatives of EEA nationals. EU law gives rights to family members to come to the UK without having to satisfy the immigration rules. In addition to spouses and minor children, the following relatives may benefit from EU free-movement rights: dependent grandparents and great-grandparents of the EEA national or their spouse; grandsons and grandaughters (and great-grandchildren) of the EEA national or of their spouse; sons, daughters, grandchildren and great grandchildren up to the age of 21, and 21 and over if they are still dependent. For more details about the rights of family members of EEA nationals ▶see pages 458-464.

These rights do not apply to relatives of most British citizens who have not travelled between countries exercising free-movement rights themselves, but they may apply to relatives of many Irish nationals in the UK or to those of other EEA nationals in the UK. The relatives themselves do not have to be EEA nationals and, as indicated above, they can be directly related to the EEA national's spouse, rather than to the EEA national. So, for example, the Colombian parents of a Colombian woman married to a German man working in the UK would qualify. Although the immigration rules do not need to be satisfied, for some people the effect of becoming a charge on public funds may terminate their free-movement rights. Workers and work-seekers must have a genuine chance of obtaining work, which means that they are less likely to require public funds.

Visitors. It may be that the applicant does not in fact want to stay permanently in the UK but only wishes to come for a visit to their relatives who they may want to see frequently. In that case, the appropriate application is for a visit entry clearance (if the applicant is a visa national). If an application is first made for settlement as a dependent relative and it is refused, it will be extremely difficult to persuade the immigration authorities, on a subsequent visitor application, that a genuine visit is intended and that the person will leave when the visit is over. However, because the Home Office has a policy of not carrying out very detailed checks when elderly dependent parents apply to settle having entered the UK (▶see below page 401), ECOs are often reluctant to grant visit entry clearances to elderly parents who appear to be alone or in need of care overseas.

Retired persons of independent means. People with 'close connections' to the UK, who are 60 or over and who have a guaranteed private annual income of at least £25,000 available to them in the UK and who are no longer intending to work, can be admitted as 'retired persons of independent means'. They will normally be given four years leave in the first instance and can apply for indefinite leave after that. It may be that, for example, a parent can satisfy this rule.

Parents and grandparents aged 65 or over

WHAT THE RULES SAY

Parents or grandparents who are coming to the UK in order to live with their adult children or grandchildren have to satisfy the following rules:

- they are widows or widowers aged 65 or over; *or*
- they are travelling together as a couple and at least one of them is 65 or over; *or*
- if they have married again, they are 65 or over and they cannot look to the spouse or children of the second marriage for support; *or*
- if they are under 65, they are living alone in the most exceptional compassionate circumstances and are mainly dependent financially on relatives settled in the UK.

Applicants have to satisfy all of the following rules:

- they are wholly or mainly financially dependent on the children or grandchildren settled in the UK who they are seeking to join;
- they have no other close relatives in their own country to whom they could turn for financial support;
- the relative they are joining is present and settled in the UK or is travelling with the applicant/s and will be admitted for settlement;
- they will be accommodated, together with any dependants, in accommodation which their relative owns or occupies exclusively without recourse to public funds; and
- they can be maintained in the UK without recourse to public funds.

Applicants can be refused if any of the general grounds for refusal apply ►see page 67. Those who are coming to the UK must obtain an entry clearance whether or not they are visa nationals.

However, applications can be made by parents or grandparents who are already in the UK for a different purpose without the applicants having to leave and apply for entry clearance. For in-country applications, Home Office instructions to its case-workers are to grant applications from elderly dependant relatives who are over 65 years old, where the sponsor has given a maintenance undertaking, without making detailed enquires into the circumstances (IDI, Ch8, s6). In-country applications are made on form SET(F) to which is attached the sponsorship declaration which states that completion of the declaration is not compulsory, but that an application will normally be refused if the sponsor refuses to complete it ►see below page 405 for more details. If an in-country application is being made, it should be clear that there has been a change of circumstances since the applicant entered, otherwise the Home Office may decide that the person always intended to settle and is an illegal entrant having obtained entry, for example, as a visitor.

If the application for entry clearance is granted, the parents or grandparents should be given an entry clearance which operates as indefinite leave to enter. Similarly, if an in-country application is accepted, indefinite leave should be given. If the entry clearance application is refused, there is a right of appeal. There is also a right of appeal against a refusal of an in-country application provided the application was made in time. There is always a right of appeal on human rights grounds, if the applicant alleges that the decision is in breach of their human rights.

WHAT THE RULES MEAN

Age requirement

The age requirement (above) is interpreted strictly and it is important to show the age of the applicants by a birth certificate if possible. There can be serious problems in countries where there was no system of registration of births when the parents or grandparents were born. Elderly people may not know exactly when they were born and may date their age from local events which are also unrecorded. When they obtained their passports, they may have given an approximate age for this purpose. The British authorities may take this as the only definite proof of age and it may be very difficult for the parents or grandparents to prove, at the time of any application for settlement, that a different date of birth is more accurate.

Prior to 1 October 1994, the rules exempted widowed mothers and grandmothers from the age requirement. Now they have to satisfy the age requirement as well. Younger parents or grandparents can still qualify but they need to show that they are 'living alone outside the UK in the most exceptional compassionate circumstances' (►see pages 406–409 below) as well as satisfying the other rules.

It is important to note that where one parent or grandparent is over 65 and one is under 65, they must be travelling together. It was recognised by the IAT in *Yambos* that this creates an unnecessary gap in the rules. This is because the rules do not provide for the situation where one parent comes to the UK alone for a visit and then decides to apply for settlement and his or her spouse has also applied for an entry clearance to come to the UK. Even though they meet all the other requirements of the rules, they could be refused on the basis that they are not travelling together. If Article 8 was raised in such a case, it would be for the Home Office to show the justification for this gap in the rules.

Wholly or mainly financially dependent

The words 'financially dependent' do not mean that money has to actually be exchanging hands. In *Bibi*, the Court of Appeal ruled that, if accommodation, clothing, food and other needs are met by the relative, then that is sufficient. The dependency must be of necessity and not created. For example, if the parent or grandparent gives away their income to other relatives and therefore relies on money sent over by relatives in the UK, this will not satisfy the rules. Applicants may also not qualify if they have already passed on property or capital to their children and no longer own it. The Court of Appeal held in *Desai* that the question of whether a person is 'mainly' financially dependent does not depend upon precise calculations; all of the circumstances have to be taken into account. Although the focus of the rules is on financial dependency, other kinds of dependence, for example, emotional dependency, may be taken into account in deciding whether the rules are met. Indeed, where there are strong and long-lasting emotional ties between the sponsor in the UK and the parent, this may help to show why the parent should not be expected to turn to other relatives for support. Support provided by a sponsor which is over and above that which is necessary to enable the parent or grandparent to have a reasonable standard of living, may not be taken into account in deciding whether a person is wholly or mainly dependent on the relatives.

The Immigration Appeal Tribunal has indicated that the rules are intended to look at the situation when the relatives are in their own country (*Kartar Kaur*). If the relatives are dependent while they are visiting the UK and make an application while here but are not dependent when they are in their own country, the requirements will generally not be satisfied.

It is demeaning for elderly people to have to show that they cannot maintain themselves. It can also be difficult to prove, as many people do not keep records of all the money they have sent to their families abroad. If money has been sent through postal orders or international money transfer agencies, people may have kept at least some of the counterfoils. If it has been sent through a bank account, the bank may have records. Registered letter slips, showing at least that something valuable was sent, can be useful. Also of use are letters from the parents which mention the receipt of remittances and which date from as far back as possible.

If money was taken in cash by visiting relatives or friends, it may be difficult to do anything more than assert this fact. It may be helpful to have letters from the couriers, confirming when and how much money they took, or letters from the parents confirming that they received the money. It may be that the money was converted into a different currency and there are regular receipts which show this. Passport stamps can also show that the person carrying the money travelled at the various times. When parents or grandparents have other means of support, for example, an occupational pension, it should be shown that the money they receive from their children is more than the pension, so that they can show they are mainly, if not wholly, dependent on them.

This requirement of the rules discriminates against people who have been thrifty, or people who live in a country where an adequate old-age pension is paid. Retired people in the United States, for example, are unlikely to be financially dependent on their children rather than on any pension or insurance. It also means that parents or grandparents who own property, for example, their own home, may not be considered dependent, even though they intend to leave the home to their children and do not wish to keep it themselves.

No other close relatives to turn to

This requirement is difficult to meet if there is more than one adult relative in the family, one or more of whom lives in the same country as the parent or grandparent. Account must be taken of cultural conditions. In parts of the Indian subcontinent, for example, it is generally accepted that it is a son's responsibility to care for his aged parents and not the responsibility of daughters because they have a corresponding responsibility to their husband's parents. So, for example, when the sons are in the UK but the daughters are in India, it can be argued that the daughters cannot usually be expected to care for their parents. In relation to this situation, the Home Office IDI (Ch8 s6 annex V) states:

'...it should be noted that this will largely depend on their culture. For example, in the Indian sub-continent, married women are unlikely to be able to provide support. Alternatively if there are several close relatives there is no reason why there cannot be a collective ability among them to support the applicant.'

The relatives who may be relied on by the immigration authorities include sons, daughters, brothers, sisters, grandchildren, uncles, aunts and even (but less likely) nephews, nieces and in-laws. If there is a relative in the applicant's own country who is able and willing to support the applicant, then the Home Office position is that it would not be unreasonable for the applicant to turn to that relative for support, even if the sponsor in the UK is financially in a better position to help. That the other close relatives must be both able and willing to provide for the applicants is clear from the High Court cases of *Bastiampillai* and *Dadibhai*. Close relatives who do not particularly care about the applicants, and who are not interested in supporting them, cannot be considered as relatives to whom the applicants can 'turn'. Account should be taken of the age and health of the applicants as well as the ability of other relatives to visit them regularly. The needs of the parents must be compared against what support is on offer.

It can also be argued that the children abroad do not have the resources to look after their parents adequately. This has sometimes been successful, for example, in some Filipino cases where there were other adult children still living in the country. Applications have succeeded by showing that the economic circumstances of the other sons or daughters are such that they cannot manage to look after their parents, or even their own families, without the financial support received from the UK. It is important to remember that an ECO may make local enquiries through unannounced 'village visits' to the parents' or grandparents' community.

The Home Office does generally accept that applications from married couples should not be refused solely on the basis that they have each other to turn to. If other close relatives with whom the parents previously lived have died, their death certificates should be produced. If circumstances have changed, so that other relatives are no longer able to care for the parents, this should also be explained.

Maintenance and accommodation requirements and undertakings

The maintenance and accommodation requirements for dependent relatives are similar to those for spouses and children (▶see pages 328-335) and similar evidence should be provided. However, dependent relatives are given indefinite leave straight away, rather than limited leave for an initial probationary period. This means that no condition can be attached to their leave which prevents them from having access to public funds (this is because no conditions can be attached to an indefinite leave). In addition, there is no other legal liability in British law for an adult to maintain his or her parents or grandparents (unlike for spouses and children). For these reasons, the immigration authorities may request that the sponsor enters into a maintenance undertaking to provide support for the applicant/s. Failure to provide an undertaking, if one is requested by the immigration authorities, is a ground for refusing the application (para 320(14), 322(6) HC395).

The undertaking should be made on the form which is attached to the prescribed form SET(F) and the form itself will then be sent to the DSS. We would suggest that, if the undertaking is not given on that form or a very similar one, then it is not effective. This is because an effective 'maintenance undertaking' is defined as one which is given 'in pursuance of the immigration rules' (see s115(1) 1999 Act) and the form to which the undertaking form is attached is a form which is itself required under the immigration rules (para 32 HC395). Home-made or notarised declarations of sponsorship will therefore not be effective. It is notable also that the IDI (Ch1, s4, annex Y, para 2.1) also state that, 'The declaration attached to form SET(F) should always be used'.

The effect of the undertaking is to deny the applicant access to non-contributory social security benefits (e.g., income support, income-based job-seekers' allowance, housing benefit) for five years or until the sponsor dies ▶for more details see pages 663, 665. It is also a criminal offence if a sponsor who has signed an undertaking refuses or neglects to provide support as a result of which the person they are supposed to support becomes entitled to asylum support (see s108 1999 Act). The DSS may also seek to recover from the sponsor any income support which is paid to the applicant as a result of their failure to honour the undertaking.

Parents and grandparents under 65 years and other relatives

The rules for parents and grandparents who are under 65 and for other dependent relatives are more restrictive than for parents and grandparents who are 65 or over. Other than the age requirement, applicants must satisfy the same requirements as above, but in addition, they must show that they are 'living alone outside the United Kingdom in the most exceptional compassionate circumstances'.

WHAT THE RULES SAY

Applicants have to show that:

- they are the parent or grandparent, adult son or daughter, sister, brother, uncle, aunt of the relative they wish to join in the UK;
- they are living alone outside the UK in the most exceptional compassionate circumstances;
- they are wholly or mainly financially dependent on their relative or relatives in the UK;
- they have no other close relatives in their own country to whom they could turn for financial support;
- the relative they are joining is present and settled in the UK or is travelling with the applicant/s and will be admitted for settlement;
- they will be accommodated, together with any dependants, in accommodation which their relative owns or occupies exclusively, without recourse to public funds; and
- they can be maintained in the UK without recourse to public funds.

WHAT THE RULES MEAN

For details of the meaning of most of these rules ▶see above.

Living alone in the most exceptional compassionate circumstances

It is difficult to satisfy this requirement, which is essentially intended to allow the admission of family members who cannot manage without the rest of their family and who are isolated without them. Where the application is being made in-country, the Home Office should consider the situation of the applicant if they were in their own country rather than in the UK. The requirement of 'living alone' does not always need to be taken literally (*Paw*). A mother living with her young baby, for example, could be counted as 'living alone'. However, in *Ibraheem*, when a father applying to join his son in the UK lived with his other son, a violent drug addict, the IAT found that he did not qualify as 'living alone' although his circumstances were compassionate.

The case of *Begum* (*Manshoora*) struck out a previous requirement of this rule, that the relative had to have a standard of living lower than the average in his or her own country. The Divisional Court agreed that this requirement was unreasonable, since the fact of receiving money from abroad at all, another requirement of the rule, could bring people above the average standard of living in several countries. However, the fact that the relative is able to send money over (as the rules require) can be taken into account in deciding whether the person is living in the most exceptional circumstances.

Before 1 October 1994, the immigration rules provided that unmarried daughters between the ages of 18 and 21 might be given 'special consideration' in coming to the UK to join their parents for settlement. They had to show they were financially dependent on their parents, they formed part of the family unit overseas, they would be left entirely on their own in the country in which they were living without any other close relatives to turn to for help, and they could be maintained and accommodated in the UK. In many countries, a young unmarried, woman living on her own is not socially acceptable and she may receive a great deal of stigma from the rest of the community. Depending on the precise circumstances, this situation may come within the present rules (*Bayar*).

When a family is applying to join a parent in the UK and the applicants include sons or daughters who are over 18, it is likely that ECOs will ask more questions about them than other members of the family. More checks will be made to be sure that she has needed to remain dependent, rather than doing so for immigration purposes. The recent case of *Begum* (*Husna*) confirms, however, that this rule must be interpreted consistently with Article 8 ECHR and that the decision of the family to migrate to the UK cannot undermine the relevance of the circumstances in which she would otherwise be left alone.

Home Office instructions state as follows (IDI, Ch8, annex V):

'Each application must be considered on the individual merits of the case. It is therefore not possible to list every possible circumstance which may arise. However, illness, incapacity, isolation and poverty are all compassionate circumstances which should be considered'.

Applications are decided on a case by case basis and all of the various elements of the case can be considered together to see if, counting them all, they amount to 'the most exceptional compassionate circumstances'. It is therefore important that the relatives applying give the fullest possible details of their circumstances to the immigration official dealing with the case, along with any evidence they can produce.

Adult sons and daughters: some other considerations

Adult sons and daughters may be able to avoid having to satisfy the restrictive rules set out above if they fall into any of the following groups.

Treated as minors under the immigration rules

It should be noted that children who have reached the age of 18 are still able to qualify under the rules relating to children if their application is made before they are 18. In some circumstances, sons and daughters who are 18 at the time of the application can also qualify under those rules. For details ▶see pages 365-366.

Relationship subsequently proved by DNA

There has been particular controversy about children, mainly from Pakistan and Bangladesh, who applied in the past to come to join their parents before they were 18 but who were refused as the authorities were not then satisfied that they were related to their parents as they claimed to be. Some were later able to make use of DNA-testing technology to conclusively prove the disputed relationship. However, by this time, they were over 18 and unable to fit into the immigration rules, unless they could satisfy the 'living alone' requirements set out above.

The Home Office has operated a policy, since 14 June 1989, that it will consider these people's cases individually to see if there are any exceptional compassionate circumstances involved (this is now in the IDI at Ch8, annex N). There must be 'some' compassionate circumstances over and above the basic injustice of having been wrongly separated from family members for many years. The young people also have to show that they have remained 'necessarily' dependent on their parents rather than dependent 'by choice' and that they are unmarried.

Special voucher scheme

An exception to the rules was usually made for children aged up to 25 of special voucher applicants if they were not themselves British nationals and would not qualify for vouchers in their own right ▶see pages 578-579 for details about the special voucher scheme. In essence, the scheme permitted some British nationals who were not British citizens and who had a connection with East Africa to come to the UK. Because of the long waiting period for people applying in India, which has reached up to eight years in the past, and which meant that many children became adults while they and their parents were waiting in the queue, children up to the age of 25 were considered as dependants.

Such people had to show that they could be maintained and accommodated in the UK by the special voucher holder, had remained financially dependent on their parents, had not been working and were not married. These requirements led to detailed inquiries being made, particularly into young women in their early twenties, as to whether they were married and therefore would not qualify as dependants. The British authorities appeared to be particularly worried about allowing in young women who may get married soon after their arrival and then try to bring their husbands to join them in the UK.

However, on 5 March 2002, the Home Office minister, Lord Rooker, announced in a written parliamentary answer that the special voucher system was to be withdrawn with immediate effect. It is understood that existing applications for vouchers will still be dealt with.

More distant relatives

More distant relatives than those covered by the immigration rules (►see above) may still make applications to come to and settle in the UK with family members. For example, cousins, nephews, nieces, half-brothers and half-sisters, mothers of *de facto* adopted children (for the policy on these applications ►see page 388) or step-mothers where there is a mother still living, are all not expressly covered by the rules.

The Home Office can grant applications outside the rules, so it may be worth trying if there are exceptional circumstances. It is important to show the immigration authorities what the strong exceptional compassionate reasons for the application are, for example, that there is a close emotional relationship between the relative and the person settled in the UK. A person who had been brought up by a great-aunt or a cousin, and who had a quasi-parental relationship with that person, will need to explain this family background, why it happened and why there were no other closer relatives who could support the person in the country of origin. If the applicant is elderly, it is more likely that exceptional compassionate reasons will be accepted. If the person has physical or mental disabilities, medical evidence to show this is required.

Although applications for other relatives are not specifically covered in the rules, it is wrong to think of them as purely discretionary since in all cases, the immigration authorities will have to apply Article 8 ECHR, which does not rigidly define which relationships fall within family life. It may be that if the sponsor in the UK is in need of care from the relative, the Home Office policy relating to carers can also be used ►see pages 289-291.

Section 6 Workers and business people

Chapter 19
Workers   413

The work permit scheme   416

Work permit free employment under the
immigration rules   426

Persons able to work outside the immigration rules   434

People who work for embassies and high
commissions   436

Chapter 20
Business purposes   438

19 Workers

This section covers the groups of people who are able to come to the United Kingdom in order to work or in order to carry out business. For nationals of the countries of the European Economic Area, the situation is much easier because European Community law provides rights of free movement for those who are economically active. The European Union also has Association Agreements with other countries which enable persons from those countries to come to the UK for self-employment/ business purposes. The free movement rights of these nationals and their family members are fully described in Section 7.

Non-EEA nationals cannot easily come to the UK in order to take up work. UK immigration law and rules are designed to protect jobs in the UK for people already allowed to live and work in this country, and to encourage investment in businesses only from people with a very substantial amount of money to invest. The 2002 White Paper, *Secure Borders, Safe Haven*, recognises, however, that there are recruitment difficulties and skills shortages within the resident and EEA workforces. It therefore maps out a plan for 'managed migration' designed to meet the current deficit in particular sectors of the UK economy. For a more detailed discussion about the 2002 White Paper and the 2002 Bill ▶see Chapter 2. The main proposals for workers and business people include:

- the Highly Skilled Migrant Programme (HSMP). This is already in operation as a pilot scheme. We look at the HSMP and innovators scheme in Chapter 20. Although those coming under the HSMP may be employed, they may also enter or stay to set up their own business;

- allowing postgraduate students to switch into employment ▶see page 320 (currently this is allowed on a concessionary basis);

- widening the scope of the seasonal agricultural workers scheme (▶see page 434) and the working holidaymakers scheme (▶see pages 294-295).

Even if all the proposals in the 2002 White Paper relating to economic migration are brought into force, it will still remain hard for non-EEA nationals to be allowed to come to the UK in order to take up work. At the present time, work permits are not issued in respect of manual occupations or for resident domestic workers, such as nannies and housekeepers (but ▶see pages 434-435 for a concession that operates outside the rules).

This chapter looks at those who are coming in order to be employed in the UK and Chapter 20 looks at the situation of those who wish to come to the UK for business.

Most people admitted in order to work or for business are entitled to have their family members join them. There are, however, some important differences in the rules relating to family members of the different workers.

It should also be noted that there are certain other categories of people who may be admitted for work-related purposes or who are able to do some work while here. They are dealt with in the appropriate part of the book:

- visitors may be admitted as business visitors and sometimes for other work-related purposes ▶see pages 280-283;
- students are generally not restricted from part-time working ▶see page 310 for more details. The chapter dealing with students also covers the rules relating to student nurses, postgraduate doctors and dentists ▶see pages 311-312, and students' union sabbatical officers ▶see page 314.

In addition, the following groups of people, although their purpose for being in the UK is not necessarily work-related, are able to work in the UK without obtaining specific permission to do so:

- people who have indefinite leave (allowed to stay permanently);
- people who have been allowed to enter or remain to be with close relatives settled in the UK, for example, husbands and wives, and have been granted leave for a year initially;
- people granted refugee status or exceptional leave;
- other people who have no restriction or prohibition on working stamped on their passports.

Those who have been granted temporary admission to the UK are prohibited from working by the immigration authorities. Their prohibition is in the form of a condition attached to their temporary admission which states that they are not permitted to work. They may, however, request that this condition is lifted. Asylum-seekers who have waited six months or more for an initial decision on their claim will be entitled to make such a request.

Consequences of working unlawfully in the UK

Where people work in the UK otherwise than as set out above and otherwise than in one of the categories set out in this chapter and the following chapter on Business Purposes, then the consequences can be severe. They:

- if they are in breach of their conditions of leave, may be removed from the UK under the Home Office's powers of 'administrative removal';

- may have any existing leave which they have curtailed (see para 323(i), HC 395);
- if they were admitted in a category in which they had to show that they did not intend to take work, may be declared an illegal entrant and removed on that basis, if it can be proved that they intended to work all along;
- may be refused any future application for entry or further leave under the general grounds of refusal (see para 320(11) and 322(3) HC 395);
- may be committing a criminal offence (s24 Immigration Act 1971);
- if they have temporary admission with a condition prohibiting work, may become an illegal entrant by breaching the condition (*Akhtar*, Court of Appeal) and are more likely to be detained.

Depending on the circumstances, if a person works in a capacity which their leave does not permit it can also result in some of the above consequences.

In addition, the Asylum and Immigration Act 1996 made it an offence for an employer to employ a person who is not entitled to work. Under section 8 of the 1996 Act, the employer will be guilty of an offence if the person employed:

- has not been granted leave to enter or remain in the UK; *or*
- has overstayed their leave; *or*
- has leave containing a condition prohibiting them from taking that particular job.

No offence will be committed, however, if the employee is an asylum-seeker who has been given written permission to work by the Home Office (see Immigration (Restrictions on Employment) Order 1996). In addition, before the employment began, if the employee produced to the employer one of the following documents, which the employer has either retained or kept a copy of and the employer did not know that they may be committing an offence, then the employer will not be guilty:

- a document containing the employee's National Insurance number issued by an agency such as the Benefits Agency or Contributions Agency or by a previous employer;
- a British passport or other passport showing that the employee has the right of abode in the UK (including passports endorsed with certificates of entitlement to the right of abode);
- a passport showing that the employee has indefinite leave or is exempt from immigration control;
- a passport, travel document or Home Office letter showing that the employee has leave which does not prohibit the employment;
- an EEA passport, identity card, residence permit or family permit;
- a registration or naturalisation certificate or other Home Office document

showing that the employee is British;

- a UK or Republic of Ireland birth certificate; or
- a Home Office letter or document showing that the employee has permission to work (e.g., an IS96W Notice of Temporary Admission, Standard Acknowledgement Letter or Asylum Registration Card appropriately endorsed.

The Nationality, Immigration and Asylum Bill 2002 proposes changes to the defence available to employers. The type of documents which the employer must have seen may be expanded. In addition, an employer may be required to prove that he or she has seen more than one document of different kinds and to be able to produce copies.

The Home Office view is that an employer can also employ someone granted bail by an adjudicator whose bail conditions do not prevent employment. This was stated by the Home Office in a letter to Gill & Co solicitors in December 2000.

We would also suggest that a person who has leave which enables them to work and has applied in time to extend that leave, is able to continue in the same work during the time it takes to make a decision and during the time of any appeal against the decision. This is because the same leave is treated as continuing during this period ▶see pages 93-95. It should be noted that the 1996 Order (above) that was introduced at the same time as employer sanctions came into force in 1997 (i.e. before the 1999 Act treated leave as continuing during appeals against refusals to extend leave), exempts employees who are appealing under the old appeals provisions if they had leave which allowed them to work at the time they appealed.

The work permit scheme

Work permits may be obtained by employers in order to enable a person from overseas whom they wish to employ to come and stay in the UK in order to work. Work permits used to be issued by the Overseas Labour Service and subsequently Work Permits (UK), which were both part of the Department of Education and Employment. From mid 2001, Work Permits (UK) has been part of the Home Office Immigration and Nationality Directorate although it remains based in Sheffield.

The granting of leave, extensions of leave and settlement to work permit holders is set out in the immigration rules and in the Immigration Directorate Instructions (IDI, Ch5, s1). Detailed guidance notes for applicants are available from the Work Permits (UK) website at www.workpermits .gov.uk. These notes describe the conditions that must be satisfied in order to get a work permit and the procedures for applying for them. It is also possible to download all the relevant application forms from this website.

The 2002 White Paper proposes changes that will allow the Home Office to charge a fee for making an application for work permits. Charging is likely to be introduced in early 2003. The Home Office has estimated that the revenue to be gained from this will be £15 million per year. This is based on about 175,000 applications being made annually.

The three main types of work permit are:

- business and commercial work permits (see below);
- training and work experience work permits ▶see pages 425-427;
- sportspeople and entertainer work permits ▶see pages 427-428.

For other work permits ▶see pages 428-429.

Business and commercial work permits

This is the most common type of work permit application and is made by employers who already have a presence in the UK and who wish to recruit skilled people from outside the EEA on a full-time basis to fill vacancies available to workers resident in the EEA.

The four basic considerations are:

1 Is there a genuine vacancy for the employment?
2 What skills or qualifications and experience are required for the employment (the 'skills' threshold)?
3 Does the person have the appropriate skills, qualifications and experience?
4 Are there suitably qualified or experienced 'resident workers' available?

Whether there is a genuine vacancy for the employment and whether the person actually has the appropriate skills are reasonably straightforward questions. Below we look at the skills threshold and the resident worker test before looking at how the procedure has been made slightly easier for some cases by the 'Tier 1' and 'Tier 2' system.

The skills threshold

In October 2000, the 'skills threshold' was lowered. Before that date, it was normally necessary for a prospective work permit holder to possess a recognised degree or equivalent professional qualification with two years post-qualification experience; or be a senior executive/administrator; or be a highly qualified technician with specialised or rare skills. At present, to meet the skills threshold an overseas national must have either:

- a UK degree level qualification; or
- a Higher National Diploma (HND) level occupational qualification which entitles a person to do a specific job; or
- a general HND level qualification plus one year's work experience doing the type of job for which the permit is sought; or

- at least three years' high-level specialist skills acquired through doing the type of job for which the permit is sought. The level of specialist skills required is equivalent to National Vocational Qualification (NVQ) level 3 or above. It includes, for example, head or second chefs, specialist chefs, paramedics, dental technicians and those with occupational skills and language or cultural skills not readily available in the EEA. Further information about NVQ level 3 jobs is available on the Work Permits (UK) website.

A person who has held a Training and Work Experience Scheme (TWES) permit, will not normally be eligible for a full work permit until they have completed a period of time working overseas (the period of time depending upon the duration of their TWES Permit).

Suitably qualified resident worker

The 'resident' workforce includes EEA nationals as well as settled non-EEA nationals. In deciding whether there is a suitably qualified resident worker available to do the job, consideration is given to the employer's recruitment methods and the reasons given for not hiring a resident worker. The general principle is that a prospective employer will be expected to 'test' the domestic labour market by advertising in the most appropriate media. This will usually be a national newspaper and/or professional journal relevant to the position in question. Where and how prominently the advert is displayed should reflect the level and nature of the position.

Any advertisement that is relied upon should not have been placed more than six months before the work permit application is submitted. Furthermore, a prospective employer should allow at least four weeks from the date the advertisement is placed before submitting an application in order to allow suitably qualified resident workers the chance to respond. If the employer believes that a recruitment search is inappropriate, an explanation of why this view is held should be given, preferably accompanied by evidence from an independent source. For certain senior level or specialist posts, Work Permits (UK) may accept the use of head-hunters. However, they will not normally accept recruitment carried out by an executive search agency that merely selects people from a pre-existing list of people registered with that agency.

Tier 1 and Tier 2 applications

From 1 October 1991, there has been a two-tier system, making it easier for employers to obtain permits to employ workers in certain circumstances.

Tier 1. Tier 1 includes:

- transfers within multi-national companies (where the employee has been employed abroad for not less than six months and the British-based company has a direct link with the overseas company by common owner-ship);

- senior board level posts (or posts at an equivalent level);
- posts that are essential to an inward investment project bringing substantial jobs and money to the UK;
- occupations where Work Permits (UK) acknowledges that suitably qualified or skilled people are in very short supply nationally. The occupations that are included in this latter category change frequently, and are set out in a list which is kept up to date on the Work Permits (UK) website. Information about the current shortage occupations can be obtained by telephoning 0114 259 4074 and for a full list of current shortage occupations ▶see pages 743-745. The shortage occupations generally fall under the engineering, information technology, healthcare and education sectors.

When an occupation is listed as falling into Tier 1 there is a simplified procedure. The employers only have to fill in part of the WP1 application form, providing details of the job, the experience and qualifications of the person concerned, and explaining how the job falls into one of the Tier 1 categories. The employer does not have to advertise the job but has to explain the commercial reasons why they need to employ the person.

Tier 2. For all other applications (Tier 2 applications), an explanation must be given as to why the employer cannot fill the post with a resident worker unless the prospective employee currently holds a work permit for the same type of work. Details of recruitment methods and responses generated should be provided, together with reasons why the employer did not employ a resident worker who was either already suitably qualified, or who, with extra training, could do the job.

Applying for a business and commercial work permit

Individuals cannot apply for a work permit on their own behalf. Work permits are issued to enable employers based in the UK to employ a named worker in a specified job at a particular rate of pay, normally on a full-time basis. Work permits are not issued to employment and recruitment agencies unless the position is in respect of a specific job within their own organisation, although certain allowances have been made for recruitment agencies employing teachers.

Application forms and guidance notes can be downloaded from the Work Permits (UK) website or from their central distribution service ▶see page 729 for relevant telephone numbers, postal and internet addresses (▶see also pages 100-101). The application form for a business and commercial work permit is WP1. A different style of WP1 form should be used depending on whether it is intended to send the application to Work Permits (UK) by post or email. The form comes with an explanatory leaflet about the work permit scheme and it is important that employers do their best to comply with the requirements or the application may be rejected out of hand.

Supporting documents. If the employer has made no application to Work Permits (UK) during the previous four years, the authorities will require evidence of the employer's physical and trading existence which could include recent accounts, recent contracts etc. For Tier 2 applications, copies of the individual's academic/professional qualifications are required as are original reference letters from previous employers confirming the precise dates of employment and the type of work undertaken. Where appropriate, copy advertisements (showing the whole page of the publication in which the advertisement was placed) and original letters from head-hunters should also be made available. The precise supporting documents to be submitted will depend on the facts of each case.

Coming to the UK after a permit has been granted

After it has been issued, the work permit is sent to the employer or their legal representative. Various conditions are printed on the back of the permit. In particular, work permits are granted to enable the employee to work in the UK for a specified period starting on the date the overseas national enters the UK. They are granted for an initial period of up to five years.

The work permit must be presented to an immigration officer on the employee's entry to the UK no later than six months from the date of its issue. If the worker is not a 'visa national', they need obtain no further documentation before travelling to the UK. However, a visa national requires an entry clearance in addition to a work permit. After a work permit has been issued, entry clearance can be obtained by applying to the employee's nearest British post provided that the job is still available. In the case of visa nationals, the work permit should be presented to the entry clearance officer within two months of the date of issue. For details about applying for entry clearance generally ►see pages 52-64. In order to obtain entry clearance, and to be admitted to the UK on arrival, the immigration authorities must be satisfied that the employee:

- is not of an age which puts him or her outside the limits for employment. Children under the age of 13 are prohibited from taking employment by the Children and Young Persons Act. Those over the age of 13 are normally issued with permits in relation to entertainment performances, but only after a licence has been obtained from the child's education authority;

- is capable of taking the employment which is named in the work permit and does not intend to take work in the UK other than the work named in the permit;

- is able to maintain and accommodate himself and any dependants adequately without recourse to public funds; and

- in the case of a person in possession of a work permit which is valid for a period of 12 months or less, intends to leave the UK at the end of the period of employment.

If the work permit holder satisfies all of the above conditions then they should be admitted to the UK unless any of the general grounds for refusing admission apply ►see page 67. One general ground which specifically applies to work permit holders is 'whether or not to the holder's knowledge' false representations were made in order to get the permit or there was a failure to disclose important information' (para 320(15), HC 395). When they arrive, work permit holders may be admitted to the UK for up to four years.

Obtaining leave to *remain* in the UK as a work permit holder

The business and commercial work permit scheme is designed primarily for workers who are overseas at the time a prospective employer submits an application for a permit, or who are already here in approved employment. Persons admitted to the UK for other purposes such as visitors, cannot normally have their immigration status varied to that of work permit holders while remaining in the UK. However, Work Permits (UK), who now also consider in-country variation of leave applications, are approving increasing numbers of such applications in line with the government's changing policy in respect of economic migration.

Applications to 'switch' status by students of graduate level and above are currently being approved for those who have obtained work-permit approved employment ►see page 320 for further details. The Home Secretary announced in Parliament on 29 October 2001 that the immigration rules will be amended formally to allow students who graduate in the UK at degree level and above to switch into work permit employment. Discretion is also being exercised in favour of Common-wealth holidaymakers who can obtain work permit approved employment ►see pages 294-295. Switching applications submitted by people who have leave in other categories will normally succeed if the post being applied for is classified as a shortage occupation, or the applicant is recognised as someone whom the employer is in 'urgent need of' due to their 'specific knowledge and skills' and in order 'to support inward investment' (IDI, Ch5, a1, annex C).

In the current climate, discretion may sometimes also be exercised in favour of those without leave to remain who can fill posts in the shortage occupation category, for example, asylum seekers. Regard will be paid to the applicant's immigration history but advisers should always consider whether the person's particular skills make it worthwhile lodging such an application.

An application to extend a permit is also treated as an application to extend the leave granted to a work permit holder and therefore must be submitted before the holder's leave expires. Because Work Permits (UK) has become part of the Home Office both matters are dealt with in Sheffield by them. Only exceptionally will Work Permits (UK) refer the application for leave to Croydon. Leave will normally be granted for the period specified in the work permit or four years, whichever is the shorter. The application should ideally be submitted by the employer between one month and three months before the expiry of the existing work permit.

To extend a work permit, it is necessary for the employer to complete Form WP1X (or WP3X in respect of entertainers and sportspeople) and provide any documentary evidence that may be necessary. For example, if the employer had been trading for a limited period of time when the initial work permit was submitted, it may have been made a condition of any extension that audited accounts of the business should be provided at the time an extension is sought. The employee may continue to work while the application is pending, provided that the request for an extension has been submitted before the expiry of the individual's current leave. It is not necessary for the employer to re-advertise the position provided the job remains the same.

The application is submitted to Work Permits (UK). This can be done by post, or by email via the Work Permits (UK) website. If emailing the application, supporting documentation must follow by post. There is no need for the employee to complete and submit any of the prescribed forms required for most other applications to extend stay. A prescribed form (SET(O)) is only required when the work permit holder and their family members are applying for *indefinite leave* (see below), in which case there is no need to extend the work permit.

Changes of employment

It is possible for a person to stop working and to remain in the UK legally during the currency of their leave to remain, but they should only *change* jobs if the new employer *first* obtains a new work permit or if the individual obtains permission to take that position in some other way.

A person who already has a work permit is allowed to take *additional* work of a similar nature on a part-time basis with a different employer outside of normal working hours. It is not necessary for either employer to seek permission from Work Permits (UK) for this supplementary employment.

Rights of work permit holders

Work permit holders pay national insurance contributions and income tax. They are therefore entitled to any benefits for which they qualify as a result of their contributions. However, they are prevented from access to non-contributory benefits as they are normally admitted with a condition that they will not have recourse to public funds. In any event, work permit holders are required to maintain and accommodate themselves without recourse to public funds. If they have paid sufficient contributions, work permit holders can get contributory benefits such as contribution-based job-seekers' allowance, which do not count as 'public funds'. However, an applicant in this position is unlikely to be able to extend their work permit.

Work permit holders also have the same rights under employment law as any other workers. The work permit does not alter any contract of employment or remove any trade union, employment or negotiating rights. However, workers who wish to continue to live in the UK may be deterred from getting into disputes with their employer or making complaints by the fact that the permit depends on the employer and their chance of remaining in the UK usually depends on extending their work permit.

Families of work permit holders

The spouse or unmarried partner (▶see pages 337-339 for who qualifies) of a work permit holder may qualify under the immigration rules to accompany or join a work permit holder in the UK (paras 295J-295L, HC395). Family members applying to come to the UK must obtain entry clearance from a British post overseas before travelling. They will have to prove their relationship to the work permit holder, that they intend to live together with the work permit holder in the UK, that they do not intend to remain longer than him or her and that there is adequate maintenance and accommodation for them in the UK without recourse to public funds.

Unmarried children under the age of 18 of work permit holders may also be admitted in line with the work permit holder, provided both parents live, or come to live, in the UK. If only one parent is in the UK, children have to meet either the 'sole responsibility' or 'exclusion undesirable' criteria ▶see pages 373-378. In 1996, the Home Office confirmed the existence of a concession outside the immigration rules for over-age (i.e. over 18) children of intra-company transferees, provided they are fully dependent on the worker and form part of the household overseas. No other relatives have any claim under the rules to join a work permit holder before he or she is granted settlement.

Persons admitted as family members of work permit holders are generally free, under their conditions of leave, to take any lawful employment without themselves requiring work permits. In order to extend their stay in the UK together with the work permit holder for a limited period, provision is made on the current application form WP1X for details of family members to be entered. No separate application form needs to be completed.

Settlement

After four continuous years lawfully working in a job or jobs for which permits have been granted, the work permit holder will be eligible to apply for indefinite leave to remain. In order to do this, near the end of the four years, the worker should make an application to the Home

Office using form SET(O), enclosing his or her passport, confirmation from the employer that the job is still continuing, and all other documents requested on the form. If there have been periods of unemployment, or periods when the person was working without a permit, these may not count towards the four years. In practice, a short period of up to three months between jobs is not usually treated by the Home Office as breaking continuity of employment. Any other family members who have been admitted to be with the work permit holder should apply for settlement in line with him or her on the same form. If the children of work permit holders who were initially granted leave as dependants, have turned 18 during the duration of the permit, they will be allowed to settle with the rest of the family. This is provided that they are still unmarried and are financially dependent upon the work permit holder.

In calculating the four-year period of continuous residence, the following guidance contained in the IDI (Ch5, a1, annex D) is applicable:

- short absences abroad will be disregarded, for example, for holidays consistent with annual paid leave or business trips;
- longer absences abroad may exceptionally be disregarded if they were for 'compelling grounds either of a compassionate nature or for reasons related to the applicant's employment or business in the United Kingdom'. Each absence should not be for more than three months. The total time spent abroad should not amount to more than six months;
- breaks in authorised employment may exceptionally be disregarded if totalling less than six months and are not longer than three months each.

If the four-year period is found not to have been reached, an extension for a year will normally be granted by the Home Office with a note advising the applicant to resubmit the settlement application the following year.

The above guidance applies not only to work permit holders but also to permit-free employees, business people and domestic servants.

Rights of appeal

In order to be entitled to appeal to an adjudicator against a refusal of entry clearance, leave to enter or leave to remain as a work permit holder, the applicant must have been issued with a work permit (see ss59(7)(8) and 62(1)(2) of the 1999 Act). However, the appeal generally concerns whether the immigration rules for work permit holders have been satisfied, for example, questions of whether the person intends to take work other than that stated in the work permit. The appeal to the adjudicator is *not* about whether the person should have been issued with a work permit under the criteria operated by Work Permits (UK).

It is possible, however, to appeal under an internal procedure against the refusal to issue a work permit. If a work permit is refused, the letter notifying the decision should explain how this is done. The appeal should be brought within 28 days and there should be a decision on the appeal within 15 working days.

TWES work permits

Work permits may also be issued to employers in respect of those wishing to come to the UK for training or work experience. Persons may come to the UK under the immigration rules for either 'approved training' or 'approved work experience'. These two categories are dealt with together in the immigration rules although the rules relating to how long a person may be admitted and for how long they may extend their stay are slightly different. Visa nationals need entry clearance as well as a work permit when they arrive in the UK. Family members (spouses and children under the age of 18 but not unmarried partners) can accompany or join a TWES permit holder in the UK and the criteria that apply are the same as for work permit holders ▶see above.

It should be noted that the lowering of the skills threshold in the main work permit scheme (e.g., to 3 years experience of using specialist skills at NVQ level 3), means that some applications previously approved under TWES are now considered under the business and commercial work permit arrangements. This applies to graduate trainees who should now apply for a business and commercial work permit and not for a TWES permit. They will therefore have to satisfy the resident labour test. The guidance notes make particular reference to overseas qualified professionals who require conversion/adaptation training, stating that this category of people should apply under the business and commercial work permit criteria.

Applications should only be submitted under TWES where the person is *additional* to normal staffing requirements. Applications should be submitted on Form WP1 and the procedure is the same as that for business and commercial work permits ▶see pages 419-420. Employment should not be commenced until after approval has been granted.

As with the business work permit scheme, a TWES work permit application must be made by an employer based in the UK. The purpose of the scheme is to enable individuals to gain skills and experience through work-based learning which builds on their previous education and training, and which they intend to use on their return to their home countries. It is not intended that those admitted for approved training or work experience will eventually settle in the UK. On their admission to the UK and each time they seek an extension, applicants need to demonstrate that they intend to leave the UK on the completion of their training or work experience. They will not normally be allowed to transfer to business and commercial work permit employment.

If the person was on a TWES permit for up to 12 months they will not normally be eligible to return for work under a business and commercial work permit until they have spent 12 months outside the UK. If they have completed more than 12 months in TWES employment, the required period of absence is 24 months (see Work Permits (UK) guidance notes on how to apply for a business and commercial work permit).

In addition to having a TWES permit, those seeking leave in this category must also:

- be within the employment age limits ▶see page 120;
- be capable of undertaking the training or work experience;
- intend to leave the UK on completion of the training or work experience; and
- be able to maintain and accommodate themselves without recourse to public funds.

TWES permits are issued where a genuine need exists for a person to undertake work-based training for a professional or specialist qualification, or for a period of work experience. Training or work experience offered should be for a minimum of 30 hours per week, excluding any time for associated studies.

There are some separate considerations which also apply to approved training and approved work experience (▶see below).

Approved training

The training should lead to a recognised professional or specialist qualification that requires an applicant to have *already* achieved at least NVQ Level 3, or its equivalent, prior to commencing the training. Normally the person should have an academic or vocational qualification at this level or above. The prospective employer should obviously be competent to provide the training. This will normally mean registration or approval by the relevant professional body. The training should be completed in the shortest possible time. The pay and other conditions of employment should be comparable to those given to a resident worker during this level of training.

Work Permits (UK) will normally issue a permit for the average time expected to complete the training up to a maximum period of five years. Those in approved training will normally be given leave for the period of the permit. Although the immigration rules stipulate that a person may only be granted leave for three years at a time, from April 2001 a TWES holder can be admitted for up to five years, in line with normal periods of training for certain professional qualifications. This reduces the need for frequent applications for extensions under this scheme (IDI, Ch4, s5). It is anticipated that the immigration rules will be amended to remove this time constraint on the period of leave which may be granted. If a permit is required for longer than this period, an extension may be granted for up to five years at a time (again, the IDI extend the three-year period of leave specified in the rules).

The authorities will expect the individual to have taken any exams at the earliest possible sitting, normally allowing two attempts for each exam. A TWES permit is not normally issued for training for a qualification that can be obtained on a full-time study basis. In those cases, the person should seek admission as a student.

Work experience

Work experience should be at managerial level or at least NVQ level 3 or equivalent. A person should normally have previous relevant experience or appropriate academic/vocational qualifications to enable them to benefit from a work experience programme at this level. A work experience programme provided by a prospective employer should describe the type and level of experience to be gained, and how it will be supervised. It is necessary to set out a detailed timetable for each stage of the programme and a description of the tasks to be undertaken. The pay and other conditions of employment should be comparable to those normally given to a resident worker undertaking this type of work experience.

Although the immigration rules specify that not more than 12 months leave to enter should be granted to those embarking on work experience programmes, the IDI state that immigration officers can grant up to 24 months' leave. If a work experience programme is likely to take longer than 12 months to complete, this should be explained in the initial application. If less than 24 months is granted, the TWES holder may apply for an extension for up to 24 months. The IDI reinforce the stipulation in the rules that those on work experience programmes cannot spend more than 24 months in total in the UK for this purpose.

Sportspeople and entertainers' work permits

The Sportspeople and Entertainers work permits scheme allows employers to employ non-EEA nationals who are established cultural artists, entertainers and sportspeople. Guidance notes and the relevant application forms, WP3 and WP3X, are available from the Work Permits (UK) website. The tests applied include a rigorous skills test and a 'resident labour' test. The following groups of people may apply providing they can demonstrate the stated skill level:

- sportspeople who are internationally established 'at the highest level' and 'whose employment will make a significant contribution to the development of that particular sport in this country at the highest level';

- entertainers who have 'performed at the highest level and have established a reputation in their profession';

- cultural artists who are 'skilled in foreign arts that are rare or unavailable in this country and can make a contribution to the arts, cultural relations and cultural awareness'; and

- technical and support staff with 'proven technical or other specialist skills' whose work is 'directly related to the employment of an entertainer, cultural artist, sportsperson or a dramatic production'.

Those coming for a specific engagement or series of appearances are generally issued with short-term work permits for 12 months. Those who have spent time in the UK on short–term work permits will not normally qualify for settlement unless they have spent four out of the last eight years in the UK, have achieved international status and intend to make the UK their main home.

Sportspeople and entertainers may also sometimes be admitted as visitors or under a number of permit-free concessions. The IDI (Ch2, s2, annex B) distinguish between 'amateurs' and 'professionals' and specify when such people may be admitted as visitors. Generally, both these categories may be admitted as visitors for personal appearances without remuneration save for reasonable expenses.

Sportspeople, both amateur and professional, competing in a single event or a series of tournaments, may be granted leave in a permit-free category outside the immigration rules (the requirements are set out in the IDI, Ch17, s8). Similarly, entertainers invited to perform at a specific event or events, may be granted leave on a permit-free basis outside the rules (the requirements that they have to meet are set out in the IDI, Ch17, s3).

Other work permits

In addition to the above work permits, there are two other types of work permit which are less frequently used. They are student internship and GATS work permits.

Student internship work permits. Under the student internship work permit scheme, employers may offer an internship to a graduate or post-graduate student, who is studying abroad, to work at their company as a trainee at N/SVQ level 3 or above for a maximum period of three months on completion of their course. Further employment in the UK will only be approved under the other work permit schemes or under any applicable permit-free employment categories in the immigration rules (set out later in this section).

'General Agreement on Trade in Services' (GATS) work permits. GATS work permits are issued to employers who do not have a commercial presence in the European Union (EU), to enable their employees to work in the UK on service contracts awarded by British organisations. The employee must have 'high level professional skills' and must work in particular service sectors specified in the guidance notes for this scheme issued by Work Permits (UK). The work permit holder will be granted leave for a maximum of three months under the scheme, which is the maximum permitted length of time for the service contract. The non-European employer must be based in a country which is a member of the World

Trade Organisation (WTO) and has signed up to the GATS agreement with the WTO.

Work permit free employment under the immigration rules

Separate from the work permit scheme, the immigration rules list a number of occupations for which work permits are not necessary. These occupations are known as 'permit-free employment' and are normally jobs which it is unlikely that someone already resident in the UK would be able to do. In order to come to the UK to work in these occupations, these people *generally* need to obtain entry clearance from a British post, but the employers do not need to apply for a work permit. The person needs to obtain confirmation of their job offer and then they need to submit application forms IM2A and IM2C to the British post and pay the requisite fee ▶see page 738. The entry clearance officer may refer the application to the Home Office in the UK to confirm details of the job or the employer before making a decision about granting entry clearance.

The following requirements are common to all categories of permit-free employment in addition to holding a valid entry clearance in that capacity:

- an intention to work full-time in that particular capacity and not to take any other form of employment;
- the ability to maintain and accommodate themselves without claiming public funds.

It is generally not possible for persons already with limited leave in the UK to switch into permit-free employment, although specific exceptions are discussed below.

Ministers of religion

A minister of religion is a 'religious functionary whose main regular duties comprise the leading of a congregation in performing the rites and rituals of the faith and in preaching the essentials of the creed'. They have to show that they will be working full-time as ministers and that they are capable of filling the position required by the religious group requesting them to come. They will be asked for evidence of any formal qualifications and of past experience of work as a minister for at least one year or, if they have been ordained as a minister, that they first undertook at least one year's full-time, or two years' part-time training. They will also be asked for details about their proposed job and the pay and conditions offered. Pay and fringe benefits such as accommodation must be sufficient to show that they and their dependants can be maintained and accommodated by the religious community or denomination that will employ them.

The entry clearance officer will require a letter from the religious group giving full details of the position offered. The core duties are normally: leading worship; providing religious education; officiating at marriages and other such occasions; offering counselling and support to members of a congregation; recruiting, training and co-ordinating the work of local volunteers/lay preachers.

Congregations may have invited priests from abroad to visit, to see if they are mutually compatible, and then decide to offer them a post. In these circumstances, it is sometimes possible for an application to be considered in the UK, and for permission to remain as a minister of religion to be granted, even though no entry clearance has been obtained.

The 2002 White Paper proposes to allow those already in the UK who are 'appropriately qualified', such as theological students, to switch into permit-free employment as ministers of religion. The thinking behind this proposal is that:

'those who have already spent some time in the UK will be able to speak some English and have absorbed something of our culture and are therefore better able to relate their faith to the context of the UK'.

Furthermore, the 2002 White Paper proposes to impose a requirement upon all overseas applicants that they demonstrate 'an appropriate command of English'. The latter requirement is not yet in force and cannot currently be used as a basis for refusal.

Missionaries

A missionary is defined as 'a person who is directly engaged in spreading a religious doctrine and whose work is not in essence administrative or clerical'. They have to show evidence of previous experience or training in missionary work, and must be sent to the UK by an overseas organisation.

Members of religious orders

A person may come to live in a community maintained by the religious order of which they are a member. If the person is intending to teach, this must only be at an establishment maintained by the order. If they are teaching in an outside school, the school must obtain a work permit to employ them. It is assumed that the religious order will be providing board and lodging for its members.

Representatives of overseas newspapers, news agencies and broadcasting organisations on long-term assignments to the UK

The permanent employment of these representatives will be with the organisation abroad. They must have been engaged outside the UK although their place of work will be in the UK for prolonged periods.

Sole representatives

'Sole representatives' are representatives of overseas firms which have no UK branch, subsidiary or other representative. The company must be based overseas and the representative must have been recruited or taken on as an employee outside the UK and be seeking entry as a senior employee with the power to make decisions and negotiate on behalf of the company. The representative must be a full-time employee and must not be a majority shareholder in the firm.

The ECO will require documentary evidence confirming the legal, physical and trading existence of the overseas firm, and a detailed explanation of why the company requires a permanent presence in the UK and why the proposed sole representative is suited for that role.

The person will be admitted for an initial period of 12 months. Any application for an extension of leave should be submitted on the prescribed Home Office application form BUS accompanied by appropriate documentary evidence. During the first year, the representative is expected to set up a registered branch or wholly-owned subsidiary of the company in the UK and to continue to run it. The sole representative can also hire local staff or apply for work permits for prospective employees overseas to join them in the UK as employees of the company.

Private servants of diplomats

Private servants of diplomats must be at least 18 years old. They must be employed full-time as a private servant of a diplomat or of a family member who forms part of the household of a diplomat. Frequently, servants falling into this category are housemaids or chauffeurs. They are not exempt from immigration control, like diplomats and others who work in embassies (▶see below), because they are employed *privately* by an individual diplomat, not by the embassy itself. It is therefore not possible for someone who is exempt from control through a job at an embassy or high commission to change status within the UK to work for an individual diplomat, as entry clearance was not granted for this purpose.

Operational ground staff of overseas airlines

Operational ground staff of overseas airlines must have been transferred to the UK to work full-time as a station manager, security manager or technical manager for an airline based overseas which operates services to and from the UK.

People employed by an overseas government or a United Nations organisation or other international organisation of which the UK is a member

These are people who are not diplomats but are based overseas and have formal contracts of employment with the international body or overseas government, but not with their embassy or high commission in the UK.

Ancestry (Commonwealth nationals with British-born grandparents)

Commonwealth citizens aged 17 or over with a British-born grandparent (paternal or maternal) can come to the UK to work or to seek work. They need to prove their descent from the person born in the UK, usually by producing the grandparent's birth certificate, the grandparents' marriage certificate, the birth certificate of their father or mother descended from the grandparent, the parents' marriage certificate and their own birth certificate. If the parents or grandparents were not married, any other evidence to show the relationship would be helpful, such as statements from people who knew them to confirm that they are the grandparents and parents of the applicant, or any evidence from school or medical records showing the family connections. An adoptive relationship is, in practice, accepted. The parent of an illegitimate child includes the father for these purposes.

People coming to the UK for this purpose need to obtain entry clearance. People already in the country, for example as visitors, may be permitted to change their status and should apply on form FLR(O). Those who qualify under this heading will be allowed to enter or remain for four years, without any restrictions on employment.

Applying for extensions of stay and indefinite leave

All the above categories of people (except for those with ancestral ties) will be admitted for one year at first. They may apply for an extension on Home Office application form FLR(O) (except for sole representatives, who must use form BUS), and at that stage have to show the Home Office that they are still working in the same job for which entry clearance was granted and that all the same requirements are met.

After four years' continuous work in the qualifying category, and provided the person is still working and the employers confirm that the person's work is still required, the worker can be granted indefinite leave to remain. The spouse or unmarried partner and children of all these people may also be allowed to join them either at the outset or during the four-year qualifying period, provided they obtain entry clearance. They need to show that they can be maintained and accommodated in accommodation owned or occupied exclusively by the family and that they do not intend to remain in the UK longer than the worker's period of permission to remain. If only one parent is in the UK, children have to meet either the 'sole responsibility' or 'exclusion undesirable' requirements (▶see pages 373–378).

Persons admitted as family members will generally be admitted without any working restrictions.

Short-term workers

In addition to members of the above categories who may eventually obtain settlement in the UK as a result of their employment, some people may be admitted for work and allowed to stay for a limited period only without needing a work permit. These categories of 'short-term' workers are as follows.

Au pairs

Young people between the ages of 17 and 27 (when first admitted to the UK), who are unmarried and have no dependants may apply as au pairs. They must be nationals of Andorra, Bosnia-Herzegovina, Croatia, Cyprus, Czech Republic, the Faroes, Greenland, Hungary, Macedonia, Malta, Monaco, San Marino, Slovak Republic, Slovenia, Switzerland or Turkey. They may come to take up arranged placements as au pairs for up to two years. Many people from EEA countries also come to the UK as au pairs but do not have to qualify formally under the immigration rules.

An au pair is supposed to be living as part of an English-speaking family with appropriate opportunities for study. It is intended that they will help in the home for not more than five hours per day, with two free days per week. In return they should receive a reasonable allowance and board and lodging. The main purpose of the au pair's stay is to learn English, although there is no obligation for an au pair to enrol on an English language course during their stay. The two-year period cannot be aggregated but runs for two years from the first date that admission as an au pair was given and no allowance is made for any time spent out of the UK during that period. Entry clearance is not compulsory for non-visa nationals although it may be advisable to obtain it. In fact, the immigration rules actually advise potential au pairs, who wish to know whether they are likely to be admitted, to apply for entry clearance (see para 90, HC395).

It is not possible to change status within the UK to become an au pair. Persons already in the country for another purpose have to leave and then return and ask to be admitted in this capacity. There is no provision for the admission of dependants of au pairs.

Teachers and language assistants

Teachers and language assistants may come to schools in the UK under official exchange schemes approved by the Department for Education, or administered by the Central Bureau for Educational Visits and Exchanges, or the League for the Exchange of Commonwealth Teachers. Two years is the maximum period they will be permitted to stay. There is provision in the immigration rules for the admission of spouses (but not unmarried partners) and minor children of those gaining leave in this category.

Seasonal workers

Seasonal workers may come to work at agricultural camps under Home Office approved schemes. These are mainly people coming to help with harvests. They must be students who are in full-time education abroad, aged between 18–25 (unless returning at the specific invitation of a farmer for whom they have worked before) and hold valid Home Office 'work cards' issued by the operator of an approved agricultural work camp scheme. They cannot be allowed to remain for more than six months or beyond 30 November of any year.

Time spent as a seasonal agricultural worker also counts as time spent as a visitor, so they cannot add to the six-month period by seeking to stay longer for a visit. There is no provision in the immigration rules for the admission of dependants of seasonal workers.

The seasonal workers scheme is promoted as a key element of the government's proposed economic migration policy (►see pages 37-38). The 2002 White Paper describes the scheme as providing much needed 'short-term casual labour' and proposes extending its remit to the non-agricultural sectors of the UK economy. It also envisages the introduction of quotas targeted at specific sectors which will be determined after consultation with employers and unions. However, the 2002 White Paper emphasises that entry will not be long-term (therefore presumably not leading to settlement).

Persons able to work outside the immigration rules

There are a number of other categories of person who can obtain admission to the UK in order to work without a work permit but they are not actually described in the immigration rules. These categories are therefore the subject of policies and practices outside the rules.

Domestic workers

There is currently no provision in the rules for domestic workers to come to the UK, other than those working for families of diplomats ►see above page 431. However, when the rules are finally next consolidated, they are expected to contain provision for domestic workers who come to the UK with their employers. Leave is currently granted as a concession to wealthy families wanting to continue to employ domestic staff who have worked for them overseas. The Home Office has formalised this concession and its operation is set out in full in the IDI (Ch5, s12 and its accompanying annexes).

Under the terms of the concession, the worker must be aged between 18 and 65 years, be currently employed as a domestic worker in a private household and have been employed by that employer for at least 12 months. The requirement that the person should undertake work at a level exceeding basic International Labour Organisation standards was dropped from October 2001 as being impractical.

The worker must have entry clearance before travelling to the UK. There has been much concern about the abuse of domestic workers. The employer must give a written undertaking to provide adequate maintenance and accommodation for the worker, and set out the main terms and conditions of employment in writing. The worker must have a copy of this statement, and must confirm that he or she agrees to it. The British post should check the type and hours of work involved, and that the worker wants to come to the UK. The British post must interview the worker, at least on the first application for entry clearance, to ensure that he or she understands the position.

When a domestic worker arrives in the UK, they will normally be given leave to enter for the same length of time as the employer. If the employer is a visitor, the domestic worker will also be granted entry for a six-month period and will be restricted to working as a domestic worker in a private household. If the employer is staying in the UK for longer than 12 months, the worker will normally be given leave to enter for up to 12 months, with the same employment conditions. The worker is expected to register with the police. The worker may apply to the Home Office to extend their leave, on form FLR(O), and the application is likely to be granted provided the worker still lives in the UK and continues to be employed as a domestic worker. The spouse and minor children of a domestic worker may be admitted and given leave in line. The dependants will not be subject to employment restrictions, unless the employer is a visitor.

The concession allows workers to change employer while in the UK. However, the worker must notify the Home Office in writing with an outline of the reasons for change. The worker is allowed to apply for further leave, even if they are with a different employer. Subsequent periods of 12 months each may be granted.

The domestic worker can apply for settlement after four years' work as a domestic worker in a private household, albeit with different employers, provided that the present employer can certify that they are still required for the employment in question. Form SET(O) should be used.

Voluntary work

The Home Office may allow people to come to the UK for voluntary work. The terms of this concession are laid out in the IDI (Ch17, s9). These people are advised to apply for entry clearance, with proof of the work they are coming to do, and each case is considered individually. Volunteers must work for a charitable organisation, receive no remuneration other than pocket money, board and accommodation. The work they do must be closely related to the aims of the charity and they must not be undertaking clerical, administrative or maintenance work. The maximum period allowed is 12 months and volunteers are expected to leave the UK at the end of that time. They are not able to take or seek long-term employment. For the ability of asylum-seekers to carry out voluntary work ▶see pages 194-195.

Other categories

People in the following employment categories may also be allowed to come to the UK outside the immigration rules.

Off-shore workers. Those working on installations at sea are not covered by UK immigration legislation. However, they will usually spend their shore leave in the UK and wish to base their family here. For this purpose they and their dependants will usually be given entry for 12 months.

Research assistants to members of parliament. These people are normally students coming to the UK to learn about British government and politics before returning abroad to resume their studies. They are normally given 12 months leave.

Rudolf Steiner establishments. These establishments (about 70 in number) are concerned with the teaching and development of children and adults, some of whom have learning difficulties. Overseas staff at these institutions will normally be granted entry for 12 months.

Japan youth exchange scheme. This scheme enables young Japanese nationals aged between 18 to 25 to spend up to 12 months in the UK on an extended visit with employment being restricted to incidental work.

Representatives of overseas insurance companies. They will normally be given 12 months' entry on the understanding that they will leave the UK to process policies gained through clients in the UK.

Jewish Agency. Employees of the Jewish Agency will be granted leave to enter for 12 months and will be expected to work in the office of the agency.

The International Association for the Exchange of Students of Technical Experience. This organisation is linked to UNESCO and sponsors students studying overseas to work in UK companies, local authorities and universities. Leave will be given for up to three months.

For other classes of business visitor and other special groups who are able to do some work while in the UK ▶see pages 280-283.

People who work for embassies and high commissions

Diplomats and others working at embassies or high commissions in the UK do not need work permits because, under international law, they are considered to be employed in the country of the mission. Their admission to the UK is therefore mainly the responsibility of the Foreign and Commonwealth Office, which is given lists by the countries concerned of their diplomatic staff. They require entry clearance explaining their status, but this will be granted on proof of their employment. The entry clearance states that they are 'exempt' from immigration control and therefore their passports are not stamped, or may be stamped only with the entry date, when they travel to the UK. They may remain as long as they are employed by the embassy or high commission. Time spent working while exempt from immigration control is taken into account under the 10-year concession (▶see pages 105-108) if the person later ceases to be exempt.

When a person who is exempt from control leaves their job at a high commission or embassy, they cease to be exempt from immigration control. They then require leave to remain in the UK. In order to prevent these people from being in 'limbo' at the point their job with the embassy ends, the 1999 Act has made special provision for what happens to them. From March 2000, when these people cease to be exempt, they are automatically treated as though they have been granted leave to remain in the UK for 90 days. If they wish to stay longer in the UK after this period, they must apply to the Home Office within this time and will be considered under the immigration rules. If they do not apply within the 90 day period, they will become overstayers.

It is not possible for people who are in the UK in another capacity to change status in order to work at an embassy or high commission. They need to leave the UK to apply for entry clearance. Occasionally, if the person has been in the UK in breach of immigration control, he or she will be refused permission to return for this type of employment as the immigration authorities cannot then control how long the person remains.

Which people at diplomatic posts are exempt?

The 'members of the diplomatic mission' who are exempt from immigration control are: the head of the mission; the diplomatic staff; and the administrative, technical and service staff of the mission, such as chauffeurs, cleaners and cooks. Private servants of individual diplomats are usually not exempt from control but may qualify under the rules ▶see page 431. If they are not diplomats, in order to be exempt, the person working for the embassy must *not* have been living in the UK when they were given their job. Not all people working for embassies will be exempt. For example, if an employee is paying local taxes, they may not be exempt from control.

Members of diplomats' families forming part of the household are also exempt from control and they include spouses, certain unmarried partners, dependent children under 18 and dependent children over 18 who are in full-time education, other relatives who formed part of the household abroad and other close relatives who have no one else to look after them.

20 Business purposes

As is the case with workers (Chapter 19), the immigration rules allow for people to come to the UK for business purposes in carefully restricted circumstances. The rights of EEA nationals and nationals of those countries which have concluded an 'Association Agreement' with the European Union are far more extensive ▶see Section 7 for their rights and the rights of their family members. There are also some circumstances in which the immigration rules relating to visitors allow people to be admitted for business purposes ▶see pages 280-283. This chapter sets out the general categories in which people may be admitted for business purposes.

Business people

Immigration policy is designed to ensure that only wealthy business people (or business people with particularly innovative ideas ▶see below) will be permitted to come to the UK to set up or to join businesses. An entry clearance is necessary whether the person is a visa national or not. Those seeking entry to the UK as a business person must show:

- they have at least £200,000 capital of their own to put into the business. This has to be readily available capital, either in the UK already or easily transferable to the UK, which can be put into the business. The immigration authorities are entitled to ask about where the money originates from, so borrowing money on a short-term basis from a wealthy friend will not be adequate. The business should also need this amount of new financial investment;

- they will be involved full-time in running the business, will be able to meet their share of any liabilities and are able to demonstrate that there is a genuine need for their time and investment. This means that they should not have any other time-consuming activities either in or outside the UK. They will not be allowed to engage in ordinary employment. This is intended to ensure that people admitted as business persons are actually needed for the business and that this part of the rules is not simply being used as a way for wealthy people who do not otherwise qualify to come to join their relatives;

- they have a controlling or equal interest in the business with a proportionate financial investment in it, showing that they are genuine owners of the business rather than its employees;

- that new, full-time employment will be created for at least two people already living in the UK as a result of the admission of the business person from abroad;

- if they are planning to set up a new business, that they are bringing sufficient funds into the country to establish the business, *and* have enough money left over after the investment of the £200,000 to support themselves and their family, without doing any other work, until the business can reasonably expect to make a profit;

- if they are joining an existing business, the applicant must be able to produce the audited accounts of the business for previous years and a written explanation of the terms on which they will be joining; *and*

- that the share of the profits they will receive is likely to be adequate to support them and any dependants without recourse to public funds.

Business people are normally granted leave to enter for a year initially and can apply to the Home Office, on form BUS, to extend this near the end of that year. If there is evidence that the business is continuing, that the money has been invested and is being used in the business, and that new employment has been created, an extension of three years should be granted. The spouse, unmarried partner and children under 18 of the business-person may be granted entry clearance to come to join him or her and will be granted an extension of stay in line with the business-person. After four years, they can all apply to settle. Settlement will be granted provided the business is still continuing and is making enough profit to support them. Full yearly accounts must be provided.

Self-employed people

Earlier versions of the immigration rules provided for a separate category of self-employed people, who had to meet most of the same criteria as business people. It was intended to provide for people wanting to set up as professionals, for example, as architects, accountants or doctors in private practice. These groups have now been subsumed into the business category. There is, however, a special concession for overseas lawyers setting up as consultants, or joining a partnership which specialises in the law of another country. They do not need to have £200,000 capital to invest, nor do they have to create employment for anyone else (see IDI, Ch6, s1, annex D).

Investors

The 1994 rules created the category of 'investor' for the first time. These are people who have at least £1 million of their own which is disposable in the UK. They must intend to bring this money with them and invest at least £750,000 in UK government bonds, or share or loan capital in active and trading UK registered companies (other than those principally engaged in property investment), and intend to make the UK their main home. They are not allowed to take employment, but may be self-employed. They need entry clearance and, like business people, may be admitted for 12 months initially and then be given an extension of three years. They can obtain settlement at the end of that time if they still meet all the requirements of these rules. The spouse, unmarried partner and children under 18 may be granted entry clearance to accompany or join an investor and be given extensions and settlement in line with them.

Retired persons of independent means

Persons who are 60 or older, who have a guaranteed income of at least £25,000 per year under their control and which is disposable in the UK, may be eligible to enter the UK as retired persons. In the past, there was no age limit for persons of independent means. Retired persons must demonstrate that they can support themselves (and any dependants) without taking employment, engaging in business, obtaining help from anyone else, or claiming public funds. The Home Office draws a distinction between overseeing business interests, which is allowed, and taking an active interest in a business, which is not. They also have to intend to make their main home in the UK and show that they have a 'close connection' with the UK. The Home Office interprets 'close connection' as having, for example, close relatives either settled or living in the UK for some time, or the applicant having spent a substantial period of time in the UK in the past.

Those intending to come to the UK under this category must obtain entry clearance. The spouse or unmarried partner and children under 18 of persons of independent means may be given entry clearance to come to join them. The retired person and their dependants will normally be given permission to stay for four years on arrival with a prohibition on working and can apply to settle near the end of that time. This will be granted as long as the money has remained available throughout the period, they have made the UK their main home and they have had no recourse to public funds.

Writers, composers and artists

There is a specific provision in the rules for self-employed writers, composers and artists to come to the UK. They do not need to have £200,000 to invest in the UK. However, in order to qualify, they must have established themselves outside the UK as a writer, composer or artist. They must have primarily engaged in producing original work which has been published (other than exclusively in newspapers or magazines), performed or exhibited for its literary, musical or artistic merit. They are not able to take any other employment in the UK but, if they also have savings or private means, they may use these funds to support themselves in addition to income derived from their art, composing or writing. They must be able in this way to support themselves and any dependants without recourse to public funds. Applicants must, for the previous 12 months, have been able to support themselves and any dependants without working except as a writer, composer or artist.

Writers will not normally include freelance journalists. Artists may include art photographers and sculptors but not performing artists, such as actors, musicians, dancers and singers, who need to obtain work permits. Writers, composers and artists will be granted entry for an initial period of 12 months and will thereafter be eligible to apply for a three-year extension on form FLR (O). Those intending to come to the UK under this category must obtain entry clearance. The spouse or unmarried partner and children under 18 may be admitted and granted extensions of stay in line, and they can all apply to settle near the end of the four-year period.

Innovators

In July 2000, the government launched a two-year pilot scheme to attract entrepreneurs. The scheme commenced in September 2000. For applicants under this pilot scheme, no minimum investment is required, third-party funding is permitted and applications are assessed in order to identify talented entrepreneurs, particularly in the field of 'e-business' and other new technology fields.

The general criteria for innovators is:

- the proposed business must lead to the creation of two full-time jobs (or the equivalent);
- the applicant must maintain a minimum five per cent shareholding of the equity capital in the business; and
- the applicant must be able to maintain and accommodate him or herself and any dependants without recourse to other employment or public funds until the business provides an income.

If these initial criteria appear to be satisfied, applications are assessed using a points system, additional points being awarded depending upon, for example, the individual's business experience and the economic benefits of the business plan.

Although entry clearance is required, the Home Office has in practice been prepared to consider in-country applications in certain circumstances. At the end of the four-year period, innovators, and persons admitted as their dependants, may apply for settlement.

Highly Skilled Migrant Workers

In January 2002, the government introduced the Highly Skilled Migrant Programme (HSMP). The programme assumes a central part of the government's new economic migration policy set out in the 2002 White Paper. The White Paper states that the overall aim of the HSMP is to attract 'high human capital individuals, who have the qualifications and skills required by UK businesses to compete in the global marketplace'. The programme is currently in pilot format and operating as a concession outside the immigration rules until at least the end of January 2003. Its operation is set out in the IDI (Ch5, s11, and accompanying annexes).

The HSMP is fundamentally different to the existing work permit and permit-free categories set out in Chapter 19 because the applicant can be given leave to enter the UK to seek work instead of having to demonstrate a pre-existing offer of employment (the only other persons who are permitted entry to look for work are those with ancestral ties, working holidaymakers and EEA nationals). Those given entry under the programme are also able to set up their own businesses in the UK, bring their families here and apply for settlement. The programme is similar to the innovators' scheme in that applications are assessed on a points-based system.

The HSMP criteria

Applicants are allocated points according to the following five criteria:

1 educational qualifications;
2 work experience;
3 past earnings;
4 achievement in a chosen field;
5 whether it is a 'priority application'.

The box on page 443 sets out the points which are available under the five criteria. Applicants need to obtain a minimum total of 75 points. One of the criteria is the applicant's existing or past level of earnings in their own country. The points system has built-in allowance for those countries where the level of salaries is generally lower as a result of the nature of the country's economy. Countries are categorised into four country 'codes'. For details of the different country codes and the income levels applicable to them ▶see pages 746-747. The income levels may, of course, change.

The following *also* need to be satisfied.

Ability to continue to work in the UK in the chosen field. Applicants must set out future career plans and must demonstrate that they have a 'good chance' of being able to continue their career. A lack of proficiency in the English language will be held to reduce the applicant's ability to find work unless the contrary can be demonstrated in the applicant's field of work. Professional qualifications must be recognisable in the UK.

Sufficient savings and/or potential income to support applicant and family without reliance upon public funds. The existence of an offer of employment will be taken into account. In the absence of a firm offer, the level of planning to obtain work will be relevant. Also relevant will be the cost of maintaining any dependent family either in the UK or abroad.

HIGHLY SKILLED MIGRANT PROGRAMME POINTS SYSTEM

A minimum of 75 points needs to be scored in total by adding together the scores under the five criteria. It is not necessary to score under each of the criteria, provided the minimum 75 points is obtained.

1 Educational qualifications   points

Ph.D.	30
masters degree	25
graduate degree	15

2 Work experience   points

5 years in graduate level job	15
Ph.D. and 3 years in graduate level job	15
senior managerial level (e.g., department head)	10
specialist position (requiring high level of expertise)	10

3 Past earnings

Earnings over the past 12 months are categorised into three income bands which determine the points which the applicant will score. Countries where the salary may have been paid are also categorised into four country codes to reflect differences in income levels across the world (▶see pages 746-747 for a full list of countries and the codes assigned to them, together with a full list of the applicable income band for each code).

Past earnings	points
Income band 1 (ranging from £15,000 for code D countries to £40,000 for code A countries)	25
Income band 2 (ranging from £35,000 for code D countries to £100,000 for code A countries)	25
Income band 3 (ranging from £90,000 for code D countries to £250,000 for code A countries)	50

4 Achievement in chosen field   points

significant achievement (have contributed significantly to development in field of work)	25
exceptional achievement (recognised beyond field of expertise and have obtained international recognition)	50

5. Priority applications   points

The only category of applicants who can currently be deemed as having a 'priority application' are those who are legally entitled to work in general medical practice in the UK	50

Intention to make the UK the main home of residence. Applicants will be required to sign a declaration on the application form that they intend to make the UK their main home.

How and from where to apply

Entry clearance is mandatory for those living abroad. Applicants will need to submit an application to the nearest British post on form IM2A and the specifically designed HSMP form which is available from the Home Office website. All applications will be referred to Work Permits (UK) in Sheffield for consideration.

'Switching' to remain in the UK on the basis of the HSMP is allowed for certain categories of people with limited leave to remain in the UK. Graduate and postgraduate students can apply on conclusion of their studies, unless they were being sponsored by an overseas government. All those who have been granted leave in the UK under a work permit or other category leading to settlement (e.g., the permit-free categories set out on pages 429-432 and those here for business purposes) are also permitted to switch. In-country applications should be made by completing both forms FLR(O) and the HSMP form referred to above.

The applicant's spouse and children can apply to join them.

Further leave to remain and settlement

Entry or leave to remain will initially be granted for 12 months. Further leave to remain for a period of three years will be granted provided all the criteria continue to be satisfied. Indefinite leave can be applied for after four-years' leave under the HSMP.

Section 7 **European rights of free movement**

Chapter 21
Background to free movement rights   447

Chapter 22
Rights of free movement in the European Economic Area   452
Who qualifies as being an EEA national?   452
When can rights of free movement be used?   453
Non-EEA national employees of businesses established in the EEA   457
Family members of EEA nationals   458
Evidence of status   464
Entry procedures   468
Decisions refusing or revoking rights   469
The effect of claiming public funds   471
Rights of appeal   472
EU rights and obtaining indefinite leave   473

Chapter23
Association and Co-operation Agreements   476
Central and Eastern European Countries (CEEC) Association Agreements   476
Turkish Association Agreement   480
Co-operation Agreements with Algeria, Morocco and Tunisia   482
The future   482

21 Background to free movement rights

This section deals with immigration rights provided by the laws of the European Union. This is quite different from human rights law under the European Convention of Human Rights, which is covered in Chapter 13. This chapter gives a background to the European Union, the European Economic Area and how the various European institutions work.

In Chapter 22, we look at the actual rights of free movement within the European Economic Area and at who qualifies for them, including which family members qualify. That chapter also considers how the rights work in practice and at appeals against negative decisions made by the immigration authorities. Chapter 23 covers the immigration rights provided by the Association Agreements and Co-operation Agreements made between the EU states and certain other countries. It also looks at possible future developments in Europe which are relevant to immigration.

Two systems of law

European Union legislation and British immigration law are not always compatible. This is not surprising because they are based on completely different premises. One of the aims of the European Union (the 'European Union' or 'EU' is the term more commonly used for the European Community since the Maastricht treaty) is to minimise barriers for EU citizens travelling between EU countries for what are defined as economic purposes. However, one of the aims of British immigration law is to strictly control and, in many cases, deter economic migration from people who are not EU nationals.

Where these two systems of law clash, EU legislation overrides individual national laws because most of the EU rules relating to freedom of movement have what is called 'direct effect', which means that they are automatically part of the law of all the member states. From 1 January 1994, the rights of free movement enjoyed in the EU have been available in what is known as the 'European Economic Area' or EEA which includes additional countries to those of the EU (▶see below).

In addition to the rights of free movement within the EEA, there are a number of agreements that exist between the EU and other countries which are relevant to determining immigration rights. There are:

- 'Association Agreements' with Bulgaria, the Czech Republic, Estonia, Hungary, Latvia, Lithuania, Poland, Romania, Slovenia, the Slovak Republic and Turkey;
- 'Co-operation Agreements' with Algeria, Morocco and Tunisia.

The impact of these agreements upon immigration rights varies greatly depending on the agreement. Some of the immigration rights given by the Association Agreements are also written into the immigration rules.

The European Union and the European Economic Area

The European Union. The countries of the EU are Austria, Belgium, Denmark, Finland, France, Germany, Greece, Ireland, Italy, Luxembourg, the Netherlands, Portugal, Spain, Sweden and the UK. Citizens of EU countries are, by and large, able to move freely between all other EU countries and the individual national immigration laws do not apply to them.

The European Economic Area. From 1 January 1994, five of the European Free Trade Association (EFTA) countries – Austria, Finland, Iceland, Norway and Sweden – joined with the EU to form the European Economic Area (EEA). Nationals of EEA countries have the same freedom of movement rights as EU citizens. Liechtenstein joined the EEA in May 1995. Switzerland decided not to join the EEA; however, it has now signed an Association Agreement which will include rights of free movement which are similar to other EEA states. This Agreement has not yet been implemented. Although Austria, Finland and Sweden joined the EU from 1 January 1995, Iceland, Liechtenstein and Norway did not, so the EEA remains a separate entity.

The way the European Union works

The European Community (EC) was set up in 1957 by the Treaty of Rome, which provided for the gradual reduction of barriers to free movement of workers, capital, goods and services between European Community countries. An amendment to the Treaty, the Single European Act (SEA), came into force in 1986. The intention of this Act was to create a single internal market in goods and services and the free movement of people within the whole European Community area, by harmonising the laws of the individual countries in specific areas.

The next European agreement, the Maastricht Treaty on European Union (TEU), was ratified and came into force on 1 November 1993. Under this treaty, the EC is called the 'first pillar' of the European Union, alongside two other pillars dealing with common security (the 'second pillar') and justice and home affairs (the 'third pillar').

Under the terms of the justice and home affairs pillar of the TEU, common policies on immigration and refugee issues are negotiated under a procedure known as 'intergovernmental co-operation' which requires the unanimous agreement of all of the member states. However, this position has been revised by the terms of the Treaty of Amsterdam in 1997. The Treaty of Amsterdam amended the European Communities (EC) Treaty (the first pillar) by putting into it a new 'Title IV', dealing with visas, asylum, immigration and other matters relating to the free movement of persons. Therefore, by these means, the immigration and asylum provisions of the justice and home affairs pillar were transferred to the EC pillar. The effect of this is that, after a transitional period (the end of 2004), asylum and immigration policies will become subject to agreement by qualified majority voting rather than requiring unanimous agreement. Three member states, Denmark, Ireland and the UK, negotiated and secured separate agreements under the Amsterdam Treaty allowing them to opt-out from the legal effect of the 'Title IV' provisions (the Irish and UK protocols contained provisions allowing these states to opt-into the measures they approved of). Despite these opt-outs, the new arrangements brought about by the Amsterdam Treaty can be expected to be the engine room for European immigration law and policy in the future.

The EU began work in earnest on the adoption of common immigration and refugee policies at a meeting of the European Council in the Finnish city of Tampere in October 1999. The Council committed itself to the adoption of a policy based on 'a full and inclusive application of the Geneva Convention', and, in particular, to 'ensuring that nobody is sent back to persecution'. In relation to the treatment of non-EU nationals who are settled in the member states, the Council called for, 'a more vigorous integration policy' aimed at granting them rights and obligations which are comparable to the rights of EU citizens. In relation to admission policies for immigrants, the Council stressed, 'the need for more efficient management of migration flows at all their stages and the development, in close co-operation with countries of origin and transit, of information campaigns on the actual possibilities for legal immigration.'

Since October 1999, the European Commission has made proposals for directives dealing with issues such as temporary protection for those fleeing danger, minimum standards of conditions of reception and procedures in relation to asylum-seekers, rights to family reunion, the rights of long-term residents of member states, and the admission of workers and self-employed people. Other proposals for common measures have been made by member states, but only a few of these have been agreed by the European Council. The majority of the new proposals are still being considered by the various EU institutions.

European institutions

There are several European institutions that debate proposed changes within the Union and provide for its implementation. They are set out in the following box.

EUROPEAN UNION INSTITUTIONS

The European Parliament. The Parliament sits in Strasbourg but also has offices in Brussels. It has directly-elected members (MEPs) from each EU country and debates proposals for change in European legislation and resolutions on particular areas. It can investigate specific aspects of policy and produce reports. The Parliament has limited powers to initiate new legislation or to propose amendments to policies recommended by the European Commission. It can receive complaints from individuals about EU policies and laws and, if necessary, make references to the European Court of Justice.

The European Commission. The Commission is based in Brussels and is the executive wing of the EU. It has 20 appointed members, representing all the EU countries, and prepares legislation for the EU. It has its own supporting bureaucracy, also recruited from all the different EU countries. The Commission is powerful because it has responsibility for proposing and drafting the majority of new EU legislation (regulations and directives). Under the current transitional arrangements operating for Title IV of the EC Treaty, it shares its right to initiate legislation with the member states. The Commission can also receive and is empowered to investigate individual complaints and is particularly useful where the complaints cover the activities of member states as to the application of EU law.

The European Council. This is also called the 'Council of Ministers'. It consists of ministers from the 15 EU countries and takes the final decisions on most legislation, having taken account of the views of the European Parliament.

The European Court of Justice (ECJ). The ECJ sits in Luxembourg and decides on legal cases brought under European law. Its interpretation of Community legislation has to be followed by individual countries. Under Article 177 of the Treaty of Rome, national courts and tribunals at any level can refer cases to the ECJ for a ruling on questions of European law. Governments of member states may also seek rulings from the Court.

The Office of the European Ombudsman. The Ombudsman was established in 1995 and is empowered to receive complaints concerning maladministration by the European institutions. Complaints might cover such issues as wrongful application of rules, abuse of power, discrimination or negligence. The right to complain is not limited to EU citizens but extends to anyone living in a member state. However the Ombudsman's powers are limited to investigating the European institutions and do not cover complaints against national or local administrations, even on matters concerning the application of European law.

European Union legislation

EU policies are given effect in legislation known as 'regulations' and 'directives'. Regulations are 'binding in their entirety and take direct effect in each member state'. This means that each country has to take immediate measures to bring them into force. There are regulations on the freedom of movement of workers, and the rights of workers to remain in a member state after finishing employment there. Directives are 'binding as to the result to be achieved', meaning that countries may use different means to bring them into force. There are directives on the right of establishment for the self-employed and service providers, and on limitations on the right of free movement for reasons of public policy, public security and public health.

European law reflected in UK legislation

The EU rights of free movement contained in the Treaty of Rome were incorporated into UK law by section 7(1) of the Immigration Act 1988, which came into force on 20 July 1994 and which states that a person does not require 'leave' to come in and stay in the UK if they have rights to do so given to them by EU law. The delay was due to the Home Office working out a way to do this which was compatible with the rest of the immigration control system.

European law concerning immigration is mainly contained in the Immigration (European Economic Area) Regulations 2000. *However*, these Regulations are not an exhaustive statement of the actual legal position as they were prepared to *reflect and describe* the rights which are granted by EU law; they are not the ultimate source of those rights. The EEA Regulations describe those who benefit from rights of free movement as 'qualified persons'. In some limited instances therefore, EU law may give greater rights than those described in the Regulations. In cases of uncertainty, advice should be obtained. Some aspects of the European law are also described in the immigration rules; in particular the rules refer to:

- the immigration rights of nationals of countries with whom the EU has an Association Agreement. However, the immigration rules do not reflect the Association Agreement with Turkey which is not described in any UK legislation (paras 211–223 HC 395);
- the right of EEA nationals to obtain indefinite leave in the UK (paras 255–257 HC395).

22 Rights of free movement in the European Economic Area

This chapter covers the rights of free movement which are enjoyed within the European Economic Area. It therefore looks at:

- which nationals actually qualify for rights of free movement ▶see directly below. This is mainly EEA nationals but their non-EEA family members and some other 'third country' nationals can also qualify;
- the circumstances in which people can make use of rights of free movement ▶see pages 453-457;
- obtaining residents permits, residence documents and family permits as evidence of exercising EEA rights of free movement ▶see pages 464-468;
- the way in which the rights of free movement apply and operate in practice ▶see pages 468-469;
- exclusions from free movement rights and the effect of claiming public funds ▶see pages 469-471;
- appeals against negative 'EEA decisions' ▶see pages 472-473;
- obtaining rights to permanent residence in the UK after exercising free movement rights ▶see pages 473-475.

The basis for the EEA and the institutions and working of the European Union are dealt with in Chapter 21.

Who qualifies as being an EEA national?

The full right of freedom of movement only extends to people who are citizens of EEA countries. The rights therefore extend to citizens of all the EU member states and to citizens of Iceland, Liechtenstein and Norway which are part of the EEA but not the EU ▶see page 448 for the list of countries. Members of the family of EEA nationals, who are not EEA nationals themselves, have rights with regard to freedom of movement which are derived from the EEA national and can rely on these rights in the circumstances discussed below ▶see pages 458-464. People who are not citizens of an EEA country are known in EU terminology as 'third country nationals'. Certain other third country nationals can also qualify ▶see pages 457-458.

The Maastricht Treaty of 1993 established the status of citizen of the

European Union. This status automatically exists for all people who are citizens of an EU member state. However, in the case of the UK the structure of nationality law is very complex and there are different categories of national, not all of which will be considered to be EU citizens for the purposes of free movement law.

The UK entered a declaration that came into effect on 1 January 1983 which states that *only* the following categories of person are UK nationals for the purposes of EU law:

- British citizens;
- British subjects with the right of abode in the UK;
- British Dependent Territories citizens who acquire that citizenship from a connection with Gibraltar.

In the recent case of *Manjit Kaur*, the European Court of Justice (ECJ) held that the UK was entitled to determine which of its nationals were EU citizens for the purposes of EU law. Mrs Kaur's status as a British Overseas Citizen (BOC) did not mean that she was entitled to the status of EU citizen. Others who are *not* entitled to free movement rights within the EEA are:

- British nationals other than those stated above;
- citizens of the Isle of Man and the Channel Islands living in those islands, because they have their own immigration and citizenship laws;
- Commonwealth citizens, even if they do have the right of abode in the UK;
- those with indefinite leave who are 'settled' in the UK.

If any of the above persons wish to travel to another country in the EEA, they have to fit into that country's immigration rules and regulations.

When can rights of free movement be used?

The rights of freedom of movement were created in order to allow the movement of workers, self-employed people and service providers and recipients. Anyone who is an EEA national (►see above) and who falls into any of the categories set out in the box below, qualifies for free movement rights within the European Economic Area. Further details about some of these categories are dealt with below. The Immigration (European Economic Area) Regulations 2000 (the 'EEA Regulations') are the UK regulations which attempt to define and describe the rights of free movement guaranteed by European law and to practically accommodate those rights into the system of UK immigration control. The EEA Regulations describe those who are entitled to free movement rights as 'qualified persons'.

Workers and work seekers

Those in work

The ECJ has ruled that the essential element of the term 'worker' is employment for a period of time in the provision of services for and under

EEA NATIONALS WITH RIGHTS TO ENTER OR REMAIN IN THE UK UNDER EUROPEAN UNION LAW

Rights to enter and remain

Any of the following people may travel to and stay in the UK:

- people who have a job to go to or to continue in the UK ('workers') ▶see pages 453, 455;
- people who, although they are not actually employed, are genuinely looking for work in the UK with a genuine chance of getting it (also seen as 'workers') ▶see pages 455-456;
- people who wish to become self-employed or establish a business in the UK;
- certain self-employed people who have stopped being economically active ▶see pages 456-457;
- people who wish to come to the UK to provide or receive services ▶see page 457.

Since 30 June 1992, three additional EU directives, on the freedom of movement of students (93/96/EEC), retired people (90/365/EEC), and other self-sufficient people (90/364/EEC) extend free movement rights to:

- students ▶see Chapter 15 pages 317-319 for further details;
- people who were previously employed or self-employed who are receiving an invalidity, early retirement or similar pension which is enough to support them without their becoming a charge on public funds and who are covered by sickness insurance ('retired' persons);
- other people who have the resources to support themselves and their families without becoming a charge on public funds, and who are covered by sickness insurance to protect them against all risks in the host country ('self-sufficient' persons).

Rights to remain

The following people have the right to stay in the UK after they have been admitted:

- people who were employed or were self-employed and who stop their economic activity because they become temporarily incapable of work as a result of illness or accident – they do not lose their rights to remain while they remain temporarily incapable of work ▶see page 456;
- people who become involuntarily unemployed – they do not lose their rights unless their unemployment becomes too prolonged and they do not have a real chance of getting further work ▶see page 455-456.

Note: The above categories are all described in the EEA Regulations which define all the people who fall into them as 'qualified persons'.

Rights of permanent residence

The following people may stay in the UK permanently after they have been admitted ▶see pages 473-475:

- anyone, other than a student, who has remained in the UK for four years lawfully in any of the above categories (or a combination of them) *and* continues to be in the UK in any of the above categories *and* who has been issued with a 'residence permit' ▶see pages 464-466, valid for five years. Family members can also benefit. The rights for people in *this* category do not derive from EU law itself but solely from the immigration rules. For the remaining categories below, although the rights are described in the immigration rules, they are rights which are given by EU law (Commission Regulation 1251/70);

Rights to enter or remain in the UK under European Union law
continued

- people who have been continuously resident in the UK for at least three years *and* who have been employed in the UK or any other EEA state for the last 12 months *and* who have reached pensionable age;
- people who have stopped working because they are permanently incapable of work because of an accident at work or an occupational disease which entitles them to a state disability pension;
- people who have stopped working because they are permanently incapable of work and who have been continuously resident in the UK for at least two years;
- family members of EEA nationals in the last three categories. These family members can still benefit if the EEA national died during his or her working life *provided* the EEA national lived in the UK for at least two years *or* the EEA national died because of an accident at work or an occupational disease.

The rights to remain permanently are all set out in the immigration rules (paras 255–257).

Note: The above carefully defined rights must be read together with the practical procedures which operate relating to the admission of EEA nationals (▶see pages 468-471).

---

the direction of another in return for remuneration (*Lawrie-Blum*). In the case of *Steymann*, the ECJ ruled that the provision of services in return for work constituted an acceptable form of payment. This case concerned a person living as part of a religious community who received food and lodging in return for work performed as a handyman for the community.

Is the status of worker affected by the kind of employment that the person has? Does employment need to be continuous or can it be temporary or casual? In the case of *Raulin*, the ECJ considered the position of workers who were on 'on-call' contracts, with a guarantee on the number of hours worked and who were paid by the hour. The Court ruled that such people could still be 'workers'. In the case of *Levin*, the Court considered whether a person with a part-time contract, earning a net income below the social security norm could qualify. The Court ruled that, provided the work performed was 'effective and genuine' as opposed to being 'marginal and ancilliary', a person on a part-time contract was also entitled to free movement rights.

Those without work but seeking work

Those who are involuntarily unemployed can continue to qualify for free movement rights. The EEA Regulations state that a person who is 'involuntarily unemployed' does not cease to qualify provided that they are registered with the 'relevant employment office' (Regulation 5(2)(b)). The position may change, however, if the unemployment is prolonged. This point was dealt with by the ECJ in the case of *Antonissen* when it considered at what point the national authorities of a member state might decide that prolonged unemployment was evidence that the individual had ceased to be active in the labour market. The Court ruled that a period of six months' unemployment should not jeopardise the status of the individual as a worker or work-seeker. At the end of six months, the onus would be on the individual to show that he or she 'is continuing to seek employment and that he has genuine chances of being engaged'. Therefore, periods of unemployment of six months or more do not necessarily extinguish the status of 'worker', providing the person concerned can show evidence of continuing efforts to place him or herself in employment for which they are suitably qualified.

Although the EEA regulations state that the unemployed person must be registered, there is no actual requirement in EU law that unemployed workers should register with the employment services of the state in which they live. The benefit of being registered, however, is that the acceptance by the employment service for registration as a person available for work will help in *demonstrating* that the person is making continuing efforts to find work. Other evidence would be copies of correspondence with prospective employers, or evidence of having attended job interviews.

Those temporarily incapable of work

The EEA Regulations state that a person does not stop being a worker while they are 'temporarily incapable of work as a result of illness or accident' (Regulation 5(2)(a)). Appropriate evidence to show that a person is incapable of work and that the incapacity is not permanent is best obtained from a doctor.

Those who become *permanently* incapable of work may still benefit from free movement rights if they satisfy certain conditions (▶see box above).

Self-employed people who have stopped economic activity

This category is very similar to those EEA nationals who are able to remain permanently (▶see box above). It consists of the following self-employed people who have stopped their business activities in the UK:

- people of pensionable age when they stop their business activity who have been in the UK for the last 12 months before they stopped and who have lived continuously in the UK for more than three years;

- people who have lived in the UK continuously for more than two years and who stopped their business activity in the UK because they became permanently incapable of work;

- people who have lived and had a business in the UK and who stopped being active because they became permanently incapable of work as a result of an accident at work or an occupational illness which entitles them to a state pension;

- people who have been continuously resident and active in their business in the UK for three years and who continue to be active in their business in *another* EEA state but whose normal place of residence remains the UK and who return home at least once a week.

For the above purposes, periods of absence of not more than three months in any year are not counted as breaking continuity of residence. In addition, periods of inactivity caused by circumstances outside the control of the self-employed person and inactivity caused by illness or accident, count as periods of activity.

Providers and recipients of services

Article 3(1)(d) of the EEA Regulations defines 'recipient of services' by reference to Article 50 of the EC Treaty. This defines services as 'activities' of an industrial, commercial, craft or professional character, which are 'provided for remuneration'. So, for example, the provision of free health care by the NHS does not entitle a person to qualify as the recipient of services. Providers and recipients of services are treated differently to workers and self-employed persons in the form of residence permit which they may obtain. The worker and self-employed person is *normally* entitled to a residence permit of not less than five years duration. According to Article 18(4) of the EEA Regulations, the validity of the residence permit issued to service providers or recipients 'may be limited to the period during which the services are to be provided.'

Non-EEA national employees of businesses established in the EEA

The rights of free movement described above only apply to EEA *nationals*. The rights of non-EEA national family members are covered below. However, in some narrow cases, it is possible for some non-EEA national workers to benefit. Where a company which is established in the EEA carries out a contract to provide services in another member state, it is entitled to take its employees with it, even though the employees are not EEA nationals. This is because EU law sees the company as the entity which is exercising free movement rights by providing services. The non-EEA national, as well as the EEA national, employees of the company therefore benefit from rights of admission and residence in the other EEA state for a temporary period while the service is being provided.

This principle was first established in the case of **Rush Portuguesa**, which concerned the residence status of Portuguese national employees of a Portuguese firm with a contract for civil engineering works in France. At the time, the transitional conditions which governed the admission of Portugal to the EU allowed freedom of movement for self-employed workers and service providers, but not for Portuguese *workers* seeking employment with employers based in France. The ECJ ruled that the status of the company as an undertaking lawfully entitled to provide services on a commercial basis in another member state was sufficient to secure a residence status for its employees who were providing those services.

In the further case of **Vander Elst**, a Belgian employer won recognition from the ECJ that the firm's Moroccan employees, who had been directed to provide services on its behalf in France, were entitled to consideration for their position in France under EU law, rather than French domestic employment law.

By these decisions, it appears that there is a right for third country national employees of a business in a member state to travel to, and trade on behalf of their company in, a second member state. The Home Office has stated that the family members of employees of companies who benefit from free movement rights in this way are admitted in exactly the same way as other family members of EEA nationals (letter from Joint Entry Clearance Unit to Kingsley Napley solicitors, 18 May 2001).

Family members of EEA nationals

'Family members' of EEA nationals who are exercising rights of free movement in another EEA country, are entitled to be admitted to and stay in that other EEA on the same basis as the EEA national. The EEA Regulations apply to these family members in the same way as they apply to EEA nationals who the regulations describe as being 'qualified persons'. This applies to family members whether they themselves are EEA nationals or nationals of other countries (known as 'third country' nationals). The best way of understanding these rights is to see them as being *derived* from the free movement rights of their family member.

If an EEA national permanently leaves a country where they were exercising rights of free movement, then the family member does not retain any rights. If the same EEA national leaves temporarily (for less than six months), then the family member retains their rights (68/360/EEC).

Who is a 'family member'?

The definition of 'family member' varies slightly depending upon the reason for the EEA national to be in the UK. The 'family' of an EEA national is defined as (see Regulation 6 EEA Regulations):

- spouse;
- sons and daughters, grandsons and granddaughters up to the age of 21, and those over 21 if they are still dependent of the EEA national or their spouse;
- dependent parents, grandparents and great-grandparents of either the EEA national or their spouse;
- other relatives may also qualify in certain circumstances ▶see page 460.

It should be noted, however, that family members of EEA nationals who only qualify for rights of free movement as students, are more restrictively defined. For students only their spouse and dependent children qualify.

Spouses

A 'spouse' in this context means a person who is formally contracted in a legal marriage. In the case of cohabitees, the ECJ has ruled that cohabiting but unmarried couples could not be included in the definition of spouse (*Reed*). However, the case also establishes that where the national law allows unmarried but cohabiting partners of its own nationals to obtain residence in the country on the basis of their relationship, it would be discriminatory not to extend that same benefit to the cohabiting partners of EEA nationals. Therefore, given that the immigration rules allow unmarried partners to be granted permission to enter and remain, unmarried partners of EEA nationals should be treated in the same way. In a letter of 15 August 2000 to Warner Cranston solicitors, the Home Office confirmed that unmarried partners of EEA nationals can be treated in the same way as the unmarried partner of a British citizen or person settled in the UK, even though the EEA national does not have a permanent right of residence and is not therefore settled in the UK (for the requirements of the unmarried partners rules ▶see pages 337-339).

The 'spouse' relationship only breaks down for the purposes of EU law when there is a divorce. A non-EEA national can still rely on his or her marriage to an EAA national even if they are separated or living in different houses (*Diatta*, ECJ).

As regards the genuineness of a marriage, there is no equivalent in EU law to the primary purpose test. The production of a valid marriage certificate is the only requirement laid down in the European legislation. The Home Office is of the view that it is entitled to investigate marriages between EEA nationals and 'third country' nationals to establish whether they have been entered into purely for immigration purposes. In a statement in May 1994 explaining the government's attitude on this question, the then Home Office minister, Lord Annaly, stated that:

'A marriage of convenience is regarded as a sham marriage which is entered into solely for immigration purposes where the partners have no intention of living with each other as man and wife in a settled and genuine relationship'.

The EEA Regulations reflect this position by stating that a person cannot be considered to be a 'spouse' if the marriage was one of 'convenience' (Regulation 2(1)). The Immigration Appeal Tribunal has adopted the same line (see *Kwong*). In order to be a marriage of convenience, the marriage must be shown to be a sham in the sense that the couple do not intend to pursue any kind of married life together.

In most EEA states, once it is accepted that a marriage is legally valid, there is no further enquiry into the nature of the marriage. In order to exclude free movement rights in this way, it is probable that EU law would require the Secretary of State to demonstrate that the marriage constituted a fraud that was sufficient to justify the exclusion of the person on public policy grounds ▶see pages 469-470 for public policy exclusions. The point is important also in determining whether a family member has a right of appeal, as only a person who can produce proof of family membership can appeal (Regulation 33, EEA Regulations).

Children

For the purposes of free movement law, 'children' are broadly interpreted to include step-children and adopted children, including children in *de facto* adoptions where there is evidence of the assumption of parental responsibility and dependency.

Other relatives

EU law also gives rights to other relatives who are not included within the above categories but who have been living 'under the same roof' of the EEA national or their spouse and who are dependent on them. 'Other relatives' is not defined in EU law but needs to be interpreted broadly, giving practical effect to the core principles of free movement. So, the definition must go beyond formal and legal relationships.

This is intended to be reflected in Regulation 10 of the EEA Regulations which states that the immigration authorities may give family permits or residence permits and documents to other relatives if 'in all the circumstances, it appears appropriate to do so' and provided that they are dependent and either were living in the EEA national's household before the EEA national came to the UK or are still living as part of that household outside the UK. This implies a wide degree of discretion for the immigration authorities. EU law itself is expressed in more positive terms stating that the admission of other relatives *shall* be 'facilitated' where they are dependent on the EEA family member, or their spouse, or lived with them in the country from which they came (see Article 10(2), 1612/68). If the immigration authorities take into consideration matters other than the specified criteria in EU law, the decision may be unlawful.

The extension of 'family member' to these other relatives does *not* apply, however, where the EEA national is a 'qualified' person on the basis of being a self-sufficient person, a retired person or a student.

Loss of free-movement rights by family members

A family member can lose their rights to freedom of movement derived from an EEA national in different ways. Firstly, a person may cease to be a 'family member'. For example, a person married to an EEA national would cease to be their family member on pronouncement of a *decree absolute* dissolving the marriage. A son who reached the age of 21 and who was no longer dependent, would also cease to be a family member. Free movement rights will also be lost when the EEA national themselves ceases to be a 'qualified person', for example by them ceasing to be economically active in any of the ways described above.

Under the regulations, an EEA national is not a qualified person when they leave the UK. Where this is for temporary reasons and the EEA national intends to return, there is unlikely to be any effect. However, where the EEA national is giving up their residence permanently, the family member also loses their rights. There is currently a case outstanding in the ECJ (*Baumbast*) which will affect the position on this.

Can family members of UK nationals use EU law? – the *Surinder Singh* case

It will be clear from the above that the prospects of family reunification under EU law are more extensive than under the domestic immigration rules. Not only are the procedures for the admission of members of the family more simple and straightforward but they also grant rights of entry and residence without having to satisfy the, often restrictive, criteria of the immigration rules. Looking at the position from the standpoint of British citizens resident in the UK, in many circumstances they will have greater opportunities to obtain family reunification in the other countries of the EEA than they do in the country of their own citizenship. This anomalous situation has given rise to a strategy for family reunification which has become known as the 'Surinder Singh' route.

The case of **Surinder Singh** was decided in the ECJ. It concerned the status of an Indian citizen who had formerly lived in Germany with his British citizen wife. His residence in Germany had been squarely within the provisions of free movement law. After a couple of years, however, the couple moved to the UK. At the time of his admission to the UK, Mr Singh was granted leave to enter under the immigration rules. After a period, the marriage got into difficulty and the couple separated. The UK then initiated action to remove Mr Singh on the grounds that he no longer had a right of residence in the UK. Mr Singh countered this by arguing that he was in fact covered by the provisions of EU law by virtue of his former residence in Germany with his British wife and that he had retained the benefit of EU law provisions when entering the UK. The ECJ agreed. A principle was therefore established which allows the third country family member of a British citizen who has lived with the British citizen in another member state to retain their rights to benefit from EU law on moving to the UK. However, the British citizen must have been genuinely exercising rights of free movement in the other state.

The government has not been easily reconciled to the implications of the **Surinder Singh** case and has attempted to limit the effect of its defeat by the provisions of the EEA Regulations. Regulation 11 states that the family member of a British citizen will only be treated in the same way as a family member of another EEA national in these circumstances if *all* the following conditions are met.

1 After leaving the UK, the British citizen resided in an EEA country and was employed there (other than on a transient or casual basis) or was established there as a self-employed person.

2 The British citizen 'did not leave the UK in order to enable his family member to acquire rights under these Regulations' and therefore evade the ordinary immigration law.

3 On returning to the UK, the British citizen would, if he or she were an EEA national, be a 'qualified person' under the EEA Regulations.

4 If the family member is a spouse, the marriage took place, and the parties lived together in an EEA country, before the British citizen returned to the UK.

With regard to the requirement that the British citizen is employed or self-employed in the second state, the Home Office Immigration Directorate Instructions advise immigration officials that this should normally be for a minimum period of six months. The EEA Regulations make no reference to the other circumstances in which EEA nationals have residence and family reunion rights. They appear to exclude the possibility, for example, of free movement rights applying to the case of a British citizen who has resided in another EEA country as a student, who marries a third country national and then brings their spouse to join them in that country, and then seeks the protection of EU law when returning together to the UK. Although *Surinder Singh* did not expressly cover other categories such as students, there is nothing in the judgement that would exclude this possibility.

The second condition, *if strictly enforced*, would close off the *Surinder Singh* route to all but a small group of families. It would be difficult, for example, to benefit from this route if an application for admission or leave to remain in the UK had been refused under the domestic immigration rules or where there were no provisions in those rules allowing entry to the UK for that category of family member and the family had decided to move to another European country in order to enjoy family life together. In practice, as far as JCWI has been able to discern, ECOs considering *Surinder Singh-type* applications for EEA family permits will generally accept a statement from a British citizen that the reason for residence in the second country was a desire to live and work in that country. However, if the British citizen were to state that their reason for moving was the wish to benefit from EEA family reunification rights, it is likely that they will be refused. In the case of *Akrich*, the Immigration Appeal Tribunal has referred to the ECJ the question of whether EU law allows free movement rights to be restricted in this way at all. It is being argued that the free movement rights cannot be limited on the basis of the particular reasons that the EEA national has for moving from one state to another.

The other conditions are not as limiting. The final condition, requiring that the marriage took place before return to the UK, reflects the fact that the rights of free movement do not generally cover the admission of fiancés and fiancées.

On being admitted to the UK, the family member in a *Surinder Singh* case would reside under the provisions of EU law and, as such, would not be required to obtain leave to remain. They could, if they wished, apply for an EEA residence document and this would be granted for a five-year period as described below.

Can family members of EEA nationals use the 'ordinary' immigration law?

As seen above, British citizens who have remained living in the UK do not count as EEA nationals for the purpose of family reunion because EU law only permits family reunion where the EEA national has actually exercised rights of free movement. Family members seeking to join British citizens and others settled in the UK are therefore usually required to use the immigration rules.

However, an EEA national (or a UK national who counts as an EEA national because they have exercised free movement rights) may, in certain circumstances, choose between using EU law or the immigration rules. Whether EEA nationals can use the rules in this way depends upon whether they are treated as 'settled'. This is because, in order to bring a family member permanently to the UK, the rules generally require the sponsor to be settled.

Until recently, there was uncertainty as to whether EEA nationals could benefit from the immigration rules on the basis that they were 'settled'. As a result of the EEA Regulations, the EEA nationals who are treated as settled are those whom the immigration rules and EU law state are entitled to remain in the UK on a permanent basis and to have their passports endorsed to that effect ▶see pages 473-475 below (and see regulation 8 EEA Regulations). Other EEA nationals are not treated as settled. Whether an EEA national is treated as settled also determines whether their children born in the UK become British citizens at birth ▶see page 570. Advice should be obtained if a person has a choice whether to use EU law or domestic law. The advantages of using EU law are:

- entry clearance (in this case, the 'EEA family permit') is issued free of charge;
- it is possible to be re-united with children and grandchildren of any age (although for those aged 21 and above, it is necessary to show dependence), dependent parents of any age and dependent members of

the same extended family;

- there may be additional requirements of the immigration rules which the family member may not be able to satisfy, for example, the 'sole responsibility' rule where there is another living parent who is not settled in the UK, or the requirement to show that the family member is 'living alone in the most exceptional compassionate circumstances' where, for example, they are a parent or grandparent under 65 or son or daughter over 18.

Where the person can qualify under the immigration rules, there are some advantages of using them in that the person will generally obtain indefinite leave either on entry or (with spouses) after a probationary period of 12 months. It takes longer to obtain permanent rights of residence if EU law is being relied on ▶ see pages 473-475.

Is it possible for a person who has entered under the provisions of the EEA Regulations to 'switch' to claim the benefit of the domestic rules where they give greater benefit? For example, can the spouse of an EEA national apply for indefinite leave to remain after completing 12 months of residence, rather than waiting the normally required four-year period? After all, EU law does require equality of treatment between EEA nationals and members of their families with nationals of the country in which they reside. This point was considered by the Court of Appeal in *Boukssid* and was rejected on the grounds that the domestic law status of indefinite leave to remain did not confer a 'social advantage' for the purposes of EU law. This is a surprising result as indefinite leave or 'settled' status is a condition for an application to naturalise as a British citizen and provides security for the third country spouse in the event of a divorce. In the case of *Kaba*, an immigration adjudicator has made a reference to the ECJ for clarification of a related legal issue.

Can people admitted under the immigration rules later use rights of free movement?

There are some cases in which a person originally admitted under the immigration rules is subsequently able to rely upon EU free movement rights. For example, a person admitted as a student under the rules might marry an EEA national who is in the UK exercising free movement rights. That student would then be entitled to assert their rights of residence as a family member and to apply for a residence document as proof of their status.

Evidence of status

Residence permits

EEA nationals may find it useful to have a document to demonstrate their status. In the UK, this is known as a 'residence permit' and is a small blue folded card which contains a photograph of its holder. The residence permit is available not only for EEA nationals who are exercising rights of free movement as 'qualified persons' but also to their family members if the family members are themselves EEA nationals. Family members who are not EEA nationals can instead apply for a 'residence document' (▶see below).

The residence permit confirms that the holder is exercising a right of residence in the UK under the provision of EU law. Its main uses are as an identity document, as an aid to gaining settlement (▶see below) and as evidence of status should the EEA national wish to be joined by family members who are not themselves EEA nationals. However, the EEA national is still entitled to all the rights guaranteed by EU law even if they have not applied for or been issued with a residence permit as these are conferred directly by the EU law and are not dependent on the approval of the national authorities (see *Royer*, ECJ).

Residence permits may be obtained from the Home Office. Article 15 of the EEA Regulations states that a residence permit 'must' be issued if the EEA national applies for one provided that they produce valid identity and proof that they are a qualified person. The form of proof requested would normally be evidence of employment, self-employment or being engaged in business activity. There is no obligation to issue a resident permit to any of the following:

- a person whom the Home Office believes ought to be excluded from the UK on grounds of public policy, public security or public health ▶see below;
- a worker on a contract of employment which is limited to three months or less;
- a worker who is employed in the UK but who actually lives in another EEA country and who returns there at least once a week;
- a seasonal worker in approved employment;
- a provider or recipient of services if the services are to be provided for no more than three months.

EU law requires that residence permits are issued as 'soon as possible' and in all cases no later than six months after the date they are applied for (see Article 5, Directive 64/221). In practice, however, there is often a substantial delay at the Integrated Casework Directorate (ICD) of the Home Office in issuing residence permits because of the volume of work in the department. Where such delay obstructs the exercise or enjoyment of any rights which the person is otherwise entitled to under EU law, or where the delay exceeds six months, the Home Office is arguably in breach of its legal obligations and may be open to claims for damages. Further, the ICD is unwilling in many instances to issue residence permits to people who are not actually working at the time they apply, even if they have previously had a lengthy record of employment in the UK. Providing the person is registered as seeking work with the employment authorities and still has a genuine chance of obtaining employment, this is arguably contrary to EU law under principles derived from the ECJ case of *Hoekstra*.

Family permits

Family members travelling with or joining EEA nationals who are exercising free movement rights are entitled to be issued, free of charge, with a family permit by an ECO. Only exceptionally are family permit applications referred back to the Home Office for further consideration. Where the family member is a visa national or they are seeking to 'install' themselves in the UK with the EEA national, then they *must* obtain a family permit before travelling. 'Installing' themselves is not defined but probably means seeking to reside in the UK as their ordinary home with the EEA national as opposed to entering for a visit or some other purpose. The family permit takes the form of a vignette which is placed in the passport and is endorsed to show that it is an EEA family permit. It is normally valid for a period of 12 months. It can be used for the purpose of entry on an unlimited number of occasions during its period of validity.

The EEA Regulations further provide that a non-EEA national can only obtain a family permit where the EEA national is either in the UK as a 'qualified person' or, if they are not in the UK, that they will be travelling to the UK with the EEA national within a year from when the application is made. According to this, a non-EEA national married to, for example, a German national and residing in Germany would therefore be issued with a family permit if they travelled with or followed their spouse to the UK; but if they travelled on their own, they would be expected to qualify under domestic immigration rules.

Non-EEA national family members who do not require a family permit (above), arriving in the UK to join an EEA national will be admitted and advised to contact the Home Office to obtain a 'residence document' which confirms an EU right of residence (below). Again, the family member is not obliged by law to do this as they can rely directly on the operation of EU law as the basis of their rights. However, in order to obtain confirmation of their status as a legal resident, it is usually advisable to obtain one as directed.

For who qualifies as a 'family member' and more details of the rights of family members of EEA nationals ▶see above.

Residence documents

Family members of EEA nationals who are not themselves EEA nationals and who are in the UK can apply for a residence document which confirms that they are entitled to reside in the country with the EEA national. In the UK, this residence document takes the form of a stamp usually placed in the family member's passport confirming their connection with an EEA national. It is valid for five years although it cannot be relied upon and may be revoked if the holder is longer entitled to it by, for example, ceasing to be a spouse through divorce. Where a family member has been issued with a residence document and travels out of the UK and returns, provided it is still valid, the residence document can be produced at the port as an alternative to applying for and obtaining a family permit.

'Right of abode' certificate

EEA nationals who are resident for a limited period in order to either receive or provide services on a commercial basis, are entitled to a special form of residence permit which is, confusingly, known as a 'right of abode' certificate (Article 4, Directive 73/148).

Applying for residence permits, residence documents and family permits

Applications for residence permits and residence documents are usually made on form EEC1 which can be obtained from the Home Office. It is not compulsory to use this form, however, and an application will be equally valid if it is made by letter enclosing relevant documents. If the person is working, the employer needs to confirm this fact. If the applicant is studying, confirmation should be obtained from the relevant educational institution. If the person is self-employed, evidence of the financial state of the business will be required. The Home Office also requires two passport-size photos and evidence that the person is an EEA national (normally a valid passport) and will then issue a residence permit.

Family members of EEA nationals applying for residence documents (or resident permits if the family member is an EEA national) require proof they are related as claimed. If the family member needed to get a family permit before they came to the UK – because they are a visa national or they came to reside indefinitely with the EEA national – then the EEA Regulations state they need also to produce their family permit. This may be unlawful as EU law relating to residence permits and documents contains no requirement that an applicant be in possession of a 'visa' which is, effectively, the function of a family permit.

Resident permits and documents are normally valid for a period of five years. However, in the case of students, they may be limited to the duration of the course, or in seasonal or short-time contract work, they may be limited to the length of the intended work or contract. In the case of a provider or receiver of services, the permit may be limited to the period during which the services are to be provided. The residence permits of retired or self-sufficient persons are sometimes limited by the Home Office to two years. There are certain circumstances in which the Home Office is not obliged to issue a residence permit at all (▶see page 465). Residence permits and documents issued to family members are given on the same terms as the EEA national whose rights they are relying upon.

Renewal of residence permits and documents

Residence permits and documents can be renewed on application. If an EEA worker has been involuntarily unemployed in the UK for over a year when they come to renew their permit for the first time, a permit valid only for one year may be granted. Where a student comes to renew their permit and the first permit was only granted for one year, future permits may also only be valid for one year.

Entry procedures

When an EEA national arrives in the UK, provided that they produce a valid passport or national identity card, they 'must' be admitted by the immigration officer without the need to obtain formal permission to enter unlike most other non-British citizens (see Reg 12, EEA Regulations). They can only be refused admission if their exclusion is justified on the grounds of 'public policy, public security or public health' ►see below.

Checking of EEA nationals at the internal borders of the EEA, other than an examination of their passports or national identity documents to show their nationality, is not permitted under EU law (68/360/EEC). It is, therefore, very unusual for EEA nationals to be refused entry. In the case of *Commission v Netherlands*, the ECJ ruled that the Dutch authorities had no right to demand any further information from a German national crossing its frontier once that person had established that they were an EEA national. Although under the EEA Regulations a person can later be removed from the UK on the ground that they are not in fact exercising free movement rights and are therefore not 'qualified persons', this will not generally arise on their entering the UK.

Non-EEA nationals who are family members of EEA nationals must also produce a national identity card issued by an EEA state *or* a valid passport. If the family member is a visa national or is coming intending to 'install' (►see above page 466) themselves, they should also have a valid EEA family permit or residence document.

Both the decision of the IAT in *Chang* and the EEA Regulations indicate that the examination of family members of EEA nationals seeking entry under the Regulations can be more extensive than for EEA nationals and can include questioning to see whether a marriage is one of convenience. If the EEA family member holds a family permit when they arrive, the family permit can be revoked by the immigration officer if revocation is justified on public policy grounds or if, in fact, the person is not the family member of a qualified EEA national.

No formal time limit can be put on the stay of EEA nationals or their family members and their passports are not normally stamped with a date of entry and should not be endorsed with any conditions of entry. They are free to remain in the UK, to work or to study, and do not need to apply for any further permission to stay, as this is an automatic right.

The ECJ agreed in the case of *Antonissen* that a failure to demonstrate that serious efforts were being made to find work might lead the national authorities to the conclusion that the individual concerned was no longer entitled to free movement rights as a worker. However, the Court ruled that the national authorities should not reach this conclusion at least until the person has not found work for six months or more.

Individual countries do have the right to restrict some jobs to their own nationals, but these areas are defined in European law. Some public service jobs, for example, may be restricted, but only those which involve the exercise of public powers or which concern national security. From 1 June 1996 the UK has restricted recruitment for higher level civil service jobs to British nationals. Prior to that, Irish and Commonwealth nationals had also been eligible.

Decisions refusing or revoking rights

The position as regards admission to the UK is set out above, but once a person has been admitted to the UK as an EEA national or as their family member, the immigration authorities can also make decisions to refuse to issue or renew a residence permit or a document or to revoke those documents after they have been issued. The Home Office can do this if it believes that this course is justified on grounds of 'public policy, public security or public health'. The Home Office can also take this course if it decides that the person is no longer exercising rights of free movement, ie is no longer a 'qualified' person or if a person has ceased to be the 'family' member of such a person. An example of the way in which an EEA national might cease to be qualified is referred to above with regard to people who cease to be treated as workers as they are no longer seeking employment with a genuine chance of obtaining it.

Public policy grounds

The exclusions on grounds of public policy, security or health have been defined very tightly. The ECJ has repeatedly held that free movement is a fundamental principle and that the public policy proviso is an exception to that which must be interpreted strictly in favour of the exercise of free movement rights.

It was established by the ECJ in *Rutili* that, while states are free to determine their own requirements of public policy, they cannot do so in a way which would undermine the fundamental principles of equality of treatment and freedom of movement for workers. In that case, the French authorities had sought to exclude an Italian trade unionist from entering the country.

Among the conditions that a person may have which would justify exclusion on grounds of public health are active tuberculosis, syphilis, infectious and parasitic diseases which the host country has provisions to protect its nationals from and other diseases which can be the subject of quarantines. Diseases and disabilities which may threaten public policy or security are drug addictions and serious mental disturbance.

As to decisions based on a person's conduct, the exclusion of an EEA national cannot be justified on grounds of general deterrence. In *Bouchereau,* the ECJ held that the person must pose a 'genuine and sufficiently serious threat to the requirements of public policy affecting one of the fundamental interests of society.' A person's past conduct, including their previous criminal convictions, are relevant only if they indicate that that person is a *present* threat to the requirements of public policy. In *Adoui* and *Cornuaille*, which concerned French nationals who were prostitutes working in Belgium, the ECJ established that member states could not consider conduct as contrary to public policy if it did not enforce genuine and effective measures against its own nationals for the same offences. The Court in that case also ruled that an application for re-admission after expulsion on public policy grounds could be made after a 'reasonable period', with the national authorities being required to take into account any material change in the circumstances of the applicant which would be relevant to an assessment of the threat they pose.

The essential characteristics of conduct which might raise public policy or public security grounds can therefore be summarised as follows:

- that it is conduct on the part of the person concerned, and not merely that she or he might be presumed to be involved with by virtue of being a member of a particular group (such as a football supporter, or someone of a particular religious persuasion);
- that the conduct is sufficiently serious to pose a genuine threat to society;
- that for conduct which has taken place in the past, there should have been no material change indicating that the danger is no longer present;
- that the conduct is dealt with in relation to nationals of the state in a serious way so as to be comparable to the serious step of denying free movement rights.

Enforcement and detention

The powers to enforce the departure of and to detain EEA nationals who do not have rights of free movement are similar to the ordinary immigration powers of enforcement and detention (▶see Section 8) and, in fact, refer to those powers. They are set out in Regulation 21 and part VI of the EEA Regulations as follows:

On arrival

A person arriving in the UK may be examined and detained while awaiting a decision as to whether to admit them if they are either:

- a non-EEA national who is claiming the right to be admitted to the UK as the family member of an EEA national; *or*
- an EEA national who the immigration authorities *suspect* may be refused on public policy grounds.

If, after their arrival in the UK, a person is refused entry because they:

- are excluded on public policy grounds;
- cannot demonstrate that they are an EEA national; or
- if they are not an EEA national, they cannot show that they are the family member of an EEA national exercising rights of free movement;

then they are treated in the same way as if they had been refused 'leave' to enter. They may therefore be detained and, subject to appeals, removed from the UK.

After entry

When the immigration authorities decide that a person, who has been admitted to the UK, is not entitled to free movement rights either as an EEA national or their family member, they are treated in the same way as an overstayer or a person who has breached their conditions of leave. They may therefore also be detained and, subject to appeal rights, removed from the UK.

When the immigration authorities decide that a person who has been admitted would be entitled to exercise rights of free movement as an EEA national or their family member but is excluded from doing so on public policy grounds, they are treated in the same way as people who are being 'deported'. They too can therefore be detained and, after exercising any appeal, removed from the UK.

The effect of claiming public funds

EEA nationals are not required to satisfy the immigration authorities that they can support themselves without recourse to public funds (although, see below). They are eligible to claim any benefit at any time provided they meet the qualifying conditions for the benefit. They are *not* defined as 'subject to immigration control' for welfare purposes by the 1999 Act. For example, EEA nationals who are signing on and genuinely looking for work are entitled to income-based jobseeker's allowance whether or not they have a residence permit.

Like all claimants, however, from 1 August 1994, EEA work-seekers have had to show that they are 'habitually resident' in the Common Travel Area of the UK, Ireland, the Channel Islands and the Isle of Man in order to get the core means-tested social security benefits (or be exempt from the test). The government's stated intention behind this test, which is discussed in more detail on pages 670-671, was to disqualify some people, in particular EEA nationals, from claiming if they had not lived in Britain for long, or had not worked here. EEA nationals who have already worked in the UK will usually be exempt from the habitual residence test.

However, although they may be able to get benefits from the Benefits Agency, if an EEA national who is exercising free movement rights as a student, a retired person or a self-sufficient person were to claim, they would cease to be qualified persons under the EEA Regulations and would lose their rights to remain in the UK under EU law. This is because, under EU law, these categories of person can only exercise rights of free movement for so long as they are not a 'charge on public funds'. Workers and work-seekers may claim benefits without ceasing to lose their rights under EU law provided that they do so temporarily and, if they are not in work, have a reasonable chance of obtaining it.

Rights of appeal

The rights of appeal which are specific to EEA nationals and members of their families are set out in part VII of the EEA Regulations. In order to be able to appeal at all a person *must* first be able to produce *either*:

- a valid national identity card or a valid passport, if they are claiming to be an EEA national; or
- an EEA family permit or some other proof that they are related as claimed to the EEA national (eg., a marriage certificate or birth certificate), if they are claiming to be a family member of the EEA national.

There are rights of appeal against what are defined in the Regulations as 'EEA decisions'. EEA decisions are decisions which concern:

- a person's rights to be admitted to the UK;
- a person's right to be issued with, to renew or not to have revoked, a residence permit or residence document;
- a person's removal from the UK.

In addition to relying upon their rights of free movement, appellants may also argue that an adverse decision is in breach of their human rights or that they have been discriminated against. Human rights claims brought in appeals against EEA decisions can be 'certified' by the Secretary of State so as to prevent a further right of appeal to the Immigration Appeal Tribunal (IAT) in exactly the same way as in ordinary human rights claims ▶see pages 203-205. Unless the adjudicator upholds a certificate, however, there is a further right of appeal to the IAT in these cases.

There is nothing to prevent EEA nationals claiming asylum and appealing under the ordinary asylum appeals system but this is very rare and claims are likely to be treated as manifestly unfounded.

Who is the appeal to?

In most cases, the appeal is to the adjudicator and then to the IAT as in other immigration cases.

In certain circumstances, however, the right of appeal is to the Special Immigration Appeals Commission (SIAC) (▶see pages 618-621), for example, if the Home Office has decided that a person's removal is conducive to the public good in the interests of national security.

Is it an in-country appeal?

A person always has an in-country appeal where the appeal is to the SIAC, or one of the grounds of appeal is that the decision breaches the person's human rights, or where the person had a family permit, a residence permit or a residence document when they arrived in the UK. If none of those circumstances apply, then the appeal is from outside the UK if the relevant 'EEA decision' is:

- to refuse to admit a person to the UK; or
- to refuse to revoke a deportation order; or
- to refuse to issue an EEA family permit.

EU rights and obtaining indefinite leave

Rights under EU law

The rights of free movement under EU law do not in themselves generally provide rights of 'settlement' except in a limited number of circumstances involving people who have ceased economic activity because of incapacity, illness or disability, in which case an EEA national is to be regarded as 'permanently resident'. These rights are guaranteed by EEC Regulation 1251/70 and the categories of people who qualify are set out in the box on pages 454-455. Although these rights of permanent residence are described in the immigration rules (para 257, HC 395), the source of the rights is EU law. Other than for the above categories of person, the EU regulations and directives only create a right to residence documentation is usually to be valid for a period of not less than five years.

Rights under the immigration rules

The UK immigration rules allow non-EEA nationals who have been admitted under the various 'economic' categories in the rules of workers, self-employed persons and business people, to be given indefinite leave after four years. The immigration rules have therefore extended the same principle to EEA nationals and members of their family who have been in the UK for four years (paras 255–257, HC395). This extension of rights is purely provided by the immigration rules, it does not derive from EU law.

Under these rules, EEA nationals and their family members who have been issued with a residence permit or document which is valid for five years and who have remained in the UK for four years 'in accordance with' the rights of free movement laid down in the EEA regulations (or the previous 1994 EEA Order) *and continue to do so*, may have their residence permit or document 'endorsed to show permission to remain in the UK indefinitely'. Students, however, are not entitled to obtain indefinite leave under these rules.

According to a Home Office letter to Clifford Chance solicitors of 4 December 2001 about these applications:

'Absences from the United Kingdom do not penalise an application. Periods spent here in exercise of a treaty right may be amalgamated. Only in the case of very long absences would consideration be given to refusing the application.'

'In accordance with the Regulations' is intended to mean the same as in accordance with free movement rights granted under EU law. So, a person who has had some breaks in their employment while in the UK but has continued to search for employment with a genuine chance of getting it, or who has been sick or on maternity leave, may still count the time when they were not working as part of the qualification period. It is also possible that a spouse who has ceased to live with, but not divorced the EEA national, will still qualify as a family member (▶see page 459). Although the rules state that a person should have been issued with a residence permit or document, in practice the Home Office generally do not insist upon this if there is clear evidence that a person qualifies. As a residence permit or document merely confirms a right of residence which already exists, it would seem unreasonable to make possession of such a document essential in order to obtain permanent settlement rights. It is also possible for the applicant to be issued with a residence permit at the same time as their right to permanent residence is granted. In this case, the residence permit may be issued simultaneously and endorsed with permission to remain indefinitely.

No application form is needed to make these applications. The applicant should produce any residence permit or document, their passport and evidence of their having been in the UK exercising free movement rights for four years. This could take the form of wage slips across the relevant period, a letter or letters from employers confirming the length of period of employment or a statement of the applicant's national insurance contributions record.

Home Office decision-making in relation to family members can be inconsistent. Sometimes, the passports of family members are endorsed to show permission to remain permanently at the same time as that of the EEA national, irrespective of the length of time that the family member has been living in the country. On other occasions, the Home

Office requires that the family members themselves have completed four years' residence.

There is no right of appeal against a refusal of indefinite leave for EEA nationals under these provisions of the immigration rules, unless the decision to refuse leave is accompanied by a requirement to leave the country. In many cases, a refusal will not be accompanied by a requirement to leave in recognition of the fact that, even if the applicant is not considered to have *yet* qualified for indefinite leave, he or she can still continue to rely on their EU rights of free movement as a basis for staying in the UK.

23 Association and Co-operation Agreements

In addition to the rights of free movement which apply within the European Economic Area ▶see Chapter 22, the European Community has agreements with some non-EEA states which provide certain immigration rights. These are looked at here.

Central and Eastern European Countries (CEEC) Association Agreements

The European Community negotiated agreements with several countries which give their nationals some advantages in migration and other matters related to work. The group of countries known as the 'Central and Eastern Europe Countries' (CEEC) have a set of Association Agreements which have become known collectively as the 'Europe Agreements'. The UK immigration rules now cover the 'Europe Agreements' with Bulgaria, the Czech Republic, Estonia, Hungary, Latvia, Lithuania, Poland, Romania, Slovakia and Slovenia.

These Agreements provide for nationals of these countries to establish themselves in the UK (and other member states) as business persons without having to have the £200,000 capital demanded of others in order to establish themselves in business. Applicants may be given leave to enter for a year initially, and an extension of stay for three years ▶see pages 438-439 for the general immigration rules relating to admission for business. They may apply for settlement after a total of four years on showing the Home Office audited accounts.

Four recent ECJ judgments (*Gloszczuk & Others*) confirm that the EU rights of establishment under the Association Agreements are 'directly effective'. This means that they are directly part of the law of the member states. However, just as the EEA Regulations seek to set out and describe rights of free movement in the EEA, the immigration rules set out the rights under the Association Agreements (see paras 211-223, HC 395). The Agreements are not all the same for all the countries and the differences in them are also reflected in the rules. Although the rights set out are for those who can all be described as 'establishing themselves in business', the rules provide separately for people who intend to 'establish themselves in a company' and those who intend to 'establish themselves in self-employment or in partnership'. The requirements for both are, however, very similar and there are some common requirements which apply to both.

In order to be admitted as a person intending to establish themselves *in a company in the UK which he or she 'effectively controls',* an applicant must meet the following requirements:

- that they are a national of Bulgaria, the Czech Republic, Estonia, Hungary, Latvia, Poland, Romania, Slovakia or Slovenia;
- that they will have a controlling interest in the company;
- that they will be actively involved in the promotion and management of the company;
- that the company will be registered in the UK and that it will be trading or providing services in the UK;
- that the company will own the assets of the business;
- where the applicant is taking over an existing company, they must produce a written statement of the agreement on which they are taking it over and the company's previous annual audited accounts; and
- that the common requirements (▶ see below) are met.

In order to be admitted as a person intending to establish themselves *in self-employment or in partnership in the UK,* an applicant must meet the following requirements:

- that they are a national of Bulgaria, the Czech Republic, Estonia, Hungary, Latvia, Lithuania, Poland, Romania or Slovakia;
- that they will be actively involved in trading or providing services on their own or as part of a partnership in the UK;
- that they, or they together with their partners, will be the owners of the assets of the business;
- if the business is a partnership, the applicant's part in the business is not employment 'in disguise';
- where the applicant is taking over or joining an existing business, they must produce a written statement of the agreement on which they are taking it over or joining it and the business' previous annual audited accounts; and
- that the common requirements (▶ see below) are met.

The *common requirements,* which all applicants must meet, are:

- the money which they are putting into the business is under their control and is enough to establish the business in the UK;
- until the business provides the applicant with an income, they have

sufficient funds to maintain and accommodate themselves and their dependants without taking employment (other than working for the business) or recourse to public funds;

- the applicant's profits from the business will be sufficient to maintain and accommodate themselves and their dependants without taking employment (other than working for the business) or recourse to public funds; and

- the applicant does not intend to seek or take any other employment in the UK other than their work for the business.

Applying under the Association Agreements

The decision of the ECJ in *Gloszczuk & Others* makes it clear that, although the rights under the Association Agreements are 'directly effective', member states are still entitled to have rules in place to control rights of entry and residence to CEEC nationals wishing to establish themselves. It was also decided that a member state is not entitled to refuse to permit a person to establish themselves on the grounds of economic considerations relating to the labour market.

In the case of the UK, the ECJ stated that the authorities are entitled to require that those persons wishing to obtain entry to establish themselves, obtain entry clearance. Therefore where a person enters the UK having made false representations, the UK is entitled to reject the application to remain as a business person and insist that they return to their country in order to make an entry clearance application. This must not prevent them from having their circumstances reviewed at a later date. The same applies to a person who has overstayed their leave, entered without the relevant entry clearance or otherwise breached the UK's immigration laws.

The immigration rules do require that all those wishing to enter in order to establish themselves must first must apply for and obtain entry clearance. When a person is admitted to the UK under the Association Agreements, they will be given leave to enter initially for 12 months with a condition restricting them to working only in the business.

It is possible, under the rules, for people who have already been admitted to the UK in another capacity to 'switch' into these categories. However, under the ruling in *Gloszczuk*, the Home Office is entitled to refuse the application if a person has overstayed or breached the immigration law in any other way. There are presently a large number of applications under the CEEC Agreements which have been pending in the Home Office for some years while the ECJ decisions were awaited. The Home Office is in the process of formulating its policy on those cases where the applicant is not in the UK with leave.

Evidence required for Association Agreement applications

In order to succeed in meeting the most substantial parts of the above rules, it is recommended that applicants obtain and submit the following documentation:

- a breakdown of the applicant's and their dependants' monthly expenditure;
- bank statements covering the previous three months;
- an estimate of how much profit the applicant will make from the business. This should take the form of a cash flow forecast and a profit and loss account and, if possible, should be prepared by an accountant;
- details of any income or savings that the applicant may rely upon until his or her business generates sufficient profit to maintain and accommodate themselves and their dependants;
- a business plan containing a statement of the applicant's plans for their activities in the UK including any qualifications he or she may have in connection with those activities and any market research they have done. This business plan is an essential part of the application.

Applying to extend stay under the Association Agreements

Those who have already been admitted to the UK can seek to extend their stay under the Association Agreements. In addition to the nationality requirements (►see above), applicants need to show that they have actually established themselves in business, that their profits are sufficient to maintain themselves and their dependants and that they will not take work outside the business. When applying, applicants must produce audited accounts to show the present financial position of the business. Applicants *also* need to show:

- *in the case of companies*, that they are actively involved in promoting and managing the company, that they have a controlling interest in it, that the company is registered in the UK and is trading or providing services in the UK and that it owns the assets of the business;
- *in the case of those who are in self-employment or partnership*, that they are actively involved in trading or in providing services either themselves or through the partnership, that they (or together with their partners) own the assets of the business and, in the case of partnerships, the applicant is not being employed 'in disguise'.

It is not necessary to use any prescribed application form. Applications should be sent to the Integrated Casework Directorate of the IND. Extensions are granted for periods of up to three years.

Settlement

After a person has been allowed to stay in the UK for four continuous years under the Association Agreements, they become eligible to apply for indefinite leave. They must show that they have met the above requirements throughout the four years, that they are still in business and they must produce audited accounts for their first three years of trading and management accounts for the fourth year.

Family members

The spouse, unmarried partner and minor children of people who are granted leave under the above rules may also be admitted and allowed to stay in line with Association Agreement country nationals. Under the rules, the dependants must have obtained entry clearance to come to the UK as a dependant in this capacity, whether they are applying to enter or to stay after they have already been admitted.

Turkish Association Agreement

The EC–Turkey Association Agreement did not give Turkish citizens rights to come to the European Community and that remains the case.

The main benefit under the Turkey Association Agreement is for those who have been admitted in a category that allows access to employment. Regulations, known as Decision 1/80 issued under the authority of the Turkish Association Council, state that after completing a period of one year in employment, a Turkish national has a right to a residence permit, allowing him or her to continue in that same employment for a further three years. On completion of the fourth year, the Turkish national acquires a right to a residence permit which will allow them to take up any employment.

These provisions only apply to those whose lawful access to the employment market is at a time when their immigration status is sufficiently 'stable and secure'. So, for example, time which is spent in employment while an asylum-seeker with temporary admission waiting for a decision on the asylum claim does not count, even if the asylum-seeker has been granted permission to work by the Home Office. The rules for admission and residence under this Agreement are not set out, either in the EEA Regulations or the immigration rules.

A good example of the circumstances in which a Turkish national can benefit from the Agreement is the ECJ case of *Kus*. *Kus* concerned a Turkish man who had been allowed to work in Germany because of his marriage to a German citizen. It established that he might continue his employment after his marriage broke down and the couple divorced. The German authorities were obliged to issue a residence permit so that he could continue this employment. The case also confirmed the direct effect of Decision 1/80 in EU law.

In a further case, *Sevince*, the ECJ confirmed that Turkish citizens who have worked legally in a job for three years are entitled to change employment in the same field and after four years may remain and work in any job. The Association Agreement could therefore be useful to a Turkish national admitted, for example, as a spouse for a 12-month period who worked during this time but whose marriage then broke down. In such cases, the person would lose the possibility of remaining on the grounds of marriage, but might get further leave as a result of the Agreement if their employers confirm that they wish to continue the employment. Similarly, a Turkish national who has completed at least one year of a work permit should not lose the right to remain even if Work Permits (UK) refuses to grant further authorisation by extending the work permit. Provided the employer wishes to continue the employment, the Home Office may be required to grant further leave to remain under the Agreement.

In the case of *Birden*, the ECJ ruled that a Turkish national engaged in Germany on a one-year employment contract provided under a state-sponsored work opportunity scheme, who had been offered an extension of his contract on a part-time basis, was entitled to benefit from the provisions of the Agreement. This suggests that a Turkish national engaged on a work experience scheme, with prospects of extension beyond one year, should also qualify to stay.

Turkish Association Agreement 'stand-still' provision

In another development under the Turkey Association Agreement, the ECJ recently decided in the case of *Savas* that the Agreement contained a 'stand-still' provision which prevented signatory states from introducing more restrictive immigration regulations for *self-employed* persons than were in place when the Agreement became effective in that member state. In the case of the UK, this means that the rights of self-employed Turkish nationals to entry and residence must be no less beneficial than they were at the date the UK was bound by the Agreement on 1 January 1973.

The full implications of the *Savas* ruling have yet to be established but it is likely that it means that the requirement to demonstrate an investment of £200,000 (which is required for business people under the immigration rules), cannot be applied to Turkish nationals. Turkish nationals also probably do not have to demonstrate that their business will employ a particular number of persons. This is because the law in 1973 did not impose these requirements, although they are contained in the present immigration rules. As a result, the rights of entry and residence for self-employed Turkish nationals may become similar to those extended to the nationals of the CEEC countries under the Europe Agreements.

Co-operation Agreements with Algeria, Morocco and Tunisia

The Co-operation Agreements with Algeria, Morocco and Tunisia were made in 1987 and are known as the 'Maghreb' Agreements. They are presently being re-drafted as the 'Mediterranean Agreements'. They do not confer any rights to enter EU member states for the purpose of employment. However, they do outlaw discrimination against nationals of the signatory countries in relation to other EU nationals 'as regards working conditions or remuneration' and in the field of social security, provided that the national of the 'Maghreb' country has been working with permission. In a ruling in the case of *Amimim Mohammed*, the Gibraltar Supreme Court decided that, having been in lawful employment, a Moroccan national could rely on the non-discrimination provisions with regard to working conditions to ensure a right to remain to pursue new employment. However, in the case of *El Yassini,* the ECJ rejected the argument that the right to non-discrimination concerning 'working conditions' covers rights of residence.

The future

As set out in Chapter 21, the EU is presently engaged in a major review of immigration policies across the member states with a view to proposing common policies to be applied with the force of EU law. To date, this has resulted in proposals for major new directives covering procedures for the consideration of asylum applications, minimum standards for the conditions of reception for asylum-seekers, a common definition of the status of 'refugee', rights to family reunification, the rights of 'third country' (i.e. non-EEA) nationals who are long-term residents in member states and the admission of third country nationals as workers or self-employed persons. Agreement has so far been reached on a small number of measures, including arrangements for people requiring temporary reception and mutual recognition of expulsion orders.

Aspects of these proposals will be of interest to supporters of individual rights of immigration and asylum in that, in some areas, they amount to improvements in those rights. The proposals for family reunion, for example, would extend the family reunion rights of persons other than EEA nationals such as long-term resident third country nationals. In addition, the rights contained in the proposed long-term residents' directive would grant a form of freedom of movement within the European Union to third country national residents who have resided in a member state for a period of five years.

Other aspects of the current range of proposals, however, do give rise to concern, particularly in the field of asylum and refugee rights. The principal areas of concern are that the proposed replacement to the Dublin Convention remains very similar to the original. As regards the proposal on asylum procedures, there is concern over the use of safe third country and safe country of origin concepts and accelerated procedures for certain types of 'unmeritorious claims'. Certain aspects of the proposal on reception conditions for asylum-seekers are causing rifts between member states, particularly as regards access to employment during the asylum procedure and whether asylum applicants can be denied freedom of movement within the member state. These proposals are, of course, all subject to negotiation and while the European Commission has tried to put forward proposals which can be broadly welcomed, there is considerable concern that member states will seek to water down the rights contained within the proposals.

The UK government has remained intent on using its opt-out protocol to block the effect of certain measures on domestic policy. It is particularly concerned about the effect upon UK border controls. Its approach to the proposals now emerging from the Tampere process ▶see page 449, is that nothing will be agreed for the UK which undermines its right to decide who can enter the UK and under what conditions. The UK government is, however, committed to opting in to the asylum proposals because it considers that the harmonisation of asylum procedures and law across the EU will be beneficial to the UK and will reduce movements by asylum-seekers within the European Union.

The process initiated by the EU in October 1999 is still in its early stages of development. Those interested in immigration and asylum rights will still have many opportunities during the period ahead to influence European policy-making in a progressive way. JCWI is actively engaged in this process.

Section 8 **Detention and enforcement**

Chapter 24
Powers of detention 487
Background to immigration detention 487
Who can be detained? 493
The limits on the power to detain 497
Who is likely to be detained? 502
Inspection of detention 509

Chapter 25
Getting people out of detention 510
Temporary admission, temporary release and
restriction orders 510
Bail from chief immigration officer or police
inspector 512
Bail from the adjudicator or IAT
Bail from Special Immigration Appeals Commission 516
Applying for bail before the Immigration Appellate
Authority 517
High Court procedures 525

Chapter 26
**Removal, deportation, illegal entry and
criminal offences** 527
Port removals 530
Administrative removal 531
Deportation 537

Illegal entry   545
The process of removal   549
How people are traced   551
Powers of arrest and search   552
Criminal offences   553

24 Powers of detention

This section looks at the use of detention by the immigration authorities as part of immigration control. It also covers the circumstances in which people can be forced to leave the UK and the means of making them leave. This chapter sets out the background to and conditions of immigration detention, the circumstances in which a person can and is likely to be detained under Home Office policy, and the limitations that there are on the powers to detain. Chapter 25 considers the different ways of getting people out of detention, including temporary admission and bail, and preventing detention in the first place. Chapter 26 then looks at the ways in which people can be forced to leave the UK; namely, the removal of 'port' applicants and illegal entrants, administrative removal and deportation. These powers of 'enforcement' are often, but not always, used together with the powers of detention.

Background to immigration detention

The powers to detain people for immigration reasons are very wide. There are no clear time limits for how long a person can be detained for immigration reasons. There is also no automatic, independent judicial oversight of detention. In criminal cases, there is a 'right' to be released on bail unless good reasons are shown for keeping a person detained while the criminal matter is decided. There is no such right for immigration detainees. The general law has always viewed restrictions upon individual liberty very seriously and, where possible, has limited the extent to which people can lose their liberty. However, as a result of the broad way in which the powers of detention are stated in the legislation, these general principles have not prevented the development of a system in which immigration detainees have been locked up for months, or even years, while awaiting the resolution of their cases.

Neither the legislation nor the immigration rules state what criteria must be applied in deciding whether to actually detain a person. It has therefore been up to the Home Office to decide which factors to take into account and it has operated various policies for deciding when to detain. The perception among many of those affected is that detention is used as a means of punishment and a disincentive to those seeking to come to the

UK. The increased use of detention, in particular for asylum-seekers, has deepened the suspicion that detention is used as a deterrent.

Until recently the Home Office published detention policy remained, at least superficially, in keeping with general principles of law concerning the liberty of the subject. The guiding principle was that detention was only used as a 'last resort', where it was necessary because a person was likely to abscond if not detained, or for similar pressing reasons. Since March 2000, however, a large number of asylum-seekers have been detained at Oakington Reception Centre, not because they may abscond, but because the Home Office says it can determine their claims more quickly and easily while they are detained there.

The most important recent developments in immigration detention are set out in the box below.

Numbers detained

There has been a relentless increase in the numbers detained in recent years. The Home Office has in particular used its powers of detention against asylum-seekers. The government has stated that there were 900 detention places available in 1997 and just under 2,800 by the end of 2001. It wishes to increase the spaces available by 40 per cent to 4,000 by early 2003.

Length of detention

During the passage of the 1999 Act, Lord Williams of Mostyn said that 'the average time spent in detention, according to my information, is about 63 days'. However, during the House of Lords debate on the Detention Centre Rules 2001, Baroness Williams of Crosby reported that a survey conducted by the Medical Foundation of detainees who were the possible victims of torture showed that 'the average length of stay of members of that group was of the order of seven and a half months'. At the beginning of 2001, the government confirmed that the longest period of detention of an asylum-seeker detained under immigration powers was over 600 days.

As at 30 September 2001, the figures for the length in detention of the 1,425 existing detainees (excluding Oakington) were:

Length of time in detention	Number of detainees
Less than 1 month	440
1 to 2 months	275
2 to 4 months	290
4 to 6 months	180
6 to 12 months	140
Over 12 months	100

DEVELOPMENTS IN IMMIGRATION DETENTION

Article 5 ECHR. Under Article 5(1)(f) ECHR, a person can only be detained for immigration reasons in order to prevent them from making an 'unauthorised entry' into the UK or where steps are being taken to enforce their departure from the country. Article 5 therefore limits the circumstances in which a person can be detained ►see pages 498-502 below.

Oakington Reception Centre. In March 2000, a detention centre was opened at Oakington in Cambridgeshire at which asylum-seekers are detained not because they are likely to abscond but on the basis that it is administratively convenient to detain them in order to determine their claims for asylum 'quickly'. Whether a person may be detained at Oakington depends upon their country of nationality and the nature of their claim to asylum. Whether detention at Oakington is lawful is yet to be finally decided ►see pages 506-509.

Detention Centre Rules. The 'Detention Centre Rules', which apply to detainees at immigration detention centres, cover matters such as giving reasons for detention, the conditions in which detainees are kept and measures for maintaining safety and security in the detention centres ►see page 491.

Expansion in detention estate. Detention places increased significantly in 2001. New detention centres were opened at Harmondsworth near Heathrow (550 places), Yarl's Wood in Bedfordshire (900 places) and Dungavel in Scotland (150 places). Yarl's Wood, however, was largely destroyed by fire in February 2002. In the 2002 White Paper, *Secure Borders, Safe Haven*, the government has stated that it wants to increase detention capacity.

Removal centres. Existing detention centres (other than Oakington) are being re-designated as 'Removal Centres' in order to re-inforce what the Home Office states is the 'key role' of detention, namely the removal of failed asylum-seekers.

Anti-terrorism, Crime and Security Act 2001. From December 2001, this Act allows the detention in the UK of those who the Home Office believes are a threat to national security because they are involved in 'international terrorism'. The legislation was prompted by the attacks of 11 September 2001 in New York and Washington. Detention can continue without a person having been convicted of any offence and even if they cannot actually be removed from the UK. The first arrests under the Act took place towards the end of 2001 ►see pages 496-497.

Places and conditions of detention

Detainees can be held at ports, prisons, detention centres, police stations and appeal hearing centres. Following the 2002 White Paper, immigration detention centres (other than Oakington) are being re-named 'removal centres'. Detainees can only be held in police cells for five continuous nights before being transferred to a prison or a detention centre and seven nights if directions for removal have been given. The aim is, however, to detain people for only one or two nights in police cells (see *Operational Enforcement Manual*, para 38.11.2). Airport holding centres are also intended for short-term detention only.

Immigration detention centres

The detention centres are (others are to be added): Campsfield House, Kidlington, near Oxford; Harmondsworth, near Heathrow airport; Tinsley House near Gatwick airport; Oakington, Cambridgeshire; Yarl's Wood in Bedford; and Dungavel in Scotland. Oakington Reception Centre is described separately below. Contact details of the principal places of detention are contained in Section 12. The Detention Centre Rules state that the purpose of immigration detention centres is to provide for the:

'secure but humane accommodation of detained persons in a relaxed regime with as much freedom of movement and association as possible, consistent with maintaining a safe and secure environment, and to encourage and assist detained persons to make the most productive use of their time whilst respecting, in particular, their dignity and the right to individual expression.' (rule 3)

Immigration service detention is intended to have a less structured regime than prisons, with easier access for visitors and longer hours of association when detainees are able to mix with each other, rather than being locked in cells ▶see the box below for the main features of the Detention Centre Rules.

The Detention Centre Rules also establish a visitors' committee for each detention centre which makes reports to the Secretary of State and which can hear complaints from detainees. Complaints relating to a person's detention can also be made to the Detention Centre manager or to the Home Office.

Detention at prisons

Prisons are inappropriate places for immigration detention. The ethos of the prison service is geared towards punishment and addressing offending. Prisons were not designed for immigration detention. Because remand prisoners are intended to be held only for a short period, prison conditions for them are often poor. The regimes emphasise the need for security and control rather than the therapeutic needs of detained asylum-seekers, who may have suffered detention and torture before.

As long ago as 1998 the government's White Paper, *Fairer, Faster, Firmer*, gave a commitment to reduce the use of prisons as places of detention. The UNHCR has commented that no other country in Europe uses prisons in this way. Despite this commitment and the already high numbers of asylum-seekers detained in prisons, at the end of 2000, the government announced that an extra 500 places for asylum-seekers had been secured from the prison service. This included 68 places at high security Belmarsh and 50 places each at Cardiff and Winchester. The government stated that these would be 'short term' measures. On 30 September 2001, a total of 1,620 persons were recorded as detained. The overwhelming

DETENTION CENTRE RULES

The Detention Centre Rules 2001 state:

- Detainees may keep their personal property while in detention, apart from cash or where allowing them to keep it would be contrary to the 'interests of safety or security' of the centre.
- Personal searches are to be carried on a person's reception at the centre and may also be carried out at other times if the Detention Centre manager thinks that it is necessary to do so.
- Written reasons for detention must be given to a person at the time of their detention and every following month while they are detained.
- If a detainee asks for an update on the progress of their case, the Home Office must provide the relevant information to them within 'a reasonable time'. This includes a progress report on an asylum claim, any other application to enter or stay in the UK, a nationality application, a claim to stay under EU law, removal or deportation from the UK, an appeal or judicial review involving their immigration case and bail applications.
- Men and women are to be provided with separate sleeping accommodation.
- Detainees may wear their own clothes and must be provided with additional clothing where it is necessary. On release, detainees must be given suitable clothing.
- Food and drink is to be wholesome and nutritious and it must meet all religious, dietary, cultural and medical needs. Alcohol is not allowed except where required for particular medical or religious reasons.
- Detainees must be able to have a bath, shower and a shave every day and be able to have their hair cut regularly.
- Detainees must have access to: physical education and recreation (at least one hour in the open air every day); a library in the centre which has books relevant to different cultures and in a range of languages and includes religious books; any paid activity which is provided by the centre.
- Ministers of the different religions are to carry out services for those detained and visits are to be arranged to individual detainees if they so wish.
- Detainees are able to write and receive letters and faxes and use the available public telephones. Where the person detained does not have the necessary funds, the Home Office may pay for a reasonable number of letters to be sent and calls to be made.
- Detainees can receive 'as many visits' as they like within 'reasonable limits'. Visits must generally take place in the view of an officer but generally *not* in the hearing of an officer. Legal visits are also to be in confidence but may be in the sight of an officer. However, the Home Office may prohibit visitors to a detained person 'for such periods of time as [it] considers necessary' in order to ensure safety and security and to prevent crime.
- Provided that they consent to it, detainees are medically examined within 24 hours of admission to the centre. The doctor must report to the Detention Centre manager any case where the detainee may have been the victim of torture, or is potentially suicidal.
- A detainee can be prevented from associating with other detainees where necessary 'in the interests of security or safety'. The authority of the Home Office must be obtained in order to remove rights of association for more than a day. In similar circumstances, detainees can be put in 'special accommodation' or under 'special control or restraint'.

majority (1,330) of those detained were asylum-seekers. Of the 1,620 recorded as being in detention, 355 were detained in an immigration detention centre, 195 were detained at Oakington Reception Centre and 1080 were detained in prisons.

The 2002 White Paper indicates that the withdrawal from the use of local prisons as places of immigration detention was completed by mid-January 2002. The Home Office has stopped using the dedicated immigration accommodation section of HMP Rochester, and the similar facilities at HMP Haslar and HMP Lindholme are to be re-designated as 'Removal Centres' and will then operate under the Detention Centre Rules. HMYOI Dover (Young Offenders' Institute) is also being re-designated as a Removal Centre.

The government does not, however, intend to stop detaining people at prisons completely. The 2002 White Paper states (para 4.79):

'It will always remain necessary to hold small numbers of immigration detainees, including asylum-seekers, in prison for reasons of safety. This would include suspected international terrorists detained under the Anti-terrorism, Crime and Security Act 2001. Any asylum-seeker who is held on suspicion of having committed a criminal offence or is serving a custodial sentence will also be held in prison'.

Costs of detention

The cost of detention to the taxpayer is high. The government has estimated that the total average cost to the immigration service of holding a detainee is slightly over £5000. A policy of detaining all asylum-seekers on arrival, as proposed by the Conservative Party during the election campaign in 2001, could cost £2 billion in start-up costs, with annual running costs of over £1 billion.

Attitudes of immigration officers to detention

In 'Deciding to Detain' (University of Cambridge, 2000), Leanne Weber and Loraine Gelsthorpe, with the co-operation of the immigration service, interviewed 35 immigration officers and 25 chief immigration officers. Each official was asked what they thought was the main purpose of detaining persons on their arrival. The response form enabled each officer to give two answers. Although 51 per cent of those interviewed thought preventing asylum-seekers absconding was a main reason for detention, 15 per cent felt that encouraging someone to withdraw their asylum application was a main purpose and 13 per cent gave deterring other people from seeking asylum as a main purpose.

Weber and Gelsthorpe's report also identified very wide disparities in the detention rates between the different ports. Of those who claimed asylum, 32 per cent of all new arrivals at Manchester Airport Terminal 2 were detained overnight, compared with 1.5 per cent of arrivals at

London Heathrow Terminal 1. Stansted detained 18 per cent of arrivals for over five days whereas Felixstowe only detained 1.5 per cent.

Automatic bail hearings

There is no specified limit on the length of time that an individual can be detained. However, the Immigration and Asylum Act 1999 does contain some measures to ensure independent control of the use of detention powers. These safeguards have never been brought into force and the 2002 Bill will repeal them so that there is no chance of them being made into law. In outline the safeguards included:

- automatic bail hearing for those detained under immigration powers after eight days and 36 days in detention. Where an immigration appeal has been lodged against a decision, the bail hearing would be heard by an adjudicator. Where a decision is still awaited or no appeal had been brought, the bail application would be heard by a Magistrates Court;

- a presumption that bail is to be granted (a 'right' to bail).

JCWI believes that it is a travesty that those detained will not automatically benefit from independent review by the courts. The reason given in the White Paper for not implementing such a measure is that it is:

'inconsistent with the need to ensure that we can streamline the removals process in particular and immigration and asylum processes more generally. The significant and continuing expansion in the detention estate since the proposals were first put forward would make the system unworkable in practice.'

By comparison, when people are detained pending criminal proceedings, they have a right to be produced before the court, usually within 24 hours, and to apply for bail. The fact that those who are detained under immigration powers are often isolated, vulnerable and often unable to access legal advice, makes automatic independent review of their detention all the more important.

Who can be detained?

As stated above, the powers of immigration detention are very wide. They are also frequently misunderstood, partly because they, and the powers to grant bail, have changed over the years. The powers of detention were changed by the Immigration and Asylum Act 1999 to fit in with the introduction of 'administrative removal' in place of deportation in many cases. The 1999 Act also enables immigration officers to detain persons if there is a 'reasonable suspicion' that they may be removed administratively, as an illegal entrant or having been refused entry at a port. Recently, the Anti-terrorism, Crime and Security Act 2001 provides additional powers to detain those suspected of being connected to international terrorism.

The boxes below set out those who can be lawfully detained and the legal power given in the legislation for their detention. The powers of detention are divided between the immigration authorities: sometimes it is an immigration officer who may carry out the detention and sometimes it is the 'Secretary of State', which is another way of referring to the Home Office. However, it should be noted that the 2002 Bill proposes to give the Home Office powers to detain in certain cases where, at present, the power is exercised by the immigration service. The proposals do not affect *who* can be detained but simply which officers can authorise detention. According to the Home Office, the purpose of this change is to allow the person at the Home Office who decides an asylum claim to also authorise that person's detention having looked at all the circumstances of their case

---

PERSONS WHO MAY BE DETAINED BY AN IMMIGRATION OFFICER

Port cases

- persons arriving in the UK pending their examination by an immigration officer to establish whether they can be admitted, and pending a decision as to whether to admit them.

  Power to detain:
  Immigration Act 1971 Sch 2 para 16(1)

- those who arrive in the UK with leave to enter given to them before they arrive and whose leave is then suspended by an immigration officer, pending their examination by an immigration officer and pending a decision whether to admit them or whether to cancel their leave.

  Power to detain:
  Immigration Act 1971 Sch 2 para 16(1A)

- those refused leave to enter and those reasonably suspected of having been refused leave to enter, pending a decision to give directions for their removal and pending their removal after those directions have been given.

  Power to detain:
  Immigration Act 1971 Sch 2 para 16(2)

Illegal entrants

- illegal entrants and those reasonably suspected of being illegal entrants, pending a decision on whether to issue removal directions and pending their removal after those directions have been given.

  Power to detain:
  Immigration Act 1971 Sch 2 para 16(2)

Administrative removal cases

- those who overstay their leave in the UK or who breach any of their other conditions of leave, those who obtained leave to remain by deception, those who are family members of a person being administratively removed; anyone who is 'reasonably suspected' of falling into any of the last three categories. All of these people may be detained pending a decision on whether to remove them and pending their removal after those directions have been given.

  Power to detain:
  Immigration and Asylum Act 1999 s10(1)(a)(b)(c),(7); Immigration Act 1971 Sch 2 para 16(2)

Crews of ships and aircrafts

- members of the crews of ships or aircraft who remain beyond the leave granted to enable them to join their ship or aircraft or who intend to remain beyond that leave, or those who abscond or intend to abscond having lawfully entered without leave, or anyone who is reasonably suspected of being in any of those categories. They may be detained pending a decision as to whether to remove them and pending their removal after those directions have been given.

  Power to detain:
  Immigration Act Sch 2 para 16(2)

PERSONS WHO MAY BE DETAINED BY THE SECRETARY OF STATE

Notice of intention to make a deportation order

- persons who have been given notice of intention to make a deportation order, pending the making of the deportation order.

The only people who may now be detained under this power are those whose presence is not 'conducive to the public good' and family members of those being deported. However under the 2002 Bill, the Home Office may begin issuing 'notices of intention' to deport to those recommended by a criminal court for deportation instead of proceeding directly to making the deportation order.

Power to detain:
Immigration Act 1971 Sch 3 para 2(2)

Recommendation for deportation

- persons who have been issued, by a criminal court, with a recommendation that they be deported following their conviction for a crime. These persons may already be imprisoned under the criminal law, but if they are not then they may be detained under the immigration detention powers unless the criminal court or the Secretary of State directs that they are to be released. These people may be detained 'pending' the making of a deportation order.

Power to detain:
Immigration Act 1971 Sch 3 para 2(1), (1A)

Deportation orders

- persons who have a deportation order in force against them, pending their removal or departure from the UK. If a person is already detained under the powers above for deportees when the deportation order is made, then they 'shall' continue to be detained unless the Secretary of State directs otherwise or unless they are released on bail.

Power to detain:
Immigration Act 1971 Sch 3 para 2(3)

Detention of 'international terrorists'

- persons whom the Secretary of State has certified as being a risk to national security and suspected of being connected to international terrorism. These persons may be detained in any of the circumstances set out above *but regardless* of whether they can actually be removed or deported from the UK.

Power to detain:
Sections 21(1)-(5), 23 Anti-terrorism, Crime and Security Act 2001; Immigration Act 1971 Sch 2 para 16, Sch 3 para 2

(see Explanatory Notes to 2002 Bill, para 100). That official would not otherwise be able to do this if the asylum-seeker's detention could (under existing powers, above) only be authorised by an immigration officer.

It should be noted that the boxes above set out the powers to detain people for *immigration* reasons. There are circumstances in which there is a power to detain people both for immigration reasons *and* for other reasons. For example, an immigration detainee may also be held while suspected of or charged with a criminal offence, or as the result of a prison sentence given for an offence or, occasionally, under the Mental Health Act. It is possible for someone to be detained for criminal reasons on suspicion of having committed an offence relating to immigration, for example, breaching conditions of leave or illegal entry, although prosecutions are rarely brought.

The Home Office has agreed that, when a person who has been recommended for deportation finishes their criminal sentence, and is *liable* to be detained under immigration powers, it will not automatically continue to detain them. The Home Office will also not operate a 'presumption' that the person will remain in detention. Instead, the Home Office must consider, usually before or on the date of release from criminal detention, whether immigration detention is justified. If detention is to be continued, reasons should be given (see **Sedrati & Others**, a High Court case which was settled by agreement between the parties in terms which confirmed this as the Home Office approach to these cases).

For the application of immigration detention powers to EEA nationals ▶see pages 470-471.

Detention of 'international terrorists'

In December 2001, the controversial Anti-terrorism, Crime and Security Act 2001 became law. The trigger for this legislation was the attacks of 11 September 2001 in New York, Washington and Pennsylvania. Shortly after the legislation became law (and before it was even published) eight people were arrested and detained under its provisions in London, Birmingham and Luton and there were further arrests in early 2002.

The legislation has important consequences for immigration detention although it is only likely to affect a small number of people. The new powers only affect foreign nationals because the powers are grafted on top of the existing powers of detention set out in the boxes above.

The 2001 Act allows the immigration authorities to detain those suspected of being 'international terrorists', even though they are not being charged with any offences. It allows them to be detained indefinitely, whether or not they can be deported or removed from the UK (s23, 2001 Act). It therefore allows the detention of a person who is claiming protection from removal under Article 3 ECHR as well as someone who has established that they cannot be removed for those reasons. It also allows for persons to be detained if there is a practical reason preventing their removal, for example, because there are no arrangements which can be made to carry out the removal.

Without the new legislation, these detentions would be in breach of the limits imposed on the powers of detention by the courts ▶see pages 497-498. The new powers are also contrary to the right to liberty under Article 5 ECHR ▶see pages 498-502. This is because a person who cannot be removed can be detained under the new powers even though deportation proceedings are not 'in progress'. Therefore, the government has had to announce that it is 'derogating' from Article 5 while the legislation is in force. The government's justification for this is that there is a 'public emergency':

'There exists a terrorist threat to the United Kingdom from persons suspected of involvement in international terrorism. In particular, there are foreign nationals present in the United Kingdom who are suspected of being concerned in the commission, preparation or instigation of acts of international terrorism...and who are a threat to the national security of the United Kingdom.' (Human Rights Act 1998 (Designated Derogation) Order 2001, 11 November 2001)

In order to detain a person under the 2001 Act, the Secretary of State has first to certify that it is believed that a person's presence in the UK is a 'risk to national security' *and* that it is suspected that the person is connected to international terrorism. Once a person has been certified, the immigration authorities may take any of the forms of immigration action listed in the boxes above which give rise to the power to detain. These forms of immigration action are usually intended to be taken when a person is to be deported or removed from the UK but in the case of 'suspected international terrorists' they may be taken *even though* the person cannot be removed for either legal or practical reasons (ss21–22 2001 Act).

The detention can continue indefinitely although those detained can obtain release by either appealing against the certificate, succeeding in a 'review' of the certificate or applying for bail. All three of these procedures must be conducted before the Special Immigration Appeals Commission (SIAC) ▶see pages 516-517. The Act seeks to also exclude the powers of the High Court to release people from detention in these cases.

These detention powers will continue initially until March 2003 but may be extended beyond then if the government thinks that it is necessary. If the government wishes to extend the powers beyond 10 November 2006, however, it would have to return to parliament and pass further legislation.

The limits on the power to detain

Although the powers of detention are set out in the legislation in very broad terms, important limitations on the powers have been imposed by:

- the courts in the UK;
- the European Convention on Human Rights.

We now look separately at how the powers have been limited in these ways.

Court limitations on detention powers

It can be seen from the boxes on pages 494-495, that the powers of detention are generally given for an identified purpose relating to immigration control. For example, persons are detained 'pending' their 'examination', or a 'decision' or their 'removal'. Where powers of detention exist, the courts have generally interpreted them narrowly so as to cause the least restriction on liberty. In *Hardial Singh*, Woolf J (as he was then) said:

'Whilst of course, Parliament is entitled to confer powers of administrative detention without trial, the courts will see to it that where such a power is conferred, the statute that confers it will be strictly and narrowly construed and its operation and effect will be supervised by the court to high standards.'

Woolf J then identified important limitations to the powers to detain which had to be implied into the powers given by the legislation. These principles were later confirmed by the Privy Council in *Tan Te Lam*, which concerned the detention by the authorities in Hong Kong of certain Vietnamese refugees. The four principles are:

1 Detention can *only* be used for the purpose of the particular immigration action for which the legislation allows it to be used ('removal' etc) and for no other reason.

2 A person may only be detained for as long as it is *reasonably necessary* to carry out the immigration action for which the power is given.

3 The immigration authorities must act with speed to ensure that the immigration action is carried out within a 'reasonable time'.

4 If it appears that the purpose cannot be carried out within a reasonable time, then detention will no longer be lawful and the person must be released.

Detention will therefore become unlawful if it is excessive, if steps are not being taken efficiently to carry out the immigration action or if it appears that the immigration action cannot be carried out at all or cannot be carried out within a reasonable time. In *Mahmod* (*Wasfi Suleman*), the High Court found that a 10 month detention in order to obtain a travel document was excessive. In *Chahal*, the court held that lengthy detention during the period taken for the judicial process to be exhausted was not necessarily unlawful and nor is extended detention brought about by a refusal to co-operate with the authorities. Although there is as yet no case law on the subject, the new powers to detain international terrorists do not appear to be restricted by the above principles. This is because the legislation itself states that persons may be detained *even though* the immigration action cannot be implemented.

ECHR limitations on detention powers

Detention must be in line with Article 5 ECHR (right to liberty) in order for it to be lawful. The European Court of Human Rights has rarely considered the nature of the protection provided by Article 5 in immigration cases. The matter arose in the Court of Appeal in *Saadi & Others* (the 'Oakington Reception Centre case'). The House of Lords heard the asylum-seekers' appeal in early May 2002 and a decision is awaited. In summary, immigration detention must not be 'arbitrary'; it must fall within either of the two 'immigration control' reasons in Article 5(1)(f); reasons for detention must be given and there must be speedy access to a court if it is alleged that the detention is unlawful.

The overriding purpose of Article 5: to prevent 'arbitrary detention'

The main purpose of Article 5 is to protect people from 'arbitrary' detention. Detention must, firstly, therefore be authorised by the law of the state. A good example is the case of *Amuur* (ECtHR) where a number of Somali asylum-seekers were detained in an airport transit zone in Paris. They could depart by aircraft but they could not enter France. The French authorities argued that they were not actually being 'detained' because they were free to leave. The court, however, held that holding the asylum-seekers in those circumstances was a 'deprivation of their liberty' under Article 5. The court also held that the detention was arbitrary and therefore unlawful because French law did not make any proper allowance for it in those circumstances. In particular, the asylum-seekers had no proper access to legal and other assistance.

Immigration detention under Article 5

Article 5 states that everyone has the right to liberty, which can only be taken away if certain limited exceptions apply. There are exceptions, for example, for those who are being prosecuted for criminal offences and those whose detention is justified as a result of their mental illness. Article 5(1)(f) contains the specific authority for a state to detain for the purposes of immigration control:

'5.1 Everyone has the right to liberty and security of person. No-one shall be deprived of his liberty save in the following cases and in accordance with a procedure prescribed by law:...

(f) the lawful arrest or detention of a person to prevent his effecting an unauthorised entry into the country or of a person against whom action is being taken with a view to deportation or extradition.'

Immigration detention is therefore justified under Article 5 in two circumstances: first a person may be detained to prevent them from entering the UK unlawfully and, secondly, a person may be detained if their departure from the UK is currently being enforced. We look at these two parts of Article 5(1)(f) separately.

The first part of Article 5(1)(f) ('to prevent his effecting an unauthorised entry'). This part is concerned with the control of people seeking to enter a state. So, for example, the detention of an asylum-seeker who arrives in the UK and claims asylum before any steps have been taken to enforce their departure should be considered under the first part of Article 5. Until recently, the meaning of the first part had hardly been considered by the courts. It has become particularly important, however, in the context of asylum-seekers seeking entry because it is impossible to make an immediate decision as to whether they are 'refugees' and therefore entitled to be admitted. The main point in *Amuur* (▶see above) was whether holding in the transit zone actually constituted detention. However, the ECtHR suggested that detention in these circumstances was only acceptable in order to 'prevent unlawful immigration'. This seems to suggest that the detention of an individual can only be justified under the first part of Article 5 where there is a risk that the person will abscond and be unlawfully at large in the UK.

If it is judged that the individual is not someone likely to abscond from temporary admission, then it might be thought that detaining that person does not 'prevent' them from entering unlawfully. This was the conclusion reached by Collins J in *Saadi & Others*. However, the Court of Appeal overturned that decision and decided that the first part of Article 5(1)(f) allowed the detention of asylum-seekers while a decision was made on their claim to asylum whether they were likely to abscond or not. The court came to this conclusion by drawing to attention the fact that established international law gives states the general right to decide whether to admit persons who are not their own nationals. The court then reasoned that Article 5 could not have been intended to force states to admit persons for a temporary period (to give them 'temporary admission' or its equivalent) simply because it would take some time to decide whether they qualified for admission as refugees.

The second part of Article 5(1)(f) ('against whom action is being taken with a view to deportation or extradition'). 'Deportation' in Article 5(1)(f) means any form of enforced departure. In the UK, it therefore includes deportation and any form of removal. 'Extradition' is, of course, a criminal procedure used for returning those who are charged with criminal offences in another country. In *Chahal*, the Secretary of State made a decision to deport an Indian national who had lived in the UK for many years on grounds of national security. Mr Chahal was also detained. Following the decision to deport, Mr Chahal made a claim for asylum. His detention therefore had to be justified under the second part of Article 5(1)(f) because deportation action was being taken. The ECtHR commented that the second part of Article 5(1)(f) did not mean that the state had to show that it was 'reasonably necessary' to detain Mr Chahal, for example to prevent him absconding or committing offences, in order to deport him. The state only had to show that action was being taken to enforce the departure of the person. The Court of Appeal has now confirmed that this is the law as far as the second part of Article 5(1)(f) is concerned (*Sezek*).

However, the court in *Chahal* also said that the deportation or removal proceedings must be 'in progress' and they must be being carried out with 'due diligence' by the state. If they are not, then the detention will be unlawful. It follows that deportation must also be 'possible' otherwise the deportation proceedings cannot be in progress (*Ali*, EComHR). The second part of Article 5 could not therefore be used as a justification for detaining a person who cannot be removed, for example, because they are permanently unfit to travel, or the country to which they could legally be removed will not accept them or because no practical arrangements can be made to effect their removal (recent examples would include nationals of Afghanistan and Kurds from the Kurdish Autonomous Region in Northern Iraq).

Excessive detention. Even if the detention satisfies all of the above, Article 5 also requires that the detention is not excessive (*Chahal*). *Chahal* was an exceptional case because Mr Chahal was a Sikh separatist leader who the Home Office was seeking to deport on the grounds that he was a threat to national security. The court held that, even though the deportation proceedings were being conducted with due diligence and that, even given the national security considerations, five years was an excessively long period of time for him to be detained. Clearly, in other cases periods of much less than five years may be considered to be excessive. In the *Oakington* case, the Court of Appeal decided that the main impact of the ECHR on immigration detention related to the length of detention. It said:

'The inroad that we believe that the European Court of Human Rights has made into the right of immigration authorities to detain aliens pending consideration of the applications for leave to enter, or their deportation, is that these processes must not be unduly prolonged'.

Of course, and as the Court of Appeal noted, detentions for excessive periods would be unlawful under the law as it was before the ECHR was incorporated ▶see pages 497-498 above.

The need for reasons for detention

Article 5(2) ECHR states:

'Everyone who is arrested shall be informed promptly, in a language which he understands, of the reasons for this arrest and of any charge against him.'

In April 1998, Lord Williams of Mostyn, speaking for the government in the House of Lords, accepted that the giving of written reasons improves decision-making and that detainees 'will know and have at least a degree of moral consolation that their detention is not an unthinking exercise of administrative power'.

Since October 1999, immigration officers have served written reasons for the decision to detain in the form of a checklist which, according to the *Operational Enforcement Manual*, should be interpreted for the applicant. The Detention Centre Rules require that detainees be given initial reasons for detention and further reasons every month (rule 9). The *Operational Enforcement Manual*, however, goes further and suggests that detention should be reviewed weekly by an immigration inspector (para 38.6). However, there have been difficulties. For example, it took the Home Office until February 2001 to add a note to the form given to Oakington detainees, which advised them that they had been detained in order to process their application for asylum quickly. For almost a year, detainees at Oakington were given inappropriate reasons for their detention with immigration officers ticking whichever of the checklist criteria could possibly apply when the detention was really for the purpose of speedy decision-making. Collins J referred to these failures on the part of the Home Office as 'disgraceful'.

'Speedy' review of detention

Article 5(4) ECHR requires that those who are detained are entitled to speedy access to a court to challenge the lawfulness of their detention. Strictly speaking, applying for 'bail' is not a review of the lawfulness of the detention. Bail can be given by the court or by an adjudicator simply because, although the detention is 'lawful', the court feels that a person can be released on bail usually under certain conditions. The *lawfulness* of a detention can only be challenged in the High Court or above in proceedings for judicial review or under a similar procedure called *habeas corpus* ▶see pages 525-526. It remains to be seen whether these procedures can be operated sufficiently quickly so as to comply with the Convention where a person has a case for saying that they are being detained unlawfully.

Who is likely to be detained?

Where a person *can* be detained for immigration reasons, it doesn't mean that they necessarily will be. Wherever a person can be detained, there is also a power to grant that person temporary admission so that they are not detained. A person who is detained may at any time be granted temporary admission and a person granted temporary admission may later be detained. For more details about 'temporary admission' ▶see pages 510-512. Within the limits of their powers, the immigration authorities therefore have a wide discretion as to when to detain.

All asylum applicants are subjected to an initial screening process. The details of the screening process change rapidly. However, one of the aims of screening is to determine whether it is appropriate to detain the person. For details about asylum procedures ▶see Chapter 10. The screening process is also designed to identify those whose claims may be processed at Oakington Reception Centre.

Detention policy

Decisions to detain are taken on the basis of criteria set out in policies developed by the immigration authorities. In December 1991 and September 1994, instructions were issued to officers setting out what was to be taken into account in deciding whether to detain. That policy was elaborated on in the White Paper *Fairer, Faster and Firmer – A Modern Approach to Immigration and Asylum* (July 1998) and the policy is now consolidated in the current *Operational Enforcement Manual*. Detention of asylum-seekers at Oakington Reception Centre is based on different criteria ▶see below.

The instructions to the immigration service staff dated 3 December 1991 and 20 September 1994 stated that detention should be authorised 'only when there is no alternative' and that 'the overriding consideration is whether the person is likely to comply voluntarily with any restrictions imposed, including any arrangements for removal'. The 1998 White Paper also confirmed that there is a presumption in favour of temporary admission or release. It stated that detention would be justified in the following circumstances:

- where there is a reasonable belief that the individual will fail to keep to the terms of temporary admission or release;
- initially, in order to clarify a person's identity and the basis of their asylum claim;
- where their removal is imminent.

The White Paper continued:

'In particular, where there is a systematic attempt to breach immigration control, detention is justified wherever one or more of those criteria is satisfied.'

The White Paper also indicated that evidence of torture should weigh strongly in favour of temporary admission while an asylum claim is being considered and that the detention of families with young children should be planned so that it is operated as close as possible to removal to ensure that families are not normally detained for more than a few days. It also states that unaccompanied minors should never be detained, other than in the most exceptional circumstances and then only overnight with appropriate care, for example, if they arrive unaccompanied at an airport. All cases of unaccompanied minor asylum-seekers should also be referred to the Refugee Council children's panel. Where reliable medical evidence indicates that a person is under 18 years of age, they are to be treated as minors.

The general policy set out in the 1998 White Paper has recently been changed in one important respect. In a letter circulated to immigration lawyers in October 2001, the immigration service announced that the new detention centres at Yarl's Wood, Dungavel and Harmondsworth contained dedicated family accommodation which ensures that family members are not separated. It was stated that the same criteria would therefore apply to families whose circumstances justified their detention, as it applied to single applicants. It was nevertheless stated that:

'In every case, the detention of a family, especially those with children, will have to be considered necessary in all the circumstances of the case. There

DETENTION POLICY

The factors which the *Operational Enforcement Manual* states must be taken into account in deciding to detain are *whether*:

- a person has an appeal pending or representations outstanding which may give them more incentive to comply with any conditions of temporary admission;
- the person has cause for reasonable expectations about the outcome of their case which provide an incentive not to abscond;
- there is the likelihood of the person being removed and, if so, in what timescale;
- there is any evidence of a previous failure to comply with conditions of temporary release or bail;
- the person has taken part in a determined attempt to breach the immigration laws (e.g., entry in breach of a deportation order, attempted or actual clandestine entry);
- there is a previous history of complying with the requirements of immigration control (e.g., by applying for a visa, or applying in time for further leave);
- the person has close ties with the UK, for example, whether there are close relatives in the UK, there are dependants who rely on the person in the UK and whether the person has a settled address or employment;
- the person is a minor (under 18);
- the person has a history of torture;
- the person has a history of physical or mental ill health.

The *Operational Manual* also states that persons who come within any of the following categories should only be considered suitable for detention in 'very exceptional circumstances':

- unaccompanied children and persons under the age of 18;
- the elderly, especially where they require supervision;
- pregnant women, unless there is the clear prospect of early removal and medical advice suggests that there is no question of their needing to be confined before removal;
- those suffering from serious medical conditions or the mentally ill;
- cases where there is independent evidence that the person has been tortured;
- people with serious disabilities.

In addition, the *Operational Manual* identifies the following people who are 'normally considered unsuitable' for detention in dedicated Immigration Service detention facilities but 'may be detained in alternative locations, such as prison hospitals or prisons with immigration detention units':

- the physically violent or emotionally disturbed;
- those with a violent or serious criminal background;
- those with suicidal tendencies;
- determined absconders.

The policy relating to these categories must also, however, be read together with the statement in the 2002 White Paper concerning detention in prisons ▶see page 492.

Special exercises

From time to time the immigration authorities initiate 'special exercises'. The immigration service has stated that these take place 'when we perceive there to be a threat to the integrity of immigration control, as, for example, when people whose asylum applications have been refused and whose appeals have been dismissed by the Immigration Appellate Authority simply return to the UK . . . and make a fresh application for asylum'. Detention may well result from a person being subject to a special exercise but the criteria are not clear and chief immigration officers will generally not comment upon them.

will remain a general presumption in favour of granting temporary admission and release. No family will be detained simply because suitable family accommodation is available'.

The 1991, 1994 and 1998 policy statements have been *consolidated* in the *Operation Enforcement Manual*, which identifies the factors which should be taken into account in exercising the power to detain and give further guidance as to when detention can be used. The policy contained in the *Enforcement Manual* is summarised in the box above.

If the immigration authorities fail to properly follow their own guidelines as to when to detain, the detention will be unlawful. The High Court has been fairly strict in ensuring that detention is carried out reasonably and in accordance with the established guidance. In *B*, by reference to the above criteria, the High Court held that the continuing detention of an asylum-seeker for two months after his identity had been established and sureties offered, was unlawful. In *AKB*, McCullough J indicated that the possession of false documents alone was not a good reason to detain an asylum-seeker and that all the factors needed to be balanced. In *Ferko*, the court dealt with the practice of detaining heads of households in order to deter other family members from absconding. That approach was held to be lawful only so long as there was a reasonable apprehension that the person who is being detained is otherwise likely to abscond. The Home Office *Operational Enforcement Manual* itself states that:

'detention for purposes such as deterrence to others where detention is not necessary for the purposes of removal of the individual is not compatible with Article 5 ECHR'.

International guidelines

Although they are not formally part of the law and therefore not binding, further useful indications of acceptable criteria for detention policy can be taken from the United Nations High Commissioner for Refugees (UNHCR) and the International Covenant on Civil and Political Rights (ICCPR).

Importantly, the Chief Adjudicator in *Bail: Guidance Notes for Adjudicators from the Chief Adjudicator* (re-issued in February 2002), states that adjudicators should have regard both to the criteria set out in the policies of the immigration authorities (▶see above) and the UNHCR Guidelines (see para 1.3 *Guidance Notes*).

The UNHCR Geneva office issued guidelines on the detention of asylum-seekers in February 1999: *UNHCR revised guidelines on applicable criteria and standards relating to the detention of asylum-seekers*. They state that regard should be had to the general principal that asylum-seekers should not be detained. The only permissible exceptions to that rule are:

• for the purposes of a preliminary interview to determine the elements on which the claim for asylum is based;

- where the applicant has destroyed or used fraudulent travel or identity documents and is failing to comply with procedures for verifying their identity;
- in order to protect national security and public order.

The UNHCR's guidelines also state that detention should not interfere with the asylum-seeker's ability to pursue their application for asylum. They also set out certain procedural protections similar to those contained in Article 5 ECHR. They suggest that asylum-seekers are entitled to: prompt communication of reasons for detention and their rights in connection with it and their rights to free legal advice. The UNHCR also advises that unaccompanied elderly persons, torture or trauma victims or persons with mental or physical disabilities, should only be detained if a qualified doctor certifies that detention will not adversely affect their health and well being.

Further guidance may be obtained from the UN International Covenant on Civil and Political Rights (ICCPR). The ICCPR is ratified by the UK but is not incorporated into UK law. It gives an indication of the approach to detention in international human rights law. Article 9 of the ICCPR is also intended to protect persons against arbitrary detention. Applying the ICCPR in relation to the detention of boat people seeking asylum in *A v Australia*, the UN Human Rights Committee stated that the detention of an asylum-seeker could be considered arbitrary if it was,

'not necessary in all the circumstances of the case, for example, to prevent flight or interference with evidence.'

Detention at Oakington Reception Centre

Oakington Reception Centre in Cambridgeshire was opened in March 2000. It is a detention centre solely for asylum applicants and operates on a completely different set of criteria to all other immigration detention. Although it is described as a 'Reception' centre, Oakington is a designated place of detention and asylum applicants referred there are detained. The doors are locked and it is not possible for Oakington 'residents' to leave of their own free will.

Oakington Detention policy

Following the establishment of this detention centre, Barbara Roche, the then Home Office Minister, announced to Parliament on 16 March 2000 that:

'[asylum] applicants will be detained at Oakington where it appears that their application can be decided quickly, including those which may be certified as manifestly unfounded ... If the claim cannot be decided in [a period of about seven days], the applicant will be granted temporary admission or, if necessary in line with existing criteria, moved to another place of detention. If the claim is refused, a decision about further detention will similarly be made in accordance with existing criteria. Thus detention in this latter category of cases will normally be to effect removal or where it has become apparent that the person will fail to keep in contact with the immigration service'.

The policy reason given for detention at Oakington is, therefore, not the risk of an asylum applicant absconding, or any similar concerns, but instead it is in order for the claim to be dealt with 'quickly'. In fact the *Operational Enforcement Manual* sets out certain categories of person who are unsuitable for Oakington and should *not* be detained there, which includes anyone who is an absconding risk (▶see below).

The most important factor in deciding whether to detain is the nationality of the applicant. In the case of some countries, any asylum-seeker who is a national of that country could be detained at Oakington. In the case of others, whether the person is suitable for Oakington depends upon the nature of the claim for asylum. For example, Turkish nationals who may be referred to Oakington are those whose claims are based on their ethnic origin, evasion of military service, the involvement of their family members in illegal organisations, membership of 'HADEP' or their religion. Iraqi asylum-seekers can be detained at Oakington but only if they are Kurds from the autonomous region who speak Sorani and who fear persecution because of their membership of one of the Kurdish political parties. Asylum applicants from Pakistan may also be detained there but not those whose claim is based upon their being Ahmadi, Christians or women because those claims are treated as being of a more complex nature. These are only examples of the criteria for individual countries.

It must be remembered that the list of nationals and the kinds of claim which may be referred to Oakington are under constant review and are likely to change. However, at the time of the last announcement (7 January 2002), applicants from the following countries could be detained at Oakington: Albania, Bangladesh, Bolivia, Brazil, Bulgaria, Cameroon, China, Congo (Brazzaville), Cote D'Ivoire, Czech Republic, Estonia, Equador, Ghana, Hungary, India, Indonesia, Iraq, Federal Republic of Yugoslavia, Kenya, Latvia, Lithuania, Macedonia, Malaysia, Nepal, Nigeria, Pakistan, Poland, Romania, Slovakia, Slovenia, Tanzania, Turkey, Uganda, Ukraine, Zimbabwe.

The following categories of applicants should *not* be referred to Oakington, even if they satisfy the nationality/claim criteria (see *Operational Enforcement Manual*):

- persons not belonging to one of the nationalities listed above;
- any case which does not appear to be one in which a quick decision can be reached;
- any case, which has complicating factors, or issues, which are unlikely to be resolved within the constraints of the Oakington process. A person whose case at first appeared to be one which could be dealt with quickly but which is later identified as being more complex, should be transferred out of the Oakington system;

- unaccompanied minors;
- cases where there is a dispute as to whether the asylum applicant is a minor, other than where there is clear and irrefutable documentary evidence that the applicant is aged 18 years or over;
- disabled applicants, save but the most easily manageable;
- any person who has special medical needs, except those whose needs can be managed within a GP surgery environment;
- any person who gives reason to believe that they might not be suitable for the relaxed Oakington regime, including those who are considered likely to abscond.

What happens at Oakington?

The purpose of Oakington is to examine and make a decision on the asylum claim within 7 to 10 days. Once detained at Oakington, those applicants who are not already represented are offered advice from either the Refugee Legal Centre or the Immigration Advisory Service. These organisations have case-workers on site to advise, be present at interviews and to make representations about the application. The applicants are interviewed about the claim and, after a further short time is allowed for further representations to be made, the case papers are given to a Home Office official for a determination of the claim. Decisions granting or refusing asylum are given to the applicants while they are at Oakington. If asylum is refused and the applicant appeals, a further decision is then taken as to whether to continue the detention. This decision is taken on the basis of the 'ordinary' criteria, ▶see the box on page 504.

About 80 per cent of Oakington detainees are released after they receive a decision and are therefore free while they appeal. The rest move on to detention at other detention facilities. Many of those released are dispersed to be supported by the National Asylum Support Service (NASS) in different places around the country. Refugee Council assistants are also on site at Oakington to help detainees make their applications for asylum support. The Refugee Legal Centre has complained about being unable to trace their clients to give them further legal advice after they have been dispersed from Oakington.

The significance of 'Oakington' detention

The Oakington centre represents a very significant change in policy towards detention both in terms of the reasons for the detention and the numbers detained. The centre has a capacity to hold approximately 400 detainees. If it operates at full capacity and the detention lasts a period of seven days, then it is capable of detaining up to 20,800 people a year, representing more than 25 per cent of the total number of asylum applicants in the year 2000. This compares with the previous figure of 1.5 per cent of asylum-seekers who were detained.

The lawfulness of detention at Oakington was challenged in judicial review proceedings (*Saadi & others,* CA). The four Kurdish Iraqi asylum-seekers' case is that their detention is contrary to Article 5 and that the centre could be operated just as well as a genuine reception centre without actually locking the asylum-seekers in. The Court of Appeal decided that the detention was lawful; a further decision is awaited from the House of Lords.

Inspection of detention

HM Chief Inspector of Prisons, Anne Owers, is currently undertaking a review of immigration detention as part of her responsibilities to inspect the conditions of people detained in the UK's prisons. There is no report yet available. The visiting committees set up under the Detention Centre Rules (▶see above) also have a duty to provide annual reports to the Home Office concerning the state of immigration detention centres.

Previous reports concerning immigration detention make disturbing reading. The former HM Chief Inspector of Prisons, Sir David Ramsbotham, following a short unannounced visit to HMP Rochester in 1999, stated:

'Most of all I must express my concern at the poor treatment and conditions of the numbers of asylum-seekers, immigration detainees and other foreign nationals who form almost half the prison population.

'Detainees were treated as if they were unconvicted prisoners. This approach seemed to be based on guidelines from the Immigration and Nationality Directorate and was adopted by prison staff in their dealings with them'.

One incident witnessed by Sir David illustrates the lack of care and sensitivity with which immigration detainees are often faced:

'A detainee who had never been in custody before, was placed in a double cell with another who was from Poland and who spoke no English. The officer escorting him addressed the Pole and said in a clear loud slow voice, "You tell him what goes on" and closed the cell door on the two people. The new arrival was from Albania and spoke no English. The Pole and the Albanian did not share a common language. We asked on what basis he had been allocated to that particular cell and found it was because of available space and the fact that both names ended with an "i". The member of staff concerned made no effort to discover whether either person had under-stood what he had just said, could communicate with each other or knew what was going to happen to them next. When we challenged this approach, the member of staff concerned assured us that this was common practice and invariably resulted in the detainees communicating at some level'.

25 Getting people out of detention

The immigration authorities never *have* to detain a person. Whenever they have a *power* to detain, they can also grant a restricted period of residence in the UK usually called 'temporary admission' (▶see below). The immigration authorities can release someone who has been detained and re-detain a person who has been temporarily admitted or released. The first means, therefore, of dealing with the powers of detention is to try to persuade the immigration authorities not to detain. The immigration authorities also have a power to grant 'bail' which is similar to temporary admission but it allows the immigration authorities to accept sureties for a person's release which they cannot otherwise do.

In most cases, people who are detained can also apply to the immigration appellate authorities to be released on bail ▶see pages 513-516. In a few cases, it may be appropriate to apply to the High Court to obtain the release of an immigration detainee in judicial review or *habeas corpus* proceedings ▶see pages 525-526.

Temporary admission, temporary release and restriction orders

'Temporary admission', 'temporary release' and admission under a 'restriction order' are all ways of allowing people who could be detained to have their freedom. They are, however, very similar. Technically, 'temporary admission' is a power normally exercised by an immigration officer instead of detaining a person. 'Temporary release' is granted by an immigration officer in order to release a person who actually is detained. Those persons who are under 'restriction orders' are people who would otherwise be detained under the authority of the Secretary of State (the Home Office), rather than an immigration officer (ie. deportation cases ▶see box on page 495). However the 2002 Bill proposes to allow the Home Office (as well as immigration officers) to detain certain people who were previously the responsibility only of the immigration service. In parallel, the 2002 Bill proposes to allow the Home Office to grant temporary admission in these cases as well. These are changes in the personnel who operate the powers of temporary admission, not the powers themselves.

The phrase 'temporary admission' is generally used as a shorthand to refer to all three powers and we will therefore refer to them all by that general term.

Applying for temporary admission

It is always possible to ask the Home Office or the immigration service to consider the temporary admission of a person who is being examined or detained under immigration powers. An attempt should be made in the first place to speak on the telephone to the official dealing with the case, requesting the reasons for detention. Representatives should try to address the criteria for detention listed in the *Operational Enforcement Manual* (▶see page 504) and explain why detention is not appropriate in the particular case ▶see pages 726-727 for contact details of ports and immigration offices. It is more likely that an individual will be released if suitable accommodation is offered. If the matter cannot be solved by a telephone call, it is important to follow up in writing the request for temporary admission and for written reasons for the detention.

Detention is supposed to be regularly reviewed. It is possible, therefore, to request release repeatedly and for it to be reconsidered over a long period of detention. New factors, like the distress caused to the detainee and his or her family, medical evidence of the effect of the detention or a new address becoming available, may all be useful.

Conditions of temporary admission

If temporary admission is granted, it will normally be subject to conditions which may include requirements to live at a particular address and report at specified intervals to the police or immigration service. It will also often include a prohibition on work. Work prohibitions are normally imposed on asylum-seekers but it is Home Office policy to lift those restrictions if there has been no initial decision on the asylum application for six months. In addition, the *Operational Enforcement Manual* states that illegal entrants and overstayers should not have work prohibitions imposed if the resolution of their case is likely to take a substantial amount of time or if the person is supporting dependants by working. Following release, an application can be made to the same authority to change these conditions. The conditions are written on the form on which the temporary admission is granted.

Importance of an address

It is difficult to obtain temporary admission without an accommodation address. Where the person is an asylum-seeker and cannot provide an address through their own contacts in the UK, they may be entitled to support from the National Asylum Support Service (NASS) ▶see Chapter 32. That support can include the provision of accommodation. There has been confusion over whether NASS and its 'assistants', such as the Refugee

Council and the Refugee Arrivals Project, can provide an address for those who are detained. However, those assistants will generally be willing to provide an offer of accommodation to detainees who are otherwise without accommodation and they can be approached to provide a letter in support.

Period of temporary admission

It is normal for temporary admission to be given for a set period of time at the end of which the person has to report to the immigration authorities. If there has been no change of circumstances in the case but the case has not resolved by that time and the conditions have been complied with, temporary admission will normally be renewed for a further period. Often this can be done in writing without the person actually having to report.

If, however, the case appears to be moving towards the stage where the immigration authorities will soon be enforcing the individual's departure, then the person may be detained when they report. Indeed, the initial period of temporary admission can often be cut short for this purpose. For obvious reasons, it is very unlikely that the immigration service will confirm in advance that they will detain someone when they report.

Induction and accommodation centres

The Home Secretary has the power, aside from the NASS system of support, to provide accommodation and board to those granted temporary admission (see s4 1999 Act). At the moment, this power is used to provide support for people who no longer qualify for NASS support but may be able to get support from the 'hard cases' fund. In the 2002 Bill, the government is proposing to set up new 'induction' and 'accommodation' centres where asylum-seekers will not be detained but will be provided with support as people with temporary admission ▶see pages 719-721 for more details.

Bail from chief immigration officer or police inspector

Wherever there is power for an immigration adjudicator or the Immigration Appeal Tribunal to grant bail (▶see the boxes below on pages 514-515), a person may also be released on bail by a chief immigration officer (CIO). In addition, where bail can be granted on the basis that there is an appeal outstanding (▶see the same boxes), bail can be granted by a CIO or a police Inspector. The 2002 Bill proposes to allow Home Office officials (i.e. not just CIOs) to be able to exercise this power to grant bail. It is likely that the power to grant bail will be with the CIO for the first eight days of a detention, following which it will transfer to the Home Office. However CIOs may still act on *behalf* of the Home Office. Again these are changes in the personnel operating the powers, not substantive changes to the powers to grant bail.

The difference between bail and temporary admission is that the CIO can accept sureties which may be sufficient to justify the grant of bail although not temporary admission. Bail is not often granted by CIOs, partly because they tend to ask for very substantial amounts from sureties before they are prepared to grant bail, but also partly because advisers often do not request CIO bail as an alternative to temporary admission. *The Operation Enforcement Manual* gives an idea of the level of surety a CIO might ask for (para 39.5.1):

'Each case should be assessed on its individual merits but a figure of between £2,000 and £5,000 per surety will normally be appropriate. Where there is a strong financial incentive to remain here, it is justifiable to fix bail (or suggest to the adjudicator that it be fixed) at a larger sum'.

If there are sureties available, it is often worth trying to get CIO bail if the application for temporary admission fails.

Bail from the adjudicator or Immigration Appeal Tribunal

The powers of the immigration appellate authorities (the adjudicators and the Immigration Appeal Tribunal) to grant bail are often confusing. The powers have changed over the years. In many cases, there are overlapping powers to grant bail. For instance, a person may be entitled to apply for bail on the grounds that they are to be removed having been refused entry but *also* because they have an appeal outstanding before the adjudicator against the decision to refuse entry. When a person is detained and he or she is eligible to apply for bail, they should be given a form by the immigration authorities (forms IS98 and IS98A) informing them of their right to apply for bail and how to apply.

At the outset of a bail hearing, adjudicators often like to identify the relevant power to grant bail. Advisers should satisfy themselves that there is a power to grant bail before applying so as not to raise false expectations as well as time and money. The relevant powers of the immigration appellate authorities to grant bail, following the amendments made by the 1999 Act, are set out in the boxes below. For the powers to grant bail in national security cases ▶see pages 516-517.

Who cannot get bail from the adjudicator or Immigration Appeal Tribunal

The box below sets out those categories of people who *can* apply for bail to the immigration appellate authorities. Anyone falling into the following groups, *who does not have an immigration appeal pending as set out below in the box,* cannot be granted bail from the appellate authorities:

1 New arrivals to the UK, who are not illegal entrants and who are detained while they are examined by the immigration officer before a decision regarding their entry is made. They cannot apply for bail *during the first seven days* following the date of their arrival. After the seven-day period, they can be granted bail.

PERSONS WHO MAY BE GRANTED BAIL BY AN ADJUDICATOR

Port cases

- new arrivals to the UK who are detained while being examined by the immigration officer *but they cannot be given bail until seven days after the date of their arrival in the UK;*

Power to grant bail
Immigration Act 1971 Sch 2 para 22(1)(a), (1A), (1B)

- those who already have leave to enter when they arrive in the UK which is suspended by an immigration officer and are detained while they are examined further or while a decision is being made as to whether to cancel the leave, or after removal directions have been set after the cancellation of leave;

Power to grant bail
Immigration Act 1971 Sch 2 paras 22(1)(aa), (1A), 34

- those who arrive in the UK and are refused leave to enter (or are suspected of being such persons) and are detained pending a decision as to whether to remove them or after removal directions have been given;

Power to grant bail
Immigration Act 1971 Sch 2 paras 22(1)(b), (1A), 34

Illegal entrants

- those detained as illegal entrants (or suspected illegal entrants), pending a decision as to whether to remove them or after removal directions have been given;

Power to grant bail
Immigration Act 1971 Sch 2 paras 22(1)(b), (1A), 34

Overstayers and others

- those detained as overstayers, persons who have breached conditions of leave, persons who have obtained leave to remain by deception (and those suspected of being any of the above), pending

a decision as to whether to remove them or after removal directions have been given;

Power to grant bail
Immigration Act 1971 Sch 2 paras 22(1)(b), (1A), 34
Immigration and Asylum Act 1999 s10 (7)

Those who have appeals pending before the adjudicator

- those who are detained under the authority of an *immigration officer* (▶see box on page 494) and have any of the following 'in-country' appeals pending: against refusal of entry, a human rights/race discrimination appeal, an asylum appeal against refusal of entry or removal as an illegal entrant, an asylum appeal against removal to a safe third country, an appeal against the lawfulness of directions for removal (as an illegal entrant, an overstayer or person who has breached their conditions of stay, a person who has obtained leave by deception or the family member of any of those people) or an appeal against the destination of removal;

Power to grant bail
Immigration Act 1971 Sch 2 para 29(1)(3)

- those who are detained under the authority of the *Secretary of State* (▶see box on page 495) and have any of the following 'in-country' appeals pending: asylum or non-asylum appeals against a notice of intention to make a deportation order, an in-country appeal against the lawfulness of directions for removal (in the same circumstances as above for those detained by an immigration officer) or an appeal against the destination of removal.

Power to grant bail
Immigration Act 1971 Sch 2 para 29(1)(3), Sch 3 para 3

PERSONS WHO MAY BE GRANTED BAIL BY THE IMMIGRATION APPEAL TRIBUNAL

- persons who appealed to the adjudicator on any of the bases set out in the box above **and** *either*:

  (a) have made an application for leave to appeal to the IAT which has not yet been decided; *or*

  (b) have made an application for leave to appeal to the IAT which has been granted.

  Note: In certain cases leave to appeal to the IAT *must* be granted: appeals against refusals of entry where the person holds a certificate of entitlement or an entry clearance (Immigration and Asylum Act 1999 Sch 4 para 7).

  Power to grant bail
  Immigration Act 1971 Sch 2 para 29(1)(4), Sch 3 para 3

- persons who are detained under the authority of an immigration officer (▶ see box on page 494) and are appealing to the Court of Appeal (or, for cases decided in Scotland, the Court of Sessions) against a decision of the IAT and who therefore have *either*:

  (a) an application for leave to appeal to the Court of Appeal outstanding; *or*

  (b) been granted leave to appeal to the Court of Appeal

  (It should be noted that bail can also be granted by a CIO, police officer or adjudicator in these circumstances).

  Power to grant bail
  Section 9A Asylum and Immigration Appeals Act 1993

2 Those detained following a recommendation for deportation by a criminal court.

3 Those detained following a notice of intention to make a deportation order (although they may well have an appeal pending or be able to make an appeal which would enable bail to be granted).

4 Those detained following the making of a deportation order.

However, the Immigration and Asylum Act 1999 Act (s54) does contain provisions which change the law so that immigration adjudicators can grant bail to people who have had a recommendation for deportation, or been given a notice of intention to deport or a deportation order. Unfortunately, like the provisions for automatic bail hearings, these powers have not been brought into force by the government. The government has, however, affirmed that it will bring these powers into effect (para 4.83, 2002 White Paper) and they are not proposed to be repealed by the 2002 Bill. Therefore, people should shortly be able to apply for bail in deportation cases from an adjudicator, even where there is no appeal pending.

In addition, people who are at present detained for immigration reasons after having been given a recommendation for deportation by a criminal court may be released by the criminal court which made the recommendation. If the person appeals against their conviction, or against the recommendation to the next criminal court (usually the Crown Court or the criminal division of the Court of Appeal), that court can order that the person is released.

Cases where there is a 'right' to bail from the IAT

The circumstances in which the IAT can grant bail are set out in the box above. In certain cases, there is a *right* to be granted bail from the IAT *unless* certain limited conditions apply. In *any* of the following circumstances, provided the applicant enters a 'recognizance' (i.e. agrees to be bound by the terms of bail) and has sufficient and satisfactory sureties, if the IAT requires them, the IAT *must* grant bail:

- the IAT has granted leave to appeal to the IAT from a decision of an adjudicator; or

- the Home Office is applying for leave to appeal or has been granted leave to appeal, from the decision of IAT to the Court of Appeal (or, in Scotland, the Court of Sessions); or

- the applicant for bail has been granted leave to appeal from the decision of the IAT to the Court of Appeal (or, in Scotland, the Court of Sessions).

Even in these cases, however, the IAT does *not* have to grant bail if the applicant:

- has previously breached conditions of bail;

- is likely to commit an offence or cause a danger to public health if released;

- is suffering from a mental disorder which makes detention necessary in the person's own interests or for the protection of others; or

- is under the age of 17 if no satisfactory arrangements for their care have been made.

In all other cases (as is the case with CIOs, police inspectors and adjudicators), the power of the IAT to grant bail is discretionary, although the above considerations are all relevant.

Bail from Special Immigration Appeals Commission

People whose detention has been certified by the Home Office as necessary in the interests of national security or who are detained having been excluded from the UK or are being deported from the UK on national security grounds, must apply to the Special Immigration Appeals Commission (SIAC) for bail (see s3 and Sch 3 Special Immigration Appeals Commission Act 1997).

If a person is detained after the Secretary of State has certified them as a 'suspected international terrorist' under the Anti-terrorism, Crime and Security Act 2001 (for details of this Act and the certificate ▶see pages 496-497), they must also apply to SIAC in order to be released on bail (see s24 2001 Act). These people may also obtain release by a SIAC review or by appealing against the certificate. SIAC must review a certificate that a person is a suspected international terrorist six months after it is issued, unless the person has appealed against the certificate in which case the review takes place six months after the determination of the appeal. After the first review, SIAC must review the certificate again every three months. SIAC may also review a certificate on the request of the applicant, or even on its own initiative if it thinks that a review should be held because of a change of circumstances (see s26, 2001 Act).

Very few cases have been dealt with by SIAC and it is essential that anyone who is certified as a national security risk or as a suspected international terrorist is referred for specialist advice.

Applying for bail before the Immigration Appellate Authority

The procedure governing bail applications before the Immigration Appellate Authority (the adjudicators and IAT), is set out in rule 34 of the Immigration and Asylum (Appeals) Procedure Rules 2000. An application for bail should be started by completing the bail application form which can be obtained from the Immigration Appelate Authority (IAA) ►see page 726 for addresses. Public funding is available for representation at bail hearings as it is for appeals. The form of public funding is 'Controlled Legal Representation'.

The application for bail

The form asks for the amount of the 'recognizance' (money) which the applicant agrees to be bound by and the names, addresses, occupations and the amounts of recognizances in which two sureties agree to be bound. The requirement for the appellant to offer recognizance is a formality and a nominal sum of say £5 can be put forward which the applicant does not have to actually produce. Although the form to apply for bail gives the impression that two sureties must be available, there is no such requirement in the law and this has been confirmed in *Bail Guidance Notes for Adjudicators from the Chief Adjudicator* (re-issued in February 2002, see para 2.2.2). In *Brezinski and Glowacka*, Kay J stated:

'Clearly it would be wrong to require sureties, if there were no need for sureties, but where one reaches a situation where one cannot otherwise be sure that the obligation will be observed, Parliament has rightly provided that that extra ammunition is available to a Special Adjudicator dealing with these matters if, in fact, that will have the consequence that a person who might not otherwise be granted his liberty will be granted it'.

In *Lamin Minteh* (8 March 1996), the Court of Appeal decided that it was unlawful for an adjudicator not to grant bail if there were no sureties regardless of whether there was evidence that the applicant was likely to abscond.

The address at which it is proposed the applicant will reside should also be stated on the form. Many bail applications are successful with no sureties or with sureties offering fairly low sums such as hundreds rather than thousands of pounds.

This completed form should then be sent to the Immigration Appellate Authority who will notify the Home Office. The Home Office will then arrange for the police to check the status of any sureties who are named on the form before the application is heard. People with criminal convictions are unlikely to be acceptable as sureties. A Practice Direction issued by the Chief Adjudicator in July 2001 states that bail applications should be listed for hearing within three working days of the application being received.

Once the security checks have been done and if the Home Office is opposing the grant of bail, written reasons for opposing bail are drawn up. This Home Office 'bail summary' is usually only produced or read out at the hearing itself, which is unsatisfactory because the applicant may not be prepared to meet all the points contained in it. The Home Office has explained that, because bail hearings are listed at short notice, it is not always possible to send out bail summaries. However, the *Operational Enforcement Manual* suggests that bail summaries should be given to representatives before the hearing if they request them (para 39.6.1.2). Also, in a letter of January 2001 to Bail for Immigration Detainees, the Home Office indicated that it is possible to see the summary before the hearing:

'Detainees now receive the reasons for detention form IS91R giving them details of why they have been detained. Unless circumstances have changed significantly between detention and the hearing, the bail summary is basically an amplification of those reasons. If representatives want to see the summary earlier, they can contact the presenting officers' unit or port concerned, but they should be aware that summaries are only drafted shortly before the hearing'.

Preparing for the bail hearing

When taking details from the detainee, regard should be had to Home Office policy on detention (▶see pages 502-506), the reasons for detention given on the form given to the applicant at the time of, or shortly after the initial detention, and any other reasons that are likely to be contained in the bail summary.

Common issues arising include:

- why did s/he enter with false documentation?
- why didn't s/he approach an immigration officer immediately on arrival?
- why not inform the immigration officer immediately when questioned that s/he wished to make application for asylum?
- why 'choose' to enter United Kingdom clandestinely?
- what reasons are there for having previously failed to comply with conditions of temporary admission?
- why did the person fail to claim asylum in a third country which they have passed through?
- does the applicant have contacts in the UK?
- does the applicant have an address?
- what prospects does the applicant have of remaining in the UK – is there an appeal outstanding which provides an incentive to comply?

Common responses are: the inability to obtain or leave the country of nationality with a valid passport; distrust of officials following experiences in the applicant's own country; the detainee was following the instructions of an agent and inability to enter the UK through legitimate means as an asylum-seeker. However, in order to convey these reasons to the adjudicator, the detainee's own response will have to be obtained prior to the hearing. In the Divisional Court in *Adimi & Sorani*, Simon Brown LJ acknowledged that failure to claim asylum at the border could be due to 'the effects of trauma, language problems, lack of information, previous experiences with authority, and feelings of insecurity.'

In *Bugdaycay*, Lord Bridge made the following comments about the circumstances of the case under consideration before the House of Lords:

'**the appellant has always put forward the explanation that he had been advised to try to gain entry as a visitor and then to seek asylum through the 'refugee office' in London, which seems not to be wholly implausible'**.

Release on bail will almost always be subject to conditions and the detainee must agree to any such conditions. It is therefore advisable for representatives to describe to the applicant the likely conditions and ensure that he or she understands and is willing to comply with them. Common conditions are signing at a police station at specified times and residing at a particular address. It is therefore a good idea to identify the nearest police station to the address at which it is suggested that the applicant will stay. A detainee (and their sureties) should also be advised that a failure to comply with the conditions is likely to lead to re-detention with little prospect of further release on bail as well as the possible loss of the sureties' money. Breach of conditions could also have negative consequences for the resolution of the person's case.

Sureties

As stated above, there is no absolute requirement for sureties. The sureties named on the bail form will be checked by the immigration authorities for unspent criminal records or having come to adverse notice in other immigration matters. If the surety comes forward after the bail application notice has been sent, the immigration authorities should be contacted directly with the details. If the surety does not come forward until the day of the hearing, adjudicators are often willing to allow a short adjournment for the presenting officer to telephone through the details of a surety so that they can be immediately checked.

There is always the potential for a conflict of interest for a representative when dealing with a detainee and their sureties. For these reasons, representatives often advise sureties that they should get independent advice if they are unsure or uncertain of the commitment that they are entering into.

Ability of surety to exercise control

In addition to the size of the amounts offered, the most important qualities of the surety are the extent to which he or she is able to exercise control over the actions of the applicant and the extent to which the applicant will be deterred from absconding from bail for fear of the surety losing their money. It is therefore always useful to take details from sureties about how they know the detainee and for how long they have known each other.

Adjudicators usually prefer a surety who will be living with or near to the bail applicant. Where the applicant is not going to live with the surety, then an adjudicator will be concerned as to how the surety will supervise the applicant and ensure that s/he is complying with conditions of bail. Details should be taken as to whether the surety could arrange a certain time to meet the applicant or make regular visits to the address where s/he will be staying or whether s/he would agree to telephone the applicant on a regular basis in order that contact is maintained. Sureties may wish to assure the court that, if the applicant were to abscond or fail to comply with conditions of bail, then s/he would immediately notify the immigration service and the applicant's solicitors of this fact.

Consideration should also be given to whether the surety can give any evidence to counter the reasons given for detention. For example, where the immigration authorities are questioning the identity of an applicant, a surety may be able to give evidence about this and produce documentary evidence such as photographs in support.

Amount and evidence of surety

The sureties should provide evidence of the money they are putting forward as the amount they are prepared to stand. Bank or building society savings statements of account are often produced for this purpose. Evidence of statements and passbooks should cover the past three months with evidence of current balances. If the money is in a savings account, then the account should be in the sole name of the surety. If the account is in joint names, then a letter should be obtained from the other account holder confirming that s/he consents to the funds being used in this way. Where a large amount of money has recently been placed in an account, an adjudicator may be suspicious as to whether the money really does belong to the surety or has simply been placed there for the purposes of the bail application and may shortly afterwards be transferred back. Details should therefore be taken as to any significant recent transactions contained in the statements. Sureties should also produce wage slips or, if self-employed, a copy of their latest set of accounts. If other assets (e.g. property) are being relied on, documentary evidence of their value and equity should be produced.

Sometimes a surety's money is paid into the solicitor or representative's account with an undertaking being given by the representative that the money will be held there to the order of the court. According to the *Guidance Notes for Adjudicators* (para 2.3.3), adjudicators in England and Wales have no power to *require* that this is done but they can agree to it if it is proposed as an additional form of security.

As to the amount of money offered by the sureties, a relatively small amount would constitute a significant loss to an individual on a low income with a family. Therefore, it is often important to convey to the adjudicator what the consequences would be for the surety if s/he were to lose the money being offered. This has been acknowledged in *Guidance Notes for Adjudicators* in which it is advised:

'Assessment of the amount of the recognizance to be taken from a surety should be based upon the means of that surety.' (para 2.3.2)

However, this consideration can cut both ways. There is a danger of an adjudicator entering into a bidding war with sureties requiring larger amounts, having regard to the surety's apparent means. It is therefore necessary to be able to anticipate any suggestion that the failure to put forward all monies available in support of the application indicates any lack of trust on the part of the surety. This can be achieved by evidence that there are good reasons why any additional savings are not being offered in support, for example the surety's children's welfare, emergencies or other financial commitments.

Other evidence required from sureties

There is no absolute requirement that a surety be a British citizen or settled in the UK despite the fact that notices sent out to applicants often state that a surety must have evidence of their 'identity and settlement' in the UK. In addition, the presenting officer may raise objections to sureties who are not settled since the *Operational Enforcement Manual* states that acceptable sureties should be 'aged 18 or over and settled in the UK' (para 39.5.2). Those with an irregular immigration position in the UK will, however, clearly be unsuitable. Sureties should therefore usually bring to court evidence of their identity, nationality and, if not British, immigration status. Evidence of their occupation is often also useful. If the applicant is to live with the surety, evidence of the surety's property ownership should be produced. If the property is rented, some adjudicators require evidence that the landlord has no objection to the applicant residing at the property.

Attendance of sureties at hearing

Where sureties are offered, an adjudicator will almost always require their personal appearance. If, however, a surety is unable to appear in person, it is possible for an adjudicator to fix the conditions of bail and the amounts to be provided by the surety with a view to the bail actually being taken before another responsible person such as an immigration officer, police officer or solicitor (paras 22(3), 29 (6) Sch2 1971 Act). This is, however, very unusual and should only be used as a last resort.

Those without sureties

For those without sureties, the 'Bail Circle', set up by the Churches Commission for Racial Justice, has a register of people who are prepared to act as sureties for detainees. If no surety can be found, applicants and advisers should not be deterred from making bail applications. Bail can be granted without sureties if the adjudicator can be persuaded that this is the right course.

The bail hearing

The *Guidance Notes for Adjudicators*, indicate that adjudicators should approach the bail application in three stages:

'First, is this a case where bail should be granted in principle, subject to suitable conditions? Second, if so are sureties necessary? Third, if so are the sureties and recognizances offered satisfactory?' (para 2.7.3)

If the Home Office is opposing bail, it will prepare a statement setting out its reasons for doing so. While it is open to the presenting officer to expand upon the reasons contained in the statement, it is usual for them to simply rely upon it with no further elaboration.

The applicant's representative will then normally be required to respond to the reasons given for continued detention. If the applicant is 'produced' at the bail hearing, their oral evidence may be called. If the adjudicator is satisfied that it would be appropriate in principle for bail to be granted, then s/he may wish to hear from any sureties who are supporting the application.

Representatives should address the reasons given by the Home Office for opposing bail as well as making any relevant submissions concerning the Home Office's own criteria relating to detention and the UNHCR guidelines. The *Guidance Notes for Adjudicators* refer to there being a 'common law presumption in favour of bail' (see para 1.4). This presumption should apply *unless* the applicant has previously failed to comply with conditions of bail, is likely to commit offences, is a danger to public health, is suffering from a mental disorder or is under 17 and no proper arrangements for their case has been made (para 30 Sch2 1971 Act). Otherwise the burden of showing that bail should not be granted lies with the Home Office. The Guidance further states that adjudicators should consider the Immigration Service Instructions to Staff and the UNHCR guidelines on detention in addition to the contents of the White Paper of July 1998, *Fairer Faster and Firmer*.

The decision of the adjudicator or IAT

The approach to bail varies considerably from one adjudicator to another. Some adjudicators continue to approach applications in the belief that two sureties, each offering a substantial sum of money, are required for an application to succeed. The approach of the majority of adjudicators however has changed enormously over the years and adjudicators will often now grant bail with no sureties at all or where sureties are offering relatively small amounts of money as recognizance. For example, in the case of a Rochester Prison hunger-striker whose bail application was refused, the adjudicator asked for two sureties with £5,000 each available. In the course of a judicial review challenge, the High Court judge accepted £300, which he described as 'ample'.

In *Brezinski & Glowacka* (High Court), it was stated:

'one only restricts a person's liberty if it is essential to do so and one judges that by having regard to all the factors that are properly to be considered'.

In *AKB*, McCullough J indicated that an adjudicator should justify his or her decision to refuse bail. It was not enough to say that there was a chance that the applicant will abscond, there had to be a 'significant risk'. As to the bail summary prepared by the Home Office, McCullough J stated:

'I am not happy that this document is an adequate statement of reasons for continuing [detention]. There is no balance in the document. It simply sets out arguments for continued detention. It does not acknowledge that there were other arguments raised against continued detention and that the two had to be considered together and balanced before a decision was reached'.

If bail is granted

If bail is granted, forms are completed which show the conditions of the bail and copies are given to the applicant, representative and the sureties. In addition to the conditions relating to residence, reporting and sureties, the adjudicator will normally fix the period of time for which bail is granted. This is done by setting a time and place for the applicant to re-appear (the 'return date') before the adjudicator or an immigration officer at a set date in the future. If there is an appeal outstanding, it is common for the return date to be the hearing date. If the case has not resolved by the time that the bail expires, an application to 'renew' (or 'continue') bail is usually made on that date.

Provided that the person has stuck to the conditions of bail and there have been no changes of circumstance, bail renewal applications are normally a formality. The bail applicant should appear before the adjudicator on each application to extend bail. Sureties should also attend unless they were previously given permission not to attend provided they confirmed in writing that they are happy to continue to act as sureties. Bail renewal hearings can also be used as an opportunity to 'vary' the bail conditions, for example, to reduce the times at which the person must report. If a change of circumstances occurs while a person is on bail, for example, if a person needs to change their address, an application to vary the conditions of bail must be made to the adjudicator in order to do this. If the person is required to report to an immigration officer on the return date, normally temporary admission will be granted when they report provided that there have been no changes of circumstance, but advisers should contact the immigration authorities about this before the person has to report.

If bail is refused

If bail is refused, further applications for bail may still be made. A different adjudicator may make a different decision. However, the applicant is required to state on the application form what change of circumstances there have been since the last application. The passage of time can count as a change of circumstance, even if there have been no other changes. When an adjudicator refuses bail, a form should be given to the applicant which explains, in brief, the reasons for the decision.

Failure to answer to bail

If bail is granted and the applicant fails to re-appear at the time and place fixed on the return date, both they and their sureties risk losing part or all of the money they have offered. The proportion which is lost is as much as the adjudicator or the IAT sees fit. The term used for this process is 'forfeiture' of the amount by which the surety is bound. A failure to comply with a residence condition or to report to a police station is not a reason for instituting forfeiture proceedings, but an adjudicator may take such a failure into account in renewing bail.

In deciding whether to forfeit all or part of the sum, the adjudicator may question sureties to see whether their trust in the applicant was well-founded, whether they were vigilant in monitoring compliance with the bail conditions and whether they could have reasonably suspected a failure to comply with bail conditions, in which case they would be expected to have alerted the authorities. Forfeiture proceedings are very rare. An immigration officer or a police officer may arrest and detain any person who they reasonably believe to be in breach or likely to breach their conditions of bail.

High Court procedures

The procedures for obtaining temporary admission and bail set out above do not require the detainee to show that their detention is unlawful. Although advisers often refer to the Home Office's own detention guidelines to try to show that internal criteria have been mis-applied, the focus of the above procedures is upon persuading the Home Office or the adjudicator that the use of detention powers is not justified in the individual case and that the individual may be trusted to comply with any conditions.

By contrast, where High Court procedures are used to obtain the release of immigration detainees, it must be shown that the detention is unlawful. There are two procedures which may be used: *habeas corpus* and judicial review. The courts have indicated that lawyers should try to use these procedures together where there appears to be an overlap rather than using them separately. They will probably eventually merge together. Technically, *habeas corpus* is used where there is no lawful *power* to detain a person. Judicial review is appropriate where, although there is a legal power, it is being used unlawfully. Chapter 24 explains in detail the powers of detention and the limitations which the courts (▶see pages 497-498) and Article 5 of the ECHR (▶see pages 498-502) place on those powers.

Habeas corpus proceedings

These applications have procedural advantages in that a high priority is traditionally given to getting the applications heard in court quickly. It is, however, unusual for immigration detainees to be able to apply for *habeas corpus* because the powers of detention are so wide. *Habeas corpus* proceedings may be appropriate when people have been detained pending removal for a long time after they have been finally refused and it does not appear that they will be removed within a reasonable time or it is not clear to which country they can be removed. In assessing whether the person has been detained for an unreasonably long time, the court will take into account all of the circumstances, including the detainee's level of co-operation. It is worth discussing the cases of people in such situations with a solicitor experienced in immigration and detention work to see if *habeas corpus* might be possible.

The main court decision in this area is the case of *Hardial Singh*. In that case, the Home Office believed that Mr Singh was an Indian citizen and wanted to deport him to India. He had no documents to prove his identity and the Indian authorities would not give him a travel document. The court held that people cannot be detained for longer than is reasonably necessary in order to carry out their removal and that, if it appears that the removal is not going to be carried out or will not be carried out within a reasonable time, there is no power to continue to detain.

The worst delays in obtaining travel documentation have occurred in cases of detainees from China, Algeria, Pakistan and India.

The same principle was applied by the High Court in *Mahmod (Wasfi Suleman)* in which the applicant had to be released because the Home Office had been unable to obtain the agreement of the German authorities to accept him back. The applicant had refugee status in Germany but had been convicted of drugs offences in the UK and had been detained for 10 months after he was eligible for parole.

Judicial review proceedings

Judicial review is appropriate where the detention is unlawful for reasons other than there being no legal power to detain. For example, there may be a power to detain a person because they are an illegal entrant or an overstayer etc, but the detention is unlawful because the power has been used unfairly without proper regard to the Home Office's own detention policy or because no adequate reasons have been given. The procedures for using judicial review are described on pages 142-144. In many of these cases, however, where it is clear that the immigration authorities should not have detained, the quickest and easiest route to obtain release, will be to make an application for bail to the adjudicator.

Bail in the course of judicial review proceedings

It is also possible to obtain bail from immigration detention in the High Court or the Court of Appeal as an additional application in the course of judicial review proceedings. For example, if a person is in the course of taking judicial review proceedings against the IAT for refusing leave to appeal against a decision of an adjudicator, the High Court has the power to release the person on bail as well as considering the lawfulness of the IAT's decision. It has the power to do this both at the 'permission' stage of judicial review proceedings and at the final stage (see *Turkoglu*, CA). Because there is a statutory right to apply for bail before an adjudicator, bail should generally be sought from the appellate authority. However, in *Kelso*, Collins J held that, where such a bail application could result in a further application for judicial review if the adjudicator refused bail or imposed unsatisfactory conditions, it was appropriate for the High Court to hear the application.

26 Removal, deportation, illegal entry and criminal offences

Those who are in the UK but who cannot establish a right to remain under the immigration rules, or otherwise, and who cannot persuade the immigration authorities to exercise discretion to allow them to stay, can be required to leave. If they do not leave, they can be arrested and detained until their 'removal' from the UK can be arranged. Detention, covered in Chapters 24-25, is one of the main weapons the immigration authorities have in enforcing immigration control. This chapter covers the different ways in which people can be required to leave, the procedures used and the criminal sanctions which may be imposed against those who breach immigration law.

The procedure which is used for requiring any particular person to leave depends upon their immigration status. The different ways in which people can be required to leave are:

Port removal ►see pages 530-531. This applies to people who arrive in the UK and apply for but are refused entry. It is easy to get these people confused with some of the categories below because, by the time they are being required to leave, they may have been in the UK for a long time on temporary admission, for example, as asylum-seekers.

Administrative removal ►see pages 531-537. People can be removed from the UK under Home Office powers of administrative removal if they have overstayed their leave, breached their conditions of leave or obtained leave to remain by deception. Until 2 October 2000, the procedure for requiring all these categories of people to leave was 'deportation'. Family members of those administratively removed can also be removed.

Deportation ►see pages 537-545. The categories of people who are 'deported' has been very much reduced as a result of 'administrative removal' (above). The remaining categories of people who are deported are those whose presence in the UK is not 'conducive to the public good' and those who are recommended for deportation by a criminal court after being convicted of an offence. Family members of deportees can also be deported.

Illegal entrants ►see pages 545-549. Illegal entrants are those people who enter the UK in breach of the immigration laws. This can be done in a number of ways including by deception.

We look at these four procedures in more detail in turn below. When a person may have immigration control enforced against them in one of these four ways, they have often (although not always) committed a criminal offence. Immigration offences generally are considered on pages 553-558. Only deportation completely prevents a person's return to the UK (until the deportation order is revoked), although enforcement under the other procedures will usually affect future immigration decisions regarding them.

The terms used

The terms which are used to describe the above procedures can be confusing. Most confusing of all is that the final stage of all the procedures is 'removal'. All of the groups are issued with 'removal directions', which are the directions given to the carrier to convey the person away from the UK. So, in addition to removals in 'port' cases and administrative removal, those who are being deported after a deportation order has been signed are 'removed' and illegal entrants are also 'removed'. This final process of removal is considered on pages 549-551.

Another term which is often used by immigration officials and lawyers is 'enforcement'. Often this term is meant to only include deportation and illegal entry (and now, possibly, also administrative removal). However, in ordinary language, the removal of people who have applied and been refused at port is just as much an 'enforcement' of their departure. The 1999 Act introduced language which defines 'enforcement action' as covering all kinds of removal (see the amended s24A(2), 1971 Act). We therefore use the term 'enforcement' to cover all four procedures.

Exemptions

Certain Commonwealth and Irish nationals who were resident in the UK on 1 January 1973 and who have long residence in the UK cannot be deported or administratively removed. Those with diplomatic privilege also enjoy exemption from being removed from the UK in certain cases. Persons in these categories should seek more detailed advice if the immigration authorities are seeking to enforce their departure.

Special Immigration Appeal Commission (SIAC) cases

The different rights of appeal of those whose departure is being enforced are mentioned below. However, in certain cases where there is a right of appeal, the appeal is to SIAC rather than to an adjudicator. This occurs in cases where the immigration authorities are enforcing a person's departure at least partly for reasons of national security. For more details about SIAC ▶see pages 618-621.

Taking a decision that a person must leave

It must never be assumed that because the conditions exist which mean that the immigration authorities have the power to enforce a person's departure, they must always automatically use it. In all cases, a decision must be made as to whether it is appropriate to carry out enforcement. The factors to be taken into account in making this decision are, in administrative removal and deportation cases, set out in the immigration rules. In other cases, although there are no factors set out in the rules, advisers can still make representations on their clients' behalf, often relying on similar factors.

In addition, in many cases, there may be human rights reasons why a person should be able to stay in the UK, in particular, because they have family life here, or removing them would expose them to torture or inhuman and degrading treatment or punishment ▶see Chapter 13 for details about human rights claims and Section 3 for asylum generally.

In addition, there may be a policy outside the immigration rules that applies to the case which may enable a person to remain, although they have no rights under the immigration rules. These policies are covered in the appropriate part of the *Handbook*. The policies most relevant to enforcement cases are:

- enforcement against people with a spouse settled in the UK ▶see pages 353-355;
- enforcement against parents whose children have long residence in the UK ▶see pages 392-393;
- long residence concessions ▶see pages 105-108;
- those who are caring for a friend or relative in the UK ▶see pages 289-291;
- those with HIV/AIDS or other serious illness ▶see pages 252-254;
- those who have been the victim of domestic violence ▶see pages 358-361.

Other forms of enforcement

In addition to the above procedures, there are some additional procedures which more rarely apply:

Removal of EEA Nationals and their family members. For details of the circumstances in which EEA nationals and family members can be required to leave and the appeal rights which they have ▶see pages 469-473.

Extradition. People who have been charged with criminal offences overseas may be extradited in order to stand trial in the foreign country. This *Handbook* does not cover extradition, which is a very complex area. For suggestions about where to find further information ▶see Section 12 under 'Further sources of information'.

Removal of those detained under the Mental Health Act. Certain patients who have been detained under the Mental Health Act can be removed from the UK in order for their medical care to be continued in their own country. The initiative for triggering the procedure lies with the hospital rather than with the Home Office. For details of the conditions which must be satisfied ▶see pages 254-255.

Repatriation

A very small number of people have taken advantage of the fund which exists to pay for people, together with their family or households, to travel to a country (usually their country of origin) where they intend to reside permanently (see s29 1971 Act). The scheme is for non-British nationals and applications are usually only granted to people who are settled in the UK but who have decided to repatriate. It must be shown that it is in the interests of the applicant to do so. The majority of people who have used the scheme have been Jamaican nationals. The scheme is operated by the International Social Service of Great Britain; for its address ▶see page 734. Those who use the scheme ought to note that, because they are travelling at public expense, if they change their mind after they have left, they could be refused re-admittance to the UK under the 'returning resident' rule ▶see page 82.

The Nationality, Immigration and Asylum Bill 2002 proposes to replace the existing scheme with a similar scheme for 'voluntary leavers'. The three proposed changes are:

- the new scheme excludes EEA nationals as well as British Citizens;
- the assistance given is expanded to include costs of settling back into the country of origin and being re-integrated;
- 'explore and prepare' visits by people who want to return to assess whether they may wish to leave permanently, can be funded.

It may be that the practical arrangements are made through other organisations funded by the Home Office, such as the International Organisation for Migration or Refugee Action. It appears that the new scheme is not intended simply for those who are settled in the UK.

Port removals

People who arrive at a port in the UK, apply for entry but are refused, can be removed through an uncomplicated procedure. 'Port removal' is not an official term but there is no other general phrase which is used to describe removal in this category. Beyond the decision that they do not qualify for entry, there is no need for the immigration officer to make any decision or declaration about their intentions (as with illegal entrants). Also, the immigration officer does not have to decide whether they fall into a category rendering them liable to one of the forms of administrative removal. Nor is there a complex two-stage process as with deportation.

However, people can ask for entry in different capacities before leaving, each of which must be considered. It is unusual for the second application to be accepted if the first is refused because the two applications are likely to be incompatible and the immigration authorities are unlikely to accept that the second stated purpose is a genuine one. For example, the fact that a person has asked for entry in a category leading to settlement would itself demonstrate that they did not intend to leave the UK and would therefore undermine a second application as a visitor or a student. The major exception to this concerns asylum-seekers. Sometimes asylum-seekers who do not fully understand the procedures for claiming asylum arrive and present a passport seeking entry in one capacity and, when refused, state their true reasons for coming to the UK.

People who return to the UK when they already have leave, for example, because it did not lapse when they left, and that leave is cancelled on their arrival, are also liable to be removed under this procedure. So too are people who arrive in the UK with an entry clearance (which now operates as leave to enter) and are refused entry, because the immigration officer cancels the leave and grants no other leave. For details of these on-entry procedures ▶see pages 68-72. For details about which leave does not lapse when a person departs ▶see pages 76-77.

People cannot be removed while they are exercising any in-country right of appeal. In the case of asylum-seekers and those making human rights claims, not only do they have in-country appeal rights against negative decisions but some time will be taken while a decision is made as to whether they qualify for entry. While a person is waiting for a decision on granting leave to enter, they may either be detained or given temporary admission.

When people are refused leave to enter, they are issued with a notice to this effect informing them of their liability to removal and of any appeal rights. Most people who hold a valid entry clearance or whose prospective employers have been issued with a valid work permit, also have an in-country right of appeal. These people can also object to being removed to the country which the immigration officer wants to return them to but must specify an alternative country which is likely to admit them. For full details about who has the right of appeal ▶see pages 601-606.

The 2002 Bill proposes that members of the family of a person who is being removed in this category can also be removed. The Home Office's particular concern in making this change (and a similar change for family members of illegal entrants – see below) is to ensure that all non-British citizen children born in the UK to those being removed in this way can also be removed. The powers of administrative removal and deportation already enable family members to be removed with the principal.

Administrative removal

Administrative removal is a new procedure, introduced from 2 October 2000, for the removal of any of the following categories of people (see s10, 1999 Act):

- those who have overstayed their leave in the UK;
- those who have breached a condition of their leave;
- those who have obtained leave to remain by deception;
- family members of a person in any of the above three groups who is being administratively removed.

Before 2 October 2000, all of the above groups would have been 'deported' from the UK. The most important consequences of the replacement of deportation by administrative removal for these people are:

- there is no effective right of appeal against administrative removal except on asylum or human rights grounds. Prior to 2 October 2000, an overstayer would be given a notice of intention to deport and could appeal against it. If the person had last entered the UK seven years or more before the time that the notice was given, they could rely upon all the compassionate and other features of their case in the appeal and argue that, on balance, the decision to deport should not have been made. If they had not been in the UK for seven years, they could only appeal on the grounds that there was no legal power to deport them (an appeal which could hardly ever succeed). In these cases, the practice was for appellants to ask adjudicators to make a 'recommendation' on compassionate grounds;

- the process is a much shorter one. There is only one stage of 'removal' (like illegal entrants and port removal cases), rather than a two-stage process which involves the notice of intention to deport followed by the deportation order.

Those who are being administratively removed will be given a notice informing them of the decision to remove them. They may also be detained or alternatively granted temporary admission. If a person does overstay or breach their conditions, or obtain leave to remain by deception, this can count against them in future applications which they make to enter or remain in the UK. This is because all of these circumstances are covered in the general grounds upon which leave can be refused under the immigration rules ▶see pages 67, 102.

Regularisation of overstayers scheme

The administrative removal procedure does not apply to people who the Home Office decided to deport before 2 October 2000. It also does not apply to those people who applied before the 2 October 2000 deadline to the Home Office under the 'Regularisation of Overstayers Scheme' which allowed people who were overstayers, or in breach of conditions, to apply to the Home Office to regularise their stay. If the decision of the Home Office is still negative then, even if the decision was made after 2 October 2000, the applicant is still treated under the deportation procedure and maintains their rights of appeal under that procedure. The regularisation scheme was not an 'amnesty' and, in fact, it enabled the Home Office to identify many long-term overstayers. However, many people have been successful in their applications.

Rights of appeal

As indicated above, there were previously important appeal rights under the deportation process for people who are now administratively removed. Those administratively removed, have no in-country right of appeal unless they claim asylum or rely on other human rights or discrimination grounds. The withdrawal of the right to make an in-country appeal on the merits of the case will often force people to make a human rights claim and obtain an appeal in order to have the circumstances of their case heard. If there are strong compassionate features which are not found to be sufficient to amount to a breach of human rights, it is still possible to ask an adjudicator to make a recommendation to the Home Office (►see pages 646-647 for further details about recommendations).

There is also an appeal which can be won if, on the facts of the case, there was no legal power for the Home Office to have made the decision to remove. On such an appeal, the appellant can only argue that they were not in fact an overstayer or in breach of their conditions etc. This will be rare; the appeal is not on the merits of the decision to remove. This right of appeal can only be exercised after the person has left the UK, unless they are also appealing on asylum or human rights grounds. Therefore, if the only challenge is to the decision that a person is an overstayer or in breach of their conditions, this can only be done before removal by judicial review.

Overstaying

Overstaying is the most common of the reasons for the Home Office to try to remove someone administratively. All limited leave has a date of expiry and a person is expected to either leave the UK or make a further application to remain within the time of their leave. If they do not, they become overstayers and can be removed. As with liability for administrative removal on the grounds of breach of conditions or being a family member of someone who is being removed, there is no need for the person to know that they are overstaying in order for them to be liable to be removed. A person can also become an overstayer if their leave is curtailed by the immigration authorities. For details of the grounds upon which leave can be curtailed ►see pages 103-104. If a further grant of leave is given after a person has overstayed, then they are no longer liable to be removed as an overstayer, unless they overstay the fresh leave.

If the person applies to the Home Office for an extension of leave before their existing leave expires, and the Home Office does not make a decision on the application before the leave expires, the applicant is treated as having been given an extension of leave until 10 days after the Home

Office makes a decision on the application. The legal provision which has this effect is section 3C of the 1971 Act which was inserted by the 1999 Act and replaces the previous provisions of the Variation of Leave Order 1976. Applicants do not become overstayers during this period. Only valid applications for extensions completed on the appropriate forms with all the required original evidence will count for these purposes.

If the decision on the extension is positive then, obviously, the applicant will have further leave. If it is negative, the applicant becomes an overstayer and liable to administrative removal unless they appeal. People who have applied for an extension of leave and are waiting for their appeal to be dealt with are treated as still having the same leave until the end of the appeals process (including any appeals beyond the adjudicator, provided applications for leave to appeal are made in time). For more details about automatic extensions of leave ▶see pages 93-95.

It should be noted that, during these periods of automatic extension, it is the old leave which is treated as continuing to have effect and so the old conditions continue. Therefore, if a person has a prohibition on claiming public funds or on working on their existing leave, this continues until they get a positive decision, even if the leave they have applied for (e.g., indefinite leave) would not contain these conditions.

If a person's conditions of leave, before it ran out, were generous, for example, they did not prohibit recourse to public funds or working, then a person loses these when they overstay. For example, a person given exceptional leave to remain for four years who fails to apply for indefinite leave in time, becomes a person 'subject to immigration control' as an overstayer and unable to obtain most social security benefits until the application for an extension is made and decided in their favour.

In addition to making someone liable for administrative removal, the other effects of overstaying are that it breaks a period of continuous lawful leave. This may have an impact on a later application for indefinite leave where there is a requirement for a continuous period of leave or for an application for naturalisation as a British citizen. It also may affect an application under the 10-year lawful residence concession.

Breach of conditions

As well as overstaying, a person is liable to administrative removal if they breach one of the other conditions of their leave. Which conditions will be imposed on the leave depends upon the category a person is admitted in. Immigration officials refer to the various different combinations of these conditions as 'codes' and the table on pages 110-111 sets out the different conditions which are normally given under the different categories of leave. Indefinite leave cannot have any conditions attached to it.

The conditions which may be imposed on a person's leave are as follows.

'Prohibition' on employment or occupation. This prevents the person from doing any kind of work in the UK, paid or unpaid. Even helping out at a friend's shop could mean that a person is in breach of their conditions. Visitors, for example, are all given a prohibition on working although the rules are interpreted flexibly for 'business' visitors and certain others ▶see pages 280-283.

'Restriction' on employment or occupation. Working restrictions are generally intended to prevent people from working other than in the job which they have been admitted to do or except in specified circumstances. They are usually expressed as restrictions preventing work other than work which they have been given permission to do. For example, a work permit holder will be able to work in the employment approved by their work permit.

Previously, students could not work without first obtaining specific permission. However, those who are given entry for more than six months are now treated as having been permitted to work for up to 20 hours per week in term-time and full-time during vacations without having to seek permission in advance ▶see page 310.

Registration with the police. Foreign nationals, aged 16 or over, of the countries which are listed on page 750, may be required to register with the police. None of the countries listed are Commonwealth countries. People will usually be required to register if they:

- have been given leave for more than six months for the purpose of employment, unless it is employment as a seasonal worker at an agricultural camp, private servant in a diplomatic household, or a minister of religion, missionary or member of a religious order; or
- have been given leave for more than six months as a student, au pair, business-person or self-employed person, investor, person of independent means or writer, composer or artist; or
- are the spouse or child of any of the above people.

The requirement to register can also be imposed on any national of the countries listed where, exceptionally, the immigration officer thinks that it is necessary to do so to ensure that the person complies with the terms of their leave.

In order to register, a person must go to their local police station within a week of the condition being imposed and provide their name, address, details of employment, marital status, photograph and pay the registration fee. Any changes in these details must be registered within a similar period of time. The police will provide the person with a 'certificate of registration'.

Maintain and accommodate themselves and any dependants without recourse to public funds. Since 1 November 1996, the immigration authorities have been able to impose a requirement that people maintain and accommodate themselves and any dependants without recourse to public funds. We suggest that this must be interpreted, in line with the immigration rules, as meaning *additional* recourse to public funds. People in many of the categories under the rules have this condition imposed on their leave. The main effect of this condition is to prevent people from getting public funds in the first place.

In addition to administrative removal, breach of conditions can lead to criminal charges and convictions. Immigration officers can also require that someone entering the UK reports to a medical officer for examination or treatment (para 7 sch 2, 1971 Act). This is infrequent and although breach of it does not seem to lead directly to 'enforcement', refusal to undergo a medical examination can lead to refusal of leave under the immigration rules.

Obtaining leave to remain by deception

A person who obtains leave to remain in the UK from the Home Office by deception can also be administratively removed. This is similar to one kind of illegal entry (▶see pages 547-549), which concerns those obtaining entry to the UK by deception. Importantly, this power can be used to deal with people who have obtained *indefinite* leave to remain when they were not entitled to it. Overstaying and breaches of conditions (above) can only apply to people granted limited leave.

The classic situation for use of this power is where the immigration authorities later discover that a spouse or unmarried partner, at the end of their probationary period, obtained indefinite leave to remain when the relationship had, in fact, broken down and they no longer had any intention of living together permanently. Before this power was introduced, the only way in which the Home Office could enforce the removal of such a person was by deporting them on the ground that their presence was not conducive to the public good. The deportee would then have full appeal rights against the decision.

It should be noted that, under the 2002 Bill, the Home Office will be able to administratively remove someone who *tries* to obtain leave to remain by deception, even if they are not successful in getting leave.

Family members of those being administratively removed

Family members (spouses and minor children) of people who have been given directions that they are being removed administratively for any of the reasons stated above, can also be removed. However, the family members must be notified that they are being administratively removed no more than eight weeks after the departure of their principal. If the family members cease to be family members before removal is carried out, for example, there is a divorce or a child has reached the age of 18, the removal directions against the family member are no longer valid.

Deciding whether a person should be administratively removed

Even though there is a power to remove a person administratively, the Home Office has to make a decision that it is appropriate to remove them given the circumstances of their individual case. In making this decision, the immigration rules must be applied (paras 364–368, HC 395). The considerations set out in the rules are exactly the same as for deportation cases. So, although people who are being administratively removed have lost important appeal rights, the Home Office itself must still apply the same factors when making its decision as to whether to force them to leave.

Under the rules, the Home Office has to consider whether removal is the right course, balancing the public interest in maintaining immigration control against the compassionate circumstances of the case. Although each case must be considered on its own merits, the Home Office must aim to come to decisions which are consistent between one case and another. Where it is a case of overstaying or of breaching conditions, removal will 'normally' be the correct decision but the Home Office has to take into account all known relevant factors including:

- the person's age;
- their length of residence in the UK;
- their strength of connections with the UK;
- their personal history, including character, conduct and employment record;
- their domestic circumstances;
- the nature of any offence which the person has been convicted of;
- the person's previous criminal record;
- any compassionate circumstances; and
- any representations received on the person's behalf.

The above factors are not the only relevant ones: any of the consequences of removal can be relied on. For example, in *Bakhtaur Singh* the House of Lords ruled that the interests of a particular community were, in principle, relevant in keeping a person who was a particularly talented performance artist in the UK. Removal of each family member must be considered separately and where a spouse or child is liable to be removed, further factors still must be taken into account to determine their cases ▶see page 392. For the special policy considerations which apply in cases of marriage and children ▶see pages 353-355, 392-393.

Deportation

The remaining cases where the Home Office uses deportation powers are as follows. They are available whether or not a person has existing limited or indefinite leave.

Recommendations for deportation. Those who are convicted of either immigration or non-immigration criminal offences can be recommended for deportation by the criminal court as part of their sentence for the offence.

Deportation conducive to the public good. People can be deported on the grounds that their presence is not 'conducive to the public good'. They may or may not have committed criminal offences in order to be liable for deportation on these grounds.

Family members of people being deported. As with administrative removal, family members of people in the above two categories can also be deported.

It should be noted that the 2002 Bill would allow for a person to have their indefinite leave 'revoked' if that person could be deported under the above rules but cannot physically be removed for 'legal reasons'. This would apply, for example, if a person had committed very serious crimes but would face torture or inhuman and degrading treatment if removed. Similar proposals are made for those who the immigration authorities believe have obtained leave by deception. The Bill also proposes that there will be a right of appeal against revocation of indefinite leave.

The effect of a deportation order when it is made and while it continues in force, is that it invalidates any existing leave and it prevents any further leave from being given. Therefore, when a deportation order is made, the person cannot return to the UK unless the deportation order has first been 'revoked' (▶see below). Deportation can be used even if the person could be removed in another way, for example, as an overstayer.

Recommendations for deportation

In criminal cases for which the maximum sentence is a prison term, the court has the power to recommend deportation as part of the criminal sentence for people aged 17 or over.

When the criminal court may make a recommendation

In 1980, in *Nazari*, the Court of Appeal gave the following guidelines for criminal courts in deciding whether to make recommendations for deportation:

- the court should consider the potential detriment to the country by the person's presence – this depends on the seriousness of the offence, the harm caused to the community by it and the risk of the person committing further offences;
- the court should also bear in mind the effect on innocent third parties of the person being deported, for example, family members who are settled in the UK and who would be separated from the deportee. Article 8 ECHR will now be an important consideration in looking at the effect on these people;

- the court should not consider the political system in the country to which the person will be sent and their future life there as this is the job of the Home Office in considering whether to act on the recommendation. Under the Human Rights Act 1998, however, it may be the case that the courts must now look at all the potential effects of the recommendation where it is alleged that a person's human rights are at stake.

The official handbook for magistrates, *The Sentence of the Court*, gives guidance on making recommendations for deportation. The person who has been convicted or their representative should be asked to address the court specifically on the question of a recommendation. The handbook states:

'Those who have committed serious offences or who have long records are suitable for recommendations, as are those who are convicted of immigration offences'.

After a recommendation for deportation has been made

The only formal appeal against the recommendation itself is through the criminal appeals system against conviction or sentence. The appeal may therefore be to either a Crown Court or the Court of Appeal. Often criminal solicitors, with little understanding of immigration law, are unaware of the possibility of a recommendation being made or of the right of appeal against it. An appeal may be brought against the recommendation, even if no other part of the sentence or the conviction is being appealed. Appeals have frequently been successful for procedural reasons, for example, because the criminal court failed to give the appellant the required seven days' notice that it is considering a recommendation so that the person can make representations, or because the court has failed to give sufficient reasons which address the relevant factors referred to in *Nazari*.

If no appeal is made, or if the appeal is unsuccessful, the Home Office then considers whether to carry out the recommendation. In most cases, the Home Office will agree with the recommendation and act upon it. Presently, unlike the other forms of deportation, the Home Office will not then issue a notice of decision to make a deportation order (against which there is a right of appeal) but will proceed directly to the making of the deportation order. Therefore, the only effective appeals which may be brought against the Home Office's decision in these cases is on asylum or human rights grounds if such claims are made. However, the 2002 Bill proposes to introduce a right of appeal before an adjudicator against a decision to deport following a court recommendation. This would mean, presumably, that the Home Office will make a decision to deport if it decides to follow a recommendation and that no deportation order will be signed while the deportee is appealing. This proposal was initially made in the early stages of the 1999 Bill but never implemented.

If a Court makes a recommendation for deportation against an EEA national and the Home Office decides to act upon it, we would suggest that the resulting Home Office decision constitutes an 'EEA decision' (▶see pages 472-473) against which there is a right of appeal. However, in cases where an EEA national is recommended for deportation, the Home Office practice has been to issue a decision to deport, therefore ensuring an appeal.

The final decision as to whether to make a deportation order rests with the Home Office which has to consider any representations made as to why it should not carry out the court's recommendation. If representations are made to the Home Office, it is important to explain any special or compassionate circumstances, or why deportation should be delayed, for example, to enable a person to complete a course of studies.

Where a recommendation has been made, the person may be detained under immigration powers while awaiting the making of the deportation order. Alternatively, the person may be released by the immigration authorities and given temporary admission.

Conducive to the public good

The Home Office may deport a person on the ground that their presence in the UK is not 'conducive to the public good'. It can do so on the basis of criminal offences even if the Court made no recommendation for deportation (▶see above) and, indeed, this is when the power is most often used. The power can also potentially be used where a person has committed offences overseas, has criminal connections which are likely to result in adverse consequences for the community in the UK, or where the person has obtained leave by deception (although the use of illegal entry or administrative removal powers is more likely in these latter cases).

As far as criminal convictions are concerned, the decisions of the courts have varied as to whether it is necessary to show that there is a risk of re-offending or whether deportation on these grounds can proceed if the offence in itself was sufficiently serious to justify deportation. In *Santillo*, the Court of Appeal suggested that the fact of a conviction alone would not be enough. In any case, the criminal conviction must be sufficiently serious to justify the decision and the kinds of conduct which have resulted in deportation are serious violent or sexual offences, robberies and the importation or supply of controlled drugs.

In all cases, the public interest in deportation must be weighed against the compassionate circumstances of the case, applying the same rules as for administrative removal (above). There is a full right of appeal against a notice of intention to deport made on these grounds, regardless of the length of time the person has lived in the UK.

Family members

The spouse and minor children of people being deported can also be deported. However, a deportation order cannot be signed against a spouse or minor child more than eight weeks (excluding any time during which the family member is appealing against the decision to make the deportation order) after the principal has been deported. A deportation order is no longer effective against a family member who ceases to be a member of the family of the principal who is deported. Family members must be given independent consideration and the factors in the rules set out above (▶see page 537), as well as those particular to spouses and minor children, must be applied.

The deportation process

The Home Office decision as to whether to make a deportation order is taken with regard to the same factors as for cases of administrative removal. In cases where deportation is on 'conducive to the public good' grounds or a family member is being deported, there is a two-stage process involving a decision to deport (also called a 'notice of intention to deport') which is given first. This initial decision is different from the deportation order itself. In cases of court recommendations following a conviction, the Home Office can proceed to make the deportation order. However, as stated above, following court recommendations, the 2002 Bill proposes to bring the procedure into line with other deportation cases.

Before issuing a decision to make a deportation order, the Home Office will normally write to the person stating that it is considering deportation proceedings and asking for any representations to be made within a certain time. If a decision to deport is made, this will be sent or given to the person. The notice of decision should include details about how to appeal, as it carries a full right of appeal. The notice of decision to deport also gives the immigration authorities the power to detain a person pending deportation. A recommendation for deportation has the same effect with regard to detention.

In the appeal against the decision to deport, the deportee can argue that:

- the decision should not have been made, applying the factors to be considered under the immigration rules (or any relevant Home Office policy) to the circumstances of the case;
- they should be deported, if at all, to a different country which must be specified by the deportee. The appellant must specify the alternative destination and, if they are not a national of that country, show evidence that they will be accepted there;
- there are human rights reasons why they should not be deported; or
- if they have claimed asylum, their removal would be in breach of the Refugee Convention.

If no appeal is brought to the adjudicator against a notice of decision to deport or to the next criminal court against a recommendation given by the criminal court, or if such appeals are dismissed, the Home Secretary can then proceed to sign a deportation order against the person. It is possible to make written representations to the Home Office again at this stage if there is relevant information which has not yet been considered or if circumstances have changed, for example, a child may have been born to the family or indeed if there has been a further substantial passage of time during which the person has become yet more established in the UK.

Although the practice of serving deportation notices 'on the file' (at the Home Office) where the Home Office has no knowledge of the whereabouts of a particular person is no longer used, notices may still have been served at a person's last known address, even when the person had a representative. People therefore still sometimes find, after living unlawfully in the UK for many years, that a notice has been given which stops the clock for the purpose of the 14-year long residence concession (►see page 107; the 10-year long residence concession depends on lawful residence anyway), or even that a deportation order has been made against them.

The same factors under the immigration rules are considered at the stage of signing the order. For cases involving recommendations for deportation, the rules are presently considered for the first time at this stage.

If a person is serving a criminal sentence, the Home Office will usually wait until near to the end of the period of the sentence before considering deportation. As soon as it is signed and before it is given to the deportee, a deportation order is effective. There are no appeal rights against the order unless human rights or asylum are being raised at that stage. The deportee only has the right to appeal against the destination country and to specify an alternative country.

However, if the deportee could have raised the same objection against destination in an appeal against the initial decision to make the order and either raised no objection at that stage or the adjudicator did not uphold the objection, they do not get a second chance to appeal against the same destination when the deportation order is made.

Alternatives to deportation

In many cases, where a person has lost their appeal against the decision to deport or against a recommendation and there are no other grounds for staying in the UK, it is in the person's interests to leave before an order is made. This is because, if the order is not signed, the person is at least eligible to return to the UK. If the order is signed, they cannot return until it is revoked.

It may take several weeks or even months for an order to be signed, which gives time for the person to make a voluntary departure. At any time, a person may make a voluntary departure from the UK by buying their own ticket and leaving. It is worth informing the immigration service of travel plans, so that it is less likely that a deportation order will be signed before they leave.

In addition, it is also possible for anyone who is liable to be deported to make a 'supervised departure' from the UK (see s5(6), 1971 Act). This is where the immigration authorities pay the travel expenses of the person and any members of their family or household who wish to leave with them.

If a voluntary or supervised departure is made after a person has been given a notice of intention to deport, then the person's passport will usually be endorsed 'served with form APP 104' to show that a deportation decision has been made. However, even if a person leaves before the decision to deport is given, future applications can still be affected. Firstly, the Home Office has stated that information about people removed under the supervised departure process is available to immigration officers and to ECOs overseas. Secondly, if people apply for entry clearance, they are required to declare their circumstances on the application form where they have had previous immigration difficulties and it is likely that the application will be referred to the Home Office to be checked against their Home Office file. The general considerations under the immigration rules allow applications to be refused, among other cases, when a person has convictions, or on the grounds of their character or conduct or because their exclusion is conducive to the public good or because they have previously obtained leave by deception.

Those convicted of criminal offences who have completed their prison sentences and who cannot obtain bail, may wish to leave the UK rather than spend further time in immigration detention awaiting the deportation process. However, people in detention are very vulnerable to suggestions and it has been alleged that sometimes immigration officers may try to persuade people to make voluntary departures and request that they sign disclaimer forms stating that they do not want to appeal. Even when this has been done, people can change their minds and lodge an appeal within the 10-day time limit or, if the time limit has passed, submit the notice of appeal out of time and explain the reasons for the delay.

Revocation of deportation orders

After an order is signed, it must be revoked before a person can return. If a person does gain entry while there is still a valid deportation order against them, they have entered illegally and can be arrested and removed as illegal entrants. There is no form designed for an application to revoke a deportation order. A deportation order will not be signed after a person has left, so if it is shown that the person had already left by the date an order was signed, it should be revoked.

It is possible to urge the Home Office to revoke a deportation order while the person is in the UK, but the application is only likely to be considered if the deportation order was signed a long time ago, there have been changes in circumstances since the order was signed and the person has only recently been traced. All the changes in the person's circumstances and any compassionate or family reasons, should be put forward.

If a person claims asylum while in the UK, then this is treated as an application for the order to be revoked and there is an in-country right of appeal against the refusal to revoke the order on asylum grounds. Human rights grounds can also be raised even though an order has been signed and an appeal can be made on this basis as well.

The immigration rules state that an order will not normally be revoked until the person has been out of the UK for at least three years after the order was signed, except in the most 'exceptional circumstances' (see paras 390-392 HC395). If an application is made sooner, it should contain full details of the exceptional circumstances justifying revocation earlier than normal. The immigration rules state that relevant factors will include:

- the grounds on which the deportation order was made;
- any representations made in support of revocation;
- the interests of the community, including the maintenance of an effective immigration control;
- the interests of the applicant, including any compassionate circumstances.

Having a spouse and children settled in the UK, who have reasons for being unable to join the deportee abroad, for example, may be strong compassionate circumstances for earlier revocation, even if they were not considered adequate to avoid removal under the policy guidelines on enforcement in cases involving marriage and children. It may be possible to argue that the continued separation of a family is contrary to Article 8 ECHR.

However, the Home Office approach to revocation concerning the category of case still dealt with by the deportation procedure, is not generous. The rules themselves state that a person may be required to be absent for a 'long term' of years where serious criminal offences were committed and, in such cases, the Home Office may be expected to refuse to revoke an order until approximately 10 years have passed. If revocation is refused, there is a right of appeal from abroad against the refusal. The full merits of the case can be raised as well as any human rights grounds.

If a deportation order is revoked, this does not give the person an automatic right to return to the UK. It merely means that there is no legal obstacle to him or her applying to return. The person will still have to fit into all the requirements of the immigration rules in the category in which he or she is seeking to return. The Home Office is likely to consider the application in great detail. Therefore, even if the person is not a visa national and is not seeking to return in a category for which entry clearance is always required, it is advisable to apply for entry clearance so as to minimise the risk of refusal at the port.

Illegal entry

Illegal entry means entering, or seeking to enter, the UK unlawfully in breach of the immigration laws. Like port removals and administrative removals (▶see above), illegal entrants can be removed from the UK in an uncomplicated process by the setting of directions for removal. Illegal entrants can be detained pending their removal. The 2002 Bill proposes that members of the family of an illegal entrant can also be removed. Currently there is no power to remove family members just because they are family members. They can only be removed if they are liable to be removed in their own right.

There is an in-country right of appeal on asylum or human rights grounds. There is another right of appeal on the grounds that, on the facts of the case, there was no legal power to remove the person as an illegal entrant. This latter right of appeal can be exercised in-country only if the appellant is also appealing on asylum or human rights grounds, otherwise it can only be exercised from abroad. Because this appeal right is generally exercised from abroad, legal challenges to a decision that someone is, in fact, an illegal entrant have traditionally been made by judicial review. In these cases, it is for the Home Office to demonstrate that the person has entered illegally. In many cases, the Home Office is alleging fraud on the part of the applicant, and this must be proved to a high degree of probability.

As with other cases where there is a power to remove, representations can be made to the Home Office concerning any compassionate or other features of the case which suggest that removal should not be carried out.

Following the introduction of administrative removal, the importance of illegal entry has diminished. This is because, previously, the effect of an illegal entry decision was to make the person liable to summary removal without the protections of the deportation system. The procedure for administrative removal is, however, just as quick as the illegal entry route.

Illegal entry decisions do, however, remain important in those cases where a person still has a substantial period of leave remaining and is not in breach of their conditions, and is therefore not liable to administrative removal. When the immigration authorities declare someone to be an illegal entrant, any leave which they have is automatically invalid from that time. In particular, it is important to note that an in-country application from someone who has been declared to be an illegal entrant, to remain as a spouse or unmarried partner cannot satisfy the rules because the applicant does not have any leave and is in breach of the immigration laws. In addition, the decision on any such in-country application would not carry a right of appeal.

A person who enters the UK in any of the following ways can be declared to be an illegal entrant:

- without seeing an immigration officer at all;
- without obtaining leave to enter when this was required;
- while there is a deportation order signed against them which is still in force;
- by deceiving an immigration officer, for example, as to their identity, nationality, or some other matter relevant to their right to enter.

We look at these four categories in turn below. The concept of illegal entry was originally designed to cover people in the first three categories but the definition has been greatly expanded by the Home Office and the courts.

Entry without seeing an immigration officer

The category of people who enter without seeing an immigration officer covers those who, for example, arrive in a small boat on a deserted beach at midnight. This is not common. Far more common among these 'clandestine' entrants, are those who arrive concealed in the back of lorries or containers who are not discovered until after they have passed through the immigration control area and who have therefore entered the UK without going through controls. Many asylum-seekers arrive in this way and, under the 1999 Act, carriers' liability sanctions were extended so that those carrying people arriving in this manner would be charged fines for each clandestine entrant. There have been court decisions about the legality of these sanctions.

If a person confesses to having entered by avoiding examination by an immigration officer, there is no way of arguing that he or she is not an illegal entrant.

Entry without obtaining leave from an immigration officer

Immigration officers are required by the Immigration Act 1971 to examine people when they arrive to decide whether they need leave to enter the UK and whether or not to give them leave. If they fail to examine someone who needs leave and instead pass them through into the UK without stamping their passports, those people can be treated as illegal entrants because they have not obtained leave. This was confirmed by the Court of Appeal in the case of *Rehal*. Mr Rehal was a British Overseas citizen whose passport was not stamped on entry because the immigration officer mistakenly assumed that he was a British citizen, who therefore did not need leave. The court accepted that he had not *deceived* an immigration officer, but decided nevertheless that he was an illegal entrant.

Entry through Ireland

It is also possible for people who enter through Ireland to be treated as illegal entrants by not obtaining leave from an immigration officer. There is no passport control between the two countries. Normally people do not require leave to travel within the Common Travel Area (the UK, Republic of Ireland, Channel Islands and Isle of Man) so they do not have to see an immigration officer. However, some people do require leave, and if they enter without it, they have entered illegally. For the categories of entrant from Ireland who are illegal entrants if they enter without leave ▶see pages 74-75.

Records are not generally kept of people entering through Ireland, so such people are only likely to be treated as illegal entrants if they apply to the Home Office for an extension or a change of status, or if they happen to come to the attention of the authorities in some other way and the Home Office then makes checks on their entry.

Entry in breach of a deportation order

If someone enters the UK while still the subject of a deportation order that has not been revoked, the entry is illegal. It would be rare for a person travelling in his or her true identity to be readmitted, so people who enter in breach of a deportation order will usually have entered with a false passport which constitutes illegal entry in itself. If there is a current deportation order, then the Home Office have a choice: they could remove the person under the deportation order, which automatically cancels any leave that the person managed to get when they arrived anyway, or it can declare the person to be an illegal entrant and remove them as such.

Deception of an immigration officer

Many of those dealt with as illegal entrants are so treated because the immigration authorities allege that they entered by deception. The deception may be by the use of false passports or a passport which is not false but which did not truly belong to the passenger who used it. However, a person may also enter by deception without misusing documents. They may appear to have been legally allowed into the country and have stamps on their own genuine passports granting leave to enter. The immigration authorities may allege, however, that they told lies or deliberately hid information when applying for leave to enter, or they may claim that the person did not give information which, if the immigration officer had known it, may have affected the decision to grant entry.

A person may also be an illegal entrant if the deception is carried out by a third party in order to gain entry for the passenger although the passenger themselves is innocent of it. This could be the case, for example, if a relative makes false representations at an entry clearance interview or in writing and entry is granted on that same basis, or if a person accompanying the passenger makes false representations about them to the immigration officer at the port.

Entry by deception has been the subject of many court cases. The most important decision came in the joined cases of **Khawaja & Khera**. In these cases, the House of Lords decided that it is for the Home Office to prove, on the balance of probabilities but to a high standard, that false representations were made to the immigration authorities and that leave to enter was granted on the basis of that false information. Mr Khera was found not to be an illegal entrant. He had applied as a child to come with his mother to join his father but had married in India while the application was still under consideration. He did not know that this made any difference and was not asked whether he was married, so it was accepted that he had not deceived the immigration authorities. Mr Khawaja, on the other hand, was held to be an illegal entrant. He had entered as a visitor saying that he would spend a week with his cousin but applied to the Home Office shortly afterwards to remain as a husband, having married his wife in Belgium before travelling to the UK and married her again in the UK during his visit. He was held to have deceived the immigration officers on arrival and therefore to be an illegal entrant.

Since then, court decisions have further widened the interpretation of illegal entry. The Court of Appeal held in the cases of **Durojaiye** and **Akinde** that merely showing a passport with a previous immigration stamp of leave to remain to an immigration officer can count as deception if the reason for which the previous leave was given is no longer current. For example, a student who decides to give up their course but has several months' extension of stay travels out of the UK with leave which does not lapse and returns to the UK within this time. If the person enters by presenting their passport with evidence of their un-lapsed student leave, they could be considered to have deceived the immigration officers on return because they are no longer in fact entitled to entry as a student.

Establishing illegal entry by deception

Where an illegal entry decision is based on misrepresentations as opposed to false documents, there is often no evidence to support the Home Office's view and the only way that the allegation can be substantiated is through the 'confession' of the person concerned.

For example, if a man who was given entry as a visitor is subsequently found working, he is likely to be questioned by immigration officers about his intentions when he first came to the UK. Had he really intended just a visit? Had he always wanted to work here? Did he know before he came that he would work? Had he always intended to stay longer than he said? If the answer to any of the questions is 'yes', immigration officers may allege that he had concealed his true intention of coming to the UK to work. If this had been revealed on entry, it would have resulted in refusal of leave to enter. Therefore, entry was gained by deception as he was never really a genuine visitor.

Most people are questioned by immigration officers after arrest, perhaps after being detained in a police station for some hours, and without advice. If they have any advice it will usually be because the police have contacted a duty solicitor on their behalf, but these lawyers will nearly always be practitioners of criminal law with little or no special knowledge of immigration procedures. The arrested person is unlikely to appreciate the reasoning behind the questions or what the officer is getting at, and will be unaware of the difference between remaining in the UK unlawfully after any leave has run out and being an 'illegal entrant'. They may make admissions in response to questions about their original intentions, believing they are talking about their current situation.

It is always important to ask the immigration office or police station concerned for a copy of its record or the tape of the person's interview, which may clarify what the person has said and whether the responses have been misunderstood. Interviews carried out at police stations will generally be tape-recorded, as with any criminal investigation, and other immigration interviews may also be recorded.

Removal and return

As with others who may be required to leave, illegal entrants who are not detained may leave the country voluntarily by buying their ticket and leaving. Those who do not wish to contest removal may explain this to immigration officers. They may be asked to sign a disclaimer, indicating that they are leaving voluntarily, particularly if other issues, such as marriage, have been raised before they go.

There are no formal procedures laid down to restrict people removed as illegal entrants from applying to return. They may apply immediately, but will have to show that they satisfy the requirements of the immigration law and rules for the category in which they are seeking to return. However, entering the UK by deception on a previous occasion is a ground for refusing an application to return under the general grounds for refusal in the rules. If a person does wish to return to the UK after having been removed as an illegal entrant, it will often be advisable to apply for entry clearance, even if this is not strictly required, so as not to risk refusal at port having paid the costs of travel.

The process of removal

'Removal' is the final practical means of enforcing the departure under any of the four main procedures described above. The directions for removal themselves are given to the captain of a ship or aircraft or to a train operator to remove the person. The directions are also notified to the person who is to be removed. Often the person will be detained. Where the person is not detained, they will normally be given a notice that they must attend at a port at a particular time in order to be removed as a condition of their existing temporary admission.

The removal itself may be carried out by force if necessary. The immigration service has been very severely criticised in the past for the inappropriate use of force. In some cases, the immigration authorities make arrangements for escorts to accompany the returnee on the journey back.

Where can people be removed to?

When people are removed from the UK, the list of countries to which they can be sent depends upon which procedure is being used to enforce their departure. In cases of port removal and illegal entry, the person can be sent to a country:

- of which they are a national; *or*
- which has provided them with a passport or another travel or identity document; *or*
- from which they embarked for the UK; *or*
- to which there is 'reason to believe [they] will be admitted'.

In cases of deportation or administrative removal, people can only be sent to a country:

- of which they are a national; *or*
- to which there is 'reason to believe [they] will be admitted'.

There are special considerations in cases where asylum-seekers are being removed on 'third-country' grounds (▶see pages 206-212) but they are additional to the above rules which apply to all cases.

If the immigration authorities are seeking to return someone to a country where there is 'reason to be believe they will be admitted', it is not enough for them to show that they ought to be admitted there. There must be evidence that they are in fact likely to be accepted.

Travel documents

Countries are bound to accept the return of their own nationals but sometimes removal to a country of which a person claims to be a national becomes impractical and is delayed because that country refuses to accept their return. In many cases of, for example, asylum-seekers who do not possess travel documents, the Home Office may seek to return them using its own one-way identity documents. However, the immigration authorities may also need to obtain travel documentation for them from their own national authorities.

Some countries, for example Algeria, have been known to be very slow to document and accept the return of their own nationals and returns can be very much delayed as a result. If a person is detained while awaiting travel documentation, then the delay may make that detention unlawful ▶see pages 497-498. As a result of these delays, in some cases the Home Office has been seeking to approach the applicant's consular authorities very early in the asylum process. Asylum applications are intended to be confidential and if this has occurred it may well be an additional ground to raise in an appeal as giving rise to a further risk to the individual.

Who meets the costs of removal?

In almost all cases it is either the Home Office or the 'carrier' who must pay for the removal. There are detailed provisions setting out when the Home Office rather than the carriers must pay. When a person is removed after a deportation order has been signed, the Home Office can try to recover the cost of removal from the deportee. It should be remembered that in deportation cases a person can opt for a supervised departure before they are removed under a deportation order.

How people are traced

The immigration authorities may come to know of people who are in breach of the immigration laws in many ways. The applicant may have been in contact with the Home Office, for example, by applying for an extension of leave which was refused, or they may have lost an appeal and remained in the UK after this trying to persuade the Home Office to allow them to stay.

If the person has not been in contact with the Home Office, but has simply stayed beyond the leave granted or worked without permission, he or she may be traced through various sources. Many authorities, such as the Benefits Agency, local authority housing departments, marriage registrars, health authorities, employers and colleges may now check on immigration status and make enquiries. Under the 1999 Act there is a duty on marriage registrars to report suspicious or 'sham' marriages to the Home Office. These are marriages which are entered into for the purpose of avoiding the effect of immigration law. Even before these developments, the courts had said that there may be a duty on housing authorities to report to the Home Office people they believe to be in the UK unlawfully (see *R v Secretary of State for the Environment ex p Tower Hamlets LBC*).

In addition, the police or the immigration authorities may have received information anonymously. The 2002 White Paper proposes the setting up of a 'hot-line' for people to report suspected immigration offenders.

The police frequently ask for evidence of identification and immigration status from those who are black or 'foreign-looking' or those who do not have English as their first language. People may come into contact with the police for entirely separate reasons: they may have been stopped on suspicion of a traffic offence, at a demonstration or they may be wanted as a witness to an accident or crime. People may call the police because of a burglary or an assault and then be asked to prove their status. If it is then suspected that the person may be in breach of the immigration laws, the police can check with the immigration service or their own records. They are then likely to hold the person 'on suspicion' of committing an immigration offence and call immigration officers to interview them who may then be able to detain them under immigration powers.

It is a criminal offence for employers to employ a person who is not permitted to work in the UK although employers have a defence to prosecution if they have carried out certain checks and kept certain documents ▶see pages 415-416. Information may be relayed back to the immigration authorities by employers. In addition, sometimes the immigration authorities conduct raids on particular premises when they have information that people who have an irregular immigration status are working there.

Some employers are prepared to collaborate with the immigration authorities but, the Home Office has indicated that, in some cases, it will not try to obtain assistance in advance from the employer because:

'...efforts to enlist the co-operation of the employer would undermine the effectiveness of a planned operation. Visits will be authorised where there is apparently reliable information that immigration offenders will be found. Particular account will be taken of whether there is a history of the premises being used by offenders.'

Detection and the 2002 Bill

The 2002 Bill proposes to make further changes to assist in detection. Under its provisions, local authorities in whose area the immigration authorities believe a person to have been living, can be required to provide information about that person. Employers may also be required to produce information about their employees if they are suspected of being illegal entrants, overstayers or in breach of their conditions. The inland revenue (tax) authorities are also to be allowed to disclose information to the immigration authorities in order to establish the whereabouts of a person who has worked in breach of conditions of leave or temporary admission. The Bill also proposes to give powers to police and immigration officers to enter business premises, in some cases without a warrant, to search for illegal entrants, overstayers and those in breach of conditions of leave or temporary admission.

Powers of arrest and search

The police and the immigration service have powers, extended by the 1999 Act, to make unannounced raids on premises to search for people. Further powers are proposed in the 2002 Bill. The 1999 Act specifically extended the powers of arrest held by immigration officers and has given them police-like powers in relation to search, entry and seizure in dealing with the immigration offences of illegal entry, obtaining leave to enter or remain by deception and breaking conditions of leave ▶see below for these and other offences. Immigration officers are permitted to use 'reasonable force' in carrying out these functions.

The aim of these powers is to decrease the dependency of the immigration service on the police by enabling them to carry out such functions without police presence as was previously required.

Immigration Service teams are being trained to carry out the powers that they have been given under the 1999 Act and teams around the UK in different regions have begun to operate. They are concentrating on arresting asylum-seekers who have exhausted their appeal rights and for whom there is no bar to removal. The intention is that there is as little delay as possible between arrest and removal, with detainees only having access to family, friends and legal representatives initially by telephone. The stepping-up of these measures is designed to meet the government's publicly stated target of removing 2,500 failed asylum-seekers and their dependants each month.

Although the Home Office has stated, 'visits to private addresses will continue to be authorised only where there is good reason to suspect that an identified person is there in breach of the immigration laws', a house may be raided in search of one person and others are then asked to prove their identity.

Amendments which were made to the Immigration and Asylum Procedure Rules 2000 and effective from 7 January 2002, provide for the service in person by the immigration authorities of certain appeal determinations of adjudicators and the Immigration Appeal Tribunal (for further details ▶see pages 649-650). This will, of course, give the immigration authorities a further opportunity to detain and swiftly remove failed asylum-seekers without they or their advisers having a proper opportunity to consider the determination and, if appropriate, challenge it in the courts.

Criminal offences

Immigration law creates many criminal offences. Because some of the offences can lead to enforced departure, in most cases the authorities are content that immigration control is enforced and people are not actually charged with the criminal offence. The most important offences created by immigration law are set out below. Certain changes to the offences and sentences are proposed by the 2002 Bill (▶see pages 556-557 below).

Overstaying and breach of conditions

When a time limit is placed on a person's leave in the UK, it is an offence to stay beyond it (s24, 1971 Act). It is also an offence to breach any of the conditions which are attached to the leave, for example, by working when forbidden to do so. People can also be prosecuted for breaching the terms of their temporary admission or bail. The criminal offence is committed by 'knowingly' overstaying or breaching conditions. For the purposes of administrative removal, however, someone can be in breach of their conditions or overstaying their leave without knowing that they are doing so although they may not be committing the criminal offence.

Overstaying is a continuing offence, running from the day after the expiry of leave until the person either leaves the UK or is given fresh leave to remain by the Home Office. Anyone who applies even a day late to the Home Office for an extension and is aware that their application has not been submitted in time, may be committing this offence, despite the fact that their application remains under consideration. This is because, even though the delay may have been a mistake, they may be overstaying 'knowingly'. The authorities will not, in practice, want to prosecute if they consider the overstaying was inadvertent.

Those whose applications for extensions are submitted in time initially, but due to certain documentation or information not being provided the application is returned and then resubmitted out of time, may or may not know that they have become overstayers.

The maximum sentence is imprisonment for up to six months and a fine.

Entry without leave or in breach of a deportation order

Persons who 'knowingly' enter the UK either in breach of a deportation order or without obtaining leave (which they need) are liable for prosecution (s24, 1971 Act). These forms of entry are illegal but do not necessarily involve deception. The maximum sentence is imprisonment for up to six months and a fine.

Deception in obtaining leave or preventing enforcement

A person who obtains or tries to obtain leave to enter or leave to remain by deception and people who, by deception, avoid any form of action to require them to leave the UK, can be prosecuted (s24A, 1971 Act).

It is important to distinguish between the criminal offences relating to illegal entry and the immigration status of an illegal entrant. It will be seen from the categories of illegal entrant set out above that, for a person to be declared an illegal entrant by the immigration authorities, it is not necessary for them to have any intention to act unlawfully or any knowledge of the unlawful act. The criminal offence requires knowledge. So a person brought unlawfully to the UK without the required degree of knowledge, and certain entrants through Ireland (▶see pages 74-75), may not be committing a criminal offence (▶see below for the prosecution of asylum-seekers for illegal entry). The maximum sentence, if tried in the Crown Court, is two years' imprisonment and a fine.

Assisting illegal entry and asylum claimants

It is an offence for a person to help (see s25, 1971 Act):

- a person who they know or believe to be intending to enter illegally to gain entry;
- a person who they know or believe intends to make an asylum or human rights claim to gain entry;
- a person to obtain leave to remain by means which the person helping knows will include deception.

The offence of assisting asylum claimants is worrying and adds to the already difficult task which asylum-seekers have of getting to the UK in the first place. The specific offence relating to asylum claimants was introduced because of the decision of the House of Lords in *Naillie*. In that case, the House of Lords held that, where those travelling to the UK claimed asylum on arrival, there was no illegal entry and so anyone helping them to come here could not commit the offence of assisting illegal entry.

The offence is aimed at racketeers who charge to help secure entry of asylum-seekers clandestinely or with false documents. The offence does not cover assistance given to people already here who have been detained or granted temporary admission on entry and it only applies to people who are giving their assistance 'for gain'. It also does not apply to anything done by a person working for a *bona fide* organisation which helps asylum-seekers. Neither of these exemptions is defined further but the government has stated that community organisations, churches and charities are generally protected from prosecution and also that the offence is not aimed at solicitors.

The maximum sentence, if convicted in the Crown Court, is 10 years' imprisonment and a fine.

'Harbouring' illegal entrants, overstayers and those in breach of conditions

It is an offence for anyone to 'harbour', which means look after or accommodate, anyone who they know or believe to be an illegal entrant, an overstayer or someone in breach of their conditions of leave (e.g. someone who is working unlawfully). The present maximum sentence is imprisonment for six months and a fine.

Offences connected with the support of asylum-seekers

In relation to asylum support, it is an offence to make false representations; to fail to notify a change of circumstances; to obstruct an officer in operating the support scheme; or, as a sponsor, to fail to maintain a person who they have signed an undertaking to support and who later claims asylum support (see s105–108, 1999 Act). The maximum punishments in most of these cases are prison sentences of up to three months and/or fines. However, for dishonest representations, a person can be sentenced, on conviction in the Crown Court, to imprisonment for seven years and a fine.

Provision of advice

Those who provide immigration advice in contravention of the rules set out in Chapter 3 may be prosecuted for an offence (s91, 1999 Act). If tried in a Crown Court, they can be sentenced to a maximum term of two years' imprisonment.

Employer sanctions

From 27 January 1997, it has been an offence for an employer to employ a person who requires, but who either does not have, leave, or whose leave prevents them from working in the job in question. Asylum-seekers who have written permission to work are exempted from this. For full details about this offence and the means by which employers can ensure that they are not prosecuted for it ▶see pages 415-416. The offence is presently punishable by a fine.

General offences

Included among the general offences under the 1971 Act which can result in imprisonment for a maximum period of six months and/or a fine are (s26, 1971 Act): refusing to be examined by an immigration officer or to produce information or documents which they have and which is required for the examination, making false representations or using false or altered documents which are required for immigration control and obstructing an immigration officer in carrying out their duty.

Proposed changes to criminal offences in the 2002 Bill

The 2002 Bill proposes that it will be an offence to assist another person in breaching the immigration laws of any EU member state (including the UK) with regard to entry, remaining or travelling in that state. This offence is intended to include harbouring a person in breach of the immigration laws. It will also be an offence to assist anyone to enter in breach of a deportation order. The maximum sentence for these offences, on conviction in the Crown Court, is 14 years' imprisonment and/or a fine. The proposals also increase the sentence for what were already offences (see above) as well as creating new offences.

The following new offences are also proposed:

- An offence of trafficking in prostitution. It will carry a maximum sentence, on conviction in the Crown Court, of 14 years and fine. This offence will be committed when a person arranges for a person to enter or leave the UK in circumstances where they will be controlled in prostitution in the UK or elsewhere.

- A range of offences concerning the Asylum Registration Card; including making a false card, altering a genuine card and possessing or using a false card. The maximum sentence, on conviction, in the Crown Court, is a two-year prison sentence and a fine.

- An offence of being in possession of an immigration stamp (the stamp used by immigration officials for issuing leave) or a replica stamping device. The maximum sentence, on conviction, in the Crown Court, is two years' imprisonment and a fine.

The Bill also proposes to allow the immigration authorities to require employers, banks and building societies to disclose information about a person's earnings and their finances where that person is suspected of having fraudulently obtained asylum support.

The prosecution of asylum-seekers

The criminal sanctions on illegal entry (above) have been used to prosecute asylum-seekers who had entered the UK illegally despite the fact that, for most asylum-seekers, there are no legitimate methods of entry to the UK available. In *Adimi*, the High Court found that to impose penalties by prosecuting refugees in this way was unlawful and contrary to Article 31 of the Refugee Convention which states that refugees should not have penalties imposed on them if they enter directly from the place they fear persecution and claim asylum without delay.

As a result of *Adimi*, the 1999 Act includes a defence for refugees who are prosecuted with illegal entry by deception and forgery offences (see s31). To benefit from the defence, the person must:

- have presented themselves to the immigration authorities in the UK without delay;

- show 'good cause' for their illegal entry;

- have made a claim for asylum as soon as was 'reasonably practicable' after arrival in the UK;

- be a 'refugee'. A defendant can still produce evidence to the criminal court to demonstrate that they are a refugee, even if the Home Office has refused the claim to asylum.

The 1999 Act also allows anyone previously wrongly convicted in the light of *Adimi*, to have their cases referred to the Criminal Cases Review Commission.

There is now a joint memorandum of good practice between the Home Office, the Crown Prosecution Service and the Law Society which indicates that, before any proceedings are initiated, consideration should be given to both Article 31 and the statutory defence under the 1999 Act. Only in the clearest of cases, where there is no suggestion of a fear of persecution, should the police proceed to charge a person with such an offence. In addition, consideration must be given to whether it is in the public interest to prosecute, which is unlikely to be the case where the person appears to be a genuine asylum-seeker at the time of his or her arrival or has been granted exceptional leave or refugee status, even where the person did not present themselves without delay.

Section 9 **British nationality**

Chapter 27
British nationality   561

Establishing citizenship   564

British citizens   567

British nationals who are not British citizens   576

Chapter 28
How to become British   583

Naturalisation   584

Registration   589

Passports and travel documents   593

Deprivation of citizenship   594

27 British nationality

This section looks at the law relating to nationality. Nationality law is different from immigration law as it deals with the country of which a person is a citizen, rather than the method of controlling the entry of people into the country. Normally countries do not impose immigration restrictions upon their own citizens. British nationality is, however, more complex than most in that it recognises different forms of British national with different rights.

This chapter covers the development of British nationality to its current state, the different forms of nationality and how to determine whether a person is British. Chapter 28 describes how people can obtain British nationality.

For a summary of the proposed changes in nationality law under the Nationality, Immigration and Asylum Bill 2002 ▶see pages 594-595. For JCWI's views on the nationality proposals ▶see pages 22-24.

Development of British nationality

British nationality law has changed greatly during the post-war period. In 1947, there was no such thing as British or UK citizenship. Instead, people born in the UK, or a British colony or dominion, were British subjects. All of them had an automatic right to enter and live in the UK. During the period 1948–83, a series of nationality and immigration laws restricted and defined those rights. The British Nationality Act 1948 created a citizenship of the UK and Colonies (CUKC) for those from the UK and those colonies not yet independent. It also recognised two residual forms of status for small groups of people, mainly from the Indian subcontinent and Africa: British Protected Persons and British subjects without citizenship.

As colonies gained independence, people from the newly independent countries normally lost CUKC status and gained citizenship of the new Commonwealth country. At first, this did not affect their right to enter the UK; all Commonwealth citizens, as well as CUKCs, continued to be classed as British subjects and as such had the right of abode in the UK (also called 'patriality'). This is much more than simply a right of residence: it means that a person is free from general immigration control and has a right to enter, live and work in the UK.

However, immigration laws between 1965 and 1971 restricted those rights, not only for citizens of independent Commonwealth countries, but also for some CUKCs who did not have connections of birth or descent with the UK. This meant that having a British passport was no indication of a right to enter or live in Britain. East African Asians, people from Hong Kong and from Montserrat were among those who found that they were unable freely to enter the country of their nationality when they wanted and needed to do so. Conversely, some citizens of independent Commonwealth countries, who were not CUKCs, retained the right of abode because, for example, a parent had been born in the UK or they had a husband who was a British citizen or had the right of abode.

The British Nationality Act 1981

The British Nationality Act 1981 (implemented on 1 January 1983) did two things. First, it changed the way people can acquire British nationality, by birth, descent or grant. Second, it tried to bring citizenship and immigration law into line. It abolished the status of CUKC and created three new nationalities:

- CUKCs who had the right of abode became British citizens;
- CUKCs who had gained that status because of a connection with an existing colony or dependency became British Dependent Territories citizens;
- CUKCs who did not fit into either of these groups became British Overseas citizens.

Neither British Dependent Territories citizenship (▶but see changes below) nor British Overseas citizenship conferred a right of abode in the UK (though some British Dependent Territories citizens with a UK connection may be British citizens as well). Citizens of independent Commonwealth countries who had the right of abode on 1 January 1983 will retain this for the rest of their lives; but no one has been able to acquire the right of abode in the UK since that date without becoming a British citizen.

Types of British nationality

There are six types of British nationality which a person with a British passport may have. These nationalities are listed below, with examples of the main (but not the only) people who may hold them.

- **British citizens:** people who gained British nationality because of a connection with the UK itself – by birth, descent, registration or naturalisation ▶see flowcharts on pages 569 and 575 to help identify who is a British citizen.
- **British Overseas Territories citizens (BOTCs) (formerly British Dependent Territories citizens (BDTCs)):** this covers people from the few remaining Overseas Territories (formerly Dependent Territories) ▶see below for their status from May 2002.

- **British Overseas citizens (BOCs):** people who were UK and Colonies citizens but do not qualify for either of the above; mainly people from minority ethnic communities from East Africa ('East African Asians') or Malaysia.

- **British Nationals (Overseas) (BN(O)s):** people from Hong Kong who applied for this status before 1997 and who did not, or could not, register as British citizens under one of the 1990–97 Acts.

- **British Protected Persons (BPPs):** people from places that were protectorates, not colonies; mainly in the Indian subcontinent and Africa.

- **British subjects** (formerly British subjects without citizenship): mainly people from the Indian subcontinent, who were born before 1948 and did not become UK and Colonies citizens or Indian/Pakistani citizens.

The last two categories are now rare, as they applied only to small numbers of people, who are now elderly or middle-aged. The middle two are also transitional statuses and will largely die out with their present holders.

Members of the first category, British citizens, have the right of abode in the UK and are not subject to immigration control ▶see below for BOTCs. Other kinds of British nationals need to fit into the immigration rules, as described in the other chapters of this book, if they want to enter or live in the UK. They may, therefore, have permission to be in the UK (e.g., as students, visitors or spouses) but they have no automatic right by virtue of their British nationality – they are treated like any other foreigner applying to enter Britain (but ▶see pages 576-577 for the right of re-admission for some BOCs).

Important changes since 1983

Since 1983, there have been three important changes to the structure set out in the 1981 Act.

- People from the Falkland Islands (originally BDTCs) were made into full British citizens after the Falklands war under the British Nationality (Falkland Islands) Act 1983.

- People from Hong Kong (also BDTCs) were given the opportunity to acquire yet another new British status, that of British National (Overseas), under the Hong Kong Act 1985, prior to Hong Kong's return to China in 1997. This status does not carry the right of abode in the UK. Some Hong Kong British nationals were, however, allowed to register as full British citizens under legislation passed between 1990 and 1997 ▶see pages 579-582.

The British Overseas Territories Act 2002

The third important change is that the British Overseas Territories Act 2002 redesignates BDTCs as 'British Overseas Territories Citizens' (BOTCs). Anyone who was a BOTC immediately before 21 May 2002 was automatically granted British citizenship and obtained the right of abode in the UK (see s3 British Overseas Territories Act 2002 and British Overseas Territories Act 2002 (Commencement) Order 2002). The dependencies themselves were redesignated by the 2002 Act as 'British Overseas Territories'. They are: Anguilla, Bermuda, British Antarctica, British Indian Ocean Territory, British Virgin Islands, Cayman Islands, Falkland Islands, Gibraltar, Montserrat, Pitcairn Islands, St Helena and Dependencies, South Georgia and the South Sandwich Islands, Turks and Caicos Islands and the Cyprus Sovereign Base Areas of Akrotiri and Dhekelia.

However, the Act excludes BOTCs from the Cyprus Sovereign Base Areas because of its special status as a military base. They do not obtain the right of abode in the UK. People who were only BOTCs by descent will become British citizens by descent. This is important because British citizens by descent cannot automatically pass their citizenship on to their children. People who become BOTCs *after* the commencement of the Act, will be able to apply to be registered as British citizens. This registration is discretionary.

The legislation is welcome as it restores some citizenship rights which were taken away in 1962. However, JCWI believes that it does not go far enough: it does not restore the rights of British Overseas citizens or bring the position of British Protected Persons, British Subjects or British Nationals (Overseas) into line with British citizens. The explanatory notes to the legislation had estimated a population of 200,000 for all the Overseas Territories and so extending rights at least to British Overseas citizens would not have had any major implications. The position is particularly acute in Kenya where the conflicting policies of the British and Kenyan governments have resulted in the children of BOCs being rendered stateless and the Kenyan government denying any form of responsibility to them.

In a letter to the Immigration Law Practitioners' Association on 4 January 2002, the Home Office indicated that it had no intentions to amend the law further so as to give full citizenship rights to the outstanding categories of British national including BOCs. It was recognised, however, that the government would reconsider the position if (as expected) Lord Redesdale brings forward a private member's bill on the subject.

Establishing citizenship

This is relatively easy for those with current passports. All passports issued since 1 January 1983 will describe the citizenship status a person acquired under the 1981 Act. It is more complicated to establish the present citizenship of those British nationals who have pre-1983 passports, or no passports at all.

Passports issued on or after 1 January 1983

These passports should describe people's nationality status on the page with their personal details: 'British citizen', 'British Overseas citizen', 'British Dependent Territories citizen', 'British subject', 'British Protected Person' or 'British National (Overseas)'.

Points to note

- There is now no endorsement on British citizen passports stating that the holder has the right of abode: that is automatic because of the holders' status as British citizens. This worries some people when they get a new passport, in case their right of abode has been withdrawn. They should be reassured that this is not the case.

- No other British nationals have the right of abode in the UK (although see above for BDTCs), except for a few British subjects (usually married women). They should have passport endorsements called 'certificates of entitlement to the right of abode' (▶see page 121 for an example), which have replaced the old certificates of patriality, issued before 1 January 1983.

- All new British passports issued now are the uniform EU passports, which are maroon-coloured and computer-readable. Some people, wrongly, believe that they are of lower status than the old blue passports.

Passports issued before 1 January 1983

Most British passports issued before 1 January 1983 describe the holder, on page 1, as a 'British subject: citizen of the UK and Colonies'. If this is the case, turn to page 5 of the passport. This usually says 'holder has the right of abode in the UK'. If this is in the passport, and has not been crossed out, it is almost certain that the holder is now a British citizen. He or she would automatically have become a British citizen on 1 January 1983 without needing to do anything about it.

If the wording on page 5 has been cancelled, then it is likely that the holder is a British Overseas citizen. The holder may also have been a BDTC ▶see above for their status following the British Overseas Territories Act 2002, which gave them the right of abode. Otherwise, if the wording has been cancelled, this will mean that he or she does not have the right of abode in the UK and will need to fit into the immigration rules to come to or stay in the UK. But it is still worth checking the points below in case this status has changed since the passport was issued, or it was issued in error.

The status of British Protected Person and British subject was not changed by the British Nationality Act 1981: passports issued before or after 1983 will show these statuses on the first page. A few British subjects (usually married women) have the right of abode in the UK; if so, it will be signalled on page 5 or as a stamp called a certificate of patriality. However, the majority of British subjects and all British Protected Persons do not have the right of abode in the UK and will need to fit into the immigration rules if they wish to come to or stay in the UK.

Points to note

- **Check that nothing has happened to change the person's status since the passport was issued.** A passport is not proof of present nationality; it is only evidence that a person had that status when the passport was issued. This is particularly relevant for people from Commonwealth countries who hold British passports which were issued before their countries became independent. At independence, most people from that country automatically lost their British nationality and gained nationality of the newly independent country; but their British passports were not recalled and they were usually not even told about their change of nationality. For people born outside the UK, without parents or grandparents born in Britain, it is therefore worth checking the date of issue of the passport against the date of independence of their country of origin ▶see page 748.

- **People from Caribbean countries which gained their independence from 1981 onwards** gain citizenship of the new country but also, if they had lived in the UK for more than five years and were settled before independence, keep their British citizenship. This has applied so far to people from Belize, St Kitts-Nevis and Antigua, Barbuda and Bermuda.

- **Some people from Hong Kong** are not any kind of British national, though they have travel documents which were issued by the Hong Kong government or the British Home Office. They are people born in the People's Republic of China, who emigrated to Hong Kong and may subsequently have come to the UK. They travel on brown documents called certificates of identity (or CIs in Hong Kong). They are, in effect, stateless people (save for having a right to Chinese nationality) and have no special rights in British immigration and nationality law.

- **Women who were Commonwealth citizens on 31 December 1982** (the day before the British Nationality Act 1981 came into force), who were married on or before that date to British citizen men, or men with the right of abode, have themselves the right of abode in the UK (although they are not British citizens by entitlement). Such women need to apply to the British high commission before they travel for a 'certificate of entitlement to the right of abode' and pay a fee (currently £110 payable in local currency). This provision does not apply to men. Nor does it apply to non-Commonwealth citizen women. Camerounian, Mozambican, Namibian, Pakistani and South African citizen women cannot benefit from this because these countries were not members of the Commonwealth in 1982.

- **Commonwealth citizens born before 1 January 1983** who had a parent born in the UK also have the right of abode in the UK.

There are special queues for people with a claim to the right of abode (which in the Indian subcontinent countries means that the queue will be much shorter) which are separate from those applying for entry clearance.

If a woman applied by mistake for an entry clearance and paid the fee appropriate to the entry clearance application, then the difference should be refunded by the ECO as they have a duty to identify which category a person falls under. In order to obtain the certificate of entitlement, the woman will need her original marriage certificate (to show the date of the marriage) and proof that her husband was either a British citizen or a Commonwealth citizen with the right of abode at the time of the marriage. It does not matter if the husband has since died.

When the certificate of entitlement is granted, it is valid for the same length of time as the passport and the person is free to travel to the UK and to return at any time during the validity of the passport. The returning resident rules (▶see pages 79-83) do not apply to them. When the passport expires, the Home Office or the British high commission will give a new certificate of entitlement in a new passport, on production of the same evidence. Such people may of course seek to naturalise to become British citizens once they have resided in the UK (▶see pages 584-589) for a certain length of time. For Commonwealth women, the length of residence required depends on whether the husband is still alive.

British citizens

Checking for British citizenship

If people have current passports which describe them as 'British citizens', then it is clear that they are British citizens. But some people do not have British passports (for example, children born in the UK, or children born abroad who have been issued with certificates of entitlement to the right of abode endorsed on their foreign passport, rather than a British passport issued overseas), or may have changed their status since their British or foreign passport was issued ▶the flowcharts contained in the boxes on pages 569 and 575 will help to identify other people who are British citizens.

Points to note

- It is not definite that people are not British citizens just because they do not fit into the flowchart; there are other, somewhat rare, ways of acquiring British citizenship.

- The flowcharts deal only with *British citizens* and not other kinds of British national.

- 'Parent' or 'father' applies to men only if they were legally married to the child's mother. If the parents married after the child's birth it depends on the law of the country where the marriage took place whether the marriage automatically 'legitimises' the child (if so this makes him or her a British citizen), or whether any special procedures have to be followed. Despite the recommendation of the Law Commission as long ago as 1986 and the introduction of DNA testing this has remained the position. A recent challenge to this rule under the Human Rights Act in the case of *Montana* (Court of Appeal) was unsuccessful. However the Home Office operates a policy on registration of illegitimate children ▶see page 591. The 2002 Bill finally proposes to abolish discrimination in nationality law against 'illegitimate' children.

- Children (under 18) who are adopted in the UK are treated as if they were born in the UK and if one or both of the adoptive parents are British at the date of adoption then the child will be treated as if he or she were British by birth. However, this will not be the case if the parent(s) are only settled in the UK. In such cases the child will need to be registered as a British citizen ▶see page 590. If the child is adopted overseas, they will not currently acquire British citizenship. However, the Adoption (Intercountry Aspects) Act 1999, which is not yet wholly in force, provides for the automatic acquisition of British nationality under section 1(5) of the British Nationality Act 1981 for adoptions abroad from countries who are signatories to the Hague Convention on Protection of Children and Co-operation in respect of Inter-Country Adoption 1993. When section 7 of that Act comes into force, whether or not the child will acquire British citizenship in this manner will depend on whether the adoption took place in a country which is a signatory to the Hague Convention. This will be a welcome change from the current position where all adopted children from abroad have to enter under 'ordinary immigration' law and then seek to register as British citizens.

- British citizens are divided into those who acquired their citizenship 'by descent' (i.e., through a parent or grandparent) and those who acquired it 'otherwise than by descent' ▶see below for an explanation of how to tell, and what difference it makes.

People born or adopted in the UK

Before 1983

Prior to 1 January 1983, everyone born in the UK (and all children adopted in the UK by a British father) were British citizens ▶see above. The only exception was the children of diplomats. The British Nationality Act 1981 does not change the status of people born before 1 January 1983 and therefore all those born in the UK before that date (except diplomats' children) remain British citizens.

Since 1983

One of the major changes in the British Nationality Act 1981 was the provision for acquiring nationality by birth in the UK. People born in the UK on or after 1 January 1983 become British citizens at birth only if one of their parents either is a British citizen or is settled (allowed to stay permanently) in the UK at the time of the birth ▶see above for children adopted in the UK since 1983.

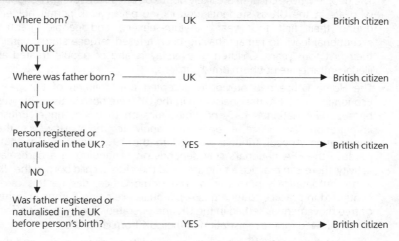

WHO IS A BRITISH CITIZEN? People born before 1 January 1983

Where born? ——————— UK ——————————————→ British citizen

NOT UK

Where was father born? ——————— UK ——————————————→ British citizen

NOT UK

Person registered or naturalised in the UK? ——————— YES ——————————————→ British citizen

NO

Was father registered or naturalised in the UK before person's birth? ——————— YES ——————————————→ British citizen

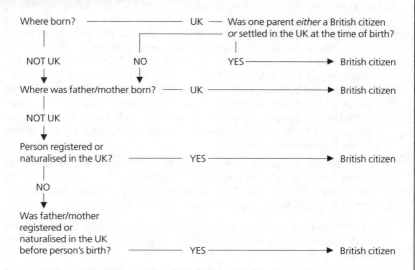

WHO IS A BRITISH CITIZEN? People born on or after 1 January 1983

Where born? ——————— UK —— Was one parent *either* a British citizen *or* settled in the UK at the time of birth?

NOT UK   NO   YES ——————————→ British citizen

Where was father/mother born? —— UK ——————————————→ British citizen

NOT UK

Person registered or naturalised in the UK? ——————— YES ——————————————→ British citizen

NO

Was father/mother registered or naturalised in the UK before person's birth? ——————— YES ——————————————→ British citizen

You cannot be sure that someone is *not* British on the basis of these flowcharts

Note: Throughout, father = father who is married to mother but the position for 'illegitimate' children will change under the 2002 Bill.

Points to note

- The people whose children are likely *not* to be British are foreign nationals who are in the UK as students, visitors, au pairs, work permit holders during their first four years, asylum-seekers, and people granted exceptional leave to remain (having been refused refugee status) within their first four years. Children of overstayers and of people treated as illegal entrants are not born British citizens.

- The Home Office had previously accepted that children of European Economic Area (EEA) nationals born in the UK were born British. This was because EEA nationals have no time limits on their stay under British immigration law, since it does not apply to them. However the Immigration Appeal Tribunal decided in the 1997 case of *Gal* that, because the EEA national's stay depends on continuing in a particular activity, there is in practice a time limit and therefore a child born in the UK is not automatically born British. The Home Office, despite this case, continued in practice to regard EEA nationals exercising European rights of free movement as settled in the UK and operated a policy to this effect which allowed for the registration of their UK-born children.

  However, the Home Office has now changed its approach on this and the European Economic Area Regulations 2000 (reg 8) confirm the Home Office view (now) which is that *most* EEA national parents who are in the UK exercising rights of free movement are to be treated as having restrictions on the period of their leave. Accordingly, they are not treated as 'settled' for nationality purposes and therefore any child born is not British. However, as the Home Office confirmed in a letter to the Immigration Law Practitioners' Association in September 2000, the change in the law only applies to children born on or after 2 October 2000. Children born to parents exercising rights of free movement before that time are British whether or not their parent had by that time established a right of permanent residence. Clearly this may lead to the anomalous situation where there is an earlier child who is born British whilst a later one may not be.

  EEA nationals exercising free movement rights who *are* regarded as 'settled' are those who EU law or the immigration rules say are entitled to permanent residence in the UK. For details of those EEA nationals who are treated as settled ▶see pages 454-455 and 473-475.

  If the British-born child of an EEA national is now refused citizenship, it is worth seeking advice and considering an application for registration in due course.

- 'Parent' in nationality law does not (presently) include the father if he is not married to the child's mother. But if the marriage takes place in the UK the child can get British citizenship from the father even if the parents marry after his or her birth ▶see pages 567-568 above.

- Children born in the UK and not born British do not have any immigration status. They cannot therefore overstay a leave to remain, as they do not have leave. However, they are not free from immigration controls. If their parent(s) are deported from the UK (on grounds that their presence is not conducive to the public good) or are being administratively removed from the UK (as overstayers, a person who has breached their conditions of leave or has obtained leave to remain by deception), non-British citizen British born children can also be removed as part of the family unit (the 2002 Bill will allow all such children to be removable when their parents are being removed from the UK). Otherwise, these children (though not necessarily their parents) can remain in the UK indefinitely. If, however, they leave the UK, they will require leave in order to return. If they are travelling with parents who obtain leave to enter the UK, the children will usually be readmitted for the same time period and on the same conditions as their parents; they will then be subject to the usual sanctions if they overstay that leave.

- Children born in the UK and not born British may be able to register as British citizens after their birth either if their parent becomes settled or if they live in the UK for ten years ▶see pages 590-593 for further details.

- If the parents want to travel and to take the children, the children have no claim to a British passport. They may be entitled to the nationality of either parent, depending on the nationality laws of their country and may be able to get a passport from the relevant high commission or embassy, or a parent may be able to have the children's names inserted on his or her passport. If the children are not able to get a passport, the parent should try to obtain the refusal in writing, or confirmation that the children are not regarded as citizens of the country. It may then be possible for the parent to obtain stateless travel documents for the children from the Home Office.

People born overseas

People born before 1 January 1983 with a British parent

Before 1 January 1983, British nationality by descent could pass only through fathers; children born overseas to British mothers and foreign fathers were not born British.

Children born outside the UK to British fathers automatically became CUKCs by descent with the right of abode, and therefore British citizens, if their father obtained that status in one of the following ways:

- by being born, or being adopted by a UK citizen father, in the UK; *or*
- by being registered or naturalised in the UK before the child was born.

If the father registered outside the UK it would give him (and possibly the child) some other kind of British nationality (▶see above) but not British citizenship. If the father became British after a child's birth, this would not retrospectively make the child British. 'Father' here applies only to men who were legally married to the child's mother. Marriage certificates or some very clear proof of marriage will be required in order to prove the citizenship of people born overseas.

Children born outside the UK before 1983 to British mothers could not inherit their mother's citizenship. However the Home Office has stated that if British-born mothers apply for children under 18 born outside the UK to be registered to become British citizens, this will be granted, provided the father (if the parents are still married) has no well-founded objection and provided that the child is still under 18 at the time of application. This dispensation therefore came to an end at the end of 2000. There is no special provision for people who are now adults born abroad to British mothers to become British citizens.

There are some circumstances in which having a British *grandfather* could result in a child born overseas before 1 January 1983 being a British citizen now. This applies if:

- the grandfather in question is the father's father, *and*
- the grandfather acquired his citizenship in the UK by birth, registration or naturalisation, *and*
- the child was born in a non-Commonwealth country (▶see page 748 for list of Commonwealth countries), *and*
- the child's birth was registered at a British consulate within a year of the birth.

People born on or after 1 January 1983 with a British parent

Since 1 January 1983, women as well as men have been able to pass on British nationality to children born overseas. Children born abroad on or after 1 January 1983 are therefore British citizens automatically if either their father or mother is a British citizen who acquired citizenship in the UK as described on page 571 above, or is a British citizen otherwise than by descent in some other way. Once again, the father's status only counts if he was married to the mother and can prove this to be the case.

This provision is not retrospective; in other words, there will be families of British women living overseas where some children (born before 1 January 1983) are not British citizens while their siblings born on or after 1 January 1983 are British citizens.

From 1 January 1983, any British citizen who acquired his or her citizenship *otherwise than by descent* (▶see below) is able to pass on that citizenship to children born abroad. Thus there is a further category of people whose children born abroad from 1983 onwards are British citizens; people who themselves were British otherwise than by descent and who had gained the right of abode by living in the UK as a UK and Colonies citizen, for five years or more, and being settled in the UK, before 1 January 1983 and before the child's birth. The parent must have been British during the five-year period and must have remained so at least until the child's birth. If the child was born before 1983, he or she will not be a British citizen.

The provisions for acquiring British citizenship for subsequent generations are set out in the flowchart in the box on ▶page 575.

People without a British parent

People born overseas who do not have a British parent or grandparent can normally only obtain British citizenship by living in the UK and meeting the residence and other requirements for registration or naturalisation ▶see Chapter 28.

British citizenship by descent

People born overseas who acquire British citizenship only because one or both of their parents is a British citizen are classified as British citizens by descent.

People who acquire British citizenship by birth in the UK, by registration or naturalisation in the UK, or by being UK and Colonies citizens with five years' residence and settlement in the UK before 1 January 1983 are classified as British citizens otherwise than by descent.

The only difference between the two kinds of British citizens is that those who are citizens by descent cannot automatically pass on citizenship to their children born abroad. However a citizen by descent cannot seek to 'upgrade' their citizenship status in order to seek to transmit their nationality to their children born abroad. It was recently confirmed by the Court of Appeal in *Ullah* that a British Citizen by descent could not become a British Citizen by naturalisation.

Before 1 January 1983 British men who had children in *non-Commonwealth* countries could pass on British nationality through numerous generations, provided that the children's births were registered at a British consulate. This would not usually make the children full British citizens after the second generation born abroad (i.e., if they did not have a grandfather born, registered or naturalised in the UK). Such children would not have the right of abode because they would not fulfil the requirements for patriality under the Immigration Act 1971 (▶see Glossary for definition of patriality) and would therefore normally have become British Overseas citizens on 1 January 1983.

Children born in *Commonwealth* countries did not acquire any form of British nationality if their father was British by descent.

After 1 January 1983 the British Nationality Act 1981 removed the difference between Commonwealth and non-Commonwealth countries but restricted the automatic transmission of British nationality to one generation. Children born abroad to a parent who is a British citizen otherwise than by descent are automatically born British. However, if the

British citizen parent is a citizen by descent, a child born abroad will not be born British. This means that British citizenship can pass automatically only for one generation to a child born abroad to British parents. However, the 1981 Act included provisions for some second-generation children to be registered abroad as British citizens.

These provisions mean that a child born overseas has the right to be registered at the British consulate as a British citizen within one year of the birth (or within six years where there are special circumstances in a particular case) provided that:

- one of the parents is a British citizen by descent;
- the British parent has a parent who is or was British otherwise than by descent;
- the British parent had at some time before the child's birth lived in the UK for a continuous period of three years, not being absent for more than 270 days in that period.

These children will become British citizens by descent. A registration form (MN1) must be completed and a fee is payable.

If the child and its parents do not fulfil all the above requirements, it is not possible for the child to be registered as a British citizen overseas. A third-generation child born overseas will never have a right to registration under the provisions above, because she or he will never be able to fulfil the second requirement ▶see box below. The only exception to this is if a parent is in 'designated service' ▶see below.

However, there is a fall-back provision if the child and both its parents return to live in the UK. Any child born overseas to a British-citizen-by-descent parent has a right to be registered as a British citizen in the UK provided that the child and both parents (unless they are divorced or one is dead) live in the UK for a continuous period of three years. In that case, the child will have a right to register as a British citizen and moreover will become a British citizen otherwise than by descent.

It is possible to use this last provision as an alternative to registration abroad; for example, if the parents have missed the one-year deadline or if they would rather wait and register the child in the UK so that the child will be able to pass on its own British nationality later without any problems. Once a child has been registered abroad as a citizen by descent, it is not possible to alter this to become a citizen otherwise than by descent, even if the family comes to live in the UK for more than three years.

There are further details about other registration and naturalisation provisions in Chapter 28.

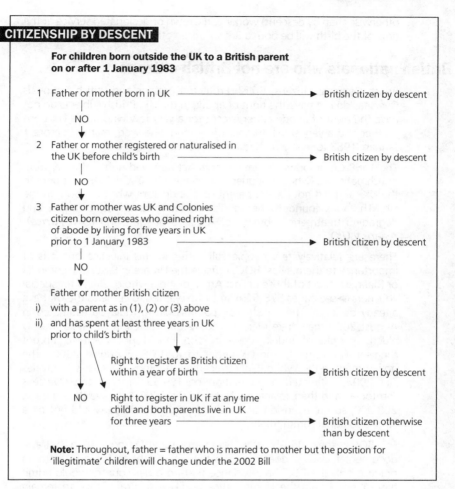

CITIZENSHIP BY DESCENT

For children born outside the UK to a British parent on or after 1 January 1983

1 Father or mother born in UK ⟶ British citizen by descent

   NO

2 Father or mother registered or naturalised in the UK before child's birth ⟶ British citizen by descent

   NO

3 Father or mother was UK and Colonies citizen born overseas who gained right of abode by living for five years in UK prior to 1 January 1983 ⟶ British citizen by descent

   NO

   Father or mother British citizen
i)   with a parent as in (1), (2) or (3) above
ii) and has spent at least three years in UK prior to child's birth

     Right to register as British citizen within a year of birth ⟶ British citizen by descent

NO   Right to register in UK if at any time child and both parents live in UK for three years ⟶ British citizen otherwise than by descent

Note: Throughout, father = father who is married to mother but the position for 'illegitimate' children will change under the 2002 Bill

Citizenship through Crown or designated service

There are special citizenship provisions for people doing certain government service jobs abroad. The work must be either Crown service (i.e., working at a British embassy or high commission abroad, or serving in the British armed forces abroad) or designated service (working outside the UK in a defined list of jobs for the British government, for example working for the British Council, the British Tourist Authority or the Medical Research Council, or working abroad for an EU or international institution, e.g., the United Nations). People in these jobs are considered as working in the UK for the purpose of passing on citizenship. A child born outside the UK to a parent who is a British citizen (by descent or otherwise than by descent) working in Crown or designated service at the time of the birth will be born a British citizen otherwise than by descent.

British nationals who are not British citizens

British Overseas citizens, British Protected Persons and British Nationals Overseas do not have the right of abode in the UK. British subjects do not have the right of abode either except for a very few who had a UK-born mother and a very small number of women who were married before 1 January 1983 to men who had the right of abode in the UK.

The 1968 Commonwealth Immigrants Act removed rights of entry from British nationals (who subsequently became BOCs) who were not born in the UK, and did not have a parent or grandparent who was born in the UK. This was found to be so discriminatory as to be inhuman and degrading treatment in breach of Article 3 of the ECHR (*East African Asians v UK*).

There are relatively few people still suffering this injustice but it is of importance to them. Most BOCs outside the UK are in East Africa or India or Malaysia. Most of those in East Africa or India who qualified for special vouchers (▶see pages 578-579) and who wanted to come to the UK have already done so. The British high commission in Malaysia estimated in August 2000 that there were 'up to 12,000' BOCs in Malaysia, mainly elderly people of Indian descent who would not want to uproot themselves and go to the UK (letter to JUSTICE, 3 August 2000). The government in the White Paper preceding the British Overseas Territories Act 2002, estimated a population of 189,531 for all the Overseas Territories, and the Explanatory Notes to the 2002 Act gave the figure as 200,000, so an extension of citizenship rights to BOCs would not be a large additional commitment.

For BOCs, their British status amounts to little more than a travel document facility. It does not give them the right to live anywhere. In practice only if a BOC had evidence that no other country would admit him or her would the Home Office be likely to grant leave to remain exceptionally outside of the Immigration Rules.

The European Court of Justice (in the case of *Kaur*) was asked to rule on the position of BOCs unable to gain entry to the country of their only nationality. It found that the matter was outside EU law. But at the hearing the court expressed concern at their position, describing them as 'Flying Dutchmen': able to travel, but with no rights to settle anywhere.

Right of readmission

British Overseas citizens who have been admitted for settlement to the UK have a right to be readmitted for settlement at any time. They may obtain a passport endorsement from the Home Office, 'Holder has the right of readmission to the UK'. This means that even if they stay away from the UK for more than two years at a time, they cannot be refused indefinite leave to remain when they return. They are not, therefore, subject to the requirements of the returning residents rule ▶see pages 79-83. In practice, this also normally applies to other British nationals except BDTCs.

Other British nationals who are not British citizens, except Gibraltarians and those who do not hold special vouchers, have to fit into the immigration rules to come into the UK for any other purpose (see the relevant chapter for details). People who enter as visitors and then apply to remain longer, because their citizenship does not entitle them to live in any other country, may be refused under the strict letter of the immigration rules. The Home Office has also made decisions to enforce their departure, usually to the country in which they were living immediately before coming to the UK, and has then put pressure on the authorities of that country to admit them. Deportation orders were enforced against two BOCs in 1994–96, but the Home Office has not stated to which countries they were sent. Immigration officers have completed application forms for visas to other countries for British Overseas citizens who have made it clear they do not wish to travel there. It is important to monitor this Home Office treatment of British Overseas citizens and to challenge attempts to enforce immigration controls against them.

Passing on nationality to children

British Overseas citizens, British Protected Persons, British subjects and British Nationals (Overseas) cannot pass on their citizenship to their children. Apart from the special provisions for Hong Kong, it is no longer possible to acquire BOC, BPP or BS status through birth or descent, so these nationalities will die out with their present holders.

There are some provisions to protect the children of British nationals who would otherwise be stateless, but these are very restrictive. Children born to a British national, other than a British Protected Person, in the UK or a dependency have a right to acquire their parent's status by registration if they would otherwise be stateless. Children born outside the UK or a dependency to such a British national parent only have a right to registration if they become settled in the UK or a dependency and have lived there for three years.

There are general discretionary provisions for the Home Secretary to register minors as British subjects and British Overseas citizens. The qualifications for this are not defined and the provisions are very rarely used.

British nationals with an East African connection

The special quota voucher scheme

The treatment of British nationals from East Africa, most of whom originated from the Indian subcontinent, is one of the most disreputable parts of British nationality law. When they came under pressure to leave countries such as Uganda and Kenya in the 1960s, the Commonwealth Immigrants Act 1968 was passed to deny them entry to the UK. Only a few were allowed entry to the UK every year, under the 'special voucher' scheme. When large-scale expulsions from Uganda took place in 1972, they had no right to live in any other country and found it difficult or impossible to enter the UK. The European Commission held that this amounted to 'inhuman and degrading treatment' under the ECHR.

As a result of the European Commission's judgement, the UK expanded the 'special voucher' scheme, supposedly to 5,000 a year. But the majority of expelled Ugandans had gone temporarily to India to await resettlement, and only 600 vouchers a year were allocated for them. The nominal quota was never reached; but during the 1980s an eight-year queue built up in India.

The special voucher scheme was abolished on 5 March 2002. Any new applications for special vouchers lodged on or after this date will presumably be refused without consideration. On 24 April 2002, the Home Secretary, however, admitted that the UK has a moral obligation towards BOCs and agreed to 'examine the possibility of an alternative arrangement.'

The voucher scheme was completely outside the immigration rules and was administered at the discretion of the Home Secretary. Vouchers were issued only to British nationals with no other nationality, who were:

- 'under pressure' to leave the country in which they were living;
- and who were 'heads of households'.

Under pressure to leave. This criterion referred to people living in the countries of East and Central Africa (Uganda, Kenya, Tanzania, Malawi, Zambia) and people who had left those countries to go to India and wait for admission to the UK. Vouchers were not normally issued to people from East Africa who went to live in other countries (e.g., to work in the Gulf States) or to British nationals living in other countries in the world, even if their immigration or other status there was very insecure.

Heads of households. Under the voucher scheme, married women were not regarded as 'heads of households' save in few circumstances. Divorced or widowed women were eligible for vouchers if they fulfilled the other requirements. An attempt to challenge this blatant sex discrimination in the British courts (*Amin*) failed although another legal challenge is currently being pursued before the High Court.

Voucher-holders' immediate family may qualify to accompany or join them in the UK. This includes spouses and dependent children up to the age of 25 (this upper age limit was introduced because the eight-year queue in India meant that children who were nearly 18 when their parents applied would reach 25 before the application was considered). In order to remain dependent, however, children must be unmarried and financially dependent on their parents (i.e., not working). ECOs may also investigate to decide whether they are dependent 'by necessity' or whether they have chosen to remain or become dependent in order to qualify to accompany the family.

Dependants have to apply in the usual way for entry clearance and pay the settlement fee at the time they apply.

British nationals from Malaysia

Besides East Africa, the other country where there are many British Overseas citizens is Malaysia. Three areas of Malaya – Penang, Melaka and Singapore – were ruled directly by Britain as the Straits Settlements and Malayan independence law provided that people who were born or whose father had been born in those areas before independence (31 August 1957) would retain their citizenship of the UK and Colonies. When Singapore became independent separately from Malaysia, this provision was lost for Singaporeans, but it still exists for people from Penang and Melaka. They are British nationals, but unless they have lived in the UK for five years and became settled before 1983, they are not British citizens, but British Overseas citizens. Since they had no connection with East Africa, they did not qualify for special quota vouchers. Malaysia does not permit people to gain any advantage from holding another nationality without forfeiting their Malaysian nationality and many Malaysians do not know that they have British nationality. People with this connection with Penang or Melaka who wish to claim their British nationality should obtain specialist advice.

British nationals from Hong Kong

Most British nationals from Hong Kong lost the right to live in the UK under the Commonwealth Immigrants Act 1962. The only citizens of the UK and Colonies (as they then were) from Hong Kong who retained the right of abode at that time, and who still have the right of abode now, are:

- people who were born, registered or naturalised in the UK;
- people with a parent or grandparent who was born, registered or naturalised in the UK;
- people who had at any time before 1983 spent five years continuously and legally in the UK and were settled in the UK at the end of that period;
- women married to a man who fulfilled any of these conditions.

This means that most people of Chinese or other Asian origin in Hong

Kong lost the right of abode in the UK and became British Dependent Territories citizens. British Dependent Territories citizenship was abolished for people from Hong Kong. Former British Dependent Territories citizens were only allowed to acquire the status of British National (Overseas) if they wished to retain British nationality.

However, there are four ways in which they may have been able, or may be able, to acquire the right of abode and become British citizens:

- by living for five years or more in the UK before 1983. Some people from Hong Kong lived in the UK as students or workers in the 1950s or 1960s. At that time, people from Hong Kong and other Commonwealth countries were technically 'settled' in the UK, because no conditions could be put on their stay if they were admitted. It is therefore worth checking if Hong Kong British nationals have lived in the UK. If they lived in the UK for more than five years, at any time before 1983, and had no time limit on their stay at the end of that five-year period, they gained the right of abode and are therefore British citizens now;

- by registering before 31 March 1994 under the quota for certain specified categories under the British Nationality (Hong Kong) Act 1990 ▶see below;

- by registering under the provisions for war wives and widows in the Hong Kong (War Wives and Widows) Act 1996 ▶see below;

- by registering after 1 July 1997 under the provisions of the British Nationality (Hong Kong) Act 1997 for those who have no other nationality than British nationality ▶see below.

British Nationals (Overseas): the Hong Kong Act 1985

Under the 1985 agreement for the return of Hong Kong to China, Britain and China agreed that British Dependent Territories citizens would be able to apply for a new status, called British National (Overseas). The status of BDTC would no longer exist for people from Hong Kong. The status of British National (Overseas) does not carry the right of abode in the UK. The Chinese authorities do not regard it as a citizenship, merely as a travel document facility.

BDTCs from Hong Kong could apply for British National (Overseas) passports until September 1997. Anyone who had not applied by the relevant date lost British nationality altogether on 1 July 1997.

Most ex-BDTCs from Hong Kong are also considered by the Chinese authorities to be Chinese citizens and now have Chinese citizenship. People who are not of Chinese ethnic origin may not be Chinese citizens, for example people of Indian origin who have lived in Hong Kong for many years or generations. JCWI and others argued that they would be left with no real citizenship after 30 June 1997. The British government conceded that they needed special treatment and they were allowed to finally register as British citizens, but only after Hong Kong was returned to China ▶see below.

Acquiring British citizenship:
The British Nationality (Hong Kong) Acts 1990 and 1997
and the Hong Kong (War Wives and Widows) Act 1996

After a great deal of pressure, and on a piecemeal basis, the British government agreed to allow three categories of British nationals from Hong Kong to register as British citizens.

The British Nationality (Hong Kong) Act 1990 provided for British citizenship to be granted to 50,000 people in certain specified categories. They were people considered necessary to Hong Kong's future but who might leave in the uncertainty leading up to the handover, particularly after the Tiananmen Square events of 1989.

Applications were decided on a points system, to identify those considered most likely to emigrate, those who had been in sensitive government service and some entrepreneurs. The final tranche of 2,400 registrations under this scheme was completed in 1997.

The Hong Kong (War Wives and Widows) Act 1996 permitted around 50 women resident in Hong Kong whose husbands fought in the Second World War to register as British citizens without the need to come to the UK. To be eligible, a woman must be able to show that the Home Office sent her a 'UK settlement letter' via the Hong Kong Immigration Department in 1994, confirming her right to enter the UK.

The British Nationality (Hong Kong) Act 1997 belatedly dealt with the position of Hong Kong British nationals who would not be eligible for any other nationality after 1 July 1997. It applied only to people who were ordinarily resident in Hong Kong on 3 February 1997 (by which time many of those affected had already left, if they could, to find a more secure status).

A right to register as a British citizen was provided to people who

* are ordinarily resident in Hong Kong at the time of application; and
* were ordinarily resident in Hong Kong immediately before 4 February 1997; and
* were BDTCs immediately before 4 February 1997; and
* are BDTCs only by virtue of their connection with Hong Kong (defined in the Schedule to the Act: in most cases due to their or their parents' birth, registration, naturalisation or adoption in Hong Kong), or were British Overseas citizens, British Protected Persons or British subjects; and
* would have been stateless but for their British nationality.

For a definition of 'ordinarily resident' ▶see page 671.

Applications can be made at any time after 1 July 1997.

People from Hong Kong who are living in the UK

The following checklist will help to decide the status of someone from Hong Kong who is living in the UK:

- **Does the person have a (brown) certificate of identity?**

  If so, the person is not a British national of any kind. He or she was born in mainland China and is probably entitled to Chinese citizenship. He or she may be able to obtain British citizenship by naturalisation if he or she fulfils the requirements ▶see Chapter 28;

- **Does the person have a British passport?**

- does the passport state 'holder has the right of abode in the UK' on page 5, or 'British citizen' on the inside back cover or on page 1? If so, the person is a British citizen, with the right of abode in the UK.

- did the person, at any time before 1 January 1983, live legally in the UK for at least five years, without any conditions on his or her stay at the end of the period? If so, and provided that the person can prove this, he or she is a British citizen with the right of abode in the UK.

- was the person born in the UK before 1983? Was the person born in the UK on or after 1 January 1983 to a parent who was British or was settled in the UK at the time of the birth? If so, the person is a British citizen.

If none of these apply, check the immigration stamp on the passport. This will show under what conditions, if any, the person has been admitted or allowed to remain. Only people with indefinite leave can apply for British citizenship ▶see Chapter 28. Students, visitors and work permit holders cannot apply and should not do so as this may prejudice future applications to remain here or return here. Some students who have been in the UK for 10 years or more may be able to obtain indefinite leave ▶see pages 105-108.

28 How to become British

This chapter explains how people living in the UK can become British citizens. Registration from outside the UK is possible for a small group of Hong Kong British nationals and for British nationals in Gibraltar and the Falkland Islands.

There are two ways in which people of other nationalities can obtain British citizenship:

- **naturalisation** is the way almost all adults (people aged 18 and over) can become British. Formally, it is always discretionary. There is no right of appeal against a refusal of citizenship;

- **registration** is the way all children (people under 18) and a very small number of adults (▶see below) can become British. It is sometimes a right which cannot be refused, but in most cases it is discretionary and without a right of appeal.

It is important to note that the Nationality, Immigration and Asylum Bill 2002 proposes significant changes to the process of naturalisation, including changes to the language test and to the oath of allegiance which must be taken. It is also proposed to extend the circumstances in which people can be deprived of their citizenship. For full details of these and other proposals ▶see pages 594-596.

The Home Office has developed and published on its website Nationality Instructions (NI) to assist in its decision-making. They are similar to the Immigration Directorate Instructions (IDI) and the Asylum Policy Instructions (API) and give further guidance on nationality and related procedures.

Points to note

- All adults (but not children necessarily) applying for British citizenship *must* be settled (have indefinite leave) in the UK at the date of application. Sometimes people who are in the UK for a limited period (e.g., as students) mistakenly believe that an application for citizenship will be a means of being able to stay in the UK permanently. Quite the reverse is true: they do not qualify for citizenship, and the Home Office is likely to interpret a citizenship application as evidence that they do not intend to leave the UK at the end of their studies and therefore may refuse an extension of leave as a student.

- Applications for citizenship will probably lead to an investigation of the whole family's immigration status. If there is any irregularity in the applicant's status or that of a close family member (e.g., if they are overstayers), they should seek advice about regularising their status before making a citizenship application.
- The Home Office now retains the whole of the citizenship fee, even if the application is unsuccessful ▶see page 738. It is therefore very important for people to check before applying that they at least fulfil the objective criteria for obtaining citizenship (i.e. residence, language) rather than risk losing money.

Naturalisation

Requirements for naturalisation

The requirements for naturalisation as a British citizen relate to:
- residence and settlement in the UK;
- language;
- good character;
- intention to live in the UK;
- taking an oath of allegiance.

The requirements (and the fees) are slightly different for people who are married to British citizens and people who are not. The former will usually find that it is easier and cheaper for them to become British. The requirement of marriage is a requirement at the time of application. However, if a couple separate or divorce after the application is made but before it is granted, the Home Office should be told of the state of the marriage. If the couple are divorced, it is likely that the application will be refused. The person may be asked whether he or she wants to apply instead on the basis of residence, by paying the extra amount of money.

Residence and settlement

People who are not married to British citizens must have been living in the UK for five years continuously, and must have been physically present in the UK on the date five years before they apply. They must not have been 'in breach of the immigration laws' during that time (see para 1, sch 2 British Nationality Act 1981). They must not have been absent for more than 450 days in total and not more than 90 days in the year immediately before they apply. They must have been settled (have had indefinite leave in the UK) for at least a year before they apply.

People who are married to British citizens must have been living in the UK for three years continuously, and must have been physically present in the UK on the date three years before they apply. They must not have been in 'breach of the immigration laws' during that time. They must not have been absent for more than 270 days in total and not more than 90 days in the year immediately before they apply. They must be settled (have indefinite leave in the UK) at the time they apply.

In relation to the requirement that a person is physically present in the UK either three or five years before the date of application, the Home Office has a 're-declaration' policy (letter to the Immigration Law Practitioners' Association (ILPA) dated 25 September 2001). If the person was not actually in the UK on that date, but was in the UK within the period of two months before or after that date, the Home Office may return the form to the applicant. The applicant is then invited to re-sign and date the form such that the requirement will subsequently be met. This means that the application is not refused and the applicant does not have to pay the fee again.

Whether people are married to British citizens or not, it used to be the case that the Home Office applied the rule about absences quite strictly, counting all the days out of the country shown by stamps in their passports. Now that passports are not stamped on leaving the country the Home Office has said that it will be more flexible about this. In particular when people travel often on business, it will look mainly at whether they remain resident here for tax purposes. The Home Office policy (NI Ch18) states 'We need to be sure, before we agree to waive a requirement, that applicants are of good character and have genuinely thrown in their lot with this country'. The 2002 White Paper also proposes a more flexible approach to residence requirements.

The Home Office has stated in a letter to Camden Community Law Centre of September 2000 that periods spent on temporary admission or in detention in the UK are not usually counted as periods of absence for the purposes of naturalisation applications provided the person was granted leave afterwards, rather than being removed or making a voluntary departure. In a further letter to John Howells solicitors in September 2001, the Home Office indicated that time spent during an automatic extension of leave following an 'in-time' application to extend leave counted as a period of lawful residence. In addition, it was indicated in a letter to JCWI, dated 3 October 2001, that where a person is in breach of the immigration laws, for example, as an illegal entrant or an overstayer, the period from the time that they *apply* to regularise their position will count as lawful residence.

The 2002 Bill proposes a definition of 'in breach of the immigration laws' for the purposes of these qualifying periods. Under that definition, those who are in the UK and who need leave but do not have it are 'in breach of the immigration laws'. It remains to be seen how this definition will affect the existing exercise of the Home Office's discretion (above) to treat those who do not have leave flexibly, and to treat those who are on temporary admission as not being absent from the UK where appropriate (see paras 2, 4, sch1, 1981 Act).

Language

People who are not married to British citizens must show that they have a 'sufficient knowledge' of English, Welsh or Scottish Gaelic. They do not need to be literate in the language, but should be able to converse in it. This test is occasionally assessed by the immigration service in London and by police forces in other areas. It is usually done by means of a visit or an interview, or occasionally by a telephone call to the applicant. It is very unsatisfactory as the people making the assessment are not trained to do so, and the people being assessed may be shocked by the arrival of a police officer, or have difficulties with telephone conversations. However, very few people are, in fact, refused on this ground. In theory, elderly or infirm applicants can be excused the language test, but this is at the discretion of the Home Office.

The new White Paper proposes significant changes to the assessment of the language test, and to include lessons on 'knowledge about life in the UK'. Also of concern is the proposal to require most applicants for naturalisation to pass the language test; currently people who are married to British citizens do not need to pass this test.

Good character

All applicants must show that they are of 'good character'. This is very ill-defined. Unspent criminal convictions are taken into account (applicants have to list these, including motoring offences, on the application form). Checks are also usually made on financial solvency. The Special Branch of the police also may be asked to comment on any alleged security risk. In addition, the local police force (or, in London, the immigration service) may be asked to run checks on the applicant, which may include an interview. This is the most subjective of the tests.

Intention to live in the UK

People who are not married to British citizens have to show that they intend to continue to live in the UK if the application is granted. Ministers have said that they want to be sure that applicants are really committed to the UK and do not simply want 'the convenience of a British passport'. It is therefore unwise, for example, to seek to speed up the processing of an application giving as a reason that there is likely to be a prolonged absence abroad.

Technically, applicants can travel overseas for as long as they like after the application has been submitted (the residence requirements refer to the period before the application was made). However, if it is clear that an applicant is no longer living permanently in the UK while the application is being considered (e.g., if it is impossible for a police interview to be arranged) the Home Office may consider this as evidence of a lack of intention to live permanently in the UK. It may then require evidence that the stay abroad is only a temporary one (e.g., contractual employment, study or caring for a sick relative) and that connections with the UK are maintained, indicating a return in the near future. People who have submitted naturalisation applications remain in any case subject to the returning residents rule ▶see pages 79-83, and will need to return within two years to secure their settled status in the UK.

People who are married to British citizens do not have to show that they intend to continue to live in the UK.

Oath of allegiance

As part of the process of becoming a British citizen and before the Home Office will issue the certificate of naturalisation, all applicants have to swear or affirm an oath of allegiance (on a form sent to the applicant) to *'Her Majesty Queen Elizabeth the Second, her heirs and successors'* before a commissioner for oaths, which may be a solicitor or a barrister who is not advising the applicant. Once this form has been returned to the Home Office duly signed and stamped by the commissioner, then the issue of the naturalisation certificate is usually a formality. There are, however, proposals in the 2002 Bill to alter the meaning and wording of the oath of allegiance. Also, the government wants a more public and ceremonial declaration before a registrar, rather than the oath being taken in a private solicitor's office.

The process of application

Applicants have to fill in Form AN, available from the Home Office Nationality Directorate ▶see page 725 or from their website (www. ind.homeoffice.gov.uk). They need to send the fee at the same time as the application. A married couple applying together pay only one fee between them. If they are applying to register their children at the same time, an additional fee is payable. However, only one additional fee is payable, even if more than one child is applying.

The Home Office has agreed to give priority to applications in certain circumstances which include those unable to make urgent journeys until they have obtained citizenship, the elderly, those who need citizenship for employment or to represent the UK internationally, or where the Home Office has been inefficient. In most cases, however, priority treatment   means that earlier enquiries by the police or immigration authorities will be started on the application.

Until April 2001, applicants did not need to send their passports with the application form, because it was taking so long to deal with applications. The Home Office would ask to see the passport when it was needed. This was so that applicants were not inconvenienced by having their documents retained in the Home Office while their applications were waiting to be dealt with.

However, because delays in processing naturalisation applications have been greatly reduced recently, procedures have changed. The Home Office application form (Form AN) now contains guidance (Guide AN) which lists the supporting documents required. These include the applicant's national passport, evidence of their residence in the UK and, where appropriate, a marriage certificate. The appropriate fee (▶see page 738) should also be enclosed. If a person wishes to travel in the near future, or needs the immediate return of any other documents, they should send in a certified copy of the relevant document. If they are sending a copy of the passport, *all* of the pages (including the blank ones) should be included.

The last published information on waiting times indicated that the average delay was just under twelve months. One reason for this may be that, as at the middle of 2001, the police and intelligence services were apparently taking between 10 and 11 months to respond to routine enquiries referred to them by the Home Office. Their previous turn around time had been five to six months. The stated aim of the Home Office is to reduce consideration times to three months by 2004.

Refusals of applications

The Home Office is not obliged to give reasons for refusal and refusal decisions cannot be appealed or judicially reviewed (s44(2)(3), British Nationality Act 1981). In the past, applicants would usually be told if their applications had failed because of a technicality; for example, a failure to meet the residence requirements, or an assessment that the applicant's language skills are inadequate. If, however, they failed the 'good character' test, reasons were not given. The Fayed brothers, who were refused without reasons, successfully challenged this in the Court of Appeal, which held that the Home Office must at least indicate the nature of its concerns before making a negative decision in order to allow the applicant to address them. In December 1997, the Home Secretary announced that the case would be conceded and that in future 'in principle' reasons for refusal of citizenship would be given.

Although the 1981 Act still prevents appeal or judicial review, this decision has opened up nationality decisions to greater scrutiny and the possibility of more effective challenge. There will have to be an opportunity, before a decision is finalised, for an applicant to challenge decisions which are factually wrong or based on irrelevant considerations. JCWI has successfully challenged refusals on language grounds where it has been perfectly obvious that the applicant can communicate effectively in English. It is also possible to argue against a Home Office assumption that an applicant who has spent long periods abroad since applying does not intend to make his or her home in the UK. Decisions refused on grounds of 'good character' are more difficult to challenge. There are fewer grounds of challenge to the Home Office's conclusions in such cases unless they have failed to address any counter-arguments put to them. Representations to reconsider decisions, or requests for further information, can be made through the applicant's MP or a legal representative.

The 2002 Bill proposes to repeal those parts of the 1981 Act which prevent the Home Office from being required to give reasons for nationality decisions and which protect those decisions from being challenged in the courts.

Crown service

A person who is not British but who is working in Crown service overseas may apply for naturalisation on the ground of a period of work rather than of residence in the UK. Crown service involves working for the British government abroad, but no length of service is stipulated. The Home Office interprets the term as people in fully-established, permanent positions, whose salaries are paid directly from government funds, for example, people in the armed forces, the civil service and the diplomatic service. The other requirements for naturalisation must be met, including the intention to continue in the service of the British government. These applications are relatively rare.

Registration

Registration of adults

There is one small group of adults able to obtain British citizenship by registration. Their applications cannot be refused. British nationals who are not British citizens (British Overseas citizens, British Protected Persons, British subjects and British Nationals (Overseas) ▶see Chapter 27 for definitions) have a right to obtain British citizenship by registration if they gain settlement rights in the UK. It is difficult for most of these people to gain settlement rights in the UK as they must first obtain indefinite leave under the ordinary immigration rules.

In order to register, they have to fulfil the following requirements:

- they must have lived in the UK legally for at least five years, and have been physically present in the UK on the date five years before they apply, and not have been absent for more than 450 days, not more than 90 of those days in the year immediately before applying; and

- they must have been settled (have had indefinite leave in the UK) for at least one year.

BOTCs who have not become British citizens (see pages 563-564) may register as British citizens at the discretion of the Home Office (see new s4A 1981 Act).

The process of application

Applicants have to fill in Form B, available from the Home Office Nationality

Directorate. Applicants need to send the fee at the same time as the application. The present waiting time is up to six months.

Registration of children

Children with a right to register

Children under 18 always obtain British citizenship by registration. Two groups of children have a right to register as British citizens.

1. Children born in the UK since 1 January 1983 and not born British

Children who were born in the UK but who did not acquire British citizenship at birth, because neither of their parents was a British citizen or settled in the UK, have a right to register as British citizens if:

- one of their parents becomes settled (is given indefinite leave to remain) in the UK; or

- the children remain in the UK for the first 10 years of their life and are not outside the UK for more than 90 days in any of those years. There is a discretion to waive the number of days if it does not exceed 180 in any one year or 990 overall. Days may in particular be waivered if the reasons for absence are outside that person's control, (see NI, Ch8, s5). There is no requirement in the law for these children to have indefinite leave to remain nor even to be lawfully resident in that period.

Some children born in the UK who are not British may not be entitled to the nationality of either parent, depending on the nationality laws of their country. Such children will be stateless. Currently, these children are entitled to register as British citizens if they are at least 10 years old but not yet 22, and have spent the five years prior to the application in the UK, being absent for no less than 450 days. Under a new proposal contained in the 2002 Bill, such children will be entitled to register as British without having to reach the age of 10.

2. Children born overseas to parents who are British citizens by descent

Children who are born overseas to a parent who is a British citizen by descent do not acquire British citizenship automatically. Such children have a right to register overseas within a year of their birth (or within six years where there are special circumstances in a particular case) where they have a parent who has lived in the UK for three years prior to their birth. However, if the child and both its parents return to live in the UK, the child has a right to be registered as a British citizen in the UK provided that the child and both parents (unless they are divorced or one is dead) live in the UK for a continuous period of three years. In *that* case, the child will become a British citizen *otherwise* than by descent. For more details of these requirements ▶see page 574.

The Home Office position is that children who apply in the above categories as minors but who have become adults at the date of the decision may have to take the oath of allegiance before their citizenship is confirmed.

Children who can apply to register at discretion

All other children can register only at the discretion of the Home Secretary. There are no specific qualifications in the British Nationality Act 1981, which simply says that the Home Secretary can register a minor child as a British citizen. In theory, this means that any child, anywhere, could be registered as British. In practice, it is rare for registration to be granted to a child living outside the UK (except those children with a right to register, described above). The Home Office has also stated that children born outside the UK before 1983 to British-born mothers (who would have automatically been born British by descent if they had been born after 1 January 1983) will be registered if the mother applies for this before the children are 18, and, if the parents are still married, if the father has no well-founded objection.

The Home Office also has a policy relating to 'illegitimate' children of British citizen fathers. Under the British Nationality Act 1981, a child cannot automatically acquire British citizenship through his or her father unless the father was married to the mother. Subsequent marriage in the UK legitimises the child (and may do for marriages elsewhere) from the date of the marriage. However, the Home Office will normally register as British the 'illegitimate' child of a British citizen father if there are no doubts as to paternity, no reasonable objections from either parent or those with parental responsibility and there are no 'good character' objections (bearing in mind, of course, the age of the child). There is no reference to the status of the mother in this policy. Until recently the Home Office policy was to require the child to be living in the UK but this has been dropped and therefore, in principle, a child living abroad could apply to the post abroad with the relevant evidence. An illegitimate child of a deceased father, even a child who was born after the death of that father, can also benefit from this policy but paternity may be difficult to prove if the father has died.

A child who is born 'illegitimate' but whose parents subsequently marry is then regarded as British by birth, without the need to register. The 2002 Bill proposes to abolish the discrimination against illegitimate children as far as nationality rights are concerned.

In other cases, if children are living in the UK, there are no specific residence or other requirements on when a child can be registered as British. The Home Office has given some guidance in the NI on the factors it takes into account which are as follows:

- the child's connections with the UK (e.g., whether the child is settled);
- where the child's future is likely to be;

- the views of the parents;
- the nationality of the parents.

In the case of 'older children, particularly those approaching 18', the Home Office will also take into consideration:

- whether the child is of good character ▶see above for definition of this;
- the length of time the child has lived in the UK.

Because the qualifications are so unclear, it is very difficult to be sure whether a child's registration application will succeed. In practice, if either of the parents is British or applying to become British, the Home Office will usually register young children and older children who have lived in the UK for some time (this is undefined, but would certainly include children who have been living in the UK for five years or more, although it would not usually include those here for less than the last two years).

In a letter to Bindmans solicitors of 26 November 2001, the Home Office stated:

'less than two years is not considered long enough to establish such ties. But we must consider the best interests of the child and be flexible within reasonable time limits'.

Examples of cases where the two year residence requirement may not be applied strictly may be cases where a child goes abroad on school trips regularly; where there was an overall aggregate two-year period which had been broken; where a child would otherwise reach 18 before the expiry of the two-year period depending on the reason why they did not come to the UK earlier; or where the child would be the only member of the family who would not become a British citizen if the application were to be refused.

If neither parent is British, or intending to become British, there may be difficulty in succeeding in registration applications. The Home Office would not normally register a child whose parents were not settled in the UK unless the child had been taken into local authority care and it was clear that there was no prospect of the parents regaining custody. However, it is not a pre-requisite that the child is settled in the UK before an application for their registration can be made.

Most children who are registered become British citizens 'otherwise than by descent'. However, children born abroad who are registered, whose father or mother was a British citizen by descent at the time of the child's birth, only become citizens 'by descent'. This does not apply to those children whose father or mother were British citizens by descent at the time of the child's birth and who registered in the UK as described on page 590. These children become British 'otherwise than by descent'. This has important significance for the child in the future because only citizens 'otherwise than by descent' will automatically transmit their nationality to any children they may have who are born abroad ▶see Chapter 27.

The process of application

Parents or guardians normally apply on behalf of a child. If an older child makes an application him or herself, the reasons for this should be explained to the Home Office. When an application is made for children on their own, it is normally on Form MN1, available from the Home Office Nationality Directorate. Parents who are applying for registration of their children at the same time as for naturalisation for themselves may add the children's names to their own AN forms. Children born in the UK who have lived here for over 10 years may apply on Form T. A single fee covers all the children in the same family if they apply at the same time, either on their own or with their parent(s). Whether or not the application is successful, the Home Office retains the fee. The waiting time is up to six months.

Passports and travel documents

When the Home Office grants an application for British citizenship, it sends the person a certificate to confirm the grant of citizenship. This certificate is then evidence of the person's citizenship status.

In order to obtain a British passport, people need to apply to the office of the Passport Agency nearest to where they live. They can get application forms for British passports from any large Post Office; there are separate forms for adults and children. The forms must be filled in and sent together with the citizenship certificate, any other documents requested and the fee, to the Passport Agency. At present, the time this takes varies with the season but the UK Passport Agency has a target time of issuing passports in a few days at any time of year. All newly-issued passports are now the uniform European Union, machine-readable, maroon-coloured British passports, rather than the old blue British ones; the colour of the passport makes no difference to the person's status and rights.

From October 1998, all children are required to hold their own passports, and may no longer be included on a parent's passport. This is partly to make child abduction more difficult. Children already on a parent's passport will not be affected until the passport is changed.

Stateless people living in the UK, for example, some children born in the UK but not born British, may apply to the Home Office Travel Documents Section for travel documents. They fill in Form TD112 and return it to the Home Office with the fee. The Home Office normally requires evidence that the person cannot get a travel document from any other country which might be expected to provide it, for example, a letter from the embassy of their parents' country confirming that the child does not have that nationality, before issuing a travel document. When it is hard to obtain this evidence, or when the parents are not prepared to contact the embassy, for example, if they have been granted exceptional leave to remain, this should be explained to the Home Office and the application submitted anyway.

Deprivation of citizenship

The Home Office has the power to make an order depriving a person of citizenship. It can do this if the citizenship had been obtained by fraud, or if the person is convicted of an offence and sentenced to imprisonment for a year or more within five years of citizenship being granted, and the Home Office decides it is not conducive to the public good for the person to remain a citizen.

This power under the British Nationality 1981 Act has been exercised very infrequently and was discussed in 1993 in the case of **Naheed Ejaz**. She had naturalised on the grounds of her marriage, but it later emerged that her husband had never been a British citizen himself. The Home Office therefore stated that she also had never been a citizen, and tried to remove her as an illegal entrant. The Court of Appeal held that because Mrs Ejaz had not been involved in any deception, the Home Office could not simply strip her of citizenship but would have to go through the formal process of deprivation. The Home Office did not do so, and she remains a British citizen.

The 2002 Bill proposes to extend the use and the scope of the power to deprive people of their citizenship (▶see box below).

PROPOSALS FOR CHANGE

The 2002 Bill sets out a proposed series of changes to nationality laws. The 2002 White Paper sets out the government thinking behind the changes, some of which are intended to be largely symbolic only. A summary of the changes and JCWI's comments can be found in Chapter 3.

Naturalisation

The Bill proposes:

- a requirement that those who apply for naturalisation have 'sufficient knowledge about life in the United Kingdom';
- regulations for determining whether or not applicants satisfy the above requirement and whether or not they possess 'sufficient knowledge of English, Welsh or Scottish Gaelic'. The 1981 Act already contains a requirement that an applicant for naturalisation needs to possess a sufficient knowledge of one of these languages. The White Paper suggests that applicants will need to produce certificates showing that they have passed a test, if necessary after attending a specified course;
- to make spouses of British citizens, who are currently exempt from the language requirement, subject to both that test and the 'sufficient knowledge about life in the United Kingdom' requirement.

Citizenship ceremony, oath and pledge

- Applicants for naturalisation and registration are already required to take a citizenship oath which obliges them to 'be faithful to Her Majesty Queen Elizabeth the Second, Her Heirs and Successors'. They will now be required to take the following citizenship pledge:

'I will give my loyalty to the United Kingdom and respect its rights and freedoms. I will uphold its democratic values. I will observe its laws faithfully and fulfil my duties and obligations as a British citizen'.

- Applicants will be required to take the above oath and pledge at a citizenship ceremony within a specified time. The White Paper indicates that these ceremonies will take place in public local authority facilities such as registrars' offices and community centres.

Deprivation of citizenship

The Home Office already possesses powers to take away the British citizenship of someone who has registered or naturalised under the 1981 Act under the following circumstances: obtaining citizenship by fraud, false representation, or concealment of a material fact; being sentenced for a crime for a term of 12 months or more within five years of being granted citizenship; unlawfully trading, associating with or assisting 'an enemy' during war; or for showing themselves to be 'disloyal to Her Majesty' through their words or actions. Although these powers have been used rarely, if at all, under the 1981 Act, the White Paper makes it clear that the proposed new powers of deprivation will be used much more regularly.

The Bill proposes:

- the replacement of the above criteria (except for fraud, false representation or concealment of a material fact) with a power to deprive a person of their status if the Home Office 'thinks that the person has done anything seriously prejudicial to the vital interests of the' UK;
- that any British citizen, not just those who obtained citizenship by way of naturalisation or registration, can be deprived of their citizenship unless deprivation would make them stateless;
- a right of appeal against the power of deprivation, unless the Secretary of State certifies that the decision was taken on the basis of information which cannot be made public on the grounds of 'national security', in the 'interests of the relationship between the UK and another country, or another matter of a political kind'.

Other proposals

The Bill also proposes:

- the removal of the exemption which permitted discrimination by a public authority in the exercise of nationality functions;
- the removal of the current distinction between the nationality rights of legitimate and illegitimate children (▶see pages 397, 567-568);
- the removal of the current provision in the British Nationality Act 1981 which states that there is no duty upon the government to give reasons for refusing citizenship and protecting Home Office decisions from being challenged in the courts;
- the removal of the minimum age requirement (currently 10) for stateless children born in the UK who can register as British citizens;
- to define the meaning of: 'in the United Kingdom in breach of the immigration laws' for the purposes of nationality applications ▶see pages 584-585.

Section 10 Appeals

Chapter 29
Rights of appeal 599
The basic appeal system 600
When can people appeal? 601
The one-stop appeal system 606
Notices of decision and of appeal 611
Particular appeals 614

Chapter 30
Conducting appeals 626
Appeal procedures 626
Powers of adjudicators in deciding appeals 642
Appeals and other challenges after the
adjudicator has determined the appeal 647
The Immigration Appeal Tribunal 651

29   Rights of appeal

This section concerns appeals from decisions made by the immigration authorities relating to people's rights to be admitted to or remain in the UK. This chapter looks at the basics of the appeal system and sets out the circumstances in which people can and cannot appeal. It also covers the notices of decision given to people when they can appeal and deals with 'one-stop' notices and the ways in which the immigration authorities can take action to prevent appeals where the one-stop procedure has not been complied with. Towards the end of the chapter, we look at the special features of certain particular kinds of appeal. Chapter 30 looks at the procedures which operate during the appeal process and gives some practical guidance on how to conduct appeals. It also looks at identifying grounds of appeal against decisions of adjudicators.

For the proposed changes to the appeal system set out in the Nationality, Immigration and Asylum Bill 2002 ▶see the box on pages 622-625.

In all cases involving appeals, it is important to make sure that the time limits under the appeals system are complied with. For a summary of the relevant time limits and the rules about how periods of time are counted ▶see the box on pages 613-614.

There are certain specialised appeals which are not covered in this chapter but are looked at in the relevant part of the *Handbook*. They are:

- appeals in asylum cases where the immigration authorities have decided that the applicant can be removed to a 'safe' third country ▶see pages 209-212;

- appeal rights for EEA nationals and their family members against 'EEA decisions' ▶see pages 472-473;

- appeals and reviews of decisions to detain people as 'suspected international terrorists' under the Anti-terrorism, Crime and Security Act 2001 ▶see pages 516-517;

- appeals to the asylum support adjudicator about refusal of asylum support ▶see pages 712-717.

Bail hearings are not strictly appeals. For full details about making bail applications and conducting the hearings ▶see pages 517-525.

The basic appeal system

The appeals system enables decisions by the Home Office, the Immigration Service and British posts abroad to be reviewed by an independent judicial body. The 'Immigration Appellate Authority' (IAA) consists of adjudicators and the Immigration Appeal Tribunal (IAT). It is independent of the Home Office and is part of the Court Service within the Lord Chancellor's Department. Its personnel are appointed by the Lord Chancellor, although until 1987 they were appointed by the Home Office.

There are two levels of appeal:

- appeals are dealt with first by an adjudicator, who generally sits alone to hear a case;

- in most cases, there is a right to make a written application for leave to appeal to a higher level, the Immigration Appeal Tribunal, which can review the adjudicator's treatment of the case. The IAT comprises a panel, usually of two or three people, at least one of whom is legally qualified. It will grant leave to appeal usually where there is a legal point at issue, or where there are other special circumstances which justify a further appeal. If leave is granted, a hearing before the Tribunal is arranged.

There is no right of appeal to the IAT in an asylum or human rights case where the appeal is certified by the Home Office under paragraph 9, schedule 4 1999 Act and the adjudicator agrees with the certificate. Usually, the way to challenge the determination of the adjudicator in such cases is to apply for 'judicial review' but this procedure can only used to overturn decisions on certain narrow grounds. For general details about these certificates ▶see pages 621-622 below and Chapter 11, pages 203-205. This kind of certificate may be abolished by the 2002 Bill.

If a person applies to the IAT for leave to appeal and is refused, there is no right of appeal against that decision. Again, in general, the way to challenge the decision is by judicial review. The new legislation may, however, prevent judicial review of the decisions of the Tribunal.

Where appeals in certified cases are dismissed and the certificate is upheld, or in cases where the IAT refuses leave to appeal, the IAA can be asked to review the decision on the grounds that there has been a procedural or administrative error. This will only be done in rare cases where, for example, it is clear that although the actual grounds of appeal had been properly sent and received by the IAT, they were not given to the chairman of the IAT who made the decision.

If the IAT grants leave to appeal but then dismisses the appeal after a hearing, a written application can be made to the IAT for permission to appeal to the Court of Appeal (or Court of Session in Scotland). If this too is refused, a renewed application for permission can be made to the Court of Appeal itself. Few cases reach the Court of Appeal and even fewer go beyond that Court to the House of Lords, which is the final level of appeal in the UK.

In certain cases, usually involving questions of national security, the right of appeal is not to the adjudicator or the IAT but instead to the Special Immigration Appeals Commission (SIAC). If SIAC dismisses an appeal, the way to challenge the decision is to ask for leave to appeal to the Court of Appeal.

Legislation

The appeals system was originally set up by the Immigration Appeals Act 1969 but it has undergone many changes since that time. In particular, the appeals system and how it works has become more complex and detailed. Before October 2000, rights of appeal were contained in part 2 of the Immigration Act 1971 and section 8 of the Asylum and Immigration Appeals Act 1993. The appeals system under the Immigration and Asylum Act 1999 came into force on 2 October 2000, the same day as the Human Rights Act 1998 took effect. Rights of appeal and limitations on appeal rights are set out in part 4 of that Act.

The practical operation of the appeals system, as opposed to who can and cannot appeal, are set out in rules of procedure. The Immigration and Asylum Appeals (Procedure) Rules 2000 also became effective on 2 October 2000 and apply to all appeals in existence on or after that date. The 2000 Rules combine the arrangements for asylum and non-asylum appeals, which in the past have been provided for by separate procedure rules.

There are separate rules about the notices which the immigration authorities must give when they make a decision which can be appealed: the Immigration and Asylum Appeals (Notices) Regulations 2000. In addition, there are rules which regulate the 'one-stop' procedure: the Immigration and Asylum Appeals (One-Stop Procedure) Regulations 2000. Separate provision is made for appeals which are to be heard by SIAC: the Special Immigration Appeals Commission Act 1987. Those appeals also have their own special procedure rules.

The 2002 Bill proposes to replace all of part 4 of the 1999 Act and the schedules of the Act which set out the structure and powers of the IAA with a re-statement of the rights of appeal and their limitations. Although the government seems to want to re-draft the legislation dealing with appeal rights, the actual proposed changes to the appeal system in the Bill are not as extensive as first appears.

When can people appeal?

The rights of appeal are set out in the box below. When the immigration authorities make a decision against which there is a right of appeal, they are also required to inform the person that there is a right of appeal: reg 5

Immigration and Asylum Appeals (Notices) Regulations 2000. The procedure for human rights cases is, however, slightly different ▶see pages 614-615 below. However, people can determine for themselves whether they will have a right of appeal by checking first of all whether the decision is one against which there is generally a right of appeal (Box 1 below). They should then look to see whether, in their case, they cannot bring an appeal because of the limitations on appeal rights set out in Box 2. Box 1 also indicates when an appeal can only be brought from outside the UK and the limitations on the *grounds* on which certain appeals can be brought.

Other than the limitations in Box 2, there are two other main circumstances in which people cannot appeal to the adjudicator under the rights set out in Box 1:

- the immigration authorities can issue certificates which prevent people from appealing at all. These certificates are most easily looked at as part of the 'one-stop' appeals procedure ▶see pages 609-611;
- in some cases, the right of appeal is to the SIAC rather than to the adjudicator where the Secretary of State has denied the applicant the right to be in the UK on conducive grounds, usually based on national security, diplomatic or political reasons. For details about SIAC ▶see pages 618-621.

Some appeals are in-country (sometimes called 'suspensive'), meaning that the person can exercise them while in the UK and that they cannot be removed from the UK while they have an appeal outstanding. The appeals set out in Box 1 below are all in-country appeal rights except where otherwise stated. It is possible to ask for entry as a visitor in order to attend an appeal hearing against a refusal of entry clearance, but while permission has been granted in the past, this is rare.

Decisions against which there is no right of appeal

Box 2 below explains when the rights of appeal listed in Box 1 are denied to would-be appellants. The following list confirms certain other circumstances in which there is no right of appeal. There is no right of appeal against the following decisions or actions:

- a decision to add conditions to a person's leave or to refuse to lift conditions, for example, if a condition prohibiting work is added by the immigration authorities;
- a refusal to issue a work permit (but ▶see pages 424-425 for internal appeals);
- the cancellation of leave to enter or remain when a person is outside the UK;
- the cancellation of an entry clearance in cases where someone arrives in the UK before the entry clearance has become effective or who seeks entry for a purpose other than that stated on the entry clearance.

BOX 1: DECISIONS AGAINST WHICH A PERSON MAY APPEAL

The immigration decisions against which a person can in principle appeal are as follows.

1 Appeals against decisions of ECOs
There is a right of appeal against:
- a refusal of an entry clearance;
- a refusal of a certificate of entitlement to the right of abode.

2 Appeals against refusal of entry
A person may appeal against the following decisions refusing entry:
- a refusal to grant leave to enter. The appeals against these decisions are only in-country if, at the time of the decision, the person held an entry clearance or their employer holds a work permit for them. If not, the appeal can only be exercised from abroad;
- a decision to 'cancel' a person's leave when they they arrive in the UK with an entry clearance (which now operates as leave to enter), or have leave which did not lapse when they last left the UK, or were otherwise granted leave before they arrived (for all these terms and categories ►see pages 68-70). These decisions are all treated as refusals to grant leave to enter to a person who has an entry clearance and so they allow in-country appeals as above;
- a decision that a person requires leave to enter.

3 Appeals against decisions to refuse to extend leave or to curtail leave
Appeals may be brought against decisions:
- to refuse to extend leave so that a person has less than 28 days' leave left remaining;
- to curtail an existing leave so that a person has less than 28 days' leave left remaining – the immigration authorities can curtail leave without any application being made to them ►see page 103 for the grounds for curtailment.

4 Appeals in deportation cases
An appeal may be brought against:
- a decision to make a deportation order. This is the initial decision, not the deportation order itself. The Home Office will make such a decision where the deportation is on grounds of 'conducive to the public good' or on the grounds that the deportee is the 'family member' of someone being deported. The 2002 Bill proposes that deportations following recommendations by criminal courts will also give a right of appeal to an adjudicator at this stage;
- a refusal to revoke a deportation order, but this appeal cannot be brought by a person who is in the UK, whether because they have never left after the deportation order or because they have returned when the order is still in force.

5 Appeals in illegal entry and administrative removal cases
An appeal may be brought against removal directions to a person on the grounds that:
- they are an illegal entrant;
- they are liable to be administratively removed under section 10 1999 Act (overstaying, breach of conditions, obtaining leave by deception or being a family member of a person being administratively removed).
A person may only appeal on the grounds that, on the facts of their case, there is no power to remove them. For example, they could argue that they are not in fact an overstayer because they did have leave at the time of the decision. People can *only* appeal in-country under these appeal rights, if they are also appealing on either asylum or human rights grounds.

6 Appeals in asylum cases

Where a person has claimed asylum under the 1951 Refugee Convention, they can appeal on the grounds that their removal would be in breach of the 1951 Convention. The right of appeal is against any one of the following decisions:

- a decision to refuse leave to enter the UK as a refugee;
- a refusal to extend or a decision to curtail leave so that the appellant has less then 28 days of leave left remaining;
- a decision to refuse leave as a refugee accompanied by a grant of limited leave to enter or remain (these are 'upgrade' appeals against decisions to grant exceptional leave rather than refugee status ►see pages 617-618 below for further details about these appeals);
- a decision to make a deportation order;
- a refusal to revoke a deportation order;
- removal directions to a person liable to be removed administratively (on grounds of overstaying etc) or as an illegal entrant.

7 Appeals in human rights and discrimination cases

A person who alleges that any decision made by the Home Office, an immigration officer or an ECO, relating to their 'entitlement to enter or remain in the UK' breaches their human rights or involves racial discrimination, can appeal.

Also, appellants can, in existing appeals, argue that the immigration authorities have breached their human rights or racially discriminated against them. For details about race discrimination generally ►see pages 270-272. For further details about human rights appeals ►see pages 614-617 below.

8. Appeals against removal to a particular destination

A person can appeal against the destination which they are to be removed to if:

- they are appealing against a refusal of entry (above); or
- they are appealing against a decision to make a deportation order; or
- they are being removed having entered the UK in breach of a deportation order (whether in these circumstances they are being removed under the deportation order or as an illegal entrant).

In all these cases, the appellant must state the alternative country which they should be removed to. If the appellant is not a national of the alternative country, they must produce evidence that the alternative country will accept them. Any additional cost in carrying out removal to the alternative destination can be taken into account. Where the immigration authorities have stated the destination country to which the appellant has an objection and they have an existing entry or deportation appeal, they *must* object in that appeal as they will not be given a second chance of raising the objection in a later appeal.

Note: None of the appeals above can be brought in-country if the appellant has claimed asylum under the Refugee Convention and the immigration authorities are proposing to remove them to a safe third country and have issued a certificate under sections 11–12 1999 Act *unless* that certificate has first been set aside by a successful human rights/discrimination appeal or appeal against a third-country removal.

Please note also that appeals against refusal of asylum in third country cases and the other special appeals mentioned above on page 599 are dealt with on the pages indicated there.

BOX 2: LIMITATIONS ON RIGHTS OF APPEAL

In the circumstances listed below, people cannot appeal under the rights set out in Box 1. Only 6 below applies to asylum or human rights/discrimination appeals.

1 Appeals against decisions that a person needs leave to enter the UK
A person who claims the right of abode so that they do not need leave to enter the UK can only appeal against a refusal of entry if they have a British passport which states that they have the right of abode or a certificate of entitlement.

Certain other persons who are exempt from needing to obtain leave can only appeal if they have specified documents – people in this position should seek advice.

2 Appeals against refusals to grant entry clearance
People refused entry clearance as visitors, students enrolled on a short course of six months or less, prospective students or dependants of anyone in these categories, cannot appeal against a refusal of entry clearance. However, 'family visitors' can appeal (for family visit appeals ▶see page 618 below).

3 Appeals against refusals to grant leave to enter
People refused leave to enter as visitors, students enrolled on a short course of six months or less, prospective students or dependants of anyone in these categories cannot appeal against a refusal of leave to enter unless they have a current entry clearance at the time of the refusal.

4 Appeals against refusals to extend leave to enter or remain
People who failed to apply to extend their leave 'in time' and whose original leave has expired (as in most cases it will have done) by the time of the decision, cannot appeal.

5 Appeals against refusals of entry clearance/refusals to grant leave to enter/ refusals to extend leave/curtailment of leave
People refused entry clearance, leave to enter, an extension of leave or whose leave is curtailed cannot appeal if any of the following apply:
- they do not hold a 'relevant document' (below) required by the immigration rules for the purpose they wish to come to the UK under the immigration rules;
- they do not satisfy a requirement of the immigration rules relating to age, nationality or citizenship (e.g., only nationals of certain countries can come to the UK as au pairs; retired persons of independent means must be at least 60 or over);
- they ask for entry for longer than is permitted by the immigration rules (e.g., visitors may only be admitted for up to six months); or
- they are the dependant of anyone in the above categories.

'Relevant documents' are entry clearances, passports or other identity documents and work permits. For who needs an entry clearance for the UK under the immigration rules ▶see pages 53-55.

6 All appeals
No appeal can be brought in any case if a person failed to make their application to the immigration authorities on the 'prescribed form' or has failed to take 'prescribed steps' in relation to the application or to take those steps within the required time. A person who does not not make their in-country extension application on the form required by the immigration rules (▶see pages 95-96) is not excluded from appealing under *this* rule. This is because the form must be prescribed under 'regulations', not the immigration rules. However, a person who fails to use the correct form for their extension will have their application rejected as invalid and may lose their appeal rights by not having made an in-time application unless they re-submit a valid application within time.

The Home Office has stated that it has no intention to use this rule to prevent appeals by asylum applicants who fail to return their statement of evidence forms (SEFs) in time or who miss an interview. Its officials have also stated in meetings with ILPA that failures to comply with the time limits for sending statements of additional grounds under the 'one-stop' procedure will not be used to deny appeals. It doesn't appear, therefore, that any relevant regulations have been made so as to prevent appeals under this rule. Failures to raise matters during the one-stop procedure can, however, mean that they cannot be raised later (▶see below).

The one-stop appeal system

An important part of the philosophy behind the appeals system set down in the 1999 Act is that people are expected to bring to the attention of the Home Office, or to appeal to an an adjudicator, all the reasons why they should be allowed to remain in the UK in one go. They should do this rather than make an application on one basis and, only if unsuccessful, then make an application on another basis. In order to achieve this, the 1999 Act requires that, in two basic circumstances, the immigration authorities must give appellants a 'one-stop' notice. This notice tells them that, if they have any other grounds upon which they wish to remain in the UK, they must state them. If they do not state those further grounds, they may not be able to raise them later. These two circumstances are:

- when a person has made an asylum or human rights claim (s75, 1999 Act);
- when a person has an in-country right of appeal (s74, 1999 Act).

The one-stop procedure does not apply to applications or appeals made from abroad nor to illegal entrants and overstayers etc who have not claimed asylum or breaches of human rights and who have no appeal rights while remaining in the UK.

The 2002 Bill proposes to simplify the working of the one-stop system but the same basic procedure is likely to remain.

One-stop notices under section 75 of the 1999 Act

A one-stop notice is issued under section 75 of the 1999 Act to any of the following categories of people who claim asylum or claim to be allowed to stay in the UK on human rights grounds:

- people who arrive in the UK without leave to enter, an entry clearance or a work permit;
- illegal entrants;
- people who have overstayed their leave in the UK;

- people who have breached their conditions of leave, or who obtained leave to remain by deception.

Family members of any of the above people also get one-stop notices. 'Family member' for these purposes covers the person's spouse, their child (or the child of their spouse), their unmarried partner who has been living with them for two of the last three years and any person who is dependent on the applicant or on whom the applicant is dependent. The purpose of serving one-stop notices on family members is to prevent them from claiming asylum after the first family member has already appealed unsuccessfully. Therefore, if a woman has applied for leave to enter as the dependent of her husband but has her own reasons to fear persecution in her country of origin, the receipt of the one-stop statement is her opportunity to say so.

The notice specifies that the applicant must state any grounds which are additional to the asylum or human rights grounds which have already been given. The notice is accompanied by a 'statement of additional grounds' which should be completed and returned within 10 working days. If an asylum statement of evidence form (SEF) has been issued, this should also be completed and returned.

If a person given a section 75 notice has their application refused, then with the notice of refusal and the appeal forms they are given another one-stop notice under section 74 of the 1999 Act (below). This is because they have an in-country right of appeal on asylum or human rights grounds. It is obviously better to raise all the grounds in the original one-stop notice so that they can be considered. This is because, although both the statements which accompany the one-stop notices indicate that the additional grounds will be considered before an appeal, the Home Office has frequently failed to do this (►see below). It is more likely that grounds put forward at the time of the asylum or human rights claim will be considered by the Home Office than those which are put forward with the notice of appeal.

One-stop notices under section 74 of the 1999 Act

Notices under section 74 of the 1999 Act are issued to those who have, for any reason, had any of the following negative immigration decisions made against them against which they have an in-country right of appeal:

- refusal of leave to enter;
- decision to refuse to allow them to remain in the UK;
- decision to make a deportation order.

Family members of a person in any of the above categories also get one-stop notices. The same definition of family member applies as for section 75 notices above.

Because these people already have in-country rights of appeal, they are given notices of decision and appeal forms at the same time that they are given their section 74 notice. So, as examples, people given notices of decision to make a deportation order, most people refused entry at a time when they hold a valid entry clearance or whose leave is cancelled when they arrive in the UK and those who are refused extensions of leave having made an in-time application, will all be given these one-stop notices.

It is not necessary for a person to have claimed asylum or made a human rights claim in order to receive a one stop notice under section 74. Therefore, the notice makes a point of stating in bold that the person must now state any human rights claim, claim for asylum or claim to have been racially discriminated against in the decision that has been made as well as any other grounds. Like the section 75 notice, this one-stop notice warns that failure to raise additional grounds in time may mean that an adjudicator is unable to deal with them. The statement of additional grounds must be returned within 10 working days. If the case involves issues of national security, the time limit for returning a section 74 notice is five working days.

Completing the statement of additional grounds

It is very important to obtain advice before completing one-stop notices so that applicants do not miss out on the opportunity to have considered by the Home Office and at any appeal, asylum or human rights issues, aspects of the immigration rules or policies operated outside the immigration rules which the appellant is not aware of. The Home Office and the adjudicator will not necessarily consider everything which may benefit the appellant or their dependants unless it is pointed out. Indeed, it may be that the immigration authorities are unaware of certain facts which could benefit the appellant but have not been put forward because the appellant did not realise that they were important.

While the 1999 Act was being discussed, the Home Office stated that detailed grounds were not expected in the one-stop statement and that it would seek further information if relevant matters were raised. The wording of the original one-stop notice sent out under section 74 of the Immigration and Asylum Appeals (One-Stop Procedure) Regulations 2000 states that the refusal will be 'reviewed' in the light of any additional grounds raised. However, the Home Office soon became dissatisfied with the failure of applicants to make clear precisely what additional grounds they wished to rely on, and in April 2001, made it clear that additional grounds will only be responded to if supported by 'arguments'. In a letter to Asylum Aid, the Home Office stated that 'arguments' do not mean lengthy or detailed submissions, but it is necessary to do more than merely cite, for instance, the Human Rights Act, or an Article under the ECHR, or refer to a particular immigration rule, if an answer is to be expected from the Home Office.

Where arguments, detailed or not, are provided, however, it is rare for any response to be given in good time (or indeed at all) by the Home Office. This is apparently because the section within the Home Office dealing with responses to statements of additional grounds is not the same as the section making the initial decisions. If further grounds of refusal are given, the appellant can give further grounds of appeal responding to the latest refusal letter within five days (see rule 9, Procedure Rules). The appeal papers are often sent to the IAA without any further comment from the Home Office. In many cases there may be no advantage in challenging this. For example, if there is a strong case that a restricted ECHR right (►see pages 236-238 for the meaning of this) is being interfered with by the immigration decision, it is up to the immigration authorities to justify the interference. Therefore, failure to respond to the additional grounds will make the Home Office's job harder at the appeal. Unfortunately, adjudicators have recently been willing to take notice of the public interest in maintaining immigration control in, for example, Article 8 cases even where no apparent consideration has been given to the question by the Home Office.

Preventing grounds being raised in existing appeals and preventing further appeals

The one-stop procedure itself contains penalties where the procedure has not been complied with by the applicant. Applicants can be prevented from bringing further appeals and prevented from raising grounds in existing appeals where the one-stop procedure has not been complied with. The general means by which the immigration authorities do this is by issuing various certificates.

It should be noted that, although the 1999 Act itself seems to apply some of the following procedures only to cases where section 74 notices have been given, they generally apply to section 75 notices as well: see regulation 5, Asylum Appeals (One-Stop Procedure) Regulations 2000.

Preventing grounds being raised in existing appeals

1 If an applicant fails to raise a ground in response to a one-stop notice and the ground is not a claim for asylum, a human rights or a discrimination claim, they cannot raise that ground in the existing appeal or a further appeal (see s76(1)–(3), 1999 Act). This only applies if:

• the person was aware of the ground at the time of the one-stop notice; and

• the Home Office considers that there is no reasonable excuse for not mentioning the ground in the statement.

So, if there is a change of circumstances or if, for other reasons, the applicant did not know that they could rely on the particular ground or had some other reason for not including it at that time, appellants can argue that they should not be prevented from raising the ground. However, experience suggests that claims to be unaware of what reasons might legitimately be offered for wanting to stay in the UK are rarely accepted as credible by the Home Office. Applicants are routinely assumed to be aware of the relevant law and practice, whether or not they have access to legal representation.

2 If a person claims asylum under the Refugee Convention after the 10-day period for returning the statement of additional grounds, the Home Office can prevent them from appealing on asylum grounds by issuing a certificate to the effect that (see s76(4)(5), 1999 Act):

- one purpose of making the claim for asylum is to delay the applicant or a member of their family's removal from the UK; and
- the applicant has 'no other legitimate purpose' for making the claim.

It is arguable that, if a person does have a sincere fear of persecution, this is a legitimate purpose in claiming asylum, even if they had failed to mention it before. However, it is likely that the Home Office would take a certain amount of persuasion on this point.

This certificate cannot be given in relation to a human rights or discrimination claim and these claims can therefore be made late if there is an existing appeal. Section 65 of the 1999 Act expressly states that human rights points can be raised during the course of an existing appeal. However, delays in raising the claim could lead to doubts about the credibility of the claim. The Home Office can, however, prevent *further appeals* being raised on human rights, discrimination (or any other) grounds where there was a failure to raise them in an earlier appeal ▶see below.

Preventing further appeals

The Home Office has the power to prevent further appeals where an original appeal has already been finally determined in the three following circumstances.

1 Where a person seeks to bring a further appeal on either human rights or discrimination grounds after they have already had any appeal which has been determined, the Home Office may prevent the person appealing by issuing a certificate to the effect that (s73(1)–(3), 1999 Act):

- the human rights or discrimination claim could reasonably have been made in a one-stop statement and was not made or the claim could have been made in the earlier appeal and was not made; and
- one purpose of the claim is to delay the applicant's or a member of their family 's removal from the UK; and
- the applicant has 'no other legitimate purpose' for making the claim.

It should also be noted that, even after the decision of the IAT in *Pardeepan*, the Home Office has tried other methods of limiting the power to hear human rights appeals after an appellant has had an earlier appeal ▶see pages 615-616 below.

2 Where a person seeks to bring a further appeal on any grounds after they have already had any appeal which has been determined, the Home Office can prevent the person appealing by issuing a certificate to the effect that (s73(7)–(9), 1999 Act):

• one purpose of the application made is to delay the applicant's or a member of their family's removal from the UK; and

• the applicant has 'no other legitimate purpose' for making the application.

3 Where a person seeks to bring a further appeal on any grounds after they have already had an appeal before which they were given a one-stop notice and which has already been determined, the Home Office can prevent the person appealing by issuing a certificate to the effect that the grounds for the further appeal were considered in the original appeal (see s73(4)-(6) 1999 Act).

Notices of decision and of appeal

Whenever the immigration authorities make a decision against which there is a right of appeal, there is an obligation on them to:

• give a notice which gives the reason for the decision;

• if the decision concerns giving directions for removal, state the country to which the person is to be removed;

• explain the right of appeal and the time limit for appealing;

• state where the notice of appeal is to be sent.

However, a person does not have a free-standing right of appeal against a decision on human rights or discrimination grounds unless and until they write to the Home Office to actually make an allegation that the decision is in breach of their human rights: regulation 4 Immigration and Asylum Appeals (Notices) Regulations 2000.

The notice of decision can be given by hand, fax or sent by post to the applicant or their representative. It will be accompanied by a notice of appeal and, if appropriate under the rules above, a one-stop notice. The applicant appeals by filling in the appeal form and returning it, together with the notice of decision and any statement of additional grounds (if any) to the address stated in the notice of decision. The notice is sent to the immigration authorities themselves rather than the court. It is the job of the immigration authorities to prepare the papers and then send them to the IAA. The notice of appeal can be given in person, sent by fax to the number given on the notice of decision or sent by post.

If it is an asylum or human rights case, in addition to the immigration decision being appealed against (refusal of leave to enter, directions for removal etc), there will be a reasons for refusal letter (sometimes known as the 'RFRL'). This should also be returned. The notice of appeal can be signed either by the applicant or their representative (if they have one) and the name and address of both the applicant and the representative should be included on it. The IAA should be told straight-away about any changes of address or of representative.

The notice of appeal should include the grounds for the appeal. In many cases, where the basis for the application is clear and there is nothing further to add at this stage, representatives often put in standard grounds of appeal. They often simply state that the decision was 'not in accordance with the law, the immigration rules and that discretion should have been exercised differently'. Where additional grounds are being raised, these should be set out in the one-stop statement.

The appeal form also asks if people will require an interpreter at the appeal. If the appellant has any concerns about understanding and speaking English, an interpreter should be requested. It is the responsibility of the IAA to book an independent interpreter in the correct language and only their approved interpreters will be used in court.

Response to the appeal form

Once the appeal forms are sent in, the Home Office is supposed to consider any matters raised in the grounds of appeal and, in particular, the statement of additional grounds. Once these matters have been considered, if the refusal is maintained, the intention is for the Home Office to send the applicant supplementary grounds of refusal, after which the appellant can amend their grounds of appeal. It is after this that the Home Office is supposed to send the relevant documents to the appellate authority although, in practice, this is often done before the five days for replying to the supplementary grounds of refusal are up.

ECOs also review their decisions in response to notices of appeal. If the ECO has clearly over-looked some important matter, pointing this out in the grounds of appeal or in representations can, sometimes, result in a reversal of the decision.

Appealing in time

It is important to appeal in time. For details of the various time limits which apply ►see the box below. If notice of appeal is not given in time, the immigration authorities can still treat it as being in time if they are satisfied that 'because of special circumstances, it is just for the notice to be treated in that way'. Therefore, if the appeal is being submitted late, it is important to explain on the appeal form, or in a covering letter, the full reasons for the delay. If the immigration authorities refuse to treat the appeal as being sent in time, the papers are still sent to the IAA for the adjudicator to decide whether to treat the appeal as in-time as a preliminary issue.

TIME LIMITS AND CALCULATING TIME

Relevant action	Period of time
• Appealing to the adjudicator:	10 days after the decision is received where the appeal is being brought by an appellant who is in the UK.
	28 days where the appellant is outside the UK. If the appellant was in the UK when the decision is made, time runs from the date of departure from the UK. If the appellant was not in the UK when the decision was made, time runs from when the decision was received.
	The above limits are extendable if there are 'special circumstances' which justify the notice being treated as in time.
• Application for review of determination of adjudicator (procedural errors):	10 days after written notice of determination is received.
	The time limit is not extendable.
• Application for leave to appeal to the Immigration Appeal Tribunal:	10 days after the appellant has received the determination of the adjudicator where the application is being made from inside the UK.
	28 days after the appellant has received the determination of the adjudicator where the application is being made from outside the UK.
	These time limits are extendable if the IAT is satisfied that, because of 'special circumstances', it is 'just' to extend the time limit.
• Application for review of determination of IAT refusing to grant leave to appeal (procedural errors)	10 days after written notice of the decision refusing leave to appeal is received by the appellant.
	The time limit is not extendable.
• Application to the IAT for leave to appeal to the Court of Appeal (England) or the Court of Session (Scotland)	10 days after receipt of the determination of the IAT.
	The time limit is not extendable.

Notes on calculating time:

(See rule 48 Immigration and Asylum Appeals (Procedure) Rules 2000)

1 When a decision or determination is sent by post, it is taken to have been received either:
   • on the second day after it was sent if sent to the appellant or their representative in the UK; or
   • on the twenty-eighth day after it was sent, if it was sent to the appellant or their representative outside the UK; or
   • if faxed or delivered by hand, it is taken to have been received on the day it was faxed or delivered.

So if a notice of decision or determination is only sent by post to an applicant outside the UK (e.g., if an ECO gives notice of decision by sending it to the applicant who is abroad), that person's time limit (above) does not start running until 28 days have passed.

However, if the notice of determination was not in fact received by the appellant at the time it should have been received or is treated under the rules (above) as having been received, with the result that an appeal or application would otherwise be late, then it is up to the appellant to prove when it was received. The 2000 Procedure Rules were drafted so as to allow appellants to prove that they had not received the relevant notice following the decision of the Court of Appeal in *Saleem*. That case declared earlier rules which had the effect of 'deeming' notices and determinations as having been received, even if they had not been, as unlawful.

2   Where notices of appeal or applications for leave to appeal are sent to the IAA, the rules are different. They are taken to have been received only on the day they actually are received.

3   In all the time limits given above, time starts running from the end of the day on which the notice of decision or determination was received. So, if a notice of an adjudicator's determination is taken as having been received on Tuesday 5 March, the first day of the 10-day appeal period is Wednesday 6 March.

4   Where the time limit given above is 10 days or less (e.g., the time limit for applying to the IAT for leave to appeal), the following days do not count towards the 10 days: Saturdays, Sundays, bank holidays, Christmas day, 27–31 December, Good Friday.

Certain refusal notices sent to people in the UK may be confusing, as they explain that if the person does not appeal, they have 28 days in which to make arrangements to leave. People sometimes misunderstand this to mean either that they have 28 days in which to appeal, instead of 10, or to mean that they should leave within 28 days even if they do appeal.

Particular appeals

Below we look, in turn, at certain appeals which have certain special features which applicants and advisers should be aware of.

Human rights and discrimination appeals

There are a number of ways of raising human rights and discrimination so that they are considered by the immigration authorities or the appellate authorities ▶see pages 266-267. What follows below applies to both human rights and discrimination claims, although there have been very few of the latter.

Human rights can be raised during the course of any existing appeal, but in order to get a free-standing human rights appeal it is necessary to actually make an allegation that a 'decision' taken under the 'Immigration

Acts' which relates to a person's 'entitlement to enter or remain in the UK', is in breach of human rights. Human rights appeals are therefore different to other appeals in that the Home Office will not, when they issue a notice of decision, state that there is or could be a right of appeal on human rights grounds. This is the case even if the decision has been made in response to a human rights claim and deals with human rights issues. An 'allegation' can be made simply by writing to the decision-taker and stating that the decision is in breach of the person's human rights. Once the allegation has been made, the immigration authorities will send out a notice of decision, appeal forms and, for in-country appeals, a one-stop notice.

There is, as yet, no time limit for this allegation to be made although this may change. The Home Office has stated that it will not remove people in this situation for 10 working days after refusal (unless they are in detention, in which case they have only two days) in order to give them the chance to make the allegation which triggers the right to appeal. There does appear to be scope for people to be removed without having had the chance to appeal, even where they have clearly stated, in advance of the refusal, that they think they would be at risk of abuses of their human rights if they were removed.

The allegation can be made against a decision of a Home Office official (in-country decisions), an immigration officer (most on-entry decisions) or entry clearance officers. The decision must also relate to the entitlement of the person to enter or remain in the UK. The actions of others, such as airline staff denying access to an aircraft or NASS officials in relation to providing asylum support, cannot therefore be raised on a human rights appeal. If these actions are in breach of the ECHR, they may be challenged by other appeals or judicial review. Human rights appeals also only cover decisions under the 'Immigration Acts'. This does not, therefore, include nationality decisions.

The decision in *Pardeepan* and raising human rights after a failed appeal

As a result of government legislation, human rights appeals or grounds cannot be raised against decisions taken before 2 October 2000, even if the appeal was still outstanding on that date. In the case of *Pardeepan*, the IAT confirmed that it was not possible to raise human rights in these cases. It did so only after being told by the Home Office that anyone in this situation would not be prevented from appealing again on human rights grounds if their existing appeal failed and they then made a human rights claim. The IAT recorded the Home Office's assurance as follows:

'We are assured by Mr Thompson, on behalf of Secretary of State, that those whose appeals are refused, for example, on asylum grounds, will be given the opportunity to raise, if they think fit, human rights objections to removal, should the Secretary of State decide to remove them. We are equally assured that the Secretary of State will not seek to argue that they do not have a right of appeal under Section 65 in respect of such a subsequent decision to remove'.

The Home Office confirmed this position in the the Court of Appeal in the case of **Ramirez**. This effectively gives most people who were refused asylum before 2 October 2000 and are still in the UK a second chance to appeal, this time on human rights grounds.

The Home Office have since tried to back-track on these undertakings, arguing, for instance, that the appeal right did not apply to people whose claims were based on matters which had already been the subject of findings of fact by the IAA which meant that the human rights claim was 'bound to fail' (statement of minister of 20 March 2001). However, following concerns expressed by the IAT itself, as well as applicants' representatives, the Home Office changed tack again. On 19 July 2001 it announced that all those who had appeals outstanding on 2 October 2000, would still be able to raise a human rights claim and obtain an appeal.

However, in relation to cases which do not fit into the strict **Pardeepan** assurance, the Home Office position seems to be that, where removal is set to take place after the dismissal of the earlier appeal, it is not bound to make another 'decision' which gives rise to a human rights appeal. It has argued that directions given for removal do not constitute such a decision and therefore, if no further 'underlying' decision is made about the person's entitlement to be in the UK, an applicant can be removed without a human rights appeal.

The High Court has come to different decisions about the correct position. In **Kariharan**, the Home Office's arguments were accepted. However in **Kumarakuparan**, Newman J held that an applicant who had been prevented from raising human rights in his asylum appeal (because of **Pardeepan**), had a right of appeal on human rights grounds against removal directions issued subsequently. His view was that the Home Office could use the certificates under section 73 1999 Act (▶see pages 610-611) to deal with abusive repeat claims. The Court of Appeal will have to decide which approach is correct. In the long run, these decisions of the court may not matter so much as the 2002 Bill proposes to clarify which immigration decisions can and cannot be appealed against.

It should also be noted that, where an applicant wishes to raise human rights by relying on the same matters which have already been dealt with in an earlier appeal, the IAT has stated that, in most cases, the next adjudicator should make their findings 'in line' with the earlier determination (**Devaseelan**). This does not mean that the human rights claim must fail because, in some cases, a human rights claim may succeed on the same facts as an asylum claim fails (▶see pages 243-244 for examples of the differences in the level of protection under Article 3 ECHR compared with the Refugee Convention).

Asylum appeals where exceptional leave has been granted

Where a person was appealing against a decision to refuse asylum but already had leave (usually exceptional leave), a problem arose of what date the adjudicator and IAT had to consider when assessing whether the asylum-seeker was at risk of persecution if returned. Should they consider the situation at the date of the appeal hearing or should they look ahead to the date when the exceptional leave ran out and the point at which the asylum-seeker might be returned?

In *Saad, Diriye & Osario*, decided in December 2001, the Court of Appeal made it clear that the right of appeal is an effective one. The IAT had earlier ruled that any appeal could not possibly succeed because it was impossible for an appellant to show that there would still be a well-founded fear if they were forced to return at the end of their period of exceptional leave in a number of years' time. In *Saad*, the Court effectively decided that an asylum appeal had to be determined on the basis of the circumstances at the date of the hearing just as with any other asylum appeal. The adjudicator does not have to guess at what may be the situation in the future in the asylum-seeker's country of origin. This is important for people who want to establish their refugee status so, for example, they can secure rights of family reunion.

Saad also considered the question of when a person may appeal even through they have exceptional leave. The case was decided under section 8 of the Asylum and Immigration Appeals Act 1993 (the old asylum appeals legislation). It held that a person who is granted leave to *enter* exceptionally as well as a person who applies to upgrade their status but is granted further exceptional leave, can still bring an effective asylum appeal. The 1999 Act makes it clear that this is the case for appeals brought under that Act (see s69(3), 1999 Act). There remain difficulties, however. For example, someone who is already appealing against directions for removal as an overstayer or illegal entrant and who is *then* granted exceptional leave, may be faced with an argument by the Home Office that their appeal must be treated as 'abandoned' under the provisions of the 1999 Act (see s58(9)).

Another situation where there may be difficulties are the circumstances which arose in the case of *Massaquoi*. In that case, there was a non-asylum and an asylum appeal lodged against a decision to make a deportation order. The non-asylum appeal was successful but the asylum appeal was unsuccessful. The appellant wanted to appeal to the IAT against the adjudicator's decision to dismiss the asylum appeal. However, the Court of Appeal held that this could not be done because the decision appealed against (the decision to make the deportation order) had itself been overturned so there was nothing left to appeal about. The best course in these circumstances is to apply to 'upgrade' status to that of refugee and to appeal any negative decision. The 2002 Bill proposes a further limitation. It proposes that where a person is granted 12 months or less exceptional leave, they will be denied an upgrade appeal.

Family visitor appeals

The only people entitled to appeal against refusal of entry clearance as visitors are those classified as 'family visitors'. The Immigration Appeals (Family Visitor) (No2) Regulations 2000 define these as those people visiting members of their immediate family up to and including first cousins as well as certain members of their step-family and in-laws. Family visitors can also be visiting their unmarried partner (heterosexual or same-sex), provided they have lived together as an unmarried couple for two of the previous three years. A fee was initially payable for the appeal, the level of which depended upon whether an oral hearing or a determination on the papers was requested. The fee has now been abolished. For full details of those family members who qualify as 'family members' and other details ►see Chapter 14 on visitors, page 286.

To give an idea of how long these appeals are taking, the Lord Chancellor's department has indicated that the average time taken to process family visitor appeals between 1 April and 31 December 2001, from receiving the appeal to determining it, was:

- just over two and a half weeks for family visitor appeals decided without a hearing;
- just under seven weeks for family visitor appeals decided with a hearing.

It seems that more appellants are opting for paper appeals rather than oral hearings: in December 2001, the IAA received 97 cases for oral hearing and 129 cases for determination without a hearing.

Special Immigration Appeals Commission (SIAC)

A very small number of people are excluded from the normal system of appeals and must use a separate appeal system. This is the case where the Secretary of State has denied the applicant the right to remain in the UK on 'conducive' grounds, usually based on national security, diplomatic or political reasons. This also applies to an asylum case where the application has been refused on national security grounds or, in some cases, where a person has been excluded from the Refugee Convention under Article 1F because of their conduct.

If a person is refused entry clearance or leave to enter the UK following a direction on conducive grounds by the Secretary of State, they also have no right of appeal to the IAA. They also have no right of appeal to SIAC unless they are relying on rights under EU law or they are seeking entry for rights of access to a child, or as a spouse, fiancé(e) or dependent relative.

The SIAC panel is made up of three people: a High Court judge, an 'immigration judge' (usually a senior adjudicator or member of the IAT) and another person who is not necessarily a lawyer but who has experience of security matters.

Why was SIAC set up?

Until 1998 there was no right of appeal against decisions to exclude people based on reasons of national security or the interests of the UK's political relations with another state. All that existed was a chance to put a case to a panel of three 'advisers' (the 'three wise men'), but with no right to be given the Home Office's reasons, or to be represented at the hearing. Even if the advisers accepted the person's case, the Home Secretary was not bound by their decision.

In November 1996 the European Court of Human Rights held, in the case of *Chahal*, that this procedure was inadequate and a decision was made to set up a special commission which would give the right of appeal but with safeguards to protect national security. SIAC's functions have now been extended to deal with appeals against decisions to detain suspected international terrorists under the Anti-terrorism, Crime and Security Act 2001 ▶see pages 496-497, 516-517.

SIAC procedures

The main differences between proceedings before SIAC and the adjudicators and IAT are as follows. Appellants are entitled to two sets of legal representatives. They are entitled to have a 'special advocate' appointed by the government who represents their interests in the part of the hearing concerning national security issues. The special advocate is able to see the 'sensitive' national security material which the Home Office is relying on and to make representations about it and cross-examine Home Office witnesses. That part of the hearing is in closed session and the appellant and the public are excluded from it and are not able to see the sensitive material. After the special advocate has seen the sensitive material, they are no longer able to have direct contact with the appellant. The appellant is also entitled to have another legal representative who remains in contact with the appellant all the way through the hearing and who represents their interests in the open part of the hearings but, like the appellant, is not allowed to see the sensitive material.

Changes to SIAC procedure made by the Anti-terrorism, Crime and Security Act 2001

Where SIAC is considering an asylum appeal, important changes to the procedure have been made by section 33 of the Anti-terrorism, Crime and Security Act 2001. If the Home Office issues a certificate that the applicant is excluded from the protection of the Refugee Convention under Article 1(F) or 33(2) (essentially because they do not deserve protection due to their conduct or because they are a danger to national security) and that their removal is conducive to the public good, then SIAC must first decide whether they agree with the certificate. If they do agree with the certificate, the appeal is to be dismissed without any consideration of whether the person does, in fact, have a well-founded fear of persecution as a 'refugee'. If SIAC does not agree with the certificate, the matter is referred back to the Home Office to decide how to proceed.

This procedure is in line with another provision of the 2001 Act which states that, whenever an asylum-seeker is being excluded on these grounds from the Refugee Convention, it is not necessary to consider how serious or grave any persecution of them would be and to balance it against the person's previous conduct or the risk that they present to national security. This part of the 2001 Act seems also to apply to decisions taken by the Home Office or the adjudicator and the IAT in any asylum case where exclusion is an issue, not just to those referred to SIAC. Exclusion from the Refugee Convention does not, however, mean that a person who faces persecution can be removed because their removal will be likely to breach Article 3 ECHR (►see below).

SIAC decisions

Very few appeals have been fully heard by SIAC. The first appeal to SIAC, *Rehman*, was a non-asylum case. Mr Rehman was a Pakistani national who had lived lawfully in the UK as a minister of religion since 1993. When he came to make an application for indefinite leave to remain in the UK in 1998, a decision was made to deport him on national security grounds. SIAC rejected the allegations that Mr Rehman had recruited British muslims to undergo military training and that he had raised funds for an organisation called the 'Lashkar Tayyaba' and decided that it had not been shown that he was a danger to national security. SIAC also decided that the interests of national security must require that the appellant's conduct was targeted at the UK, its people or at least be targeted against a foreign power in circumstances where that government was likely to take reprisals against the UK which would affect its security.

The case went to the Court of Appeal, and then reached the House of Lords, which held that, although the individual's presence had to result in a real possibility of an adverse effect on the UK, there was no need for that effect to be direct or immediate. The Law Lords also held that SIAC must pay great respect to the government's assessment of whether an applicant posed a threat to national security and could only disagree with that assessment on very narrow grounds. The effect of the decision is also that the Home Office does not have to 'prove' each individual allegation but that it and SIAC must look at all the information globally as well as to the potential activities of the individual person to see whether there is a real possibility of activities harmful to national security. The judgments in the *Rehman* case were largely written before the events of 11 September 2000 in New York. However, their Lordships acknowledged that those events re-inforced the decision reached.

The first asylum case to be heard by SIAC, *Singh & Singh*, concerned two Sikh asylum-seekers who were involved in the movement for 'Khalistan', an independent homeland for Sikhs in Punjab. SIAC found that they were connected to proposed violent activities on the Indian sub-continent and that, following *Rehman* (which had, by that time, only been decided in the Court of Appeal in a decision which was similar to that of the House of Lords), they were a danger to the broad meaning of national security, which also applied to asylum cases under the Refugee Convention. The applicants were excluded from protection under the 1951 Convention but, because SIAC agreed that they faced a risk of torture if they were returned to India, their appeal under Article 3 ECHR was allowed and they were permitted to stay in the UK.

Appeals certified to prevent appeals to the Immigration Appeal Tribunal

The 1993 Act introduced the concept of claims which are certified as 'without foundation' as a way of dealing more rapidly, although not more fairly, with asylum appeals. These certificates must be distinguished from the certificates (▶see pages 609-611) which prevent any appeal, limit the grounds of appeal or require that the appeal can only be exercised abroad. The principal effect of this kind of certification is that the appellant's right of appeal to the IAT is removed if the adjudicator agrees with the certificate.

The 1996 Act extended this category of certificate and they are presently provided for in paragraph 9, schedule 4 of the 1999 Act, which enables claims under either the Refugee Convention or the ECHR to be certified. One well-publicised change in the 1999 Act was to remove the so-called 'white list' of countries in relation to which the government had decided that there was, in general, no serious risk of persecution. There remain numerous other circumstances in which claims may be certified, some of which do not have much bearing on the strength of the claim in question. The certificate itself normally takes the form of a paragraph in the reasons for refusal letter. The government is considering abolishing this form of certificate on the grounds that it over-complicates the appeal process.

For more detailed explanation of the grounds for these certificates and how the certificates work ▶see pages 203-205. In brief, claims can be certified if there is no evidence to show a reasonable likelihood that the applicant has been tortured in their country of origin *and* either:

- the applicant, on arrival in the UK, failed, without reasonable explanation, to produce a valid passport when required to do so by an immigration officer, or produced a passport that was not valid and failed to inform the officer of that fact; *or*

- a person is claiming asylum under the Refugee Convention but their fear of persecution is not, in the Secretary of State's opinion, for one of the five reasons listed in the Convention: race, religion, nationality, membership of a particular social group or political opinion; *or*
- a fear of persecution is considered 'manifestly unfounded or the circumstances which gave rise to the fear no longer subsist'; *or*
- a claim under the ECHR 'does not disclose a right' under the ECHR, or where the claim is manifestly unfounded; *or*
- the claim for asylum is made after the applicant has been refused leave to enter the UK, has been notified of a decision to deport them or to remove them as an illegal entrant, or has been recommended for deportation by a court; *or*
- a claim under either Convention is classified as 'manifestly fraudulent, or the evidence adduced in its support is manifestly false'; *or*
- the claim is 'frivolous or vexatious'.

The Home Office is also entitled to certify racial discrimination claims but only on the grounds that they are 'manifestly unfounded'. In those cases, the certificate does not have to also state that there is no evidence of torture. The effect of the certificate is the same.

At the hearing, the adjudicator will have to make a decision on the certificate as well as on the merits of the appeal. If the adjudicator upholds the certificate, there is no right of appeal to the IAT against a dismissal of the main appeal. If the certificate is not upheld, the right of appeal to the IAT is reinstated. Needless to say, the Home Office has the right of appeal to the IAT in all cases.

PROPOSED CHANGES TO APPEALS SYSTEM

The Nationality, Immigration and Asylum Bill 2002, the White Paper *Safe Havens, Secure Borders*, together with written Home Office statements on future plans, propose possible changes. Not all may be realised. Although the provisions in the Bill are lengthy, many of them replace the provisions of the 1999 Act but without changing the effect of them. There are, however, significant proposed changes which are set out below.

Appeals against decisions that a person needs leave to enter. Appeals against decisions that a person needs leave to enter the UK may no longer exist independently. If there is a dispute about whether an applicant is exempt from immigration control or that they have the right of abode in the UK, they can raise those grounds in an appeal against a refusal of leave to enter or a refusal to issue a certificate of entitlement to the right of abode.

New appeal rights. If a court makes a recommendation for deportation which the Home Office decides to follow, rather than proceeding directly to signing a deportation order, it will make an initial 'decision to make a deportation order' (as in other deportation cases) against which there will be a new right of appeal. There will also be a right of appeal against the decision to 'revoke' an indefinite leave. The power to revoke indefinite leave is itself a new proposal ▶see page 168. These two new appeal rights will be 'suspensive', that is, they can be brought while the applicant is in the UK and the applicant cannot be removed while the appeal is outstanding.

Define decisions which allow a human rights appeal. The Bill tries to specifically define the 'immigration decisions' which give rise to human rights and discrimination appeals. Since the human rights appeal was introduced, there have been conflicting decisions in the High Court as to which decisions are included ▶see page 616 above. The intention is to make clear that the issuing of later removal directions which flow from an earlier immigration refusal of entry, decision to deport, decision to remove as an illegal entrant, overstayer etc, will not give rise to a right of appeal. The Home Office intention is to allow only the earlier 'underlying' immigration decision to give a right of appeal so as to prevent applicants from getting further rights of appeal every time removal directions are given.

Connected to this change is the likely introduction of a time limit for making a human rights allegation which will give rise to a right of appeal.

Re-structuring and simplification of the 'one-stop' system. The working of the 'one-stop' system has confused all involved with it. The intention is to clarify it and remove the unnecessary repetitions in its processes but to retain the operation of the same system requiring disclosure by applicants and those who are appealing of all their grounds for entering or staying in the UK and preventing them from raising grounds late by a system of certificates.

The Bill indicates that the system will be extended so that, at the application stage, any applicant, not just those who make asylum or human rights claims, can be given a one-stop notice.

The penalties for failing to comply (▶see pages 609-611) are proposed to be extended in two ways:

- an applicant can be prevented from appealing where they have not actually had an appeal but had the opportunity of appealing but did not do so;
- a person can be prevented from appealing on grounds which they could have raised earlier even though they have left the UK and returned.

Asylum appeals where the applicant is given exceptional leave. In response to the decision of the Court of Appeal in *Saad & Others* ▶see pages 617-618, the Home Office intend to restrict the right of appeal on asylum grounds to those who are given exceptional leave for more than one year. Presumably, those given leave for 12 months or less will have to wait until their next application is refused or they are granted leave for more than a year before they will have a right of appeal.

New circumstances arising after the decision. At present an adjudicator can have regard to evidence about new circumstances and facts which come into existence between the date of the decision of the immigration authorities and the hearing only in asylum appeals and cases raising Article 3 ECHR. It is proposed to allow adjudicators to take into account new circumstances in all appeals. However, in appeals against refusals of entry clearance and certificates of entitlement to the right of abode, the Bill proposes that adjudicators will only be able to take into account evidence which was made *available to the ECO*. This is a restriction on the existing position because, although adjudicators presently cannot take into account evidence about new circumstances arising after the ECO's decision, they can, in any case, look at further evidence which relates to the circumstances at the time of the decision.

The Bill would prevent, therefore, bank statements showing the availability of funds existing at the date of the decision being taken into account by the adjudicator when deciding whether an applicant can be maintained without recourse to public funds, unless those statements had been produced to the ECO. It would also prevent evidence of 'intervening devotion' in marriage or unmarried partners cases – that is evidence that the couple have continued to show affection for each other after the decision which is relevant to their intentions at the time of the decision.

Appeals where the application is for a purpose not covered by the immigration rules. The Bill proposes that, where an applicant is refused on the grounds that they are seeking to enter or remain for a purpose not covered by the rules, they will have no right of appeal. The present position is that, although these applications may be refused under the rules, if a person is not granted leave outside the rules, they may still succeed on an appeal by showing that a decision is 'not in accordance with the law'. For example, if a policy outside the rules has not been properly applied the appeal may be allowed on this basis. This is a potentially very wide-ranging restriction which would prevent all such people from appealing at all.

Discrimination appeals to be 'non-suspensive'. The Bill proposes that, where a person appeals solely on grounds of race discrimination, they will not be able to appeal while they remain in the UK.

Appeals in third country cases on human rights grounds. Third country cases are proposed to be dealt with in much the same way although it is expected that, at some stage, the Dublin Convention will be supplemented or replaced by other agreement(s) between the EU member states. The existing legislation is wide enough to allow removals under the same procedures but in line with other agreements between states. The Bill proposes that the certificate which is issued to prevent a person from having an in-country appeal right against removal on human rights grounds will have its label changed. The Home Office will certify that the human rights claim is 'clearly' rather than 'manifestly' unfounded.

Adjournments and 'closure' date for appeals. The government believes that many appeals are subject to multiple adjournments, the purpose of which is to delay the outcome. The Bill allows for new procedure rules to prevent adjournments except in strictly specified circumstances and to have a final closure date by which time an adjourned appeal must be determined.

Setting aside decisions. The Bill allows for procedure rules which will enable adjudicators to set aside their own determinations, or those of other adjudicators, and gives a similar power to the IAT in relation to determinations of the IAT. To what extent the new rules will enlarge on the existing ability of the chief adjudicator or the IAT to set aside certain decisions on the grounds of procedural errors, remains to be seen.

Allegations of forgery. The Bill also paves the way for procedure rules to allow for hearings in the absence of applicants where it is alleged that a document which is relied on is a forgery and it would be contrary to the public interest for the applicant to see the evidence which the Home Office relies on to show how it has detected the alleged forgery. The existing powers which allow this to be done only relate to passports, travel documents, certificates of entitlement, entry clearances or work permits. The proposed powers cover all documents. So, for example, the Home Office may allege that an arrest warrant produced by an asylum applicant is a forgery and seek to produce evidence showing the forgery to the adjudicator in private.

Appealing to the Immigration Appeal Tribunal. It is proposed that both an applicant and the immigration authorities will only be able to appeal to the IAT if they can show that the decision of the adjudicator was wrong 'on a point of law', which means that they must be able to show that the decision is legally wrong. There is no such restriction at present. It is also proposed that the IAT will have an additional power of remitting a case to an adjudicator to hear additional evidence in an appeal with a view to the appeal still being determined by the IAT.

Judicial review of the adjudicator and Immigration Appeal Tribunal. The government's view is that applicants and their advisers abuse the appeal system and the availability of judicial review by making unfounded judicial review applications to delay removal. Currently, if an appellant applies for leave to appeal against a decision of an adjudicator to the IAT and the IAT refuses leave to appeal, the person may challenge that decision to refuse leave to appeal by judicial review. Applicants also judicially review determinations of adjudicators who dismiss appeals and uphold the Home Office certificate which prevents an appeal to the IAT.

The government has made a number of proposals which were not in the first draft of the Bill but which it may still include in the legislation to change the system:

- to make the IAT into what is called a 'Superior Court of Record' whose decisions are not open to judicial review (White Paper); or
- to implement a statutory review process which does not involve judicial review by the High Court but which is able to review the refusal of the IAT to grant leave to appeal and determinations of adjudicators where there is no right of appeal to the IAT; or
- to have only one level of appeals in asylum cases.

Ending of certification of appeals preventing appeals to the IAT. The White Paper announced that the appeals process would be simplified by removing the system of certification of asylum and human rights claims to the effect that a right of appeal to the IAT is denied if the adjudicator agrees with the certificate. It is odd that, in January 2002, the government introduced the system of personal delivery by the Home Office of determinations in certified cases (▶see pages 649-650) which, in the next month, it proposed to abolish. It is unclear whether it will finally be abolished.

It should be noted that the original commitment was only to ending the certificates which prevent a further appeal to the IAT not those certificates which prevent appeals at all, or those which restrict the grounds of appeals, or those which require that human rights appeals against third country removals are exercised from abroad.

Further proposals. As the Bill has progressed, the Home Office has developed further proposals in relation to appeals including requiring appeals to be brought from outside the UK in cases where the asylum claim is 'clearly unfounded'. It has also proposed a system which will prevent representatives from being paid by the LSC if they assist in bringing cases which have no merit.

Increasing capacity for hearing appeals. The government intends to increase the capacity for the hearing of appeals by adjudicators by 50 per cent. The intention is to increase the numbers of cases heard each month from 4,000 to 6,000 by November 2002.

For JCWI's views on the proposals in the Bill and the White Paper ▶see Chapter 2.

30 Conducting appeals

This chapter looks at the procedures which operate when an appeal comes before the Immigration Appellate Authorities (IAA). It also gives some practical guidance about conducting appeals and taking appeals to the Immigration Appeal Tribunal , including identifying grounds of appeal against decisions of adjudicators. The powers of the IAA in considering and deciding appeals are also covered. For details about rights of appeal, the notice of decision which gives rise to the appeal itself and giving notice of appeal and the one stop procedure, see Chapter 29 above. For details about time limits ▶see the box on pages 613-614.

The time taken for an appeal to go through the process has fluctuated greatly over time depending upon the numbers of appellants and the available resources of the IAA. To give an idea of the approximate time-scales, figures released by the Lord Chancellor's department concerning appeals between April and December 2001 show that the average time taken for an adjudicator to determine an appeal from the date it was received by the IAA was (written parliamentary answer, 23 January 2002):

- nearly 20 weeks for asylum appeals;
- nearly 18 weeks for other immigration appeals.

The rules which regulate the procedure for all current appeals, whether immigration, asylum or human rights appeals and whenever the appeal was begun, are the Immigration and Asylum Appeals (Procedure) Rules 2000. In this chapter, we refer to them as the 'Procedure Rules' or the 'rules'.

Appeal procedures

Parties

The person appealing is known as the appellant and the Secretary of State (the Home Office), the immigration officer or entry clearance officer who made the decision which is being appealed is called the respondent. The appellant and the respondent are the 'parties' to the appeal. In asylum appeals, the UNHCR is entitled to become a third party to the appeal. This is rare; the UNHCR only becomes a party where there are important standard-setting principles at issue in the case which will have an effect on the wider development of the law.

Representation

People who are appealing are always best advised to obtain representation. The law and procedures can be very complex, particularly in asylum appeals. A significantly higher proportion of appeals which are represented are successful. Specialist representatives not only have substantial experience and knowledge of the law and procedures in immigration cases but also have access to evidence and reports.

Those who have legal representatives and who are wishing to appeal should ask their representative, immediately on receiving any negative decision, who will represent them at the hearing and who will pay for this. Adjudicators are increasingly reluctant to postpone appeal hearings where there has been a last minute change of representative because of problems with fees. Since 1 January 2000, Controlled Legal Representation (CLR), a form of legal aid, has been available to enable immigration advice providers to represent or arrange for representation at appeals if they hold a contract or a franchise from the Legal Services Commission (LSC). This depends on the appellant passing both a means and a merits test. The Refugee Legal Centre (in asylum/human rights cases) and the Immigration Advisory Service (in all cases) can also provide free representation. Some charitable or local authority funded advice agencies also provide free representation at appeals.

In common with other immigration advice, non-lawyers must be exempted or registered under Part 5 of the 1999 Act if they are to represent people at appeals. For those registered or exempted by the Immigration Services Commissioner (OISC), only those practising at Level 3 (the highest level) are allowed to do appeals work, including lodging the appeal. This means that any voluntary sector adviser or paid consultant practising at a lower level needs to pass the case to a solicitor, the IAS or RLC, or a level 3 practitioner immediately a refusal is received. For full details about immigration advice and representation ▶see Chapter 3.

Hearings

Hearings in most cases are in public although private hearings can be requested ▶see page 631. The hearings take place at the designated hearing centres although there is provision in the Procedure Rules for hearings to be conducted by video link. This does not yet seem to be available in practice but may be in the future.

In the following circumstances, appeals can be determined without an oral hearing at all: the IAA have decided to allow an appeal; the appellant is outside the UK or it is not possible to give them notice of hearing and they have no representative; there is a preliminary question as to whether there is a right of appeal; the appellate authorities believe the appeal can be justly determined without a hearing; there has been a failure to comply with directions or the Procedure Rules themselves; no party wants an oral hearing; it is a family visitor appeal where the appellant does not want an oral hearing or the same issues involving the same appellant (or one of their family members) have already been dealt with in an earlier appeal. In most of these cases, the IAA must give the parties an opportunity of making written representations before deciding to deal with the appeal without a hearing.

Travel while awaiting an appeal

It is not safe to travel out of the UK while an in-country appeal is outstanding. If a person leaves the country while an appeal is pending, the appeal is taken to have been abandoned.

Before the main hearing

Documents

After notice of appeal has been given, it is the duty of the immigration authorities to prepare the papers for the appeal and to send them to the IAA. There are often delays in doing this in cases of appeals against entry clearance refusals. The documents sent to the IAA, which will form the 'appeal bundle' (or the 'Home Office bundle') should include all the documents which have been considered by the Home Office in making the decision. This includes notes of interviews (these must be included in asylum cases, and would normally be expected in others), written statements from the appellant, letters from their representative and any supporting evidence which has been submitted. Also included in the bundle will be the notice of decision, reasons for refusal, notice of appeal with the grounds of appeal, any statement of additional grounds which the appellant has filed under the 'one-stop' procedure and any further grounds of refusal (▶see below). The appellant will receive a copy of the appeal bundle. It is not uncommon for important documents to be left out of the Home Office bundle and appellants should check that everything has been included.

With the appeal forms there should be included a form for notifying the IAA of any change of the address of the appellant or change of representatives. It is vital that changes of address should be passed on, and it is important not to assume that a change of address notified to the Home Office or Immigration Service will be passed to the IAA, particularly after the appeal bundle has been sent out.

Explanatory statement/reasons

Other than in asylum or human rights cases, the reasons for the negative decision are unlikely to be explained in any detail at the time of the notice of decision. Detailed reasons are likely to be put in the form of an 'explanatory statement' after an appeal is lodged; this will also form part of the appeal bundle prepared by the Home Office. In in-country applications, the explanatory statement may go into some detail about the person's immigration history in the UK, from the Home Office point of view. There may be details about the application that has been refused, the checks carried out by the Home Office, the information it has gathered and the reasons why it believes that the person does not qualify to remain. There are often delays of several months before the statement is prepared. If the appeal is against refusal of entry at port, the explanatory statement is prepared by an immigration officer and is usually much shorter and prepared more quickly.

If the appeal is against refusal of entry clearance, the explanatory statement is normally prepared by an ECO at the overseas post. It frequently includes a record, in question-and-answer form, of the interview between the ECO and the appellant, and anyone else who was interviewed, and then an explanation of the reasons for the refusal. Some posts have their own forms for asking details about the appellant's family tree and, in family settlement cases, this is also attached to the statement. The time taken to prepare the statement varies between posts. Where there is little immigration work, it may be only a few days or weeks but it may be much longer from countries where there are delays. If the post referred the case to the Home Office for decision, the explanatory statement is written by the Home Office.

Those refused asylum will, in contrast, be informed at the time of refusal why the Home Office does not accept that they should be given asylum. This takes the form of a reasons for refusal letter (RFRL), which is separate from the formal notice of refusal which gives notice of the immigration decision appealed against. The RFRL is likely to set out in detail (if not always accurately) the basis of the claim, the response of the Home Office to individual claims made by the applicant and the Home Office's understanding of the situation in the person's country of origin. The Home Office will also state its position on the legal issues raised by the case. Above all, the reasons for refusal usually focus on the credibility of the claims which have been made. The Home Office's usual approach is to state that it does not believe the account given, often for reasons which asylum-seekers find surprising or upsetting.

When there is no right of appeal

If the immigration authorities are alleging that there is in fact no right of appeal, for example, on the grounds that one of the limitations set out in Box 2 on pages 605-606 applies, or on the grounds that the appeal was not made in time, the Home Office must prepare an explanatory statement which raises that issue and explains all the facts and circumstances. The appellant may send in a written statement in reply explaining why there is a right of appeal. The question is then likely to be decided by the adjudicator as a 'preliminary issue'. Obviously, if the adjudicator rules that there is no right of appeal then s/he will not go on to consider the other matters in the appeal.

Arranging the appeal hearing

Once the Home Office has sent the appeal bundle to the IAA, a date will be arranged for the appellant to attend a hearing. Hearings are usually arranged in the closest hearing centre to the appellant's home address. An increasing number of courts are now in operation outside the London area. For a list of the addresses for the IAA ▶see page 726. Travel costs to attend hearings can be met from asylum support. In many cases the IAA arrange a 'first' hearing (below) rather than proceeding directly to the main hearing. The Procedure Rules do not specifically provide for this process or 'fast-track' hearings (▶see also below).

Advisers need to be aware that many of the practicalities of the hearing process are from time to time changed by the IAA. For example, from approximately September 2001, the hearing centre at Hatton Cross, London piloted a new system which may be introduced more widely. Both the President of the IAT and the Chief Adjudicator can issue 'practice directions' which set out the practice and procedure which is to be followed in relation to appeals.

Directions

The Procedure Rules refer to directions as being part of the process for ensuring the 'the overriding objective' of the conduct of appeals, which is to 'secure the just, timely and effective disposal of appeals', and it is the adjudicator's responsibility to see that this happens. Directions are intended to help achieve this, although at times they are applied with a lack of flexibility which seems to value timeliness or administrative convenience above fairness.

When the first notice of hearing is sent out, the IAA will also send out a list of standard directions which the parties have to comply with (see Practice Direction of Chief Adjudicator of 27 July 2001). The standard directions for the appellant are that they file with the IAA by a specified time:

- witness statements of the appellant and all other witnesses who will be called to give evidence at the hearing. The witness statements should contain all the evidence that the witness is to provide;
- a bundle containing all the documents which the appellant wants to refer to at the hearing;
- a schedule that indicates all of the essential passages in the bundle of documents which the appellant wants the adjudicator to pay particular attention to;
- a skeleton argument which sets out all the relevant issues and claims and which states any decided cases which the appellant wants to refer to;
- a chronology of events.

Translations must be provided of documents which are not in English. The Home Office usually only has to comply with the direction relating to the bundle of documents. The Home Office hardly ever calls witnesses and its case is supposed to be fully set out in the RFRL or in the explanatory statement. For the penalties for failing to comply with directions ▶see page 638. Where an appellant is not represented, the appellate authorities are not allowed to give directions unless they are sure that the appellant will be able to comply with them.

Sometimes an appellant may wish to ask the adjudicator to make certain directions which can be requested in writing or at a first hearing (below). An appellant might want to ask for any of the following:

Exclusion of the public from the hearing. Appeal hearings are open to the public, unless the adjudicator directs otherwise (rule 40). The public generally, or particular members of the public, can be excluded from a hearing if the adjudicator thinks that it is necessary in the interests of 'morals, public order, or national security', or if the interests of minors or the protection of an appellant's private life require it, or if it is necessary in the interests of justice. Sometimes, in cases of minors or victims of particularly serious abuse such as rape, where the appellant would find it difficult or distressing to have to give evidence in public, advisers ask for private hearings. Similarly, if the issues in the appeal affect very sensitive areas of the person's private life, the public can be excluded. This has happened, for instance, in cases involving HIV/AIDS infection. Although decisions of adjudicators and the IAT are public documents, in some cases they have agreed to only identify the appellant by an initial so as to protect their identity.

Further details of the Home Office case. It may be that the RFRL or explanatory statement is unclear about what the Home Office's case is on certain issues and the appellant does not know whether a particular requirement of the rules or some other matter is in dispute. Before spending time and effort in dealing with the point and if the Home Office will not respond directly, in some cases it may be appropriate to ask for a direction for 'further particulars' of the Home Office position (see rule 31(4)(c)(iii)). This rule or rule 36 (witness summons) could also be used to get the Home Office to produce documents which are relevant to an appeal and which the Home Office clearly has, but has not produced. It is a criminal offence for a person to fail to comply with a witness summons. Witness summons are, however, rarely made and appellants should always consider whether, tactically, it is best to ask for further evidence or particulars when they do not know exactly what may be produced.

Combined hearings. The IAA can join together appeals where similar questions arise and it seems desirable that the appeals are heard together (rule 42). This may occur, for example, where there are separate appeals relating to members of the same family where the events overlap with each other and where they could be witnesses in each others' cases. However, because of the large number of appeals, often the Home Office and the IAA will not have linked the cases. Great care should be taken before applying for cases to be linked. Representatives should be sure that they have seen everything that has already been said in the other case before advising their clients on applying to have cases joined.

First hearing

It is now usual practice to arrange a first hearing in all cases except those allocated to a 'fast-track' (▶see below). First hearings are also known as 'mega-list' hearings because a large number of appeals are listed before the same adjudicator on the same day. Appellants and their representatives do not have to attend the first hearing unless they are unable to comply with the standard directions (above) and state that they are ready to proceed with the hearing. If the appellant is unable to comply with the directions, is not ready or wishes to obtain further directions, they should attend the first hearing.

If they cannot comply and do not attend the hearing to explain why, the hearing could be dealt with in their absence. Appeals can also be heard at the first hearing if the appellant is not intending to give any oral evidence or if the appeal is not going to be contested and a recommendation (▶see pages 646-647) only will be requested.

The main purpose of this procedure is to ensure that the appeal is ready to go ahead and that the appellant has arranged for legal representation. The adjudicator will also wish to ensure that a convenient date is set for the hearing, that an interpreter in the correct language will be available and that enough time is set aside to complete the hearing. If the hearing is not ready to proceed, it may be that the best course is to ask for another short hearing (sometimes called a 'for mention' hearing), in order to take stock of progress in the case.

Fast-track hearings

Appeals placed in the 'fast-track' do not have a first hearing but, instead, a full hearing is arranged immediately. According to the Practice Direction of the Chief Adjudicator of 11 September 2000, appeals placed in the fast-track are:

- asylum appeals where the claim has been 'certified' (i.e., issued with a certificate which, if upheld by the adjudicator, denies an appeal to the IAT);
- appeals where the appellant is in detention;
- appeals remitted for re-hearing after judicial review proceedings;
- asylum appeals where the appellant has dependent family members with them in the UK – this assists the government in reaching its time targets for handling asylum claims by families;
- family visit appeals which are to be heard orally. For an idea of waiting times for family visit appeals ▶see page 618;

- cases where a person is appealing against refusal of entry when they arrived with a valid entry clearance;
- appeals listed for hearing in Belfast.

Adjournments

Getting an adjournment of a hearing is always difficult. Adjudicators are under pressure not to adjourn and the 2002 Bill makes way for new rules to limit the power to adjourn to specified circumstances and also to set a date by which an adjourned hearing must be dealt with. The present Procedure Rules state that the IAA should not adjourn unless the appeal cannot be determined 'justly' without an adjournment (rule 31). They also state that, whenever a party applies for an adjournment it must show a good reason why it is necessary and provide any evidence in support of that reason. They should also offer a new date for the hearing. So, if, for example, the reason is because of a vital medical or other important appointment that cannot be changed, evidence should be produced. Similarly, if the appellant is waiting for vital evidence, evidence should be produced of the attempts to get it and of when it is likely to be available.

According to the Chief Adjudicator's Practice Direction issued on 27 July 2001, applications for adjournments should be made by 4.00pm one clear working day before the date of the hearing. This means that, for example, if a case is listed for hearing on Friday, the written application for an adjournment must be made by 4.00pm on Wednesday. The application and supporting documents should be copied to the Home Office presenting officer. It is a good idea to get the presenting officer to support the application. If they agree to support it, there is more chance that the application will be granted. If it is not possible to make the application within this time, it is almost certain that the appellant and their representative will have to attend to make the application to adjourn. Of course, if the application to adjourn is refused in writing before the hearing, there is no reason why the application cannot be made again orally, perhaps with more evidence, on the day of the hearing. It should never be assumed that an appeal will be adjourned. Up until an appeal is adjourned, appellants and their representatives must continue to prepare as though the hearing will proceed.

Preparing for hearing

Most appeals are won and lost at the preparation stage. The kind of evidence which is required for an appeal depends on the nature of the case and is the same as the evidence required for applications referred to throughout the *Handbook* for the various different categories of applicant. If the evidence was not produced for the application, it can still be produced at the hearing. For example, in a marriage case in which the 'intention to live together' requirement of the rules is disputed and in which the appellant has, since the refusal, produced a bundle of letters between themselves and their spouse, the letters can be used in the appeal. However, the 2002 Bill will allow for rules which may exclude this evidence in entry clearance cases. Where an asylum-seeker has not yet produced medical evidence to show, for example, that they have been tortured, they can obtain a report to put before the adjudicator. Some of the most respected medical reports are provided by the Medical Foundation for the Care of Victims of Torture ▶see page 735 for address.

The appellant's representative must have a thorough knowledge of the evidence put in both by themselves and the Home Office and be prepared to refer to it quickly. They should also be prepared to answer all the points raised in the letter of refusal or explanatory statement and be able to anticipate any additional points that may arise at the hearing and that they may be asked by the adjudicator.

Witnesses and witness statements

In most appeals, the evidence given by the appellant is of critical importance. Often it is the only direct evidence of the facts which are in dispute and the credibility of the appellant is therefore central. It is not so important, however, in cases where the only issue is a question which depends largely on documentary evidence. For example, the ability to maintain and accommodate without recourse to public funds can usually be dealt with by evidence such as bank statements, letters from employers or pay slips.

Although in most cases, much of the preparation of the appeal will involve preparing the statements of the appellant and any witnesses, the appellant's side should not think that they automatically have to call oral evidence. If, for example, the essential facts upon which the claim or application is based are accepted by the immigration authorities but the application has been refused for legal reasons, there may be no point in calling witnesses. In addition, occasionally, in asylum and human rights cases, the appellant is so traumatised that they are not able to give proper evidence to further explain their circumstances. In these cases, it is important to obtain medical evidence to demonstrate this.

The witness statement, particularly in the case of the appellant, will generally need to be more detailed than any interview notes which may have been produced by the Home Office, and will need to address points made about the appellant's credibility in the RFRL or the explanatory statement. Witness statements, if well prepared, are very helpful to appellants. They give them the opportunity of instantly presenting to the adjudicator a comprehensive account of what is often a complex set of events, which might otherwise be difficult for them to recount step by step.

Other witnesses in an asylum appeal may be family members, friends of the asylum-seeker who may be aware of what the appellant has experienced in the past, political party colleagues or experts on the country in question. In family cases, the sponsor or relative being joined or visited is usually called to give evidence.

Witnesses can be useful in corroborating the evidence of the appellant but care must be taken. For example, in asylum cases in particular, witnesses can be asked about matters spanning a great number of years and there is a good deal of scope for witnesses to contradict each other. Inconsistencies arise, not necessarily because witnesses are not telling the truth but because memories of certain events differ. Even so, adjudicators and presenting officers may take this as showing that the witness or the appellant or both, are not being truthful.

The appellant and their witnesses should be well prepared. Before the hearing, they should be fully familiar with their own witness statements and can also read each others' statements as well as the other important papers in the case. They should also have explained to them what the issues are in the case as this will help them to understand the purpose of the questions they are asked in the hearing and to give more effective evidence. Often appellants and witnesses are bewildered when they give evidence because they do not really understand why certain questions are being asked or where these questions are leading.

The appellant should meet with the person who is going to represent them before the hearing in order to discuss the case and to enable the representative to explain the procedure at the hearing. Some appellants like to actually visit a hearing centre before their own hearing and observe some hearings so that they know what to expect and will be less nervous on the day.

Country and expert evidence

An important part of the evidence in many asylum and human rights cases relates to the conditions in the appellant's country of origin. The Home Office has prepared country reports as background information for use in asylum appeals. Often, despite the directions, the Home Office do not actually produce their assessment until the day of the hearing. It is therefore important that the appellant or their representative is aware of the contents of the report beforehand. Country reports are available on the Home Office website ▶see pages 197-198 for more details about these reports.

The Home Office reports have been criticised as painting a rosy picture of the countries of feared persecution, of selectively quoting their primary sources so that the most critical passages are left out and of concentrating on the past history or political constitution of the country, to the exclusion of the most common issues arising in asylum appeals. It is, therefore, often important that information from independent sources is produced in these appeals as part of the appellant's bundle and the adjudicator's attention drawn to the most relevant passages. Sources of material to which appellants can turn are set out in the box below.

COUNTRY MATERIAL

It is often useful to refer to the country material at the time of the application so that it can be taken into account by the Home Office in their decision. The Legal Services Commission rules require firms with immigration contracts to keep country information for the main nationalities they represent. A lot of up-to-date information can now be downloaded from the internet.

The following sources can be investigated:

- **Amnesty International** has detailed information about most countries of the world and its researchers may be able to provide references or information to support what the asylum-seeker has said. It publishes a yearly review, with brief details about each country and many detailed briefings and bulletins which are invaluable.

- **The United States State Department country reports** are published on the internet annually. These are very detailed and great weight is attached to them by the Home Office and adjudicators. Much of the detail in the Home Office country assessments is taken from them. However, they may reflect US political bias towards some countries.

- **The Minority Rights Group** publishes in-depth studies of particular groups which are very helpful.

- **The Refugee Legal Centre** may have comprehensive up-to-date information about the Home Office's current practice with regard to particular countries and considerable information about those countries, but most of it is only available to other organisations or individuals if they subscribe through the RLC's information service.

- **Human Rights Watch** produces reports on the human rights situation in particular countries, mainly in Africa, Asia and the Middle East.

- **The Immigration Law Practitioners' Association** has published a directory which identifies academic and other experts on different countries who may be able to provide background and corroborative evidence. Expert evidence is particularly useful in cases where the particular circumstances described by the appellant are not covered in the other general country reports.

- **The United Nations High Commissioner for Refugees** may offer support in particular cases or give its views on the situation in particular countries. It produces a regularly updated CD-ROM of collated material relevant to asylum claims, called *Refworld*.

- **The Electronic Immigration Network** has set up a series of bulletin boards and a database of immigration and asylum decisions and other relevant information for subscribers.

- **ICCID (the Immigration Consortium Country Information Database)** has recently been launched and is a CD-based source of country information for subscribers.

Appellants may also use expert evidence in support of their cases. Usually the expert does not come to the hearing but will provide a written report. The expert should be provided with at least the appellant's statement and the reasons for refusal. Their reports must be prepared from an independent perspective: experts are not there to act as 'cheerleaders' for appellants but to give a truly professional assessment which helps the adjudicator come to their decision. Experts can often give an explanation of why, given a certain set of facts, a person is at risk in a particular country. Where credibility is challenged, experts can also sometimes help by painting the background to a person's claim which can then be used to explain why what they are saying is plausible in the light of the conditions in that country.

At the full hearing before the adjudicator

Appeals are supposed to be an informal process but, in practice, many of those attending will find them a formal and even intimidating experience. The adjudicator has control of the conduct of proceedings and usually sits on a slightly raised desk. The appellant's representative normally sits at one side of the room, and the Home Office presenting officer, representing the official who made the decision, sits at the other. The appellant or other person giving evidence will usually sit in the middle, directly opposite the adjudicator. If there is an interpreter, he or she will usually sit next to the witness. If there are any other witnesses to be called, the practice of most adjudicators is to require them to wait outside until it is their turn to give evidence. After they have given evidence, they can remain to watch the rest of the hearing.

Appeals are usually listed to start at 10am and the appellants and representatives for every case on the list should be at the hearing room ready to begin at that time. Although there will be an order in which the cases are listed, adjudicators will not always begin with the first case and finish with the last. It is up to the adjudicator which order to take the cases in. The adjudicator will normally first run through the list to check who has arrived, who is ready to start and deal with any initial problems or applications for adjournments.

Dealing with the presenting officer

It is always a good idea to speak to the Home Office presenting officer or other representative before the hearing in order to check that both sides have got all the evidence which has been put in by the other. Sometimes, it is possible to more closely define the issues in the appeal so that both sides know what they have got to deal with. In some cases, there is the possibility of negotiation – it may be that the presenting officer is prepared to concede certain issues, for example, that a certificate which is particularly weak should not stand.

Preliminary matters

At the outset of the hearing, it is a good idea to ensure that the adjudicator has all the material which has been filed. Documents sometimes go missing at the IAA and it is important that the adjudicator has an appreciation of all the important documents before the hearing starts. If there is any evidence which is being produced on the day, it should be handed to the adjudicator at the beginning of the hearing, not during or after it. If there are any preliminary issues, for example, as to whether the adjudicator has the power to hear the appeal, then that issue is dealt with first.

In certified cases, some adjudicators also like to consider the certificate at the outset. If the dispute about the certificate is part and parcel of the main issues in the appeal, for example, if it concerns only whether there is evidence of a likelihood of torture, this is often best dealt with after hearing all of the evidence in the appeal. However, where the issue is more neatly separated from the other issues, for example, whether a passport was produced on arrival, or there was reasonable excuse for not producing one, it *may* be easier to deal with the certificate at the start of the hearing.

Dealing with a failure to comply with directions

If, at the hearing, it is clear that either party has failed to comply with the directions at all or within the time limits for complying with them, the adjudicator can take a number of courses of action. In order of the most severe, they are:

- treat the appeal as abandoned (rule 32);
- allow or dismiss the appeal without considering the merits (rule 33(2)(a));
- determine the appeal without a hearing (rules 33(2)(b) and 43);
- exclude witness statements, documents and other evidence which has not been filed in accordance with the directions (rule 33(2)(c)).

If the adjudicator indicates that he or she is considering taking action, appellants or their representatives at the hearing should be ready to fully explain all failures and delays and address the extent to which the Home Office has been prejudiced (often the presenting officer will only have picked up the file very late in the day and there will be little or no prejudice). If a penalty is to be imposed, representatives should argue for the least severe option.

Evidence given by the appellant and witnesses

Both sides have the right to call witnesses, although it is almost always only the appellant's side which does so. The appellant and any other witnesses need to be confident about what they are saying and to have organised their thoughts in advance. In asylum appeals in particular, the 'credibility' of the appellant's account of past events is of central importance. When an interpreter is used, it is important that the witness and interpreter first confirm that they can understand one another. Sometimes appellants have their own interpreters sitting in the hearing room who are able to pass a note to the representative if they feel that critical matters are being mis-interpreted.

In most cases, a witness statement will have been prepared in advance and, under the standard directions (▶see above) the witness statement is supposed to 'stand' as evidence-in-chief: that is, as the evidence that the appellant's representative wishes to call from that witness. However, most adjudicators are sympathetic to allowing a representative to ask some supplementary questions of the appellant and other witnesses. It can be unnerving for an appellant to begin their evidence by being questioned by the Home Office representative. Provided that the witness statement is reasonably detailed and full, representatives will usually focus on anything which needs to be clarified from the witness statement and any changes of circumstance which have occurred since the witness statement was made which might include commenting on documents produced by either side since the statement.

Cross-examination of the appellant is the next stage of the hearing. The purpose is to test the truth of what the appellant is saying but it often takes the form of questioning about matters which are not directly concerned with the important issues in the appeal. Asylum appellants are often questioned about their route to the UK and the circumstances in which they claimed asylum, rather than the central question of what they fear and why. Cross-examination of the appellant, in particular, is likely to be the most time-consuming part of the appeal.

Although adjudicators tend to give presenting officers some leeway and to allow them to ask about matters relating to credibility even if not directly raised in the refusal letter, cross-examination is not intended to give the Home Office an opportunity to conduct a 'fishing expedition' into the appellant's background, covering all sorts of matters not raised in the appeal so far in the hope that something negative to the appellant's case will be revealed. Nor is cross-examination an opportunity for the Home Office to ask the appellant to re-count all of their evidence again, like an interview, in the hope that they make some mistake so that there will be an inconsistency which is relevant to credibility. If the presenting officer begins to ask questions of this nature, then it is open to appellants' representatives to object. They can also object to questions which are too vague or complex so that the witness (especially through an interpreter) will not be able to understand them or questions which the witness cannot be expected to know the answer to. For example, witnesses are often asked to explain why the authorities in their country of origin have behaved in a particular way or to explain the motivations of other people which, depending on the context, they cannot know.

The adjudicator can intervene to ask questions at any time. Usually, the adjudicator will ask some questions to clear up various matters of particular concern to them after the presenting officer has finished asking questions. The adjudicator is not supposed to 'enter the ring' and cross-examine the witness.

Following the presenting officer's and the adjudicator's questions, the appellant's representative is invited to ask any further questions in 're-examination' of the witness. The purpose of this is to clarify matters arising out of the questions which have been asked in cross-examination or by the adjudicator. It is not an opportunity to raise new matters but a chance for the appellant's representative to repair any damage which has been caused by cross-examination if they think that the witness could have performed better on some of the matters they have been asked about.

Normally the appellant gives their evidence first which is then followed by their other witnesses, although there are no hard and fast rules. The appellant and their representative can choose the order.

Submissions

After all the witnesses have given their evidence, first the presenting officer and then the appellant's representative have the chance to make oral submissions to the adjudicator. The 'submissions' are a speech to the adjudicator summing up the appellant's and the respondent's case and trying to persuade the adjudicator to allow or dismiss the appeal.

It is always useful for representatives to have planned at least the basic structure of their submissions beforehand. In cases where the appellant's submissions have been set out fully in the skeleton argument and no real new issues have arisen, the oral submissions will be shortened. The structure of submissions for any case depends on the style which the representative has developed and the particular issues in the case. Representatives must be prepared to accommodate any new issues which have arisen in the appeal and to deal with the way the oral evidence has come out. If the evidence has been somewhat different to what was expected, the representative must be prepared to think quickly and to modify their submissions to meet the circumstances.

The following is a suggested list of the matters which should be covered:

- set out what the appeal/s or grounds for appealing are and identify the essential immigration rules or legislation with which the appeal is concerned;
- deal with the certificate if the case is certified;
- identify the other basic issues between the parties in the appeal;
- set out and make submissions on any legal issues in the appeal, including submissions about the Home Office's approach to the law;
- set out the essential facts that the adjudicator is being asked by the appellant to find;
- remind the adjudicator of the evidence which supports the facts, namely,
  - the appellant's evidence,
  - the particular evidence that supports the appellant, for example, from other witnesses or from specific documents;

- set out and deal with any matters relied on by the Home Office for doubting the appellant's credibility both raised in the refusal letter and any further matters raised on the day;
- for asylum and human rights cases, if the basic facts are accepted, explain what the risk is to the person if they are returned to their country of origin;
- present any background country material in support of the case and identify the parts which are most essential for the adjudicator to consider (these may well have already been drawn attention to in the schedule prepared following the standard adjudicator's directions ▶see page 630);
- ask for the appeal to be allowed with any appropriate directions ▶see page 646.

During submissions the adjudicator may ask questions on certain aspects of the evidence, or may indicate his or her thinking on certain particular issues and ask to be addressed on certain matters. After submissions, the adjudicator will end the hearing and will normally 'reserve the determination' which means that an immediate decision is not made and that the determination in writing will be sent out to the parties by post in a few weeks. Occasionally, adjudicators indicate their decision on the appeal on the day and state that the full reasons for the decision will be set out in the written determination which is to follow.

Appeals where one party does not attend the hearing

If either party has had proper notice of the hearing but fails to attend, the adjudicator can either:

- proceed to deal with the appeal in the absence of that party and to determine it on the existing evidence (rule 41); or
- treat the appeal as having been abandoned in which case the adjudicator will simply send out a notice to the parties stating why it is being treated as abandoned and no determination is issued (rule 32).

The usual course is the first one, namely, for the adjudicator to consider the appeal in the absence of the party and then to decide whether to allow or dismiss the appeal. The adjudicator can, of course, adjourn the appeal without any specific application having been made, but this is rare.

In some cases, the Home Office fails to send a representative to the hearing and, rather than asking for an adjournment, is happy for the appeal to go ahead in its absence. In *MNM*, the IAT agreed guidelines as to the approach which adjudicators should take in these cases. The most important points are:

- the adjudicator is not to treat the decision as withdrawn or to automatically allow the appeal just because the Home Office does not attend;
- the adjudicator should take care to read all the evidence in the papers before the hearing, even if this means adjourning for a short time;

- where the appellant's credibility is raised in the refusal letter, the adjudicator should ask the appellant's representative to deal with those questions in the evidence called from the appellant or in submissions;
- where there are matters which are of concern to the adjudicator relating to credibility or other issues which have not been raised by the Home Office in the refusal letter, the adjudicator should ask the representative to deal with those matters in the evidence called or in submissions;
- the adjudicator should not take over the role of the Home Office in the appeal by acting as the appellant's opponent or by conducting a detailed investigation into the appellant's circumstances beyond the evidence which has been put before them;
- where the adjudicator wishes to refer to country material which is in the public domain, such as US State Department reports, Amnesty International reports or the Home Office country reports, the adjudicator should state this to the representative and ask for their comments;
- an adjudicator should only adjourn an appeal in these cases in exceptional circumstances, where he or she feels that the issues cannot properly be dealt with in the absence of the Home Office.

An adjudicator can also consider an appeal in the absence of one of the parties where that party is not in the UK, is suffering from a communicable disease or mental disorder, cannot attend the appeal as a result of illness or accident, cannot be found so that notice can be given to them of the hearing or if the party has told the IAA that they do not want to attend the hearing. In any of these cases, if the adjudicator dismisses the appeal, there is still a right to make an application for leave to appeal to the IAT.

Powers of adjudicators in deciding appeals

When an appeal must be allowed

When an appeal comes before an adjudicator, they must decide whether to allow or dismiss it. They must allow the appeal if the decision appealed against is wrong for any of the three reasons set out below.

If none of the grounds are made out, the appeal will be dismissed. The 2002 Bill proposes to describe the grounds on which an appeal can be brought in more detail but in a way which continues to reflect the basic grounds below. If the appeal is allowed, the adjudicator will consider whether any directions or recommendations should be given (▶see below).

1 **Not in accordance with the immigration rules.** If the immigration authorities have decided that an appellant does not satisfy the rules when, in fact, they are satisfied, then the appeal is to be allowed. The immigration authorities may have misunderstood the relevant rules or the relevant facts of the case.

2 **Not in accordance with the law.** The higher courts have accepted that the 'law' for these purposes is wider than just the immigration rules and legislation. The highest authority for this is *Bakhtaur Singh* where the House of Lords accepted that, in a case decided under the deportation immigration rules, the Home Office and the IAA were bound to have regard to the effect on the community of a person's deportation where it was alleged that there would be a significant impact. They held that this followed not just from the immigration rules but also from the general principles of public law which require all relevant matters to be taken into account.

In a case involving the Somali family reunion policy, the Home Office accepted, and the Court of Appeal proceeded on the basis that, 'not in accordance with the law' included all 'established principles of common or administrative law' (*DS Abdi*). The most important use of this power is in relation to cases outside the immigration rules where there is an established policy which has not been properly applied, or the decision is procedurally unfair or in breach of a person's reasonable expectations of how the immigration authorities will act, or if relevant matters have not been taken into account. An important application of these principles by the IAT was in their ruling in another case involving family reunion outside the immigration rules, *Onen*.

3 **Discretion should have been exercised differently.** The adjudicator can only 're-exercise' the discretion of the immigration authorities if it is a discretion exercised *within* the immigration rules. For example, the immigration rules normally state that leave 'may' be granted if a set of conditions are satisfied. The word 'may' involves a discretion which could be exercised against the appellant if any of the general grounds of refusal apply. Application of the general grounds themselves usually involves an exercise of discretion because they also state that, where certain conditions are satisfied, leave will 'normally' be refused. Further, the rules about curtailing leave state that it 'may' be curtailed if the conditions are satisfied. All of these exercises of discretion can be reconsidered by the adjudicator. However, the immigration authorities also have a general discretion to waive the rules and to grant leave outside them. The exercise of that discretion cannot be re-exercised by the adjudicator.

Restrictions on grounds on which an appeal can be allowed

It must be noted that, although the above grounds are contained in the adjudicator's (and the IAT's) general powers in considering appeals, some of the individual rights of appeal are themselves restricted by the specific legislation which gives that right of appeal.

For example, asylum appeals are restricted to considering whether removal of the appellant would involve a breach of the Refugee Convention; human rights appeals are restricted to a consideration of the rights incorporated by the ECHR and non-asylum appeals against removal of illegal entrants or overstayers can only be brought on the grounds that the person is not, in fact, an illegal entrant or an overstayer ▶see Box 1 page 603.

However, where a person is given a one-stop notice and is allowed to raise any additional grounds, it appears that the adjudicator is able to consider any additional grounds raised under their general powers, even if the appeal would otherwise be restricted. This would fit with the whole purpose of the 'one-stop' appeal system. The legislation is not entirely clear as to what grounds can and cannot be considered in these circumstances, but where there remains uncertainty, representatives should not feel constrained from pressing ahead with all their grounds at appeal.

Power of adjudicators to consider the facts of the case

Adjudicators are not generally restricted to considering whether the Home Office has made some technical legal mistake (lawyers often call this 'errors of law' or 'misdirections of law'), but rather they can consider all of the facts of the case again and assess whether a different decision should be arrived at.

In non-asylum appeals and in human rights cases not involving Article 3 ECHR, the adjudicator is only concerned with the situation at the date of the decision of the immigration authorities. This is not as restrictive as it sounds for two reasons:

- the adjudicator can take into account evidence or facts which were not known to the person who made the decision;
- the adjudicator can also take into account evidence arising after the decision which sheds light on the situation at the time of the decision. For example, continued devotion between a couple in a lengthy period between the decision and date of hearing helps to show their intention to live together permanently at the time of the decision.

In asylum cases or cases raising Article 3 ECHR, the adjudicator must also take into account evidence about any *changes* of circumstance which have taken place between the decision and the hearing so that they are considering the situation as at the time of the hearing. This was decided by the Court of Appeal in *Ravichandran* but has also since become part of the legislation (see s77, 1999 Act). This makes sense as the adjudicator considers whether, if a person were to be returned in present circumstances, they would face a risk of persecution or torture. The 2002 Bill proposes that non-asylum/Article 3 appeals should be treated in the same way. This will be a welcome change. The present position, and in particular the singling out of Article 3 from among the other rights contained in the ECHR, leads to the kind of situation where an adjudicator will have to pretend that an appellant has not (for instance) got married in between the decision and the appeal on an asylum claim, and therefore that there are no potential breaches of family life under Article 8 to be considered at the hearing. Again, the only option here would be for the appellant to re-apply for permission to stay on the basis of Article 8 if the asylum appeal was dismissed, or to ask the adjudicator for a discretionary 'recommendation' (▶see below).

However, the 2002 Bill also contains a very negative proposal to treat entry clearance appeals more restrictively than at present. It is proposed that, in those cases, the adjudicator should be restricted to considering only the evidence which was available to the ECO.

Burden and standard of proof: immigration cases

The standard of proof which the adjudicator must apply in non-asylum cases is the balance of probabilities. Generally, the burden is on appellants to make their case and to establish the truth of what they say (rule 31). There are, however, instances where the onus rests with the immigration authorities, for instance, where the Home Office is alleging that documentary evidence is forged.

Burden and standard of proof: asylum cases

In asylum appeals, the burden of proof is still on the appellant, but the standard of proof is a lower one. Appellants must show that there is 'a reasonable degree of likelihood' or 'real risk' of harm. This reflects the wording of the Refugee Convention, which defines a refugee as a person with 'a well-founded fear of being persecuted'. This definition is intended to allow for the possibility that people will qualify for refugee status even when their fate is far from certain. This was decided by the House of Lords in the case of *Sivakumaran*, which concerned six Sri Lankan Tamils who had been refused asylum and returned to Sri Lanka.

The application of the standard of proof to the assessment of past facts (for example, what is asserted to have happened to an appellant previously) was developed in the case of *Kaja*, where the IAT, despite the dissent of one of its members, stressed that the lower standard applies to *all* aspects of the decision-making process. The IAT stated that it was important for the adjudicator in any determination to make clear:

- that the assessment of whether a claim to asylum is well-founded is based on the evidence as a whole (relevant to the past, present and future) and is according to the criterion of 'reasonable degree of likelihood';
- the evidential foundation for the decision; and
- how the adjudicator has moved from the evidential foundation to the conclusion.

The essential approach in *Kaja* was approved and developed by the Court of Appeal in *Karanakaran*, putting to rest the attempts of some presenting officers and adjudicators to argue that a higher standard (balance of probabilities) applied to the assessment of historical facts in asylum cases.

Burden and standard of proof: human rights cases

The IAT held in the case of *Kacaj* that the standard of proof in appeals under Article 3 of the ECHR is the same as that in asylum appeals, in spite of efforts by the Home Office to argue that the standard of proof in such cases was a very high one. The IAT concluded, understandably, that it would be strange, given the similarity of the issues arising in asylum and Article 3 cases, if the same facts had to be decided to a different standard of proof. The burden of proof in human rights cases is also normally on the appellant. However, where the appellant shows that there would be an interference with a restricted right, such as Article 8 ECHR, the burden is on the Home Office to show that the extent of the interference is justified.

Directions where appeal is allowed

When an appeal is allowed, it is the job of the adjudicator to give directions which they think are required to 'give effect' to the determination. The adjudicator may also make 'recommendations with respect to any other action' which they think it is appropriate for the immigration authorities to take. These recommendations, which are covered by the legislation, must be distinguished from the recommendations which may be given when appeals are dismissed (▶see below). Commonly, directions will be given that the immigration authorities grant leave or grant an entry clearance.

However, it may be that, even if a decision is wrong so that the appeal has to be allowed, there is still some matter which remains for the immigration authorities to consider. This may be the case if the immigration authorities have simply not considered the application under the correct immigration rules, or if they have not properly considered an applicable policy outside the immigration rules but where the policy itself contains a discretion whether to admit someone if certain conditions are satisfied. In those cases, the direction may simply be that the immigration authorities reconsider the matter in a particular way according to the law.

The 2002 Bill proposes to modify the power to give directions so that they only need to be given where the adjudicator thinks they are appropriate. Because the present requirement is to only give those directions which give effect to the substance of the determination, it is unclear why there needs to be any change to the legislation.

Recommendations where appeal is dismissed

If an appeal seems to have limited prospects of success yet there are strong compassionate circumstances which suggest that the Home Office should allow the appellant to stay in the UK outside the immigration rules, an adjudicator might be persuaded to make a 'recommendation' to the Home Office. It may be that the circumstances amount to human rights grounds for remaining in the UK which the adjudicator can consider as part of the appeal.

The other situation in which recommendations have traditionally been considered in non-asylum cases is where the immigration rules were not satisfied as of the date of the decision of the immigration authorities but have subsequently become satisfied. For example, where a person could not necessarily have been maintained without recourse to public funds as of the date of the decision but could if they were admitted at the time of the hearing. A recommendation might also be appropriate in cases where an unmarried partner has been living together with their partner for two years by the date of the hearing but not by the date of the decision. Recommendations in these circumstances may become more important if the government is successful in its proposal in the 2002 Bill that, in entry clearance cases, only evidence which was made available to the ECO can be taken into account.

Recommendations grew out of the restriction of rights of appeal in deportation cases imposed by the Immigration Act 1988. That Act restricted many deportation appeals to the question of whether there was a 'power in law' to deport people and so adjudicators were prevented from considering all of the other factors in the rules as to whether it was right to deport the appellant. These appeals may still arise where a person is refused under the 'regularisation of overstayers' scheme and that person last entered the UK less than seven years before the date of the notice of intention to deport.

At the time of the 1988 Act, the Home Office policy on when to follow recommendations was generous. It stated that the Home Office would 'invariably' follow recommendations made by adjudicators. Since then, the Home Office has, step by step, watered down its policy so that recommendations are now acted on (API, Ch13, s3):

'...only where the determination and/or recommendation discloses clear exceptional compassionate circumstances which have not previously been considered and which would warrant the exercise of the Secretary of State's discretion outside the immigration rules'.

This does not, of course, cover all of the circumstances mentioned above but there is no reason why representatives should not ask for a recommendation where they think it is appropriate. The ability to make recommendations in dismissed appeals is not part of the adjudicator's official functions and is not covered in the legislation. They are, therefore, entirely discretionary, do not form part of the 'determination' of the appeal itself and a failure to give one cannot usually be appealed (see *Chavrimootoo*, High Court).

Appeals and other challenges after the adjudicator has determined the appeal

The determination of the adjudicator will be sent by the IAA to the appellant's representative (if they have one) or to the appellant. A typical determination will set out what the nature of the appeal was, what happened at the hearing, including who the representatives were and who attended to give evidence, a summary of the evidence and documents before the adjudicator, what conclusions the adjudicator has reached on the main questions of fact and the reasons for those conclusions, and a summary of what legal principles apply. The determination will conclude by stating whether the appeal is allowed or dismissed and what directions or recommendations (if any) are given.

If the determination of the adjudicator is that the appeal is allowed, then the immigration authorities have the right of appeal to the IAT. If they do not appeal, they will usually be required to give the appellant leave to enter or remain in the UK, or grant the entry certificate or entry clearance which was in dispute. There have been very great delays by the Home Office in actually implementing favourable determinations by adjudicators, which often lead to appellants having no immigration status in the meantime and therefore being unable to access benefits and other welfare services for months ▶see page 219 for details of how to deal with this problem.

If a certified appeal is dismissed and the certificate is upheld by the adjudicator so that the there is no right of appeal to the IAT, the means of challenging the decision on the appeal and/or the decision on the certificate is judicial review. The immigration authorities retain the right of appeal to the IAT in any certified case. New procedures were introduced on 7 January 2002 for giving the appellant and their representatives notice of these determinations ▶see below. If there is a 'procedural' or 'administrative' error in these determinations, the Chief Adjudicator may be asked to review the determination and to direct a re-hearing.

If a non-certified appeal is dismissed, or if a certified appeal is dismissed but the adjudicator does not uphold the certificate, the appellant has the right to apply for leave to appeal to the IAT. This is done by a paper application on the form which will be sent out with the determination. The form states which documents must be returned with the form. There is space on the form for stating what the grounds of appeal against the determination are, but usually representatives like to set out the grounds on separate pages which can then be attached to the form. For details about preparing grounds of appeal ▶see pages 651-653. If new evidence is being submitted, it should be sent as early as possible and ideally with the application for leave to appeal.

Once the application for leave to appeal has been sent in, the appeal is treated as continuing so that the immigration authorities cannot take any action to enforce the departure of the appellant. The appeal should be given within the time limits which apply ▶see box pages 613-614. There is provision for extending time if the circumstances justify it. If a person does not appeal against the decision, then it is usually extremely difficult to obtain further appeal rights covering the same matters. However, if in an asylum case there are later genuinely new circumstances which arise, it may be that the person can make a 'fresh' claim to asylum ▶see pages 220-221. The question of bringing further human rights appeals has become very complex ▶see pages 220-221.

If leave to appeal is not granted, the appellant will not be able to appeal to the IAT. The appellant will receive a short (usually two-page) decision refusing to grant leave which can only be challenged by judicial review. The 2002 Bill may prevent judicial review of these decisions of the IAT ▶see pages 622-625. If the refusal to grant leave to appeal results from an administrative or procedural error, the IAT can be asked to set aside the refusal of leave itself and reconsider the decision.

A grant of leave to appeal by the IAT is, in effect, acceptance that there is at least an arguable case that the adjudicator's decision was defective in some way. If leave to appeal is granted, a short determination saying so, followed by a notice of hearing before the IAT, will be sent to all parties. The IAT may give a summary of its reasons for granting leave, although this is not required to be as detailed as when leave is refused, and will often simply state that the grounds of appeal merit consideration. Sometimes the IAT limits the grounds on which a person can appeal (see rule 18(9)).

Home Office personal service of certain determinations

On 7 January 2002, the government introduced a system under which:

- determinations of appeals by adjudicators dismissing appeals and against which there was no further right of appeal (because the adjudicator had agreed with the Home Office certificate); *and*
- refusals of the IAT to grant leave to appeal;

would be passed by the IAA to the Home Office for them to pass on to the appellant either personally or by post: see the Immigration and Asylum Appeals (Procedure) (Amendment) Rules 2001. The Home Office justification for this is that:

'Previously, the appellant has been notified at the same time as the Home Office allowing a high level of absconding on receipt of the determination'.

This rule is probably unique in giving one party the right to be told the outcome of an independent court decision before their opponent and to decide for themselves when and how to let the other party know the result. It is an affront to the principle of equality before the law. The practical concern has been that the Home Office will be able to require the personal attendance of the appellant in order to receive the determination, which provides an opportunity to detain and remove them, while representatives do not receive the determination until some time later through the post, when it may be too late to give considered advice and to decide whether there should be a judicial review challenge to the determination. The Home Office response to these criticisms has been that appellants will always be able to make contact with their representatives. The Refugee Legal Centre and ILPA requested that the IAA continue to send representatives the determination at the same time as they send them to the Home Office. However, both the Chief Adjudicator and the President of the IAT (letters of 21 and 24 January 2002) have stated that they cannot do this as they are bound by the new rules only to send the determinations to the Home Office.

In response to the concerns raised, Rosie Winterton, minister in the Lord Chancellor's Department, stated to the House of Lords on 30 January 2002:

'The Home Office has undertaken to serve decisions within a maximum of six weeks. That is a firm undertaking. The target is to issue the majority of postal decisions within two working days...There is an undertaking to deliver decisions in person within six weeks. If they are not delivered within that time, they will be sent by post and delivered within two weeks wherever possible...

'...in all cases under the rules the appellant's legal representative will be sent a copy of the appeal determination. Again, that will be prompt. In cases of personal delivery, the decision will be faxed to the legal representative within 24 hours of delivery of the decision to the appellant. When delivery is by post, the legal representative's copy will be sent out at the same time as the appellant's.'

The numbers of appellants affected should not be underestimated. In a written parliamentary answer given on 23 January 2002, the minister revealed that 494 determinations of adjudicators had been passed to the Home Office for service by the IAA in the first two weeks of the operation of the new rule. The Home Office proposes to review this system and to consider expanding it to include all appeal determinations.

Judicial review

There are two circumstances identified above in which judicial review rather than appealing is the way to challenge a decision: dismissed certified appeals where the certificate is upheld by the adjudicator, and refusals of leave to appeal to the IAT. Judicial review is a complex procedure under which the 'Administrative Court', which is part of the High Court, can intervene in a decision made by any public body including an appeal body like the IAA. The court will only intervene on very narrow grounds concerning the legality of the decision and the orders it can make are usually limited to requiring that the decision be taken again on a correct legal basis, which means that the same ultimate decision may be arrived at again.

For a summary of the basic procedures for judicial review ▶see pages 142-144. Appellants should always obtain legal advice about claims for judicial review. Usually it is necessary to involve both a solicitor and a barrister. Barristers are contacted through a solicitor. Legal funding is available if the applicant can pass strict merits and means tests. The government is considering including measures in the 2002 legislation to prevent judicial review of the decisions of the IAA.

The Immigration Appeal Tribunal

The IAT has broadly the same powers as adjudicators when it is deciding appeals. The IAT can make any decision which could have been made by the adjudicator and give any directions or recommendations which the adjudicator could have made. However, because the IAT is hearing an appeal from a decision already made by an adjudicator, there are inevitably some differences in how it operates. The IAT's first concern is to determine whether it ought to interfere with the conclusions that the adjudicator has reached. No appeal can be brought to the IAT unless the IAT first grants leave to appeal, and in persuading the IAT to do this in the application for leave to appeal, it is necessary to show where the adjudicator may have gone wrong.

Preparing grounds of appeal to the IAT

The Procedure Rules state that an application for leave to appeal to the IAT will only be granted where (see rule 18(7)):

- the IAT believes that the appeal would have a 'real prospect of success'; or
- there is some other compelling reason why the appeal should be heard.

The IAT is not restricted, therefore, to granting leave to appeal where there is a legal error by the adjudicator but it is usually necessary to show that there is some arguable legal error. This is because leave will be granted if there is a real prospect of success and the IAT will not normally allow an appeal on the basis of a disagreement with findings made by the adjudicator, that is, simply because another person or adjudicator could have come to a different view of the case. The 2002 Bill proposes to restrict appeals to the IAT to points of law only. Cases in which there is a compelling reason why the appeal should be heard are not defined but could include:

- asylum or Article 3 cases in which there has been a change of circumstances since the hearing;
- cases in which further evidence has come to light which was not before the adjudicator but which could have a major impact on the case – wherever this is the case, appellants should fully explain why the evidence was not produced earlier, otherwise the IAT may refuse to consider it (see rule 18(11)); or

GROUNDS OF APPEAL TO THE IAT: IDENTIFYING LEGAL ERRORS

Common questions for the person preparing the grounds of appeal to ask themselves when considering whether there are any legal errors in the determination of the adjudicator include the following:

- Has the adjudicator considered and dealt with all the relevant appeals and grounds of appeal that were brought?

- Has the adjudicator applied the correct burden and standard of proof? ▶see pages 645-646.

- Has the adjudicator identified the correct date for making findings of fact? (*Ravichandran, Kotecha*) ▶see pages 644-645.

- Has the adjudicator made an error in understanding or failing to apply the law set out in the immigration rules, the legislation, the Refugee Convention or ECHR, a policy or in the case-law interpreting them?

- If the adjudicator has found against the appellant on grounds of credibility, was the determination prepared in a reasonable time after hearing the evidence? The rule of thumb has been that if the determination is prepared over three months after the hearing, the evidence will have gone stale in the adjudicator's mind and the findings may be unsafe (*Subaskaran*).

- Did the adjudicator refuse a request for an adjournment or otherwise conduct the proceedings unfairly? If an adjournment request was refused, were adequate reasons given for the refusal? (*Sesay, Cabrera*).

- Does the determination make proper findings of fact and give sufficient reasons for the decision? In the case of *Amin*, Schiemann J stated, in relation to a non-asylum appeal, that an adjudicator must state with clarity what evidence is accepted, what evidence is rejected and what evidence, if any, an adjudicator cannot make their mind up about. In an asylum or human rights case, the findings and reasons must be particularly well set out and, if there is evidence which the adjudicator is uncertain about, the adjudicator must bear in mind the low standard of proof and the positive role which, the courts have decided, must be given to any uncertainty.

- Were there any facts which the Home Office did not contest or challenge or were not contested or challenged by cross-examination, which the adjudicator has found against the appellant?

- Were there any matters on which the adjudicator drew negative inferences as to an appellant or their witnesses' credibility but which were not in the Home Office's grounds of refusal or put to the appellant or their representative in order for them to deal with? The decision will be unfair if the adjudicator gives reasons for dismissing an appeal which the appellant has had no chance of answering (*Bahar, Gaima, Mayisokele*).

- Has the adjudicator taken into account all relevant evidence which was put before them? The determination may be flawed if, for instance, the adjudicator has failed to have regard to:
  - evidence of witnesses;
  - background evidence of country conditions (*Horvath, Danleu*);
  - statements in support of the case even if the witnesses were not called;

- expert reports;
- medical evidence. Careful and specific consideration should be given to medical reports (*Swaleh Mohammed*);
- warrants or documentary evidence of charges or membership of a party.
- Has the adjudicator rejected an appellant's credibility:
  - because it has not been supported by other sources? (*Kasolo*)
  - because the account given is implausible in the view of the adjudicator but that implausibility, in reality, reflects assumptions made by the adjudicator based on their own perspective, rather than on what may be the case in the very different conditions of the appellant's country of origin? (*Mendes, Adebizi*)
  - solely because the appellant has not given live evidence? (*Coskuner*)
- Has the adjudicator rejected a witness' credibility solely because they are related to the appellant or has some other interest in the appeal? (*Ahmed* (*Kalem*))
- Has the adjudicator misunderstood the basis of the claim, the appeal or important evidence in the case?
- Has the adjudicator inaccurately recorded evidence given at the appeal leading to incorrect findings?
- In an asylum case, where the adjudicator has accepted part, although not all, of an appellant's account, has the adjudicator properly considered whether they are at risk in their country of origin on the basis of the facts accepted by the adjudicator?
- In a case where the Home Office presenting officer did not attend the hearing, has the adjudicator followed the guidelines set down for such cases in *MNM*? (▶see above pages 641-642).

Note: the above is not an exhaustive list of errors which the adjudicator may have made.

- cases where the appellant or their representative, for no fault of their own, did not attend the appeal hearing and the appeal was dismissed in their absence.

When preparing the grounds of appeal to the IAT, it is often best to begin by explaining, as briefly as possible, what the appeal is about and the essential reasons why the adjudicator dismissed the appeal. Determinations of adjudicators can be very long but most are now set out in numbered paragraphs. This has become a general judicial trend to make it easier to refer to particular parts of the determination. Therefore, where appropriate, the grounds should cross-refer to the paragraphs in the determination so as to make it easier for the IAT to identify the points which are being made.

It is then necessary to identify any legal errors made by the adjudicator. The person preparing the grounds should read the determination through very thoroughly and know exactly what documentation was before the adjudicator when the appeal was dealt with. A checklist of legal errors is set out in the box above.

Before the IAT hearing

Details of the procedure before the IAT is set out in some detail in a practice direction issued by the President of the IAT on 4 October 2000, just after the 2000 Procedure Rules came into force. The essential points made in the direction and in the Procedure Rules are as follows.

Further evidence. Further evidence which was not before the adjudicator and which is submitted with the application for leave to appeal must be accompanied by the reasons why it was not put before the adjudicator. New evidence which is not being submitted with the application for leave to appeal but after the IAT has granted leave, should be sent to the IAT and the Home Office as soon as possible (rule 22(5)(6)).

Time in which application for leave will be decided. The IAT used to be required to decide applications for leave to appeal within 10 working days and, although that requirement is no longer in the rules, it will still attempt to meet that time-scale.

Amending grounds of appeal. If an appellant wishes to change the grounds of appeal after leave is given, this should be done in writing at least 21 days before the hearing. The other party to the appeal can object to the grounds being changed.

Before the hearing. The IAT will normally send the appellant a form asking for a time estimate for the appeal and asking whether they wish to call any witnesses. The form states that the IAT will only automatically have before them the Home Office refusal letter or explanatory statement, the adjudicator's determination, the notice of appeal to the IAT and the decision of the IAT to grant leave to appeal. Any additional material which the appellant wishes the IAT to have for the hearing needs to be placed into a bundle and filed with the IAT and the other party at least 14 days before the IAT hearing. Three copies of the material need to be filed as the panel which hears the case will have up to three people on it. The party which is not appealing must, at least seven days before the hearing, file any material which they want the IAT to have which is not in the bundle prepared by the appellant.

Using case law. Where a party wants to rely on a decided case which is not reported in the Immigration Appeal Reports (the 'green books') or the Immigration and Nationality Law Reports (the 'blue books'), copies of the full decision must be provided to the IAT and to the other party.

Adjournments. Requests for adjournments should be notified to the IAT at least 48 hours before the hearing. Of course, if the reasons for the adjournment arise later than the 48-hour deadline, applications can still be made and must be considered under the Procedure Rules ▶see page 633.

At the IAT hearing

At the hearing before the IAT, the appellant is unlikely to be asked to give further evidence in person. The hearing will be before two or more members of the IAT, at least one of whom, the chairman, will be legally qualified; the others may be 'lay members'. Where a case raises particularly important legal or procedural issues, two or three members may be legally qualified, and the decision may be 'starred'. Starred decisions are intended to give authoritative guidance to adjudicators and to avoid the problems from which the IAT has often suffered in the past, namely that different chairmen would come up with different interpretations of the law or of the situation in a particular country. Adjudicators are expected to abide by decisions of the IAT, whether starred or not.

Hearings before the IAT are usually shorter than before the adjudicator and focus firstly upon the alleged failings of the adjudicator's determination. If the IAT is satisfied that the adjudicator has made an error, it may proceed to either consider the appeal itself, in which case representatives need to be prepared to make submissions on all aspects of the case, or it may send the appeal back to the adjudicator to be determined again by the same or a different adjudicator (known as 'remittal'). The IAT rarely hears further oral evidence although it has the power to do so.

The 2002 Bill proposes to the give the IAT a new power to remit an appeal to an adjudicator for the purpose of hearing further evidence yet with a view to the IAT still deciding the appeal after the further evidence has been taken.

Representatives should make a decision before the hearing about what they are trying to achieve in the appeal: are there enough favourable findings of fact made by the adjudicator to enable the IAT to allow the appeal outright, or is it necessary to have further findings made by another adjudicator? If it is the Home Office that is appealing, representatives, as well as defending the determination of the adjudicator, should consider what reasons there are to avoid remittal to a different adjudicator if the factual findings in their favour are strong.

After the determination of the IAT

Following the determination of the IAT, either side has a right of appeal to the Court of Appeal (in England) or Court of Session (in Scotland). Before a party can appeal, they need to obtain leave to appeal. Applications for leave to appeal are made initially to the IAT on paper by filling out the form which will be sent with the determination and stating the grounds for appealing. Leave to appeal will only be given if the determination of the IAT involves an arguable error of law important to the basis of the decision.

Where the IAT considers that there are grounds for a further appeal, instead of giving leave to appeal, it can alternatively set aside the original determination and direct that the appeal is re-heard by the IAT (see rule 27(5)). If the IAT refuses leave to appeal, the application can be made again to the Court of Appeal or Court of Session. Appellants must seek advice about procedures for doing this.

Section 11 Welfare

Chapter 31
Welfare benefits, housing, health and social services 659
'Subject to immigration control' test 660
Welfare benefits 664
Housing 674
Social services 678
Children Act 1989 685
Health care 687

Chapter 32
Asylum support 689
Who is entitled to asylum support? 690
Which asylum-seekers get NASS support and which asylum-seekers get interim support? 695
NASS asylum support 696
Interim asylum support 708
Asylum support appeals 712
'Hard cases' support 717
Proposed changes 718

31 Welfare benefits, housing, health and social services

This chapter looks at the effect of immigration status upon access to various different forms of welfare and support. Access to welfare entitlements has been progressively eroded from the mid-1990s. The Immigration and Asylum Act 1999 introduced a new definition of 'subject to immigration control' for the purposes of defining who is excluded from certain entitlements. The 1999 Act also introduced a new 'asylum support' scheme intended to provide for the needs of destitute asylum-seekers. Asylum support provided both by the National Asylum Support Service (NASS) and local authorities, together with asylum support appeals, is dealt with in Chapter 32.

In this chapter, we look first at the welfare definition of 'subject to immigration control' contained in the 1999 Act. We then look separately at access to welfare benefits, local authority housing, support from a local authority social services department, support under the Children Act and, finally, at access to health care. The Children Act still forms the basis for the support of unaccompanied minor asylum-seekers. The box on pages 719-721 summarises the proposals for change to the asylum support and welfare system under the 2002 Bill, including the introduction of induction and accommodation centres.

Education

Access to grants and loans for both fees and support in order to study at colleges and universities is dealt with in Chapter 15 on pages 314-316. Immigration status does not presently affect the duties of local education authorities to provide education for children of school age. Local authorities are required to provide schooling to children who are living in their area either temporarily or permanently. However, there are proposals under the 2002 Bill to relieve local authorities of these duties for children of asylum-seekers who are placed in the new 'accommodation' centres. These children will receive separate education which will be provided in the accommodation centre itself.

The importance of 'public funds' under the immigration rules

Under the immigration rules (para 6, HC 395), certain welfare provision is defined as 'public funds'. For most categories of admission under the rules, there is a requirement that the applicant will be able to maintain and accommodate themselves without recourse to public funds. Public funds are defined as: attendance allowance, child benefit, council tax benefit, disability living allowance, disabled person's tax credit, family credit, housing benefit, income support, income-based job-seekers allowance, invalid care allowance, severe disablement allowance, working families' tax credit and housing provided by local authorities.

The requirements of the immigration rules do not themselves determine who is and who is not entitled to obtain the public funds listed. This chapter is about access to welfare; it does not deal with whether the immigration rules relating to maintenance and accommodation are satisfied. For whether the immigration rules are satisfied and Home Office policy regarding those rules ▶see pages 328-335. However, a condition can be attached to leave which prohibits the person having recourse to public funds.

Where an applicant needs to satisfy the 'maintenance and accommodation without recourse to public funds' parts of the immigration rules, they will generally have a 'public funds' condition attached to the leave (▶see the box on pages 110-111). Those with indefinite leave cannot have a public funds condition attached, even if they needed to satisfy the maintenance and accommodation requirements in order to get it. It is the *condition* which makes a person 'subject to immigration control' under the 1999 Act and which can exclude a person from access to welfare support.

In most of the cases where claiming public funds would harm an applicant's immigration position, they will not be able to actually obtain those public funds in the first place, for example because they have a 'public funds' condition attached to their leave. There are exceptions to the general exclusions from entitlement to public funds which, for welfare benefits, are set out below in the box on pages 665-667. It *may* be that the Home Office will not normally treat a person, who has evidence from the Benefits Agency that they were eligible for benefit under the regulations relating to the European Convention on Social and Medical Assistance or the Social Charter (▶see below), as having recourse to public funds (see letter to UKCOSA of 5 December 2000). In cases where claiming may have an impact on a person's immigration status or applications they may make in the future, advice should be obtained.

'Subject to immigration control' test

Before the Immigration and Asylum Act 1999, immigration lawyers used the phrase 'subject to immigration control' to describe people who needed leave to be admitted to the UK. Indeed, there is another definition of 'subject to immigration control' in the Immigration and Asylum Act 1996 (s13) which states exactly this. Under section 115 of the 1999 Act, a special definition of 'subject to immigration control' is given which is used to determine access to most social security benefits and support under certain social services or 'community care' legislation. It is also used in relation to access to local authority housing, but there the situation is more complex. In general terms, people who are 'subject to immigration control' under the 1999 Act are denied access to these services (▶see Box 'Subject to Immigration Control': the general rule below). There are important exceptions to this which are considered when we look at each of those forms of support in turn.

First, it is necessary to decide whether a person is 'subject to immigration control' within the meaning of the 1999 Act. No British citizen or EEA national is subject to immigration control. Before the 1999 Act, regulations tried to exclude EEA nationals from certain welfare benefits if the immigration authorities had 'required' the person to leave the UK. However, in *Remilien & Wolke*, the House of Lords ruled that the letters written never actually compelled people to leave and it was clear that they were being written essentially for benefit purposes. They were, therefore, found to be ineffective for the purposes of ending entitlement. However, although the 'required to leave' letters have been abolished, becoming a 'charge on public funds' can still harm the immigration position of certain EEA nationals ▶see pages 471-472.

The following people are 'subject to immigration control':
- those who need leave to enter or remain in the UK but who do not have it;
- people who have leave but which has a condition attached to it that they will not have recourse to public funds;
- people given leave as the result of a 'maintenance undertaking' (otherwise known as a 'sponsorship' agreement); and
- people who have leave but only because they are appealing against a refusal to extend leave.

Another way of understanding the 'subject to immigration control' test under the 1999 Act is to consider who satisfies it, namely, any of the following:
- those with the right of abode in the UK (mainly British citizens);
- EEA nationals;
- non-EEA national family members of EEA nationals provided they qualify for free movement rights. This can be demonstrated if the Home Office has issued a residence document to them;
- those exempt from the requirement to obtain leave (e.g., diplomats);
- those who have leave which is not subject to a condition that they will not have recourse to public funds. Those granted exceptional leave are not generally given a public funds condition;
- those with indefinite leave, provided that their leave was not granted as a

result of a maintenance undertaking. Those recognised as refugees are, in practice, granted indefinite leave although the immigration rules do not say so.

The various categories of people defined as 'subject to immigration control' are considered below.

People without leave

Aside from British Citizens and other EEA nationals, those who do not need leave are a small number of Commonwealth nationals who have the right of abode (►see pages 566-567) and certain categories of people who are exempt from having to obtain leave, including diplomats and their families and members of visiting armed forces (►see pages 15, 436-437). Of those who need leave, those who do not have leave should be easy to identify. They include:

- overstayers;
- those declared to be illegal entrants;
- those with temporary admission or detained under the 1971 Act;
- those who have had a deportation order signed against them;
- those who have had their leave 'curtailed' while they are in the UK or 'cancelled' on their arrival;
- those who never obtained leave in the first place.

In order to determine whether a person has leave, the first place to check is the person's passport. Examples of the various stamps indicating leave, its length and conditions are set out in Chapter 7. That chapter also gives examples of documents such as notices of temporary admission, illegal entry and deportation orders. Many people have become confused about how long leave lasts for when it is granted as a result of an entry clearance operating as leave to enter, and have become overstayers as a result. For an explanation of the operation of entry clearances ►see pages 56-59.

Passport stamps are not always conclusive. For example, a person still has leave if they make an in-time application to extend their stay in the UK, even if there is no decision from the Home Office before their leave would otherwise have run out (s3C, 1971 Act). Leave is automatically extended until 10 days after the decision on the application although the only evidence of this may be recorded delivery confirmation that an application was delivered, or the Home Office acknowledgement of the application combined with evidence of the length of the previous leave.

Condition prohibiting 'recourse to public funds'

Those who have a condition imposed as part of their leave that they will not have recourse to public funds are also 'subject to immigration control'. Two points must be remembered:

'SUBJECT TO IMMIGRATION CONTROL': THE GENERAL RULE

The general rule is that those subject to immigration control cannot obtain the following forms of welfare support.

1 Non-contributory social security benefits
Those subject to control generally cannot get:
- attendance allowance;
- child benefit;
- council tax benefit;
- disability living allowance;
- disabled person's tax credit,
- housing benefit;
- income-based job-seeker's allowance (JSA);
- income support;
- invalid care allowance;
- non-contributory incapacity benefit (for those who become incapable of work in their youth);
- severe disablement allowance (abolished for new claims from 6 April 2001);
- social fund payments;
- working families' tax credit.

For the exceptions ▶see box below 'Exceptions to "Subject to Immigration Control" test'.

2 Housing
The 'subject to immigration control' test under the 1999 Act is referred to in the legislation concerning the duties of local authorities to provide housing for the homeless and the arrangements they must make to allocate housing accommodation from the housing register. However, as set out below (▶see pages 674-678), there is a different 'subject to immigration control' test set out in the Immigration and Asylum Act 1996 which is more relevant to the housing duties.

3 Social Services
Those subject to control generally cannot:
- obtain 'residential accommodation' and the board and services which go with it under section 21 of the National Assistance Act 1948;
- have arrangements made for them under the duty to promote the 'welfare of old people' under section 45 of the Health Services and Public Health Act 1968;
- have arrangements made for them under the duty of authorities to prevent illness or to provide care and after care under paragraph 2, schedule 8 to the National Health Service Act 1977.

For full details and exceptions ▶see pages 678-685.

Note: The provision of some of these forms of welfare comes under different legislation in Scotland and Northern Ireland, which are not covered in the *Handbook*.

- in order to exclude someone from welfare provision, it is not enough that they have been admitted under requirements of the rules which meant that they had to show that they could support themselves without recourse to public funds. All the categories of the rules have maintenance and accommodation requirements save for the following: refugees and their dependants, transit visitors, returning residents, special voucher holders (from 4 March 2002 the voucher scheme has been abolished), bereaved spouses and unmarried partners, non-British citizen children asking for leave to remain. Those given leave in other categories are likely to have a public funds condition attached to their leave. However, unless a condition is *actually given*, the person is *not* subject to immigration control;
- no conditions of any kind, including public funds conditions, can be attached to an indefinite leave. Those with indefinite leave can, however, be 'subject to control' if they are admitted under a maintenance under-taking (▶see below).

People given leave as a result of a maintenance undertaking

Those given leave to enter or remain in the UK as the result of a maintenance undertaking are 'subject to immigration control'. These are undertakings given by a sponsor in the UK that they will maintain and accommodate the applicant so that they will not have to have recourse to public funds. In order to be effective for these purposes, the undertaking must be 'in writing' and given 'in pursuance of the immigration rules'. We suggest, therefore, that informal sponsorship declarations will not be sufficient and that the undertaking should be in a form at least similar to that which is prescribed by the rules as an attachment to Form SET(F). Those who are most likely to be asked to provide an undertaking are people who are being granted indefinite leave to join relatives who are settled in the UK ▶see page 405.

People who have leave but only because they are appealing

People who are appealing against a decision to refuse to *extend* their leave where they made an in-time application for further leave (sometimes called 'variation' appeals), are treated as continuing to have leave while the appeal remains outstanding (see para 17(1) sch 4, 1999 Act). Whether or not the leave that they originally had was subject to a public funds condition, if they only have leave as a result of the automatic extension while they are appealing, they are 'subject to immigration control'.

Welfare benefits

This handbook does not set out the general conditions which claimants need to satisfy in order to claim the many different benefits as this is a huge subject. For sources of further information on benefits, as well as other topics ▶see Section 12 under 'Sources of further information'. We deal only with the exclusions from benefits which are based upon immigration status.

Benefits affected by the 'subject to immigration control' test

The social security benefits which are affected by the 'subject to immigration control' test (as well as the other welfare entitlements affected by this test) are those which are set out in the box 'Subject to immigration control: the general rule' above. They are all 'non-contributory' benefits, namely benefits which do not depend on the person having made a certain amount of national insurance contributions before they can be claimed.

There are, however, certain claimants who, even if they cannot satisfy the subject to control test, can still obtain these welfare benefits. These exceptions are set out in the 'Exceptions' box below. Most are self-explanatory, the concept of lawful presence is considered in more detail below as is the question of claiming asylum 'on arrival' although the latter now helps very few claimants.

Even if a claimant satisfies (or is exempted from) the 'subject to control' test for certain of the non-contributory benefits referred to above, they still need to satisfy other tests which are affected by immigration status. Most notable among these is the 'habitual residence' test which must be

---

EXCEPTIONS TO 'SUBJECT TO IMMIGRATION CONTROL' TEST FOR BENEFITS

Income-based JSA, income support, social fund payments, housing benefit, council tax benefit

The following people are able to claim the above benefits even if they are subject to immigration control:

1 People who had to satisfy the immigration authorities, under the immigration rules, that they can maintain and accommodate themselves without recourse to public funds and who are 'temporarily' without funds because there has been a disruption in funds received from abroad. There must be a 'reasonable expectation' that the supply of funds will begin again.

2 People who were granted leave on the basis of a maintenance undertaking where the sponsor who gave the undertaking has died or where the claimant has been living in the UK for five years. The five-year period begins running from the date of the person's entry into the UK or the date on which the maintenance undertaking was made, whichever is the later.

3 People who are nationals of states which have ratified either the European Convention on Social and Medical Assistance (ECSMA) or the Council of Europe Social Charter (CESC) and who are 'lawfully present' in the UK (for further details ▶see below pages 667–668).

4 Asylum-seekers who claimed asylum on or before 2 April 2000 either 'on arrival' in the UK (for details of this test ▶see page 668) or within three months of either of the 'declarations of upheaval' made in relation to Zaire (now the Democratic Republic of Congo) on 16 May 1997 or Sierra Leone on 1 July 1997. In either case, benefit entitlement ends as soon as the Home Office record the claim to asylum as

having been determined (this is as soon as the claim is determined by the Home Office) or the person abandons the claim to asylum. If the asylum decision is negative and the applicant appeals, they will become eligible for asylum support (see Chapter 32). There will be few people left in this situation.

5 Asylum-seekers who claimed asylum (on arrival or otherwise) before 5 February 1996 whose claims had not been finally decided by that date and who were entitled to these benefits immediately before 5 February 1996. They will only be entitled if they have not received the next decision on their claim, whether from the Home Office or appellate authorities, after 5 February 1996. There are very few remaining people in this category. A break in the claim to benefit does not bring this transitional protection to an end (*Yildiz*, Court of Appeal).

6 People who were granted leave on the basis of a maintenance undertaking made before 5 February 1996 and who were also entitled to these benefits before that time.

Note that 4, 5, 6 above and 4 below are exemptions which provide what is called 'transitional' protection. In other words, their purpose is to allow people who have an existing entitlement to benefit to continue claiming even though changes have been introduced which would otherwise exclude them. 5 and 6 above do not apply to income-based JSA which had not come into being by February 1996.

Attendance allowance, severe disablement allowance, invalid care allowance, disability living allowance, social fund payments, child benefit, noncontributory incapacity benefit, working families' tax credit and disabled person's tax credit

The following people are able to claim the above benefits even if they are subject to immigration control:

1 Non-EEA national family members of EEA nationals. 'Family members' is not defined for these purposes but probably includes all those who are family members for the purposes of EU rights of free movement ▶see pages 458-459 (EEA nationals themselves are never treated as subject to control). Non-EEA national family members who are benefiting from EU rights of free movement should not be 'subject to control' in the first place as they do not require leave.

2 Nationals of the following countries which have made an agreement with the EU which provides for the 'equal treatment of workers...in the area of social security': Algeria, Morocco, Slovenia, Tunisia, Turkey. They must be 'lawfully working' in Great Britain and their family members who are living with them are also exempted from the 'subject to control' test for the purpose of these benefits.

3 People given leave to enter or remain on the basis of a maintenance undertaking. This re-entitles those people who would otherwise be 'subject to control' and excluded from benefit for this reason.

4 People who were entitled to these benefits before 5 February 1996 (7 October 1996 for child benefit). Entitlement continues until the person's claim to asylum (if they have made one) is recorded as determined by the Home Office, or until the social security authorities revise the award of benefit, for example, because there is a relevant change of circumstances. A break in the claim to benefit brings this transitional protection to an end.

- The exemption in 4 above does not apply to working families tax credit, disabled person's tax credit or non-contributory incapacity benefit.
- The exemption in 3 above only applies to working families' tax credit and disabled person's tax credit if the sponosr who gave the maintenance undertaking has died or if the claimant has been living in the UK for five years or more. The five-year period begins on the date of entry to the UK or the date when the undertaking was given, whichever is the later.

Note:

- Both of the two sets of exemptions apply to those seeking help from the social fund.

- Most of the exemptions summarised above are in regulations 2, 12 and the schedule to the Social Security (Immigration and Asylum) Consequential Amendments Regulations 2000.

- The exemption for non-contributory incapacity benefit is in regulation 16, Social Security (Incapacity Benefit) Regulations 1994 (as amended).

- The exemptions for working families' tax credit and disabled person's tax credit are in regulations 3(1)(e)(f),(1A) Family Credit (General) Regulations 1987 and 5(1)(e)(f),(1A) Disability Working Allowance (General) Regulations 1991. The way in which the exemptions work in these regulations is not as straight-forward as for the other benefits, but the intention to exempt certain classes from the 'subject to control' test seems to be the same (note that these regulations have kept their original name, even though the benefits have been re-designated as 'tax credits' by the Tax Credits Act 1999).

satisfied for income-based JSA, income support, housing benefit and council tax benefit. The additional tests are all set out on pages 670-672

For other benefits which are not affected by the 'subject to immigration control test' at all ▶see pages 672-673.

Nationals of certain states who are 'lawfully present' in the UK

There is an exemption from the subject to control test for certain benefits (▶see box above) for nationals of states which have ratified either the European Convention on Social and Medical Assistance (ECSMA) or the Council of Europe Social Charter (CESC) and who are 'lawfully present' in the UK. In addition to the EEA states (EEA nationals are not 'subject to control' anyway), the following countries have ratified either the ECSMA or the CESC: Cyprus, Czech Republic, Hungary, Malta, Poland, Slovakia and Turkey. Nationals of these countries who are 'lawfully present' can claim income-based JSA, income support, social fund payments, housing benefit and council tax benefit. A person who has any kind of leave will generally be 'lawfully present'. Of course, applicants may well be cautious about claiming because, if they need to satisfy the maintenance and accommodation requirements of the rules, then even though they can obtain benefit, claiming may harm their immigration position.

The more difficult question is whether this exemption can help, for example, an asylum-seeker who is not an overstayer or an illegal entrant but who has arrived at port, claimed asylum and been granted temporary admission – a perfectly lawful status. Applying the same test to an exemption in housing law, in *Kaya*, the Court of Appeal decided that such persons were not 'lawfully present' because they were not *present* in the UK at all. This seems a surprising result and advisers should watch out for any further developments in this area.

Claim for asylum made 'on arrival'

There has been much discussion about what is meant by a claim to asylum 'on arrival' (►see 'Exceptions' box above). It will be seen from the box above that, since the introduction of asylum support, the issue is now only relevant to a small number of people who claimed asylum on or before 2 April 2000 and have still not received a decision on their claim from the Home Office.

The position of the government has always been that, in order to claim on arrival, a person must claim 'while clearing immigration control'. That position is supported by decisions of the Social Security Commissioners in certain cases, for example, in *CIS/3867/98* and *CIS/259/99*. Other Commissioners have applied a more flexible approach, while still requiring compelling circumstances if a claim not made at the immigration control desk is to be accepted as being made 'on arrival'. According to this approach, claims made by returning to the desk shortly after passing through controls would more easily qualify (see the decisions of the Commissioners in *CIS/4117/97* and *CIS/4439/98*).

Benefit rates of income-based JSA/income support and claiming for dependants

Certain people who are 'subject to control' but who are exempted from this test, can only claim income-based JSA and income support at the 'urgent cases' rate. This rate is 90 per cent of the usual amount. This applies to those who are exempted from the 'subject to control' test for any of the following reasons (►see 'Exceptions' box above):

- transitionally protected asylum-seekers;
- those temporarily without funds from abroad who reasonably expect the supply to begin again;
- those who have not been living in the UK for five years but whose sponsor or other person who gave a maintenance undertaking for them has died.

Even in these cases, the full personal allowance for any child is still paid. Although persons in the above three groups only obtain benefit at the reduced rate, because they are obtaining 'urgent cases' payments, they are also able to claim benefit for their spouse and children, even if those dependants are 'subject to immigration control'. Although the drafting of the regulations relating to this after April 2000 has led to some uncertainty, this was always previously the rule and it should still be argued that dependants of those on urgent cases are covered.

By contrast, those who are entitled to these benefits at the ordinary rates, for example, those who are settled or British citizens, cannot usually obtain benefit for their dependants if those dependants are 'subject to control'. However, where both partners are not subject to immigration control, they can claim benefit for a child who is subject to control. Similarly, a lone parent who is not subject to control can claim benefit for a child who is subject to control.

In some cases, therefore, where one partner is entitled to 'urgent cases' payments, it may be better for that partner to claim for both (even though the rates are lower), rather than rely upon the benefit entitlement of the partner who is not subject to control but who can only claim for themselves.

Refugees and back-dating claims for benefit

There are often significant delays in Home Office decision-making and therefore people who are finally recognised as refugees have often had to wait a long time. Even when an adjudicator agrees to allow an appeal, there have been very serious delays in obtaining the actual grant of leave which have led to applications for judicial review. Those who are granted refugee status can apply for the back-dating of their benefit entitlement. The rules described below apply to entitlement to income support but there are similar rules for housing benefit and council tax benefit if, indeed, the asylum-seeker had any rent or council tax liability. The rules are different depending on whether the claim to asylum was made before or after 2 April 2000.

Asylum claim made on or before 2 April 2000. In these cases, refugees are entitled to back-dated benefit paid at the urgent cases rate (90 per cent) from the date the claim to asylum was originally refused, if the claim was made on arrival. If the claim was made in-country, benefit is paid from the date of the claim, or from 5 February 1996, if that was later. The refugee must claim income support and back-dating within 28 days of being notified that the Home Office has recognised them as a refugee.

Asylum claim made on or after 3 April 2000. These refugees must also claim income support and back-dating within 28 days of being notified that the Home Office has recognised them but they are entitled to back-dated benefit at the full rate from the date of their claim to asylum. However, for these claimants, the award of benefit is deducted by the value of any asylum support received during the period of the back-dating. This may cancel out much of their back-dated entitlement.

Additional tests for certain benefits affected by the 'subject to immigration control' test

Even if a person satisfies (or is exempted from) the subject to control test as described above, for some benefits to which this test applies, there are additional hurdles which affect those coming to the UK. These additional tests are set out below. It should also be noted that most of the benefits require that the claimant is present in the country in order to claim.

Income-based JSA, income support, housing benefit and council tax benefit: the 'habitual residence' test

Claimants of income-based JSA, income support, housing benefit and council tax benefit must satisfy, or be exempted from, the test that they are 'habitually resident' within the Common Travel Area (▶see glossary). Whether a person is habitually resident is a question of fact which depends on all the circumstances of the case. A person must, however, have a settled intention to live in the UK either for a temporary period or permanently. A person who has brought with them their essential possessions, has made no travel arrangements to leave and has nothing to tie them to the country which they have left, will find it easier to establish their habitual residence more quickly.

The House of Lords in *Nessa* agreed with the Social Security Commissioner who originally decided in that case that an 'appreciable' period in the UK was necessary before a person is habitually resident. However, the House of Lords also accepted that this period could be as short as a month, depending on the circumstances of the case and there does not, therefore, seem to be a minimum 'appreciable' period of time. Special considerations apply to people who have been habitually resident in the UK who leave and return after a temporary absence. They may never have lost their habitual residence in the UK when they went abroad and be treated as habitually resident as soon as they return.

British citizens and EEA nationals must also satisfy the test. However, the following people are *exempt* from having to show that they are habitual resident:

- refugees;
- those with exceptional leave;
- most of those exercising rights of free movement under EU law but not people who are seeking work who have never worked in the UK (the law relating to this exception is complex and advice should be sought in individual cases where benefit is refused);
- people who left Montserrat after 1 November 1995 because of the volcanic eruptions there;
- people who are in the UK because they have been removed here from another country and who are not 'subject to immigration control' – this

last exemption applies only for the purposes of income support and income-based JSA.

It should be noted, that a person who is actually in receipt of income support or income-based JSA cannot be refused housing benefit or council tax benefit on the basis of the habitual residence test.

Working families' tax credit and disabled person's tax credit

People claiming either of the tax credits need to be 'ordinarily resident' in Great Britain (GB); Northern Ireland has its own similar benefit regime for these and certain other benefits. Ordinary residence is not defined but there is case-law which explains its meaning. In *Shah*, the House of Lords decided that a person's ordinary residence is their:

'**abode in a particular place or country which he has adopted voluntarily and for settled purposes as part of the regular order of his life for the time being, whether of short or long duration**'.

Ordinary residence may, depending on a person's circumstances, begin on their arrival in the country and it can also continue during periods of temporary absence. A person here for a temporary purpose, for example, to study, is still here for the time being for a settled purpose and can, therefore, be 'ordinarily resident'. It is also possible to be ordinarily resident in more than one country at the same time.

Social fund

Although there are no *independent* additional hurdles for those who wish to make claims from the social fund, many of the possible claims on the social fund are linked to entitlement to other benefits, so the additional tests (above) apply.

Maternity expenses payments can be claimed only by those entitled to income support, income-based JSA or one of the tax credits. Funeral expenses payments can only be claimed by those entitled to income support, income-based JSA, housing benefit, council tax benefit or one of the tax credits. Cold weather payments are available only to those entitled to income support or income-based JSA. However, winter fuel payments (for those aged 60 or over) are available regardless of entitlements to other benefits. Eligibility for community care grants, budgeting loans and crisis loans is generally restricted to those entitled to income support or income-based JSA. There is some flexibility for crisis loans.

Disability benefits: disability living allowance, attendance allowance, invalid care allowance and non-contributory incapacity benefit

Claimants for these benefits must be 'ordinarily resident' (▶see above) in Great Britain. They must have been present in GB for at least 26 of the last 52 weeks. There are exemptions for serving members of the armed forces, mariners and offshore workers. In certain circumstances, people may be treated as present for the purposes of the 26-week qualifying period when they are temporarily absent during that time.

Child Benefit

In order to be entitled to child benefit, it is necessary that:

- the person claiming benefit for the child has been in GB for more than 182 days in the last 52 weeks (six months of the previous year); and
- either the child or one of the parents of the child has been in GB for more than 182 days in the last 52 weeks.

There are certain quite complex exceptions to these rules and there are special rules for people who are working overseas, including civil servants and serving members of the armed forces. For the exceptions and details of the related 'Guardian's allowance' for a carer when the child's parents are dead ►see Section 12 under 'Further sources of information'.

Benefits which are not affected by the 'subject to immigration control' test

Access to the contributory benefits, for which national insurance contributions are required, does not depend on immigration status. However, a person's immigration status may indirectly mean that they are unable to obtain these benefits simply because they have not been in the UK long enough to have made sufficient contributions. These benefits are:

- contribution-based job-seeker's allowance;
- contribution-based incapacity benefit;
- maternity allowance;
- the 'bereavement' benefits;
- category A and B retirement pensions.

Category D pensions are non-contributory but entitlement does depend on whether the claimant was 'ordinarily resident' (►see above) in the UK on the day they reached 80 or the later date that the pension was claimed. The claimant must also have been resident for at least 10 years in any continuous period of 20 years before they reached 80.

Access to the industrial injuries benefits (disablement benefit, reduced earnings allowance, constant attendance allowance, exceptionally severe disablement allowance) also does not depend on immigration status, although the claimant must have been working in GB when the accident or illness arising from the work occurred.

The schemes for statutory sick pay and maternity pay are practically operated by employers. Statutory sick pay is paid to people for up to 28 weeks if they are unable to work through sickness. Statutory maternity pay is a minimum payment to employees who take time off as a result of pregnancy or child-birth. There are no special rules about residence or immigration status although the rules for these benefits do focus on whether the person has been employed in GB (or another EU country).

Links between the Home Office and benefit authorities

The most important authority is the Department of Work and Pensions which operates through the Benefits Agency. There are links between the social security and immigration authorities. Sometimes enquiries about a person's immigration status are made by telephone to the Home Office and sometimes they are made by sending a special enquiry form to the Home Office Immigration Status Enquiry Unit.

The claim form for income support and income-based JSA asks whether the claimant or any member of their family has come to the UK in the last five years. If the answer is 'yes', further questions are asked. Checks with the Home Office have also been known to be triggered when a benefits claim is made by other factors such as a 'foreign' name or lack of fluency in English or not having a national insurance number. The effect of checks with the Home Office may be to alert the Home Office to a benefits claim with the result that an application may be refused on the grounds that a person is not able to maintain and accommodate themselves without recourse to public funds. It may also enable the Home Office to identify the whereabouts of people who it has lost contact with but who have no legal basis for remaining in the UK and whom it intends to remove.

Further benefit rights for EEA nationals

EEA nationals and their family members are entitled to further rights in relation to benefits under European community law. Like the rights of free-movement, these are laws which apply directly even if they are not written down in UK law. Both EEA nationals and their family members who are not EEA nationals can benefit from these rights. Community law gives rights in two areas: the co-ordination of benefits within the EEA and rights in relation to the free movement of workers. If it appears that these further rights may be relevant, one of the books mentioned in Section 12 under 'Further sources' should be referred to or specialist benefits advice obtained.

The European rights to free movement mean that, if a person is economically active by exercising free movement rights in order to take up employment, self-employment or to provide or receive services in another EEA state, they are entitled to the same tax, housing and social 'advantages' as nationals of the member state. It has been settled by the courts that social security benefits are part of these advantages.

As far as the co-ordination of benefits is concerned, the EC Regulation which provides for this is 1408/71. It protects those people who pay or have paid national insurance contributions. It also protects non-EEA nationals who are refugees or stateless persons. Regulation 1408/71 prohibits discrimination on grounds of nationality in social security; allows a person to count periods of employment, residence and contributions in one EEA state towards entitlement in another; and allows a person to take certain benefits abroad to another EEA state. This means that an EEA national may straight away satisfy the additional residence (▶see above) or contributions requirements for some benefits.

Incapacity benefit, retirement pensions, bereavement benefits and industrial disablement benefit can all be received abroad in another EEA state. 'Unemployment benefits' (contribution-based JSA is the only benefit the government accepts as meeting this description, although income-based JSA may also count) can only be taken abroad for three months.

Reciprocal agreements

The UK has certain reciprocal agreements with other countries relating to social security. The effect of the reciprocal agreements is limited – it is similar to European community law in helping a person qualify for certain benefits by allowing periods of residence and contributions which are paid in one state to count in the other. Although there are agreements with other EEA countries, the protection given by community law (▶see above) is generally just as wide and so it is not necessary to rely upon them. It is, therefore, only really necessary to consider the agreements with non-EEA states, for example, Australia, Barbados, Canada, Israel, Mauritius, New Zealand, Turkey, USA. All the agreements are different in their terms and a range of benefits is covered by them.

Housing

The housing duties of local authorities can be split into two:

Housing for the homeless. Where a person approaches a local housing authority and it appears that he or she may be homeless (or threatened with homelessness), the local authority should carry out investigations into their circumstances. The authority must determine whether the person is 'eligible' for housing assistance, homeless, in 'priority need', intentionally homeless and whether they have a 'local connection' with the area of the authority. Depending on the result of these investigations, the authority may be required to provide housing for them. Whether a person is 'eligible' for this assistance can depend on their immigration status (▶see under 'Effect of immigration status' below read with 'Eligibility for housing for the homeless' box also below).

Allocation of housing accommodation. Local authorities are required to maintain a housing register which consists of 'qualifying persons'. The local authority then allocates accommodation to people who are on its register. This is done in accordance with the authority's 'allocation scheme', which is normally based on a points system. Whether an applicant is a 'qualifying person' depends on their immigration status

(▶see under 'Effect of immigration status' below read with 'Qualification for the housing register' box also below).

The effect of immigration status: an overview

We do not explain here the details of the housing duties themselves nor the homelessness requirements such as 'priority need' nor the way in which authorities operate their allocation schemes. For details on all these matters, one of the further sources referred to in Section 12 should be consulted. Set out below are the circumstances in which an applicant's immigration status can prevent them from being eligible for assistance as a homeless person or from qualifying to be included on the housing register.

The current provisions are contained in parts VI and VII of the Housing Act 1996. Applicants are excluded from both duties if they are 'subject to immigration control' within the meaning of the Asylum and Immigration Act 1996 (see s13(2)). This is a much wider exclusion than the exclusion under the 1999 Act. Under the 1996 Act, a person is subject to immigration control if they need leave to enter or remain in the UK. This, therefore, applies to everyone other than:

- those with the right of abode in the UK (mostly British citizens and some Commonwealth citizens ▶see pages 566-567);
- EEA nationals and their family members exercising rights of free movement;
- those exempt from having to obtain leave (▶see pages 15, 436-437).

There are then regulations which 're-include' certain classes of people even though they are 'subject to control' within the meaning of the 1996 Act (▶see below). For the duties to the homeless, the regulations are the Homelessness (England) Regulations 2000 and for allocation of accommodation, the relevant regulations are the Allocation of Housing (England) Regulations 2000. As a result of separate regulations, both of these regulations also apply in Wales.

The 'subject to immigration control' test in the 1999 Act is mentioned in the housing legislation but it confuses the position. At present, the easiest way to understand the provisions is to see who is primarily excluded by the test used from the 1996 Act (▶see above) and then see who is re-included. It should be noted that the 1999 Act also seeks to prevent those who are 'subject to control' (within the 1996 Act definition) from obtaining security of tenure in any housing which they are given and from benefiting from protection from eviction rights.

The Homelessness Act 2002

The Homelessness Act 2002, passed by parliament in February 2002, makes changes to both the scheme providing for homelessness and to the arrangements for the allocation of local authority housing. The homelessness provisions of the 2002 Act are likely to come into force in July 2002, and the allocations provisions in January 2003.

Whether there are any changes which affect immigration status will depend on regulations made under the Act. However, the government has indicated that it does not intend to alter the classes of people who are re-included, so the position set out below is likely to remain the same or very similar.

Habitual residence test in housing

Persons who are not 'subject to immigration control' may still be ineligible for housing as a homeless person and may still not be able to qualify for a local authority's housing register or allocations scheme if they are not 'habitually resident' in the Common Travel Area (CTA) (▶see glossary for meaning). The habitual residence test itself is explained on pages 670-671.

Those who are exempted from the habitual residence test for housing purposes are:

- most of those exercising European rights of free movement but not people who are seeking work who have never worked in the UK (the law relating to this exception is complex and advice should be sought on individual cases where benefit is refused);
- people who left Montserrat after 1 November 1995 because of the volcanic eruptions there.

For the homelessness duty, but not for allocation of accommodation, an applicant is also exempt from the habitual residence test if they are receiving income support or are entitled to income-based JSA.

Housing for the homeless

Those who are 'subject to immigration control' within the meaning of the test set out on page 675 can still be eligible for housing as a homeless person. The classes of applicant who are still eligible are set out in the 'Eligibility for housing for the homeless' box (below). A person who is themselves prevented from eligibility for housing as a homeless person by their immigration status cannot be counted in order to determine whether another applicant is homeless, threatened with homelessness or in 'priority need'. This often occurs when there is a child of the household who would otherwise bring the family into the 'priority need' category but cannot because the child's immigration status requires the local authority to discount them. These people do, however, continue to be treated as part of a homeless applicant's household for the purposes of what accommodation is reasonable for the applicant and his or her family to occupy. So, if an applicant is eligible for homeless assistance, but all of his or her three children are ineligible, the children cannot confer priority need on the applicant, but, if a duty is accepted, accommodation will be provided on the basis that his or her household includes three children.

ELIGIBILITY FOR HOUSING FOR THE HOMELESS

Those who are eligible for housing even though they are 'subject to immigration control' within the meaning of the 1996 Act are:

1 People 'recorded' by the Home Office as refugees (Class A).

2 People who have been granted exceptional leave which is not subject to a condition that they maintain and accommodate themselves without recourse to public funds (exceptional leave is not generally given with this condition) (Class B).

3 People who have indefinite leave and who are habitually resident in the CTA *except* people who were given leave on a maintenance undertaking in writing in pursuance of the immigration rules who have not been in the UK for five years (beginning on the date of entry or the date when the undertaking is made, whichever is the later) and whose sponsor is still alive (Class C).

4 People who left Montserrat after 1 November 1995 because of the volcanic eruptions there (Class D).

5 A person who is habitually resident within the CTA and is either:

• a national of a state which has ratified ECSMA or the Social Charter and is lawfully present in the UK (►see pages 667-668) (Class E); or

• a person who was owed a duty by the local authority under the homelessness provisions before 3 April 2000, is still owed a duty and is a national of a state which has *signed* ECSMA or the Social Charter (note: there are additional states which have *signed* these agreements as opposed to having actually ratified them; *in addition* to the EEA states and those countries which have ratified at least one of the agreements (►see pages 667-668), states which have signed one of these agreements are: Croatia, Estonia, Latvia, Macedonia, Romania, Slovenia, Switzerland and Ukraine) (Class E).

6 A person who claimed asylum before 3 April 2000 on their arrival in the UK and whose asylum application has not either been decided by the Home Office or been abandoned (Class F).

7 A person who claimed asylum before 3 April 2000 who was in GB at the time when the Home Office made an 'upheaval' declaration in relation to their country of origin, who claimed asylum within three months of the date of the declaration, and whose claim has not either been decided by the Home Office or been abandoned (Class G).

8 A person who claimed asylum on or before 4 February 1996, who was entitled to housing benefit on 4 February 1996 and who has not received a further negative decision on their claim since 4 February 1996, either from the Home Office or, if there was an appeal outstanding on that date, from the immigration appellate authorities (Class H).

9 A person who is receiving income support or is entitled to income-based JSA and is entitled to those benefits *other than* on the basis of the exemption from the 'subject to immigration control test' for those benefits, that he or she is 'temporarily without funds because the supply from abroad has been disrupted' (►see 'Exceptions' box on page 665) (Class I).

Allocation of housing accommodation

Those who are 'subject to immigration control' within the meaning of the test set out on page 675 can still qualify to be included on the housing register and to be allocated accommodation. The classes of applicant who qualify are set out in the 'Qualification for the housing register and to be allocated accommodation' box (below).

QUALIFICATION FOR THE HOUSING REGISTER AND TO BE ALLOCATED ACCOMMODATION

Those who may still qualify for inclusion on the local authority's housing register and be allocated accommodation even though they are 'subject to immigration control' within the meaning of the 1996 Act are:

1 People 'recorded' by the Home Office as refugees (Class A).

2 People who have been granted exceptional leave which is not subject to a condition that they maintain and accommodate themselves without recourse to public funds (exceptional leave is not generally given with this condition) (Class B).

3 People who have indefinite leave and who are habitually resident in the CTA *except* people who were given leave on maintenance undertaking in writing in pursuance of the immigration rules who have not been in the UK for five years (beginning on the date of entry or the date when the undertaking is made – whichever is the later) and whose sponsor is still alive (Class C).

4 People who left Montserrat after 1 November 1995 because of the volcanic eruptions there (Class D).

5 A person who is habitually resident within the CTA and is either:

• a national of a state which has ratified ECSMA or the Social Charter and is lawfully present in the UK (▶see pages 667-668) (Class E); or

• a person who was owed a duty by the local authority under the homelessness provisions before 3 April 2000, is still owed a duty and is a national of a state which has signed ECSMA or the Social Charter (note: there are additional states which have *signed* these agreements as opposed to having actually ratified them ▶see 'Eligibility for housing the homeless' box above) (Class E).

Social services

In February 1996, the government introduced severe restrictions on benefit entitlement for those coming to the UK. Those claiming asylum were denied benefit unless they claimed 'on arrival' or within three months of a declaration of upheaval being made in relation to their country of origin. JCWI brought court proceedings against the government which resulted in the regulations being struck down as, by reducing asylum-seekers to destitution, they prevented them from properly pursuing their claims for asylum in the UK. The government responded by passing the Asylum and Immigration Act 1996 which gave firm grounding for the same regulations. It was at that stage that asylum-seekers in particular began turning to social services departments of local authorities in order to obtain support under their community care responsibilities. As a result, for a few years, many destitute asylum-seekers were supported by local authorities under section 21 of the National Assistance Act 1948. Local authorities contested this on the basis that the National Assistance Act was never meant to apply to asylum-seekers as this issue did not even arise in the 1940s when the legislation was introduced. In *MPAX* (also known as the '*Westminster*' case), the Court of Appeal held that local authorities did indeed have a duty, in most cases, to support destitute asylum-seekers in this way.

From 6 December 1999, the asylum support scheme was introduced (▶see Chapter 32), with the intention that the majority of asylum-seekers would be supported under the new scheme. Local authorities responsibilities under the community care legislation were amended at the same time so that, in most cases, access to social services support was restricted by the 'subject to immigration control test' under the 1999 Act. This is the same test which applies to certain welfare benefits and it is dealt with in detail above ▶see pages 660-664.

Clearly, not all those who fall within the 'subject to control' test are asylum-seekers, which leaves a gap in the support system for those who are overstayers, or otherwise fail the 'subject to control' test but do not have any other form of support. There is also a gap in provision for childless asylum-seekers who have exhausted their appeals but who are taking judicial review proceedings or pursuing further representations. They may try to obtain support under the 'hard cases' arrangements ▶see pages 717-718. Below, we look at when it may still be possible to obtain support from social services. Support under the Children Act is covered on pages 685-687.

Immigration status restrictions on community care services

Until recently, there was nothing in the community care legislation which specifically excluded people from assistance on the basis of their immigration status. At one stage, the courts were willing to imply restrictions. In *D*, the High Court ruled that assistance could generally not be provided under section 21 of the National Assistance Act to those who entered the country unlawfully or who overstayed their leave. The reason for this was that it was said to be contrary to 'public policy' for persons of an unlawful immigration status to be able to obtain support. The decision in *D* did not apply to asylum-seekers regardless of their immigration status. In *O and Bhikha*, the Court of Appeal overruled this case law. It stated that immigration status does not easily lend itself to distinctions based on 'legality' and that local social services authorities should not refuse people on this basis.

'Subject to immigration control' test

Following the 1999 Act, access is denied to the following forms of assistance for people who are 'subject to immigration control' within the meaning of that Act (s116-117, 1999 Act):

- 'residential accommodation' and the board and services which go with it under section 21, National Assistance Act 1948;
- arrangements for the 'promotion of the welfare of old people' under section 45, Health Services and Public Health Act 1968;
- 'arrangements by local authorities for the prevention of illness and for care and after-care' under paragraph 2 schedule 8 to the National Health Service Act 1977.

However, assistance is only denied on this basis if the person would otherwise qualify for it *solely*:

- because they are destitute; or
- because of the physical effects, or anticipated physical effects, of their being destitute.

It should firstly be noted that section 21 of the National Assistance Act requires local authorities to provide residential accommodation for two classes of people who do not otherwise have support available to them:

1 people who are aged 18 or over and who are in need of care and attention by reason of age, illness, disability, or 'any other circumstance'; and

2 expectant and nursing mothers who are in need of care and attention.

The 'subject to control' restriction applies only to the first class. Nursing or expectant mothers who are subject to control, may, therefore, still be able to obtain accommodation and support under this provision.

'Destitute' for these purposes has the same meaning as for asylum support, namely, a person who is without adequate accommodation or the means to obtain it or who is unable to meet their essential living needs. The government's intention was to reverse the effect of the *Westminster* case so that most asylum-seekers and others who are subject to immigration control are not entitled to community care services unless they are able to show that their needs do not arise solely because of their lack of resources or the effect of their lack of resources.

The first main case to consider the meaning of 'solely because [he or she] is destitute' was *O and Bhikha*, which was a case concerning section 21 1948 Act support. The two applicants in that case were not asylum-seekers and so would not be entitled to asylum support but would have been on the streets if they were not assisted. They also had fairly pronounced illnesses and so, they argued, their needs for care and attention were not caused 'solely' by their destitution. They said that they should be able to add the fact that they had no resources to the fact of their illnesses which, in combination, resulted in the authority being required to provide support for them. The Court of Appeal agreed. It stated that in order to satisfy the test, it is not necessary that the person's needs arise completely independently of their destitution. Therefore, they do not have to show that, even if they were not destitute, they would still qualify for assistance. It was accepted that it was enough if the applicant could show that their needs were made materially 'more acute' by reasons other than lack of resources, for example, age, illness or disability. A person who is significantly disabled will be likely to have a more 'acute' experience of homelessness and be less well able to fend for themselves than an able-bodied person.

The next question is whether this reasoning also applies to asylum-seekers who would not be destitute if they were not provided with section 21 assistance because they would then be entitled to asylum support instead. In two cases in the High Court, *Murua* and *Mani, Tasci and J*, the Court applied the same reasoning and test in *O and Bhikha* to asylum-seekers. The result is that certain elderly, ill, disabled etc asylum-seekers remain the responsibility of local authorities rather than that of NASS under the asylum support scheme. The result, for some, is that they are likely to remain housed in their own area rather than being dispersed or placed in one of the government's proposed 'accommodation' centres.

It is possible that the above position will change. In *NASS v Westminster*, which is due to be heard in the House of Lords, the local authorities are battling with NASS over whether *any* asylum-seeker should be supported by local authorities because asylum support is always available to them. NASS won this battle in the Court of Appeal.

What services or assistance can be obtained?

'Community care services' is an umbrella term for services provided under the National Assistance Act 1948 together with the Chronically Sick and Disabled Persons Act 1970, the Health Services and Public Health Act 1968, the National Health Services Act 1977 and the Mental Health Act 1983. The legislation is supplemented by government circulars and directions. The circumstances in which people may be considered eligible for assistance and the support they can receive are set out below. It must be remembered that, unlike social security benefits, there is no absolute entitlement to services if certain conditions are satisfied. The availability of certain assistance is restricted by the 'subject to control' test (►see above).

Where a person may be eligible for any community care services, the local authority is required to make an assessment under the National Health Service and Community Care Act 1990 (►see pages 684-685 below).

Section 21 National Assistance Act 1948

The basic conditions for qualifying for support from any particular local authority under this provision are that the applicant is:

- in 'need of care and attention' which is 'not otherwise available'; *and*
- either 18 years or over and in 'need of care and attention' by reason of age, illness, disability *or* 'any other circumstance' or an 'expectant' or 'nursing' mother; *and*
- 'ordinarily resident' in the area of the local authority approached for assistance, or of no settled residence, or not ordinarily resident in the area of that local authority but in 'urgent need' of accommodation.

The requirement that the care and attention is 'not otherwise available' indicates that the service is one of last resort. Aside from the case of expectant or nursing mothers, the 'need for care and attention' must arise for one of the given reasons. The reason of 'age' is generally applied to the elderly. There is no definition of ' illness' or 'disability' for these purposes. Under guidance issued by the government, 'some other circumstance' includes alcoholics and drug dependants and also those suffering from a mental disorder. For the meaning of 'ordinarily resident' ▶see page 671.

As indicated above, in the *MPAX* case, the Court of Appeal held that asylum-seekers deprived of other means of support and who become destitute may satisfy the requirements of needing 'care and attention' for 'some other circumstance' because of their complete lack of resources and their vulnerability. A local authority must always assess the real and practical obstacles that an applicant may face. In *Hong Cui*, a local authority was criticised for denying support under section 21 to a Chinese woman who had permission to work but who was experiencing difficulty in obtaining further work as a result of her deteriorating psoriasis and who could obtain access to food in a soup kitchen only if she walked all day to and from the different kitchens.

The main purpose of section 21 is the provision of residential accommodation, although other support such as food, laundry and personal hygiene facilities may be provided as part of a package with the accommodation. The High Court has decided that an authority has no power to provide other services and support, for example, food or vouchers, without also providing accommodation (*Gorenkin*). In the same case, it was indicated that a person does not need to be imminently homeless in order to become eligible for accommodation and the support connected to it under section 21. Where, for example, a person has no resources, continues to have a roof over their head but not the means to be able to continue to pay their rent or otherwise provide for themselves, an authority is bound to consider whether, looking at their overall position, they should take responsibility for the person by providing them with alternative accommodation and services. Authorities are only able to provide support in kind or vouchers, they are not able to provide cash.

Section 29 National Assistance Act 1948

In order to qualify for services under this provision, a person needs to be:

- over 18; *and*
- ordinarily resident (►see page 671) in the area of the authority approached for help; *and*
- blind or deaf or dumb or suffering from mental disorder of any description; or substantially and permanently handicapped by 'illness, injury, congenital deformity'; *and*
- in need of services to 'promote' their 'welfare'.

There is no restriction for people 'subject to immigration control'. Services which may be provided include:

- advice and social support;
- facilities for social rehabilitation and adjustment to disability;
- occupational, social, cultural and recreational facilities, and, where appropriate, payments for work undertaken by the service users;
- holiday homes;
- free or subsidised travel;
- assistance in finding accommodation;
- hostel accommodation and board and other amenities for those undertaking occupational activities in a workshop provided as part of occupational facilities.

Section 2 Chronically Sick and Disabled Persons Act 1970

In order to qualify for services under this provision, the person needs to be:

- ordinarily resident (►see page 671) in the area of the authority approached for services; *and*
- blind or deaf or dumb or suffering from mental disorder of any description; or substantially and permanently handicapped by 'illness, injury, congenital deformity'; *and*
- in need of any of the services listed below.

The services which may be provided include the following: practical assistance in the home (cleaning, cooking etc); provision of or assistance with getting TV, radio, library facilities, hi-fi, or computers; recreational/ educational facilities; assistance with travel; adaptation of the home to make it more safe and comfortable for the person's needs, assistance in taking holidays (including funding the cost of the holiday in appropriate cases); provision of meals at home or elsewhere; provision of or assistance with obtaining a telephone and any special equipment needed to operate it (loud bell, flashing signal etc).

There is no restriction for people 'subject to immigration control'. People may qualify for support under this provision regardless of their age.

Section 117 Mental Health Act 1983

In order to qualify for support under these provisions, the person may be of any age and must have been detained under the Mental Health Act. The services which may be provided are unlimited but are directed towards after-care until the local health authority or social services authority decides that the person is no longer in need of services. There is no restriction for people 'subject to immigration control'.

Section 45 Health Services and Public Health Act 1968

The purpose of this provision is to make services available to promote 'the welfare of old people'. 'Old people' is not defined but typically provided for are the housebound, those living alone, bereaved, about to be discharged from hospital, and other persons aged over 75 and living in the community. The services which may be provided include meals and recreational facilities, assistance in finding accommodation, social work support and advice, home help and adaptation of property. Other services may be provided with the individual approval of the Secretary of State. The 'subject to immigration control' restriction applies but those who qualify are likely anyway to pass the test that they are not in need of assistance 'solely' because they are destitute (▶see above pages 680-681).

Schedule 8 National Health Service Act 1977

Services may be provided for people in order to prevent their illness, to care for people suffering from an illness and to look after them after they have been suffering from illness. Services include day centres, social services support, and recreational facilities. The 'subject to immigration control' restriction applies but those who would qualify for help are likely not to be in need of assistance 'solely' because of their destitution.

Procedures: community care assessments

Where the circumstances of a person who may be in need of any of the above community care services comes to the attention of a local authority, the authority is under a duty to (s47(1), National Health Services and Community Care Act 1990):

- carry out an assessment of the needs of that person for community care services; and
- having regard to the assessment, decide whether the needs 'call for' the provision of any services.

In recognition of the fact that many of the people who community care law is designed to help are less able to be aware of their rights and less capable of accessing them, the duty to make an assessment does not depend on a person having made an approach or an application to the local authority concerned. In practice, however, many of the persons provided with services come to the attention of the authority in this way. Depending on the circumstances of the particular potential service user, the extent of their needs and the number of other people it may be necessary to consult, the process of assessment may be simple or it may be more complex.

Normally, the authority will conduct an interview with the person and the information obtained from them will include details of all the needs which they have, their preferences as to how those needs could be met and the difficulties that the person may face if the needs are not met. The needs which are assessed are the needs for community care services, not needs generally.

Having identified a person's needs for services, those services are not automatically provided. The authority must then move on to determine separately whether to provide services and, if so, what provision should be made. In deciding on what provision, if any, should be made, the authority must have regard to the nature and extent of the need identified and may also have regard to the priorities of the community more generally. To a more limited extent, an authority may also have regard to its own resources. There are some situations where the consequences of not making provision to meet the need are so severe for the person concerned that an authority could not reasonably fail to provide the service.

Once the process of assessment has been completed and it has been decided what services should be provided, the arrangements for making those services available are set out in a 'care plan'. It should be noted that, if the need for services is urgent, as may be the case for asylum-seekers, then it is possible for those services to be provided on an emergency basis before the process of assessment and the drawing up of a care-plan has been completed (see s47(5), 1990 Act).

Children Act 1989

Many families who are in the UK who are subject to immigration control have, in the absence of social security benefit, sought services from local authorities under the Children Act 1989. Those who qualify as asylum-seekers for asylum support purposes no longer need to rely on the Children Act as they continue to be treated as asylum-seekers while they and their child dependants remain in the UK, even after the conclusion of the asylum appeals process (▶see pages 692-693). Unaccompanied child asylum-seekers and other unaccompanied children continue to be supported under the Children Act but families who are not claiming asylum may also seek support. An unaccompanied minor asylum-seeker will continue to be accommodated by a local authority until they reach the age of 18, when they become entitled to asylum support.

There is no set way in which an application must be made to the local authority. A local authority to which representations are made about a child, should make an assessment to see whether they are 'in need' and, if so, what support should be provided in order to meet those needs.

The provision of support

Section 17 of the Children Act requires local authorities to 'safeguard and promote' the welfare of children within their area who are 'in need' by providing a range and level of services which are appropriate to the child's needs. Section 20 of the Children Act allows a local authority to provide accommodation for a child who is in need as a result of their being no person with parental responsibility to care for them, their being lost or abandoned or the person who was caring for them being prevented from providing the child with suitable accommodation. This duty will continue until the child is 18. Beyond that stage, if the local authority provided assistance to a child when they were aged between 16–18, it still has a responsibility to provide advice and some limited forms of assistance until the person becomes 21, and, in some cases, till they are 24.

The reason why local authorities have provided services for the family of the child as well as the child, is that section 17 of the Act also places local authorities under a duty to promote the upbringing of children in need by their families where that is consistent with promoting the child's welfare. Section 17 also states that any service which is provided under it may be provided for family members of the child as well.

A child is 'in need' if he or she is disabled, or if it is the case that, unless services are provided:

- the child is unlikely to achieve or to maintain, or to have the opportunity of achieving or maintaining, a reasonable standard of physical or mental health or development; or
- the physical or mental health or development of the child is likely to be significantly impaired or further impaired.

The 'development' of the child can mean the child's physical, intellectual, emotional, social or behavioural development. Clearly, a child whose parents are destitute and who is without other means of support, is likely to satisfy the above criteria unless support is provided by the local authority. A child is 'disabled' for these purposes if he or she is 'blind, deaf or dumb or suffers from mental disorder...or is substantially and permanently handicapped by illness, injury or congenital deformity'.

The support which may be provided under the Children Act to the child in need and to the family of the child includes both accommodation and support to meet living needs. The assistance may be by giving assistance in kind or the authority may provide cash.

Restrictions on the powers to provide support

There is no requirement that either the child or the parents of the child have any particular immigration status before they are entitled to obtain services under the Children Act . Children Act support is also not restricted by the 'subject to control' test. However, the High Court in *Damoah* and the Court of Appeal in *G* both indicated that, depending on the circumstances, it may be open to a local authority to carry out their duties under the Children Act by providing assistance to the family to return to the country from which they have come where financial assistance is available in that country.

There are also conflicting decisions in the Court of Appeal (*A, W*) about whether a local authority can be put under any duty at all under section 17 to provide accommodation to a child *and* their parent/s and the nature of the local authorities' duties. Both *G, A* and *W* are likely to go to the House of Lords, so there may well be developments in this area in the near future.

In some cases, in the absence of assistance under the Children Act, it may be that support from a local authority can be obtained from changes made to the Housing Act 1996 by the Homelessness Act 2002. These changes require a local housing authority, where it has decided that there is no duty to an applicant because they are intentionally homelessness, to ensure that accommodation is made available for applicants who have children living with them for as long as they are requested to do so by the social services authority. It should also be remembered that nursing or expectant mothers who are 'subject to immigration control' may still be able to obtain support under section 21 of the National Assistance Act 1948 ►see page 680.

Health care

A person who is an 'overseas visitor' can be charged for treatment received from the National Health Service. The provisions dealing with this are the National Health Service (Charges to Overseas Visitors) Regulations 1989 (as amended by 'Amendment' regulations of the same name of 1991 and 1994). 'Overseas visitors' are defined as people who are 'not ordinarily resident'.

In *Reffell*, the Court of Appeal indicated that the meaning of 'ordinarily resident' for these purposes had to be looked at in the context of the regulations relating to charges and that the meaning given to it in *Shah* (►see page 671) could not be applied in the same way. *Reffell* involved a young Nigerian who had come to the UK as a medical visitor for a kidney transplant and further dialysis in the meantime. The private funds dried up but the court rejected the argument that, because the patient was residing in the UK for the settled purpose of obtaining medical treatment, he was ordinarily resident and had therefore ceased to be an 'overseas visitor'.

However, certain NHS treatment is exempt from being charged for and certain people are exempt from being treated as overseas visitors.

NHS treatment which is exempt from charges are the following services:

- accident and emergency treatment in hospital casualty departments;
- the treatment of certain diseases such as malaria, TB, whooping cough,

family planning services, sexually transmitted diseases, cholera, food poisoning, diagnosis of HIV and AIDS and treatment under the Mental Health Act.

Included among those who are not treated as overseas visitors are:

- people in the UK for the purposes of employment, certain volunteers, students where the course of study involves periods of industrial experience within the first year, and those taking up permanent residence in the UK;

- people who have lived in the UK for one year immediately before the time when the services are provided;

- asylum-seekers and those accepted as refugees;

- persons detained under the Immigration Act 1971;

- nationals of countries with which the UK has a reciprocal agreement. These agreements vary and most only cover treatment for conditions which have arisen during the visit or where people have been specifically referred to the UK for treatment for a particular illness. There are also limited exemptions for certain people whose need for medical treatment only arose in the UK, including nationals of countries which are parties to the European Convention on Social and Medical Assistance (▶see page 667).

In addition to the above rules, EEA nationals in possession of form E128 are eligible to free NHS treatment of all kinds together with their family members.

Even where there is no exemption from charges, the court in *Reffell* did accept that a health authority always has a discretion whether to withhold treatment if payment, or an undertaking to pay, is not made in advance. In a case where lack of treatment will inevitably lead to the need for more expensive emergency treatment (which the health authority must provide ▶see above), then a failure to provide the initial treatment may be challengeable by judicial review.

General practitioners are not subject to the above rules about charging for treatment and both they, dentists and opticians, can treat people who would otherwise be liable for charges free of charge on a discretionary basis. Asylum-seekers on a low income can qualify for free optical and dental treatment and prescriptions by completing Form HC1 (and ▶see page 706). The British Medical Association has indicated that it is not ethical to refuse to register a patient because they may need expensive treatment.

For the rules relating to those who are coming to the UK for private health care as medical visitors ▶see page 293. In certain cases, the Home Office grants exceptional leave to people in the UK on humanitarian grounds which then entitles them to all forms of health care. For the human rights aspects to cases such as this and for Home Office policy in relation to those with life-threatening illnesses and HIV/AIDS ▶see pages 252-254. For Home Office policy relating to the grant of exceptional leave to those caring for relatives or friends in the UK ▶see pages 289-291.

32 Asylum support

There are two schemes of asylum support which we describe below as 'NASS' support (provided by the National Asylum Support Service) and 'Interim' support (provided by local authorities). Asylum support is intended as a replacement for both welfare benefits, social services support and local authority housing for those who are claiming asylum. A small group of asylum-seekers, however, have remained the responsibility of local authorities under their duties to provide community care under the National Assistance Act rather than being provided with asylum support ▶see pages 680-681. The two schemes are very similar, the basic conditions of entitlement contained in the 1999 Act apply to both of them. They do, however, have their own separate sets of regulations, the regulations for the NASS scheme being more detailed.

The interim support scheme was introduced on 6 December 1999 at which point it was only intended to continue in existence until 1 April 2002. By that time it was hoped that NASS would be able to provide for all asylum-seekers. However, that has not proved possible and the interim scheme will now continue in existence until at least 5 April 2004 (see reg 3, Asylum Support (Interim Provisions) (Amendment) No 2 Regulations 2002).

This chapter, looks at the basic conditions that need to be satisfied which are common to both NASS and the interim scheme and considers which asylum-seekers are the responsibility of NASS and which are the responsibility of the local authorities under the interim scheme. Each scheme and its procedures are then considered separately. The Chapter also covers the asylum support appeals process which applies only to NASS support. Towards the end of the chapter, we look at the 'hard cases' fund intended to provide support for certain asylum-seekers who have exhausted the appeals process and who are no longer able to obtain asylum support.

Certain changes are expected to be made to the asylum support scheme under the 2002 Nationality, Asylum and Immigration Bill. Significantly, the scheme is to be modified in order to allow for support to be provided in the experimental new 'accommodation' centres which are being set up to house asylum-seekers. There is also a proposal to end the ability of asylum-seekers to obtain help with their essential living needs only, namely, without also being provided with accommodation. For these and other proposals in the Bill ▶see the box on pages 719-721.

Who is entitled to asylum support?

In order to be entitled to asylum support under either scheme, a person must be:

- an 'asylum seeker' or the 'dependant' of an asylum seeker; and
- 'destitute' or 'likely to become destitute'.

Who counts as an 'asylum seeker'?

An asylum-seeker for these purposes is a person who is:

- 18 years of age or older;
- has made a 'claim for asylum';
- the claim for asylum has been 'recorded' by the Secretary of State; and
- the claim for asylum has not been 'determined', unless there is a child in the asylum-seeker's household.

Each of these elements is considered in turn below. It should be noted that unaccompanied minor asylum-seekers are provided with support not by either of the asylum support schemes but by local authorities under the Children Act 1989 ▶see pages 685-687.

Claim for asylum

A 'claim for asylum' means a claim that it would be a breach of the UK's obligations under either the Refugee Convention or Article 3 ECHR for the person to be removed from or required to leave the UK. An Article 3 claim to asylum may entitle a person to support even where that person had previously exhausted all appeals against an earlier refusal of asylum under the 1951 Convention. Making claims under the Refugee Convention and under the ECHR is dealt with in detail in Section 3.

As to how the claim must be made, the case law of the Social Security Commissioners as to what amounts to a 'claim for asylum' for welfare benefit purposes indicates that it is not necessary to go through any formal process or to complete any particular forms (*CIS/4341/98*). They have also held that 'an indication of a desire to claim asylum is itself a claim for asylum' (*CIS/4439/98*, *CIS/3867/98*). For other purposes, immigration law has also recognised that what is necessary to amount to a 'claim for asylum' is to be seen very broadly. This is reflected in the internal instructions which state (API, Ch 1, s1, para 1.2):

'Many applications are made by applicants or representatives who specifically apply for asylum but this is not always the case. Not all applicants have an awareness of the UN Convention and it is not necessary for the terms "asylum" or "refugee" to be used'.

If a potential applicant expresses an unwillingness to return to his or her country of nationality or habitual residence because of some perceived danger, an asylum application must be deemed to have been made. If the reason is one clearly not covered by the Convention, this may be a reason for refusing the application in due course but the claim must be considered substantively.

Claim for asylum has been 'recorded by the Secretary of State'

It is necessary that the claim to asylum has been 'recorded by the Secretary of State'. There are no rules which define when a claim to asylum has been 'recorded'. There is some case law under the old social security benefit regulations concerning the slightly different question of when a claim to asylum is 'recorded by the Secretary of State as having been determined'. The effect of those cases is that, in order for such a 'record' to exist, there needs to a reliable document (*Karoui & Abbad*, High Court) constituting a clear decision that the claim has been determined, regardless of whether the applicant had been notified or not (*Salem*).

The case law of the Social Security Commissioners relating to the 'record' of a claim to asylum for benefit purposes, can also be applied to the recording of claims for asylum support purposes. In one case, a Commissioner held that there was 'no specified way in which a [claim for asylum] should be recorded' and used a letter from the Home Office in response to a complaint as to how a person had been treated on entry to the UK as either sufficient itself as a record of the claim or, alternatively, as secondary evidence of a Home Office record (*CIS/4439/98*). In another case, the Commissioner accepted that a record of the claim to asylum had been made during the course of a telephone conversation between the asylum applicant and an immigration officer before the applicant was subsequently issued with the Standard Acknowledgment Letter (SAL) (*CIS/3867/98*, and see *CIS/259/99*).

The most useful evidence of having made a claim for asylum to be able to present to a local authority or NASS in connection with support is clearly a SAL or an Application Registration Card which are currently replacing SALs.

Claim for asylum has not been determined

A person remains an 'asylum-seeker' for support purposes until the claim for asylum 'has been determined'. Unless there is a child dependant in the household (in which case ▶see below), the claim for asylum is treated as having been determined, and asylum support ceases, following a grace period after either:

• the Home Office notifies the applicant of the decision on the claim to asylum (this notice must be in writing); *or*, if the applicant appeals against the decision of the Home Office;

• the expiry of the time limit for applying to appeal further following the determination of the adjudicator.

If there are further appeals following the original one (i.e. to the IAT or Court of Appeal), the claim is treated as not determined throughout the appeals process.

The grace period, which is triggered when there is no longer either an application or an appeal or an ability to appeal again was initially set at 14 days. One of the purposes of having a period of grace was, in cases where the decision or appeal is successful, to enable the asylum-seeker to continue to be supported until they have been formally granted leave by the immigration authorities which allows them to access mainstream welfare support. However, there have been very serious delays in granting leave to successful appellants and, as a result, the Home Office extended the grace periods.

With effect from 8 April 2002, applicants continue to be entitled to asylum support for *28 days* following (see reg 3, Asylum Support (Amendment) Regulations 2002, and reg 4 Asylum Support (Interim Provisions) (Amendment) Regulations 2002):

• notification of a decision to grant asylum; or

• notification of a decision to refuse asylum but to grant exceptional leave; or

• the allowing of an appeal against the decision of the immigration authorities.

In all other cases, the grace period is *21 days*. These grace periods still provide a very short period compared to the delays which occur at the Home Office. Where an applicant is bringing a judicial review against a decision of the adjudicator or IAT after an unsuccessful appeal or application for leave to appeal to the IAT, there is no ongoing entitlement to asylum support. The grace periods are certainly not long enough to allow applicants to be supported during the time taken for judicial review and neither are they intended to. During this period, applicants should therefore consider making an application to NASS for 'hard cases' support which is basic accommodation and board ▶see pages 717-718.

Households including a child

If the asylum-seeker has within their household a child under the age of 18 who is their dependant, then entitlement to asylum support continues even after the asylum application and any appeal has been determined. It continues while the asylum-seeker remains in the UK or until the child becomes 18 or leaves the UK or the household. Provided these conditions are met, the child does not actually have to be the asylum-seeker's child. Because the Home Office is concerned that some asylum-seekers claim to be under 18 when they are not, the Home Office has a specific power to make enquires about and to decide the age of anyone who it is claimed is a child.

Who counts as the 'dependant' of an asylum-seeker?

Dependants of asylum-seekers are also entitled to asylum support. There are some minor differences in the definition of dependants for the two schemes. The box below sets out who counts as a dependant.

DEPENDANTS OF ASYLUM-SEEKERS

A person is the dependant of an asylum-seeker for the purposes of the interim scheme if the person they are claiming to be a dependant of is an 'asylum-seeker' as set out above and they are related or connected to the asylum-seeker in one of the following ways:

1 spouse of the asylum-seeker;

2 child of the asylum-seeker or a child of the spouse of the asylum-seeker who is both under 18 and dependent on the asylum-seeker;

3 a person who is under 18 and a member of the asylum-seeker or their spouse's 'close family', there is no definition provided for the meaning of 'close family';

4 a person who is under 18 and has been living as part of the asylum-seeker's household either for at least six of the 12 months before the claim for support was made or since birth;

5 a person who is in need of care and attention from the asylum-seeker or a member of their household by reason of a disability and either:
• they are a member of the asylum-seeker's or their spouse's close family; or
• they have been living as part of the asylum-seeker's household for six of the 12 months before the claim to support was made or since birth;

6 a person who has been living with the asylum-seeker as a member of an unmarried couple for at least two of the three years before the claim to support was made;

7 a person who is living with the asylum-seeker as part of their household and who was receiving assistance from a local authority under section17 of the Children Act immediately before 6 December 1999;

8 a person who is being treated by the Home Office as the dependant of an asylum-seeker for the purposes of the asylum claim. Under the immigration rules, only the spouse and minor children of asylum-seekers are considered as dependants on the asylum claim but the immigration authorities have a discretion to treat other family members as dependants (▶see pages 192-193);

9 where it is the dependant of an asylum-seeker who has claimed support, the person is the asylum-seeker.

A person is a dependant of an asylum-seeker under the NASS scheme if they fall into any of the above categories with the following minor differences:
• in categories 2, 3 and 4 above a person counts as a dependant if they are under 18 or they were under 18 either:

- at the time the application for support for them was made; or
- if they joined the asylum-seeker in the UK while they were already here, at the time when they joined them;

- in category 6, a person qualifies if they were living with the asylum-seeker as an unmarried couple for at least two of the three years before the time when the application for support was made *or* the date they joined the asylum-seeker in the UK. Also in this category, in the NASS scheme an 'unmarried couple' is given a definition: a man and woman who, though not married to each other, are living together as if married. No definition is provided for 'unmarried' couple in the interim scheme and so it could be argued that a same-sex partner, where the couple are living together in a relationship akin to marriage, would qualify as a dependant under the interim scheme;

- *in addition* to the categories referred to for the interim scheme, a person qualifies as a dependant under the NASS scheme if they are living as a part of the asylum-seeker's household and, immediately before 3 April 2000, they were receiving support from a local authority in Scotland or Ireland under the equivalent provisions of the Children Act. This is because the interim scheme, unlike the NASS scheme, never applied in Scotland and Ireland and so this category is intended to ensure that dependants in Scotland and Ireland are provided for by NASS rather than by social services.

If a person falls into the above categories, they qualify as a dependant. They do not need to satisfy any additional tests showing, for example, that they are emotionally or financially dependent on the asylum-seeker (*Dirrshe,* High Court).

'Destitute' or likely shortly to become 'destitute'

In order to obtain support under either scheme, asylum-seekers and their dependants have to be either destitute or likely shortly to become destitute.

A person is destitute if either:

- they do not have 'adequate accommodation' or any means of getting adequate accommodation; or

- they have adequate accommodation or the means of getting it but cannot meet their other 'essential living needs'.

For the rules about what can and cannot be taken into account in determining whether a person has adequate accommodation or can meet their essential living needs ▶see pages 697-699 (NASS support) and page 708 (interim support). The 2002 Bill proposes to change the definition of destitution ▶see page 719.

Which asylum-seekers get NASS support and which asylum-seekers get interim support?

There has been much confusion over which asylum-seekers and their dependants are entitled to apply for interim support and which asylum-seekers and their dependants are entitled to apply for the support provided by NASS. The main reason for this confusion is that the 1999 Act itself does not say who is entitled to which and neither do the regulations.

The division of responsibility between NASS and local authorities is set out in a series of 'directions' given by the Home Office under the 1999 Act which are summarised in the box below. The effect of the directions is to treat the 'interim period' as having come to an end for certain classes of asylum-seeker. Under current law, those who became entitled to interim support, will remain entitled to interim support rather than NASS support for as long as they remain asylum-seekers for support purposes, or until the end of the interim period, which is now set to end on 5 April 2004.

NASS SUPPORT OR INTERIM SUPPORT?

Those who fall into any of the categories below are entitled to NASS rather than interim asylum support.

1 **Post 2 April 2000 port or 'declaration' asylum-seekers; Oakington Reception Centre detainees; cases in Scotland and Northern Ireland**

From 3 April 2000, the following asylum-seekers were ineligible for interim support but able to apply for NASS support.

(a) People who apply for asylum on or after 3 April 2000 who either claim asylum:
- on their arrival in the UK; or
- within three months of a declaration by the Home Office that their country of origin is subject to such a fundamental change of circumstances that the Home Office would not normally order their return to that country (there have been no further 'declarations' since the ones made concerning the Democratic Republic of Congo on 16 May 1997 and Sierra Leone on 1 July 1997).

(b) Persons who make a claim to asylum other than in (a) above (i.e., those who claim in-country) on or after 3 April 2000 and who are, any time after making that claim, detained at Oakington Reception Centre.

(c) Persons who claim asylum in-country on or after 3 April 2000 and are living in Scotland or Northern Ireland (the interim support scheme never applied in those places so the government was keen to introduce the NASS scheme as soon as possible).

2 **Pre 3 April 2000 port or declaration refused asylum-seekers**
People who made claims to asylum before 3 April 2000, either on arrival or within three months of a declaration of fundamental change, and who had their claim to asylum recorded as decided by the Secretary of State on or after 25 September 2000. This category is often described as 'dis-benefitted' asylum-seekers because

until such time as their claim for asylum is determined, they were able to obtain social security benefits.

Special arrangements were made for 'disbenefitted' asylum-seekers in Kent or Medway to ensure NASS had responsibility for them after 17 April 2000.

3 In-country asylum seekers

Those who make in-country applications for asylum after the relevant date for the region in which they were living are entitled to NASS rather than interim asylum support. The relevant dates for the different regions are shown below. All the local authorities in England and Wales are covered in the regions given.

Area	Relevant date
Kent and Medway	17 April 2000
London	24 July 2000
North East, Yorkshire, Humberside, Wales	31 July 2000
North West, East Midlands, Eastern, South West and South Central	14 August 2000
West Midlands and Sussex	29 August 2000

Who remains eligible for interim asylum support?

All *new* asylum-seekers are now entitled to obtain NASS rather than interim support, whether they claimed on arrival, within three months of a declaration of fundamental change or in-country. The persons who are still entitled to get interim support rather than social security benefits or NASS support are the following:

1 asylum-seekers who claimed asylum before 3 April 2000 at port, or within three months of a declaration of upheaval and who were recorded as having their claim to asylum determined by the Secretary of State before 25 September 2000, except those who were living in Kent or Medway who received their decisions on or after 17 April 2000;

2 asylum-seekers who claimed asylum in-country at any time before the relevant date (▶see above) for the region in which they were living;

3 asylum-seekers with dependent children who, under the above rules, have been entitled to interim support and who make a further asylum application. These asylum-seeking families remain the responsibility of local authorities.

NASS asylum support

The National Asylum Support Service (NASS) is a part of the Home Office. Although it has responsibility for ensuring that certain destitute asylum-seekers are provided for, it does not have to provide support directly itself. NASS support can also be provided by local authorities by arrangement with NASS or by local authorities together with other private contractors in 'consortia' or by companies formed by local authorities.

Much of the detail of the NASS scheme is set out in the Asylum Support Regulations 2000. Further practical and policy details about the scheme are contained in NASS Policy Bulletins which can downloaded from websites such as www.asylumsupport.info or the Home Office website.

Important examples, are the Policy Bulletins dealing with:

- 'mixed households', namely, where some members of the family are entiled to other forms of support such as welfare benefits or housing (Bulletin 11);

- allegations of racial and other harassment and domestic violence (Bulletin 18);

- dispersal policy (Bulletin 31);

- maternity payments (Bulletin 37);

- dispersal of pregnant women (Bulletin 61);

- arrangements for 'dis-benefitted' cases, namely those in which the asylum-seekers ceased to be entitled to welfare benefits (Bulletins 27, 51–53);

- essential travel costs (Bulletin 56);

- travel, and cases where people have failed to travel to dispersal accommodation (Bulletins 17, 25, 28 and 57);

- applications for support from those who are detained (Bulletin 64);

- travel expenses to asylum or asylum support hearings, interviews, Medical Foundation appointments for those receiving temporary NASS support (Bulletin 66);

- how NASS recovers overpayments (Bulletin 67).

Determining destitution under the NASS scheme

For the basic conditions for obtaining asylum support ▶see page 690. In short, to be entitled, a person must be a 'destitute' asylum-seeker, or the dependant of an asylum-seeker whose claim has not been 'determined' under the above rules (together with the exception relating to cases where there is a child in the asylum-seeker's household). If a group applies together, NASS will consider whether the group taken as a whole are destitute or likely to become destitute.

Factors in determining whether a person has adequate accommodation and can meet their essential living needs

In considering whether an applicant does have adequate accommodation and whether they can meet their essential living needs, NASS takes into account:

- any income which the applicant or their dependants have or may reasonably be expected to have;

- any other support which is available, or which may reasonably be expected to be available to the applicant or their dependants; and

- any of the following assets which are available to them or which they might reasonably be expected to have available: cash, savings, investments, land, vehicles, goods for trade or business.

The government intends that the above might include support from friends and relatives in the UK or from voluntary sector organisations. NASS must, however, not count any assets which are not in the list above. The notes which accompany the NASS 1 application form state that NASS will ignore items of jewellery, personal clothing, bedding and medical or optical items (e.g., wheelchairs). However, NASS requires applicants to state in the application form for support any items of jewellery or watches belonging to them and their dependants which are worth over £1,000 at the current market value, and to inform NASS immediately if any of those items are subsequently sold and how much they were sold for. The intention is that NASS may then take into account the money received as a result of the sale.

Further factors in deciding whether a person can meet their essential living needs

Whether a person has the means to obtain items such as food, toiletries, and clothing, is relevant in determining whether they can meet their essential needs for living. In deciding whether a person's needs are met regarding clothing, NASS cannot take into account personal preferences regarding clothing but it can take into account a person's 'individual circumstances' regarding clothing.

Further factors in deciding whether a person has adequate accommodation

Where an applicant already has some form of accommodation, NASS must decide whether the existing accommodation is 'adequate'. In deciding whether accommodation is 'adequate', NASS must take into account whether:

- it is 'reasonable' for the applicant to continue to occupy the accommodation;
- it is affordable;
- the applicant can gain entry to the accommodation;
- if the accommodation is a house-boat, a caravan or some other moveable structure which may be lived in, whether the applicant has a place where they can lawfully place it;
- whether the applicant will be able to live in the accommodation together with their dependants; and
- whether the applicant is likely to suffer harassment, threats or violence if they continue to live in the accommodation.

There are also certain matters which cannot be taken into account in determining whether a person has adequate accommodation. These are:

- that the applicant does not have a legal right to stay in the accommodation, although NASS will not consider that the accommodation is adequate if the applicant has actually been required to leave the accommodation, for example, by the owner or as a result of a court order for possession;

- that the accommodation (or part of it) is shared with others;
- that the accommodation is temporary; and
- the location of the accommodation.

What support is provided under the NASS scheme?

NASS can provide support in any of the following ways:

- support to meet essential living needs;
- accommodation which is adequate for the asylum-seeker and their dependants;
- expenses, other than legal expenses, which the asylum-seeker has in connection with the asylum claim;
- expenses that the asylum-seeker has or their dependants have in attending bail hearings;
- services in the form of education, English language lessons, sporting and other developmental activities;
- if the circumstances of the particular case are exceptional, any other form of support which NASS thinks is necessary.

These forms of support are considered further below. In deciding the level and kind of support which it will make available to an asylum-seeker, NASS will take into account similar factors as are relevant in deciding destitution: income or support which the applicant has or might reasonably be expected to have and assets such as cash, savings, investments, land, vehicles, goods for trade or business. NASS is also entitled to take account of whether the applicant has breached any conditions on which support has been or is being provided. NASS can disregard any preference which the asylum-seeker has as to how to provide for or to arrange the provision of support.

Excluded items

Certain items are excluded from being provided as essential living needs by the Asylum Support Regulations. They are (see reg 9 (4)):

- the cost of sending or receiving faxes, photocopying or buying or using computer facilities;
- travelling expenses (except for expenses in travelling to take up accommodation but ▶see page 703);
- toys and other recreational items; and entertainment expenses.

Providing for essential living needs

When the scheme originally came into force, under the 1999 Act, NASS had to provide the majority of a person's support other than by providing them with cash. Following the government's internal review of the support system, and in particular the effectiveness of voucher support, that provision of the 1999 Act was repealed from 8 April 2002 (see Asylum Support (Repeal) Order 2002).

In addition, the Asylum Support Regulations 2000 (reg 10(6)) themselves initially laid down that, as a general rule, NASS support would involve a person getting vouchers exchangeable for *cash* only to the extent of £10.00 per week per person. That rule has also been abolished and the standard amounts that are to be provided to each asylum-seeker and any dependants is now stated to be 'in the form of vouchers redeemable for cash' (see reg 4, Asylum Support (Amendment) Regulations 2002).

While for the time being vouchers may be given which can be exchanged for cash, the government has stated that it intends to phase vouchers out altogether by the end of 2002.

NASS ASYLUM SUPPORT RATES

Person/s	Amount
Married or unmarried couple at least one of whom is 18 or over but where neither is under 16:	£59.26
Lone parent aged 18 or over:	£37.77
Single person aged 25 or over:	£37.77
Single person aged at least 18 but under 25:	£29.89
Person aged at least 16 but under 18 (except a member of a married or unmarried couple as referred to above):	£32.50
Person aged under 16:	£33.50

The amounts are about 70 per cent of income support levels which the Home Office justifies on the grounds that asylum-seekers will have the costs of their utility bills, council tax and certain other expenses already met through the provision of accommodation.

In the above table:
- to count as a married couple, the couple must be a man and a woman who are married to each other and who are members of the same household;
- to count as an unmarried couple, the couple must be a man and a woman who, although not married, are living together as though they are married;
- a 'lone parent' is a person who is not a part of a married or unmarried couple who is the parent of a child who is under 18 and support is being provided for that child;
- a 'single person' is a person who is not either a member of a married or unmarried couple or the parent of a child under 18 for whom support is being provided.

Additional Single Payments
In addition to the above, after every period of six months during which asylum support has been provided, every supported person is entitled to an additional 'single payment'. This was previously provided in the form of vouchers exchangeable for cash to the value of £50.00. From 8 April 2002, it can be made as a cash payment of £50.00. An application to NASS should be made in order to obtain the additional cash payment.

Part of the reasons for having single payments is to acknowledge that the resolution of the asylum application, including any appeal, has been delayed beyond Home

Office targets. However, if in NASS's view the applicant is, without reasonable excuse, responsible for the delay in determining the claim for asylum, NASS may extend any of the six-month periods by the period caused by the applicant's delays.

Maternity Payments

A single, one-off payment to the value of £300 may be made to asylum-seekers who are being supported by NASS to help with the costs of a new born baby (see NASS Policy Bulletin 37). Generally, an application must be made in writing to NASS between a month before the estimated date of delivery and two weeks after the birth. If the application is being made after the birth, the birth certificate should be submitted, otherwise medical evidence of the estimated delivery date should be provided.

As a general rule, the total weekly amount provided through NASS will be as set out in the box above. The amounts shown in the box were uprated from 8 April 2002 in line with increases in the rates of income support.

It should be noted that the amounts shown in the table above may be reduced if NASS is providing accommodation as part of the support package and included with the accommodation is some provision for essential living needs, for example, if bed and breakfast is provided. At present, it is possible to obtain support for essential living needs only but this 'voucher only' option may not be possible following proposed changes under the 2002 Bill.

Providing accommodation – 'dispersal'

The ability of NASS to make arrangements with other agencies for the provision of support rather than providing support directly is a crucial part of the dispersal scheme. It enables NASS to arrange for local authorities and others up and down the country to provide support. The 2002 Bill will enable the provision of NASS support in 'accommodation centres' (▶see box on pages 719-721). Trial centres will be opened in the first instance and, depending upon their viability, accommodation centres may become the main form of NASS accommodation rather than dispersal to the various different 'cluster' areas which the government has so far developed. At least in the initial stages, however, accommodation centres and the existing dispersal scheme will operate alongside each other.

Under the dispersal scheme, in deciding upon the location and nature of the accommodation, NASS has regard to:

- the fact that accommodation is only being provided temporarily during the period of the asylum claim; and
- the desirability of providing accommodation for asylum-seekers in those areas where there is a good supply of accommodation, for example, areas outside London. It is the government's view that there is an acute shortage of accommodation in the London area.

In making the decision about where an asylum-seeker is to be located, NASS is not entitled to take into account any of the following matters:

- the area in which the asylum-seeker wishes to be accommodated;
- the nature of the accommodation which is to be provided; and
- the nature and standard of the fixtures and fittings in the accommodation.

However, despite this, in deciding where and what kind of accommodation will be provided, NASS can still take into account the asylum seeker's 'individual circumstances' as they relate to their accommodation needs (see reg 13(2) Asylum Support Regulations). For example, in a case decided under the similar provisions of the interim scheme, *Mahdia*, the High Court held that location close to a mosque was not just a matter of choice or preference but was connected to the applicant's religious and emotional needs and was therefore relevant to their 'welfare'. According to the notes which accompany the form on which NASS support can be applied for, a person's relevant individual circumstances include:

- their ethnic group and/or religion. NASS should identify an area where there is an existing community of people of similar culture together with support organisations which are sensitive to the asylum-seeker's cultural background and needs;
- the applicant's medical or psychological conditions or any disabilities which they have and any treatment they are receiving for those conditions; and
- any special dietary needs of the asylum-seeker and their dependants.

NASS policy generally is to disperse asylum-seekers to accommodation outside London and the South East of the country. However, according to NASS Policy Bulletin 31 ('dispersal guidelines'), NASS may be persuaded not to disperse a person if:

- they have family connections of an exceptional nature which make dispersal inappropriate; or
- they have children who have been resident in the area for 12 months or more and attending school or pre-school classes during that time; or
- the area where the asylum-seeker is residing is the only area in which they can properly worship.

The above examples are all stated by NASS to be circumstances in which the asylum-seeker's human rights would be infringed by dispersal; in particular the right to respect for family life and home, the right not to be denied an education and the right to freedom of religion. NASS has also indicated that it will be sympathetic to cases where the applicant has been accepted for treatment by the Medical Foundation for the Care of Victims of Torture which is in London (NASS Policy Bulletins 19–21).

Where a person is being dispersed, after a period of temporary or 'emergency' NASS accommodation, it is likely that a condition of the support will be that the asylum-seeker travels to the new accommodation so that people may lose support if they fail to travel. There have been serious and well-documented cases of people who have left dispersed accommodation because they have been the victims of racial harassment and domestic violence. A person can be excluded (▶see below) from further NASS support if they leave their NASS accommodation but this is not automatic; NASS will consider whether there is evidence that someone has been the victim of an assault or there is good reason to believe that they may be.

People can also be excluded on grounds of breaching conditions of their support in failing to travel back to accommodation provided by NASS. In deciding whether asylum-seekers have a reasonable excuse for breaching conditions in these circumstances, the asylum support adjudicators (ASA) have stated that the degree, frequency, persistence and organisation of any harassment and its effect on the asylum-seeker are all relevant. They have also indicated that the effectiveness of the local police in dealing with harassment is relevant.

Expenses in connection with asylum claims

NASS can meet expenses which are connected with an asylum claim. These expenses do not include 'legal' expenses so NASS would not, for example, meet the costs of paying a lawyer to prepare the case and represent the applicant. These can be met through the Community Legal Service ▶see Chapter 3, as can travel to meet with a legal representative. Included expenses may be travel expenses in attending appeals or medical or other examinations in connection with a claim or attending immigration interviews. They also might include expenses such as preparing and copying documents and sending letters and faxes in order to obtain further evidence. Travel costs to attend bail hearings are expressly covered. It will be noted that there is a clash between items which appear to be covered under this head and certain items which are expressly excluded (▶see page 699 above).

Services

In terms of services, NASS is able to provide both education (including English language lessons) and sporting or other development activities. These services are not necessarily provided automatically to those receiving NASS support but can be provided in order to 'maintain good order' among supported asylum-seekers.

Exclusions from NASS support

The following people may be excluded from getting NASS support.

1 People not excluded from getting welfare benefits (income support, income-based job-seekers' allowance, housing benefit and council tax

benefit) by their immigration status (►see 'Exceptions to "Subject to immigration control" test' box on pages 665-667 for those who can get these benefits even though they are 'subject to immigration control').

2 People who are not being treated as the dependants of asylum-seekers for immigration purposes.

3 People applying as part of a group where every person in the group is excluded under (1) or (2) above, or on the basis that they are able to get interim support.

4 People who are reasonably suspected of having breached the conditions upon which support was given. The conditions must be given in writing. Conditions may, for example, be given that the asylum-seeker does not sub-let the accommodation.

5 People who are reasonably suspected of having committed a criminal offence connected with asylum support. Criminal offences in relation to asylum support include giving false information, failing to notify to NASS of a change in circumstances relevant to the support provided, obstructing NASS in administering the scheme, failing to provide information when required, and failing to maintain a person in respect of whom the applicant gave a maintenance undertaking.

6 People who are reasonably suspected of having 'intentionally' made themselves and their dependants destitute. A person is intentionally destitute if they, or any of their dependants, do or fail to do something, without reasonable excuse, which leads to them becoming destitute.

7 People who are absent from their address provided by NASS (or if not provided with NASS accommodation, the address notified to the immigration authorities as the place where they are living – normally the address where the applicant will be living as a condition of temporary admission) for seven days and nights in a row, or for more than 14 days and nights in any six-month period, without the permission of NASS.

8 People who have stopped living at their address (as in (7) above) permanently.

The persons listed in categories 1–3 above *cannot* be provided with NASS support. NASS has a discretion whether to exclude a person from support if they fall into categories 4-8 above. In addition, for people in categories 4-8 it is not automatic that support is ended indefinitely as NASS may either 'discontinue' or 'suspend' the support. For example, NASS could decide to suspend the provision of support on the basis of a 'reasonable suspicion' of the conduct referred to in categories 4-6 until such time as it can confirm its suspicions or it is satisfied that they should not in fact be excluded.

Procedures for getting NASS support

The NASS scheme incorporates the services of various voluntary sector agencies – the Refugee Arrivals Project, Migrant Helpline, Refugee Action, the Refugee Council and the Scottish and Welsh Refugee Councils – in order to help identify applicants for support and to assist them in making their applications and producing relevant information to NASS. They are referred to as 'assistants' and temporary NASS support (►see below), in particular, is provided through them.

The application

NASS support is applied for using the 'NASS1' form which is attached to the Asylum Support Regulations or available from the above assistants who should help the asylum-seeker to complete it. Only one form needs to be used for an applicant and their dependants. If a person wishes to obtain support as the dependant of a person who is already being supported by NASS, it is not necessary to complete the application form again; NASS will consider providing additional support for that person if they are notified of their existence.

There are detailed notes attached to the Asylum Support Regulations which give further information about procedures and also give guidance about how to fill out the form. The form asks for details of the asylum-seeker and their dependants. If a person is applying as the dependant of an asylum-seeker, the form asks for details of the asylum-seeker themselves and their other dependants. The form also asks for details of the stage which the asylum claim has reached, the kind of support needed, details of current accommodation, any other kind of support which the applicant has (including support from friends or relatives, cash, savings, investments or other property, employment, state benefits), and also about any disabilities or special needs.

The details of any assistant from the voluntary organisations or a solicitor or other representative who helped to make the application should also be given on the form. In relation to many of the details asked, NASS requires documents to confirm what has been stated. It also requires four passport-size photographs of the person applying for support. In order to save time and for the application to be considered as soon as possible, the form can be sent to NASS by fax, otherwise it can be sent by post. If the form is sent by fax, the original is also to be sent by post ►see page 725 for NASS's fax number. NASS may then make further enquiries of the applicant in connection with any of the details contained in the application form.

Awaiting the decision from NASS

There are no time limits in the regulations which require that NASS make a decision within any particular time although it is intended that NASS makes a decision within two working days of receiving the application. However, in practice it often takes much longer than this. If no decision has been made within seven days of making the application, NASS should write to the applicant explaining the delay.

Temporary or 'emergency' NASS support

While the applicant is waiting for NASS to make a decision on the application, the applicant should be provided with temporary NASS support which will normally be provided directly by one of the assistants referred to above although it is actually paid for by NASS. The legislation states that temporary support may be provided to an asylum-seeker or the dependant of an asylum-seeker who it appears may be destitute. As with full NASS support, temporary support can be provided subject to conditions given in writing. If NASS refuses support, temporary support ends at the same time. There are no rules setting out what can and cannot be provided for by temporary support. Support should clearly be appropriate to the emergency needs of the asylum-seeker and their dependants.

NASS decision

If NASS decides to provide support, it will write to tell the applicant that the application has been accepted and to inform them of the package of support which will be provided. Although there are no rules requiring NASS to give reasons for its decisions, a brief explanation is usually given for a refusal and NASS will inform the person of any appeal rights ▶see pages 712-717. If support is being provided by way of accommodation and vouchers/cash rather than 'voucher'-only support, the applicant will be notified about the place where the accommodation is located and any arrangements for travel to dispersal locations.

Support is subject to conditions which must be stated in writing. If the asylum-seeker is being dispersed, one condition is normally that they attend at the relevant time and place to travel to the accommodation. Other conditions may concern practical arrangements about using the accommodation itself. Breach of conditions may lead to withdrawal of support.

National Health Service prescriptions/dental treatment/sight tests

If the application for support is accepted, NASS will also issue the applicant with a certificate (HC2) enabling them to get free NHS prescriptions, dental treatment, sight tests and wigs. It may also be possible to get vouchers towards the cost of glasses and contact lenses and money back on the costs of travel to and from hospital for NHS treatment. The HC2 certificate itself tells the applicant how it can be used and what it can be used for. If the applicant has already paid for any of the above items or travel, they may be able to claim the money back. There is a table attached to the end of the notes to the Asylum Support Regulations which explains what the applicant needs to do in order to claim back the expenses for each of the different items.

Changes of circumstances

Those who are provided with support must notify NASS of relevant changes of circumstance. Relevant changes are if either the asylum-seeker or their dependants:

- are joined in the UK by a dependant;
- receive or get access to any money or savings, investments, land, cars or other vehicles, goods for the purposes of trade or other business which have not previously been declared to NASS;
- become employed;
- become unemployed;
- change their name;
- get married;
- begin living with another person as their spouse;
- get divorced;
- separate from a spouse or from a person with whom they have been living as if married to that person;
- become pregnant;
- have a child;
- leave school;
- begin to share their accommodation with another person;
- move to a different address or otherwise leave the accommodation;
- go into hospital;
- are sent to to prison or some other form of custody;
- leave the UK;
- die.

After NASS has obtained all the necessary information about any change, it may make a decision changing the nature or level of the existing support or withdrawing support.

Further applications for support and appeals

If an applicant is refused support, in most cases there is nothing to prevent them from making another application at any time and NASS must consider any application which is made. The only circumstances in which the rules allow NASS not to 'entertain' an application for support are if it is not made by properly completing the application form, or where a person has previously had their support suspended or discontinued, or where a further application for support is made after an appeal to the ASA is dismissed. In the last two cases, NASS must still consider a further application for support if there has been a material change in circumstances.

Interim asylum support

The interim scheme for the support of asylum-seekers by local authorities came into effect on 6 December 1999. It was intended as a temporary measure until the NASS scheme could be applied to all asylum-seekers. The scheme was intended to end in April 2002 but has in fact been extended to April 2004. Asylum-seekers who are the responsibility of local authorities under the interim scheme (►see the box on pages 695-696 for which asylum-seekers are entitled to interim rather than NASS support) will remain their responsibility until that time. It is possible, of course, that the Secretary of State will issue further 'directions' before April 2004 with the effect of transferring certain groups of asylum-seekers to NASS before that time.

The interim scheme does not extend to Scotland or Northern Ireland and asylum-seekers in those areas were able to continue to obtain support from social services until the introduction of the NASS scheme in April 2000. The local authorities which can be required to provide support are therefore:

- in England – a county council, metropolitan district council, a district council, a London Borough Council, the Common Council of the City of London and the Council of the Isles of Scilly;
- in Wales – a county council or a county borough council.

Unlike under the NASS scheme, there is no right of appeal against refusals to provide interim support or withdrawals of support. The only legal means of challenging decisions of local authorities about decisions concerning support is by judicial review.

Deciding whether a person qualifies for interim support

Because it is only intended as a temporary measure, the interim scheme is much less detailed than the NASS scheme. The basic conditions which need to be satisfied, namely, that a person must be a destitute asylum-seeker or the dependant of an asylum-seeker, are the same ►see page 690. As well as the provisions in the 1999 Act, the interim scheme is regulated by the Asylum Support (Interim Provisions) Regulations 1999.

There are no special or additional rules under the interim scheme for what should be taken into account in deciding whether a person can meet their essential living needs. In determining whether a person has adequate accommodation, no account can be taken of:

- the fact that they do not have a legal right to stay in that accommodation;
- the fact that they share the accommodation or part of it with other persons;
- the fact that the accommodation is temporary; or
- the location of the accommodation.

Providing interim support

If an applicant is entitled to interim support, the local authority is required to provide:

- accommodation which is adequate for the asylum-seeker and their dependants (if any);
- support to meet the essential living needs of the asylum-seeker and their dependants; and
- if the person is an asylum-seeker, support to meet their reasonable travel expenses in attending the hearing of their asylum appeal and any interview concerning their claim to asylum which has been requested by the immigration authorities.

Providing both accommodation and support for essential living needs

Under the regulations, the local authority must provide both accommodation and support to meet an asylum-seeker's essential living needs. Only if the circumstances of a particular case are 'exceptional', can support be provided in terms of *either* accommodation *or* support to meet essential living needs (see reg 5(4) Asylum Support (Interim Provisions) Regulations 1999). In addition, where the circumstances are 'exceptional', the authority is not restricted to the forms of support set out above but is to provide support in any way 'necessary' in order for a person and their dependants to be 'supported'.

It doesn't seem to make any sense for an authority to be restricted like this although this is also the position under section 21 of the National Assistance Act 1948 which, before the interim scheme came into force, had been the mainstay of support for asylum-seekers where benefits were not available. The government is now considering extending this restrictive regime to the NASS system.

Where however a person is eligible for interim support and their household includes a child who is under 18 and is their dependant, the local authority is not restricted in the same way and can provide either accommodation or support for essential living needs or both.

Deciding on the level of support and where it is provided

In deciding what should be provided in terms of accommodation and essential living needs, the local authority must have regard to:

- the income which the asylum-seeker has or may reasonably be expected to have;
- assets which the asylum-seeker has or which might reasonably be expected to be available to them;
- the welfare of the asylum-seeker; and
- the cost of providing support.

As with the NASS support scheme, the arrangements under the interim scheme were amended from 8 April 2002 to remove the requirement in the regulations that asylum-seekers can only be provided support by way of cash of up to £10.00 per person each week (see reg 5, Asylum Support (Interim Provisions) (Amendment) Regulations 2002). Authorities may now provide all such support in cash.

Unlike under the NASS scheme, however, there are no set rates for the levels of support that should be provided to asylum-seekers. Comparison may be made with NASS rates in order to determine the levels which can be expected, although it should be remembered that the table of rates assumes that NASS are paying for the household bills and that there will be a £50.00 per person additional payment every six months. The High Court case of *Bajric* is useful for demonstrating that the levels of support provided under the interim scheme should not be greatly different from under the NASS scheme. The judge stated:

'...although there are now two schemes in operation, they are both under the same principal Act and both aim to achieve the same legislative purpose, and there cannot be anything in the suggestion that consideration of the two schemes should give rise to different results in respect of otherwise identical cases only to be distinguished by the day when a person became entitled as an asylum-seeker to benefit'.

In providing accommodation, the authority cannot take into account a person's expressed preferences as to the location or nature of the accommodation. As with the NASS scheme, however, this does not mean that the local authority can ignore the asylum-seeker's interests in deciding where to accommodate them. This is because the local authority, in providing any form of support, is bound to have regard to the welfare of the supported person and their dependants (see reg 6(1)(c) Asylum Support (Interim Provisions) Regulations 1999). It may well be that the welfare of the individual claimant can only be properly safeguarded if they are located near to appropriate medical facilities, certain other family members or the school to which the children of the household have been admitted and have already settled.

The accommodation which is provided must be 'adequate'. When this phrase has been interpreted by the Immigration Appeal Tribunal for the purposes of the immigration rules, it has been determined that it must be accommodation which is not statutorily over-crowded nor unfit for human habitation within the meaning of housing law. We suggest that it is not sufficient for the authority to simply meet these tests because the wording of the regulations is that the accommodation must be adequate 'for the needs of the assisted person'. This means that the local authority must address any individual or particular need which the asylum-seeker has.

Exclusions from interim asylum support

Even if they meet the basic conditions, asylum-seekers and their dependants may be excluded from asylum support under the scheme if they:

1 have made themselves 'intentionally destitute'. This is the case if they are destitute as a result of a deliberate act or failure to do something without any reasonable excuse;

2 have made a claim for support to another local authority (unless the claim for support is 'transferred' from the first authority to the second one, ▶see below);

3 are claiming support from a local authority which is different from a local authority to which they have made a claim to support in the previous year for assistance under section 21 of the National Assistance Act 1948 or section 17 of the Children Act 1989;

4 are not prevented from getting income support as a result of their immigration status ▶see 'Exceptions' box on pages 665-667;

5 are not an asylum-seeker or are not being treated by the Home Office as the dependent of an asylum-seeker;

6 fail to comply with the conditions on which the support is provided;

7 leave the accommodation in which support is provided for more than seven days.

Categories 6 and 7 apply to people who have already been granted asylum support by the local authority. For either of these categories, even if all of the conditions for excluding a person from support are satisfied, including there being no 'reasonable excuse' for the breach of condition or leaving the accommodation, the authority still has a *discretion* whether to exclude them from support. In addition, for these two categories, it is not automatic that support is ended indefinitely as the local authority may either 'discontinue' or 'suspend' the support. For example, an authority might suspend the provision of support until the asylum-seeker has put the breach of conditions right or returned to the accommodation.

If a person falls into any of the other categories of exclusion, the local authority has no discretion, it 'must' refuse support.

Procedures for getting interim support

The interim support regulations themselves do not provide any particular procedures for applying for and getting support or for how decisions relating to entitlement to support should be reviewed. Many asylum-seekers are referred to the authority by an adviser or representative. The asylum support teams within local authorities have largely been connected to social services departments. It is probable that a local authority has a duty to assess those who come to its attention and who may qualify for support to determine whether they are eligible.

While an authority is making a decision on the application, it should provide adequate temporary support. Unlike in the NASS scheme, there are no rights of appeal to an independent body against decisions refusing to grant or terminating interim support. It is, therefore, essential that local authorities proceed with care and thoroughness in making these decisions.

There are no regulations dealing with how the support provided may be reviewed owing to a change in a person's circumstances after they have been awarded support. However, it is implicit that an authority may review a person's situation if there is a change in circumstances, for example, if the asylum-seeker obtains employment.

Transferring claims for support

In certain circumstances, the local authority to which the claim for support is made may transfer the claim for support to another local authority. The local authority to which the claim is transferred then has the responsibility for determining whether the asylum-seeker is eligible for support and for providing support if they are eligible.

The circumstances in which local authorities are able to transfer claims for support are not set out in the regulations themselves but instead the local authorities are able to make their own agreed arrangements for the circumstances in which they may transfer. Because no new asylum-seekers are now the responsibility of local authorities under the interim scheme, these transfers will now generally have already taken place. The agreement reached by local authorities complemented the general NASS policy of dispersing asylum-seekers away from London and the South East wherever possible.

Asylum support appeals

Rights of appeal

There are no rights of appeal against interim support decisions and there are only limited rights of appeal against NASS decisions. A person may appeal if:

- after they have made an application for asylum support, NASS decides that they are not entitled to any support at all; or
- NASS decides to stop providing all asylum support to them.

In relation to any other decision relating to asylum support or any decision relating to interim support, the only other means of legally challenging the decision will be by judicial review. The right of appeal is to the asylum support adjudicators (ASA) who are based at Christopher Wren House in South London. Further information about how they operate can be obtained from their website (asylum-support-adjudicators.org.uk) which also contains copies of all of the decisions made by the adjudicators. Any appellant who wishes to contact the ASA about their appeal or to get further information about the appeals process can contact them on their freephone number: 0800 3897913.

The number of appeals dealt with by the ASA, is much less than those heard by the Immigration Appellate Authority which hears immigration and asylum appeals. The number of appeals is still, however, significant. According to the ASA's figures, they received 896 appeals in the three months from January to March 2002.

Appeal procedures

The appeal procedures operated by the ASA (and referred to below) are set out in the Asylum Support Appeals (Procedure) Rules 2000. The emphasis of these rules is to deal with appeals with the minimum of delay. The appeal procedures set out in the rules are not detailed but the adjudicator has a general power to give directions on matters connected with the appeal where the adjudicator considers that it is in the interests of justice to do so.

The time-table for the various stages of the hearing and determination of appeals is summarised in the box below. It should be noted that there is currently a review of the Procedure Rules taking place and it may be that

---

TIME TABLE FOR NASS APPEALS

Day	Event
Day 1	Notice of appealable decision is received by asylum-seeker (the appellant)
Day 3 (latest)	Notice of appeal must be received by ASA
Day 3 or Day 4	ASA faxes notice of appeal to NASS
Day 4	Assuming NASS fax notice of appeal on Day 3, NASS send appeal bundle to ASA by fax/hand and to appellant by first class post or by hand
Day 5	ASA: • decides whether to hold an oral hearing; • gives notice of details of any oral hearing; • if no oral hearing is to be held, if possible, ASA proceeds to determine the appeal' • if there is no oral hearing and the appeal is determined, the asylum-seeker and NASS are sent both the notice of decision and the statement of reasons for the decision
Day 9	Oral hearing is held; the appeal is determined straight after the hearing. ASA notifies the decision to the appellant and NASS at the hearing or if they are not present, sends notice to appellant or NASS of the decision

Day	Event
	Last day for determining the appeal if no oral hearing
	ASA sends the notice of decision and statement of reasons for the decision to the appellant and NASS
Day 11	Last day for ASA to send the stateiment of reasons for the decision to the appellant and NASS if an oral hearing was held

Note that, in applying the above table and the description of the procedures which follows below, it is important to remember that the following rules regarding timing and sending documents apply:

1 unless otherwise stated in the table above or below, all notices or documents to be sent by either NASS or the appellant should be sent by first-class post, fax or given by hand;

2 where a notice or another document is sent by first-class post by NASS or by the ASA, it will be assumed that the asylum-seeker has received it two days after the day on which it was sent, unless they can prove that they did not in fact receive it;

3 where a notice or a document is sent other than by first-class post, there is no assumption made about when it was received, it is treated as having been received on the day on which it was in fact received;

4 where a time limit expires on a number of days after a particular event, time begins running at the end of the day on which the event occurs;

5 where a time limit covers a Saturday, Sunday, bank holiday, Christmas Day or Good Friday, that day is not counted for the purpose of the time limit. Similarly, if the time limit expires, or the rules say that a particular act is to be carried out, on one of those days, the rules are still complied with if the act is done on the next working day.

the time limits set out are relaxed. In particular, amending rules may extend the time limit for appealing and the time granted to NASS to prepare the appeal bundle.

Notice of appeal

Any decision against which an asylum-seeker has a right of appeal to the ASA must be communicated to that person in a letter from NASS. Notice of appeal must be sent to the ASA so that it is received by them no later than two days after the day on which the notice of the decision was received.

The ASA can be requested to extend the time limit for appealing and may do so either before or after the time limit has expired but only if:

• it is in the interests of justice to extend the time limit; and

• the appellant (or their representative) could not comply with the time limit due to circumstances beyond their control.

Preparation of the appeal bundle

On the same day as the ASA receives the notice of appeal or, if that is not reasonably practicable, as soon as possible on the next day at the latest, the ASA must fax a copy of the notice of appeal and any supporting documents which have been sent in with the appeal form to NASS.

On the day after the day that the ASA received the notice of appeal (the last day on which the ASA had to fax the notice of appeal to NASS), NASS must fax or deliver by hand to the ASA, and either fax or send by first-class post to the asylum-seeker, copies of the following documents (known as the 'appeal bundle'):

- if the appeal is against a decision to refuse to provide support rather than a withdrawal of support, the form on which the appellant claimed support and any supporting documentation which is attached to that form;
- the decision letter refusing support; and
- any other evidence which NASS took into account in refusing support.

Decision of the ASA whether to hold a hearing of the appeal

On the day after NASS sends to the ASA the above documents, the ASA must consider the documents and decide whether to hold an oral hearing of the appeal or whether the appeal is going to be determined without a hearing. Whether the ASA decides to hold an oral hearing or not, the ASA must set the date for when the appeal is going to be determined. If the ASA decides to hold an oral hearing, they must, on the same day, send a notice to NASS and to the appellant of the time, date and place of the hearing. The ASA must decide to hold an oral hearing of the appeal if:

- the appellant has requested an oral hearing in their notice of appeal; or
- the ASA thinks that it is necessary, in order to fairly decide the appeal, that there is an oral hearing.

The adjudicator may also decide to hold an oral hearing of the appeal for any other reason. Where the adjudicator decides to hold an oral hearing, the hearing must be held and the appeal determined four days after the day on which the ASA makes the decision whether to hold a hearing. If the ASA decides not to hold an oral hearing, it must determine the appeal either on the same day as it makes that decision or 'as soon as possible' after that day, which must be within four further days.

Further evidence before determination of the appeal

Prior to the determination of the appeal, the asylum-seeker or NASS may submit further evidence to the ASA. Copies of all such evidence should also be forwarded to the other party. It should be noted that, if no oral hearing is to be held, the appeal will be determined within days after notice of appeal was given which means that asylum-seekers and their representatives must act very quickly if they wish to provide further evidence. In particular, the appellant may wish to rely upon evidence which shows a change in their circumstances after the date of the NASS decision.

If the appellant has not requested an oral hearing initially, but subsequently wishes to do so in the light of the bundle of evidence or further evidence submitted by NASS, the ASA should be notified of this as soon as possible by fax or telephone.

Oral hearings

If an oral appeal hearing is to take place, NASS may be asked to pay for the appellant's reasonable travelling expenses to the place of the hearing. However, there is no public funding for legal representation at the hearing. A solicitor may be able to help with the preparation of the appeal and it is possible that other agencies such as law centres may be able to provide free representation at the appeal itself.

There are no rules which set out the procedure which must be adopted at the oral hearing of the appeal and the precise procedure will be for the adjudicator at the hearing to determine. Normally, however, appellants are able to give oral evidence and either they or their representative will have the opportunity of directly addressing the adjudicator as to what decision s/he should make and of commenting on all of the evidence which has been given or submitted.

If the adjudicator has decided to hold an oral hearing, the hearing may be heard in the appellant's absence in the following circumstances:

- if the appellant stated in the notice of appeal that they did not want to be present or be represented at an oral hearing; or
- the appellant did state in the notice of appeal that they wanted to be present or represented at an oral hearing and they were sent a notice of the date, time and place of the hearing but have not attended.

Decisions on appeals

Whether an appeal is dealt with orally or without a hearing, the adjudicator must give reasons for her/his decision in writing. Where an oral hearing is held, the adjudicator must state the decision which has been reached at the end of the hearing. If the appellant does not attend, notice of the decision will be sent out subsequently, on the same day as the appeal is heard. In addition, whether the appellant attended the hearing or not, not later than two days after the day of the hearing, the ASA must send a written statement containing reasons for the decision.

Where the adjudicator does not hold an oral hearing, the notice of decision, together with the reasons for the decision, must be sent out on the same day as the appeal is determined.

Powers of ASA in deciding appeals

In deciding the appeal, the adjudicator is able to take into account any changes of circumstance which take place between the date on which the decision of NASS was made and the date of the determination of the appeal. There are, however, no rules which deal with who bears the burden of proof in asylum support appeals. Applying ordinary legal principles, the person who makes a particular contention must prove it. So, while it may be for the asylum-seeker to demonstrate that they are destitute overall, if there are any particular contentions which NASS is making, then NASS may bear the burden of proving them. For example, if NASS believes that the appellant has an income from other sources it may be for NASS to demonstrate this. If NASS is seeking to exclude someone from support on the basis, for example, that they have breached their conditions upon which support was provided, the burden would lie with NASS to demonstrate the necessary facts.

On deciding the appeal, the adjudicator can do one of three things:

- make NASS reconsider its decision;
- substitute their own decision for the decision which was made by NASS;
- dismiss the appeal so that the NASS decision stands.

Ending the appeal by withdrawal

The appellant may at any stage decide to withdraw the appeal. In addition, NASS may at any time decide that they wish to withdraw the decision against which the applicant has appealed. If that happens, NASS must give to the appellant and the adjudicator notice of the withdrawal as soon as possible. In either of these two circumstances, the appeal is treated as having come to an end. If NASS withdraws the decision, it is of course required to make a further decision on the application for support. If that decision is of a kind which is appealable (►see above), and the person is dissatisfied with the second decision, they may of course appeal against it again.

'Hard cases' support

In order to deal with certain cases in which a person's claim to asylum has been 'determined' and they are no longer an asylum-seeker for support purposes, NASS operates a 'hard cases' fund under which some people can obtain accommodation and full board which is provided outside London. The basis for this form of support is section 4 of the 1999 Act which gives a broad discretion to provide support for people who are:

- temporarily admitted to the UK;
- released from detention by the immigration authorities;
- released on bail from immigration detention.

The 2002 White Paper and Bill propose to extend hard cases support to ensure that all those who are not detained but given some form of temporary admission are eligible to apply – at present it does not cover those released from deportation detention powers (▶see box on page 720).

The policy which is operated by NASS as to who in practice will be able to access this form of support is restrictive. Under the policy, to be eligible a person should satsisfy all the following conditions:

- their claim to asylum (under the Refugee Convention or Article 3 ECHR) has been determined;

- they have been supported previously by NASS or by a local authority under the interim scheme;

- they are no longer an asylum-seeker for asylum support purposes so that they are no longer able to obtain asylum support;

- they 'appear' to NASS to be destitute – the same definition as for asylum support purposes applies (▶see pages 694, 697-699); and

- they have no other avenue of support available (e.g. friends, family, NHS or community care services).

The policy states that, although each case is considered individually, even if an applicant satisfies all the above conditions, support will still not be available unless *any* of the following conditions apply:

- he or she is genuinely unable to leave the UK by reason of a physical impediment to travel, for example, through illness or a pregnancy which is in its late stages. A further example would surely be that the applicant cannot practically be removed to their country of origin because there is no established route of removal; *or*

- the circumstances of the case are exceptional and he or she is taking all reasonable steps to leave the UK and is fully co-operating with efforts to remove him or her; or

- the applicant has been granted permission to apply for judicial review of any determination in respect of their application for asylum or has brought an application for permission to apply for judicial review and the Home Office does not think that the application is 'wholly unmeritorious'.

The judicial review may, for example, be of a decision of the Immigration Appeal Tribunal refusing to grant leave to appeal or of a certificate issued by the Home Office denying a person a further right of appeal. Given the broad power to provide support, any rigid and inflexible application of NASS's criteria may be open to challenge by judicial review.

Proposed changes

The government originally announced a review of the asylum support system in late 2000. NASS published its *Report of the operational reviews of the voucher and dispersal schemes* in October 2001. Some of the recommendations made are reflected in the changes to the system proposed in the present White Paper and the Nationality, Immigration and Asylum Bill 2002. There are, however, other significant proposed changes. The important proposals are set out in the box below.

PROPOSED CHANGES TO THE ASYLUM SUPPORT AND WELFARE SYSTEM

The proposed changes under the 2002 White Paper and the Nationality, Immigration and Asylum Bill 2002 to the system for supporting asylum-seekers are as follows.

No 'cash only' option. The Bill changes the definition of 'destitute' so that in order to be entitled to get any asylum support, an asylum-seeker must be without both accommodation and food and other essential items. The new definition applies to asylum support both in and outside the new 'accommodation centres' (▶see below). The Bill also paves the way for NASS to refuse to provide cash or voucher-only support for food and essential living items to anyone who qualifies for NASS support under the new definition but who chooses to accept cash or vouchers without accommodation. This will obviously be applied in the accommodation centres but may be used in non-accommodation centre cases as well.

An end to vouchers. Although it may not be possible in the future to get support for food and essential living needs only, the government intends to phase out vouchers towards the end of 2002. Vouchers are to be replaced by cash. It is understood that NASS has begun issuing either cash or vouchers redeemable for cash rather than for goods. The necessary legislative changes are described in the text above (▶see page s 700, 710) and were introduced on 8 April 2002.

Induction and accommodation centres
* **Induction centres.** Asylum-seekers and dependants will initially be referred to an 'induction centre' where asylum procedures and the system of support will be explained to them and they will be given basic health screening. Under the Bill, asylum-seekers can be required to reside (for up to 14 days) at an induction centre whether or not they have other accommodation and support available to them. A residence requirement can be imposed as a condition of their temporary admission.

The government has indicated that the likely periods of residence in the induction centres are as follows. Those who do not need asylum support are likely to only remain in the induction centre for one day and will then move to their agreed address under conditions of temporary admission. Those who are to be referred to an accommodation centre are likely to stay in the induction centre for about two days while arrangements for them to be transferred are made. Others applying for NASS support will remain in the induction centre for about 7 to 10 days while their application for support is processed. Induction centres are intended to house 200-400 asylum-seekers and their dependants. The first trial induction centre opened in Dover on 21 January 2002.

* **Accommodation centres.** These centres are to be introduced on a trial basis and will house a proportion of those people who are eligible for NASS support, on temporary admission conditions. In the White Paper, the government indicated that criteria for referral to an accommodation centre would be developed and are likely to include consideration of the asylum-seeker's language (there will be limited core

languages at each centre), their family circumstances and the port of arrival. It was also stated that there will be a discretion to exempt people from referral to accommodation centres in exceptional circumstances, even where they otherwise meet the criteria. However, the 2002 Bill (▶see below) allows for no account to be taken of a person's personal circumstances in deciding whether to provide support in an accommodation centre or otherwise.

At the accommodation centre, people will be provided with support in the form of food, money, other essentials, transport, education and training, medical facilities and facilities to enable them to observe their religion. It is intended that children of asylum-seekers will receive education in the accommodation centre; they will not attend schools run by the local education authority. The government has indicated that where a family has been in a centre for six months, an assessment will be carried out to see if the child should be moved to a school.

People can be required to reside at an accommodation centre as part of their conditions of temporary admission. Asylum-seekers may also have conditions of residence imposed on them requiring them to be present at the centre at certain times. If they are absent or breach other conditions of residence, they can be required to leave the centre and refused other forms of support. People referred to accommodation centres will be required to reside at the centre throughout the processing of their applications and will be required to report regularly within the centre. The government hopes to use accommodation centres to tightly manage the asylum interview and decision-making process and, therefore, to reduce determination times. Information about voluntary returns will be given to those refused asylum.

As of February 2002, the Home Office had identified eight potential sites for accommodation centres, namely in Worcestershire, two in Lincolnshire, Cardiff, Cheshire, Oxfordshire, Edinburgh and Nottinghamshire. Of those, three are former RAF premises.

Extension of the 'hard cases' fund. The Bill proposes that all those who are no longer entitled to asylum support because they have stopped being asylum-seekers or the dependants of asylum-seekers (because they have exhausted their rights of appeal), will be potentially eligible for support under the hard cases fund. In the 1999 Act there is a gap which prevents some people who have been detained under deportation powers and who are released by the immigration authorities from obtaining assistance. This does not, however, necessarily mean that Home Office policy on who will actually *get* hard cases support (▶see pages 717-718) will be made more generous.

No choice as to type of support. The Home Office will be able to decide what kind of support to offer a person, whether it is support in or outside an accommodation centre or 'hard cases' type support. Where support of any of these kinds has already been offered, NASS may refuse to provide any of the other forms of support. It is proposed that, in deciding what kind of support to offer, for example, whether to put someone in an accommodation centre, NASS does not have to consider a person's personal circumstances. This may lead to decisions which are contrary to Article 8 ECHR in individual cases.

Level of support. The level of support provided by way of vouchers/cash was raised to keep to pace with increases in income support. The new levels of support (▶see pages 700-701) were introduced on 8 April 2002.

Extension of notice period. Under the regulations originally introduced as part of the asylum support scheme, an asylum-seeker without children ceased to be entitled to asylum support 14 days after the asylum decision or, if the asylum- seeker appeals against the Home Office refusal, 14 days after time ran out for appealing further (until the appeals process had been exhausted). There have been serious delays in providing people with their grant of status after favourable decisions are made. As a result, people have been unable to either access welfare benefits or asylum support. The notice period has therefore been extended from 14 days to:

- 28 days for those who are to be granted asylum or given exceptional leave; and
- 21 days for failed asylum-seekers (in force: 8 April 2002).

Temporary admission conditions linked to support. The Bill proposes that a condition of temporary admission (►see pages 510-512) can also be made into a condition of support. This means that breach of conditions of temporary admission, in particular reporting conditions, can lead to a termination of asylum support. The Home Office will meet the travel costs of asylum-seekers who have to travel to a reporting centre to report.

Extension of appeal rights. Where a person is refused support in an accommodation centre or that support is terminated and no other asylum support is to be provided to the asylum-seeker, then they may appeal to an asylum support adjudicator as in other NASS asylum support cases. There is an indication in the Bill that the government is considering extending the rights of appeal to enable people to appeal against dispersal decisions in non-accommodation centre cases.

'Benefit shopping'. The government states that it has identified a new problem of 'benefit shopping' whereby people who have refugee status in other countries come to the UK and claim benefits or support from local authorities. It has stated that it intends to bring in measures to prevent this.

Section 12 **Information**

Useful addresses and telephone numbers 725

Visa nationals, fees and overseas posts 737

Work-related applications 743

Commonwealth countries 748

Registering with the police 750

Countries whose adoption decisions are
recognised in the UK 751

Abbreviations 752

Further sources of information 755

Glossary 757

Useful addresses and telephone numbers

Home Office

Immigration and Nationality Directorate

Lunar House, 40 Wellesley Road, Croydon, CR9 2BY
Website: www.ind.homeoffice.gov.uk

Application Forms
tel   0870 2410645

General Enquiries
tel   0870 6067766

Leaflet Line
tel   020 8649 7878

Public Caller Unit (PCU)
Same address as above for lodging urgent applications by hand which may be dealt with on the day
Opening times: 9am–4pm Mon–Fri excluding public holidays

Nationality Directorate
3rd floor, India Buildings
Water Street, Liverpool L2 0QN
tel   0151 237 5200
application forms 0151 2370143/0163
fax 0151 237 5385

National Asylum Support Service
Voyager House
30 Wellesley Road
Croydon
CR0 2AD
tel   0845 602 1739
fax 0845 601 1143

Home Office regional Public Enquiry Offices (PEOs)

Belfast
Olivetree House, Fountain Street
Belfast BT1 5EA
tel   02890 322547

Birmingham
Dominion Court, 41 Station Road, Solihull, B91 3RT
tel   0121 606 7345

Glasgow
Dumbarton Court, Argyll Avenue
Glasgow Airport, Paisley PA3 2TD
tel   0141 887 2255

Liverpool
Reliance House, Water Street,
Liverpool L2 8XU
tel   0151 237 0473

Home Office Presenting Officers

1st Floor, 2308 Coventry Road,
Sheldon,
Birmingham B26 3JS
tel   0121 700 1616
fax 0121 706 1696

Presenting Officer's Unit
Hanover House, Plane Tree Crescent,
Feltham, Middlesex TW13 7JJ
tel   020 8917 2039
fax 020 8890 6489

10th Floor, Eagle Building
215 Bothwell Street, Glasgow G2 7ED
tel   0141 221 4218
fax 0141 204 5987

Presenting Officer's Unit
2nd Floor Springfield House,
76 Wellington Street, Leeds LS1 2AY
tel   0113 244 4205
fax 0113 245 3472

2nd floor, Building 1, Angel Square
1 Torrens Street, London EC1V 1SX
tel   020 7239 1701
fax 020 7239 1702

Presenting Officer's Unit
15th Floor West Point, 501 Chester Road,
Old Trafford, Manchester M16 9HU
tel   0161 877 6322
fax 0161 877 5955

Immigration Appellate Authority

General queries: asylum issues
Loughborough Support Centre
PO Box 6021, Loughborough
Leicestershire LE11 2YT
tel 0845 600 0877
fax 01509 221444/221540/221423
text 0845 606 0766
website www.iaa.gov.uk/

Leaflets and customer complaints
Customer Service Team
4th Floor, Cardinal Tower
12 Farringdon Road
London EC1M 3HS

Main Appeal Centres

7th floor, Lancashire House
5 Linenhall Street, Belfast BT2 8AA
(queries to Glasgow office)

2nd floor, Sheldon Court
1 Wagon Lane,
Birmingham B26 3DU
tel   0121 685 3300

Bromley Magistrates Court
1st Floor, 1 London Road, Bromley
Kent BR1 1RA
(queries to Taylor House, London)

Cardiff Civil Court Centre
2 Park Street, Cardiff CF1 1ET
(queries to Birmingham office)

York House, Duke's Green Avenue
off Faggs Road, Feltham
Middlesex TW14 0LS
tel 020 8831 31000

5th floor, Eagle Building
215 Bothwell Street, Glasgow G2 7EZ
tel   0141 221 3489
fax 0141 221 3532

4th floor, Coronet House
Queen Street, Leeds LS1 4PW
tel 01132 449898

Taylor House, 88 Rosebery Avenue
Islington, London EC1R 4QU
(queries to Loughborough Support Centre)

Field House
15 Bream's Buildings
London EC4A 1DZ

3rd floor, Aldine House
New Bailey Street, Manchester M3 5EU
tel   0161 837 1162
fax 0161 839 3793

Asylum Support Adjudicators ►see page 736.

Immigration Service Enforcement Units
(some incorporated within Ports of Entry – see below)

Becket House
66–68 St Thomas' Street,
London SE1 3QU
tel   020 7238 1300
fax 020 7378 9110/9107

Midlands Enforcement Unit
Dominion Court, 41 Station Road
Solihull, B91 3RT
tel   0121 606 7300
fax 0121 606 7325

North West Enforcement Unit
Units 1–2 Dallas Court
South Langworthy Road
Salford Quays
Salford L5 2GF
tel   0161 888 4100
fax 0161 888 4119

South-East Ports Surveillance Team
Dover Hoverport
Dover, Kent
CT17 9TF
tel   01304 200 400
fax 01304 216303

UK Immigration Service
Eton House
581 Staines Road
Hounslow
TW4 5DL
tel   020 8814 5060
fax 020 8814 5345

Ports of Entry

Belfast International Airport
tel   02894 422500
fax 02894 459211

Birmingham International Airport
tel   0121 606 7350
fax 0121 782 0006

Bristol City
tel   01275 815020
fax 01275 818680

Bristol Airport
tel/fax 01275 472843

Cardiff City
tel   02920 764474
fax 02920 764014

Cardiff Airport
tel   01446 710485
fax 01446 710606

Cheriton (Channel Tunnel)
tel   01303 282645
fax 01303 282610

City Airport (London)
tel   020 7474 1395
fax 020 7511 2363

Dover East Immigration
tel   01304 244900
fax 01304 213594

Dover Harbour Police Station
Detention Centre
tel   01304 216370
fax 01304 204316

East Midlands Airport
tel   01332 812000
fax 01332 815131

Edinburgh
tel   0131 344 3330
fax 0131 348 4029

Gatwick South Terminal
tel   01293 502019
fax 01293 501022

Gatwick North Terminal
tel   01293 567282
fax 01293 507097/263

Glasgow Airport
tel   0141 847 5300
fax 0141 887 1566

Gravesend
tel   01474 352308
fax 01474 534731

Harwich Immigration
tel   01255 509700
fax 01255 509718

Heathrow Terminal 1
tel   020 8745 6800
fax 020 8745 6828

Heathrow Terminal 2
tel   020 8745 6850
fax 020 8745 6867

Heathrow Terminal 3
tel   020 8745 6900
fax 020 8745 6943

Heathrow Terminal 4
tel   020 8745 4700
fax 020 8745 4705

Hull
tel   01482 593980
fax 01482 219034

Leeds City (also serving airport)
tel   0113 3865733
fax 0113 386 5756

Liverpool
tel   0151 236 8974
fax 0151 236 4656

Luton
tel   01582 439030
fax 01582 405215

Manchester Airport Terminal 1
tel   0161 489 6188
fax 0161 489 5779

Newcastle
tel   0191 214 2700
fax 0191 214 2707

Sheffield City Airport
tel   0114 201 5316
fax 0114 201 5317

Stansted Airport
tel   01279 680118
fax 01279 680145

Waterloo International Terminal
tel   020 7919 5910
fax 020 7919 5918

Passport Agency

Website www.passport.gov.uk
National Call Centre: 0870 521 0410
Application Form hotline: 0901 4700 110
National Textphone (for deaf customers):
0870 240 8090

Offices:

Globe House, 89 Eccleston Square,
London SW1V 1PN
(NB Attendance by appointment only
Mon–Fri 7.45am–6.45pm /
Sat 9.15am–3.15pm)
fax 020 7271 8403
email London@ukpa.gov.uk

Hampton House, 47–53 High Street
Belfast, BT1 2QS
fax 02890 246065
email Belfast@ukpa.gov.uk

Millburngate House
Durham, DH97 1PA
fax 0191 370 7175
email Durham@ukpa.gov.uk

3 Northgate, 96 Milton Street
Cowcaddens, Glasgow G4 0BT
Area covered: Scotland
fax 0141 331 2696
email Glasgow@ukpa.gov.uk

5th floor, India Buildings
Water Street, Liverpool L2 0QZ
fax 0151 471 2949
email Liverpool@ukpa.gov.uk

Olympia House, Upper Dock Street
Newport, NP20 1XA
fax 01633 463899
email Newport@ukpa.gov.uk

Aragon Court, Northminster Road
Peterborough PE1 1QQ
fax 01733 343094
email: Peterborough@ukpa.gov.uk

Detention Centres

Campsfield House
Langford Lane, Kiddlington,
Oxford, OX5 1RE
tel 01865 845700 (switchboard)
tel 01865 377712 (detainees)
fax 01865 377723
Social visits 2pm–5pm, 6pm–9pm
Legal visits 9am–12pm, 1.30–5pm,
7pm–9pm

Dungavel Detention Centre
Dungavel House Immigration Centre
Strathaven
South Lanarkshire ML10 6RF
Social and Legal visits 1.30pm–4.30pm
(Mon–Fri)

Harmondsworth Detention Centre
Colnbrook Bypass
Longford, West Drayton
Middlesex UB7 0HB
tel 020 8283 3850
fax 020 8283 3851
Social Visits 2pm–8.30pm
Legal Visits 9am–9pm
(7 days a week)

Haslar Holding Centre
2 Dolphin Way, Gosport,
Hants PO12 2AW
tel 02392 580381 (switchboard)
tel 02392528636 (immigration office)
fax 02392 510266
Social and Legal visits 1.30pm–4pm
(open all week excluding Wed)

Lindholme Detention Centre
Bawtry Road,
Hatfield Woodhouse,
Doncaster DN7 6EE
tel 01302 848666
fax 01302 848620
Social visits 1.45–4pm (7 days a week)
Legal Visits Book a time in the morning or
afternoon except between 12pm–1.45pm
(Mon–Fri)

Rochester Detention Centre
HMP Rochester, 1 Fort Road
Rochester, Kent ME1 3SQ
tel 01634 838100
fax 01634 838101
Social visits 2pm–4.30pm (Mon–Fri),
2pm–3pm, 3.30–4.30pm (Sat)
Legal Visits 9am–11.30am, 2pm–4.30pm
(Mon–Fri)
Legal visits limited availability, book 1 week
in advance by phone or fax.

Tinsley House Detention Centre
Perimeter Road South, Gatwick Airport,
West Sussex RH6 0PQ
tel 01293 434800
fax 01293 423221
Social visits 2pm–9pm
Legal Visits 9am–12.30pm, 1pm–9pm.
Arrange by faxing letter in advance.

Yarl's Wood Immigration Detention Centre
Twinwoods Road, Clapham,
Bedfordshire MK41 6HL
tel 01234 821000
fax 01234 821196
Social visits 2pm–9pm
Legal visits 9am–9pm

Government Offices

Department of Social Security
Benefits Agency Overseas Branch
Tyneview Park, Whitley Road,
Benton, Newcastle-upon-Tyne, NE98 1BA
tel 0191 218 7777
website www.dss.gov.uk

Joint Entry Clearance Unit / UK Visas
London SW1A 2AH
tel 020 7008 8438 (general)
tel 020 7008 8308 (forms and leaflets)
fax 020 7008 8359/8361
email visas.foruk@jecu.mail.fco.gov.uk
website www.ukvisas.gov.uk

Home Office (Minister's Private Office)
Queen Anne's Gate, London SW1H 9AT
tel 020 7273 4604
fax 020 7273 2043

House of Westminster
(House of Commons and House of Lords)
London SW1A 2PW
tel 020 7219 3000

Overseas Visitors' Records Office
180 Borough High Street,
London SE1 1LH
Metropolitan Police Service Information Line
020 7230 1208 (recorded information)

Treasury Solicitor
Queen Anne's Chambers
28 Broadway, London SW1H 9JS
tel 020 7210 3000
fax 020 7222 6006

Work Permits (UK)
Immigration and Nationality Directorate
Home Office, Level 5, Moorfoot
Sheffield S1 4PQ
tel 0114 259 4074
fax 0114 259 3776
website: www.workpermits.gov.uk

Legal help and assistance

England and Wales:

Approved private solicitors' firms and not-for-profit sector advice agencies:
Community Legal Services
Directory Call Centre: tel 0845 608 1122
'Just Ask!' website www.justask.org.uk

**Approved non-solicitor agencies
(including not-for-profit advisors):**
Office of the Immigration Services
Commissioner (OISC):
Helpline: 0845 000 0046
'Adviser finder' Website:
www.oisc.org.uk/adviser_finder

Scotland:

Solicitors' firms (not approved but usually able to apply for legal aid funding):
The Law Society of Scotland
tel 0131 226 7411 (Records dept)
Website www.lawscot.org.uk

Non-solicitor agencies:
OISC website and helpline (see above)

Northern Ireland

Solicitors that operate the legal aid scheme (not immigration specifically):
Law Society of Northern Ireland
Legal Aid Department
3rd Floor, Bedford House
16–22 Bedford Street
Belfast, Northern Ireland BT2 7FL
tel 028 90 23 16 14

Non-solicitor agencies:
OISC website and helpline (see above)

Law Centres

For full details of all law centres contact:
The Law Centres Federation
Duchess House, 18–19 Warren Street,
London W1P 5DB
tel 020 7387 8570
email info@lawcentres.
website www.lawcentres.org.uk

Complaints about advisors

Throughout the UK:
Office of the Immigration Services
Commissioner
6th Floor, Fleet Bank House
2–6 Salisbury Square
London EC4Y 8JX
Helpline: 0845 000 0046

England and Wales only:
The Office for the Supervision of Solicitors
Victoria Court, 8 Dormer Place,
Leamington Spa
Warwickshire, CV32 5AE
tel 0845 608 6565

Scotland only:
Law Society of Scotland
Client Relations Office
26 Drumsheugh Gardens
Edinburgh, EH3 7YR
tel 0131 476 8137

Northern Ireland only:
Law Society of Northern Ireland
98 Victoria Street
Belfast, BT1 3JZ
tel   028 90 23 16 14

British High Commissions and Embassies abroad

Full list (including opening hours) on
Foreign & Commonwealth website at
www.fco.gov.uk

Algeria
British Embassy
6 Avenue Souidani, Boudiemaa, BPO8,
Alger-Gare 16000, Algiers
tel   (213) (21) 230068
fax   (213) (21) 230067/230751

Bangladesh
British High Commission
Immigration Section,
United Nations Road
P.O. Box 6079, Baridhara, Dhaka 12
tel   (880) (2) 882 2705
fax   (880) (2) 882 3437
fax   (880) (2) 882 3666/2819 (immigration)
email immigration@dhaka.mail.fco.gov.uk
website www.ukinbangladesh.org

Barbados
British High Commission,
Lower Collymore Rock, PO Box 676,
Bridgetown
tel   001 246 430 7800
fax   001 246 430 7851
email britishhc@sunbeach.net
website www.britishhc.org/

Brazil
British Embassy,
SES Quadra 801,
Lote 8 Cj K Brasilia DF, Av das Nações,
70408–900
tel   55 61 225 2710
fax   55 61 225 1777
email britemb@terra.com.br
website www.reinounido.org.br

Chile
British Embassy, Av. El Bosque Norte 0125,
Las Condes, Santiago
tel   56 2 370 4100
fax   56 2 370 4170
email embsan@britemb.cl
website www.britemb.cl

China
British Embassy
11 Guang Hua Lu, Jian Guo Men Wai
Beijing 100600
tel   8610 6532 1961
fax   8610 6532 1937
email visamail@peking.mail.fco.gov.uk
website www.britishembassy.org.cn/

Colombia
British Embassy, Edificio ING Barings,
Carrera 9, No 76–49
Piso 9, Bogotá
tel   57 1 317 6690/6310/6321
fax   57 1 317 6401 (consular/visa)
email britain@cable.net.co
website www.britain.gov.co

Cyprus
British High Commission,
Alexander Pallis Street,
(PO Box 21978), Nicosia
tel   357 2 861100
fax   357 2 861200
email infobhc@cylink.com.cy
website www.britain.org.cy

Ecuador
British Embassy,
Citiplaza Building,
Naciones Unidas Ave.
and República de El Salvador
(Consular section 12th floor)
PO Box 17–17–830, Quito
tel   593 2 970 800/801
fax   593 2 970 807 (visa/consular)
email britembq@impsat.net.ec
website www.britembquito.org.ec/

Ethiopia
British Embassy,
Fikre Mariam Abatechan Street,
Addis Ababa (P O Box 858)
tel   251 1 612354
fax   251 1 614154 (consular/visa section)
email b.emb4@telecom.net.et

France
British Embassy
35 rue du Faubourg,
St Honoré
75383 Paris Cedex 08
tel   331 44 51 31 00
fax   331 44 5131 28 (visa section)
website www.amb-grandebretagne.fr/

Ghana
British High Commission, Osu Link
off Gamel Abdul Nasser Avenue,
PO Box 296, Accra
tel   233 21 221665; 7010650 (24 hours)
fax 233 21 7010655; 221715 (visa section)
email
high.commission@accra.mail.fco.gov.uk

Guyana
British High Commission,
44 Main Street,
PO Box 10849,
Georgetown
tel 592 226 5881/2/3/4
fax 592 225 0671 (Consular/immigration)

Hong Kong
British Consulate General
No 1 Supreme Court Road, Central
Hong Kong
(PO Box 528)
tel 852 2901 3000
fax 852 2901 3347
email visa@britishconsulate.org.hk
website www.britishconsulate.org.hk/

India
British High Commission, Immigration
Section, Chanakyapuri
New Delhi 1100-21
tel   91 11 68 72161
fax 91 11 68 70060
email visqry.newdelhi@fco.gov.uk
website www.ukinindia.com

British Deputy High Commissioner
Maker Chambers IV
222 Jamnalal Bajaj Road
PO Box 11714, Nariman Point
Bombay 400 021
tel   91 22 2830517/2832330/2833602
fax 91 22 2027940
email postmaster@bombay.mail.fco.gov.uk

British Deputy High Commissioner
1A Ho Chi Minh Sarani
Calcutta 700 071
tel   91 33 288 5172-76
fax 91 33 288 3996 (visa section)
email postmaster@calcutta.mail.fco.gov.uk

British Deputy High Commissioner
24 Anderson Road
Chennai (Madras)
600 006
tel   91 44 827 3136/3137
fax 91 44 827 5130 (visa section)
email Consular@madras.mail.fco.gov.uk

Iran
British Embassy
143 Ferdowsi Avenue, Tehran 11344
(P O Box No 11365-4474)
tel   98 21 6705011/19
fax 98 21 6700720 (visa section)

Jamaica
British High Commission
PO Box 575, Trafalgar Road
Kingston 10
tel   001 876 926 9050
tel   001 876 926 1022/3 (visa enquiries)
fax 001 876 960 3287 (visa enquiries)
email bhckingston@cwjamaica.com

Jordan
British Embassy, P.O. Box 87
Abdoun Amman 11118
tel   9626 5923100
fax 9626 5923759
website www.britain.org.jo

Kenya
British High Commission
Upper Hill Road, Nairobi
P O Box 48543 Nairobi
tel   254 2 714699
fax 254 2 719110 (visa section)
email bhcinfo@iconnect.co.ke
website www.britain.or.ke

Lebanon
British Embassy
Autostrade Jal El Dib,
Coolrite Building, PO Box 60180,
Jal El Dib Beirut
tel   961 4 715900/01/02/03 (visa section)
fax 961 4 715904
email britemb@cyberia.net.lb
website www.britishembassy.org.lb/

Malawi
British High Commission, PO Box 30042
Lilongwe 3
tel   265 772 400
fax 265 772 657
email bhc@wiss.co.mw

Morocco
British Consulate-General
43 Boulevard d'Anfa
BP 13762 Casablanca 01
tel   212 0 22 22 17 41
fax 212 0 22 26 57 79 (visa section)
email british.consulate@casanet.net.ma
website www.britain.org.ma

Nigeria
British Deputy High Commission
11 Walter Carrington Crescent
Victoria Island, Lagos
tel   234 1 261 9531/9537/9541/9566
tel   234 1 2625930/7 (visa/consular)
fax   234 1261 4021/2625941 (visa)
email visa@lagos.mail.fco.gov.uk

Pakistan
British High Commission, Diplomatic
Enclave, Ramna 5, PO Box 1122, Islamabad
tel   92 51 2206071/5 & 2822131/5
fax   92 51 2824728 (immigration)
email bhctrade@isb.comsats.net.pk
website www.britainonline.org.pk/

British Deputy High Commission,
Shahrah-E-Iran, Clifton, Karachi 75600
tel   9221 582 0016 (visa)
fax   9221 587 4328 (immigration)
email: visaenquiries.karachi@fco.gov.uk

Philippines
British Embassy, 15–17 Floor, LV Locsin
Building, 6752 Ayala Av, corner of Makati
Av, 1226 Makati (PO Box 2927 MCPO)
tel   632 816 7116
fax   632 810 2745 (visa)
email uk@info.com.ph
website www.britishembassy.org.ph/

Sierra Leone
British High Commission, Spur Road,
Freetown
tel   232 22 232961
fax   232 22 232070
email bhc@sierratel.sl

Sri Lanka
British High Commission, 190 Galle Road,
Kollupitiya, PO Box 1433, Colombo 3
tel   941 437336/43
fax   941 335803 (consular/visa)
email bhc@eureka.lk

Thailand
British Embassy, 1031 Wireless Road,
Bangkok 10330
tel   662 305 8374 (visa section)
fax   662 254 9579 (visa section)
email info.bangkok@fco.gov.uk
website www.britishemb.or.th/

Trinidad and Tobago
British High Commission, 19 St Clair
Avenue, St Clair, Port of Spain, Trinidad
tel   868 622 8960/2748
fax   868 622 628 3064 (Consular)
email csbhc@opus.co.tt

Turkey
British Consulate-General, Mesrutiyet
Caddesi no. 34, Tepebasi, Beyoglu,
Istanbul 80072
tel   90 212 334 6500 (visa)
fax   90 212 334 6504 (visa)
email
istanbul.visa.enquiries.istanbul@fco.gov.uk

Uganda
British High Commission
10/12 Parliament Avenue
P O Box 7070 Kampala
tel   256 41 257054/9
fax   256 41 344084 (visa)
email bhcinfo@starcom.co.ug

Zambia
British High Commission, 5210
Independence Avenue, PO Box 50050,
15101 Ridgeway, Lusaka
tel   260 1 251 133
fax   260 1 252 842 (visa/consular)
email brithc@zamnet.zm

Immigration, asylum and nationality organisations

AIRE Centre (Advice on Individual Rights
in Europe)
Third Floor, 17 Red Lion Square,
London, WC1R 4QH
tel   020 7831 4276 /
advice: 020 7831 3850
fax   020 7404 7760
email aire@btinternet.com
website www.airecentre.org.uk

Amnesty International UK
99–119 Rosebery Avenue
London EC1R 4RE
tel   020 7814 6200
fax   020 7833 1510
email information@amnesty.org.uk

Association of Visitors to Immigration
Detainees (AVID)
Mrs Helen Ireland, Secretary
Box 7, Oxted RH8 09T
tel   01883 712713
email secretary@aviddetention.org.uk
website www.aviddetention.org.uk

Asylum Aid
28 Commercial Street,
London E1 6LS
tel   020 7377 5123
fax   020 7247 7789
email info@asylumaid.org.uk
website www.asylumaid.org.uk

Asylum Rights Campaign
46 Francis Street,
London SW1P 1QN
tel   020 7798 7027
fax 020 7798 9010

Bail for Immigration Detainees (BID)
28 Commercial Street, London E1 6LS
tel   020 7247 3590
fax 020 7247 3550
email
bailforimmigrationdetainees@yahoo.co.uk

Bosnian Information &
Refugee Centre
60–62 Mill Lane, London NW6 1NJ
tel   020 7433 3834

British Agencies for Adoption and
Fostering (BAAF)
Skyline House, 200 Union Street
London SE1 0LX
tel   020 7593 2000
fax 020 7593 2001
email mail@baaf.org.uk
website www.baaf.org.uk

Campaign to Close Campsfield
email info@closecampsfield.org.uk
website www.closecampsfield.org.uk

Children's Legal Centre
University of Essex, Wivenhoe Park,
Colchester, Essex CO4 3SQ
advice 01206 873820
admin 01206 872466
fax 01206 874026
email clc@essex.ac.uk
website www2.essex.ac.uk/clc

Chinese Information
Advice Centre
1st Floor, 53 New Oxford Street
London WC1A 1BL
tel   020 7692 3471
fax 020 7692 3476

Christian Action for Justice in
Immigration Law
c/o Iona Community Peace Institute
Govan, Glasgow G51 3UU
tel   0141 445 4561
Email ionacomm@gla.iona.org.uk

Commission for Racial Equality
Elliot House, 10–12 Allington Street
London SW1E 5EH
tel   020 7828 7022
fax 020 7630 7605
website www.cre.gov.uk

Detention Advice Service
308 Seven Sisters Road
London N4 2AG
tel   020 8802 3422
fax 020 8802 0684
email das@das.ndirect.co.uk

East European Advice Centre
Room 209, Palingswick House, 2
41 King Street
London W6 9LP
tel   020 8741 1288
fax 020 8741 8388
Email eeac@btopenworld.com

Educational Grants
Advisory Service
501–505 Kingsland Road,
London E8 4AU
tel 020 7254 6251
fax 020 7249 5443
email egasenquiry@fwa.org.uk

Electronic Immigration Network
The Progress Centre, Charlton Place,
Ardwick Green, Manchester M12 6HS
tel   0161 273 7515/0845 458 4151
fax 0161 274 3159/0845 458 0051
email info@ein.org.uk
website www.ein.org.uk

Ethnic Minorities Advice Project
Ethnic Minorities Representatives Council
(EMRC), c/o Brighton Islamic Mission
8 Caburn Road, Hove, Sussex BN3 6EF
tel   01273 722438
fax 01273 326 051
email ajsajid@hotmail.com

Foundation for Public Service Interpreting
1 St Clements Court, London EC4N 7HB
tel   020 7626 0220
fax 020 7283 3678
website www.nisuk.co.uk

Free Representation Unit
Peer House, 8–14 Verulam Street
London WC1X 8LZ
tel   020 7831 0692
fax 020 7831 2398

Gatwick Detainees Welfare Group
225 Three Bridges Road
Three Bridges, Crawley RH10 1LG
tel   01293 434 350
fax 01293 434 351
email
GDWG@gatwickdetainees.freeserve.co.uk

Greater Manchester Immigration
Aid Unit
400 Cheetham Hill Road
Manchester M8 9LE
tel 0161 740 7722
fax 0161 740 5172
email gmiau@ein.org.uk

Haslar Visitors Group
All Saints Centre
Commercial Road
Portsmouth PO1 4BT
tel/fax 0239 283 9222
email info@haslarvisitors.org.uk

Human Rights Watch
2nd floor, 33 Islington High Street
London N1 9LH
tel 020 7713 1995
fax 020 7713 1800
website www.hrw.org

Immigration Advisory Service
General website www.iasuk.org

Regional IAS offices

3rd Floor, King Edward House,
135a New Street
Birmingham B2 4QJ
tel 0121 616 3540
fax 0121 616 2444

211A City Road, Roath
Cardiff CF2 3JD
tel 02920 496662
fax 02920 496602

115 Bath Street, Glasgow G2 2SZ
tel 0141 248 2956
fax 0141 221 5388
email glasgow@iasuk.org

71 Grove Road, Hounslow
Middlesex TW3 3PR
tel 020 8814 1115
fax 020 8814 1116/1578

Basement Suite, Coverdale House,
14–15 East Parade Leeds LS1 2BH
tel 0113 244 2460
fax 0113 243 1006
email leeds@iasuk.org

Toxteth Town Hall
15 High Park Street, Liverpool
L8 8DH
tel 0151 475 1628
fax 0151 475 1629
email ias_liverpool@hotmail.com

County House, 190 Great Dover Street,
London SE1 4YB
tel 020 7357 6917
fax 020 7378 0665
email advice@ias.org
website www.iasuk.org

Suite 7B, 7th floor
Lower Ground Floor Suite, Cloister House,
Riverside, New Bailey Street,
Salford, ME3 5AG
tel 0161 834 9942
fax 0161 832 9322

Immigration Law Practitioners' Association
Lindsey House
40/42 Charterhouse Street
London EC1M 6JN
tel 020 7251 8383
fax 020 7251 8384
email info@ilpa.org.uk
website www.ilpa.org.uk

Institute of Race Relations
2–6 Leeke Street, London WC1X 9HS
tel 020 7837 0041/0207 833 2010
fax 020 7278 0623
email info@irr.org.uk
website www.irr.org.uk

Interights
Lancaster House, 33 Islington High Street
London N1 9LH
tel 020 7278 3230
fax 020 7278 4334
email: ir@interights.org
website www.interights.org

International Social Service of Great Britain
Cranmer House, 39 Brixton Road
London SW9 6DD
tel 020 7735 8941
fax 020 7582 0696
email issuk@charity.vfree.com

Justice
59 Carter Lane,
London EC4V 5AQ
tel 020 7329 5100
fax 020 7329 5055
email admin@justice.org.uk
website www.justice.org.uk

Law For All
PO Box 230, Brentford, TW8 9FL
tel 020 8758 0668
fax 020 8758 0669
email info@lawforall.co.uk

Legal Action Group
242 Pentonville Road
London N1 9UN
tel   020 7833 2931
fax 020 7837 6094
email lag@lag.org.uk
website www.lag.org.uk

Liberty
National Council for Civil Liberties
21 Tabard Street, London SE1 4LA
tel   020 7403 3888
fax 020 7407 5354
email info@liberty-humanrights.org.uk
website www.liberty-humanrights.org.uk

London Detainee Support Group
77 Holloway Road, London N7 8JZ
tel   020 7700 0606
fax 020 7700 4433

Medical Foundation for the Care of Victims
of Torture
96–98 Grafton Road, London NW5 3EJ
tel   020 7813 7777
fax 020 7813 0011
website www.torturecare.org.uk

Midlands Refugee Council
5th Floor Smithfield House, Digbeth
Birmingham, B5 6BS
tel   0121 242 2200
fax 0121 242 6650
email info@refugeecouncil.org.uk

Migrants Resource Centre
24 Churton Street, London SW1V 2LP
tel   020 7834 6650
fax 020 7931 8187
email migrantrc@gn.apc.org.uk

Minority Rights Group
379 Brixton Road, London SW9 7DE
tel   020 7978 9498
fax 020 7738 6265
email minority.rights@mrgmail.org
website www.minorityrights.org

National Association of Citizens' Advice
Bureaux
Myddleton House
115–123 Pentonville Road, London N1 9LZ
tel   020 7833 2181
fax 020 7833 4371
website www.nacab.org.uk

National Coalition of Anti-Deportation
Campaigns
110 Hamstead Road
Birmingham B20 2QS
tel   0121 554 6947
fax 0870 055 4570
email ncadc@ncadc.org.uk
website www.ncadc.org.uk

National Union of Students
461 Holloway Road, London N7 6LJ
tel   020 7272 8900
fax 020 7263 5713
email nusuk@nusuk.org.uk

North of England Refugee Service
1st floor, 19 Bigg Market
Newcastle-upon-Tyne NE1 1UN
tel   0191 222 0406
fax 0191 222 0239

Praxis
Pott Street, London E2 0EF
tel   020 7729 7985
fax 020 7729 0134
email admin@praxis.org.uk

Refugee Action
3rd Floor, Old Fire Station
150 Waterloo Road, London SE1 85B
tel   0207 654 7700
fax 0207 401 3699

Refugee Arrivals Project
41b Crosslances Rd, Hounslow, TW3 2AD
tel   020 8607 6888/6900
fax 020 8607 6851

Refugee Council
3 Bondway, London SW8 1SJ
Switchboard 020 7820 3000
Info 020 7820 3085
fax 020 7582 9929
email info@refugeecouncil.org.uk
website www.refugeecouncil.org.uk

The Panel of Advisors for Unaccompanied
Refugee Children, Refugee Council
240–250 Ferndale Road
Brixton, London
SW9 5BB
tel 020 7346 6770
fax 020 7346 6778

Refugee Legal Centre
Nelson House, 153–157 Commercial Road,
London E1 2EB
tel   020 7780 3200 (administration)
tel   07831 598057 (emergencies)
fax 020 7780 3201

Royal College of Nursing Immigration
Advisory Service
Immigration Dept., 20 Cavendish Square,
London W1M 0AB
tel   020 7647 3874
email immigationadvice@rcn.org.uk
website www.rcn.org.uk

Runnymede Trust
Suite 106
The London Fruit and Wool Exchange
Brushfield Street
London E1 6EP
tel   0207 377 9222
fax 0207 377 6622
website www.runnymedetrust.org

Scottish Refugee Council
Edinburgh Office, 1st floor, Wellgate House
200 Cowgate Street, Edinburgh EH1 1NQ
tel   0131 225 9994
fax 0131 225 9997

Glasgow Office
98 West George Street, Glasgow G2 1PG
tel   0141 333 1850
fax 0141 333 1860

Southall Black Sisters
52 Norwood Road, Southall
Middlesex UB2 4DW
tel 020 8571 9595 / fax 020 8574 6781
email sbs@leonet.co.uk

Stonewall Immigration Group
C/o Central Station, 37 Warfdale Road
Islington, London N1 9SE
tel   020 7713 0620
fax/admin 020 7713 8864
email info@stonewall-immigration.org.uk

UKCOSA, The Council for International
Education
9–17 St Alban's Place, London N1 0NX
tel 020 7226 3762, fax 020 7226 3373
website www.ukcosa.org.uk

European and international organisations

Council of Europe
www.coe.int

December 18
Attention Ms Myriam De Feyter
Postbus 22
B – 9820 Merelbeke (Belgium)
Fax: 0032/9/3519762
Email: info@december18.net
www.december18.net

European Union
http://europa.eu.int/

International Organisation for Migration
www.iom.int/

United Nations
www.un.org/

United Nations High Commission
for Refugees
21st floor, Millbank Tower
21–24 Millbank, London SW1P 1QP
tel 020 7828 9191
fax 020 7630 5349
email gbrlo@unhcr.ch

Asylum Support Adjudicators
Christopher Wren House
113 High Street
Croydon
CR0 1QG
tel 020 8688 3977
fax 020 8688 6075

Visa nationals, fees and overseas posts

VISA NATIONALS

Visa nationals are people who always need to get entry clearance in advance of travelling to the UK, for whatever purpose. Countries whose citizens are visa nationals include:

Afghanistan
Albania
Algeria
Angola
Armenia
Azerbaijan
Bahrain
Bangladesh
Belarus
Benin
Bhutan
Bosnia-Herzegovina
Bulgaria
Burkina Faso
Burma
Burundi
Cambodia
Cameroon
Cape Verde
Central African Republic
Chad
China
Colombia
Comoros
Congo
Croatia
Cuba
Democratic Republic of Congo (formerly Zaire)
Djibouti

Dominican Republic
Ecuador
Egypt
Equatorial Guinea
Eritrea
Ethiopia
Fiji
Gabon
Gambia
Georgia
Ghana
Guinea
Guinea-Bissau
Guyana
Haiti
India
Indonesia
Iran
Iraq
Ivory Coast
Jordan
Kazakhstan
Kenya
Kirgizstan
Korea (North)
Kuwait
Laos
Lebanon
Liberia
Libya

Macao Special Administrative Region
Macedonia
Madagascar
Maldives
Mali
Mauritania
Mauritius
Moldöva
Mongolia
Morocco
Mozambique
Myanmar (Burma)
Nepal
Niger
Nigeria
Oman
Pakistan
Palestinian Authority
Papua New Guinea
Peru
Philippines
Qatar
Romania
Russia
Rwanda
Sao Tomé e Principe
Saudi Arabia
Senegal

Sierra Leone
Slovak Republic
Somalia
Sri Lanka
Sudan
Surinam
Syria
Taiwan
Tajikistan
Tanzania
Thailand
Togo
Tunisia
Turkey
Turkish Republic of Northern Cyprus
Turkmenistan
Uganda
Ukraine
United Arab Emirates
Uzbekistan
Vatican City (service and emergency passports only)
Vietnam
Yemen
Yugoslavia (Socialist Republic of and present Yugoslav authorities)
Zambia

SELECTED FEES, FROM 1 JULY 2002

The Home Office or Foreign and Commonwealth Office may raise fees at very short notice. It is advisable to check the current fees with them or the local British embassy, consulate or high commission.

Applying for entry clearance

All entry clearance fees are non-refundable and are usually payable in the local currency.

Visitors; students; working holidaymakers; work permit, permit-free and self-employment for six months or less; returning residents; au pairs:

Multiple Entry – six months £36

Multiple Entry – one year £60

Multiple Entry – two years £70

Multiple Entry – five years £88

Multiple Entry - ten years £150

Transit visas (airside, not entering UK) £27

Work permit, permit-free and self employment for over six months £75

Family members of all the above persons accompanying them or coming to join them pay the same fee

Settlement

To accompany or join a relative settled in the UK £260

Non-entry clearance applications from abroad

Certificate of Entitlement £110

British passport (up to 32 pages) £49

British passport for those under 16 £29

Other fees in the UK

Fee for a police registration certificate £34

Certificate of Entitlement £20

British passport (up to 32 pages) £30

British passport for those under 16 £30

British passport submitted in person £60

British passport for those under 16 submitted in person £60

Home Office travel document
Refugees £30
People granted exceptional leave £67
Stateless people £30

Applying for British Citizenship

Registration (for children under 18 and other kinds of British nationals applying for British citizenship) £120

Application for registration as a citizen under s1 British Nationality (Hong Kong) Act 1997 £250

Naturalisation on the grounds of marriage to a British citizen £120

Naturalisation on the grounds of residence in the UK £150

Renunciation of British citizenship £20

BRITISH POSTS OVERSEAS

Some British high commissions and embassies abroad are designated to offer a full entry clearance service and some only a partial service, mainly for diplomatic/official, medical and business visit visas, and refugee family reunion only. The following list was correct as at March 2002. Up-to-date details are available from:

Joint Entry Clearance Unit (now UK Visas)
89 Albert Embankment
London SE1 7TP
Tel: 0207 238 3821
Fax: 0207 238 3760

Those applying for a visit visa can apply to any designated post offering a full entry clearance service and some offering a limited service. Any non-visit application must be made to the designated post in the country where the applicant is living. Where there is no such post, the applicant must apply to the appropriate designated post outside the country where s/he is living.

Designated posts which offer a full entry clearance service

Country	Post	Country	Post
Albania	Tirana	Colombia	Bogota
Angola	Luanda	Costa Rica	San Jose
Argentina	Buenos Aires	Croatia	Zagreb
Australia	Canberra	Cuba	Havana
Austria	Vienna	Cyprus	Nicosia
Bahamas	Nassau	Czech Republic	Prague
Bahrain	Bahrain	Democratic Republic of Congo	Kinshasa
Bangladesh	Dhaka		
Barbados	Bridgetown	Denmark	Copenhagen
Belarus	Minsk	Dominican Republic	Santo Domingo
Belgium	Brussels	Ecuador	Quito
Belize	Belmopan	Egypt	Cairo
Bermuda	Hamilton (Bermuda Dept of Immigration)	El Salvador	San Salvador
		Estonia	Tallinn
		Ethiopia	Addis Ababa
Bolivia	La Paz	Falklands Islands	Stanley (Falklands Islands Dept of Immigration)
Bosnia Herzegovina	Sarajevo		
Botswana	Gaborone		
Brazil	Rio De Janerio		
Brunei	Bandar Seri Begawan	Fiji	Suva
		Finland	Helsinki
Bulgaria	Sofia	France	Paris
Burma	Rangoon	Gambia, The	Banjul
Cameroon	Yaounde	Georgia	Tbilisi
Canada	Ottawa	Germany	Dusseldorf
Chile	Santiago	Ghana	Accra
China	Peking	Gibraltar	Gibraltar (Dept of Immigration)
China	Shanghai		
China	Guangzhou	Greece	Athens

Country	Post	Country	Post
Guatemala	Guatemala City	Nigeria	Lagos
Guyana	Georgetown	Norway	Oslo
Honduras	Tegucigalpa	Oman	Muscat
Hong Kong	British Consulate General, Hong Kong	Pakistan	Islamabad
		Pakistan	Karachi
		Pakistan	Lahore
Hungary	Budapest	Panama	Panama City
Iceland	Reykyavik	Papua New Guinea	Port Moresby
India	New Delhi	Peru	Lima
India	Bombay	Philippines	Manila
India	Calcutta	Poland	Warsaw
India	Chennai (Madras)	Portugal	Lisbon
Indonesia	Jakarta	Qatar	Doha
Irish Republic	Dublin	Romania	Bucharest
Israel	Tel Aviv	Russian Federation	Moscow
Italy	Rome	Russian Federation	St Petersburg
Ivory Coast	Abidjan	Russian Federation	Ekaterinberg
Jamaica	Kingston	Saudi Arabia	Jedda
Japan	Tokyo	Saudi Arabia	Riyadh
(Jerusalem)	Jerusalem	Senegal	Dakar
Jordan	Amman	Seychelles	Victoria
Kenya	Nairobi	Sierra Leone	Freetown
Korea	Seoul	Singapore	Singapore
Kuwait	Kuwait	Slovak Republic	Bratislava
Latvia	Riga	Solomon Islands	Honiara
Lebanon	Beirut	South Africa	Pretoria
Lesotho	Maseru	Spain	Madrid
Libya	Tripoli	Sri Lanka	Colombo
Lithuania	Vilnius	Sudan	Khartoum
Luxembourg	Luxembourg	Swaziland	Mbabane
Macedonia	Skopje	Sweden	Stockholm
Madagascar	Antananarivo	Switzerland	Geneva
Malawi	Lilongwe	Syria	Damascus
Malaysia	Kuala Lumpur	Tanzania	Dar es Salaam
Malta	Valletta	Thailand	Bangkok
Mauritius	Port Louis	Tonga	Nuku'alofa
Mexico	Mexico City	Trinidad and Tobago	Port of Spain
Mongolia	Ulaanbaatar	Tunisia	Tunis
Morocco	Casablanca	Turkey	Istanbul
Mozambique	Maputo	Turkmenistan	Ashgabat
Namibia	Windhoek	Uganda	Kampala
Nepal	Kathmandu	Ukraine	Kiev
Netherlands	Amsterdam	UAE	Abu Dhabi
New Zealand	Wellington	UAE	Dubai
Nicaragua	Managua	United States	Chicago
Nigeria	Abuja		

Country	Post	Country	Post
United States	Los Angeles	Vietnam	Hanoi
United States	New York	Yemen	Sana'a
United States	Washington	Yugoslavia	Belgrade
Uruguay	Montevideo	Zambia	Lusaka
Vanuatu	Port Vila	Zimbabwe	Harare
Venezuela	Caracas		

Limited service

The following countries offer a limited entry clearance service only. Prospective applicants are advised to contact the post directly (contact details are available on the Foreign & Commonwealth Office website www.fco.gov.uk). Those applying for visit visas may apply at any post in another country designated to offer a full entry clearance service. The posts in the countries of the former USSR normally accept applications only from residents of that country.

Country	Post	Other visa categories
Algeria	Algiers	Bangkok
Armenia	Yerevan	Nairobi or Dar es Salaam
Azerbaijan	Baku	Tunis/Paris
Cambodia	Phnom Penh	Moscow
Iran*	Tehran	Moscow/Istanbul
Kazakhstan	Almaty	
Rwanda	Kigali	
St Helena	St Helena (Ascension Islands)	
Taiwan	British Trade and Cultural Office (BTCO) Taipei	
Uzbekistan	Tashkent	

*Full service from 1 April 2002

Countries where there is no entry clearance service

People applying for visit visas may apply at a post in another country designated to offer an entry clearance service. Non-visit applicants should apply at the posts listed.

Country	Post	Country	Post
Afghanistan	Islamabad	Central African Republic	Yaounde
Andorra	Madrid		
Anguilla*	Bridgetown	Chad	Lagos or Abuja
Antigua & Barbuda*	Bridgetown	Comoros	Antananarivo
Benin	Lagos	Congo	Kinshasa
Bhutan	Calcutta	Dominican Republic*	Bridgetown
British Virgin Islands*	Bridgetown	Djibouti	Addis Ababa
Burkina Faso	Abidjan	Equatorial Guinea	Yaounde or most accessible post
Burundi	Should apply to most accessible post	Eritrea	Addis Ababa
		Gabon	Yaounde or most accessible post
Cape Verde	Dakar		
Cayman Islands	Kingston	Grenada*	Bridgetown
		Guinea	Dakar

Country	Post
Guinea-Bissau	Dakar
Haiti	Santo Domingo
Iraq	Amman
Kiribati	Suva
Kyrgyzstan	Almaty
Laos	Bangkok
Liberia	Abidjan
Liechtenstein	Geneva
Macao	Hong Kong
Maldives	Colombo
Mali	Dakar
Marshall Islands	Suva
Mauritana	Casablanca
Micronesia	Suva
Moldova	Bucharest
Monaco	Paris
Monserrat*	Bridgetown
Nauru	Suva
Netherlands Antilles	Amsterdam or Caracas
North Korea	Peking
Niger	Abidjan

Country	Post
Palau	Apply to most accessible post
Paraguay	Buenos Aires
San Marino	Rome
Sao Tome and Principe	Luanda
Sikkim	Calcutta
Slovenia	Zagreb
Somalia	Nairobi or Addis Ababa
St Kitts and Nevis*	Bridgetown
St Lucia*	Bridgetown
St Vincent and the Grenadines*	Bridgetown
Surinam	Georgetown
Tajikistan	Tashkent
Togo	Accra
Tuvalu	Suva
Western Samoa	Wellington

*ECO Bridgetown visits these islands periodically

Work-related applications

SHORTAGE OCCUPATIONS LIST

The following occupations are acknowledged by Work Permits (UK) as being in short supply. Employers of prospective employees who qualify under the following list may obtain work permits under a simplified procedure and do not have to advertise the post ►see page 419. The following list is correct as at April 2002.

A current list is available from the Work Permits (UK) pages of the Home Office website www.ind.homeoffice.gov.uk.

ENGINEERS

Electronic and opto-electronic engineering
Electronic Engineers and Physicists of IENG (or equivalent) level in the following specialist areas:
Cellular Phone Systems Development
Integrated Circuit Design
Opto-Electronics
Photonics
Systems Integration
Telecommunications Systems Development
Video and Audio Systems Development
Radio Frequency and Microwave System and Component Design
Design and Development of Electronic Systems with Embedded Software

Railway engineers
For jobs that are listed below the person must have a degree with at least two years relevant experience from a civil, structures or electrical background:
Railways Planner or Engineer
Railways Modeller
Railway Track Design or Permanent Way Engineer
Signaling Engineer, Communications Engineer
Power Supply Engineer or Electrification Engineer
(Senior positions in the above posts would be expected to have at least five years relevant experience)

Structural/bridge engineers
For jobs that are listed below the person must have a degree with at least two years relevant experience from a structures background:
Structural Engineer
Infrastructure Engineer or Buildings Engineer
Bridge Engineer or Highways Structural Engineer
(Senior posts would generally require appropriate chartered status and a minimum of five years relevant experience)

Transportation and highways engineers

For jobs that are listed below the person must have a transport related degree or a degree with at least two years relevant experience from a civil background:

Traffic Engineer or Transport Planner

Transport Modeller or Transport Economist (the applicant would be expected to have experience in multi-model studies and modelling software such as TRIPS, EMME2, QVIEW, SATURN, PEDROUTE or Microsimulation)

Transport Signal Engineer

Highways Design Engineer or Highways Planning Engineer

Highways Maintenance Engineer

HEALTHCARE SECTOR

Doctors

Consultant posts in the following specialist areas:

Accident and Emergency

Audiological Medicine

Clinical Pharmacology and Therapeutics

Diagnostic Radiology (Radiology)

Morbid Anatomy and Histopathology

Nuclear Medicine

Occupational Medicine

Old Age Psychiatry

Ophthalmology

Orthopaedic Surgery (Trauma and Orthopaedic Surgery)

Paediatrics

Palliative Medicine

Radiotherapy (Clinical Oncology)

Urology

General

Audiologist

Audiological scientist

Clinical Psychologist

Dietician

Occupational Therapist

Pharmacist

Physiotherapist

Speech and Language Therapist

Social Worker

Biomedical Scientist / Medical Laboratory

Scientific Officer

Nurses

All registered nurses and midwives

INFORMATION TECHNOLOGY

For jobs which are listed below, the person must have the relevant skills and experience listed on a separate webpage linked to the information technology list in the Work Permits (UK) web pages.

Occupation	Technology area
Architects in senior positions only	Java
	Java Script
Business Analyst	In any technology area
Network Specialist	In any technology area
Analyst Programmer	Active server Pages/Activex
Database Specialist	C and C++ programming languages
Software Engineer	Cool:gen
	Peoplesoft
	SQL Server
	XML
	DHTML
	Broadvision E-Commerce Tools
Software Engineer (cont.)	All customer relationship Management (CRM) and Computer technology (CTI) packages (especially Siebel, Clarify and Oracle CRM)

OTHER OCCUPATIONS

Actuary
CAA Licensed Aircraft Engineers
Teacher – all posts in England covering compulsory schooling
Veterinary Surgeon

HIGHLY SKILLED MIGRANT PROGRAMME
INCOME BAND/COUNTRY LIST

Category A countries	Category B countries
Income band 1: £40,000	Income band 1: £25,000
Income band 2: £100,000	Income band 2: £60,000
Income band 3: £250,000	Income band 3: £150,000

Category A countries

Andorra
Antigua
Antilles
Argentina
Aruba
Australia
Austria
Bahamas
Bahrain
Belgium
Bermuda
Brunei
Canada
Cayman Islands
Channel Islands
Cyprus
Denmark
Faeroe Islands
Finland
France
French Polynesia
Germany
Greece
Greenland
Guam
Hong Kong
Iceland
Ireland
Israel

Italy
Japan
Kuwait
Liechtenstein
Luxembourg
Macao
Malta
Monaco
Netherlands
New Caledonia
Northern Mariana Islands
New Zealand
Norway
Portugal
Puerto Rico
Qatar
Singapore
Slovenia
South Korea
Spain
Sweden
Switzerland
United Arab Emirates
United Kingdom
United States
Virgin Islands

Category B countries

American Samoa
Barbados
Belarus
Belize
Botswana
Brazil
Chile
Costa Rica
Croatia
Czech Republic
Dominica
Estonia
Gabon
Grenada
Hungary
Latvia
Lebanon
Libya
Lithuania

Malaysia
Mauritius
Mayotte
Mexico
Oman
Palau
Panama
Poland
Saudi Arabia
Seychelles
Slovakia
South Africa
St Kitts
St Lucia
St Vincent
Trinidad & Tobago
Turkey
Uruguay
Venezuela

Category C countries

Income band 1: £20,000
Income band 2: £50,000
Income band 3: £125,000

Albania	Macedonia
Algeria	Maldives
Bolivia	Marshall Islands
Bosnia	Micronesia
Bulgaria	Morocco
Cape Verde	Namibia
Colombia	Paraguay
Cuba	Peru
Dominican Republic	Philippines
Ecuador	Romania
Egypt	Russia
El Salvador	Samoa
Equatorial Guinea	Surinam
Fiji	Swaziland
Guatemala	Syria
Iran	Thailand
Iraq	Tonga
Jamaica	Tunisia
Jordan	Vanuatu
Kazakhstan	West Bank & Gaza
Kiribati	Yugoslavia

Category D countries

Income band 1: £15,000
Income band 2: £35,000
Income band 3: £90,000

Afghanistan	Lao PDR
Angola	Lesotho
Armenia	Liberia
Azerbaijan	Madagascar
Bangladesh	Malawi
Benin	Mali
Bhutan	Mauritania
Burkina Faso	Moldova
Burundi	Mongolia
Cambodia	Mozambique
Cameroon	Myanmar
Central African Republic	Nepal
Chad	Nicaragua
China	Niger
Comoros	Nigeria
Congo	Pakistan
Congo (Democratic Republic)	Papua New Guinea
	Rwanda
Cote D'Ivoire	Sao Tome
Djibouti	Senegal
Eritrea	Sierra Leone
Ethiopia	Soloman Islands
Gambia	Somalia
Georgia	Sri Lanka
Ghana	Sudan
Guinea	Tajikistan
Guinea Bissau	Tanzania
Guyana	Togo
Haiti	Turkmenistan
Honduras	Uganda
India	Ukraine
Indonesia	Uzbekistan
Kenya	Vietnam
Korea, Dem Rep.	Yemen
Kyrgyz Republic	Zambia
	Zimbabwe

Commonwealth countries

COMMONWEALTH COUNTRIES

Citizens of the following countries are Commonwealth citizens, as are British citizens, British Dependant Territories citizens, and British Overseas citizens. The country names are followed by the dates of independence, or – where relevant – dates of joining:

Antigua and Barbuda	1.11.81	India	15.8.47	St Christopher & Nevis	19.9.83

Antigua and
  Barbuda   1.11.81

Australia   1.1.01

Bahamas   10.7.73

Bangladesh   26.3.71
  as East Pakistan 15.8.47

Barbados   30.11.66

Belize   21.9.81

Botswana   30.9.66

Brunei
  Darassalam   1984

Cameroon joined 1.11.95

Canada   1.7 31

Cyprus   16.8.60
  joined 13.3.61

Dominica   3.11.78

Fiji   left1987
  rejoined 1997
  suspended from the
  councils of the
  Commonwealth 2000

The Gambia   18.2.65

Ghana   6.3.57

Grenada   7.2.74

Guyana   26.5.66

India   15.8.47

Jamaica   6.8.62

Kenya   12.12.63

Kiribati   12.7.79

Lesotho   4.10.66

Malawi   6.7.64

Malaysia   31.8.57

Maldives   1982

Malta   21.9.64

Mauritius   12.3.68

Mozambique
  joined 14.11.95

Namibia   joined 21.3.90

Nauru   31.1.68
  joined 31.1.80

New Zealand   26.9.07

Nigeria*   1.10.60
  suspended 11.11.95
  rejoined 29.5.99

Pakistan*   15.8.47
  left 1972,rejoined 1989
  suspended from the
  councils of the
  Commonwealth 1999

Papua New Guinea 16.9.75

St Christopher &
  Nevis   19.9.83

St Lucia   22.2.79

St Vincent and the
  Grenadines   27.10.79

Samoa   1970

Seychelles   29.6.76

Sierra Leone   27.4.61

Singapore   3.6.65

Solomon Islands   7.7.78

South Africa   1931
  left 1961
  rejoined 31.5.94

Sri Lanka   4.2.48

Swaziland   6.9.68

Tanzania   9.12.61

Tonga   4.6.70

Trinidad and
  Tobago   31.8.62

Tuvalu   1.10.78

Uganda   1962

Vanuatu   30.7.80

Zambia   24.10.64

Zimbabwe   18.4.80

Commonwealth nationality is no longer as significant as it once was, but remains relevant in immigration law in four circumstances:

- only Commonwealth citizens can have the right of abode;
- only Commonwealth nationals (plus citizens of the Republic of Ireland) can be exempt from deportation on the basis of their residence in Britain since before 1973;
- working holiday status is only available to Commonwealth nationals; and so is
- the right to work and to settle here on the basis of UK ancestry.

These categories are covered in more detail in the chapters of this book.

*Pakistan's withdrawal from the Commonwealth meant that Pakistani citizens were not considered as Commonwealth nationals for that period. They were unable to take any of the advantages of Commonwealth nationality, even if they had been ordinarily resident in the UK since before Pakistan's withdrawal. Nigeria's suspension, on the other hand, means that Nigerians remain Commonwealth citizens, and can, for example, qualify as working holidaymakers.

Registering with the police

Those who are required to register with the police as a condition of their entry or stay in the UK have been restricted to certain nationals of the following countries (▶see page 535 for who is required to register and how. The requirements are contained in the Immigration Rules at paras 324A–326):

Afghanistan	Colombia	Lebanon	Sudan
Algeria	Cuba	Libya	Syria
Argentina	Egypt	Moldova	Tajikistan
Armenia	Georgia	Morocco	Tunisia
Azerbaijan	Iran	North Korea	Turkey
Bahrain	Iraq	Oman	Turkmenistan
Belarus	Israel	Palestine	United Arab Emirates
Bhutan	Jordan	Peru	
Bolivia	Kazakhstan	Qatar	Ukraine
Brazil	Kirgizstan	Russia	Uzbekistan
China	Kuwait	Saudi Arabia	Yemen

Certain stateless people and those travelling with a non-national travel document, rather than a recognised passport, may also be required to register.

Countries whose adoption decisions are recognised in the UK

Adoptions in the following designated countries are recognised in the UK (SI 1973/19):

Commonwealth Countries

Anguilla
Australia
Bahamas
Barbados
Belize
Bermuda
Botswana
British Virgin Islands
Canada
Cayman Islands

Cyprus
Dominica
Fiji
Ghana
Gibraltar
Guyana
Hong Kong
Jamaica
Kenya
Lesotho
Malaysia

Malawi
Malta
Mauritius
Monserrat
New Zealand
Nigeria
Pitcairn Island
Rhodesia (now known as Zimbabwe)
St Christopher and Nevis

St Vincent
Seychelles
Singapore
Sri Lanka
Swaziland
Tanzania
Tonga
Trinidad and Tobago
Uganda
Zambia

Non-commonwealth Countries

Austria
Belgium
Denmark (including Greenland and the Faroes)
Finland
France (including Reunion, Martinique, Guadeloupe and French Guyana)

Germany
Greece
Iceland
Ireland
Israel
Italy
Luxembourg
Netherlands (including the Antilles)
Norway

Portugal (including the Azores and Madeira)
South Africa (including Namibia)
Spain (including the Balearic and Canary Islands)
Surinam
Sweden

Switzerland
Turkey
United States
Yugoslavia.

Abbreviations

GENERAL TERMS

API	Asylum Policy Instructions (by Chapter, section, paragraph; and in some cases, annex)
ARC	application registration card
ASA	asylum support adjudicator
ASU	Asylum Screening Unit
BC	British citizen
BDTC	British Dependent Territories Citizen
BN(O)	British National (Overseas)
BOC	British Overseas Citizen
BOTC	British Overseas Territories Citizen
BPP	British Protected Persons
BS	British subject
CESC	Council of Europe Social Charter 1961
CIPU	Country Information and Policy Unit
CLR	Controlled Legal Representation
CLS	Community Legal Service
CTA	common travel area
CUKC	Citizens of the United Kingdom and Colonies
EC	European Community
EU	European Union
ECHR	European Convention of Human Rights
ECO	entry clearance officer
EComHR	European Commission on Human Rights
ECSMA	European Convention on Social and Medical Assistance 1953
ECtHR	European Court of Human Rights
EEA	European Economic Area
EIN	Electronic Immigration Network
ELR	exceptional leave to remain
EU	European Union
GB	Great Britain

GATS	General Agreement on Trade in Services
HMO	Houses in Multiple Occupation
HSMP	Highly Skilled Migrants Programme
IAA	Immigration Appellate Authorities
IDI	Immigration Directorate Instructions (by Chapter, section and paragraph; and in some cases, annex)
ICD	Integrated Casework Directorate
IFA	internal flight alternative (also 'IPA' internal protection alternative)
IND	Immigration and Nationality Department
JECU	Joint Entry Clearance Unit (now UK Visas)
LSC	Legal Services Commission
NASS	National Asylum Support Service
NI	Nationality Directorate Instructions (by Chapter, section and paragraph; and in some cases, annex)
OFSTED	Office for Standards in Education
OISC	Office of the Immigration Services Commissioner
PTSD	post-traumatic stress disorder
Refugee Convention/ 1951 Convention	Convention Relating to the Status of Refugees 1951
SAL	standard acknowledgement letter
SEF	statement of evidence form
TA	temporary admission
TEU	Maastrict Treaty on European Union
UASC	unaccompanied asylum seeking child
UDHR	Universal Declaration of Human Rights
UK	United Kingdom
UKCOSA	The Council for International Education
UNHCR	United Nations High Commissioner for Refugees
2002 White Paper	*Secure Borders, Safe Haven: Integration with Diversity in Modern Britain*, 7 February 2002 (Home Office)
1951 Convention/ Refugee Convention	Convention Relating to the Status of Refugees 1951

LEGISLATION

1971 Act	Immigration Act 1971
1981 Act	British Nationality Act 1981
1988 Act	Immigration Act 1988
1993 Act	Asylum and Immigration Appeals Act 1993
1996 Act	Asylum and Immigration Act 1996
1997 Act	Special Immigration Appeals Commission Act 1997
HRA	Human Rights Act 1998
1999 Act	Immigration and Asylum Act 1999

2001 Act	Anti-terrorism, Crime and Security Act 2001
2002 Bill	Nationality, Immigration and Asylum Bill 2002
HC 395	Current statement of immigration rules made under the Immigration Act 1971
EEA Regulations	Immigration (European Economic Area) Regulations 2000
Procedure Rules or Rules	Immigration and Asylum Appeals (Procedure) Rules 2000 (Chapters 29-30)

Other sources of information

GENERAL: IMMIGRATION, NATIONALITY AND ASYLUM

Butterworths Immigration Law Service (Butterworths) (updated approx three times per year)(Butterworths)

Immigration Law & Practice (2001), Jackson and Warr (Sweet & Maxwell) - now a service

Macdonald's Immigration Law & Practice 5th Edition (2001), Macdonald and Webber (Butterworths)

ADOPTION

Immigration and Adoption (1994), Claudia Mortimore (Trentham Books Limited)

ASYLUM AND REFUGEES

Statements of Principle of the Immigration Appeal Tribunal (1999) (Refugee Legal Centre) – a digest of cases

The Law of Refugee Status (1991), James C. Hathaway (Butterworths)

The Law Relating to Asylum in the UK (forthcoming), Symes and Jorro (Butterworths)

The Refugee in International Law 2nd Edition (1996), Guy S. Goodwin-Gill (Clarendon)

The State of the World's Refugees: Fifty years of humanitarian action (2000) (UNHCR)

CHILDREN

Putting Children First: a guide for immigration practitioners (2002), Coker, Finch, Stanley (Legal Action Group)

CRIME AND IMMIGRATION

Immigration Advice at the Police Station 2nd Edition (2001), Brennan (The Law Society)

EUROPEAN FREE MOVEMENT

A Practitioners' Guide to the EC-Turkey Association Agreement (2000), Rogers (Kluwer Law International)

Free movement of persons in the European Union (1996), Martin & Guild (Butterworths)

The Legal Framework and Social Consequences of Free Movement of Persons in the European Union (1999), Guild (Kluwer Law International)

EXTRADITION

Jones on extradition and mutual assistance (2001), Jones (Sweet & Maxwell)

HUMAN RIGHTS

Blake and Fransman: Immigration, Nationality and Asylum under the Human Rights Act 1998 (1999) Blake, Fransman (Butterworths)

European Human Rights Law (1999), Starmer (Legal Action Group)

LEGISLATION

Butterworths Handbook on Immigration Law (2001), Cotran et al (Butterworths)

Immigration Law Handbook 2nd Edition (2001), Phelan (Blackstone Press)

NATIONALITY

Fransman: British Nationality Law 2nd Edition (1998), Fransman (Butterworths)

WELFARE

Homelessness and Allocations (1997) 5th Edition, Arden and Hunter (Legal Action Group)

Migration and Social Security Benefits Handbook 3rd Edition (2002), (Child Poverty Action Group) (due August 2002)

Support for Asylum Seekers (2001), Willman, Knafler, Pierce (Legal Action Group)

The Homelessness Act 2002: A Special Bulletin (2002), Luba and Davies (Jordan Publishing)

Welfare Benefits Handbook 4th Edition (2002-2003), (Child Poverty Action Group)

WORK AND BUSINESS

Immigration Employment & Business Practice 2nd Edition, Devine

PERIODICALS AND UPDATES

Immigration, Asylum and Nationality Law & Practice (Tolleys Publishing) – quarterly review.

Immigration Law Digest (Immigration Advisory Service)

International Journal of Refugee Law (Oxford University Press)

Legal Action (Legal Action Group) – contains periodic 'recent developments' in immigration

LAW REPORTS

Immigration Appeal Reports (Imm AR) (HMSO)

Immigration and Nationality Law Reports (INLR) (Jordan Publishing)

Glossary

This section is intended for quick reference. It introduces many of the commonest and the most technical terms encountered in immigration and refugee law. Many of the items dealt with here are covered in more detail in the text, and may be found through the index. Terms found elsewhere in the glossary are marked with an asterisk. **Note:** Not all the terms set out below are used in the *Handbook* but may be used by immigration officials or other advisers and are included for that reason.

Accreditation: solicitors, and those whose casework is supervised by a solicitor, can have the standards of their work approved by the Law Society, so that they can become accredited members of a 'panel' of expert immigration practitioners. This helps to identify appropriate solicitors to take on immigration or asylum cases.

Accommodation centre: accommodation centres are proposed by the 2002 Bill as places where asylum-seekers may be required to reside under the terms of their temporary admission (they are not 'detained'). Support will be provided to asylum-seekers in the accommodation centre. The accommodation centres are to be introduced on a trial basis initially.

Adjudicator: the person who hears and decides an immigration appeal at first instance. Adjudicators hear cases on their own, in centres around the country. For many years appointed by the Home Office, they are now appointed by the Lord Chancellor's Department.

Administrative removal: this is the form of *enforcement used to remove those who have breached their conditions of leave, overstayed their leave or who have obtained leave by deception. Before the 1999 Act, people in these categories were 'deported' but they are now subject to a summary, quick form of removal like illegal entrants.

Appellant: a person who brings an appeal. In the first place this will always be an individual who has been refused something they were applying for (entry clearance, a certificate of entitlement, leave to enter, a variation of leave, asylum, a residence permit), or has been refused revocation of a deportation order, or against whom the Home Office has taken action (such as removing them as an illegal entrant or deciding to make a deportation order). Since it is possible for most people who lose an appeal to an adjudicator to apply again to the *Immigration Appeal Tribunal, the appellant at this second stage may be the Secretary of State, or an *entry clearance officer.

Application forms: since November 1996 a change to the immigration rules has meant that nearly all applications to the Home Office to extend *leave or to change the category of leave must be made on a standard form, supplied by the Home Office. This includes applications made outside the rules, and the only exceptions are applications: for asylum, to stay as an *EEA national or family member under the terms of the European treaties, for a work permit or applications to vary leave made on entry to an immigration officer by a person who has leave when they arrive.

Application registration card (ARC): these are replacement forms of identification for those who have claimed asylum to replace *standard acknowledgement letters (SALs)**. They have been issued at the Home Office Asylum Screening Unit in Croydon since January 2002. They are biometric smart cards with personal details including fingerprints and employment status.

Assistants: this is the term used to refer to the various voluntary agencies (such as the Refugee Council and Refugee Action) who help asylum-seekers to complete their applications for asylum support and pass them to *NASS. They also arrange for the provision of temporary accommodation for asylum-seekers on behalf of NASS until such time as a decision is made as to whether they qualify for *asylum support.

Association Agreement: a treaty signed between the European Community and another country, which gives the other country preferential access to the countries of the *EEA. Some only give advantages for trade, but the most important allow nationals of the other country to enter mainly as self-employed or business people.

Asylum: the leave to enter or remain given to a person recognised as a refugee under the 1951 United Nations Convention. The rights that go with it mostly also stem from the Convention. Asylum used to be granted for a four year period, but a grant of asylum is now coupled with a grant of *indefinite leave.

Asylum Screening Unit: the Home Office department which registers people applying for asylum after entering the UK, and carries out fingerprinting and identity checks.

Asylum-seeker: a person requesting asylum or refugee status in the UK, whose application has not yet been decided. For *asylum support purposes, 'asylum-seeker' also includes a person who has made a claim under Article 3 ECHR.

Asylum support: this is the form of support given to asylum-seekers as a replacement for the old system of support through welfare benefits or under the National Assistance Act 1948. It was introduced in April 2000 under the 1999 Act. An 'interim' asylum support scheme has been in operation since December 1999 whereby local authorities provide asylum support under a similar framework to certain asylum seekers. Only asylum-seekers who are 'destitute' (without adequate accommodation or the means to meet their essential living needs) can obtain this support.

Asylum Support Adjudicator (ASA): asylum support adjudicators hear appeals from decisions made by the *National Asylum Support Service (NASS) that a person is not entitled to asylum support or that their *asylum support is to be terminated.

Benefits Agency: the administrative branch of the Department of Social Security (DSS), which makes benefits payments.

British citizens: there are two kinds of British citizens: British citizens otherwise than by descent and British citizens by descent. The difference is that the first group can pass British citizenship on automatically to their children born outside the UK and the second cannot.

British Dependent Territories citizens: these are people who are British because of their connection with a place that is not yet independent. They may have been born, adopted, registered or naturalised in that colony and can retain British Dependent Territories citizenship as long as the colony continues. When the colony gains independence or ceases to exist as a separate territory, people lose British Dependent Territories citizenship. This form of British nationality left people requiring leave to enter and remain in the UK, and gave no right of abode anywhere other than the particular dependent (or overseas) territory with which it is connected. However, under the British Overseas Territories Act 2002, BDTCs were re-designated as '*British Overseas Territories Citizens' (BOTCs) who became 'British citizens' with the *right of abode on 21 May 2002.

British Nationals (Overseas): this status was created for British Dependent Territories citizens from Hong Kong, who are able to keep this British nationality status now that Hong Kong is again part of China. However, the status no longer gives a right to anything more than a passport which functions as a travel document.

British Overseas citizens: these are people who were born in a place that used to be a British colony but who did not qualify for citizenship under the law of the new independent country or of any other country and therefore retained their British nationality. They require leave to enter or remain in the UK, and have no right of abode anywhere through this citizenship. Many were able to obtain *'Special Vouchers' but these have been abolished for those applying after 4 March 2002.

British Overseas Territories: these territories were previously known as British Dependent Territories, hence the name of the citizenship associated with them. The remaining territories under British rule are Anguilla, Bermuda, British Antarctica, British Indian Ocean Territory, Cayman Islands, Falkland Islands, Gibraltar, Montserrat, Pitcairn Island, St Helena, Turks and Caicos Islands, Virgin Islands, Cyprus sovereign base areas.

British protected persons: these are people who are from a country which used to be a British protectorate, protected state or trust territory rather than a colony, and who did not gain the citizenship of the new independent country or of any other country.

British subjects: these are people who are from a country which used to be a British colony, who never became citizens of the UK and Colonies under the British Nationality Act 1948 and who did not gain citizenship of the new independent country or of any other country. Before 1983, the term 'British subject' meant exactly the same as *'Commonwealth citizen' but it is now only used for this small group of people. This status (it is not strictly a form of citizenship) automatically ceases on acquisition of any other nationality.

Certificate of entitlement: Commonwealth citizens who have the *right of abode must prove their right either by obtaining a British citizen passport (if they are entitled to one, and depending on the rules about dual citizenship), or by having a certificate of entitlement placed in their passport. The certificate is a type of visa sticker, but unlike other entry clearances it can also be applied for within the United Kingdom.

Certified case: under the Immigration and Asylum Act 1999 the Home Secretary may 'certify' some asylum applications. The effect of these certificates is that, if the adjudicator agrees with the certificate there is no further right of appeal to the *Immigration Appeal Tribunal. These certificates cannot apply to a case where the evidence shows a 'reasonable likelihood that the appellant has been tortured in the country to which he is to be sent', and it is a defence to a certificate to show such evidence at an appeal. There are other certificates which can be issued in asylum and human rights cases which have a different effect. In *third country cases, the Home Office may issue a third country certificate (see Chapter 11). In other cases, the Home Office may try to prevent appeals (or certain grounds being raised in an appeal) by issuing a certificate (see Chapter 29).

Commissioner's decisions: decisions made on social security appeals, at an equivalent level to the *Immigration Appeal Tribunal. They are cited as CIS (if an 'income support' case)/reference number/year. Cases which are considered particularly significant are known as starred decisions.

Common Travel Area: comprises the *UK, Republic of Ireland, Isle of Man and the Channel Islands. There are no immigration controls at the borders between them and people's passports are not stamped with leave to enter.

Commonwealth citizens: most ex-British colonies when they gained independence decided to join this loose group of countries, headed by the British monarch, to retain contacts, trade preferences etc. Commonwealth citizens still retain a few immigration-law advantages over others. All categories of British nationals, except ***British protected persons**, are Commonwealth citizens.

Community Legal Service: the Community Legal Service is a scheme established by the Access to Justice Act 1999 to co-ordinate and rationalise the provision of funds for civil legal and advice services in a way that will effectively meet the needs of individuals.

Convention: in refugee law 'the Convention' invariably means the United Nations Convention Relating to the Status of Refugees, Geneva, 1951, with its Protocol, New York, 1967. The original Convention was restricted in scope by reference to events that had occurred in Europe prior to 1951, but the Protocol removed both the geographical and historical restrictions, to apply the Convention conditions to any refugees. Not all countries have signed and ratified the Convention, and there are still a few of those that have not signed up to the Protocol, and so retain restrictions in their definition of refugees. Following the Human Rights Act 1998, 'the Convention' may also be used to refer to the European Convention on Human Rights and Fundamental Freedoms (ECHR).

Convention grounds: an asylum-seeker will qualify for asylum under the Refugee Convention if they can show that their case fits within the criteria of the 1951 Convention. They must show (i) that they have a fear, which is (ii) objectively well-founded, that if they were returned to their country of origin (iii) they would face persecution, (iv) on grounds of their race, religion, nationality, membership of a particular social group, or political opinion. These motives for persecution are the only ones that count. If a person shows that they would face persecution for any other reason, or that they cannot be returned to their country for any other reason, the Home Office should normally grant exceptional leave to remain instead.

Council of Europe: a larger and much looser grouping than the European Union or the EEA, the Council of Europe comprises some 40 member states. Best known in Britain as the source of the ***European Convention on Human Rights**.

Council of Europe Social Charter: although made in 1961, the significance of the Charter on the benefit entitlement of nationals of its member states has only become apparent with the increasing restrictions on eligibility for income support, income-based JSA and housing benefit/council tax benefit in recent years.

Curtailment of leave: the Home Office has certain narrow powers to cut short a person's leave to enter or remain in the UK if, for example, a person has made false representations in order to obtain the leave in the first place. When the Home Office does this, it 'curtails' the leave. It does not often occur.

Deportation: sending a person out of the UK under an order signed by the Home Secretary. This process of ***'enforcement** is now only used if a person has been convicted of a serious criminal offence, or because the Home Secretary has decided on public policy or national security grounds that the person's presence is 'not conducive to the public good'. The person cannot return unless the order has first been revoked.

Determination: the judgements of the ***Immigration Appellate Authority** are known as determinations. While these decisions may be given orally at the end of the hearing, it is unusual for this to occur in practice, except sometimes in ***certified** asylum appeals and some cases before the ***Immigration Appeal Tribunal**. It is much more common for written determinations to be sent out some weeks after the hearing. Time limits then apply in the case of an application to appeal further.

Directions: this is used in at least two distinct senses:

i) **removal directions:** when people are to be expelled from the UK, the immigration authorities make arrangements for them to be sent either to the country of their nationality, the country which issued their travel document (if different), the country from which they embarked to come here, or another country where they would be admitted. A notice of these arrangements, specifying the destination and flight details (or ferry or Channel Tunnel train) is served in advance.

ii)**appeal directions:** before the full hearing of an *asylum case it is usual for the *adjudicator to order that various procedural steps are completed within times specified. A standard form is usually given, dealing with the production of documentary evidence, a chronology of events, a 'skeleton argument' and other issues. Representatives complain that nearly all the burden of these falls on appellants, and the Home Office are rarely required to take similar steps.

Directorate: the immigration work of the Home Office is the responsibility of the *Immigration and Nationality Directorate. Within this the *Immigration Service has a specific structure of its own.

Dis-benefitted asylum-seekers: this is the phrase often used to refer to asylum-seekers who were entitled to welfare benefits because they claimed asylum on arrival before 3 April 2000 and who then receive a negative decision on their asylum application after that time so that they are no longer entitled to welfare benefits. They then become entitled to asylum support if they are destitute. Generally, if the asylum decision was made on or after 25 September 2000, they are entitled to *NASS support, otherwise, they are entitled to *'interim' asylum support from a local authority.

Dispersal: this is the government policy operated by NASS under which it attempts to place asylum-seekers in accommodation outside London and the South-East into 'cluster' areas of asylum-seekers where there is a ready supply of low-cost accommodation available. It remains to be seen to what extent the system of *accommodation centres under the 2002 Bill will replace the dispersal system. For the time being it seems that they will operate side by side.

DNA: since 1989 the government has operated a scheme to provide DNA testing free of charge to first time applicants for settlement if there are doubts as to the relationship between applicant and sponsor. Entry clearance officers cannot force people to undergo tests, but are likely to refuse anyone who declines to do so, just because they 'cannot be satisfied' about the relationship. The scheme is supposed to be self-financing by recovering costs through general visa fees. It is available world-wide but is mainly used in a few posts (Addis Ababa, Lagos, Istanbul and across the Indian sub-continent) and above all in Dhaka.

Domicile: the country to which people feel they belong and in which they intend to spend the rest of their life. Normally people are considered to have a 'domicile of origin', usually the country in which they were born and grew up. This can only be changed by a conscious decision to settle and stay in another country and thus acquire a 'domicile of choice'. Questions asked to determine the domicile of people who have left their countries of origin often include where they hope to die and be buried/cremated. Domicile is important in deciding which countries' laws affect a particular person, for example in deciding whether a person is capable of contracting a polygamous marriage, or of adopting a child in a particular country. People's immigration status has no direct connection with their domicile.

Dual citizenship: some people may qualify for the nationality of more than one country if for example they are born in one country to parents who hold the citizenship of another. Or they may marry, or live somewhere else, and become eligible to naturalize. Whether or not they can hold more than one nationality depends on the laws in each country. Britain expressly recognizes dual (or multiple) nationality, and so do all the commonwealth Caribbean states, Bangladesh and Pakistan. India, and most of the African common-wealth, do not. In many cases possession of more than one passport is tolerated, even though a country's law may not permit recognition. Children are generally permitted to retain dual nationality, and then opt for one or the other on becoming adults, if the law of one of those countries does not generally permit holding more than one passport. It is possible to be both a *British Overseas Citizen and a *British citizen at the same time.

Dublin Convention: this agreement was negotiated between all the member states of the EU, but as an inter-governmental measure, rather than part of community law, so the institutions of the EU have no say in its operation. It is intended to determine which state should take the responsibility for dealing with an asylum claim, and came into force on 1 September 1997. The government intends to re-negotiate the the Dublin Convention.

Electronic Immigration Network: after some years of development and lobbying for funds, the Electronic Immigration Network was launched in June 1998. It provides on-line access to a large number of links of interest to immigration advisers and others. It also carries, for subscribers, the full text of a large selection of immigration case judgements, including many not published anywhere else.

Enforcement: this is a term which, in the past has been used to refer to the *deportation and *illegal entry methods of requiring people to leave the UK. In the *Handbook* we use the term to refer to *all* of the standard ways in which people can be forced to leave including those who are removed having been refused leave to enter the UK and those who are in breach of their conditions or who *overstay. The 1999 Act also uses the term to refer to all of these methods of forced departure (see s28 inserting s24A 1971 Act).

Entry clearance officers: officials at British posts overseas who deal with immigration applications there. In a 'visa national' country, they may be known as visa officers, in a non-visa Commonwealth country as entry certificate officers. In larger posts there will also be a senior rank of officer known as the Entry Clearance Manager.

European Convention on Human Rights (ECHR): an international instrument agreed by the Council of Europe. It has now been largely incorporated into UK law by the Human Rights Act 1998 (HRA). This has had a large impact upon immigration and asylum law in the UK.

European Economic Area: covers the countries of the European Union (EU – previously the European Community) and three other European countries, Iceland, Liechtenstein and Norway. The countries of the EU are Austria, Belgium, Denmark, Finland, France, Germany, Greece, Ireland, Italy, Luxembourg, the Netherlands, Portugal, Spain, Sweden and the UK. Nationals of all these countries have free movement in all 18 countries.

Exceptional leave to enter or remain: people who apply for refugee status in the UK and are refused may be granted exceptional leave to enter or remain in the UK if the Home Office considers that it would not be safe for them to be returned to their country of origin. If people are allowed to remain in the UK on human rights grounds, the Home Office still treats the leave which they are given as leave which is given 'exceptionally'. 'Exceptional leave' is also used in a broader sense to refer to anyone who is granted leave outside the immigration rules even if no asylum application has been made.

Extradition: this procedure is not covered in the *Handbook*. It refers to the means by which a person can be sent to another country to stand trial for a criminal offence. It is a complex area and anyone who is being subject to extradition proceedings should be referred for specialist advice.

Extra-territorial effect: this is a term which has been used to describe an argument about the true extent of the *ECHR rights incorporated by the Human Rights Act 1998. The Home Office have tried to argue that, if a person is to be sent to another country, they can only complain about a breach of their human rights on the basis of what will happen to them in that country if they face treatment contrary to Article 3 (torture or inhuman or degrading treatment or punishment). This is because the Home Office say that the ECHR does not have 'extra-territorial' effect in relation to the other Articles under the Convention. In a starred decision (*Kacaj*), the IAT rejected this Home Office argument.

Family life: this often refers to the 'right to respect for family life' under Article 8 ECHR which is one of the rights incorporated by the Human Rights Act.

Family visitor: under the 1999 Act, a right of appeal against refusal of entry clearance was re-introduced for 'family visitors'. The definition of 'family visitor' is contained in the Immigration Appeals (Family Visitor) (No 2) Regulations 2000. It includes the visitor's: spouse, father, mother, son, daughter, grandfather, grandmother, grandson, granddaughter, brother, sister, uncle, aunt, nephew, niece or first cousin. It also includes the father, mother, brother or sister of the visitor's spouse and the spouse of the visitor's son or daughter. In addition, it includes the visitor's stepfather, stepmother, stepson, stepdaughter, stepbrother or stepsister. Finally, it includes a person who the visitor has lived with as a member of an unmarried couple for at least two of the three years before the day on which the application for entry clearance is made.

Fees: under the Consular Fees Act 1980 fees can be charged for all entry clearance applications and para 30 HC 395 states that an entry clearance application is not validly made until the fees are paid. The level of fees is set in sterling by the Consular Fees Orders, but they must be paid at the entry clearance post in the local currency. The Home Office has the power to set charges for settlement applications in the UK as well but has never done so.

Freedom of movement: the framework of the European Union is said to rest on four 'freedoms' – of goods, services, capital, and people. People are given the freedom to move around the countries of the European Union (and now the EEA) as workers, or to provide or receive services. The scope of these provisions, and the limitations on free movement, are not detailed in the Treaties, and much depends on interpretations from the European Court of Justice.

Great Britain: the UK excluding Northern Ireland, that is England, Scotland and Wales. It does not include the Isle of Man or the Channel Islands.

Green books: the popular name for the Immigration Appeals Reports.

Habeas Corpus: this is a High Court procedure under which a person who is detained can challenge their detention on the basis that there is *no legal power* to detain them.

Habitual residence: a term used in social security law in order to exclude some people from eligibility for income-based jobseeker's allowance, income support, housing benefit and council tax benefit and from local authority housing.

Hard cases support: 'hard cases' support is the support which, in certain cases, is made available to those who are no longer entitled to *asylum support because they have exhausted the appeals process. It is provided in the form of accommodation and board. The legal power to provide this support is contained in section 4 of the 1999 Act.

Highly Skilled Migrants Programme (HSMP): the Highly Skilled Migrants Programme was introduced by the government in January 2002 as part of its economic migration policy referred to in the 2002 White Paper. Applicants are allocated points based on their educational qualifications, work experience, past earnings, achievements in a chosen field and whether it is a 'priority' application.

HC 395: whenever *immigration rules are changed or replaced, completely or in part, the paper published is always entitled 'Statement of Changes in Immigration Rules'. What distinguishes them most easily is the issue number. The present rules are set out in HC 395 which was issued in May 1994 and in force from 1 October 1994; although it has been repeatedly amended since.

Illegal entrant: a person who immigration officers believe has entered the UK illegally; either by by-passing immigration control altogether, or by deception as to his or her identity or reasons for coming to the UK, or by entering in breach of a current deportation order.

Immigration Appeal Tribunal (IAT): this is the second tier of the *Immigration Appellate Authority (IAA)** (the first being the adjudicators) to which people can appeal if their immigration appeal is dismissed by the *adjudicator**. When hearing appeals, it consists of a two or three member panel. Before a person can appeal to the IAT, they must obtain the IAT's 'leave' (permission) to appeal which is granted or refused on a consideration of written grounds of appeal.

Immigration authorities: used in the *Handbook* to refer to those officials responsible for immigration control: Home Office officials, *immigration officers**, *entry clearance officers**.

Immigration Appellate Authority: since it was set up in 1971, the Immigration Appellate Authority has functioned as a two stage appeals body. Where there is a right of appeal, it will usually be heard in the first place by a single *adjudicator**. If either the appellant or respondent is unhappy with the adjudicator's determination, they can apply to the *Immigration Appeal Tribunal**, but they will have to show that there are strong enough grounds to be given leave to appeal.

Immigration officer: usually an official at a British port of entry dealing with immigration applications who decides on granting and refusing leave to enter, and what conditions should be attached to any leave granted.

Immigration Service: any member of the Immigration Service may be referred to as an immigration officer. The operational ranks of the service are immigration officer, immigration Assistant (below immigration officer, and will not handle casework directly), Chief Immigration Officer, who will be required to approve refusal and detention decisions, and Inspector.

Immigration and Nationality Directorate: the department of the Home Office responsible for handling all applications concerning immigration, nationality and asylum, as well as for enforcement and developing policy in these areas of law.

Immigration rules: the rules of practice, published by the Home Office as to the conditions which various different categories of applicant have to satisfy in order to be admitted to the UK. If they are published while Parliament is sitting, they are called House of Commons papers, such as *HC 395**; if in a Parliamentary recess, they are Command papers, such as Cm 3365. They are frequently amended. It is always open to the immigration authorities to waive the rules and grant leave exceptionally.

Indefinite leave: leave to enter or remain in the UK without any time limit. If there is no time limit, no other immigration conditions can be put on the person's stay either. A person who has indefinite leave to enter or remain is generally accepted as being *settled** in the UK.

Induction centre: induction centres are to be introduced in order to give asylum-seekers a basic introduction to and understanding of the asylum process when they arrive. Applicants will not be 'detained' there but can be required to reside there for a very limited period under the terms of their *temporary admission** even if they do not require any support.

Innovators scheme: this scheme was introduced as a two-year pilot operation in September 2000 in order to attract entrepreneurs to the UK. It is particularly targeted at those in the field of 'e' business and other new technology fields.

Interim (asylum) support: this is a form of *asylum support** provided to certain asylum-seekers by local authorities rather than by *NASS**.

Internal flight: sometimes referred to as internal flight alternative, or IFA. If an asylum-seeker claims that they would be at risk in a particular region of their country of origin the Home Office may reply that they could be safe elsewhere in that country. So they may refuse a Tamil from the Jaffna area of Sri Lanka, saying that they would be safe in Colombo, or a Kurd from south-eastern Turkey, on the assention that he or she could live peaceably in the west of the country. The issue may sometimes arise only in the course of an appeal. In each case the decision should be subject to a test of reasonableness.

International terrorists: 'International terrorist' is a term taken from the Anti-terrorism, Crime and Security Act 2001 to refer to certain people who are connected with international terrorism who can be detained by the immigration authorities even though they have not been charged with or convicted of an offence and even though they cannot (legally or practically) be *removed from the UK.

Judicial review: a means of asking the High Court to rule on the legal validity of decision-making by a public body. It may be the only way of contesting an immigration refusal when there is no right of appeal.

Leave to enter/remain: permission given by immigration officials for people to enter or remain in the UK. It may be indefinite or limited.

Legal Services Commission: the Legal Services Commission is a public body created by the Access to Justice Act 1999. It is responsible for carrying out functions in relation to the Community Legal Service and the Criminal Defence Service as required by statute.

Limited leave: permission to enter or remain in the UK which has a time limit, and may have other conditions attached to it.

Maintenance undertaking: a formal statement signed by a person living in the UK that he or she will support a relative applying to come to or to remain in the UK. It means that the relative is not eligible to claim non-contributory welfare benefits for five years after it was signed, or after the person was given leave to enter or remain in the UK on this basis, whichever is the later, unless the signatory to the undertaking dies.

National Asylum Support Service (NASS): this is the name of the part of the Home Office which is responsible for operating the national scheme of *asylum support.

Naturalisation: a process of applying for British nationality. The application is formally at the discretion of the Home Office and can be made on the basis of residence in the UK, marriage to a British partner or Crown service. Naturalisation and *registration are both ways of gaining British citizenship; the citizenship obtained is the same whichever process is used.

'One-stop' procedure: the one-stop system of appeals was introduced by the 1999 Act to ensure that people raise all of their grounds (particularly asylum and human rights grounds) for staying in the UK at the same time so that they can be considered altogether by the Home Office and determined in one appeal. There are penalties for not complying with the procedure. The system is likely to be clarified and simplified by the 2002 Bill.

Ordinary residence: this is defined in the case of *Shah* in the House of Lords as the place where someone is normally living for the time being. If a person is not legally in a country, that period does not count as ordinary residence. Reasons for residence can include 'education, business or profession, employment, health, family or merely love of the place'. People can be ordinarily resident in the UK without being settled here, for example students, work permit holders and au pairs. It is not an immigration status and has no direct connection to this; the term is also used in other areas of law, including the National Health Service and some benefits regulations. Ordinary residence may change; the Home Office could argue that several months' residence abroad, particularly if the person had taken a job or given up a home in the UK, had broken ordinary residence in the UK.

However, it is possible to be ordinarily resident in more than one country at a time, so such decisions can be challenged.

Overseas Territories: see British Overseas Territories.

Overstayer: a person who was allowed into the UK for a limited period but who has remained longer than the time allowed without permission from the Home Office.

Patriality: another word for *right of abode. It was first used in the Immigration Act 1971 but was replaced by the term 'right of abode' in the British Nationality Act 1981.

Permit-free employment: a list of jobs which people may come to the UK to do without the employers needing to get work permits.

Person from abroad: a term first used by the Department of Social Security Benefits Agency meaning a person who is not eligible to claim certain welfare benefits. It has now been largely replaced by the definition of persons who are 'subject to immigration control' under s115 of the 1999 Act. Those who are required to pass the 'habitual residence' test in order to obtain certain benefits, are excluded as being 'persons from abroad' if they cannot pass this test.

Pillars: one way of explaining the significance of the Maastricht Treaty on the European Union is to consider the Union as the roof of a building, supported by three pillars. One pillar is the European Community (which includes economic policy and the free movement of EEA nationals), the second is the Common Foreign and Security Policy (CFSP) and the third, Justice and Home Affairs matters (which includes *third-country national migration).

Police registration certificate: the certificate provided by the police to those non-Commonwealth, non-EEA citizens who are required to register with them.

Political asylum: another term used for refugee status (see below).

Pre-sift: at certain diplomatic posts which receive large numbers of applications for visit visas there is a system of weeding out those applications which look likely to fail, and recommending to the person that they withdraw. The advantage to the applicant is that if they withdraw they keep the fee, but if they persist and are refused, they lose it. People cannot be obliged to withdraw an application, and must be told of their right to continue. They should also be given a notice explaining what has happened, but as their application has not been considered in full this notice does not explain the reasons for the failure.

Private life: this refers to the 'right to respect for private life' under Article 8 *ECHR which is one of the rights incorporated by the Human Rights Act 1998.

Probationary period: this refers to the period which a spouse or *unmarried partner of a person settled in the UK has to serve with limited leave before becoming entitled to apply for settlement. The probationary period is 12 months for spouses and 24 months for unmarried partners. The 2002 White Paper proposes to change the rules so that spouses also have a probationary period of 24 months.

Proportionality: this is a legal term which is used in various different contexts. For our purposes, it is most often used to describe the balancing exercise which must be carried out to determine whether a 'restricted' human right under the *ECHR (like Article 8) can be interfered with in the interests of the community so that the right as a whole is not violated by government action. For example, the Home Office will often try to justify some interference with the right to respect for family life under Article 8, on the grounds that the interference is 'proportionate' when measured against the need to maintain a proper immigration control.

Public funds: public funds for immigration purposes are attendance allowance, child benefit, council tax benefit, disability living allowance, disabled person's tax credit, working families' tax credit, housing benefit, income-based jobseeker's allowance, income support, invalid care allowance, severe disablement allowance, and housing as a homeless person or from the local authority housing register.

Quality Mark: Quality Mark is a standard that all providers of legal and advice services must achieve in order to be part of the *Community Legal Service scheme.

Recommendations: when an appeal is dismissed by an *adjudicator but there are strong compassionate reasons why a person ought to be allowed to remain in the UK, representatives often ask adjudicators to make a 'recommendation' to the Home Office that *exceptional leave is granted. Whether to make a recommendation and whether the Home Office will follow a recommendation are both discretionary decisions. Making recommendations is not part of the formal powers of adjudicators.

Refoulement: the central obligation of the UN *Convention is that of 'non-refoulement', in Article 33. This is the provision requiring a state not to 'expel or return a refugee in any manner whatsoever to the frontiers of territories where his life or freedom would be threatened on account of his race, religion, nationality, membership of a particular social group or political opinion', unless it can be shown that he or she is a danger to the security of that state.

Refugee: according to the UN *Convention is a person who is unwilling or unable to return to the country of their nationality or former habitual residence because of a well-founded fear of persecution on specified grounds (the *'Convention grounds'). When the Home Office recognises people as refugees, it grants them asylum in the UK, and *indefinite leave.

Registration: there are three distinct immigration/nationality law uses of this term.

1 A process of applying for British nationality. The word is now used for any child applying for British nationality and for a person who holds any other kind of British nationality applying to become a British citizen. Registration and *naturalisation are both ways of gaining British nationality; the nationality obtained through either process is the same.

2 Registering the birth of a child at a British post overseas. A child born outside the UK to a *British citizen parent who was not him- or herself born in the UK may be registered within one year of birth to become a British citizen by descent.

3 Registering with the police. Citizens of some countries who are over 16 and who have been allowed to remain in the UK for more than six months but are not settled may be required to register with the police. This means going to the local police station, or the Aliens Registration Office in London, with the passport, two passport-sized photos and details of address and occupation, registering these details with the police and paying a fee.

Regularisation of overstayers scheme: this is the scheme by which people who were overstayers could make applications to the Home Office to 'regularise' their stay in the UK before 1 October 2000. If they made the application under the Immigration (Regularisation Period for Overstayers) Regulations 2000, then, if the application was later refused, they kept their rights of appeal which existed under the Immigration Act 1971 for those who were *deported as overstayers rather than those who are to be removed from the UK *administratively under section 10 of the 1999 Act. There have been delays in making decisions for those who have made these applications.

Removal: the final process by which the *immigration authorities expel a person from the UK.

Residence document: the term used in European law to refer to the documents which must be provided to the family member of an EEA national where that member is not him or herself a national of the EEA but who is entitled to be in the UK as the family member of the EEA national.

Residence permit: a document issued by the Home Office to EEA nationals to confirm their right to live in the UK.

Respondent: in an appeal, the person against whom the case is brought is the respondent. Typically this will be the Secretary of State at the Home Office. Immigration officers at the ports and *entry clearance officers at posts abroad, however, can legally take decisions in their own names and so may become respondents (see also *appellant).

Returning residents: people who are *settled in the UK and are returning to the UK to settle once more. They should be admitted for an indefinite period, provided the immigration officers are satisfied that they intend to return to stay permanently.

Right of abode: being free of immigration control and able to enter the UK freely at any time, after no matter how long an absence. It is more than simply having the right to live in the UK, or the right to stay indefinitely. All *British citizens have the right of abode. So do some *Commonwealth citizens – people who were born before 1 January 1983 and had a parent born in the UK (when the parent is the father, he must have been married to the mother), and women who were Commonwealth citizens before 1 January 1983 and were married before that date to a man who was born, registered or naturalised in the UK, or who is a Commonwealth citizen with a parent born in the UK, as above.

Right of readmission: the right of British nationals who are not British citizens, but who have been given *indefinite leave to enter or remain in the UK, to return for settlement after any length of absence.

Schengen group: this comprises all EU countries except the UK, Ireland and Denmark. The group has planned since 1988 to establish a common immigration policy and common border controls, with no internal border checks. The agreement came into effect on 26 March 1995 for seven countries. The Schengen 'acquis' or agreement is now incorporated within the framework of the European Union by the Treaty of Amsterdam, except for those countries which have opted out.

Settled: someone who is *ordinarily resident in the UK without any restrictions on the time they are permitted to remain here. British citizens and those with indefinite leave who usually live in the UK are, therefore, all generally accepted as being 'settled'.

Special quota voucher: the permission granted to certain *British nationals, who are not *British citizens, to come to settle in the UK. The system was set up in 1968, after the Commonwealth Immigrants Act 1968 removed the rights of British people without a connection by birth or descent with Britain itself to come to Britain. In order to qualify under the scheme, people must have no other nationality but British; be 'heads of households'; have some connection with East Africa and be under pressure to leave the country in which they are currently living. Special vouchers were abolished on 4 March 2002.

Special Immigration Appeals Commission: until 1998 whenever the Home Secretary decided to expel someone and cited reasons of national security there has been no right of appeal but only an opportunity for a very limited review. This procedure was considered inadequate by the European Court of Human Rights, leading to the creation of this Commission to provide a meaningful appeal.

Sponsor: a friend, relative or other person who supports an applicant's application to come to the UK. In some cases, they are asked to sign a *maintenance undertaking.

Standard acknowledgement letter (SAL): a letter which used to be issued by the Home Office or immigration service to people seeking asylum. People who applied for asylum on entry to the UK had a document called SAL1 and people who applied after entry had a SAL2. SALs are now being replaced by *Application Registration Cards.

Subject to immigration control: this is a term which advisers and the Home Office often use to refer to people who need *leave to enter or remain in the UK (i.e. people who do not have the *right of abode and who are not exercising European rights of free movement and are not exempt from immigration control). The 1996 Act (s13(2)) gives this definition to this term. The 1999 Act gives a different definition for this term which is used to define who is not able to access certain forms of welfare provision (s115(9) 1999 Act). To avoid confusion, in the *Handbook*, we have only used the term as it is used in the 1999 Act for welfare purposes (see Chapter 31).

Switching: 'switching' is a term used to describe applications made for people who have leave to be in the UK on one basis (for example as a visitor) and who then wish to apply for leave to remain in a different capacity (for example as a spouse). The *immigration rules severely restrict the circumstances in which people may 'switch'.

Temporary admission (TA): a kind of limbo state, used as an alternative to detention. While immigration officers are considering whether to allow someone in at a port of entry, or after refusal of entry and before removal, or when a person is being treated as an illegal entrant, he or she may either be detained or released on temporary admission. If released, the person has not been granted formal leave to enter the UK, and can be recalled and detained at any time. Asylum-seekers may be on temporary admission for long periods. For a fuller description, see the beginning of Chapter 25.

Temporary protection: one reason given by governments for the decline in the proportion of asylum-seekers granted asylum is the inflexibility of the status set up by the Convention. It is said that this makes it unsuitable as a response to emergencies, and there is increasing discussion – particularly within the EU – of other forms of status. Decisions can be made quickly to provide for whole groups of displaced people, but the individual cases will not be considered in detail, and the rights that are given will be much more limited. In particular there will be no expectation of eventual settlement. The UK government has already experimented with special measures for Bosnian detainees and some Sierra Leoneans.

Third country: this term is usually used to refer to a country, other than the one which an asylum applicant is a national of, but which the Home Office may wish to send an asylum applicant to, rather than considering their application for asylum in the UK. There are criteria set out in the 'Dublin Convention' for determining which state in Europe is responsible for determining an asylum claim made by an asylum-seeker within their territories. 'Third country nationals' is a term used to refer to non-EEA nationals in the conrext of EU rights of free movement.

Travel documents: although this may refer to any document of identity provided for the purpose of international travel, it is generally used to mean the non-national documents issued to refugees, stateless persons and those granted exceptional leave. The Home Office (*Immigration and Nationality Directorate) has a specialist Travel Documents Section: blue 'Convention travel documents' are issued to people recognised as refugees; brown 'certificates of identity' are issued to some people with exceptional leave. Brown documents are not recognised in some countries, and almost all require holders of brown documents to obtain visas.

UNHCR: the United Nations High Commissioner for Refugees maintains offices with responsibility for each country which is a signatory to the Convention. They have an interest in ensuring consistency in the application of the Convention, and can be joined to an asylum appeal as a party. They also produce the Handbook on Procedures and Criteria for Determining Refugee Status.

United Kingdom: comprises Great Britain together with Northern Ireland. British immigration law applies equally throughout the UK.

United Kingdom and Islands: this refers to the UK together with the Crown Dependencies of the Isle of Man and the Channel Islands. Certain provisions in law apply to this area as a whole. The Islands have their own immigration arrangements, but these are closely integrated with the UK controls.

Unmarried partners: this term is used in the immigration rules to refer to couples (heterosexual or same-sex) who have been together for two or more years, are in a relationship 'akin to marriage' and who cannot marry according to law (i.e. because they are a same-sex couple, or because one of them is already married). It does *not* include people who cannot marry because one or both parties is too young or because they are too closely related. The 2002 White Paper suggests that the government may allow couples who are not legally prohibited from marrying but who do not wish to marry for other reasons to also come within the definition.

Visa nationals: people who always need to get entry clearance in advance of travelling to the UK, for whatever purpose, unless they are *returning residents or are returning within a period of earlier leave granted for more than six months. Countries whose citizens are visa nationals are listed in an Appendix to the immigration rules, which is amended from time to time, usually to add fresh countries.

Voluntary departure: people liable to deportation may decide to leave before an order is signed. The Immigration Service will usually permit this if the person buys his or her own ticket.

Work permits: the permission gained by employers to employ a worker from overseas who does not otherwise qualify to come to live in the UK. Work Permits (UK) issues permits to employers, not to workers, to employ a named person in a specific job. Any change of job means the new employers must apply for a new permit.

Alphabetical list of cases

Many of the following decisions are to be found on the database of the Electronic Immigration Network (EIN).

Cases shown only as 'CIS' are Social Security Commissioners decisions. Named cases followed only by a number in round brackets are unreported decisions of the Immigration Appeal Tribunal. A '*' denotes a starred decision of the IAT, which must be followed by other decisions of the IAT and adjudicators. Those shown with a citation 'Imm AR' are reported in the Immigration Appeal Reports (Green Books); INLR cases are in Jordans Immigration and Nationality Law Reports.

'AC' is a reference to 'Appeal Cases'; WLR refers to the Weekly Law Reports; 'All ER' is a reference to the All England Law Reports; 'QB' is a reference to the Queens Bench law reports; 'BHRC' refers to 'Butterworths Human Rights Cases; 'HLR' refers to the Housing Law Reports'. 'CCLR' is a reference to the Community Care Law Reports; 'INLP' is a reference to Immigration and Nationality Law & Practice; 'LS Gaz' refers to the Law Society Gazette and 'Sol Jo' is a reference to the Solicitor's Journal.

'EWHC' and 'EWCA' are 'neutral citation references' used by the courts to number decisions of the High Court and Court of Appeal. They are not references to a separate series of law reports.

The 'EHRR' are the European Human Rights Reports; 'ECR' are the European Case Reports; 'CMLR' is a reference to the Common Market Law Reports; 'DR' is a reference to the Decisions and Reports series of European human rights cases.

A

A v Australia
  [1997] 4 BHRC 210   506

A and A v Netherlands
  (1992) 72 DR 118   258

A, R (on the application of) v Lambeth LBC
  [2001] 4 CCLR 486 CA   687
  [2002] HLR13

Abdadou v SSHD
  [1998] SC 504, OH   355
  Butterworths ILS Vol III, section 3D, 91

Abdi (DS)
  [1996] Imm AR 148, CA   228, 643

Abdulaziz, Cabales and Balkandali v UK
  Series A No 94,   235, 256,
  (1985) 7 EHRR 471   257, 258,
               259

Adan and Aitsegeur, R v SSHD ex p
  [2001] INLR 44, HL   153, 208

Adebizi (15514)   653

Adimi, R v Uxbridge Magistrate's Court, ex p
  [1999] 4 All ER 520,
  [2000] 3 WLR 434,
  [1999] Imm AR 560,   195, 519,
  [1999] INLR 490   557

Adoui and Cornuaille v Belgium:115-116/81
  [1982] ECR 1665,
  [1982] 3 CMLR 631   470

Advic v UK
  [1995] 20 EHRR CD 125   257

Ahmed v Austria
  [1997] 24 EHRR 278   243

Ahmed (Ishaque) (CA) (12292) –
  consent order not published 334

Ahmed and Patel, R v SSHD, ex p
[1998], INLR 570, CA 367

Ahmed (Kaleem)
[1995] (12774) IAT 653

Ajayi v UK
Applcn 27663/95
20th June 1999 (unreported) 255

AKB, R v SSHD, ex p
[1996] 3 ILD 2 506, 523

Akhtar
[1993] Imm AR 423 CA 415

Akinde v SSHD
[1993] Imm AR 512, CA 549

Akrich (IAT) C - 109/01 462

Ali v Switzerland
Applcn 24881/94 EComHR 500

Amimim Mohammed
(Gibraltar Supreme Court)
[1992] 3 CMLR 481 482

Re Amin
[1983] 2 AC 818,
[1983] 2 All ER 864, HL 578

Amin, R v IAT ex p
[1992] Imm AR 367 652

Amuur v France
[1996] 22 EHRR 533, ECtHR 499, 500

Antonissen, R v IAT, ex p: C-292/89
[1991] ECR I-745,
[1991] 2 CMLR 373, ECJ 455, 469

Arman Ali, R v SSHD, ex p
[2000] Imm AR 134, 58, 81,
[2000] INLR 89 235, 334

Asante v SSHD
[1991] Imm AR 78 IAT 157

Ashley v SSHD (01/TH/1837) IAT 249

Awuko (4220) IAT 376

Aydin v Turkey
[1997] 25 EHRR 251 242

Azam (Abrar) v ECO Islamabad)
(11704) (30/12/94) IAT 330

B

B (adoption order: nationality), Re
[1998] Imm AR 324,
[1998] INLR 505, CA; revsd
[1999] 2 AC 136,
[1999] 2 All ER 576,
[1999] 2 WLR 714,
[1999] Imm AR 277,
[1999] INLR 125, HL 390

B, R v Special Adjudicator and SSHD ex p
[1998] Imm AR 182
[1998] INLR 315 505

Bahar (R Othman) v Immigration Officer
[1998] Imm AR 534 IAT 652

Bajric, R v Derby City Council, ex p
(CO 1139/2000) (14 August
2000, unreported) 710

Balkandali, see Abdulaziz, Cabales and
Balkandali v UK

Bastiampillai, R v IAT, ex p
[1983] 2 All ER 844,
[1983] Imm AR 1 404

Bayar (12380) IAT 407

Begum (Hasna) (15629) IAT 334

Begum (Husna)
[2001] INLR 115, CA 407

Begum (Manshoora) R v IAT, ex p
[1986] Imm AR 385 407

Begum (Momotaz) (18699) IAT 330

Begum (Zabeda) (16677) consent order
before the Court of Appeal 334

Belgian Linguistic Case (No 2)
[1968] 1 EHRR 252 ECtHR 238

Beldjoudi v France
[1992] 14 EHRR 801 ECtHR 259, 263

Bensaid v UK
[2001] INLR 325, 241, 249,
[2001] 33 EHRR 205 ECtHR 252

Berrehab v Netherlands
[1988] 11 EHRR 322, ECtHR 257, 259, 379

Bibi [2000] Imm AR 385 CA 402

Bibi (Sonor) (19199) IAT 334

Bibi v UK
[1992] Applcn 19628/92
EcomHR 258

Bidar [2002] High Court –
ECJ reference 318

Binbasi, R v SSHD ex p
[1989] Imm AR 593 159

Birden v Stadtgemeinde Bremen: C-1/97
[1998] ECR I-7747,
[1999] 1 CMLR 420, ECJ 481

Bostanci, R v SSHD ex p
[1999] Imm AR 411 184

Botta v Italy
[1998] 26 EHRR 241 ECtHR 266

Boughanemi v France
[1996] 22 EHRR 228 ECtHR 257

Bouchereau
[1977] ECR,
[1978] QB 732 470

Boukssid v SSHD
[1998] Imm AR 270,
[1998] INLR 275, CA 464

Boultif v Switzerland
[2001] 33 EHRR1179 ECtHR   260

Bouzagou, R v Goverener of Ashford
Remand Centre, ex p
[1983] Imm AR 69   74

Boyle v UK
[1994] 19 EHRR 179 EComHR   257

Brezinski and Glowacka, R v SSHD ex p
19th July 1996, unreported   517, 523

Bugdaycay v SSHD, Musisi Re
[1987] AC 514,
[1987] 1 All ER 940,
[1987] WLR 606,
[1987] Imm AR 250   519

C

Cabales, see Abdulaziz, Cabales and
Balkandali v UK

Cabrera (17123) IAT   652

Camenzind v Switzerland
16th December [1997]
ECtHR   254

Campbell and Cosans v UK
[1982] 4 EHRR 293   245

Chahal v UK
[1996] 23 EHRR 413 ECtHR   168, 240,
                                   243, 498,
                                   500, 501, 619

Chang (01 TH00100) [2001] IAT   468

Chavrimootoo, R v IAT, ex p
[1995] Imm AR 267   647

Cicek v Turkey
(2001) App No 25704/94
27 February 2001 ECtHR   241

Clavijo-Hoyos (00/TH/02131) IAT 185

Commission v Netherlands (ECR) (C/68/89)
[1991] ECR-I-2637   468

Cobo (01TH2903) IAT
16th October [2001]   265

Corte (Dela Vina)
(12708) [1996] 10 INLP   339

D

D, R v Brent LBC ex p
[1998] 31 HLR 10   677,.679

D v UK
[1997] 24 EHRR 423   251, 253

Dadibhai, R v IAT, ex p 24th October 1983,
(unreported)   404

Damoah, R v London Borough of
Hammersmith and Fulham, ex p
[1998] 31 HLR 786,
[1999] 02 LS Gaz 28,
[1999] 2 CCLR 18   686

Danian
[2000] Imm AR 96
[1999] INLR 553, CA   201

Danleu (21500) IAT   652

Demirkaya
[1999] Imm AR 498,
[1999] INLR 441 CA   168

Derouiche v SSHD
[1998] INLR 286   98

Desai
[2000] INLR 10, CA   403

Devaseelan (Justin Surendran) v SSHD
[2002] UKIAT 00702   221, 240
*13/3/02 IAT   616

Dhima, R (on the application of) v IAT
[2002] EWCH 80 Admin
6th February 2002   244

Diatta v Land Berlin: 267/83
[1985] ECR 567,
[1986] 2 CMLR 164, ECJ   459

Durojaiye (Remi Adekola) v SSHD
[1991] Imm AR 307   303, 548

Dzhygun (00 TH 00728) IAT   159

E

East African Asians v UK
[1973] 3 EHRR 76, EComHR   576, 245

Ejaz, R v SSHD ex p
[1994] QB 496,
[1994] Imm AR 300 CA   594

Ejon, R v SSHD, ex p
[1998] INLR 195   199

El Yassini v SSHD: C-416/96
[1999] All ER (EC)   193,
[1999] INLR 131, ECJ   482

F

Fadele v UK
[1990] 1 CD 15, 70 DR   159,
HRCL Digest Vol 1 (1) 15   252, 260

Fadli, R v SSHD, ex p
[2001] 02 LS Gaz 40, CA   241

Fatemeh (Miriam)
(00 TH 00921) IAT   159

Ferko (Andrej), R v SSHD, ex p
(CO 4205/1997) (1997)   506

Foughali (00 TH 01513/4)
[2000] IAT — 164

G

G,R (on the application of) v Barnet LBC
[2001] 4 CCLR 128 CA33
[2001] HLR 649 — 686, 687

Gaima v SSHD
[1989] Imm AR 205 CA — 652

Gal (10620) INLP Vol 8 (2)
[1994] p 69 IAT — 570

Gamelsid
(13261) 29th April 1996, IAT — 225

Gangadeen and Jurawan v SSHD
[1998] INLR 206,
[1998] Imm AR 106, CA — 367

Gashi and Nikshiqi v SSHD
[1997] INLR 96 — 156

Gashi, R v SSHD ex p
[1999] Imm AR 231
[1999] INLR 276 reversed
[1999] Imm AR 415 CA — 208

Gaskin v UK
[1989] 12 EHRR 36 — 257

Gavira, R v SSHD
[2001] INLR 577
[2002] Imm AR 163 — 205

Gill (Sukhjit)
(01TH02884)
IAT 6th December 2001 — 264

Gloszczuk & Kondova, Re
C-63, 235/99
27 September 2001 ECJ — 476, 478

Glowacka and Brezinski, R v SSHD ex p
19th July 1996, unreported — 517, 523

Golchin (7623) IAT — 159

Golder v UK
[1979-1980] 1 EHRR 524 — 238

Gomez
[2000] INLR 549 IAT — 158

Gorenkin, R v Newham LBC , ex p
[1997] 30 HLR 278,
[1997] 23 LS Gaz 27,
141 Sol Jo 138,
[1998] 1 CCLR 309 — 682

Green, R v SSHD, ex p
(29 October 1996) unreported;
on appeal (31 January 1997,
unreported), CA — 291

Gul v Switzerland
[1996] 22 EHRR 93 — 257, 259

H

Haddad (Ali)
[2000] INLR 117 IAT — 206

Hashim, R v An Immigration Officer, ex p
(CO/2052/1999)
12th June 2000 — 356

Haughton (4889) IAT — 376

Hernandez (12773) IAT — 158

HLR v France
[1997] 26 EHRR 29, ECtHR — 244

Hoekstra (nee Unger) 75/63
[1964] ECR 177,
[1964] CMLR 319, ECJ — 466

Holub and Holub v SSHD
[2001] INLR 219 CA — 240, 255

Hong Cui, R v Southwark LBC, ex p
[1998] 31 HLR 639,
[1998] 2 CCLR 86 — 682

Horvath v SSHD (UNHCR intervening)
[1999] Imm AR 121,
[1999] INLR 7; affd
[2000] Imm AR 205,
[2000] INLR 15, CA; affd
[2000] 3 All ER 577,
[2000] 3 WLR 379,
[2000] Imm AR 552, — 161, 162,
[2000] INLR 239, HL — 244, 652

I

Ibraheem (11788) IAT — 406

Ibrahim
[2001] Imm AR 430,
[2001] EWCA Civ 519 — 210, 244

Iqbad Ali, R v IAT, ex p
[1994] Imm AR 295, CA — 377

Ishaq v SSHD
[1996] Imm AR 80 — 83

Isiko, R v S SSHD ex p
[2001] INLR 109, CA — 353, 367

Ireland v UK
[1978] 2 EHRR 25 ECtHR — 242, 245

Islam v SSHD, R v IAT & SSHD ex p Shah
[1999] 2 AC 629
[1999] INLR 144 HL,
[1999] Imm AR 283 — 159, 165

J

J, Re [1998] INLR 424, CA — 388, 390

Jain [2000] Imm AR 76,
[2000] INLR 71, CA — 159, 249

Jama (Zainab Ali) R v ECO, Addis Ababa, ex p
(CO 3338/1999) — 224

Jarmillo v UK
Applcn 24865/94 [1995]   255
Jeyakumaran, R v SSHD ex p
[1994] Imm AR 45   162
Johnston v Ireland
[1986] 9 EHRR 203, ECtHR   257

K

Kaba v SSHD: C-356/98
[2000] All ER (EC) 537, ECJ   464
Kacaj, SSHD v
(01/TH00634)* [2001] INLR   240, 241,
[2002] Imm AR 281 IAT   242, 244,
    249, 255,
    646
Kagema
[1997] Imm AR 137, CA   156, 243
Kaja v SSHD
[1995] Imm AR 1   645
Karanakaran v SSHD
[2000] 3 All ER 449,
[2000] Imm AR 271,   161, 239
[2000] INLR 122, CA   645
Kariharan, R (on the application of) v SSHD
[2001] EWHC Admin 1004
5th December 2001
[2002] Imm AR 281   616
Karoaglan, Hadavi and Bashiri –
consent order; CO/4634/2000;
CO/409/2001 ; CO/1040/2001
3 May 2001   206
Karoui & Abbad, R v SSHD, ex p
[1997] Times, 11 March   691
Kasolo (13190) [1996] IAT   653
Kasuji
[1988] Imm AR 587   331
Kaur, Balwinder (IAT) (12838)   334
Kaur (Kartar) (IAT)11549
15 November 1994   403
Kaur (Manjit) R v SSHD, ex p,
ECJ (C-192-99)
20 March 2001, unreported   453, 576
Kausar
[1998] INLR 141 (IAT)   333, 387
Kaya v Haringey LBC
[2002] HLR1
[2001] EWCA Civ677 CA   668
Keegan v Ireland
[1994] 18 EHRR 342,
[1994] 3 FCR 165, ECtHR   257
Kelso, R v SSHD, ex p
[1998] INLR 603   526

Kerkhoven v Netherlands (Commission)
19th May 1992 (unreported)   256
Khan (9416) IAT   328
Khan (Dewan) (00TH02531) IAT,
30th November 2000   330
Kharrazi, R v CIO Gatwick Airport, ex p
[1980] 1 WLR 1396   302
Khawaja & Khera
[1984] AC 74 (HL)   548
Khokhar
[1981] Imm AR 56   81
Kotecha, R v IAT, ex p
[1983] 2 All ER 289,
[1983] 1 WLR 487,
[1982] Imm AR 88, CA   652
Kumarakuparan
[2002] EWCH 112 Admin
24th January 2002   616
Kus v Landeshauptstadt Wiesbaden: C-237/91
[1992] ECR I-6781,
[1993] 2 CMLR 887, ECJ   480
Kwong (Yee-Kee) (10661)
IAT, 11 February 1994   459

L

Lawrie-Blum v Land Baden-Wurttemberg: 66/85
[1986] ECR 2121,
[1987] 3 CMLR 389,
[1987] ICR 483, ECJ   455
Lawson, R v SSHD, ex p
[1994] Imm AR 58   184
Levin v Secretary of State for Justice: 53/81
[1982] ECR 1035,
[1982] 2 CMLR 454, ECJ   455
Livingstone (10964) [1994] IAT   356
Lizarzaburu (10848) IAT   356
Lubetkin v SSHD
[1979-80] Imm AR 162   97, 370

M

Maaouia v France
[2001] 33 EHRR 1037
9 [2001] BHRC 205 ECtHR   248
Mahdia, R v LB Islington, ex p CO/2519/2000
14 August 2000   702
Mahmood (Amjad) v SSHD
[2001] Imm AR 229,
[2001] 1WLR 84D   352, 355
Mahmod (Wasfi Suleman), Re
[1995] Imm AR 311   498, 526

Mahmood and Isiko R (Isiko v SSHD)
(C/2000/2937) CA 2000 IAT   256, 260
                             261, 262

Mani, Tasci and J
[2002] EWHC 735 (Admin),
18 April 2002   681

Massaquoi [2001] Imm AR 309
(affd (C/2000/0622))
[2001] Imm AR 309 CA   174, 617

Marckx v Belgium
[1979] 2 EHRR 330 ECtHR   257

Mayisokele (13039)
(1996, unreported), IAT   652

Mbanza
[1999] Imm AR 508, CA   201

Meharban (Mohd)
[1989] Imm AR 57   337

Mendes (12183) IAT   653

Mersin, R v SSHD ex p
[2000] INLR 511   219

Miller
[1988] Imm AR 358, CA   212

Mindoukna (Romouald Andela)
(01TH02635) IAT
8th November [2001]   265

Minteh, Lamin R v SSHD, ex p
(396/5400/D) (8 March 1996,
unreported), CA   518

Minton v SSHD
[1990] Imm AR 199;
[1989] Imm AR 496   67

MNM v SSHD
[2000] INLR 576   641, 653

Modi (9714) IAT   334

Modinos v Cyprus
[1993] 16 EHRR 485   249

Mohammed (Swaleh) (12412)
(4 August 1995,
unreported), IAT   653

Mohammed, R (on the application of
Mohammed and Others) v SSHD
[2000] EWHC 57 (Admin)
22 January 2001   210, 244

Montana, R v SSHD, ex p
[2001] 1 WLR 552   568

Moustaquim v Belgium
[1991] 13 EHRR 802 ECtHR   257, 263

MPAX, R v Westminster City Council and Others
[1997] 1 CCLR 85   679, 680,
                            682

Murua (HC) CO/2463/01
25 October 2001   681

Musisi, Re; Bugdaycay v SSHD
[1987] AC 514
[1987] WLR 606,
[1987] Imm AR 250
[1987] 1All ER 940   173, 519

N

Naillie
[1993] AC 674,
[1993] Imm AR 462   555

NASS v Westminster
[2001] EWCA Civ 512, CA
[2001] 4 CCLR 143,
[2001] 33 HLR 938   681

Nazari, R v
[1980] 3 All ER 880   538

Nessa v Chief Adjudication Officer
[1998] 2 All ER 728, CA; affd
[1999] 4 All ER 677,
[1999] WLR 1937, HL   670

Nhundu and Chiwera
(01TH00613) IAT
1st June 2001   266

Nmaju [2000] 36 LS Gaz 41,
[2001] INLR 26, CA   376

O

O [1995] Imm AR 494 CA   164

O and Bhikha (CA)
[2000] 1 WLR 2539   679, 680,
                            681

Ofori, R v SSHD, ex p
[1994] Imm AR 34   107

Omoruyi
[2001] Imm AR 175, CA   157

Onen (TH/43596/94 (22101; R1450)
4 February 1997 (IAT)   229, 643,

Onibiyo, R v SSHD ex p
[1996] QB 768
[1996] Imm AR 370 CA   220

Osman v UK
[1998] 29 EHRR 245
5 BHRC 293 ECtHR   241

Ouanes v SSHD
[1998] INLR 230,
[1998] Imm AR 76, CA   160

Ozgur Gundem v Turkey
[2001] 31 EHRR 1082, ECtHR
Judgement 16/03/2000   251

P

Pardeepan
[2000] INLR 447   28, 221,
                            615, 616

Patel, R v ex p
  [1993] Imm AR 392   108
Pattuwearachchi
  [1991] Imm AR 341   301
Paw (4328) IAT   406
Poku v UK
  [1996] 22 EHRR CD 94,   379
Popatia, R v SSHD, ex p
  [2001] Imm AR 46,
  [2000] INLR 587   107

Q

Quaquah, R v SSHD, ex p
  [2000] 03 LS Gaz 36,
  [2000] INLR 196   266
Quijano (Fabian Martinez)
  [1997] Imm AR 227, CA   158

R

Ramirez [2002] Imm AR 240 CA 616
Ramos (Suzara) v IAT
  [1989] Imm AR 148, CA   375
Raulin v Minister van Onderwijs en
  Wetenschappen: C-357/89
  [1992] ECR I-1027,
  [1994] 1 CMLR 227, ECJ   455
Ravichandran
  [1996] Imm AR 97   156, 163,
                             243, 247,
                             644, 652
Reed, A.F. v Netherlands 59/85
  [1986] ECR 1283;
  [1987] 2 CMLR 448   356, 459
Reffell, R v Hammersmith Hospitals NHS Trust,
  ex p
  [2000] 55 BMLR 130,
  [2000] 36 LS Gaz 42, DC   687, 688
Rehal v SSHD
  [1989] Imm AR 576, CA   546
Rehman [2002] INLR 92,
  [2002] Imm AR 98,
  [2001] UKHL 47, HL   621
Remilien & Wolke
  [1997] 1 WLR 1640,
  [1998] INLR 238 HL;
  reversing [1996] All ER
  (EC) 850 CA   661
Robinson v SSHD
  [1997] Imm AR 568
  [1997] INLR 182, CA   153, 166
Royer, Re:48/75
  [1976] ECR 497,
  [1976] 2 CMLR 619, ECJ   465

Rudolph (Dilskish Antoinette Hayley)
  [1984] Imm AR 84   374, 376
Rush Portuguesa Lda v ONI: C-113/89
  [1990] ECR I-1417,
  [1991] 2 CMLR 818, ECJ   457
Rutili v Minister for the Interior: 36/75
  [1975] ECR 1219,
  [1976] 1 CMLR 140, ECJ   469

S

Saad, Diriye & Osario
  [2002] INLR 34   30, 218, 219,
                             617, 623
Saadi & Others (the 'Oakington' case)
  [2002] 1 WLR 356,   498, 500, 501
  [2001] 4 All ER 961,   508,
  [2002] Imm AR 121   509
Saleem v SSHD
  [2000] 4 All ER 814,
  [2001] 1 WLR 443,
  [2000] Imm AR 529
  [2000] INLR 413, CA   614
Salem, R v SSHD, ex p
  [1999] QB 805,
  [1999] 2 WLR 1, CA; affd
  [1999] 1 AC 450,
  [1999] 2 All ER 42,
  [1999] 2 WLR 483, HL   691
Saluguo (18815) IAT   376
Santillo; R v SSHD, ex p
  [1981] QB 778
  [1981] 2 All ER 897 CA   540
Savas: C-37/98, R v SSHD, ex p
  [2000] 1 WLR 1828,
  [2000] All ER (EC) 627,
  [2000] INLR 398, ECJ   481
Savchenkov
  [1996] Imm AR 28, CA   159
Sedrati & Others
  (High Court) – consent order 496
Selmouni v France
  [2000] 29 EHRR 403 ECtHR   242
Sen v Netherlands Applcn 31 465/96
  21 December 2001 ECtHR   264
Senga, R v IAT ex p
  (9 March 1994, unreported) 201
Sepet and Bulbul
  [2000] Imm AR 455,
  [2001] INLR 376 CA,   164, 165
  [2001] EWCA Civ 681   250
Sesay (14142) IAT   652

Sevince v Staatsecretaris van Justitie: C-192/89
[1990] ECR 1-3461,
[1992] 2 CMLR 57, ECJ   480

Sezek R (on the application of) v SSHD
[2002] 1 WLR 348,
[2001] INLR 675, CA   500

Shah v, Barnet LBC
[1983] 2 AC 309 (HL)   671, 687

Shah, R v IAT & SSHD ex p, Islam v SSHD
[1999] 2 AC 629
[1999] INLR 144 HL,
[1999] Imm AR 283   159, 165

Shirreh, R v SSHD (CO2194/1997)
(15th August 1997,
unreported)   229

Singh & Singh (Mukhtiar and Paramjit)
31 July 2000 (SIAC)
Butterworths ILS Vol II,
Section 81-148 [51]-[101]   169, 621

Singh, Baktaur
(HL) [1986] WLR 910
[1986] Imm AR 352   537, 643

Singh, Hardial
[1983] Imm AR 198;
[1984] 1 WLR 704   498, 526

Singh (Pawandeep)
(18465) (16th March 1999), IAT
Singh (Pawandeep) v ECO and IAT
2nd December 1999
SLJ 99/6971/4   388
Singh (Pawandeep) v UK (ECtHR)

Singh, Surinder
[1992] 3 All ER 798
[1992] Imm AR 565   323, 461,
                                       462, 463

Sivakumaran, R v SSHD ex p
[1998] AC 958
[1998] Imm AR 147   154, 160,
[1997] NLJ Rep 1206 HL   645

Slimani
(01 TH 00092),
unreported, IAT   190

Soering v UK
[1989] 11 EHRR 439   240, 248

Soloot (AHR)
(01TH01366) IAT
10th August 2001   266

Sorabjee v UK Commission
Applcn 239938/93
[1995]   255

Steymann v Staatssecretaris van Justitie: 196/87
[1998] ECR 6159,
[1989] 1 CMLR 449, ECJ   455

Storozhenko v SSHD
[2001] EWCA Civ 896,
15th June 2001, CA   160

Subaskaran (18892) IAT   652

Subramaniam, R v IAT, ex p
[1977] QB 190, Imm AR 155   93

Suthendran v IAT
[1977] AC 539, Imm AR 44   93

T

Tan Te Lam v Superintendent of Tai A Chau
Detention Centre
[1997] AC 97,
[1996] 4 All ER 256,
[1996] 2 WLR 863   498

Tas v Turkey
[2001] 33 EHRR 15   241

Thirukumar, R v SSHD ex p
[1989] Imm AR 270
[1989] Imm AR 402, CA   173

TI v UK (2000) INLR 211   210, 244

Tiongson, Wilbert and Others
(11467) IAT
25 October 1994   376

Tower Hamlets LBC, R v Secretary of State for
the Environment ex p
[1993] 3 All ER 439;
[1993] Imm AR 495   551

Turkoglu, R v SSHD, ex p
[1988] QB 398,
[1987] 2 All ER 823,
[1987] WLR 992,
[1987] Imm AR 484, CA   526

U

Ullah,
[2001] EWCA 659,
10 May 2001 CA   573

Uvovo (00 TH 01450)
IAS 2000 Vol 3, No 15   330

V

Vallaj, R (on the application of) v A Special
Adjudicator
[2001] INLR 455 High Ct (Dyson J),
[2001] INLR 342, CA
[2001] EWCA Civ 782,   162, 205

Vander Elst v Office des Migrations
Internationales: C-43/93
[1994] ECR I-3803,
[1995] 1 CMLR 513, ECJ   458

Vrachiu (11559) IAT   159

W

Westminster *see* MPAX   679, 680,
                                682

Williams
   (16574) 15 February 1998   375

X

X v France
   [1991] 14 EHRR 483   257
X and Y v UK
   [1993] 16 EHRR CD, EComHR 256
X, Y and Z v UK
   [1997] 24 EHRR 143   258

Y

Yambos (IAT) 00TH 21723,
   22 June 1999   402
Yogathas & Thangarasa
   [2001] EWCA Civ 1611,   210, 211,
   21 September 2001 CA   244
Yousaf (9190) IAT   334

Young, James and Webster v UK
   [1981] 4 EHRR 38
   [1982] 5 EHRR 201   250

Z

Z v SSHD (01/TH/2634)
   8th November 2001 IAT   249
Zaitz
   [2000] INLR 346 CA   164
Zakrocki, R v SSHD, ex p
   [1996] 32 BMLR 108,
   [1996] COD 304,
   [1996] 16 LS Gaz 31,
   140 Sol Jo LB 110   291
Zenovics (01TH 00631), IAT;
   [2002] EWCA Civ 273
   (7th March 2002) CA   203
Zia v SSHD
   [1993] Imm AR 404   331
Ziar
   [1997] Imm AR 456
   [1997] INLR 221   204

Index

For cases referred to in the text please see Alphabetical list of cases, pages 771–780

A

abode, *see* right of abode
academic visitors 281
accommodation
  adequate 331
  houses in multiple occupation (HMO) 332
  overcrowding 331
  spouses/partners/fiancé(e)s 331
accommodation centres 24, 26, 171, 512
  education provision 26
accountancy training 311
adjudicators
  appeals 600
  determinations 647
  powers to grant bail 28
  powers in deciding appeals 642
Administrative Court 142, 144
administrative removal 18, 527, 531
  breach of conditions 534
  deception 536
  detention 494
  exemptions 528
  family members 536
  notice to person subject to: example 127
adoption 377, 384
  adopted children
    applying for entry 385
    family life 257
  applying to enter UK for adoption 388
  by competent authority or court 369, 386
  countries whose adoption decisions are
    recognised 751
  informal (*de facto*) adoption 377, 388
  inter-country adoptions 105
  inter-family adoption cases 377
  reason for adoption 387
Adoption (Intercountry Aspects) Act 1999
    382, 385-386, 390, 568
Adoption of Children from Overseas
    Regulations 2001 390
adoptive parents
  family life 257
advice, offering

offences 556
Afghan hijacked aircraft case 212
Afghanistan 147, 197, 218, 271, 292
agents 202
AIDS 252
airline liaison officers 34, 52
Albania 197, 271
Algeria 197, 252, 260
  Co-operation Agreement 448, 482
Aliens Act 1905 4
amateur entertainers and sportspeople 282
Amnesty International 636
ancestral ties 432
Andorra
  au pairs from 433
Angola 197
Anson, Lady Elizabeth 285
Anti-terrorism, Crime and Security Act 2001
    19, 151, 168, 489, 496, 516, 619
  Special Immigration Appeals Commission
    (SIAC) 619
appeals 18, 599
  adjudicator 600
  after the adjudicator has determined the
    appeal 647
  against administrative removal 533
  against deportation 603
  against port removal 531
  against recommendation for deportation
    539
  against refusal of asylum 214, 617
  against refusal of entry clearance 71, 131
    for adoption 389
    children 372
    spouses, partners, fiancé(e)s 344
    students 304
    visitors 285, 618
  against refusal of extended leave 603
  against refusal of leave to enter 135, 285,
    603
  against refusal of leave to remain 94
    spouses, partners, fiancé(e)s outside the
      rules 358

appeals *continued*
  against refusal of re-entry 77, 83
  against refusal to grant settlement to
    spouses and partners 347
  against refusal under the domestic violence
    concession 360
  against removal 603
    to a particular destination 604
  asylum cases 604
  asylum support 707, 712
  burden and standard of proof: asylum cases
    645
  burden and standard of proof: human rights
    cases 646
  burden and standard of proof: immigration
    cases 645
  certified appeals 600
  certified as 'without foundation' 621
  change of circumstances 32, 644
  combined hearings 631
  country and expert evidence 635
  country material 636
  Court of Appeal 655
  Court of Session (in Scotland) 655
  decisions by ECOs 30
  decisions which can be appealed 603
  directions 630, 646
  discrimination cases 614
  documents: appeal bundle 628
  documents: translations 630
  EEA nationals 472
  explanatory statement/reasons 628
  failure to comply with directions 638
  family members
    against refusal of entry clearance 228
  following a recommendation to deport 31
  grounds for appeal to IAT 652
  hearings 627
    adjournments 32, 633
    exclusion of the public 631
    fast-track 632
    first hearing 632
    full hearing before the adjudicator 637
    where one party does not attend 641
  Home Office presenting officer 637
  human rights 30, 614
    human rights grounds 267
  Immigration Appeal Tribunal (IAT) 600, 651
    preparation 654
  immigration decisions giving right to appeal
    214
  in human rights and discrimination cases
    604
  in illegal entry cases 603
  in-country rights of appeal 71
  judicial review 650
  late claims for asylum
    effect on appeal 610
  legislation 601
  limitation of right to appeal 605
  notices of appeal 611
  one stop appeals 30, 606
  one-stop notices
    statement of additional grounds 608
  outside the immigration rules 31
  personal service of certain determinations of
    adjudicators 649
  powers of adjudicators 642
  preparing for an appeal 633
  preventing further appeals 609
  procedure 626
  procedures 626
  proposed changes 622
  race discrimination 271
  'recommendation' to the Home Office 646
  representation 627
  Special Immigration Appeals Commission
    (SIAC) 618
  speed of 32
  spouses, partners, fiancé(e)s
    against refusal to grant settlement 347
    against refusal of entry clearance 344
    outside the rules applications 358
  structure 31
  submissions 640
  'suspensive' 602
  system of appeals 600
  third country appeals 207
  time limits 612-613
  travel while awaiting an appeal 628
  'upgrade' appeals 32
  visitors
    appeal against refusal of entry at port
     287
    against refusal of entry clearance 285,
     618
  when an appeal must be allowed 642
  when asylum claim is refused but exception
    leave 218
  when people can appeal 601
  where there is no right of appeal 602, 629
  White Paper 2002 29
  witnesses 634, 638
  work permit holders 424
  see also Immigration Appeals Tribunal
appellants
  bail 514
  seeking re-admission to attend appeal
    hearings 281
appellate authorities 513
application forms 16, 59, 95
  see also forms

Application Forms Unit 95
Application Registration Cards (ARC) 24, 171, 178, 181
  permission to work 194
applying for leave to enter
  applications from overseas
    visa nationals 737
  EEA applications 101
  fiancé(e)s 326
  same sex partners 326
  spouse 326
  spouses, unmarried partners, same sex partners 346
  unmarried partners 326
applying to stay in the UK 90
  outside the rules 357
archaeological excavations 281
architecture training 311
armed forces, members of 15, 65
arrest 140, 552
Article 3 see European Convention on Human Rights
artists 440
Association Agreements 13, 17, 101, 448, 476
  applying for entry 478
  applying to extend stay 479
  Central and Eastern European Countries (CEEC) 476
  family members 480
  settlement 479
  the future 482
  Turkish Association Agreement 480
  'stand still' provision 481
asylum 12, 24
  appeals
    burden and standard of proof 645
    change of circumstance 644
  applications 100
  applications from abroad 177
  definition of asylum claim 151
  legal advice 130
  legal basis under refugee convention 150
  procedures 173
  refugee law 147
  'third country' asylum cases 136
  see also refugees
Asylum Aid 214
Asylum and Immigration Act 1996 6, 150, 415
  third country cases: judicial review 207
Asylum and Immigration Appeals Act 1993 5, 12, 150, 279
  third country appeals 207
Asylum Appeals (One-Stop Procedure) Regulations 2000 601, 609

Asylum Appeals (Procedure) Rules 2000 626
Asylum Appeals Policy Directorate 167
Asylum Policy Instructions (API) 151
Asylum Registration Card (ARC)
  examples of 122
Asylum Screening Unit (ASU) 179, 181
asylum-seekers 152
  agents 202
  Application Registration Cards (ARCs) 178, 181
  applying for asylum 152
  applying for asylum: screening questionnaire 180
  applying from overseas 174
  applying in person 179
  Asylum Registration Card (ARC)
    examples of 122
  asylum support 138
  backlog clearance 220
  benefits 27
  certified claims 203
  children of 26, 192
    adult children of 193
  claiming asylum 71
    in more than one country 202
    'on arrival' 668
  close connection with another country 212
  course for 316
  credibility 198
    inconsistent activities 201
  definition for asylum support 690
  definition of asylum claim 151
  delay in applying 199
  dependants 192, 693
    fingerprinting 181
    permission to work 194
  dispersal 6, 184, 701
  Dublin Convention 208
  evidence
    medical reports 190
    arrest warrants 190
    court documents 190
    expert reports 190
    from political organisations 190
    witnesses' letters 190
  exceptional leave 216
  false claims and false evidence 200
  false passports 200
  family reunion 222, 224
  fingerprinting 181
  fresh claims 220
  grounds for issuing a certificate 204
  Home Office decisions 197
  how to apply for asylum 174
    evidence 189

asylum-seekers *continued*
  illegal entrants 179
  'in-country' applications 179
  increased reporting 171
  interim support 695
  interviews 184
    at port of entry 178
    'fit and well' 185
    interpreter 184
    interpreters 186
    preparation 185
    representation 184, 185
    same gender interviewer 184
    signed declaration 186
    viewing scars 184
  invitation to withdraw claim 213
  judicial review 219
  late claims 200
  liability for detention 180
  'manifestly unfounded' cases 199, 205
  medical reports 189
  NASS support 695
  notice of refusal 214
  number of applications 26
  number of applications 147
  numbers of 12
  'one-stop' procedure 187
  'one-stop' notice 178, 214
  overstayers 179
  part of a group 202
  permission to work 194
  port applications 177
  postal applications 179
    asylum support 179
    postal applications 179
  procedures 173
  prosecution of 557
  refusal of asylum claim 213
  refusal of entry clearance
    family members 228
  refusals
    non-compliance 205
  spouses 192
  Standard Acknowledgement Letters (SALs)
      122, 178
  Statement of Evidence Form (SEF) 178
    'SEF-less' procedure 180
  temporary admission 71
  third country cases 206
  travel 222
  unaccompanied minors 172, 191
  voluntary work and 194
  vouchers 6
  ways of discouraging asylum-seekers
      195-196
  White Paper 2002 and 21

  women 165
  written permission to work 415
  see also asylum
asylum support 26, 138, 679, 689
  'claim for asylum' 690
  accommodation centres 24
  additional single payments 700
  adequate accommodation 697-699
  appeals 707, 712
    oral hearings 716
    time table 713
  asylum support adjudicators (ASA) 712
  change of circumstances 707
  dental treatment 706
  dependants of asylum-seekers 693
  destitution 678, 694, 697
  dispersal 701
  essential living needs 698-699
  excluded items 699
  exclusions 703
  expenses 699
  expenses in connection with asylum claims
      703, 717
  hard cases 717
  households with children 692
  how to claim 704
  maternity payments 701
  NASS support 24, 695
    or interim support 695
    rates 700
  NHS prescriptions 706
  offences 555
  proposed changes 718
  temporary admission 25
  temporary or 'emergency' support 706
  vouchers 25
  ways of discourage asylum-seekers 195
  who is entitled 690
  see also interim support
Asylum Support 2000 Regulations 139
Asylum Support Adjudicators (ASA) 712
  see also asylum support
Asylum Support Appeals (Procedure) Rules
      2000 713
au pairs 9, 55, 433
  switching status 92
aunts
  family life 257
  visit to see 286, 399
Australia 295
Austria
  EFTA 448
  EU country 448
Authority to Carry scheme 34-35
automatic bail hearings 27, 493
  see also bail

B

backlog clearance 220
bail 19
  appellants to the adjudicator 514
  automatic bail hearings 493
  failure to answer to bail 524
    who cannot get bail 513, 514
  from adjudicators
    who can get bail 513, 514
    who cannot get bail 513, 514
  from chief immigration officer or police
    inspector 512
  from Immigration Appeals Tribunal 515
  hearing 522
  High Court procedures 525
    habeas corpus 525
  illegal entrants 514
  Immigration Appellate Authority 517
  in the course of judicial review 526
  overstayers 514
  port cases 514
  Practice Direction 518
  preparing for bail hearing 518
  right to bail from IAT 516
  Special Immigration Appeals Commission
    (SIAC) 516
  sureties 513, 520
  when bail is granted 524
  when bail is refused 524
Bail Circle 522
Bail for Immigration Detainees 518
Bangladesh 197, 340
Bar Council 40
Bar Council of Northern Ireland 40
Barbados 295
Barbuda
  British citizenship 566
barristers 40
Belgium 54
  EU country 448
Belize
  British citizenship 566
benefits *see* welfare benefits
bereaved spouses 358
'bereavement' benefits 672
Bermuda
  British citizenship 566
biometric technology 34, 52
birth certificate 55
bona fide private education institutions 298,
  299
border controls
  White Paper 2002 and 34
Bosnia-Herzegovina 176
  au pairs from 433
Bradford, Oldham and Burnley uprisings 22

breach of conditions of leave
  administrative removal 532
British Accreditation Council for Independent
  Further and Higher Education 299
British citizens 8, 65, 562, 567
  acquiring British citizenship 581
  born before 1983 568
  born in 1983 and after 568
  British nationals who are not British citizens
    576
  by adoption 568
  by birth 568
  by descent 571, 573
    children 571
    flow chart 575
  chart 567, 569
  children
    adoption 568
  Crown or designated services 575
  naturalisation 584
  otherwise than by descent 572
  right of abode 7
British Council 301, 575
British Dependent Territories Citizens (BDTCs)
  78, 562
British Excursion Documents 79
British Medical Association 27
British nationality 561
  changes since 1983 563
British Nationality Act 1948 561
British Nationality Act 1981 6, 8, 23, 29, 562,
  568
British Nationality (Hong Kong) Act 1990
  580-581
British Nationality (Hong Kong) Act 1997
  580-581
British nationality law
  development of 561
British Nationals (Overseas) (BN(O)s) 78, 563,
  576, 580
British nationals from Malaysia 579
British nationals with an East African
  connection 578
  special quota voucher scheme 578
British Overseas Citizens (BOCs) 78, 563,
  576
  long-residence concession 108
  right of readmission 576
British Overseas Territories
  list of countries 564
British Overseas Territories Act 2002 563
British Overseas Territories Act 2002
  (Commencement) Order 2002 564
British Overseas Territories citizens (BOTCs)
  562
British posts overseas 52, 739

British Protected Persons (BPPs) 78, 561, 563, 576
British Red Cross (BRC) 175
British subjects 78, 563
    without citizenship 561
British Tourist Authority 575
British Visitor's passport 78
brothers 399
    visit to see 286
brothers-in-law
    visit to see 286
Bulgaria
    EU Association Agreement 448, 476
Burundi 197
business person 438
    children of 439
    retired person of independent means 440
    self-employed 439
    spouses and partners 363
    spouse of 439
    switching status 92
    unmarried partner of 439
business purposes 438
    highly skilled migrant workers 441
    innovators 441
    investors 439
business visitors 280
    'transact business' 280

C
Camden Law Centre 349
Cameroon 197, 265
Campsfield House 490
Canada 137, 158, 207, 211, 295
carers 282, 289
    exceptional leave 105
    HIV/AIDS 254
carriers' liability 196
    sanctions 546
cash payments 25
categories of entry 9
    au pair 9
    investor 9
    refugee 9
    spouse 9
    student 9
    unmarried partner 9
    visitor 9
    work permit holder 9
Central Bureau for Educational Visits and Exchanges 433
Central Council for Nursing, Midwifery and Health 311
certificate of entitlement to the right of abode 55, 77, 467, 566
    example of 121
certificate of identity 230
'certified' cases 203
Channel Islands 314
    Common Travel Area 17, 72
Channel Tunnel
    entry through 34, 72, 74
Channel Tunnel (International Arrangements) Order 1993 74
Channel Tunnel (Miscellaneous Provisions) Order 1994 74
Chief Adjudicator's Practice Direction 633
chief immigration officer 71, 133
child benefit 329, 672
child minders for relatives 281
Child Poverty Action Group 27
children
children 365
    access to following relationship breakdown 362
    administrative removal 536
    adopted children: family life 257
    adoption see adoption
    age dispute cases 192
    applying for settlement 373
    artificial insemination 366
    born in the UK 396
    born in the UK and not born British 570
        stateless 571
        on, or after 1 January 1983 397
        before 1 January 1983 396
    born or adopted before 1983 568
    born or adopted in 1983 or after 568
    Children Act 1989 685
    death of parent 373
    deportation of 541
    DNA testing 372
    entitlement to state education 306
    entry clearance 61, 371
    EU Association Agreements 480
    exclusion undesirable 374, 376
    family life 257
    fingerprinting 181
    fostercare 394
    human rights and 367
    in schools 395
    joining a lone parent 373
    joining a person who is not a parent 378
    joining both parents 368
    joining parents who have limited leave 382
    leading an independent life 225
    local authority care 393
    maintenance and accommodation 370
    married 370
    NHS medical treatment 372
    not leading an independent life 370

children *continued*
  of asylum-seekers 192
  of business people 382, 439
  of diplomats 367
  of EEA nationals 367, 460
  of investor 440
  of investors and innovators 383
  of overstayers and illegal entrants 354
  of refugees 222-223
  of retired persons of independent means
    382
  of students 305, 364, 383
    child benefit 307
    permission to work 330
    right to settle 319
  of teachers and language assistants 384
  of TWES permit holder 425
  of retired persons of independent means
    440
  of work permit holders 382, 423
  of workers 382
  of working holidaymakers 295, 384
  over 18 365
  over-age children of refugees 225
  parents 369
  passing on nationality to 577
  settlement 61
  sole responsibility for 373, 374
  state education 372
  support under Children Act 139
  unaccompanied asylum-seekers 191
  'Unaccompanied Children's Module' 191
  unaccompanied minors 391, 393
  'under-12' concession 377
  under 18 370
  who are British citizens 366
  whose parents may be forced to leave 391
Children Act 1989 360, 685
Children and Young Persons Act 420
China 147, 197, 271, 292
Chronically Sick and Disabled Persons Act
  1970 section 2 683
Churches Commission for Racial Justice 522
Citizen of the United Kingdom and Colonies
  (CUKC) 4, 561
Citizens Advice Bureaux (CAB) 130
citizenship *see* British nationality
civil war 162
claim for asylum
  recorded by Secretary of State 691
CLS Directory 45
Co-operation Agreements 448, 476
  Mahgreb Agreements 482
  the future 482
Colombia 196-197, 292
common problems 130

Common Travel Area (CTA) 17, 51, 72, 75,
  304
Commonwealth citizens
  right of abode 7, 77-78
  women 55
  who were Commonwealth citizens on
    31 December 1982 566
  wives of British citizens 324
  working holidaymakers scheme 294
Commonwealth countries 748
Commonwealth Immigrants Act 1962 5
Commonwealth Immigrants Act 1968 5,
  576
Commonwealth nationals with British-born
  grandparents 432
communicable disease 293
community care assessments 684
community care services
  immigration status restrictions 679
community health services 311
Community Legal Service (CLS) 40, 43, 47,
  130
  controlled legal representation 44
  Directory 45
  funding 43
  general help 43
  general help including casework 43
  legal help scheme 44
  Quality Mark 39, 41
  specialist help 43
composers 440
conditions of leave
  code 1 no recourse to public funds 110
  code 1A no conditions 110
  code numbers 109
conducive to the public good 18
conscientious objectors 164
  human rights and 250
contribution-based incapacity benefit 672
contribution-based job-seeker's allowance
  672
Controlled Legal Representation (CLR) 627
Council for International Education UKCOSA
  306
Council of Europe 232
  Agreement on the Abolition of Visas for
    Refugees 1959 54, 230
  Committee of Ministers 226
  Social Charter (CESC) *see* Social Charter
council tax benefit 670
  students 306
Country and Information Policy Unit (CIPU)
  197
couples
  intention to stay together permanently 327
  maintenance and accommodation 328

couples *continued*
   maintenance undertakings 335
   people who want to stay after a relationship
      has broken down 358
   probationary period: permission to work
      330
   relationship breakdown after settlement
      361
   third party support 334
Court of Appeal 18
cousins 409
crews of ships and aircrafts 65
   detention 494
Criminal Cases Review Commission 557
Criminal Defence Service 140
criminal offences 354
criminal record 108
Croatia 292
   au pairs from 433
curtailment of leave to remain 103
   'subject to immigration control' 103
Cyprus 249
   au pairs from 433
Czech Republic 147, 197, 272
   au pairs from 433
   EU Association Agreement 448, 476
   pre-clearance checks 52

D

daughters 399
   visit to see 286
daughters-in-law
   visit to see 286
death
   of spouse or unmarried partner 358
death penalty
   abolition of 234
   allowance in time of war 234
deception 554
   obtaining leave by deception, administrative
      removal 532
   of an immigration officer 547
delays 219
Democratic Republic of Congo 147, 197, 292
Denmark 54, 177, 356
   EU country 448
dental students 311
Department for Education and Skills (DfES)
   26, 100, 310
Department of Health 311
Department of Work and Pensions 16
dependants
   'abuse' of the dependants rule 193
   asylum-seekers 192
   claiming asylum in their own right 193
   permission to work 194

dependent relative rules 399
deportation 18, 527, 537
   alternatives to 542
   appeal against recommendation for
      deportation 539
   children 541
   conducive to the public good 18, 538,
      540
   deportation orders 495
      example of 127
   detention 495
   exemptions 528
   family members 18, 538, 541
   notice of intention to make a deportation
      order 495
   of spouse 541
   power of adjudicators to grant bail 28
   recommendation for deportation 18, 495,
      538
   revocation of order 543
   the process of 541
   threatened deportation 140
deprivation of citizenship
   appeal 22
derogations and reservations 235
destitution 360
   see also interim support
   see also asylum support
detention 11, 27, 140, 196, 487
   administrative removal cases 494
   Anti-terrorism, Crime and Security Act 2001
      489
   Article 5 ECHR 247, 489
   asylum-seekers 180
   background to 487
   Campsfield House 490
   costs of 492
   crews of ships and aircrafts 494
   deportation orders 495
   Detention Centre Rules 2001 12, 488,
      489-90, 491
   detention centres 489
   detention
      by an immigration officer 494
   Dungavel 490
   ECHR and 498
   excessive detention 501
   getting people out 510
   habeas corpus 525
   Harmondsworth 490
   HMP Haslar 492
   HMP Lindholme 492
   HMP Rochester 492
   HMYOI Dover 492
   illegal entrants 494
   inspection 509

detention *continued*
  international guidelines 505
  'international terrorists' 495
  judicial review 526
  length of 488
  limitations on powers 497
  notice of intention to make a deportation
    order 495
  numbers detained 488
  Oakington Reception Centre 488, 490,
    506
  Operational Enforcement Manual 503
  orders: by Secretary of State 495
  places and conditions 489
  policy 502, 504
    Oakington Reception Centre 506
  port cases 494
  prisons 28, 490
  removal centres 489
  restriction orders 510
  special exercises 504
  temporary release 510
  Tinsley House 490
  when an immigration officer cannot make
    an immediate decision 71
  who can be detained 493
  who is likely to be detained 502
  Yarl's Wood 490
Diplomatic Privileges Act 1964 66
diplomats 15
  and people who work for embassies and
    high commisions 436
  children of 367, 396
  family members 15
  leave to enter 66
  private servants of 431
disability benefits 671
  students 306
disabled person's tax credit 671
discrimination
  against 'illegitimate' children 21
  see also race discrimination
dispersal 6, 184, 701
displaced families 228
Djibouti 228
DNA testing 372, 408
doctors
  coming for PLAB tests 282
  medical students 311
  postgraduate 297
domestic violence concession 105, 358
domestic workers concession 105, 434
dual nationality 77
Dublin Convention 137, 170, 179, 208
  family member 208
  third country removals 209

Dungavel 28, 489-490
duty solicitor scheme 140

E

East Africa 576
  British nationals with an East African
    connection 578
EC Directive 93/96 317
EC Regulation 1612/68 318
EC Treaty 14
economic migration 37
Ecuador 196, 197, 292
education 395
  bona fide private education institutions
    299
  children of students 305
  definition of education institutions
    299
  definition of full-time studies 300
  entitled to state education
    children of students 306
  right to 255
Education (Fees and Awards) Regulations 1997
  314
Education Act 1944 298
Education Act 1996 299
Education and Library Board in Northern
  Ireland 316
EEA countries
  au pairs from 433
EEA family permits 54
EEA nationals
  'right of abode' certificate 467
  applying for permits 467
  benefit rights 673
  children of 367, 460
  children of: born in UK 570
  claiming public funds 471
  decisions refusing or revoking rights 469
  enforcement and detention 470
  entry procedures 54, 468
  evidence of status 464
  family members 54, 323
    residence documents 101
    who is a family member 458
  family permits 54, 466
  habitual residence test 471
  HIV/AIDS 254
  leave to remain 101
  other relatives 460
  recommendation for deportation 540
  relatives of 14, 399
  renewal of residence permits 468
  residence documents 466
  residence permits 101
  rights of free movement 14, 73

EEA nationals *continued*
  rights to enter and remain in UK 454
  spouses of 14, 459
  students 9, 317
  welfare benefits 138
  who qualifies 452
EEA workers
  spouses of
    students 319
  students fees, grants and loans 318
Electronic Immigration Network 636
ELR, ELE 148, 217
  see also exceptional leave
emergencies 130
employees in the service of foreign
      governments 15
  family members 15
employers
  duty of disclosure 33
endorsements
  by entry clearance officers 110
  by immigration officers 113
  by the Home Office 118
  arrival without entry clearance 114
  cancellation of leave 117
  confirmation of existing leave 117
  date stamp 115
  exceptional leave 124
  for refusal of extension of leave 288
  indefinite leave to enter 116
  indefinite leave to remain 120
  illegible stamps 72
  open date stamp 66
    example of 115
  refusal of leave to enter 117
  Home Office refusals 120
  registration with police 116
  students 304
  variation of leave stamp
    example of 116
enforcement 18, 529
  2002 Bill and 27
  administrative removal 18
  definition 528
  deportation 18
  illegal entry 18
  port removal 18
'enforcement action' 353
entertainers
  work permits 427
entry clearance 17, 52
  appeal against refusal 71, 131
  applicants with criminal convictions 60
  application forms 60
  applications made outside the UK 52
  applications to come to the UK to work 63

au pairs 55
cancellation of 69
cancellation: change of circumstances 69
children 61, 368
  evidence in support 371
  interview 371
countries offering a limited service 741
countries where there is no entry clearance
    service 741
date stamp
  example of 115
definition 52
delayed departure 59
ECO decisions 63
EEA nationals and 54
effective date 53, 57, 342
endorsement codes 110
endorsements:
  arrival without entry clearance or 114
examples of 112
  old style 113
expiry date 53, 57
family members of refugees 223, 226
family reunion 223
family settlement 61
fees 60
  refugees 224
fiancé(e)s 326, 339
for diplomats 65
for settlement 53
for work 53, 63
general grounds for refusal 67
HIV/AIDS 253
how entry clearances work 57
how to apply 59
investors 63
long-term 58
'non-visa nationals' 53
old-style 53
operating as leave to enter 56, 58
optional entry clearance 55
people who do not need entry clearance 54
people who have entry clearance when they
    arrive 68
people who need entry clearance 66
procedures on arrival 133
refusal on entry 133
refusal of entry clearance overseas 64, 131
  appeal 131
  judicial review 132
refusal stamp 113
retired person of independent means 63
returning residents 79
revocation of 64
same sex partner 326. 339
spouse 326, 339

entry clearance *continued*
  stateless people 53
  students 298, 303
  time limits 66
  transit visitors: waiver 292
  TWES permits 55
  unmarried partner 326, 339
  variation of leave stamp: example of 116
  visa nationals 73, 275
    283
  visas 52
    example of 112
  visitors 52, 58, 275, 284
  which do not operate as leave to enter 70
  work permits 55
  working holidaymakers 53, 294
entry clearance officers (ECOs) 16
  endorsements by 109
Eritrea 197, 292
Estonia
  Association Agreement 448, 476
Ethiopia 197, 228, 292
EU nationals
  student fees, grants and loans 318
'Europe' Agreements 14
European Agreement on the Transfer of
    Responsibility for Refugees (EATRR)
    176
European Commission 255, 449-450
European Convention for the Protection of
    Human Rights and Fundamental
    Freedoms *see* ECHR)
European Convention of Human Rights (ECHR)
    12, 63, 147, 231, 232, 447
  absolute rights 236
  Article 2 (the right to life) 233, 241
  Article 3 (on torture or inhuman or
    degrading treatment) 12, 13, 30,
    139, 149, 163, 168, 201, 210, 233,
    242, 496
  Article 4 (prohibition against slavery and
    forced labour) 26, 233, 245
  Article 5 (right to liberty and security) 12,
    233, 246, 496
    preventing arbitrary detention 499
  Article 6 (right to a fair trial) 233, 247
  Article 7 (protection from retrospective
    punishment) 233, 248
  Article 8 (respect for private and family life,
    home and correspondence) 12, 27,
    29, 35, 149, 175, 192-193, 222, 225,
    229, 231, 233, 248, 255, 323, 367,
    379
    the *Mahmood* case 265
  Article 9 (freedom of thought, conscience
    and religion) 234, 250

Article 10 (freedom of expression) 234, 250
Article 11 (freedom of assembly and
    association) 234, 251
Article 12 (right to marry and found a
    family) 234
Article 14 (prohibition on discrimination)
    234-235
Article 17 238
claims for protection 239
derogations and reservations 235
detrimental effect of return 239
extra-territorial effect 240
family or other connections 239
impact of incorporation in domestic law
    149
interests of society 261
limitations on detention powers 498
and polygamous marriages 335
Protocol 1
  Article 1 234
  Article 2 26, 234, 255
  Article 3 234
Protocol 6
  Article 1 234
  Article 2 234
public emergency threatening the life of the
    nation 235
removal 251
reservations 235
restrictions on rights 236
rights into which restrictions can be implied
    238
rights which can be restricted in specifically
    defined circumstances 237
rights which can be restricted in the
    interests of society 237
European Convention on Establishment 106
European Convention on Social and Medical
    Assistance 138, 660, 667
European Council 450
European Court of Human Rights (ECtHR)
    168, 231-232
  'interim measures' 270
  legal funding for cases 270
  procedure for making an application 268
  Strasbourg 232
  taking a case to Europe 268
European Court of Justice (ECJ) 450
European Economic Area (EEA) 14, 413, 448,
    452
European Free Trade Area 14
European Parliament 450
European rights of free movement 14, 254,
    323, 400, 413, 447, 452
  Association Agreements 13
  EEA nationals 13-14

European rights of free movement *continued*
   family members 458
  exclusions 14
  family permits 466
  incorporation in UK law 451
  indefinite leave and 473
  leave to enter 66
  loss of rights by family members 460
  Non-EEA national employees of businesses
    in the EEA 457
  providers and recipients of services 457
  refusing or revoking rights 469
    public policy ground 469
  residence permits 464
  seeking work 455
  self-employed people 456
  temporarily incapable of work 456
  workers: definition 453
European Union (EU) 447-448
  harmonisation of law 153
  institutions 450
  law 447, 450
    directives 450
    regulations 450
evidence
  expert reports 190
  from political organisations 190
  medical reports 189
  witnesses' letters 190
exceptional leave 148, 216
  and human rights 13
  certificate of identity 230
  concessions 105
  criteria following refusal of asylum claim
    217
  family reunion 227
  foreign travel and 230
  Home Office letter: example of 125
  how to apply 104
  human rights and 217
  letter granting leave 218
  long residence concessions 105
  numbers granted exceptional leave 216
  people who do not qualify under ECHR
    149
  period of leave 218
  refugees and 148
    other family members 225
  students: fees 315
  to remain 148, 217
  travel documents 88
  unaccompanied minors
    no reception facilities available 191
exclusion 76
exclusion undesirable 376
extradition 529

F
Faculty of Advocates in Scotland 40
Falkland Islands 563
false claims 200
false evidence 200
family court procedures 395
family life 256
  adopted children 257
  adoptive parents 257
  adult siblings 257
  aunts 257
  children 257
  definition 256
  foster children 257
  grandchildren 257
  grandparents 257
  interference with 258
  interference with: grounds for 261
  nieces and nephews 257
  parents 257
  polygamous marriages 258
  relationships which amount to family life
    257
  spouse 257
  transsexuals 258
  uncles 257
  unmarried partners 257
family members
  administrative removal 536
family permits 466
family reunion 222
  children 223
  exceptional leave 227
  exclusion 225
  four-year rule 227
  human rights 255
  maintenance and accommodation 228
  other family members 225
  sponsor 227
  spouse 223
  Surinder Singh case 461
family reunion concession 105
Faroes, the
  au pairs from 433
fathers 567
  visit to see 286
fathers-in-law
  visit to see 286
Federal Republic of Yugoslavia 197, 292
fees 738
  students: refugees 315
fiancé(e)s 323, 325
  additional rules 335
  applying to enter 326
  children of 368
  definition 335

fiancé(e)s *continued*
  entry clearance 339
  family life 256
  length of leave 343
  maintenance and accommodation 328
  maintenance undertakings 334
  proof of age over 16 341
  proof of freedom to marry 341
  refusal of entry clearance 344
  switching status 92
  switching to become 351
  work 343
fingerprinting 181
  children 181
  dependants 181
Finland 54, 177, 356
  EFTA 448
  EU country 448
first cousins
  visit to see 286
Foreign and Commonwealth Office 16, 198, 295, 327
  designated posts 59
Foreign Press Association 153
foreign travel
  exceptional leave and 230
  refugees and 229
forms and documents
  (FLR (S) 308
  APP104 127
  BUS 96, 383, 439
  EEC1 101, 467
  ELR 96, 105
  FLR (M) 96
  FLR (O) 441
  FLR (S) 96
  FLR(M) 343, 349, 351, 357
  FLR(O) 96, 105, 289, 351, 363, 381, 383, 432, 444
  GV3 224
  ICD0716 218
  ICD0725 215
  IM2A 60, 444
  IM2B 60
  IM2C 60
  IM2D 60
  IM2E 60
  IM2F 60
  IM2G 60
  IM2S 60
  IS 151A 127
  IS 151B 128
  IS 82 128
  IS 96 NW 126
  IS 96(W/NW) 126
  IS118 129
  IS96 178
  IS98 513
  IS98A 513
  MN1 574
  N461 142
  RON 117 389
  SET(F) 96, 373, 401, 405, 663
  SET(M) 96, 346
  SET(M) 373
  SET(O) 96, 105-106, 360, 383, 422, 424
  Statement of Evidence Form (SEF) 181
  TD112 89
  WP1 419, 425
  WP1X 100, 383, 422
  WP3 427
  WP3X 422, 427
foster children
  family life 257
fostercare 394
'fourteen-year' long residence concession 107
France 54, 208
  EU country 448
freedom of assembly and association 234, 251
freedom of expression 234, 250
freedom of thought, conscience and religion 234, 250
fresh claims
  asylum 220
full-time studies 300

G

gay men 159
  Article 8 ECHR and 249
  refugee status: membership of a particular social 158
Gelsthorpe, Loraine 492
General Dental Council 311
General Medical Council 311
General Register Office 356
Geneva Convention *see* Refugee Convention
Germany 54, 177, 208, 211
  EU country 448
getting married 356
Ghana 197, 292, 295
Gibraltar 577
Gill, Professor Guy Goodwin 158
grandchildren
  family life 257
  visit to see 286
grandfathers 572
  visit to see 286
grandmothers
  visit to see 286
grandparents
  family life 257

grants
  students 314
Greece
  EU country 448
Greenland
  au pairs from 433

H
habeas corpus 525
habitual residence test 670, 676
Hague Convention on Inter-Country Adoption
  1993 568
half-brothers and sisters 409
hard cases 139
Harmondsworth 28, 489-490
Hathaway, Professor James
  hierarchy of human rights 155
HC (House of Commons paper) 8
  HC395 8
health 659
health care 687
Health Services and Public Health Act 1968
  section 45 684
heartbeat sensors 52
Highly Skilled Migrant Programme (HSMP) 37,
  413, 441
  income band/country list 746
  points system 443
  'switching' status 444
Hindu Marriage Act 341
HIV/AIDS 105, 252
  carers 254
  EEA nationals and family members 254
  entry clearance applications 253
  entry into the UK 253
  leave to remain 253
HM Chief Inspector of Prisons 509
Home Office
  Application Forms Unit 95
  Asylum Screening Unit 179
  country information and reports 197,
    635-636
  Country Information Policy Unit (CIPU) 190
  decisions 101, 197, 212
    backlog clearance 220
    curtailment of leave to remain 103
    delays 219
    discretion 102
    human rights and 101
  Immigration and Nationality Directorate
    16, 231
  Integrated Casework Directorate (ICD) 173
  interpreters 186
  links with benefit authorities 673
  notice of decisions 104
  officials, powers of 28

  passport endorsements 118
  presenting officer 637
  Public Enquiry Offices 181
  Public Enquiry Unit (PEO) 99
  Research, Development and Statistics
    Directorate 61
  'Third Country Unit' 208
  Work Permits (UK) 16
homelessness 674, 676
Homelessness Act 2002 675
homosexuality 159
  Article 8 ECHR and 249
  see also gaymen, lesbians, same-sex
    partners
Hong Kong
  British citizenship 566
  British Nationals (Overseas) 580
  British nationals from 579
  certificate of identity 582
Hong Kong (War Wives and Widows) Act 1996
  580-581
Hong Kong Act 1985 563, 580
House of Commons 8, 141
  Information Office 142
House of Lords 18, 153
housing 659, 674
  allocation of housing accommodation 674,
    678
  effect of immigration status 675
  eligibility for the homeless 677
  habitual residence test 676
  homelessness 674, 676
  Homelessness Act 2002 675
  houses in multiple occupation (HMOs) 332
  overcrowding 331
  qualification for housing register 678
Housing Accommodation and Homelessness
  (persons subject to immigration control)
    Order 1996 307
housing benefit 670
  students 306
human rights 12, 231
  and asylum claims 267
  appeals: burden and standard of proof 646
    change of circumstance 644
  children 367
  claims for protection 239
  derogations and reservations 235
  exceptional leave 13
  exceptional leave and 217
  independent applications 266
  making a claim 266
  one-stop notices 267
  refugees and 148
  see also European Convention on Human
    Rights (ECHR)

Human Rights Act (HRA) 1998 6, 12, 39, 63,
    149, 231, 233, 539
  ECHR Articles not incorporated 234
  key points 233
Human Rights Act 1998 (Designated
    Derogation) Order 2001 497
Human Rights Watch 636
Hungary
  Association Agreement 448, 476
  au pairs from 433

I

ICCID (the Immigration Consortium Country
    Information) 636
ICD Complaints Unit 219
Iceland 54
  EFTA 448
  European Economic Area (EEA) 14
illegal entrants 74, 179
  asylum-seekers and: joint memorandum of
      good practice 557
  bail 514
  children 354
  children of 570
  deception of an immigration officer 547
  detention 494
  entry in breach of a deportation order 547
  entry without obtaining leave from an
      immigration officer 546
  entry without seeing an immigration officer
      546
  'harbouring' illegal entrants 555
  marriage 353
  power to remove family members 28
  removal 545
    of family members 29
  removal and return 549
  unmarried and same sex partners 355
illegal entry 18, 527
  appeals 603
  assisting illegal entry and asylum claimants
      555
  entry through Ireland 547
  notice of: example 127
illegible passport stamps 72
illegitimate children 23, 568
  discrimination against 21
Immigration Act 1971 5-7, 39
Immigration Act 1988 5, 335, 451
immigration advice 39
  Code of Standards 40
  complaints 41
  definition 41
  exemption from registration 40
  Immigration Services Commissioner 40
  levels 40

registration 40
  fee 40
regulation of advisers 39-40
seeking advice
  in England and Wales 45
  in Northern Ireland 46
  in Scotland 46
solicitors, barristers and legal executives
    40
Immigration Advice at the Police Station 140
Immigration Advisory Service 508, 627
Immigration and Asylum Act 1996 7
Immigration and Asylum Act 1999 6-7, 17,
    29, 39, 52, 64, 75, 79, 150, 151, 196,
    330
  automatic bail hearings 493
  effect on immigration control 51
  immigration advice 40
  leave to remain: delayed decisions 93
  major changes 148
  repeal of Part III 28
  schedule 9 para 4: certified cases 203
  sections 74 and 75 'one-stop' notices 187
  'subject to immigration control' 138
  third country cases 209
Immigration and Asylum Act 1999
    (Commencement No 6 and
    Consequential Provisions) Order 2000
    103
Immigration and Asylum (Appeals) Procedure
    Rules 517
Immigration and Asylum Appeals (Notices)
    Regulations 2000 132, 601-602, 611
Immigration and Asylum Appeals (Procedure)
    (Amendment) Rules 2001 203
Immigration and Asylum Appeals (Procedure)
    Rules 601
Immigration and Asylum Procedure Rules 2000
    553
Immigration and Nationality Directorate (IND)
    16, 231
  see also Home Office
Immigration and Nationality Law Reports 654
Immigration Appeal Reports 654
Immigration Appeal Tribunal (IAT) 18, 30,
    516, 600, 651
  grounds of appeal 651
  hearings 655
  Refugee Convention and 152
Immigration Appeals (Family Visitor) (No 2)
    Regulations 286
Immigration Appeals (Procedure) Rules 2000
    132
Immigration Appeals Act 1969 5, 601
Immigration Appellate Authority 18, 600, 626
  applying for bail 517

immigration authorities 15
Immigration (Carriers' Liability) Act 1987 196
Immigration (Control of Entry through
    Republic of Ireland) 1972 73
immigration control
  landing card 65
  on arrival 65
  operation of 15
  the system 7
Immigration Directorate Instructions (IDI) 277
Immigration (European Economic Area)
    Regulations 2000 14, 451, 453
Immigration Law Practitioners' Association
    (ILPA) 564, 570, 636
  Breaking down the barriers (April 2000)
    184
Immigration (Leave to Enter and Remain)
    Order 2000 57, 70, 85
immigration officers 16, 133
  powers of arrest and search 552
Immigration (Restrictions on Employment)
    Order 1996 194, 415
immigration rules 8
  and credibility 198
  discretion 68
  general grounds for refusal of leave 68
  marriage 324
  on returning residents 80
  on switching status 90
  recognition of refugee status 215
  Refugee Convention and 151
  relatives 399
  removal or deportation of family members
    392
Immigration Services Commissioner *see* Office
    of the Immigration Services
    Commissioner
Immigration Services Tribunal 42
Immigration (Variation of Leave) (Amendment)
    Order 2000 94
Immigration (Variation of Leave) Order 1976
    (VOLO) 93-94
income support 670
  benefit rates 668
  students 306
income-based jobseeker's allowance 670
  students 306
  benefit rates 668
indefinite leave 10, 79
  'returning residents' rules 79
  EEA nationals 473
  long residence concessions 105
  returning residents 82
  returning residents rule 11
  travel 79
independent fee paying schools 298-299

India 147, 159, 197
induction centres 24, 171, 512
inhuman treatment
  definition 245
Initial Consideration Unit 97
injunctions 144
Inland Revenue 552
  duty of disclosure 33
innovators 441
  dependants 441
Institute of Legal Executives 40
Integrated Casework Directorate (ICD) 97, 465
intention to leave 277
intention to stay together permanently 327
interim support 27, 689, 708
  accommodation 709
  dependants of asylum-seekers 693
  destitution 360, 694
  essential living needs 709
  exclusions 711
  procedures 711
  transferring claims 712
  who qualifies 708
internal flight alternative 166
International Association for the Exchange of
    Students of Technical Experience 436
International Covenant on Civil and Political
    Rights 1996 148, 157
International Covenant on Civil and Political
    Rights 505
International Organisation for Migration 530
International Social Service of Great Britain
    530
International Social Services of the United
    Kingdom 82
'international terrorists' 169
  derogation of human rights 235
  detention 495-496
interpreters 61
interviews
  settlement 61
investors 9, 439
  family members 440
  switching status 92
invitation to withdraw asylum application 213
Iran 147, 159, 197, 266, 271, 292
Iraq 147, 197, 218, 271, 292
Ireland 14, 54, 195
  Common Travel Area 17, 72
  entry through 72, 547
  EU country 448
  travel to Ireland and return to UK 74
  travel to the UK 73
Irish citizens
  family members 15
  indefinite leave 14

Isle of Man 314
   Common Travel Area 17, 72
Israel 212
Italy 54, 177, 260
   EU country 448

J

Jamaica 159, 340
Japan youth exchange scheme 436
Jewish Agency 436
Joint Entry Clearance Unit (JECU) 16, 59
judicial review 30-31, 132, 142, 526, 600,
     650
   application form 142
   asylum claims 219
   full hearing 142
   permission 142
   urgent cases 144
   urgent cases: Practice Statement 144
   waiting time 142

K

Kenya 5, 197, 578
Khartoum 196
Kosovo 162, 176
Kurdish Autonomous Region of Northern Iraq
    166

L

landing cards 65
   example of 113
language test 22
Latvia
   Association Agreement 448, 476
law
   immigration law 7
   nationality law 7
Law of Refugee Status (1991) 155
Law Society 140
Law Society of Scotland 46
lawyers
   overseas lawyers 439
   training: permission to work 311
League for the Exchange of Commonwealth
    Teachers 433
Learning and Skills Council of England 316
leave 8, 9
   applying to vary leave on entry 70
   cancellation of 76
   code numbers 109
   concessions 10
   conditions of leave 11, 109
   extensions of 90
   granted outside the rules 66
   leaving and returning 75
   'non-lapsing' leave 76, 83, 85

   outside immigration rules 10
   people who do not require leave 65
   people who require leave 66
   people whose leave lapses when they
      depart 84
   refusal of 11
   temporary admission 11
leave to enter 16, 65
   cancellation of leave on arrival 69
     change of circumstances 69
   diplomats 66
   EEA nationals and 66
   entry clearance 56
   general grounds for refusal 67
   people who have leave when they arrive
     68
   people who require leave 66
   persons who do not require leave 65
   refusal before arriving in UK 64
   time limits 66
leave to remain 16
   application forms 95
   applications from outside the UK 99
     or on entry 101
   applications made in person 99
   applying to stay 90
   Association Agreements 101
   automatic extensions 95
   changing conditions of leave 104
   curtailment 103
   deception 536
   delays in decisions 99
   EEA nationals 101
   exceptional leave to remain 104
   general grounds for refusal 102
   Home Office decisions 101
   how to apply 95
     24 hour and 48 hour priority service 98
     application forms 96
     interpreters 99
     validity of application 97
   'in-time' applications with a delayed
     decision 93
   limited leave 10, 83
   'subject to immigration control' 94
   successive applications 95
   'switching' status 90
   time limits 91
   'Third Party Applicants' (TPAs) 98
   work permit applications 100
   work permit holders 421
leaving and returning
   people who left the UK before 30 July 2000
     85
   people who qualify to return 77
   with limited leave 83

leaving the UK before a decision
  return of passport while application is
    outstanding 86
  travelling while an appeal is outstanding 86
Lebanon 197
Legal Aid (Scotland) Act 1986 46
Legal Aid Board 40
legal executives 40
Legal Services Commission (LSC) 40, 372, 627
  compulsory contracting 183
  Criminal Defence Service 140
  Legal Representation 45
Libya 292
Liechtenstein 54
  EEA 448
  European Economic Area (EEA) 14
Lithuania 197
  Association Agreement 448, 476
loans
  students 314
local authorities
  duty of disclosure 33
local authority accommodation 331
local authority care 393
long residence concessions 105
  10-year long residence concession 106
  14-year long residence concession 107
  British Overseas Citizens (BOCs) 108
  continuity 108
  refusal of 108
Lord Chancellor's Department 600
Luxembourg 54
  EU country 448

M

Maastricht Treaty on European Union (TEU)
  447, 448, 452
Macedonia
  au pairs from 433
maintenance and accommodation
  accommodation 331
  adequate maintenance 329
  children 370
  who the rules do not apply to 328
maintenance undertakings 334
Malawi 578
Malaysia 576
  British nationals from 579
Malta 54
  au pairs from 433
'managed migration' 21
marriages
  'akin to marriage' 337
  arranged marriages 37, 328, 337
  breakdown 336
    after settlement 361

divorce 336
DP/2/93 353, 355
DP/3/96 353
immigration rules 324
maintenance and accommodation 328
marriage breakdown 339
proposed 'no switching' rule 35-36
probationary period 35
'sham' marriages 350, 357
'switching' status 348
White Paper 2002 35
marriage breakdown
  access to children 362
marriage visits 282
maternity allowance 672
Medical Foundation for the Care of Victims of
  Torture 183, 189, 634
medical reports 189
Medical Research Council 575
medical students 311
medical visitors 293
Member of Parliament (MP) 141
  complaints to 219
  Members of Parliament Correspondence
    Section (MPCS) 141
  research assistants 436
members of religious orders 430
members of the armed forces 65
membership of a particular social group
  definition 159
Mental Health Act 1983
  removal 254, 529
  section 117 684
Mental Health Review Tribunal 255
Mexico 158
ministers of religion 429
Minority Rights Group 636
missionaries 430
Monaco
  au pairs from 433
Morocco 260
  Co-operation Agreement 448, 482
mothers
  visit to see 286
mothers-in-law
  visit to see 286

N

NASS support 316
  see also asylum support
National Assistance Act 1948 679
  section 21 681
  section 29 682
National Asylum Support Service (NASS) 19,
  24, 27, 511, 659, 689
National Health Service 372

National Health Service *continued*
  charges 687
  dental treatment 706
  prescriptions 706
  sight tests 706
National Health Service (Charges to
    Overseas Visitors) Regulations 1989
    687
National Health Service Act 1977
  schedule 8 684
National Refugee Integration Forum 172
nationality 7
  types of British nationality 8
  see also British citizens
Nationality, Immigration and Asylum Bill 2002
    (2002 Bill) 20, 39, 97, 416
  changes to asylum and human rights
    170
  children 366
  deportation of family members 531
  deprivation of citizenship proposals 22
  detection 552
  detention 510
  IAT appeals 651
  'illegitimate' children 568
  language tests 22
  new offencesa 33   summary main
    proposals 20
  'one-stop' process 29
  powers to remove family members 391
  proposed changes to criminal offences
    556
  'social integration' 22
  summary main proposals 20
  right of appeal 29
  temporary admission 510
  'voluntary leavers' 530
naturalisation 8, 23, 584
  Crown Service 589
  proposed language tests 23
  proposal to shorten waiting times 23
  refusals 508
  requirements 584
nephews 409
  visit to see 286
Netherlands, the 54, 177, 260, 356
  EU country 448
New Zealand 295
nieces 409
  visit to see 286
nieces and nephews
  family life 257
Nigeria 197, 220, 260, 292, 336
non-lapsing leave 17, 76, 83, 85
'non-refoulement' 150
Northern Ireland

Legal Aid, Advice and Assistance (Northern
    Ireland) Order 1981 46
  legal help 47
Norway 54, 137, 177, 207, 211, 356
  EFTA 448
  European Economic Area (EEA) 14
notices of
  administrative removal 127
  illegal entry 127
  one-stop appeals 137, 179, 606
  temporary admission 126
nurses
  student nurses 311

O

Oakington Reception Centre 178, 180, 196,
    488-490
  detention 11, 506
  list of countries whose nationals are likely to
    507
off-shore workers 436
offences 527, 553
  2002 Bill and 33
  assisting illegal entry and asylum claimants
    555
  connected with the support of asylum-
    seekers 555
  deception 536, 554
  deception of an immigration officer 547
  duty of disclosure 33
  employer sanctions 415, 556
  entry without leave or in breach of a
    deportation order 554
  general offences 556
  'harbouring' illegal entrants and overstayers
    555
  illegal entry 553
    for the purposes of adoption 390
  overstaying and breach of conditions
    553
  prosecution of asylum-seekers 557
  provision of advice 556
  unauthorised workers 552
Office of the European Ombudsman
    450
Office of the Immigration Services
    Commissioner (OISC) 38-39, 40, 98,
    130
  code of standards 41
  Immigration Services Tribunal 42
OFSTED 26
one-stop appeals 29, 606
one-stop notices 179, 606
  who they apply to 187
one-stop procedure
  asylum-seekers 187

Operational Enforcement Manual 503
operational ground staff of overseas airlines
431
ordinarily resident 314, 325
Overseas Labour Service (OLS) 100
overstayers 93, 179, 347, 532-533
    administrative removal 532
    bail 514
    children 354
    children of 570
    marriage 353
    offences 555
    unmarried and same sex partners 355
Owers, Anne 509

P

Pakistan 147, 197, 261
parents 567
    access to children: settlement 382
    adoptive parents 369
    death of a parent 373
    definition 369
    family life 257
    foster parents 369
    from abroad seeking access to children
        380
    joining a child with whom they have contact
        379
    settled in the UK 369
    'sole responsibility' for child 373
    with limited leave seeking access to children
        381
parents and grandparents 399
Parliamentary Ombudsman 219
part-time work
    students 297
passports
    British passports issued before 1973 78
    British Visitor's passport 78
    Declaration of Identity documents 89
    destruction of 201
    false passports 200
    issued before 1 January 1983 565
    issued on or after 1 January 1983 565
    people without passports 88
    return of passport while appeal is
        outstanding 86
    return of passport while application is
        outstanding 86
    right of abode 565
    stateless persons 89
    see also endorsements
Passport Agency 78
passport stamps *see* endorsements
people employed by an overseas government/
    international organisation 431

persecution
    past or future 163
Philippines 336, 340
Poland 197, 272
    Association Agreement 448, 476
police registration 11
    list of countries 750
    registration with 535
polygamous marriages 335
    children of 368
    family life 258
port cases
    bail 514
port medical officer 68
port removal 18, 527, 530
    and asylum-seekers 531
Portugal 54, 177
    EU country 448
postgraduate doctors and dentists 297
powers of arrest and search 552
Practice Direction of the Chief Adjudicator
        630, 632
Practice Statement
    judicial review, urgent cases 144
pre-clearance checks 34, 52
prescribed forms
    applications not on prescribed forms
        100
primary purpose rule 328
    abolition 6
prisons 28, 490, 509
probationary period
    claiming benefits 345
    partner 345
    removal for couples co-habiting for five
        years or more 35
    spouse 345
    White Paper 2002 36
Procedure Rules 626, 651, 654
prohibition
    against slavery and forced labour 245
    on discrimination 234
    on retrospective punishment 233, 248
    on slavery and forced labour 233
    on torture or inhuman or degrading
        treatment or punishment 233, 242
    see also under European Convention on
        Human rights
prohibition on work
    breach of conditions 535
prospective students 298
provider of services 457
Public Enquiry Offices 99
Public Enquiry Unit (PEO) 99
public funds 11, 659
    'additional' recourse to public funds 329

public funds *continued*
   child benefit 329
   definition 329
   'no recourse to public funds' condition 110
   without recourse to 535
public schools 299
publicly-funded institution of further or higher
   education 298-299

Q

Quality Mark (Community Legal Service) 41

R

race discrimination 270
   authorisations to discriminate 270
      statistical justifications 271
   first authorisation 270
   reviews of authorisations 271
   rights of appeal 71, 271
   second authorisation 271
Race Relations (Amendment) Act 2000 270
Race Relations (Immigration and Asylum) (No
   2) Authorisation 2001 270
Race Relations (Immigration and Asylum)
   Authorisation 2001 270
Race Relations Act 1976 232, 270
radiographer 294
raids on premises 552
Ramsbotham, Sir David 509
recipient of services 457
recognizance 517
recommendation for deportation 495, 538
recommendation to the Home Office 646
Red Cross 25
Redesdale, Lord 564
refoulement 154
Refugee Action 530
Refugee Arrivals Project 512
Refugee Convention 1951 8, 12, 54, 150
   1967 Protocol 150
   and Article 3 ECHR 243
   Article 31 200
   Article 33 150
   as part of UK law 151
   interpretation 153
   legal basis for asylum 150
   refugee status 153
Refugee Convention 1946
   travel documents 54
Refugee Council 192, 508, 511
Refugee Council Panel of Advisers for
   Unaccompanied Minors 192
Refugee Legal Centre 130, 508, 627, 636
Refugee Women's Legal Group (RWLG) 165
refugees 9, 122, 170
   '10 or more' plan 175

applications from oveseas 154
ceasing to qualify 167
children of 222-223
   leading an independent life 225
civil war and 162
conscientious objection 164
Convention reason for fear of persecution
   157
definition 153
definition of persecution 155
dependants 215
exceptional leave and 148
exclusion from Convention protection 168
family members arrival without entry
   clearance 226
family reunion 222
   entry clearance 223
fear of prosecution 164
foreign travel and 229
group refugees 176
Home Office letter granting leave: examples
   of 123
homosexuality 159
human rights and 148
indefinite leave 10
internal flight alternative 166
legal definition 153
letter recognising refugee status 215
mandate refugees 175
membership of a particular social group
   158
military service 164
nationality 157
'non-refoulement' 150
non-state agents 161
numbers granted refugee status 216
other family members 225
over-age children 225
persecution 155
   past or future 163
political opinion or belief 157
procedure for claiming asylum 173
race 157
recognition of refugee status 215
refoulement 154
refugee status 153
religion 157
same-sex partners of 225
'singling out' 162
spouse of 222-223
   not part of pre-existing family 227
standard of proof 160
stateless persons 154
sur place 163, 199
temporary protection 176
third country cases 206

refugees *continued*
   threat to life or freedom 154
   transfer of status 176
   travel abroad 216
   travel documents 152, 229
     examples of 124
     fees 229
   welfare benefits 669
   well-founded fear of persecution 153-154
   who 'do not deserve international
     protection' 169
refusal of asylum
   'one-stop' notice 214
   appeals 214
   notice of refusal 214
   reasons for refusal letter 213
refusal of entry 133
refusals
   non-compliance 205
registrars 6
registration 8
registration with the police 535
Regularisation of Overstayers Scheme 532
regulation of immigration advisers 39-40
relatives 399
   adult sons and daughters 407
     DNA testing 408
   dependent relative rules 399
   grandparents over 65 401
   more distant relatives 409
   of EEA nationals 399
   other relatives
     living alone in the most exceptional
      compassionate circumstances 406
     other than parents and grandparents
      aged over 65 406
   parents/grandparents over 65 401
     maintenance/accommodation 405
     age requirement 402
     no other close relatives 404
     financially depende 402
   special voucher scheme 408
removal 527
   administrative removal 527, 531
   Article 3 ECHR and 251
   Article 8 ECHR and 251
   costs 551
   definition 528
   Mental Health Act 1983 254, 529
   port removal 527
   removal directions 528
   the process 549
   threatened removal 140
   travel documents 550
   where people can be removed to 550
removal centres 28, 172, 489

   Dungavel 28
   Harmondsworth 28
   Yarl's Wood 28
removal directions 528
   example of 128
   for those refused leave to enter 128
   for those who have had a deportation order
     signed 129
   illegal entrants and those subject to
     administrative removal 128
repatriation 530
   public funds to leave 82
representation
   importance of 130
representatives of overseas insurance
     companies 436
research assistants to Members of Parliament
     436
residence permits 101, 464
respect for private and family life, home and
     correspondence *see* European
     Convention on Human Rights
     Article 8
restriction on employment or occupation
   breach of conditions 535
restriction orders 510
retired persons of independent means 400,
     440
   switching status 92
retirement pensions 672
returning residents 11, 79
   appeals against refusal of entry 83
   indefinite leave 82
   limited leave 83
   refusal of entry 82
   settlement 81
   what happens on arrival 82
returning residents rules 11, 80, 79
revocation of entry clearance 64
revocation of deportation order 543
right not to be denied an education 255
right of abode 8, 55, 65, 77, 565
   British citizens 7
   certificate of entitlement 55, 77, 467, 566
     example of 121
   Commonwealth citizens 7
   EEA nationals 14
right of appeal 214, 599
   human rights and 71
   limitations 605
   race discrimination and 71
   when there is no right 629
   see also appeals
right to a fair trial 233, 247
   see also European Convention on Human
     Rights (ECHR)

right to liberty and security 12, 233, 246
  see also European Convention on Human
      Rights (ECHR)
right to life 233, 241
  see also European Convention on Human
      Rights (ECHR)
right to marry and found a family 234
right to respect for private life, family, home
      and correspondence 231, 248
  see also European Convention on Human
      Rights
Roche, Barbara MP 180, 226
Romania 159, 197
  Association Agreement 448, 476
Rudolf Steiner establishments
  overseas staff 436
Russia 197
Rwanda 197

S

same sex partners 323, 325
  additional rules 337
  'akin to marriage' 327, 337
  applying to enter 326
  applying to settle 345, 346
  applying outside the immigration rules
      352
  entry clearance 339
  family life 256
  maintenance and accommodation 328
  of students 306
  'switching' status 348
  two year requirement 337
  unable to marry 338
San Marino
  au pairs from 433
Scotland
  legal help 47
Scottish Further Education Council 317
Scottish Legal Aid Board 46
search 65
  powers 552
seasonal agricultural workers' scheme 37,
      287, 413
secondary legislation 7
Secure Borders, Safe Haven: Integration with
      Diversity in Modern Britain 2002
  see White Paper 2002
self-employed 439
  switching status 92
self-employed people 456
serious illnesses 252
servants
  of diplomats 431
settlement 10, 327, 423, 479
  children 61, 373

  interviews 61
  definition 325
  documents required 62
  family settlement 61
  indefinite leave 79
  maintenance and accommodation rules 63
  marriage or relationship breakdown after
      361
  returning residents 81
  third party support 63
ship and aircrews 15
short-term workers 433
  au pairs 433
  seasonal agricultural workers 434
  seasonal workers 434
  teachers and language assistants 433
shortage occupations list 743
SIAC see Special Immigration Appeals
      Commission
Sierra Leone 147, 197, 295
Single European Act (SEA) 448
'singling out' 162
sisters 399
  visit to see 286
sisters-in-law
  visit to see 286
skill shortage 21
skills threshold 417
Slovak Republic, the 292
  Association Agreement 448
  au pairs from 433
Slovakia 196
  Association Agreement 476
Slovenia
  Association Agreement 448, 476
  au pairs from 433
Social Charter 138, 660, 667
social fund 671
social services 659. 678
sole representatives 430
solicitors 40
Somalia 147, 162, 197, 218, 228, 272, 292
  Somali Family Reunion Policy 228
sons 399
  visit to see 286
sons-in-law
  visit to see 286
Southall Black Sisters 358
Soviet Union 53
Spain 54, 177
  EU country 448
Special Immigration Appeals Commission
      (SIAC) 19, 169, 473, 497, 516, 528,
      601, 618
  procedures 619
  why SIAC was set up 619

Special Immigration Appeals Commission Act
  1997 6, 151, 516, 601
special quota voucher scheme 578
  head of household 578
  under pressure to leave 578
sponsor
  family reunion 227
sportspeople 282
  work permits 427
spouse 9, 323-325
  access to children 362
  additional rules 335
  administrative removal 536
  applying for settlement 345-346
  applying to enter 326
  applying to stay outside the immigration
    rules 352, 357
  arranged marriages 328, 337
  Association Agreements 480
  bereaved spouses 358
  common-law spouses 335
  definition 335
  deportation of 541
  divorce 336
  domestic violence concession 358
  DP/2/93 353, 355
  DP/3/96 353
  entry clearance 339
  family life 257
  intention to stay together permanently 327
  maintenance and accommodation 328
  maintenance undertakings 334
  marriage breakdown 336, 339
  of asylum-seekers 192
  of business person 439
  of deportees 538
  of EEA nationals 459
  of investors 363, 440
  of refugee 222-223
    not part of pre-existing family 227
  of retired people of independent means
    363-364, 440
  of students 364
    permission to work 330
  of TWES permit holder 425
  of work experience permit holders 364
  of work permit holders 423
  of workers and business people 363
  polygamous marriages 335
  probationary period 10, 342
    claiming benefits 345
    permission to work 330
  proof of age over 16 341
  proof of freedom to marry 341
  proof of marriage 340
  refusal of entry clearance 344

  same-sex partners and 335
  settlement 62
  'sham' marriages 350, 357
  'switching' status 92, 348
  third party support 334
  visit to see 286
Sri Lanka 147, 197, 211, 292, 295
St Kitts-Nevis and Antigua 251
  British citizenship 566
stamps/endorsements
  cancellation of leave 117
  confirmation of existing leave 117
  endorsements by the Home Office
    example of 118
  exceptional leave: example of 124
  exit stamps
    example of 118
  indefinite leave to enter 116
  indefinite leave to remain 120
  refusals 117
    example of 120
  registration with police 116
  variation of leave stamp: example of 116
Standard Acknowledgement Letters (SALs)
    24, 122, 178
standard of proof 160
state education 306, 372
statelessness 53
  travel documents 89
Statement of Evidence Form (SEF) 178, 179
  further evidence 182
  interviews 182
  practical problems 183
  process 181
step-brothers
  visit to see 286
step-fathers 369
  visit to see 286
step-mothers 369
  visit to see 286
step-mothers and adoptive mothers 409
step-sisters
  visit to see 286
step-sons
  visit to see 286
Straits Settlements 579
Straw, Jack MP 153
strong countervailing factors 108
student nurses 297
students' union sabbatical officers 312
students 9, 297
  '10-year' long residence concession 309
  ability to follow the course 301
  appeal against refusal of entry clearance
    304
  asylum-seekers 316

students *continued*
  bona fide private education institutions
    299
  change of status 319
  child benefit 307
  children of 305, 383
  dependants 301
    permission to work 306
  EEA students 317
    EC Directive 93/96 317
    EC Regulation 1612/68 318
    fees, grants and loans 318
  entry clearance 298, 303
    forms 60
  extension of stay as a visitor 287
  extending leave 307
  family dependants 305
  family members 297
  fees 300
    family members of 315
    refugees 315
  fees, grants and loans 314
  full-time studies 300
  grant support 315
    family dependants 315
  Home Office concession 302
  housing 307
  independent fee paying schools 299
  intention to leave the UK 302
    concession relating to students 302
  loans 315
  maintenance and accommodation
    299-300
  nurses 297, 302, 311
  overseas students 300
  part-time work 297
  passport stamps 304
  permission to work 310
    after studies 320
  postgraduate doctors and dentists 297,
    302
  prospective students 298, 303
  publicly-funded institutions of further or
    higher education 299
  re-sitting examinations 297, 312
  refusal of entry 304
  regular attendance 308
  same sex partners 306
  sandwich course students 301
  satisfactory progress 308
  short courses 308
  spouses and children of 364
  spouses of 305
  student internship 428
  students' union sabbatical officers 297,
    314
  switching status 92, 302, 307, 309
  switch to work-permit employment 37
  third party support 301
  travel outside the UK 320
  unmarried partners of 306
  welfare benefits 306
  work 310, 414
  writing up a thesis 297, 313
Students Awards Agency in Scotland 316
'subject to immigration control' 7, 138, 659,
    680
  application for leave to remain 94
  council tax benefit 670
  exceptions 665
  general rule 664
  given leave as a result of a maintenance
    undertaking 663
  housing benefit 670
  income support 670
  income-based JSA 670
  people with leave because they are
    appealing 663
  people without leave 662
  'recourse to public funds' 662
  test 660
  welfare benefits 665, 670
Sudan 165, 196, 197
sur place refugees 163, 199
sureties 29, 517, 520
  amounts 520
  exercise of control 520
Surinder Singh case 461
Sweden 54, 177, 356
  EFTA 448
  EU country 448
switching status 90
  changes allowed under the immigration
    rules 92
Switzerland 54, 137, 177, 207, 211, 259-260
  Association Agreement 448
  au pairs from 433

T

Tampere 449
Tanzania 578
teachers and language assistants
  spouse of 364
temporary admission 11, 71, 510
  accommodation address 511
  asylum support 25
  conditions of 511
  duration 512
  how to apply 511
  notice of: example 126
  permission to work 194
ten-year long residence concession 106, 309

terrorism
  deprivation of citizenship 22
  see also 'international terrorism'
Terrorism Act 2000 151, 170
Thailand 340
'Third Party Applicants' (TPAs) 98
  24 hour and 48 hour priority services 98
  straightforward applications 98
third country cases 136, 206
  appeals – 1993 Act 207
  Dublin convention 208
  EU states 207
  human rights and 210
  judicial review 207
  non-Dublin convention 211
  removals 209
  the 1999 Act 209
third party support 63, 334
Tinsley House 490
torture
  definition 242
tracing people in breach of immigration laws
      551
  Home Office 'hotline' 551
trafficking in prostitution 556
Training and Work Experience Scheme (TWES)
      55, 418, 425
  permits 418
  approved training 426
  work experience 427
transit visitors 196, 291
  appeal against refusal of entry 292
  direct airside transit 292
  entry clearance 292
transsexuals
  family life 258
travel 75, 222
  general rules 75
  one-way travel document 224
  visitors 296
  while appeal or application is outstanding
      86
  while awaiting an appeal 628
travel documents 550
  1951 Refugee Convention 88
  applying for 89
  Declaration of Identity 89
  destruction of 201
  exceptional leave 88
  stamps/endorsements 109
Treaty of Amsterdam 449
Treaty of Rome 5, 448
Treaty of the European Community 39
Trinidad 158
Tunisia
  Co-operation Agreement 448, 482

Turkey 147, 164, 197, 251, 292
  Association Agreement 448
  au pairs from 433
  EU Association Agreement 14, 480
Turkish Republic of Northern Cyprus 159, 292
TWES permits see Training and Work
      Experience Scheme (TWES)

U

Uganda 5, 197, 262, 292, 295, 578
United Kingdom (UK)
  EU country 448
UK nationals for the purposes of EU law 453
'UK Visas' 16, 59, 68, 224
Ukraine 197
unaccompanied minors
  asylum-seekers 25, 191
  Refugee Council Panel of Advisers 192
  where no reception facilities are available
      191
uncles 399
  family life 257
  visit to see 286
UNHCR Handbook 152, 155, 183, 199
  guidance on asylum procedure 173
United Nations Convention Against Torture
      and Other Cruel, Inhuman or
      Degrading Treatment or Punishment
      1996 148, 242
United Nations Convention on the Elimination
      of All Forms of Racial Discrimination
      157
United Nations Convention on the Rights of
      the Child 367
United Nations Convention on the Status of
      Refugees 12
  Protocol 12
United Nations High Commissioner for
      Refugees (UNHCR) 25, 153, 505, 636
United Nations International Covenant on Civil
      and Political Rights (ECCPR) 506
United States of America (USA) 137, 158,
      207, 211
  State Department country reports 636
Universal Declaration of Human Rights 1948
      150
unmarried partners 9, 323, 325
  additional rules 337
  akin to marriage 327, 337
  applying for settlement 345-346
  applying to enter 326
  applying to stay outside the immigration
      rules 352
  Association Agreements 480
  bereaved partners 358
  entry clearance 339

unmarried partners *continued*
family life 257
maintenance and accommodation 328
of business person 439
of investor 440
of retired persons of independent means
440
of students 306
of work permit holders 423
of workers and business people 363
probationary period 10, 342
proof of
inability to marry 341
previous relationship breakdown 341
relationship has lasted for two years 341
refusal of entry clearance 344
removal of 'unable to marry' provision 35
switching status 92, 348
two year requirement 337
'unable to marry' 21, 338
visit to see 286

V

Vietnamese refugees 228
village visit 371
visa nationals 17, 52, 73, 275, 737
entry clearance 53
visits 283
schoolchildren 54
students 298
switching status 309
visas 52
Uniform Format Visas (UFVs) 52, 112
see also entry clearance
visit entry clearances, example 112
visitors 9, 85, 275
academic visitors 281
admission of 275
advisers, consultants, trainers, trouble-
shooters 281
amateur entertainers and sportspeople 282
appeals 285
against refusal of entry at port 287
against refusal of entry clearance 286
appellants seeking re-admission to attend
appeal 281
application made outside the immigration
rules 287
applying for entry 283
archaeological excavations 281
business visitors 280, 414
carers 282, 289
carers concession 289
change of status 288
child minders for relatives 281
coach drivers 280

conference speakers 280
credibility 278
doctors coming for PLAB tests 282
duration of leave 276
entry clearance 52, 284
'pre-assessment sift' 283
requirements 276
extensions of leave 287
family members 276
family visitors
appeal against refusal of entry 286
definition 286
intention to leave 277
'mere suspicion' 278
job interviews 282
lorry drivers 280
maintenance and accommodation test 279
marriage visits 282
medical visitors 293
'monteurs' 281
parents of children under 12 years 283
previous refusal of entry 279
refusal of entry clearance
insufficient means 279
right to appeal 279
relatives 400
representatives of computer software
companies 281
representatives of foreign machine
manufacturers 281
seeking visas for other countries 282
'special classes' of visitor 280
switching status 92
temporary admission 285
tour group couriers 280
transit visitors 291
travel outside the UK 296
VOLO (*see* Immigration (Variation of Leave)
Order 1976)
voluntary assisted returns programme 172
voluntary work 435
expenses 194
vouchers 6, 25
abolition of 26

W

Weber, Leanne 492
welfare benefits 138, 659, 663
back-dating 669
'bereavement' benefits 672
child benefit 672
claim for asylum made 'on arrival' 668
claiming for dependants 668
contribution-based incapacity benefit 672
contribution-based job-seeker's allowance
672

welfare benefits *continued*
  council tax benefit 670
  disability benefits 671
  disabled person's tax credit 671
  'habitual residence' test 670
  housing benefit 670
  income support 668, 670
  income-based JSA 668, 670
  maternity allowance 672
  public funds 659
    definition 329
  reciprocal agreements 674
  refugees and 669
  social fund 671
  students 306
    dependants of 306
  'subject to immigration control' 660, 665
  working families' tax credit 671
well founded fear of persecution
  Convention reason 157
  definition of persecution 155
  objective and subjective fear 154
White Paper 2002 20, 25, 35, 52
  accommodation centres 26
  appeals 29, 172
  asylum 24
  biometric technology 52
  border controls 34
  cash payments 25
  changes to asylum and human rights
    170
  citizenship 22
  detention and enforcement 27
  economic migration 37
  Highly Skilled Migrant Programme (HSMP)
    37
  'hotline' 551
  'illegitimate' children 21
  increased reporting 171
  induction, accommodation and reporting
    centres 24
  legitimate gateways for refugees 25
  marriage: probationary period 35
  NASS accommodation 27
  naturalisation 23
  power of adjudicators to grant bail 28
  pre-clearance checks 52
  probationary period for spouses 345
  proposals on family relations 324
  seasonal workers 37
  skills shortage 21
  summary of main proposals 20
  'switching' status 91, 348
  targets for removals 171
  terrorism 22
  unable to marry 338

unaccompanied asylum-seeking children
  25
unaccompanied minors 172
unmarried partners 21
visitors: switching to stay 289
workers and business people 413
White Paper 1998, *Fairer Faster and Firmer*,
  150, 523
Williams of Crosby , Baroness 488
Williams of Mostyn, Lord 488
Windrush 4
without recourse to public funds 9
  breach of conditions 535
women
  asylum-seekers 165
  refugee status
    membership of a particular social 158
work
  business person 438
  business purposes 438
  prohibition on 11, 535
  restriction on employment or occupation
    535
  seeking work 455
  students, permission to work 310
  working unlawfully
    consequences 414
  outside the immigration rules 434
workers 413
  definition under Treaty of Rome 453
  seeking work 455
  spouses and partners 363
  temporarily incapable of work 456
working families' tax credit 671
working holidaymakers 9, 294
  children of 295
  entry clearance 294
  proposed changes in rules 295
  statistics 295
  switching status 92
  White Paper 2002 proposals 38
work permit
  applications 100
  approved training 426
  business and commercial 417
    applying 419
  changes of employment 422
  charging for work permits 38, 417
  cultural artists 427
  entry clearance 53
  example of 121
  families of work permit holders 423
  General Agreement on Trade in Services
    (GATS) 428
  leave to remain 421
  rights of holders 422

work permit *continued*
  settlement of holders 423
  shortage occupations list 743
  skills threshold 417
  sportspeople and entertainers' 427
  student internship 428
  suitably qualified resident worker 418
  switching status 92
  tier 1 and tier 2 applications 418
  TWES permits 418, 425
  White Paper 2002 38
  work experience 427
  Work Permits (UK) 16, 53, 63, 100, 294,
    320, 416
work permit free employment 429
  applying for extensions of leave 432
  Commonwealth nationals with British-born
    grandparents 432
  members of religious orders 430
  ministers of religion 429

  missionaries 430
  news agencies and broadcasting
    organisations 430
  private servants of diplomats 431
  representatives of overseas newspapers,
    news agencies and broadcasting
    organisations 430
  sole representatives 430
writers 440

Y

Yarl's Wood 28, 489-490
Yugoslav Republics, former 147
Yugoslavia, former Socialist Federal Republic of
  53

Z

Zambia 578
Zimbabwe 147, 197, 249

 **training**

Since 1981, JCWI has been providing high quality training to advisers and practitioners and is now recognised as one of the leading organisations in this field. Our trainers place great emphasis on the actual practice of law and our courses have a degree of participatory content which is unique to JCWI.

All courses are accredited by the Law Society for continued professional development (CPD) points. The courses are recommended by the Legal Services Commission and the Office of the Immigration Services Commissioner.

A comprehensive user-friendly training pack is provided to all participants. The packs are used by participants as up to date reference guides when they are back at work. Wherever appropriate, our trainers use case studies and role-play in order to enhance the learning experience.

JCWI is committed to taking positive action to fight discrimination in all areas of work, and specifically in its provision of training. As an anti-racist organisation, JCWI is particularly committed to increasing opportunities for groups traditionally disadvantaged by reason of race, colour, ethnic or national origin.

Our training is based on:

- practical experience of undertaking casework and providing advice to more than 5,000 people per annum
- policy work and lobbying to influence the UK's immigration, nationality and asylum laws and practices

JCWI training takes place at its London training venue and also nationwide.

The programmes range from half-day courses to two-day courses and are delivered at basic, intermediate and advanced levels.

Contact JCWI Training on 020 7251 8708 or email: training@jcwi.org.uk For full details of our training programme, please see our web site at: http:/www.jcwi.org.uk.

membership services

JCWI's strength is rooted in the diversity and support of its membership. It is striving to widen its membership base to face the challenges of the ever-changing nature of immigration law and policy.

JCWI is now needed more than ever to campaign on behalf of those affected by unfair and discriminatory laws and practices.

Membership benefits include:

- free quarterly JCWI Bulletins
- Annual Report
- selected discounts on publications
- substantial discounts on training
- election of the Executive Committee

- influence over JCWI's policy objectives
- knowledge that you are directly helping to strengthen JCWI's ability to effect change in policy and practice in this field

Membership rates are:

£40   small voluntary organisation (annual income less than £100,000)

£75   medium voluntary organisation (annual income over £100,000 to £ 1 million)

£100 voluntary organisation (annual income from £1 million to £2 million)

£200 large voluntary organisation (annual income more than £2 million)

£100 commercial organisation (solicitors'/barrister practices)

£30   individuals (excluding practising lawyer)

£50   individuals (practising lawyer)

£20   unwaged (inc.students and pensioner without income)

Currently our members range from individuals and legal practitioners through to refugee community organisations and groups representing settled ethnic communities across the UK.

publications

JCWI *Bulletin*

Relaunched in 1998 the JCWI Bulletin is a comprehensive journal targeted at everyone who needs to keep up to date in this rapidly changing field.

The Bulletin includes:

– Leading articles on important and topical matters

– Features on current topical news items

– Articles about developments in the law and practice

– Legal decisions including digest of important Immigration Appeal Tribunal cases

– Articles on campaigns and actions

– Parliamentary round-up

– European policy and legal update

– News about JCWI's services and developments

The Bulletin is published quarterly costing £5 per copy and is free for members. For membership or subscription details contact JCWI on 020 7251 8708 or email public@jcwi.org

 **publications**

Immigration factsheets

JCWI's revised factsheets provide up-to-date and practical information on specific immigration issues.

Each factsheet is concise, instructive and easy to understand and use.

The factsheets are an invaluable source of information for the individual and lawyer alike, as well as community organisations, advisers, students and visitors

Factsheets:

1 How to sponsor your husband, wife or fiancé(é) for settlement

2 How to sponsor children for settlement

3 How to sponsor dependent parents and grandparents for settlement

4 How to sponsor your unmarried partner for settlement

5 How to sponsor someone wanting to visit the UK

6 How to apply for asylum

7 A guide to studying in the UK as an international student

8 A guide to entry and settlement rights for EEA nationals and family

9 A guide to public funds benefits

10 Useful addresses and telephone numbers

11 Marriage breakdown

12 How to obtain British citizenship

Pack price £16.00 for members
Pack price £17.50 (plus £1·00 p&p) for non members
Also available singly for £2.75 each or £7 for three.

To order factsheets, please contact JCWI on Tel: 020 7251 8708

Other publications

JCWI Manifesto for the Reform of British Immigration Policy

£2.50, published May 2001. Available for free download on website.

A detailed exposition of JCWI's policy stance on every aspect of immigration, nationality and refugee law.

Migrant Workers – a TUC Guide

£6.50, published January 2002

Jointly published with the TUC, this 70-page guide sets out both the employment rights and immigration rights of workers in the UK who do not have settled status. It also examines the particular problems they face and analyses the reasons behind economic migration.